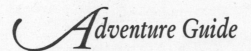
Adventure Guide

Tuscany & Umbria

Emma Jones

HUNTER

HUNTER PUBLISHING, INC,
130 Campus Drive, Edison, NJ 08818
☎ 732-225-1900; 800-255-0343; fax 732-417-1744
www.hunterpublishing.com

Ulysses Travel Publications
4176 Saint-Denis, Montréal, Québec
Canada H2W 2M5
☎ 514-843-9882, ext. 2232; fax 514-843-9448

Windsor Books
The Boundary, Wheatley Road, Garsington
Oxford, OX44 9EJ England
☎ 01865-361122; fax 01865-361133

ISBN 1-58843-399-4
© 2005 Hunter Publishing, Inc.
Manufactured in the United States of America

Cover photo: *On the Piazza della Vittoria, Montichiello, Italy*
(Terry Donnelly)
Maps by Toni Carbone © 2005 Hunter Publishing, Inc.
Index by Nancy Wolff
4   3   2

Contents

Introduction

From Tuscany and its "gentler sister" Umbria come some of Italy's most photographed landscapes. This is the countryside of a thousand postcards, and the images they depict – pole-straight cypress trees, olive groves, fields full of vibrant sunflowers and luscious vines, bottle-green rolling hills and medieval villages perched on rocky spurs – are as much an attraction as the artistic heritage of Florence, Siena and Pisa. But while these cities can be overrun in the busy summer season, the surrounding countryside has more than enough un-trampled wilderness to break your walking shoes in.

The broad arc of the Apennine mountain range marks Tuscany's northern borders, sweeping east and south into Umbria. Inside its northern boundary, shining like snow above the beaches of the Versilia Coast, lie the jagged crests of the marble-veined Apuane Alps and the gentler greener slopes of the Garfagnana. Farther east, there are horse-riding trails aplenty in the thick, woody uplands of Mugello and the National Park of the Casentino Forests. To the south, Chianti and its rolling hills full of intoxicating vineyards reach down to Siena, where the breathtaking chain of fortified hill-towns can be seen at their most splendid.

Sun-lovers should head to the miles of beach on Tuscany's coast and its nearby offshore islands – the seven sisters of the Tuscan Archipelago. While Viareggio and Forte dei Marmi may be the trendiest of the seaside resorts, in Maremma to the south you'll find some of the wildest coastline in the country, its sandy dunes protected from the tourist scramble by a Regional Park of maquis, hills, dune and coastal pinewoods.

Landlocked Umbria, "the green heart of Italy," may not completely match Tuscany's geological variation, but it comes close. This small, hilly and fairly untouched region occupying Italy's core (Narni is the country's geographical center) is crammed full of walking, rafting, caving, hang-gliding and climbing opportunities, not to mention a rich artistic and architectural heritage left over the centuries by Etruscans, Umbrians, Romans and then by scholarly monks.

Hikers seek out the Apennines, which in Umbria's eastern margins, become more rugged and soar to great heights in the savage peaks of the Monti Sibillini. Close by lie Piano Grande's prairie-like expanse, and the plush green of the Valnerina, home to the Marmore Falls (the highest in the country) and an eerie labyrinth of canyons cut out over centuries by the Nera River. Water sports are best at Lake Trasimeno, the largest body of water on the Italian peninsula.

History

■ Tuscany

The Etruscans

Remnants of prehistoric tribal settlements can be found throughout Tuscany, but it was the more advanced Etruscan civilization, making their mark from the first century BC, that has left a far larger mark in the region. Their very existence is steeped in mystery with scholars still in dispute about their exact roots. Some believe they arrived by sea from the Far East, some argue they came over land from northern Europe, while many believe they are descended from the so-called "Pre-Italians" of the Bronze Age. All are agreed, however, when it comes to their historical importance. The Etruscans formed the first consistent civilization in the area, and their growth can be traced from the original settlements around the Arno and Tiber rivers, to their later expansion up as far as the current region of Liguria to the north and down to Umbria and Lazio in the south.

Part of this steady progression was due to the Etruscan civilization's skills in construction and agriculture. They built an extensive network of roads throughout Tuscany and beyond; began to clear swamps and marshlands; set up trading networks; farmed and mined; and even headed out to sea. Add to this a legacy of exquisite art works, jewelry and surviving tombs and necropolises, and you can begin to understand what the archeologists and historians have written so excitedly about.

But you don't have to stick your head in dusty old books to enjoy the best of this intriguing civilization. Ancient Etruscan settlements such as Cortona, Arezzo, Fiesole (close to Florence), Chiusi and Volterra are still very much alive in Tuscany today and well within the visitor's reach thanks to Tuscany's extensive transport networks.

The Romans

Incursions by the Greeks, Gauls and Carthaginians heralded the beginning of the end of the glorious Etruscan civilization, but it was the might of Rome that placed the final nail in the Etruscan coffin at the beginning of the third century BC. They absorbed the Etruscan ruling class and bustling conurbations, founded their own rival cities – Lucca, Pisa, Siena and Florence, among others – and brought to  Tuscany a long period of relative peace and increasing cultural and economic prosperity. This was an extensive period of construction and modernization – roads, aqueducts, drainage, villas, theaters and entire new settlements all appeared in the Romans' wake.

Roman rule lasted until the fifth century, when their crumbling authority finally disintegrated under a flurry of barbarian invasions. The barbarians (particularly the Goths) left the territory in a state of flux until the Longobards arrived in the sixth century, setting Lucca up as their capital and slowly extending their domination throughout Tuscany.

The Middle Ages

The Middle Ages brought Tuscany prosperity as the Via Francigena (the Francigena Road), which traverses it, became a popular pilgrimage route between France and Rome. In its wake, churches, taverns and towns sprang up, but also rivalry and bitter conflict as Guelph (siding with the Pope) and Ghibelline (siding with the Emperor and feudal rulers) diversions tore the countryside in apart. But, despite the constant battles, it was also a time of financial and artistic prosperity that saw the formation of the increasingly wealthy – but politically turbulent – Tuscan Communes of Pisa, Lucca, Siena, Arezzo and Florence.

Each of these powerful Communes had their time of domination and control: Pisa, the principal port, held power for a while; Siena took over thanks to its wealth from banking; and Lucca grew rich on silk and banking. But it was Florence that ultimately came out on top, thanks to commerce and the beginning of the cultural and artistic movement known as the Renaissance.

This "rebirth" also marked the end of the Middle Ages, and the beginning of the Italian nation, as Florence set about extending its reign over the entire Tuscan region. Freed from bitter feuds, Florence – and by extension Tuscany – became the creative hub of cultural ideas and inventions. It was an era of unrivalled beauty and splendor, to a great extent thanks to the most famous native dynasty: the Medici.

The Medici

The rise of the Medici clan saw the beginning of an era of unrivalled beauty and splendor that shaped the glorious towns we see today – especially Florence. Many locals believe the city has yet to move on culturally from the Renaissance, which lives on in Florence's Duomo and the works of the giants of painting and sculpture from Michelangelo to Raphael. Under Cosimo I, the Medici become the Grand Dukes of Tuscany, which passed to the Austrian Dukes of Lorraine before being absorbed into the new Italian State.

The founder of the Medici fortune was Giovanni di Bicci, a skillful banker and businessman, but it was his elder son, **Cosimo Il Vecchio** (Cosimo the Elder), who was the first to place the family's immense economic power at the service of his political ambitions. This was to make life-long enemies of the city's other merchant bankers – the Strozzi, the Pazzi, the Acciaioli and, above all, the Albizzi. But, although they succeeded in exiling Cosimo in 1434, he was called back by the city just one year later, and went on to govern for 30 years.

The brief rule of Cosimo's successor Piero, later called Piero Il Gottoso (Piero the Gouty), preceded that of his eldest son Lorenzo (born in 1449). Considered the most significant of the Medici rulers and one of the greatest leaders of Italy in his time, he became known as **Lorenzo Il Magnifico** (Lorenzo the Magnificent), left, thanks to his patronage of artists (most famously Leonardo da Vinci and Michelangelo), which produced the artistic flourishing in Florence and then Italy, that became known as the Renaissance.

After Lorenzo's death, his eldest son Piero, called Il Sfortunato (the Unfortunate) ruled for only two years before being exiled from Florence for his political "incapacity" and it wasn't until 18 years later that the Medici family returned to Florence. Their return, in 1512, came under **Giuliano**, the youngest son of Lorenzo Il Magnifico (later called the Duke of Nemours). He governed the city on behalf of his brother Giovanni, who then still a cardinal, was elected Pope Leo X one year later.

Giuliano died childless in 1516 and **Lorenzo, Duke of Urbino** (son of Piero Il Sfortunato) took over the rule. He married the French Madeleine de la Tour d'Auvergne, but both died very young, leaving the newborn Caterina de' Medici who, at the age of 14, went on to become Dauphine and then Queen of France. On his death, the acknowledged head of the Medici family was **Cardinal Giulio,** the illegitimate son of Giuliano (brother of Lorenzo Il Magnifico). He is best known for his tumultuous rule as Pope Clement VII in a time where the conflict between

Francis I of France and Charles V of Spain brought about the Sack of Rome in 1527.

Following the Sack of Rome, Florence declared itself a "Republic-city" no longer under the control of the Medici. But less than three years later, Charles V of Spain elevated another family member, Alessandro (the illegitimate son of Giulio), to power. When he was assassinated in 1537, **Cosimo I** (descended from Giovanni di Bicci's younger son Lorenzo) took control of the city. He was the first true Duke of Florence, later made Grand Duke by Pope Pio V, and it was he who laid the foundations of the unified state of Tuscany that the Medici went on to rule without interruption for the next two centuries.

In 1587, **Ferdinando I**, the younger son of Cosimo I, succeeded to the throne after his brother Francesco I died without male heirs. Second to his father Cosimo, he was undoubtedly the wisest of the Medici Grand Dukes, ruling with his wife, Christine of Lorraine, until his sudden death in 1609. He was replaced by his son **Cosimo II**, whose reign is characterized by the political conflict between his wife Maria Magdalena (Austrian) and his mother Christine (French), which manifested itself in both the indecision of Cosimo II and that of his succeeding son, Ferdinando II.

After his death, the subsequent 53-year rule of **Cosimo III** (1642-1723), left, was even more of a disaster for both the State of Tuscany and the Medici dynasty, as artists and scientists left a Tuscany caught in the stranglehold of the clergy. His stormy marriage to Marguerite Louise of Orléans, cousin of Louis XIV, the Sun King, produced three children: Ferdinando, Anna Maria Luisa and Gian Gastone. The eldest died, leaving Gian Gastone to take over the rule, himself forced into an unhappy and childless marriage with Anna Maria Franziska.

His death made **Anna Maria Luisa** (herself a childless widower) the last of the Medici family. Her greatest achievement was the "Treaty or Convention of the Family," concluded with her successors the Grand Dukes of Lorraine in 1737, which left all the art treasures belonging to the Medici family to the city of Florence.

A Unified Italy

Tuscany entered into a united Italy in 1860, with Florence immediately establishing itself as a vital center of an undivided nation – it became the temporary capital of Italy from 1865 to 1870 and, in 1861, hosted the first Italian exhibition of industry and manufacturing. But this power didn't last long and Rome soon took over and remained as Italy's capital.

Since then, Florence and Tuscany have dragged their heels to some extent when it comes to social change. An explosive population growth in the 20th century brought unrest – which contributed to Tuscany's submission to Fascist rule in 1922. They were badly hit in World War II as a result – the River Arno at one time forming the battle's front line – but much has been reconstructed since then.

I've heard locals complain that Florence and much of Tuscany is yet to move on from its Renaissance heyday, but that is somewhat unfair. Tourism does play a heavy part in the local economy, but the territory has also grown wealthy thanks to its wine, olive oil, cheese and meat production. Although hampered by low employment levels, the territory continues to expand and modernize; hanging on to the best of the old and striving to establish the technology and resources needed to bring in the new.

■ Umbria

The Etruscans & the Romans

Although often known as "Tuscany's quieter sister," landlocked Umbria has played a strategic role in Italy's busy history. Numerous archaeological finds have unearthed a human presence in Umbria dating back to Palaeolithic and Neolithic periods; flints and arrowheads have been found on several river plains and around the shores of Lake Trasimeno; burial chambers close to Spoleto date to the time between the Bronze and Iron Ages.

The main settlers, however, arrived around 1000 BC. This tribe, thought to be of Indo-European origin, became known as the Oscan-Umbrians and is credited with establishing the towns and cities of Terni, Todi, Spoleto, Assisi, Gubbio and Città di Castello. The Umbrians arrived soon after, building an astonishing legacy of tombs, monuments and cultural artifacts, and leaving almost as suddenly with the arrival of the Romans about 309 BC. To the Etruscan remains – the necropolis and Tempio Etrusco at Orvieto, the extraordinary Eugubine Tablets in the Museo Civico at Gubbio, traces in Todi, Betton and Perugia – the Romans added amphitheaters, arches, aqueducts, temples and walls, from Città di Castello to Todi and from Perugia to Orvieto.

As in Tuscany, the Barbarian hordes ended the Roman Empire in Umbria, inaugurating decades of famine, disease and unrest in their place. The tumult started to settle at the end in the fourth century when the Christian Church emerged as a cultural and spiritual figurehead. Further peace arrived with the Longobards, who took possession of large parts of eastern Umbria, eventually establishing the autonomous and prosperous Duchy of Spoleto. This and the rest of Umbria became part of the Papal State in the 11th century, when, like Tuscany, Umbria became a flourishing region with merchants and artisans acquiring respect and positions of authority.

The Middle Ages

The medieval era saw Umbria surge as a religious and commercial center thanks to local-born religious greats such as St Francis of Assisi, right. He particularly is credited with transforming the Italian religious world and setting up Umbria as a center of pilgrimage, not just for everyday believers, but also for the bishops and popes – they adopted the land as their own in the risky years following the Church's move to Avignon, and continued to keep a base here even when the Church had returned to Rome.

The Middle Ages were also a time of great artistic innovation. Painters such as Pinturicchio created such celebrated works that artists such as Raphael, Giotto, Signorelli and Lorenzetti were drawn here to work on the great churches of Assisi, Perugia and Orvieto. The region also established itself as a center of learning thanks to numerous Benedictine and Franciscan monasteries, and the establishment of the University of Perugia in 1308.

To a Unified Italy

From this point on Umbria followed a similar fate to that of Tuscany – internal conflicts (notably Guelph versus Ghibelline) along with steady economic, artistic and spiritual growth up until the 16th century. Despite greater control from the Church, Umbria too joined the Italian State in 1860, settling happily into this new kind of rule.

The Industrial Revolution began to bring Umbria into the 20th century with extensive urban construction (and reconstruction after the Second World War) dotting what is still primarily a rural area. Like Tuscany, it gains much of its wealth from traditional agriculture and tourism. Etruscan wonders, Roman remains and medieval towns and hilltop villages bringing an increasing number of tourists to the region.

Chronology

900 BC	Etruscans arrive on the Island of Elba
700 BC	Commerce begins with Greece
600 BC	Confederation of Etruria's 12 most important cities (the "Dodecapolis")
508 BC	Lars Porsena, the Etruscan King of Chiusi leads a failed attack against Rome
395 BC	Rome takes the Etruscan city of Veii in Lazio
205 BC	Rome controls all of Tuscany and Umbria
59 BC	Roman army veterans found Florentia (Florence)
250	Oriental traders introduce Christianity to Florence
313	Christianity is made the official religion under Constantine
552	Goths attack Florence
570	Lombards conquer the north of Italy
774	Charlemagne, King of the Franks successfully campaigns against the Lombards
800	Charlemagne (Charles the Great) is made Emperor of the Holy Roman Empire
1062	Pisa takes Sicily and becomes the first Mediterranean port
1063	The first brick of Pisa's Duomo is laid
1152	Holy Roman Emperor Barbarossa invades Italy
1186	Siena Duomo is constructed
1215	Conflict between the Guelphs (pro-Pope) and the Ghibellines (pro-Emperor)
1220	Holy Roman Emperor Frederick II of Germany crowned
1224	St Francis of Assisi receives the stigmata at La Verna
1260	Siena beats Florence at Monteaperti
1284	Beaten by Genova, Pisa declines as a port
1294	Construction of Florence's Duomo
1300	Giovanni Pisano sculpts the pulpit for Pisa Cathedral
1302	Dante, exiled during the Guelph-Ghibelline conflict, begins *The Divine Comedy*
1345	Construction of Florence's Ponte Vecchio
1348-93	The plague kills half the Tuscan population
1350	Leaning Tower of Pisa finished and Boccaccio begins the *Decameron*
1377	Sir John Hawkwood named Captain of Florence
1419	Brunelleschi constructs the Spedale degli Innocenti
1426-1427	Massaccio frescoes the Cappella Brancacci
1434	Cosimo Il Vecchio returns from exile

1469	Laurent Il Magnifico inherits power
1478	The failed Pazzi conspiracy
1494	Charles VII attacks Florence, the Medici flee and Savonarola takes power
1498	Savonarola executed on the Piazza della Signoria
1502	Piero Soderini elected *gonfalonier* (chancellor of the new republic-city of Florence)
1504	Michelangelo finishes *David*
1509	Pope Giulio II starts to chase the French out of Italy
1513	Giovanni de' Medici becomes Pope Leo X
1521	Giulio de' Medici becomes Pope Clement VII and Medici retake power in Florence
1527	Imperial troops sack Rome, the Florentine Republic is reborn
1530	Florence under siege by the Pope and the Emperor
1531	Alessandro de' Medici becomes the first Duke of Florence
1532	Posthumous publication of *The Prince* by Machiavelli
1537	Cosimo I elected Grand Duke of Florence
1570	Cosimo I takes the title of Grand Duke of Tuscany
1575	The port of Livorno is created by Cosimo I
1633	Galileo Galilei is excommunicated
1737	End of the Medici and the transfer of power to the Lorraine Dynasty
1743	Death of Anna Maria Luisa, the last of the Medici
1765	Reforms by the Grand-Duke Leopoldo I
1790	Napoleon's first Italy campaign
1799	Defeat in Austria, Louis de Bourbon and then Elisa Baciocchi, govern Tuscany
1814	Napoleon exiled on the island of Elba
1814-1821	Stendhal's visit to Italy
1815	Waterloo
1865	Florence becomes the capital of Italy
1871	Capital returns to Rome
1896	First performance of Puccini's *La Bohême*
1915	Italy enters in WWI
1922	Mussolini directs first fascist government
1940	Italy enters WWII
1944	Tuscany suffers as the Nazis retreat
1946	Italy becomes a republic
1953	Italy joins NATO
1957-1965	Italian industrial boom
1966	Florence is flooded
1987	*Il Sorpasso* (the overtaking); the Italian economy becomes one of the strongest in Europe, briefly replacing the UK as the world's fifth-largest economy.
1993	A terrorist bomb damages the Galleria degli Uffizi
1994	Silvio Berlusconi becomes Prime Minister
1999	Italy adopts the Euro (the European Single Currency)

■ Architectural Styles

Romanesque (fifth to mid-13th centuries): A style that developed from Roman architecture and is characterized by the richly-decorated façades of 12th century churches and cathedrals in both Pisa (Pisan-Romanesque) and Lucca (Lucchese-Romanesque).

Gothic (13th to mid-15th centuries): The French Cistercians introduced the Gothic style to Tuscany when they built the Abbazia di San Galgano (1218, Siena province). It reached its zenith in Siena's Duomo. Often it can be seen mixed with previous Romanesque styles (such as in Assisi's Basilica di San Francesco) or influenced by the region (as in Pisan Gothic).

Renaissance (15th and 16th centuries): Tuscany returned to the principles of classic Roman architecture when Brunelleschi designed Florence's Spedale degli Innocenti (1419-24). The epitome of the style can be seen in the city's Palazzo Strozzi, with its arched windows, cornices, and level markers.

Baroque (late 16th to 17th centuries): A theatrical style, much appreciated by the Roman popes. San Stefano dei Cavallieri in Pisa is one of the best examples of a Tuscan Baroque façade, with columns, curved door arches, decorated windows and playful combinations of straight lines and curves.

Liberty (19th century): The Italian term for Art Nouveau, seen at its best in Montecatini Terme, Viareggio and Livorno. It was named after Liberty's (the shop) in London, which helped originate the style in the decorative arts and crafts that it sold.

■ Artistic Styles

The home of one of the most important artistic revolutions in history, Tuscany's art cities (Florence, Siena, Lucca, Pisa and Arezzo), contain works of art from the Middle Ages to the High Renaissance.

Medieval: Art designed for the support of prayer and contemplation, often featuring the Madonna (patron of many Tuscan towns and cities). The style is epitomized by Duccio's *Maestà* (1308-11, Museo dell'Opera del Duomo, Siena).

Renaissance: An artistic (and architectural) revolution that conquered all of Europe from the 15th century, the Renaissance took its first breath in Tuscany under the patronage of rich supporters such as the Medici. Its first bold steps into the use of perspective are epitomized by Masaccio's *Trinity* (1427, Chiesa di Santa Maria Novella, Florence) and his frescoes in the Cappella Brancacci (Florence).

Mannerism: Characterized by its intense colors, elongated bodies and deliberate poses, this style breathed new life into traditional biblical subjects under the careful hands of Andrea del Sarto (considered the first Mannerist), Pontormo and Rosso Fiorentino.

Macchiaioli: The Italian face of Impressionism, which took off in the 19th century, the style is well represented in Florence's Galleria degli Uffizi and in Livorno's Museo Civico with a collection dedicated to Giovanni Fattori, considered the style's biggest exponent.

The Big Names

1220-1284 Nicola Pisano
1241-1302 Cimabue (*Maestà* in the Uffizi, Crucifix in the Museo di Santa Croce)
1245-1301 Arnolfo di Cambio
1250-1314 Giovanni Pisano
1260-1318 Duccio di Buoninsegna (*Maestà* in the Uffizi, *Maestà* in the Museo dell Duomo in Siena)
1266-1337 Giotto di Bondone (*Maestà* in the Uffizi, frescoes in the Chiesa di Santa Croce)
1270-1348 Andrea Pisano
1284-1344 Simone Martini

1290-1348 Ambrogio Lorenzetti (frescoes of the *Effects of Good and Bad Government* in Siena's Palazzo Pubblico)

1308-1368 Andrea Orcagna (frescoes of *The Last Judgement* in the Chapel Strozzi at the Chiesa di Santa Maria Novella)

1374-1438 Jacopo della Quercia

1377-1446 Filippo Brunelleschi (the cupola of Florence's Duomo, the loggia of the Spedale degli Innocenti, the Chiesa di Santo Spirito, the central part of the Palazzo Pitti and, as a sculptor, the crucifix in the Chiesa di Santa Maria Novella)

1338-1447 Tommasso Masolino (frescoes in the Cappella Brancacci)

1378-1455 Lorenzo Ghiberti

1386-1466 Donatello (*David* and *St George* in the Bargello, the *Cantoria* and *Madeleine* in the Museo dell'Opera del Duomo)

c.1400-1455 Fra Angelico (frescoes in the Museo di San Marco)

1396-1472 Michelozzo

1397-1475 Paolo Uccello (frescoes in the Green Cloister at Santa Maria Novella, the *Battle of San Romano* in the Uffizi)

1400-1482 Luca della Robbia

1401-1428 Masaccio (*Trinity* in Santa Maria Novella and frescoes in Cappella Brancacci)

1406-1469 Fra Filippo Lippi

1420-1492 Piero della Francesca (*The Legend of the True Cross* in the Chiesa di San Francesco, Arezzo)

1420-1497 Benozzo Gozzoli (Chapel of the Magi in Palazzo Medici-Ricardi)

1435-1488 Verrocchio

1445-1510 Botticelli (*Spring* and *Birth of Venus* in the Uffizi and frescoes of St Augustin in the Chiesa di Ognissanti)

1449-1494 Ghirlandaio (frescoes in the choir of Santa Maria Novella, *The Last Supper* in Chiesa di Ognissanti and works in the Museo di San Marco and the Chiesa di Santa Trinità)

1452-1519 Leonardo da Vinci

1457-1504 Filippino Lippi

1475-1564 Michelangelo (*David* in the Galleria dell'Accademia, works in the Bargello and the Uffizi, with his only painting *Tondo Doni*, the New Sacristy of San Lorenzo and Casa Buonarroti)

1477-1549 Il Sodoma

1483-1520 Raphael

1486-1530 Andrea del Sarto

1494-1557 Jacopo Pontormo (portrait of Cosimo Il Vecchio in the Uffizi, frescoes and painting at the altar of Santa Felicità)

1495-1540 Rosso Fiorentino

1500-1571 Benvenuto Cellini (*Perseus* on the Loggia dei Lanzi)

1503-1572 Il Bronzino

1511-1574 Giorgio Vasari

1511-1592 Bartolomeo Ammannati

1529-1608 Giambologna

UNESCO World Heritage Sites

According to UNESCO, two-thirds of the world's historical artistic heritage can be found in Italy, Tuscany itself with more listed sites than the whole of Spain (the second-ranking country). Tuscany's UNESCO sites are:

- The historical center of **Florence** (see page 33)
- Pisa's **Piazza dei Miracoli** (see page 286)
- The historical center of **San Gimignano** (see page 160)
- The historical center of **Siena** (see page 143)
- The historical center of **Pienza** (see page 178)

Geography

The **Tuscan** region stretches south from the slopes of the Tosco-Emilian Apennines and along the Tyrrhenian Sea to Lazio in the south. It totals 18,000 square miles, including the seven islands of the Tuscan Archipelago. A mainly mountainous and hilly countryside inland, the coastline ranges between inhospitable rocks and long sandy expanses. The main cities are Florence, the capital, and the provincial capitals of Siena, Pisa, Arezzo, Pistoia, Prato, Lucca, Livorno, Grosseto and Massa Carrara.

The **Umbrian** region, 6,700 square miles, is adjacent to Tuscany's southeastern border and the only of Italy's regions not to border the sea. Located exactly in the center of the Italian Peninsula with its remaining borders marked out by Marche (east) and Lazio (south), it is mostly mountainous, with deep valleys running off the slopes of the Apennines that cut through its east. The regional capital and major city is Perugia; Terni is the capital, but the Umbrian territory also includes the other important cities of Assisi, Gubbio, Orvieto, Todi and Spoleto.

Mountains

Inside the confines of the towering **Apennines**, Tuscany has a range of mountainous terrain from the **Apuan Alps** in the Lucca and Massa Carrara provinces, the **Pratomagno range** shared between Florence and Arezzo, the **Chianti hills**, the Colline Metallifere on the border of Grosseto and Siena, the **Argentario**, a former island off the Grosseto coast and **Monte Amiata**. Linking through the Apennines, the most important of Tuscany's passes are the Passo della Cisa (Massa Carrara to La Spezia), the Passo dell'Abetone (between Pistoia and Modena), the Passo della Futa (linking Florence to Bologna) and the Passo dei Mandrioli (linking eastern Tuscany with Romagna).

Umbria is also dominated by the Apennines, especially the Monti Sibillini (now a national park) with its range of peaks over 2,000 m/6,560 ft (Monte Vettore the highest at 2,476 m/8,121 ft). It also includes the **Gubbio Apennines** (peaking with Monte Pennino, 1,570 m/5,150 ft), the **Monti Martani** (in the central and southern part of the region), the lower **Monti Amerini** in the west and **Spoleto mountain range** (both under 1,000 m/3,280 ft).

Parks

Tuscany

 Tuscany has two National and three Regional Parks: the National Park of the Tuscan Archipelago, the National Park of the Casentino Forests, the Apuan Alps Regional Park, the Maremma Regional Park and the Migliarino-San Rossore-Massaciuccoli Regional Park (found along the Lucchese and Pisan coasts).

National Park of the Tuscan Archipelago: How big is it? 17,887 ha/50,083 acres (plus 56,766 ha/140,232 acres of water).

Where is it? Out to sea on the islands of Elba, Gorgona, Capraia, Pianosa, Montecriso, Giglio and Giannutri.

Where can I find out more? Via Guerrazzi 1, Portoferraio, Elba, ☎ 0565-919411, www.islepark.it.

National Park of the Casentino Forests: How big is it? 38,118 ha/92,730 acres.

Where is it? An immense expanse of woods rich in flora and fauna on the border between Tuscany and Emilia-Romagna .

Where can I find out more? Via G. Brocchi 7, Pratovecchio, ☎ 0575-50301, www.parks.it/parco.nazionale.for.casentinesi.

Apuan Alps Regional Park: How big is it? 20,598 ha/57,674 acres.

Where is it? Between the Apennines and the Versilia Coast in an area known as the "marble mountains" for its rich mineral deposits.

Where can I find out more? Via Corrado del Greco 11, Seravezza, ☎ 0584-75821, www.parcapuane.toscana.it.

Maremma Regional Park: How big is it? 19,800 ha/55,440 acres.

Where is it? On Grosseto's coast, the territory includes both a California-style swampland with *butteri* (cowboys) herding wild cattle, and the more mountainous territory of Uccellina.

Where can I find out more? Loc. Pianacce, Alberese, ☎ 0564-407111, www.parks.it/parco.maremma.

Migliarino-San Rossore-Massaciuccoli Regional Park: How big is it? 23,115 ha/64,722 acres.

Where is it? A mix of dunes and wetland, the park runs alongside the Versilia Coast down into the province of Pisa.

Where can I find out more? Via Aurelia Nord 4, Pisa 050-525500, www.parks.it/parco.migliarino.san.rossore.

Umbria

Umbria has one National and six Regional Parks: the Monti Sibillini National Park and the Colfiorito, Monte Cucco, Monte Subasio, River Tiber, Lake Trasimeno and River Nera Regional Parks.

Monti Sibillini National Park: How big is it? 70,000 ha/196,000 acres

Where is it? In the center of Italy in the Kingdom of the mythic Sibilla, peaking at 2,476 m/7,400 feet (Monte Vettore).

Where can I find out more? Largo Gian Battista Gaola Antinori 1, Visso, ☎ 0737-972711, www.sibillini.net.

Colfiorito Regional Park: How big is it? 338 ha/946 acres.

Where is it? An immense plateau in the mid-western section of the Apennine chain.

Where can I find out more? Via Adriatica, Colfiorito di Foligno, ☎ 0742-681011, www.parks.it/parco.colfiorito.

Monte Cucco Regional Park: How big is it? 10,480 ha/29,344 acres.

Where is it? The northeastern territory of Umbria and the highest point of the Apennine Ridge (Monte Cucco 1,566 m/4,500 feet)

Where can I find out more? Villa Anita, Sigillo, ☎ 075-9177326, parco.montecucco@tiscalinet.it.

Monte Subasio Regional Park: How big is it? 7,442 ha/20,837 acres.

Where is it? In the middle of Valle Umbra dividing Assisi, Spello and Novera Umbra.

Where can I find out more? Cà Piombino, Assisi, ☎ 075-815181, parco.montesubasio@tiscalinet.it.

River Tiber Regional Park: How big is it? 7,925 ha/22,190 acres.

Where is it? Along the hill of Todi.

Where can I find out more? Civitella del Lago, Baschi, ☎ 0744-950732, parcotevere@libero.it.

Lake Trasimeno Regional Park: How big is it? 13,200 ha/36,960 acres.

Where is it? The largest lake in the Italian peninsula in the north of Umbria near the border with Tuscany.

Where can I find out more? Viale Europa, Passignano sul Trasimeno, ☎ 075-828059, parco.trasimeno@parks.it.

River Nera Regional Park: How big is it? 2,120 ha/5,936 acres.

Where is it? Called the "park of water" for its location along the Velino and Nera rivers and the Cascata delle Marmore, a hydroelectric station feeding Terni.

Where can I find out more? Via del Convento 2, Montefranco, ☎ 0744-389966, parconera@libero.it.

Coasts & Islands

The Tuscan coast ranges from the low, uniform and sandy beaches of the northern Apuan and Versilia coastlines (Lucca province) past the high and rocky bays of Livorno, down to the wide and sandy shores of the Piombino and Monte Argentario promontories (Grosseto province), the latter characterized by "tomboli" (cordons of sand). The Tuscan Archipelago (Elba, Gorgona, Capraia, Giglio, Pianosa, Montecristo and Giannutri) is characterized by high rugged coastlines and sandy bays.

Rivers & Lakes

Tuscany's most important river is the **Arno**, the longest in Italy, which descends from Monte Falterona through the north of the province to the sea. Secondary rivers include the **Magra** (Lunigiana), the **Serchio** (Garfagnana), the **Sieve** (Mugello) and the **Ombrone** (which flows into the Maremma). The territory's largest lake is **Lake Massaciuccoli**, running alongside the Versilia Coast.

The **Tiber River** crosses the entire region of Umbria from the north to its southwest; other important rivers include the **Nera** (the second-longest) and the

Velino (the tributary that forms the **Marmore Falls**, the highest in Europe at 160 m/525 ft). **Lake Trasimeno** is its most important lake, with **Piediluco**, the second-largest, followed by the man-made lakes of **Corbara** and **Alviano**.

Spas

Tuscany is one of Italy's most important spa regions, with springs used in Roman times still popular today. **Chianciano Terme** is the most visited (1,860,0000 people a year) with **Montecatini Terme** (at 1,700,000) close behind. Other important sites include the grotto-spas of **Monsummano Terme** and the hot springs of **Bagni di Lucca**, **Bagni San Filippo**, **San Carlo**, **San Casciano dei Bagni**, **San Giuliano**, **Caldana**, **Montepulciano**, **Petriolo**, **San Giovanni** and **Saturnia**. Umbria has three major spas at **Acquasparta**, **San Gemini** and **Fontecchio**.

Climate

 Tuscany and Umbria have a continental climate characterized by hot summers and cold winters. In the Tuscan Apennines, the snowfall allows for a winter sports season.

AVERAGE DAYTIME TEMPERATURES (°F)											
Jan	Feb	Mar	Apr	May	Jun	July	Aug	Sept	Oct	Nov	Dec
Umbria											
49	48	52	60	68	71	85	84	73	68	49	48
Tuscany											
52	55	61	66	73	81	86	86	81	72	61	54

Flora & Fauna

 **A**lthough it may not seem that way, Tuscany's natural vegetation has been greatly modified by the land reclamation work of previous generations. Man added much of the current coastal pine forests to shield the seaside from sea erosion; the much-photographed lines of cypress trees to protect the inland fields from the wind; and drained the swampland that once existed around Grosseto to enable the building of cities and roads there. And that's not even taking into account the acres of vineyards and olive groves that cover Tuscany's low-ground.

Natural vegetation does, of course, still exist. South along the coast, you'll find aromatic evergreen scrub and what remains of the original pinewood forests, while in the wide Alpine pastures of the north, there are beautiful white oak and chestnut woods to be explored. Add to this the towering silver firs and majestic old beeches of the Casentinesi Forests in the Arezzo region, and it comes as no surprise to learn that Tuscany has far more woodland than any other Italian region. In fact, it has such an extensive range of chestnut groves that it is currently ranked as one of the most important chestnut producers in the country.

By far the most interesting area of flora and fauna is in the Maremma on the southern Tuscan coast. Its unique strawberry bush scrub is thick with heather and juniper, evergreen oak and majestic cork, and there's also plenty of wildlife – wild boar, roe deer and porcupines on the ground, and birds of prey, such as harriers, soaring above. A visit to any natural park in a woodland area of Tuscany will uncover a rich wildlife. Even among the marble caverns and dizzy heights of the Apuan Alps, marmots and pine voles, and the indigenous Apuan newt have been recorded.

Economy

While the standard of living in Tuscany is higher than the national average, the agriculture-driven rural areas predictably drag behind the fortunes of the towns and cities. **Wine** and **olives** still make up the bulk of the products (mainly from Chianti, Lucca and Maremma), followed by **wheat** (Chianti), **vegetables** (Pisa and Empoli), **flowers** (Pescia and Viareggio), some **livestock** (the native breeds of cattle in Chianina, Pisana, Maremma), and the output of the declining mining industry (Grosseto, Valdarno, Campiglia Marittima, Volterra and the Apuan Alps). Industry is otherwise centered on metallurgy, engineering, chemicals, textiles, food, printing, tanning and glass-making, as well as traditional art and crafts (ceramics, lace, rush-weaving, wrought-iron). **Tourism** from the Versilia seaside resorts and the art cities (especially Siena and Florence) constitute an important part of the region's economy.

Tourism is equally important in Umbria, with Assisi, Spoleto, Perugia, Orvieto, and Castiglione representing the biggest draws. **Farming** (cereals, grapes, sugar beets, olives and cattle), **hydroelectrics** (from plants on the Nera at Terni), **chemicals**, **iron** and **steel**, **processed food**, and cotton and woolen **textiles** are all important factors to the region's economy.

Top Attractions

1. **Galleria degli Uffizi**: The best of the Renaissance in one huge art Florentine gallery (see page 38).
2. **Piazza del Campo**: Gently sloping site of Tuscany's plushest town hall and most famous event (see page 143).
3. **Basilica di San Francesco**: Home to Piero della Francesca's *Legend of the True Cross* fresco cycle (see page 436).
4. **The Maremma**: Wild hills and untouched beaches (see page 345).
5. **Pianosa**: Goats and quiet repose on the "Devil's Island" (see page 338).
6. **Lucca ramparts**: These Bourbon-remodeled avenues were once the venue for car races (see page 239).
7. **Pisa's Leaning Tower**: Get up there while it's still standing (see page 288).
8. **Vie Cave**: Mysterious hollow roads with walls as high as 60 m/197 ft (see page 355).
9. **Brunelleschi's Cupola**: The crowning glory of Florence's most recognizable attraction (see page 33).
10. **Grotta del Vento**: Rated as Italy's best cave, a treasure trove of stalactites and stalagmites, crystal-encrusted lakes and subterranean streams (see page 263).

11. **Pienza**: Pope Pius II's ideal city built by Bernardo Rosellino to Alberti's theories (see page 178).

12. **Statue-stele**: Stone idols from Lunigiana dating back over 4,000 years (see page 282)

13. **Face to Fresco**: A rare opportunity to get close up to the frescoes of Filippo Lippi (see page 114)

14. **The Torre Grossa**: The best known of Tuscany's medieval towers for its not-to-be-missed views over San Gimignano and the Val d'Elsa (see page 164-65).

15. **Going Underground**: A labyrinth of caves and tunnels hidden in the soft volcanic rock of the Etruscan Velzna (see page 383).

16. **The Marmore Falls**: The highest waterfalls in Italy (see page 398-99).

17. **Orvieto Duomo**: The pinnacle of Italian Gothic architecture (see page 382-82).

18. **Eugubine Tablets**: Gubbio's prized Etruscan possession (see page 442).

19. **Galleria Nazionale**: Perugia's important Gothic art collection (see page 363).

CONCESSION PRICING

Throughout this guide, you will see alternate admission prices labelled "conc." for various attractions. These are discounted prices that apply for special groups such as students, seniors or children.

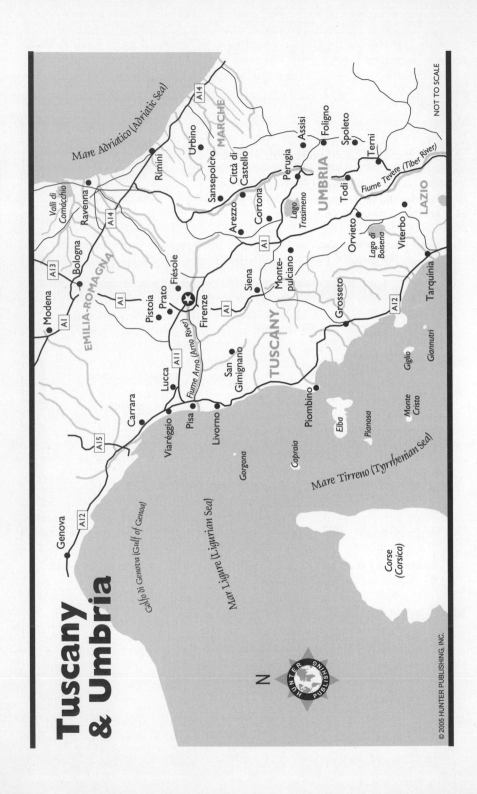

Tuscany & Umbria

NOT TO SCALE

Mare Adriatico (Adriatic Sea)

MARCHE

Urbino

Sansepolcro

Citta di Castello

Rimini

Valli di Comácchio

Ravenna

A14

Bologna

A13

EMILIA-ROMAGNA

Modena

A1

A1

Arezzo

Cortona

Perugia

Assisi

Foligno

Spoleto

Terni

UMBRIA

Todi

Lago Trasimeno

Fiume Tévere (Tiber River)

LAZIO

Orvieto

Lago di Boisena

Viterbo

Tarquinia

A12

Pistoia

Prato

Fiésole

Firenze

Siena

Monte-pulciano

TUSCANY

Grosseto

Lucca

A11

Fiume Arno (Arno River)

San Gimignano

Piombino

Viaréggio

Pisa

Livorno

Carrara

A15

Gorgona

Capraia

Elba

Pianosa

Monte Cristo

Giglio

Giannutri

Genova

A12

Golfo di Genova (Gulf of Genoa)

Mar Ligure (Ligurian Sea)

Mare Tirreno (Tyrrhenian Sea)

Corse (Corsica)

N

HUNTER PUBLISHING

© 2005 HUNTER PUBLISHING, INC.

Travel Information

■ Population

Tuscany: Approximately 3,500,000 inhabitants mostly concentrated in the cities of Florence (351,300), Livorno (147,700), Pisa (85,100), Pistoia (83,700), Arezzo (91,300) and Lucca (79,600).

Umbria: Approximately 813,400 inhabitants with by far the biggest concentrations in the cities of Perugia (148,200) and Terni (103,700).

■ Major Cities

Tuscany: The regional capital is Florence, with provincial capitals, Arezzo, Grosseto, Livorno, Lucca, Massa, Carrara, Pisa, Pistola, Prato and Siena.

Umbria: The regional capital is Perugia, also the capital of one of the region's two provinces (the other provincial capital being Terni).

■ Time Zone

Central European Time (GMT+1 hour), daylight savings from end of March to end of October, CET + 1 hour.

■ Money

The lira has been replaced by the euro (€), made up of 100 cents (in 1, 2, 5, 10, 20 and 50 eurocent pieces). The euro itself comes in coins (€1 and €2) and bank notes (€5, €10, €20, €50, €200 and €500). Credit cards are widely accepted with a daily Visa withdrawal limit of €250 in most banks and ATMs (Bancomat).

> **Exchange rates** as the time of writing are US$1.34 and GB£0.78 to €1 (€0.75 to US$1 and €1.45 to GB£1).

■ Banks

Banks are generally open Mon to Fri, 8:35 am-1:35 pm and 3-4 pm (closed on weekends). Travelers checks can be exchanged at most hotels, shops and foreign exchange offices.

■ Tipping

Although Italians themselves seem rarely or minimally to tip (service charges and state taxes being included in the price), tipping among tourists is common practice. Many tourist restaurants already suggest another 10% on top of your bill (much to the chagrin of locals). Your best bet is to play it by ear and tip for service (generally five to 10%) and not by obligation. Keep in mind that hotels have already added a service charge of 15-18% (included in the quoted price). All restaurants already figure a *pane e coperto* ("bread and cover") charge of anything from €1 and a 15% service charge into your bill. And you are already paying a bumped up price for your cappuccino if you drink it on the terrace with waiter service. That said, if you book a sightseeing guide or driver, or socialize in predominantly touristy areas, tipping is as obligatory as it is back home.

■ Language

English and French are widely understood in all tourist cities. However, locals do appreciate it when tourists make an effort to speak the local lingo even in its most basic form (see page 453 for some helpful phrases).

LEXICON	
Abbazia	abbey
Borgo	`quarter or village
CAI	Club Alpino Italiano
Campanile	church bell-tower usually detached
Cappella	chapel
Cenacolo	convent
Chiesa	church
Chiostro	cloister
Cortile	interior courtyard
Collegiata	collegiate church
Largo	street
Duomo	cathedral (from dome)
Loggia	arcaded ground floor
Lungarno	river quay (of the Arno)
Palazzo	palace
Piazza	quare
Piazzale	large square
Piazzata	small square
Pieve	parish church
Pro loco	local tourist office
Torre	tower
Via	road
Viale	avenue
Vicolo	alley

■ Religion

Although currently in decline, Italy's dominant religion is **Roman Catholicism** (80% of inhabitants). Churches are generally open from 7 am-noon and from 4:30-6 pm.

English-Language Services
Santa Maria del Fiore (Piazza del Duomo, Florence, Sat, 5 pm)
Chiesa di San Giovanni di Dio (Borgo Orgnissanti 16, Florence, Sun and holidays, 10 am)
St James American Episcopal (Via B. Ruccellai 9, Florence)

Church of England (Via Maggio 16, Florence)
Florence Synagogue (Via Farini 4)

■ Electricity

The electric current is 50Hz 220V, with two-hole round-pronged plugs (adaptors are necessary).

■ Opening Times

Normal opening hours for **shops** run from 9 am-1 pm and 3:30-7:30 pm, although some large city shops stay open through the lunch break. Sun closing is still common practice outside the major cities. **Post offices** are open Mon-Fri, 8:30 am-5 pm, Sat, 8:30 am-noon.

■ Communications

Mail: Stamps (*francobolli*) can be purchased at *tabacchi* (tobacco and newspaper shops) or at the Post Office; specify the destination before you purchase.

Phone: Public telephones accept coins, cards (*carta telefonica*, available from newsstands, tabacchi and some caffès in denominations of €5 and, increasingly, credit cards. In major cities, you'll also find phone shops, with rates to match the telephone cards but with the added benefit of noiseless and private cubicles. The code to reach Italy is +39 but, unlike some European countries, here you do not drop the first "0" of the city or provincial code. You must always dial the city code (for example Florence is 055) even if you are in the city itself. Traditionally, phone numbers with six digits after the city code denote home phones, while those with five digits belong to businesses.

Internet: It's becoming increasingly easy to find Internet cafés in Tuscan cities, most charging a flat hourly rate (€2) and usually within walking distance of the major attractions. Florence, for example, has four cafés just off the Piazza del Duomo. You can check up on options before you depart at http://cafe.ecs.net.

> **Tip:** Many Internet cafés also rent laptops and mobile phones while their notice-boards are an incomparable source of information on rooms to rent and local events.

Newspapers: Most newsstands in larger cities offer an extensive range of English-language publications.

■ When to Go

Both Tuscany and Umbria are at their best in the cooler spring and autumn months. Summer brings an often-unbearable heat as well as the worst of the tourist crowds, which are at their peak during the Easter months. May and June are the best times for flora and fauna, as well as local events. The **events** calendar is full to the brim in many Tuscan towns and villages, especially in the lead-up to St. John the Baptist Day (24th June), while the wine and truffle-hunting festivities start off in September. August is the time to avoid, when Tuscans themselves flee their cities for a bit of fresh air by the sea, leaving restaurants, bars and shops shut in their wake (a holiday known as *ferragosto*). The quietest season is during the chilly winter months when there are fewer tourists on the streets and cheaper hotel prices to match (the low season typically runs November to March).

NATIONAL HOLIDAYS			
January 1	New Year	June 2	National Day
January 6	Epiphany	August 15	Assumption (start of *ferragosto*)
April 23	Easter Sunday	November 1	All Saints Day
April 24	Easter Monday	December 8	Immaculate Conception
April 25	Liberation Day	December 25	Christmas Day
May 1	Labor Day	December 26	Boxing Day

■ Required Documents

Valid passports are required for all visitors, with the exception of citizens from the EU for whom a valid identity card will suffice. US visitors do not require a visa but are limited to a stay of 90 days. Visas are required for other non-EU citizens. Check with your embassy on current requirements prior to travel. Tourists must register within three days of arrival with the local police (any booked accommodation will complete this formality for you).

Foreign Consulates in Florence

Austria (Lungarno Vespucci 58, ☎ 055-2654222, fax 055-295474, Mon-Fri, 10 am-noon)

Belgium (Via dei Servi 28, ☎ 055-282094, fax 055-294745, Mon-Fri, 9 am-noon)

China (Via dei della Robbia 89, ☎ 055-5058188, fax 055-5520698, Mon-Fri, 9 am-1 pm, 4-7 pm)

Denmark (Via dei Servi 13, ☎ 055-211007, fax 055-289333, Mon-Fri, 9-11 am)

Russian Federation (Corso Italia 8, ☎ 055-2608940, fax 055-2740710, by appointment only)

Finland (Via degli Strozzi 6, ☎ 055-293228, fax 055-28052, Mon-Fri, 9 am-1 pm, 3:30-7 pm)

France (Piazza Ognissanti 2, ☎ 055-2302556, fax 055-2302551, Mon-Fri, 9 am-12:30 pm, 2-4 pm, by appointment only)

Germany (Lungarno A. Vespucci 30, ☎ 055-294722, fax 055-281789, Mon-Fri, 9 am-12:30 pm)

Great Britain (Lungarno Corsini 2, ☎ 055-284133, fax 055-219112, Mon-Fri, 9:30 am-12:30 pm, 2:30-4:30 pm)

Greece (Via Cavour 38, ☎/fax 055-2381482, Mon-Fri, 9 am-1 pm)

Luxembourg (Via Palestro 4, ☎ 055-284232, fax 055-2676050, Mon-Fri, 9 am-1 pm, 2-6 pm)

Mexico (Via A. della Lana 4, ☎/fax 055-217831, Mon/Thurs, 9:30 am-noon)

Norway (Via G. Capponi 26, ☎ 055-2479321, fax 055-2342629, Mon-Fri, 9 am-noon, 2:30-6 pm)

Portugal (Corso Tintori 3, ☎ 055-2343543, Mon-Fri, 9 am-1 pm, 2:30-7 pm)

Spain (Via Lamberti 2, ☎ 055-2608606, Tues/Thurs, 10 am-1 pm)

Sweden (Via B. Lupi 14, ☎ 055-499536, fax 055-471858, Mon-Fri, 10 am-noon, Wed, 4-6 pm, emergencies only)

Switzerland (Hotel Park Palace, Piazzale Galileo, ☎ 055-222434, fax 055-220517, Tues/Fri, 4-5 pm)

USA (Lungarno A. Vespucci 38, ☎ 055-2398276, fax 055-284088, Mon-Fri, 9 am-noon, 2-3:30pm)

■ Value Added Tax & Tax-Free Shopping

Non-EU citizens can claim tax refunds for goods intended for personal use either in the shop itself or in the airport prior to travel. For further information on refunds, see www.agenziadogane.it/italiano/dcagp/iva/iva-inglese.htm. Some shops, displaying the "tax-free shopping" sign, enable you to purchase products without paying tax if you show a valid passport.

■ Health

No vaccinations are required to enter Italy or to reenter the US, Canada, Great Britain and other countries in the EU. While European citizens are covered by the E111, US, Canadian and many other non-EU citizens do not benefit from a recip-rocal agreement and are advised to take out an insurance policy before traveling. In the event of a medical emergency, hospital emergency rooms (*pronto soccorso*) offer a free service (charges may apply if your case is not deemed an emergency), while medicines can be obtained only from a pharmacy (whether by prescription or over the counter). General pharmacy opening hours are Mon to Sat, 8:30 am-12:30 pm and 3-7:30 pm, with 24-hour service common inside major train stations.

EMERGENCY TELEPHONE NUMBERS	
112	Carabinieri (a branch of the police)
113	Police
115	Fire Department
116	ACI (Italian Automobile Club)
118	Ambulance
176	International telephone inquires

■ Accommodation

Costs & Types of Accommodation

 While Italy has a generic star-classification system for **hotels**, most star categoriesfrom the deluxe five-star down to the most basic one-star – are fixed with the provincial tourist office and quality and prices can vary considerably between provinces. Prices are generally lower during the off-season months (November to March) and even hotels that enforce a set price throughout the year can be bargained down during this time. Prices include taxes, service, heating and/or air-conditioning.

HOTEL PRICE CHART	
Rates are per room with private bath, based on double occupancy, including breakfast.	
$	Under €40
$$	€41-€85
$$$	€86-€140
$$$$	€141-€210
$$$$$	Over €210

Italian **B&Bs** should not be confused with the British version; most are simply one- and two-hotels offering rooms on a bed-and-breakfast basis.

At a lower price than hotels, *affitacamere* are rooms for rent in private homes throughout Italy. Although they don't rate them, the tourist office is your best point of reference for *affitacamere* in town. Reservations for private rooms in Tuscany can also be made through AGAP (Associazione Gestori Alloggi Privati, Piazza San Marco 7, ☎/fax 055-284100, www.agap.it).

Accommodation is also available in **convents, monasteries** and other **religious institutions**. Information, including any curfew details, is available from relevant tourist offices.

Agriturismi are farm-based houses generally rented out by the week but increasingly shorter terms (minimum two nights) are becoming available. For information on farm holidays, contact **Agriturist** (Via degli Alfani 67, Florence, ☎ 055-287838, fax 055-2302285, agritosc@confagricoltura.it), **Terranostra** (Via della V. Demidoff 64d, Florence, ☎ 055-3245011, fax 055-3246612, www.terranostra.it/toscana) or **Turismo Verde** (Via Verdi 5, Florence, ☎ 055-20022, fax 055-2345039, www.turismoverde.it).

Youth hostels, while generally run by the Associazione Italiana Alberghi per la Gioventù (Via Cavour 44, Rome, ☎ 06-4871152, fax 06-4880492), are springing up in major cities as a budget equivalent to even the cheapest hotels. Unlike traditional youth hostels, they do not impose a curfew or age limit, or require you to be a YHA member.

Camping in Italy is a popular pastime and more luxurious than in some other European countries, with 1,700 official campgrounds ranging from a no-star to three-star basis and often including an outdoor swimming pool and sports facilities. A complete list of campgrounds is available from the **Federazione delle Associazioni Italiane dei Complessi Turistico-Ricettivi dell'Aria Aperta** (FAITA, Via Properzio 5, Roma, ☎ 06-3574308, 06-3574217).

The CAI (Club Alpino Italiano) runs the majority of the **mountain huts** in Italy, publishing a yearly guide with information on access and rates as well as location. The contact details of local branches are listed in each regional chapter.

■ Dining

Meals

The Italian **breakfast**, *colazione*, tends to be a light affair with a *pasta* (a sweet pastry such as a chocolate-filled croissant) accompanied by a *cappuccino* (coffee with milk), a simple *caffè* (an espresso, a short black coffee) or a *caffè lungo* (a double espresso), and is often taken standing at the caffè bar. In larger cities, you can also order an *americano* (an espresso with hot water); as the name suggests, this is a recent addition for non-espresso-loving tourists. Most Italians can't see the point of adding hot water to a perfectly good coffee! You may also provoke some raised eyebrows if you order a cappuccino after dinner (it is traditionally drunk only in the morning or afternoon) or a *caffè latte* at any time of the day (in Italy, it is a kids' breakfast drink).

DINING PRICE CHART	
Price per person for an entrée, including house wine &cover.	
$	Under €20
$$	€21-€40
$$$	€41-€60
$$$$	Over €60

The Italian **lunch**, *pranzo*, while traditionally the long and leisurely meal of the day, is increasingly becoming a more hurried affair, especially in larger cities where the evening **dinner**, *cena,* has become the major meal (generally eaten from 8 pm). Both menus consist of an *antipasto* (starter), a *primo piatto* (the first course, generally pasta, rice or soup), a *secondo piatto* (the main course of meat or fish) accompanied by a *contorno* (vegetable or salad side-dishes), finished with *dolci* (sweet dessert) or *frutta* (fresh fruit), then an espresso and a *grappa* or *amaro* (bitter herb-based digestive). Most Italians do not generally eat a dish from each course, usually opting for an *antipasto* then *secondo* with *contorno*, or *primo* then *secondo* with *contorno*.

The Locales

The traditional venue for dining is the **ristoranto** (restaurant), but cheaper and less formal meals (especially those derived from local specialties) are at a **trattoria** and **osteria**.

Pizzerie, although specializing in pizzas, also offer a trattoria-like menu with dishes generally as good as their pizza range at a lower price. Cheaper still – although increasingly difficult to find in touristy areas – are **rosticceria**, which serve simple meals (generally roasted meats with a vegetable *contorno*) on a sit-down or take-out basis. You can also opt for a cheap slice of pizza at a **pizza taglie** (hole-in-the-wall pizza counters).

Enoteche (wine bars) often serve a light range of meals to accompany your wine choice, while many bars offer free *antipasti* (serve yourself from the counter) when you order an aperitif. If you want a light lunch or snack, most bars and caffès offer a range of pre-prepared *panini* (flat-bread sandwiches). But for top-quality, get yourself to a **panineria**, which makes sandwiches for you.

> **Tip:** In caffès you should pay first at *la cassa* and then take your ticket (*lo scontrino*) to the bar, unless you're being served from the terrace where prices are higher to reflect the waiter service (up to twice the bar price; check on the wall menu inside before you order).

Travel Information

■ Transportation

By Air: Domestic service between Italian airports is mainly offered by **Alitalia** (☎ 800-050350, www.alitalia.com), which provides flights to Tuscany and Umbria's main airports at Pisa and Florence. Visitors arriving via Rome Fiumicino or Bologna will find convenient train and bus links into both Tuscany and Umbria.

By Rail: The Italian railway network is managed by the **Ferrovie dello Stato** (FS, ☎ 848-888088, www.trenitalia.it) with connections throughout Italy and into France, Switzerland, Austria and the rest of Europe. While its service is by no means extensive in the rural Tuscan and Umbrian areas, it does offer a convenient and generally reliable means of travel at a very reasonable price. Rates are calculated based on the distance traveled, enabling you to pick up kilometer tickets (in denominations of 10) if you don't wish to get in line each time you jump on a train.

All tickets must be validated in the platform ticket machines (generally yellow) prior to travel to avoid fines. Supplements, unless holders of a Euro-rail or BTLC pass, are cheaper for certain fast trains (see below) and for the transportation of bicycles (from €3.62 to €5.16 dependent on train type) on trains marked with the bicycle symbol. You can pick up a timetable for the whole of Italy (known as *Il Pozzorario*, €4) from station newsstands. Discounts are available for tourist groups, families and travelers over 60 or under 26 years of age.

TRAIN TYPES

- **ES Eurostar**: International express trains also linking major domestic towns. Reservations and supplementary fare required.
- **EC Eurocity**: International express day train (its nocturnal equivalent is the **EN Euronight**). Reservations and supplementary fare required.
- **IC Intercity**: Rapid trains covering both domestic and international destinations. Supplementary fare charges may apply.
- **EX Espresso**: Express trains.
- **IR Interregionali**: Interregional trains stopping at all major (if not all) stations.
- **REG Regionali**: Regional trains generally stopping at all stations.

By Bus: Good coach and bus services link Italian cites and towns throughout Tuscany and Umbria. Their contact details are listed in the *Getting Here* sections of each chapter. As in the case of trains, bus tickets should be validated in the ticket machine once on-board.

By Car: Italy has an extensive and well-maintained road network, free but for the major *autostrade* (highways, indicated by the letter "A"), which charge minimal rates for usage (tolls are generally paid in cash). Autostrade route-planning maps and toll information is available online (www.autostrade.it). Italian road distances are in kilometers. As a general guide, one km is equivalent to 0.621 miles and one mile to 1.609 km.

Speed limits are set at 50 km/30 miles) per hour in built-up areas, 90 km/ 55 miles per hour on secondary roads, 110 km/70 miles per hour on main roads and 130 km/80 miles per hour on highways. As in all of continental Europe, vehicles drive on the right. Seatbelts must be worn both in the back and the front and the use of handheld portable telephones by the driver is prohibited. You must have held a driving license for over a year to rent a car in Italy.

Most service stations provide regular leaded gasoline (*benzina*), unleaded (*senza piombo*) and diesel (*gasolio*) pumps, and stations in smaller towns still offer pump service. Outside station hours (7:30 am-12:30 pm, 3-7 pm), you can fill up by entering your credit card or bank notes into the vending machine and choosing the fuel of choice on the keypad.

■ Information Sources

Information & Maps: The Italian tourist office in the UK (1 Princes Street, London, W1B 2AY, ☎ 020-74081254, fax 020-73993567) and the two offices in the USA, located in New York (630 Fifth Avenue, Suite 1565, New York, NY 10111, ☎ (212)-245-4822, fax (212)-586-9249) and Los Angeles (12400 Wilshire Boulevard, Suite 550, Los Angeles, CA 90025, ☎ (310)-8200098/8209807, fax (310)-8206357) are invaluable sources of information. Check out www.enit and www.italiantourism.com. The provinces of Tuscany and Umbria also have their own portals, www.turismo.toscana.it, www.umbria.org and www.umbria2000.it. More local offices are listed under the *Information Sources* section of each regional chapter.

Visitors with Disabilities: ANTHAI (Associazione Nazionale Tutela Handicappati ed Invalidi, Corso V. Emanuele 154, Rome, ☎ 06-68219168, fax 06-68892684, Mon-Fri, 9 am-1 pm, 2-8 pm) provides general information and assistance.

Travel Information

Going Metric

GENERAL MEASUREMENTS

1 kilometer = .6124 miles

1 mile = 1.6093 kilometers

1 foot = .304 meters

1 inch = 2.54 centimeters

1 square mile = 2.59 square kilometers

1 pound = .4536 kilograms

1 ounce = 28.35 grams

1 imperial gallon = 4.5459 liters

1 US gallon = 3.7854 liters

1 quart = .94635 liters

TEMPERATURES

For Fahrenheit: Multiply Centigrade figure by 1.8 and add 32.

For Centigrade: Subtract 32 from Fahrenheit figure and divide by 1.8.

Centigrade	Fahrenheit
40°	104°
35°	95°
30°	86°
25°	77°
20°	64°
15°	59°
10°	50°

Tuscany

Florence

Visitors have been drawn to Florence's architectural and artistic treasures for centuries – and for good reason. But, with an historical center of only half a square-mile, it can be hard to see the sights through the crowds. The throng on the Duomo steps, the lines for the Uffizi and the jostling for photos on Piazzale Michelangelo all require a good dose of patience, especially under the blistering summer heat. Fortunately, early evening offers a respite; the quieter streets and softer lighting at that time bring out the colors of the marble-clad cathedral topped by Filippo Brunelleschi's archetypal dome, the sheer immensity of the Palazzo Vecchio and the charm of the medieval Ponte Vecchio, with its shops latched shut for the night. But avoiding the lines when you enter the buildings and museums takes some preparation, especially if you arrive in the busiest and hottest summer months when the only option is to drag yourself out of bed at sunrise to beat the crowds to the 8:15 am openings.

NOT TO BE MISSED

- **Piazza del Duomo**: Famous address of the Duomo, Campanile and Battistero (see page 33-34).
- **Galleria degli Uffizi**: The most select picture gallery in the world and potent symbol of Medici power (see page 38).
- **Palazzo Vecchio**: Medieval town hall architecture at its most forceful (see page 37).
- **Galleria dell'Accademia**: Home to Michelangelo's *David* (see page 48).
- **Via dei Tornabuoni**: Even if you can't afford to buy, you'll enjoy the window-shopping on this luxury-laden street (see page 67).
- **Piazza Repubblica**: The 19th century makes its mark (see page 42).
- **Museo Nazionale del Bargello**: Florence's national sculpture museum (see page 52).
- **Giardino di Boboli**: Sculpture-packed gardens behind the museum-packed Palazzo Pitti (see page 55).
- **The Oltrano**: A warren of narrow streets filled with artisan workshops and some great restaurants (see page 52).
- **Piazzale Michelangelo**: The classic Florentine view (see page 56).

Florence

- **The churches**: Santa Maria Novella, San Lorenzo, Orsanmichele, Santa Croce, Santo Spirito and San Miniato al Monte are just some of the delights on offer.
- **The markets**: Shopping the Florentine way (see page 67).
- **Ponte Vecchio**: Medieval bridge architecture at its most splendid (see page 41).
- **Le Murate**: Atmospheric ex-convent and ex-prison now the venue for Firenze Estate events (see page 67).

Getting Here

 By Air: Most visitors arrive via Pisa's **Aeroporto Galileo Galilei** (☎ 050-849202, www.pisa-airport.com), from which hourly trains run directly to Florence (€9.80 round-trip; buy tickets in the Arrivals hall).

From Florence's ever-growing **Aeroporto Amerigo Vespucci** (☎ 055-3061700, www.safnet.it) three miles to the northwest of the city center, **Sita** (☎ 800-373760, www.sita-on-line.it) and **ATAF** (☎ 800-424500, www.ataf.net) jointly run a *vola in bus* (airport shuttle) service to Florence's main Santa Maria Novella train station (9:15 am-11 pm, every 30 mins, €4 one-way, buy on board), while the less comfortable ATAF city Bus #62 runs every 25 mins (6 am-11 pm, €1 one-way) to the same location. Taxis to the center cost around €15.

You can also fly to **Milan** (www.sea-aeroportimilano.it), **Rome** (www.adr.it) or **Bologna** (www.bologna-airport.it), all of which are connected by regular trains to Florence Santa Maria Novella (Firenze S.M.N.).

 By Train: The majority of trains (☎ 848-888088, www.trenitalia.it) arrive at Florence's main Santa Maria Novella train station (Firenze S.M.N.) in the center of town. City buses and licensed taxis can be picked up from just outside. If your train stops at outlying stations such as Campo Marte and Rifredi, there are frequent train and bus connections into the center of town (ATAF buses #12 and #13 from Campo Marte, #5 from Rifredi).

 By Bus: The main bus company serving Florence from destinations within Italy is Sita (☎ 800-373760, www.sita-on-line.it), which drops you off in the bus station on Via S. Caterina da Siena, just across the road from Firenze S.M.N. It is also served by Rama (☎ 0564-25215, www.griforama.it) with service from Grosseto and the south and LAZZI (☎ 055-215155, www.lazzi.it) from Lucca and the west.

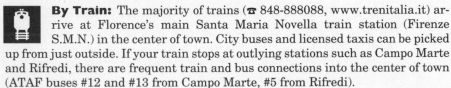 **By Car:** The main A1 Rome-Bologna-Milan highway skirts the west and south of Florence with the Firenze Nord and Firenze Sud toll-paying exits being the easiest and best signposted routes of arrival. From Pisa Airport, it's best to head north to join the A11 Livorno-Pisa-Florence approach.

> **Tip:** Parking in the city can be difficult. It's best to leave your car a little outside of the center in the parking spaces at Fortezza da Basso (behind Firenze S.M.N.). Check out **Firenze Parcheggi** (☎ 055-5001994, www.firenzeparcheggi.it) for up-to-date information on parking in the city.

Getting Around Town

With such a compact historical center, Florence is easy to navigate. Firenze S.M.N. is only a five-minute walk from the Duomo (you'll see the cupola as soon as you step out of the station), which stands more of less in the center of all the main sights. Walking is the best way to get around despite the crowded streets but, if you do need to use public transport, hop onto one of the frequent electrical ATAF buses which pilot the center's narrow streets at an impressive speed.

Addresses in Florence can be a bit confusing, with two methods of street numbering: black and red. Black numbers are traditionally meant for residences, while the red, followed by the letter "r" (short for *rosso*) denotes shops and other commercial premises such as restaurants and hotels. Be aware that the two sets of numbers do not always follow in an obviously logical pattern and 1r (red) is not necessarily next to the ordinary 1 (black) or even the 3r (red).

By Bus: ATAF (Piazza Stazione, ☎ 800-424500, www.ataf.net) lines A, B, C and D are the most useful central bus routes (7:50 am-8 pm, every 10 minutes). Bus #A runs from Firenze S.M.N. past Piazza Repubblica and Orsanmichele to the northeast; B takes you back and forth along the Arno past the Uffizi; C traverses the two sides of the river from Piazza San Marco in the north to the Ponte Vecchio in the south; as does D, this time on the west of the city taking in Piazza Carmine and Piazza Santo Spirito before returning to Firenze S.M.N. Tickets can be bought from the ATAF desk at Piazza Stazione (☎ 800-424500, 7 am-8 pm) or from most bars and tabacchi, and must be validated in the bus ticket machine. The exception is from 9 pm-6 am, when tickets must be bought on board at the higher price of €2; exact change required. Choose between the standard 60-minute (€1), the three-hour (€1.80), the *multiplo* (equivalent to four 60-minute tickets, €3.90), the 24-hour (€4), the two-day (€5.70), the three-day (€7.20) and the seven-day (€12) passes.

THE CARTA ARANCIO (ORANGE CARD)

*If you plan to travel extensively by bus or train in the province of Florence (and Prato), save money on fares with the seven-day **Carta Arancio** (€21.69), available from train stations or bus company ticket offices), valid on all buses and REG or regional trains.*

By Taxi: Taxis line up outside the station and at major tourist hubs such as Piazza Repubblica, Piazza San Marco and Piazza Santa Croce. All rides are metered. If you want to call a cab, **Radiotaxi** (☎ 055-4390/4499/4798/4242) offers swift and reliable service, telling you the exact time your cab should arrive (usually within five minutes).

By Car: Although indispensable for exploring the surrounding Tuscan countryside, navigating Florence by car isn't recommended. It really makes little sense to bring a car into the badly signposted one-way system, to spend hours circling the city looking for parking spaces or to pay the extra surcharge for garage spaces at your hotel when you can cross the historical center in less than half an hour on foot. If you do rent a car in order to head out of town, it is considerably cheaper to do so with one of the big names before arrival. If you book

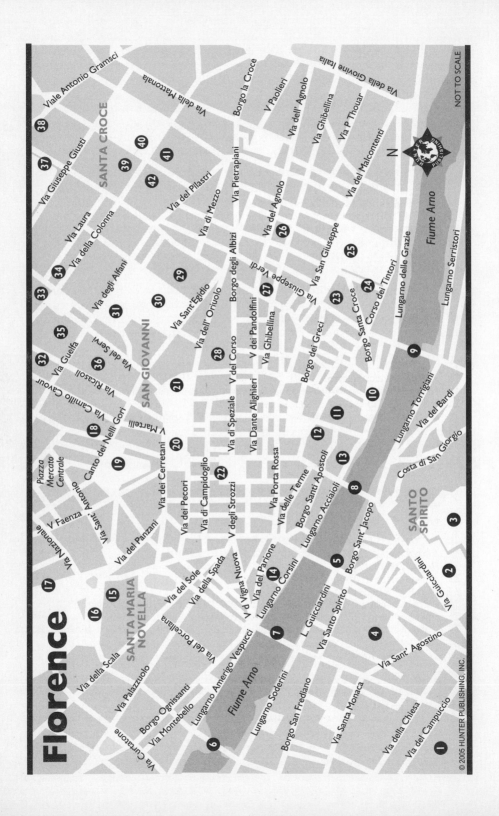

Florence

SANTA CROCE

SANTA MARIA NOVELLA

SAN GIOVANNI

SANTO SPIRITO

Viale Antonio Gramsci

Via Giuseppe Giusti

Via della Mattonaia

Borgo la Croce

V Paolieri

Via dell' Agnolo

Via Ghibellina

Via P Thouar

Via della Giovine Italia

Via Laura

Via della Colonna

Via del Pilastri

Via Pietrapiani

Via del Agnolo

Via del Malcontenti

Via degli Alfani

Via di Mezzo

Via San Giuseppe

Via Giuseppe Verdi

Via Sant'Egidio

Via dell' Oriuolo

Borgo degli Albizi

Via dei Pandolfini

Borgo Santa Croce

Corso dei Tintori

Via del Servi

Via dei Servi

Via Ricasoli

V dei Corso

V Ghibellina

Borgo dei Greci

Lungarno delle Grazie

Via Guelfa

Via Camillo Cavour

V Martelli

Via di Speziale

Via Dante Alighieri

Via Nelli Gori

Via dei Cerretani

Via di Campidoglio

Via Porta Rossa

Borgo Santi Apostoli

Costa di San Giorgio

Piazza Mercato Centrale

V Faenza

Via Sant'Antonio

Via dei Pecori

V degli Strozzi

Via delle Terme

Lungarno Acciaioli

Lungarno Torrigiani

Via del Bardi

Via Nazionale

Via del Panzani

Via del Sole

Via della Spada

V d Vigna Nuova

Via del Parione

Lungarno Corsini

Borgo Sant' Jacopo

Via Curtatone

Via della Scala

Via del Porcellana

Via Palazzuolo

Borgo Ognissanti

Via Montebello

Lungarno Amerigo Vespucci

Lungarno Soderini

Borgo San Frediano

L. Guicciardini

Via Santo Spirito

Via Sant' Agostino

Via Santa Monaca

Via della Chiesa

Via del Campuccio

Fiume Arno

Lungarno Serristori

Fiume Arno

Via Guicciardini

N

NOT TO SCALE

© 2005 HUNTER PUBLISHING, INC.

Florence Key

1. Giardino Torrigiani
2. Palazzo Pitti
3. Giardino di Boboli
4. Santo Spirito, Casa di Bianca, Palazzo Ridolfi
5. Palazzo Frescobaldi, Santo Jacopo Sopr'arno, Ponte S. Trinita
6. Ponte Amerigo Vespucci
7. Ponte alla Carraia
8. Ponte Vecchio
9. Ponte alla Grazie
10. Borsa
11. Galleria degli Uffizi (*Uffizi Gallery*)
12. Loggia della Signoria
13. Santo Stefano, Corridoio Vasariano
14. Palazzo Corsini, Santa Trinita
15. Santa Maria Novella
16. Stazione Centrale di Santa Maria Novella
17. Air Terminal
18. Palazzo Medici Riccardi
19. Cappelle Medicee, Santo Lorenzo, Biblioteca Laurenziana, Santo Giovanni
20. Battistero, San Salvatore del Vescavo
21. Duomo, Palzzo Niccolini, Museo dell'Opera del Duomo, Palazzo Guadagni
22. Piazza della Repubblica, Palazzo Vecchietti
23. Casa dell'Antella
24. Palazzo Corsini, Palazzo Rasponi
25. Santa Croce, Biblioteca Nazionale
26. Casa Buonarotti
27. Teatro Verdi, Palazzo Quaratesi
28. Museo di Antropologia, Santa Maria in Campo, Teatro Stabile, Palazzo Altovitti, Palazzo Albizi
29. Santo Egidio
30. Teatro della Pergola
31. Piazza Brunelleschi, Ospedale Santa Maria Nuove
32. Piazza San Marco
33. Università, S.S. Annunziata
34. Museo Archeologico
35. Accademia di Belle Arti, Officio della Pietre Dure, Palazzo della Regione
36. Palazzo Gerini, Palazzo Niccolini, Palazzo Pucci
37. Orto-Botanico, Giardino della Gherardesca
38. Cimitero degli Inglesi
39. Palazzo Paneiatichi Ximenes
40. Piazza Massimo d'Azeglio
41. Chiesa Israelitica
42. Santa Maria dei Pazzi

while here, go for a smaller locally based company for the best deal (usually around €65 a day, €355 per week).

Car Rental

Pisa Airport

Auto Europa (☎ 050-506883, www.sbc.it)
Avis (☎ 050-42028, www.avisautonoleggio.it)
Easy Car (☎ 050-2201219, www.easycarspa.com),
Europcar (☎ 050-41081, www.europcar.it)
Hertz (☎ 050-43220, www.hertz.it)
Liberty Rent International (☎ 050-48088, www.libertyrent.it)
Maggiore (☎ 050-42574, www.maggiore.it)
Sixt (☎ 050-28101, www.e-sixt.it)
Thrifty (☎ 050-45490, www.italybycar.it)

Florence Airport

Avis (☎ 055-315588, www.avisautonoleggio.it)
Europcar (☎ 055-318609, www.europcar.it)
Hertz (☎ 055-307370, www.hertz.it)
Maggiore (☎ 055-311256, www.maggiore.it)
Sixt (☎ 055-309790, www.e-sixt.it)
Thrifty (☎ 055-300413, www.italybycar.it).

Florence

Auto Europa (Via Il Prato 47r, ☎ 055-213333, www.sbc.it)
Avis (Via B. Ognissanti 128r, ☎ 055-213629, www.avisautonoleggio.it)
Easy Car (Via della Scala 53r, ☎ 055-284366, www.easycarspa.com)
Europcar (Via B. Ognissanti 53r, ☎ 055-290437, www.europcar.it)
Excelsior (Via Lulli 76, ☎ 055-3215397, www.excelsiorent.it)
Happyrent (Via B. Ognissanti 153r, ☎ 055-2399696)
Hertz (Via M. Finiguerra 33r, ☎ 055-2398025, www.hertz.it)
Maggiore (Via M. Finiguerra 31r, ☎ 055-21038, www.maggiore.it)
Maxirent (Via B. Ognissanti 155r, ☎ 055-2654207)
Program (Via B. Ognissanti 135r, ☎ 055-282916)
Sixt (Via Il Prato 80r, ☎ 055-2382480/1, www.e-sixt.it)
Travel Car (Via B. Ognissanti 108r, ☎ 055-210202, www.travelcar.it)

Information Sources

? **T**he very helpful **Agenzia per il Turismo (APT) di Firenze** (Florence tourist office, www.firenze.turismo.toscana.it) has offices on Piazza Stazione (☎ 055-212245, fax 055-2381226, Mon-Sat, 8:30 am-7 pm, Sun, 8:30 am-1:30 pm), Via Cavour 1r (☎ 055-290832/3, fax 055-2760383, Mon-Sat, 8:30 am-6:30 pm, Sun, 8:30 am-1:30 pm), Via Manzoni 16 (☎ 055-23320, fax 055-2346286, Mon-Fri, 9 am-1 pm) and Borgo Santa Croce 29r (☎ 055-2340444, fax 055-2264524, Mon-Sat, 9 am-7 pm, Sun, 9 am-2 pm).

For information on the latest events and entertainments, pick up the monthly listings magazine *Firenze Spettacolo* (€1.55), which has some text in English, or one of the city's two free papers (*Leggo* and *City*) from outside the Firenze S.M.N. forecourt.

Sightseeing

With too many attractions to take in on one day, explore Florence by quarter with these four city walks. The first takes you around the historical center, with visits to the religious attractions on Piazza del Duomo, the civic monuments on Piazza della Signoria and a tour of the city's best-known art gallery, the Galleria degli Uffizi. The second itinerary visits the quarter of Santa Maria Novella and includes the luxury shopping street of Via dei Tornabuoni as well as some of the city's most attractive palazzi and churches. It naturally leads onto the third walk, a tour through the Medici-rich quarters of San Lorenzo and down past the city markets to the vibrant Piazza Santa Croce. The final route is across the Arno River, in a district known for its artisan heritage and trendy nightspots. In the Palazzo Pitti and Boboli Gardens, it also includes some of Florence's most-visited sights. For those that don't have the four days to spend in the city, this last tour can easily be picked up from the Galleria degli Uffizi for a pleasant evening stroll at the end of the day.

■ The Historical Center

Piazza del Duomo – Chiesa di Orsanmichele – Piazza della Signoria – Galleria degli Uffizi – Ponte Vecchio

Start your tour of Florence's main central sights on **Piazza del Duomo**. You won't find it hard to get to the square; the red ochre of Brunelleschi's majestic cupola dominates Florence's skyline from all vantages. Walk through the winding streets and you'll see both Giotto's Campanile suddenly loom up beside it and the brilliance of the richly decorated marble-clad exterior of both the cathedral and the baptistery suddenly come into view. I've seen visitors approach open-mouthed and you'd be wise to similarly make the most of your first approach if you are to manage the awaiting traffic noise, the hordes of tourists and the length of the lines with the patience needed.

**Cupola del Duomo** (Piazza del Duomo 1, Mon-Fri, 8:30 am-7 pm, Sat, 8:30 am-5:30 pm, closed Sun, €6): Start with the earlier-opening Cupola (the earlier the better, to avoid the worst of the inevitable lines) for an insight into one of the most impressive engineering feats of the 15th century. Brunelleschi worked on the project from 1418 to 1434, solving the enormous difficulty of how to place such a large dome (at 41.5 m/136 ft in diameter, it was of a size not seen since Rome's Pantheon) on top of the already-constructed cathedral by laying the bricks in so intricate a manner that the dome supported itself as it grew. By engineering the crowning of the dome (although it was not actually placed until after his death), now over 100 m (328 ft) above ground level, with Verrocchio's gilded ball and cross, Brunelleschi again proved wrong those critics who couldn't believe the structure would be strong enough to support the weight. A climb of 463 steps takes you to the top, alongside Giorgio Vasari and Federico Zuccari's 16th-century fresco cycle *The Last Judgment*, time enough to appreciate the architect's skill and well worth it for the views over Florence and surrounding countryside.

Duomo (Cattedrale di Santa Maria del Fiore, Piazza del Duomo 1, Mon-Wed, Fri, 10 am-5 pm, Thurs, 10 am-3:30 pm, Sat, 10 am-4:45 pm, Sun, 1:30 am-4:45 pm, free): From the climb to the top of the Cupola, you'll already have a good idea of the size of this vast and luminous cathedral, at 153 m (502 ft) long and 38 m (125 ft) wide at the nave, the fifth-largest in the world after St Peter's in Rome, Yamoussourkro Basilica on the Ivory Coast, St Paul's in London and Milan Cathedral. It was built to replace the original fifth-century Chiesa di Santa Reparta. It had been enlarged and modified since the eighth century until it was finally decided in the 13th to replace it with something bigger and better. The remains of the original church, including Brunelleschi's tomb, were discovered in the 1960s and they can be visited during Duomo opening hours, €3.

The new building, dedicated to Santa Maria del Fiore, was designed by Arnolfo di Cambio to reflect the city's increasing style and ambition, but it was a succession of architects who carried out the work of his original and partly unexplained plan after Arnolfo died. The size and nakedness of the interior are all the more apparent in contrast to the detail of the exterior façade, which, though in the style of the time, dates only from the end of the 19th century and uses the same marble from Carrara (white), Maremma (red) and Prato (green) that is used inside. Look for the frescoed tributes on the wall of the left aisle to the two equestrian condottieri (mercenary commanders), the first *Niccolò da Tolentino* (1456) by Andrea Castagno, followed by the earlier *Giovanni Acuto* (1436) by Paolo Uccello (in reality showing the English commander John Hawkwood). Uccello also created the clock depicting four Evangelists on the entrance wall and a couple of the stained glass windows below the dome (Ghiberti, Castagno and Donatello are responsible for the remainder).

Just beyond the horsemen can be seen Michelino's representation of Dante, Florence and his *The Divine Comedy* (1465), while the terracotta lunettes above the two sacristies on either side of the altar are the work of Luca della Robbia (a Resurrection above the North Sacristy and an Ascension above the Sacrestia dei Canonici); he also created the bronze doors of the North Sacristy.

MURDER AT THE CATHEDRAL

One of Florence's most horrendous assassination attempts, the end of Mass, 26 April 1478, saw killers under the employ of the rival Pazzi family aim their knives at the ruling Medicis, Lorenzo Il Magnifico and his brother Giuliano. Egged on by conspirator Pope Sixtus IV, the wealthy banking family engineered a plot designed to replace the Medici Dynasty with papal, and Pazzi, rule but all did not go according to plan. While the attack was fatal for Giuliano, Lorenzo managed to escape, seeking refuge with his men in the cathedral sacristy. His allies had their revenge, hanging Francesco de' Pazzi and Pope Sixtus IV from the windows of the Palazzo dei Priori (now called the Bargello) before torturing to death all the remaining perpetrators.

Campanile di Giotto (Piazza del Duomo 1, daily, 8:30 am-7:30 pm, €6): A stunning example of the Gothic bell-tower style, the 85-m-high (279-ft) quadratic campanile, standing detached next to the Duomo (as is the Italian tradition), was constructed between 1334 and 1359 to the same three-tiered marble design as the Duomo. Although it is named after the artist Giotto, only the first storey of the tower was built under his direction. Andrea Pisano and then Francesco Talenti took over the reigns after his death. Pisano is also to be thanked for the sculpted bas-reliefs depicting the Creation of Man, now replaced with copies (the originals are in the Museo dell'Opera del Duomo). Stairs inside the campanile allow you to reach the top.

Battistero del Duomo (Piazza del Duomo, Mon-Sat, noon-7 pm, Sun, 8:30 am-2 pm, €3): The octagonal baptistery stands in ornamental and geometrical sobriety opposite the entrance to the Duomo. Dated somewhere between the end of the ninth and the start of the 10th century, it was considered to be the most beautiful monument, not just in the city, but in the entire world during the Middle Ages when the white and green marble was added to its exterior. The bronze doors date to the 14th and 15th centuries, their creation interrupted by the financial crisis and Black Plague in the 14th century.

The South Door, mostly illustrating scenes from the life of St John the Baptist (patron saint of the city), was the first to be added by Andrea Pisano between 1330 and 1336 when it was thought that the wooden doors were no longer worthy of an otherwise lavish baptistery. Ghiberti, with the help of apprentices such as Donatello, created the North Door to the same 28-panel design after beating greats such as Brunelleschi in a general design free-for-all in 1401. But it took him 20 years to accomplish the reliefs, hence there are some quite obvious changes in style. On its completion, Ghiberti was immediately commissioned to do the East Door (facing the Duomo), which an impressed Michelangelo named "The Gates of Paradise." The panels here depicting scenes from the Old Testament are reproductions; the originals are on display in the Museo dell'Opera del Duomo.

Once inside, run your eyes up the ancient Roman columns from the zodiac-decorated floor to discover one of the most important medieval mosaics in Italy. This cupola ceiling is magnificently decorated with narratives from Genesis, the story of Joseph, the life of Christ and that of St John the Baptist with a particularly bleak *The Last Judgment* shown below a glorious Jesus.

SCOPPIO DEL CARRO

If you're in Florence on Easter Sunday, get to the Piazza del Duomo for the midday Scoppio del Carro (the Explosion of the Cart). This raucous festival, which celebrates the exploits of the Florentine Pazzi family during the Crusades, begins with an historical parade from Porta del Prato, the old city gate. From here, revelers in traditional costumes follow a cart crammed full of fireworks as it is dragged to the Duomo by huge white oxen. Once it arrives – and this is where events take a decidedly strange turn – the fireworks are detonated by a plastic dove that hurtles down a wire joining the cart to the cathedral's main altar.

Museo dell'Opera del Duomo (Via della Canonica 1, ☎ 055-2302885, fax 055-2302898, www.operaduomo. firenze.it, Italian only, Mon-Sat, 9 am-7:30 pm, Sun, 9 am-1:40 pm, €6): A must for those enthralled by the Duomo, this museum charts the progress of its construction from the very first designs and tools used. It also houses the most precious works of art from the Duomo, Baptistery and Campanile, including the initial bas-reliefs decorating the Campanile, four of the panels of the Baptistery's "Gate of Paradise" and the marble *cantorie* (choir lofts) by Donatello and Luca della Robbia, formerly in the Duomo. The museum also has a few great sculptures, including works by Arnolfo di Cambio (origi-

nally intended for the Duomo façade), Michelangelo's uncompleted *Pietà*, right, and Donatello's wooden figure of a tormented Mary Magdalene. There is also St John's Altar, its silver and enamel coating perfected by the best of the 14th and 15th centuries' artists and silversmiths, including Michelozzo, Verrocchio, Antonio del Pollaiolo and Bernardo Cennini.

IMITATION, THE SINCEREST FORM OF FLATTERY

If the Piazza del Duomo's most precious works of art are installed in the Museo dell'Opera del Duomo, then where do the copies that replace them come from? Satisfy your curiosity with a visit to the cathedral restoration workshop, also known as the Stonecutter's Workshop (La Bottega degli Scalpellini, Mon-Fri, 8 am-9:30 pm, Sat, 8 am-2 pm, visits by appointment through the Museo dell'Opera del Duomo), hidden away in a narrow street just a stone's throw from the Duomo. If you haven't booked a visit, a peak through the window will offer a quick glimpse of the authentic stonecutter restorers at work, some of whom are still using copies of the typical Renaissance tools that crafted the works in the first place.

Once you've satisfied your interest in the treasures of Piazza del Duomo, head down Via dei Calzaiuoli, a large pedestrian street that links it to the second great square of ancient Florence: the Piazza della Signoria. This thoroughfare is also worth a stroll in the early evening, gelato in hand, when the boutiques and jewelry shops close. It's then that street performers and vendors take over the pavements with the usual array of knickknacks and counterfeit designer wear, plus the odd opera-singing busker.

To your right you'll see the 19th-century **Piazza della Repubblica** (see page 42), a good place to stop for a quick espresso on one of its large caffè terraces. Just past the square (still on Via dei Calzaiuoli), coming as a bit of a surprise between the street's shops and caffès, you'll find one of Florence's most charismatic churches.

Chiesa di Orsanmichele (Church of Orsanmichele, Mon-Fri, 9 am-noon, 4-6 pm, Sat-Sun, 9 am-1 pm, 4-6 pm, free): What a history this church has. It starting off as a storehouse for grain in the 13th century, hence the defensive structure of its tower and the chutes for loading grain still visible under the northwest arch. It was the vast market loggia with its thought-to-be-miraculous Virgin Mary, which led to its transformation into a church. The façade was one of the most impressive in the city when in possession of its original sculptures – Verrocchio's *St Thomas* (Via dei Calzaiuoli), Donatello's *St George* (Via Orsanmichele) and

The facade and cupola of Florence's Duomo (APT Florence)

The matching marble facades of the Duomo and adjacent Campanile di Giotto
(Tom Johnston / Emma Jones)

ove: Battistero di San Giovanni seen through the Loggia del Bigallo (APT Florence)

Below: Della Robbia's cantoria in the Museo dell'Opera del Duomo (APT Florence)

Michelangelo's David in the Cortile degli Uffizi

Ghiberti's *St Mathew* and *St Stephen* (Via dell'Arte della Lana, beside the church's entrance). Replicas are currently being restored in their place.

Once inside, it is Andrea Orcagna's 14th-century glass and marble tabernacle that takes pride of place. It frames a *Madonna* painted by Bernardo Daddi in 1347 to replace the original miraculous Virgin Mary that was lost in a fire in 1304. A museum occupies the remains of the medieval granary on the first and second floors (reached via the palazzo on Via dell'Arte della Lana, free). It houses many of the original sculptures, including those by Donatello, Ghiberti, Verrocchio and Nanni di Banco.

You'll quickly arrive from here onto the **Piazza della Signoria** (also called Piazza dei Priori), a square that draws mixed reaction. Although DH Lawrence once named it the most perfect square in the world (it has changed considerably since his day), many consider it a bit of a letdown – the scruffiness of its form and the blandness of the pizza places that run onto it unworthy of the sights it contains. Worse still, many of the buildings that surround it, including the tower of the Palazzo Vecchio, seem permanently covered in scaffolding, making it difficult to imagine the Piazza at its best. But aesthetics aside, you can't take away the power of the attractions that it holds. Yes, most of the best sculptures are now replaced by copies – Michelangelo's *David* (original in the Galleria dell'Accademia), Donatello's *Marzocco* (original in the Museo Nazionale del Bargello) and his *Judith and Holofernes* (original in the Palazzo Vecchio). But the glorious marble creations on show in the statue-lined Loggia dei Lanzi, Ammannati's much-loved (and much-hated) Neptune Fountain, the grandeur of the Palazzo Vecchio and the stately approach to the Uffizi cannot be denied.

GIROLAMO SAVONAROLA (1452-1498)

Savanorala was the famous inflammatory preacher opposed to what he saw as the frivolous and often immoral Renaissance lifestyle led under the Medici. Then Prior of San Marco, he went on to install a theocratic republic in Florence in 1494 after the Medici fled the approaching French King, Charles VIII. It was then that he held the "Bonfire of the Vanities" in which all vain, worldly processions were burnt in a huge bonfire on the Piazza della Signoria. Four years later, forbidden to preach because of his anti-papal support for the French King, excommunicated for continuing to preach and then disowned by public opinion, he was finally executed on the same square. Beside the fountain, you'll find a plaque marking the spot.

Loggia dei Lanzi (also known as the Loggia della Signoria): Created in the 14th century as a ceremonial spot for the Palazzo Vecchio, the loggia became the open-air sculpture gallery you see today in the 18th century, with the addition of works such as Benvenuto Cellini's bronze *Perseus* and Giambologna's *Rape of the Sabine Women* (1583).

Palazzo Vecchio (☎ 055-2768465, fax 055-2625984, www.palazzovecchio.it, website under construction at the time of writing, daily, 9 am-7 pm, Thurs, 9 am-2 pm, €5.70): Marked by its 94-m/308-ft tower, Arnolfo di Cambio's military-style town hall, shown at left, has been an important building in the history of Florence since the first years of the 14th century. It was built in massive fortress-like dimensions to house the *Signoria*, the highest ranks of the city's republican government. Changes in Florence's political makeup, especially with the return of the Medici, saw many transformations, especially to the interior, where fresco after fresco describes the history of the family, mainly by favored architect Vasari. He also added the frescoes to the regal Salone dei Cinquecento (the Room of the Five Hundred), which at once time housed Savonarola's republic government and still houses Michelangelo's *Genio della Victoria*.

In contrast to all this grandeur, **Studiolo** next door was the workspace of the alchemy- and astrology-fascinated Francesco I (as can be seen from the instruments on display). It seems more like a tiny broom closet. Look for wall illustrations on the themes of earth, water, air and fire. On the second floor, the ceiling of the **Sala dei Gigli** (the Room of Lilies, the city's symbol) was fashioned by brothers Giuliano and Benedetto da Maiano with frescoes by Domenico Ghirlandaio on the walls. It links to the **Cancelleria**, the former office of Machiavelli and also to the map room whose 53 maps produced by Fra' Ignazio Danti depict all that was known of the world in the 16th century.

Something for the Kids

Workshops, experiments, historic re-enactments and tours around the Palazzo Vecchio's secret passageways in the company of actors and animators are just some of the fun events on offer to eight-year-olds and over at the **Museo dei Ragazzi** (Children's Museum, Palazzo Vecchio, ☎ 055-2768224, www.museoragazzi.it, free with entrance to the Palazzo Vecchio). The play area "di Bia e Garcia" is suitable for younger kids. Booking recommended.

The tools of ancient warfare can be explored at the **Museo e Parco Stibbert** (Stibbert Museum and Park, Via Stibbert 26, ☎ 055-486049, www.museostibbert.it, €5, conc. €2) with its fascinating collection of ancient weapons, medieval standards and samurai swords.

Natural history comes alive at the **Museo di Storia Naturale "La Specola"** (La Specola Museum of Natural History, Via Romana 17, ☎ 055-2288251, www.unifi.it/unifi/msn, €5, conc. €2.50) with its rich collection of anatomical waxworks and over 5,000 animal specimens sure to intrigue youngsters.

Perfect for all bookworms, the **Biblioteca dei Ragazzi Santa Croce** (Children's Library in Santa Croce, ☎ 055-2478551, www.comune.fi.it/streghetta, free) has a great selection of books, including English-language titles and a range of activities from book-readings to puppet shows.

Smaller kids will love the indoor play area at the **Ludoteca Centrale** (Children's Recreational Center, Piazza SS. Annunziata, free).

Galleria degli Uffizi (Loggiate degli Uffizi 6, ☎ 055-2388651, fax 055-2338699, www.uffizi.firenze.it, Tues-Sun, 8:15 am-6:50 pm, €8.50): Florence has a telephone booking service for tickets to the Uffizi (Firenze Musei, ☎ 055-294833, fax 055-264406, www.sbas.firenze.it, reservations cost €1.55). Although intended as a means to avoid those long entrance lines, these days the lines to pick up tickets (if you can even get through) are just as long. In my experience, unless you're intending to see absolutely everything (in which case you should arrive at the crack of dawn in peak tourist season), it's best to arrive late in the day when the lines have started to dwindle and the interior is at its quietest. Limit yourself to one gallery, one school or one artist if you want to exit with your calm still intact. There are works here from not only the Florentine and Tuscan school, but from movements all over Italy and Europe – and that's not to mention the Roman sculptures in the museum corridors. If there's something you particularly wish to see, check in advance to make sure the room is open; they are sometimes closed.

ORIGINS OF THE UFFIZI

Cosimo I commissioned the structure you see today as a seat for the offices ("uffizi") of the city magistrates, but it is Vasari who can be thanked for the unusual horseshoe design. Picking up the project in 1560, Vasari worked on its construction until his death in 1574 when Bernardo Buontalenti took over. Buontalenti's pièce de résistance, the octagonal Tribuna, once home to the celebrated *Medici Venus*. It was the succeeding Medici Francesco I who started moving the Medicean art collection here, an idea that proved so popular all subsequent Medici (and the Lorraines who followed) continued to enrich it with spoils from many of Tuscany's formerly art-laden monasteries and churches.

Leonardo, Portrait of an Old Man

The East Gallery - Rooms 2 to 7: Start with the Tuscan Primitives in Rooms 2 to 4; the first, entitled "Giotto and the 13th century," presents two startling *Maestà* (Madonna enthroned with Child and Angels); Giotto's grandiose *Ognissanti Madonna* (about 1310), created for the church of the same name in the sacred yet naturalistic style he championed; and Cimabue's *Santa Trinità Madonna* (1280-90), taken from the altar of the Church of Santa Trinità and with visible roots in the formerly prevalent Byzantine style. Room 3 displays works by 14th-century Sienese artists such as Pietro and Ambrogio Lorenzetti, including a *Maestà* (1340) created by the former, and Simone Martini's *Annunciation* (1333) taken from Siena's Duomo and depicting a rather timid-looking Madonna surprised reading by the arriving angel. Further trecento artists follow in Room 4, this time from the Florentine school (Bernardo Daddi, Taddeo Gaddi, Jacopo del Casentino, Giottino, Nardo di Cione and Andrea Orcagna, among others).

Move on to Rooms 5 and 6 for works by Florentine Gothic artists from the end of the 14th and the start of the 15th century, such as Lorenzo Monaco, Fra Angelico and Gentile da Fabriano, whose emphasis on detail and gilded decoration in the *Adoration of the Magi* (1423) is representative of this pictorial period known as International Gothic. Room 7 is dedicated to the first masters of the Renaissance with exploratory creations by Fra Angelico, Masolino, Masaccio, Piero della Francesca and Uccello (including his *The Battle of San Romano*, circa 1453, which, depicting the decisive combat in the wars between Florence and Siena, is said to have once hung in the bedroom of Lorenzo Il Magnifico).

The East Gallery - Rooms 8 to 14: Room 8 is devoted to Filippo Lippi, his *Madonna and Child with Two Angels* (circa 1460) the best known of the 11 works

Florence

on show here. Room 9 contains works by Antonio del Pollaiolo and his brother Piero, along with the first works of Sandro Botticelli – *The Return of Judith* and *The Discovery of the Murder of Holophernes* (probably created together around 1472 as a gift for Bianco Cappello, the second wife of Francesco I). Botticelli also claims the four following rooms where his famous mythological creations, *Allegory of Spring* (1478), *Birth of Venus* (left, around 1485) and *Pallas and the Centaur* (1480), can be seen.

The East Gallery - Rooms 15 to 24: Room 15 is dedicated to Verrocchio and pupils Perugino, including a beautiful *Madonna Enthroned with Child* (1493), and Leonardo da Vinci. Works by the latter in his formative years include a *Baptism of Christ* (1470-75) worked on by himself and Verrocchio, a spectacular *Annunciation* (1472-75) and an unfinished *Adoration of the Magi* (1481-82). Later works by Perugino, along with those of Signorelli, can be seen in Room 19.

There's a bit of a break in Room 16, the Map Room, which has a display of charts depicting the state of Florence under Grand Dukes Francesco I and Ferdinando I. In Room 20 you'll find works by Dürer and German artists (Lukas Cranach the Elder, Hans Baldung Grien and Hans Suss von Kulmbach) before Giambellino and Giorgione in Room 21 (as well as Giovanni Bellini's *Sacred Allegory* and *The Lamentation over the Dead Christ,* around 1495), and Flemish and German Painting in Room 22. Room 24 features the famous Medici collection of miniature portraits assembled by Grand Duke Cosimo I around 1550.

The West Gallery - Rooms 25 to 28: The 16th century starts in Room 25 with Michelangelo's *Holy Family* (1505-07), his only completed oil painting, thought to have been painted on the birth of Agnolo Doni and Maddalena Strozzi's first daughter. Florentine Classicism in the form of Raphael and Andrea del Sarto occupy Room 26, with Raphael's *Madonna of the Goldfinch* (currently under restoration and replaced by a copy), touted as the best example of this period for its serene landscape of diffused light. Also watch for his *Portrait of Giulio II* (1512), a work currently under much discussion after the discovery of an identical portrait (now on show at the National Gallery in London) – the copy, probably carried out by his workshop under his direction, has yet to be identified. Florentine Mannerists occupy Room 27 with Rosso Fiorentino's seminal *Moses Defending the Daughters of Jethro* (around 1523), along with works by its other figurehead, Pontorno. Titian's notorious *Venus of Urbino* (1538) justifiably claims most of the limelight in Room 28, alongside works of Sebastiano del Piombo and Palma Il Vecchio.

The West Gallery - Rooms 29 to 45: Rooms 29 and 30 feature artists from the Emilian School (Dosso Dossi, Garofalo, Mazzolino and Parmigianino – his famous *Madonna with the Long Neck* dates from around 1540). Venice and the Veneto (Moroni, Jacopo Tintoretto and Paolo Veronese, including a splendidly understated *Martyrdom of St Justine*, 1573) can be found in Rooms 31-32. Rubens and Van Dyck appear in Room 41 (with Rubens' *Triumphal Entry of Henry IV into Paris*, 1625). Caravaggio is in Room 43 (*The Sacrifice of Isaac, Bacchus* and, in temporary exhibition, *Medusa*) and some of Rembrandt's best portraits, including his splendidly morose *Self-Portrait of an Old Man* in Room 44. Room 45 introduces the 18th century.

The Corridoio Vasariano (Vasari's Corridor, €28,50): Built by Vasari to link the Palazzo Vecchio to the Palazzo Pitti (see page 54) through the Uffizi, the Corridoio Vasariano winds its way over the Ponte Vecchio and into the Giardino di Boboli. The route offers incomparable views over the city (and into the old Chiesa di Santa Felicitá), as well as hidden art surprises (works by Andrea del Sarto, Vasari, Rubens, Rembrandt and Fattori lining the corridor). Only recently restored from damage caused by the 1993 Uffizi bombing, access to this half-mile covered passageway is difficult at the best of times, with no consistent yearly pattern in opening hours and days. At the present time, it opens twice a day on Fri and Sat (10:30 am and 3 pm), but as this is set to change; check with the tourist office or on the booking line (☎ 055-2654321) on arrival.

DO YOU HATE LINES?

If the lines for the Uffizi are out of control, come back another day and opt instead for the **Museo di Storia della Scienza** around the back of the Uffizi's East Gallery (The Science Museum, Piazza dei Giudici 1, ☎ 055-265311, fax 055-288257, www.imss.fi.it, Mon-Fri, 9:30 am-5 pm, Sat, 9:30 am-1 pm, €6.50.) Inaugurated in 1930, it has a collection of scientific instruments from the Medici (15th to 17th centuries) and Lorraine (18th to 19th centuries) eras, including those used for mathematical and astronomical purposes by Galileo Galilei. Examples are the lens he used to discover the four moons of Jupiter and other remnants of his scientific academy, Accademia del Cimento (Academy of Experiment), formerly in the Palazzo Pitti.

From the windows of the Uffizi's West Gallery you should already have gotten a good look at the legendary bridge where this tour ends but, for the best pedestrian approach, return to Piazza della Signoria and take Via Vacche Reccia onto Via Por Santa Maria. Here, to your right, you'll see the 16th-century loggia of the **Mercato Nuovo** (the New Market, Mon-Sat, 8 am-7 pm).

Il Porcellino: These days, the bronze boar of the fountain found in the center the Mercato Nuovo attracts as much attention as its stalls (most selling tacky souvenirs and leather goods). As it is thought to bring good luck, passersby inevitably stop to throw a coin into the fountain.

To your left, the **Ponte Vecchio** (the Old Bridge, shown at right) should be coming into sight. Designed by Taddeo Daddi in 1345, it was constructed to replace an even older bridge that had been dragged away by an angry Arno in 1333. The Arno attempted to do likewise in 1966, but the bridge managed to survive both this and the earlier Nazi retreating attacks in 1944 (the only bridge in Florence to have done so). The butchers who

Florence

originally occupied it were replaced at the end of the 17th century by the jewelry traders you still see today (Ferdinando I de' Medici couldn't stand the smell of the butcher shops along the Corridoio Vasariano). You can easily understand from its design what a bridge represented to locals in the Middle Ages.

> **Tip:** For the best views of the Ponte Vecchio, visit the Ponte Santa Trinità at nightfall when, with the light playing with its reflection, the old bridge can be seen at its medieval best.

■ The Santa Maria Novella Quarter

Piazza Repubblica – Piazza Santa Trinità – Piazza D'Ognissanti – Piazza Santa Maria Novella

Start your day off with an espresso and a *pasta* (pastry) on the vast **Piazza della Repubblica**. Although these days frequented almost solely by tourists, its four large caffès - Donnini, Gilli, Giubbe Rosse and Pazzkowski – were a veritable institution in their early 19th century, when they were patronized by the top writers, artists and intellectuals. But impressive as this piazza is, it's a little disheartening to remember that its construction (under the snobbish orders of Florence's 19th-century bourgeoisie) annihilated some of the most atmospheric medieval quarters in town, including the site of the ancient Roman forum. Fortunately, public uproar staved off further destruction. The local town planners did not understand the protest, as the inscription on the arch above Via degli Strozzi testifies: "L'antico centro della citta da secolare squallore a vita nuova restituto" (The ancient center of town given a new life after centuries of squalor).

The area to the south and east of Piazza Repubblica is crammed full of luxury shops (see page 67 for the spoils you can expect on Via dei Tornabuoni and Via della Vigna Nuova) and sumptuous palazzi. The latter were created by the wealthiest of bankers and businessmen from as early as the mid-13th century as a sign of their monetary power and, later, to show their favor with the Medici. Nearly impossible for one family to manage, these days their rooms are often rented out and ground floors occupied by many of the city's first-class shops, banks and restaurants, making them hard to enter for solely sightseeing purposes. Fortunately on Via Porta Rossa (head south from the piazza down Via Pellicceria) you can find a palazzo museum, which not only takes you inside an early example of its type but also explains the fundamentals in its design and use.

Museo di Palazzo Davanzati (Davanzati Palace Museum, also known as Museo della Casa Fiorentina Antica, the Old Florentine House Museum, Via Porta Rossa 13, ☎ 055-388610, www.sbas.firenze.it/davanzati, closed for repairs at the time of writing, free): The architecture of this mid-14th-century gem is amazing and its museum containing common household items from the 14th and 15th centuries offers a valuable insight into the way of life at that time. Each room is furnished in predominantly medieval style using genuine artifacts, and the architecture – siege-resistant doors, huge storerooms, floor hatches through which to bombard attackers – shows the lengths to which the rich felt they had to go to protect themselves from the marauding masses.

PALAZZO EXTERIORS

Replacing the medieval fashion for fortress-like tower-houses (originally favored by local nobles out of a need to defend themselves from rival families and constrained in design by a lack of urban space), these new gargantuan displays of might and wealth really took off during the 14th and 15th centuries in a Florence depopulated by the plague. Most are easy to recognize by their sheer size, but you should also look out for the "rusticated" boulders of local *pietra forte* (a steel-gray stone) that generally decorate the lower levels and the *sgraffiti* (a popular Renaissance technique in which colors of the underlay show through the top coat) that decorate the upper floors. For the archetypal Medicean palazzo **Medici Riccardi**, see page 47, for **Palazzo Pitti**, see page 54.

Overwhelming boulder-covered walls, vast windows and a symmetry of structure taken to its extreme, **Palazzo Strozzi** (at left, Via degli Strozzi on the corner of Via dei Tornabuoni, not open to the public), one of the largest palaces built in the 15th century, is definitely hard to miss. Begun around 1489 to the plans of Benedetto da Maiano when the fortunes of banker Filippo Strozzi were at their peak, legend has it the family never inhabited the construction, exiled before its completion for unwisely taking an anti-Medici stance.

The Medici heraldic emblems on the frieze ordaining the more classical **Palazzo Rucellai** (Via della Vigna Nuova 16, not open to the public) show that this was a family that chose to stay on the right side of the Medici. The palazzo-home belonged to a family made rich from the import of red dye. Constructed from 1446 on, the loggia opposite the palazzo was added in celebration of the wedding of Bernardo Rucellai to the sister of Lorenzo Il Magnifico.

Imposing not just for its external staircase and vast Gothic windows, the 13th-century **Palazzo di Parte Guelfa** (Piazza di Parte Guelfa, not open to the public) still echoes with the fierce rivalry between the Guelphs and the Ghibellines, which divided much of central Italy in the 12th and 13th centuries. It was created in 1268 after the Guelphs' decisive victory and was funded by wealth confiscated from their spoils. It exhibits a well-preserved example of *sgraffiti*. Brunelleschi designed the additions to the top storey in 1531, while Vasari, who carried out the works, also added the elegant staircase and the small loggia on Via di Capaccio.

You can enter the imposing 14th-century **Palazzo Spini-Ferroni** (along Borgo Santi Apostoli on Piazza Santa Trinità); it now houses Ferragamo, shoemaker to the stars, with shop and museum inside (page 68).

The mid-17th-century **Palazzo Corsini** (Lungarno Corsini, entrance on Via del Parione, not open to the public) occasionally rents out its Arno-facing gardens for business bashes. Rumor has it that British author Sue Townsend also rents a room here and that the kitchen is the humble home of an original Luca della Robbia terracotta (we can only imagine what delights can be found in the more palatial rooms).

Carry on along Via Pellicceria to enter a warren of some of Florence's best-preserved medieval streets marked by Via Porta Rossa in the north and the Arno in the south – linked by eight or so tiny *chiassi* (passages). By taking Chiasso

Florence

delle Missure (right in front of you), you'll reach Borgo Santi Apostoli, where a right leads you to **Piazza del Limbo**, so-called because it formerly hosted the city's cemetery for unbaptized children. It is also the site of **Chiesa di Santi Apostoli** (pm only, free), an 11th-century church (considerably reworked in the 16th) well worth a quick peak for its magnificent terracotta tabernacle from the della Robbia school, one of few of its artworks to survive damage in the 1966 flood. From here, continue along Borgo Santi Apostoli to your next port of call on Piazza Santa Trinità.

Chiesa di Santa Trinità (Piazza Santa Trinità, ☎ 055-216912, Mon-Sat, 8 am-noon, 4-6 pm, Sun, 4-6 pm, free): An 11th-century church with a 16th-century *pietra forte* façade (the work of Buontalenti) and a 14th-century Gothic interior of cross-vaulting and pointed arches, this church has a little bit of everything. Inside, you'll find some noteworthy frescoes by Simone Martini and Ghirlandaio, whose *Scenes of the Life of St Francis* on the right in the Sassetti Chapel offer a fascinating insight into the hectic everyday life found then on both Piazza di Trinità and Piazza della Signoria. The adjoining chapel also displays the miraculous crucifix taken from San Miniato al Monte (see page 56).

Known predominantly for its glorious views over the Ponte Vecchio, **Ponte Santa Trinità**, which links the Santa Maria Novella quarter with the Oltrano, is itself considered one of Florence's most beautiful bridges. Constructed by Ammannati (although its design is attributed to Michelangelo) to replace the original wooden edifice in 1557, the bridge you see today is a reconstruction of the original, which like almost all of Florence's bridges was destroyed by the retreating Nazis in 1944. Before you head back, look out for Buontalenti's mischievous gargoyle fountain on the other side of the Arno (across the road on the left).

THE ORIGINAL ICE CREAM

Florence has a lot to thank Bernardo Buontalenti for, as an architect of unquestionable skill and the inventor of ice cream. He is thought to have put together the concoction (a frozen mix of milk, butter, eggs, honey and fortified wine) for a Medicean grand banquet of visiting Spanish gentries. In tribute, Florentine *gelaterias* or ice cream sellers to this day sell a flavor akin to the original recipe and named after the great Renaissance man.

■ **Where to Buy**

Considered the best ice cream maker in Florence (if not all of Italy), **Vivoli** (Via Isola delle Stinche 7r, closed Mon), between the Duomo and Santa Croce, should be your first port of call.

You'll get ice cream the Sicilian way at **Carabè** (Via Ricasoli 60r, closed Mon) on the road from the Duomo to the Accademia.

Just off Piazza della Repubblica, you could spend hours in **Festival del Gelato** (Via del Corso 75r, closed Mon) choosing from its wide range of toppings.

Between Piazza del Duomo and Piazza della Signoria, **Perché No!** (Via dei Tavolini 19r, closed Tues) has a range of scrumptious healthy options.

Over in the Oltrano, **Bar Richi** (Piazza Santo Spirito 9r, closed Sun) knows how to pile its traditional flavors onto its cones.

■ **How to Buy**

To avoid confusion when buying, follow this simple process. First decide what you want – a cone (*un cono*) or a pot (*un coppetta*) – and in which size – usually from €1.50 to €3.50. Pay first at the register. Hand your receipt (*il scontrino*) over to the server and specify which and how many toppings you require (generally two or three, depending on the size of your purchase).

From here it's a pleasant stroll west along Lungarno Corsini, past the palazzo of the same name to arrive at Piazza d'Ognissanti.

Chiesa di San Salvatore a Ognissanti (Borgo Ognissanti 42, ☎ 055-2398700, free): This 13th-century church stands in an area historically tied to the wool cloth trade, which bolstered Florence's economy in medieval times. Its Baroque façade didn't go down well with Florentines when it was added in the 17th century, but nonetheless remains one of the best examples of this then-erupting style. Inside, look for Chapel Vespucci (family member Amerigo giving his name to the continent he helped discover); it is decorated with frescoes by Ghirlandaio (*Madonna della Misericordia* over the second altar on the right) and Botticelli (*St Augustine*), whose tomb can also be found here. More Ghirlandaio works can be found in the **Cenacle of Ghirlandaio** (adjacent to the church, in the former monastery refectory, same opening hours, free), including his incredibly well-preserved *Last Supper* fresco.

From Borgo Ognissanti, a left up Via della Porcellana and a right down Via della Scala will take you to Piazza Santa Maria Novella, a rather languid square that houses one of Florence's most famous churches.

Chiesa di Santa Maria Novella (Piazza Santa Maria Novella, ☎ 055-215918, daily, 9:30 am-5 pm, closed Fri am, €3): Begun in 1246 as the Florentine base of the Dominican faith, the first thing to strike you about Santa Maria Novella is its bright white and green marble façade added by Leon Battista Alberti in the 15th century. This is said to be Michelangelo's favorite church. The Gothic interior – with its almost hypnotic pattern of black and white marble – houses a wealth of mas-terpieces including a *Trinity* (1427) by Masaccio (one of his last works), frescoes by Filippino Lippi and Ghirlandaio depicting *The Life of St John the Baptist* (Chapel Tornabuoni) and a commentary on Dante's *The Divine Comedy* by Nardo di Cione (Chapel Filippo Strozzi). Two famous crucifixes are shown, the first by Giotto and the second by Brunelleschi. Legend has it that Brunelleschi created the crucifix after a challenge from his friend Donatello who was peeved at Brunelleschi's criticisms of his own efforts. The entrance to the museum (included in the ticket price) is to the left of the church. Here, in the Green Cloister you'll see the famous – albeit sadly damaged – fresco cycle of scenes from the Old Testament created between 1432 and 1448 by Uccello and apprentices. In the Spanish Chapel is Andrea Buonaiuto's allegory, *The Church Militant and Triumphant*, part of a glorious fresco cycle celebrating the Dominican order.

Officina Profumo Farmaceutica di Santa Maria Novella

This much-hyped pharmacy a short distance from the church (Via della Scala 16), on the spot of an earlier Dominican pharmacy, is worth a visit for its range of toiletries, herbal medicines and fragrances, made and sold in a Neo-Gothic setting.

■ From San Lorenzo to Santa Croce

Piazza San Lorenzo – Piazza San Marco – Galleria dell'Accademia - Piazza SS. Annunziata – Piazza Santa Croce – Museo Nazionale del Bargello

You'll discover an equally fascinating side of history and art in the Renaissance-rich quarters of San Lorenzo (traditionally known as the Medici quarter), San Marco and Piazza SS. Annunziata. Traditionally the domain of the Medici, this is the quarter that most bears the imprint of Cosimo Il Vecchio, whose passion for urban architecture saw the construction of many churches, palazzi and libraries by the best artists and architects of the time. These are also the centers of much of Florence's contemporary life with the bustle of the Mercato Centrale (the central market) and the University keeping the streets moving. Just a little apart from the historical center, the area of Santa Croce to its southeast is the centerpiece of a web of medieval streets leading to another of Florence's popular museums, the Museo Nazionale del Bargello.

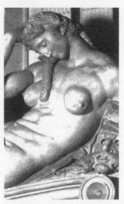

Chiesa di San Lorenzo (Piazza San Lorenzo, ☎ 055-216634, Mon-Sat, 10 am-5 pm, €2.50): Start your tour outside the unfinished façade of San Lorenzo, easily missed by the lively market stalls that cover the square before it. At one time the city's cathedral, this is one of the oldest sanctuaries in town and best reflects the pretensions of Cosimo I, who employed the biggest artists of the Renaissance to modify and restructure it in the 15th century. Brunelleschi can be thanked for its elegant geometric architecture. His superb cubic Sagrestia Vecchia (Old Sacristy), decorated by Donatello, flanks the left side and is considered one of his best works. Michelangelo is responsible for the Cappelle Medicee (Medici Chapel), made of marble and studded with semi-precious stones. This Medici family mausoleum adjoins the church (Piazza Madonna degli Aldobrandini 5, ☎ 055-2388602, www.sbas.firenze.it/cappellemedicee, 8:15 am-5 pm, closed Mon, €6). It is also home to some of Michelangelo's principal sculptures (above) with the frosty figures of *Day and Night* on the tomb of Giuliano, Duke of Nemours, and those of *Dawn and Dusk* on that of Lorenzo, Duke of Urbino. It is also the resting place of Lorenzo Il Magnifico and brother Giuliano, who met his end during the ill-fated Pazzi Conspiracy (see page 34). To the left of the church is the Laurentian Library, also the work of Michelangelo, and home to the Medici's fine collections of books and manuscripts. It offers lovely views over the adjacent 15th-century cloister designed by Manetti.

> **Market Stop:** The area between here and the train station is both the crudest and liveliest part of central Florence, its hub centered around the **Mercato Centrale** (Mon-Sat, 7 am-2 pm). The vast covered food hall built in stone, iron and glass by Guiseppe Mengoni at the end of the 19th century and one of the most authentic and tastiest places to visit for picnic ingredients.

Palazzo Medici Riccardi & the Cappella dei Magi (Via Cavour 3, ☎ 055-2760340, fax 055-2760451, www.palazzo-medici.it, daily, 9 am-7 pm, closed Wed, €4): Via dei Gori takes you right from Piazza San Lorenzo to Via Cavour alongside the famous paradigm of Florentine Renaissance palaces, Palazzo Medici Riccardi, whose "rusticated" stonework, was the inspiration for the design of both the Palazzo Pitti and the Palazzo Strozzi (see page 54). Constructed under orders of Cosimo Il Vecchio between 1444 and 1462 by Michelozzo to serve as a family home near to the family church, it passed to the Riccardi family in the 17th century. They renovated and enlarged it to the extent that only the chapel remains intact of the original work, fortunately
retaining the Benozzo Gozzoli fresco of the *Journey of the Magi* (above, 1460). Today the building is the home of Florence's Prefecture. You can visit the palazzo's peaceful inner courtyard and its 17th-century first-floor lobby, which has a Fra Filippo Lippi *Madonna and Child*.

Museo di San Marco (Piazza San Marco, ☎ 055-2388608, fax 055-2388704, www.sbas.firenze.it/sanmarco, Tues-Fri, 8:15 am-1:50 pm, Sat, 8:15 am-6:50 pm, Sun, 8:50 am-7 pm, €4): Head north along Via Cavour and you can't miss the Dominican convent and church that dominates the top of the square, again constructed by Michelozzo for Cosimo Il Vecchio, this time between 1437 and 1446. Now a museum, it is essentially dedicated to Fra Angelico (also known as Fra' Giovanni da Fiesole), whose frescoes in the cloister and in the dormitory corridor constitute some of the most important of his works. The tour takes you from the 20 or so paintings found in the large hall to the right of the entrance (best known for *The Last Judgment* and *Deposition*) past an impressive *Crucifixion* fresco (1441-42) in the Sala Capitolare, up the stairs to a stunning *Annunciation* (above, circa 1445) and into the cells where frescoes depict scenes from the *Life of Christ* and figures from the Dominican order. The cells, once the living quarters of Savonarola, the prior here (see page 37), are decorated with a number of artifacts from his time, including the famous portrait by Fra' Bartolomeo, above.

CLOISTERS WORTH A DETOUR

In the cloister and old convent refectory, **Cenacolo di Sant'Apollonia** (Via XXVII Aprile 1, ☎ 055-2388607, Tues-Sun, 8:15 am-1:50 pm, free) you can see one of Andrea del Castagno's most unsettling masterpieces, the 15th-century *The Last Supper* framed by scenes of *Resurrection, Crucifixion* and *Deposition*.

The lesser-known **Cloister Dello Scalzo** (Via Cavour 69, ☎ 055-2388604, Mon-Sat, 8:15 am-2 pm, free) is well worth a visit for its monochrome frescoes by Andrea del Sarto portraying *Scenes from the Life of St John the Baptist* and the two *Allegories of Virtue*.

Galleria dell'Accademia (Via Ricasoli 60, ☎/fax 055-2388609, www.sbas.firenze.it/accademia, 8:15 am-6:50 pm, closed Mon, €8.50): Head south from Piazza San Marco along Via Ricasoli to reach Florence's second-most-visited museum. Housed in Florence's Academy of Painting, Sculpture and Architecture, established in the 16th century, the collection on display in the Galleria dell'Accademia, just off Piazza San Marco, was acquired from the 18th century on, originally as a means of tutoring its students. Although home to an impressive range of paintings (Benozzo Gozzoli, Uccello, Botticelli, Filippino Lippi, Fra Bartolomeo, Perugino and others), it is  best-known for its seven marble sculptures by Michelangelo – *David*, above, brought here in 1873, just after the Unification of Italy to save it from further storm damage; the four incomplete *Prigioni* intended for the Vatican mausoleum of Pope Guilio II; *St Mathew,* designed but not finished for the Duomo façade; and *Pietà di Palestrina*, one of his last sculptures. In line with today's high-tech expectations, the museum has added a clever and informative touch-table display depicting not just how the sculptures were carved but also how the ravages of time, the weather and misguided attempts at cleaning and maintaining them have all taken their toll.

MICHELANGELO: THE EARLY YEARS

 Sculptor, painter and architect, Michelangelo excelled as all three. Active in both Florence and Rome, he gained his education in the former. His early works – two marble bas-reliefs, Madonna of the Stairs (c.1490) and Battle of the Centaurs (left, 1490-92) – are on display with the family's collection at **Casa Buonarroti** (Via Ghibellina 70, ☎ 055-241752, fax 055-241698, www.casabuonarroti.it, 9:30 am-2 pm, closed Tues, €6.20).

Retrace your steps to Piazza San Marco and take a right along Via Cesare Battisti to arrive on Piazza SS. Annunziata. Its Renaissance arcades are animated by a lively student population year-round, but are at their best during the summer festival *Firenze Estate*, when the Piazza becomes the city's main site for live jazz (see page 66).

Chiesa di SS. Annunziata (Piazza SS. Annunziata, ☎ 055-2398034, daily, 7:30 am-12.30 pm, 4-6:30 pm, free): Founded in 1250 and then expanded over the centuries, if you love tales of miracles, you'll love this Michelozzo-designed church. It houses a painting of the *Virgin Annunciate* from which the church takes its name. According to local legend, an unknown 14th-century monastic painter finished the piece, except for the Virgin's face, which an angel completed during his slumber. Suitably impressed, locals

Pontormo, Visitation *(detail)*

flocked here to pay their dues, later establishing a Cloister of the Voti where they would burn wax effigies of themselves in an act of devotion. Unfortunately, no effigies remain, but you should still visit both it and the Cloister of the Morti for their 16th-century frescoes created by Andrea del Sarto (his best known *Birth of the Virgin and Madonna del Sacco*), Rosso Fiorentino and Pontormo. The first two chapels on the left also contain works by Andrea del Castagno, including *The Vision of St Jerome* and *The Trinity*.

Spedale degli Innocenti (Hospital of the Innocents, Piazza SS. Annunziata 12, ☎ 055-23491708, fax 055-2037323, daily, 8:30 am-2 pm, closed Wed, €3): Constructed by Brunelleschi in 1419, the construction features swaddled babes of varnished terracotta (the work of Andrea della Robbia) its loggia that give a good indication of this building's original function as a hospice for abandoned newborns. Its well-proportioned structure and porticoed façade (novelties in civil architecture of the time) are considered the major architectural catalysts of the Renaissance, with architect after architect attempting to emulate Brunelleschi's lucid style in the *pietra serena*, the gray stone of the Florence area that he favored. Inside, you'll find two cloisters of note – Chiostro degli Uomini (Men's Cloister) with an *Annunciation* by Andrea della Robbia and a holy water font by Antonio Rossellino, and the Chiostro delle Donne (Women's Cloister) – plus a gallery containing a museum of painting, which includes Ghirlandaio's *Adoration of the Magi* (1488), Luca della Robbia's *Madonna with Child* (1450) and works by Piero di Cosimo and Botticelli (including a *Virgin and Child with St John the Baptist* created around 1460, above).

Museo Archeologico (Archeological Museum, Via della Colonna 38, ☎ 055-23575, www.comune.firenze.it/soggetti, Sat/Mon, 2-7 pm, Tues/Thurs, 8:30 am-7 pm,

Florence

Terracotta head from Arezzo (second century BC, Museo Archeologico)

Wed/Fri/Sun, 8:30 am-2 pm, €4): Head east out of the square and you'll arrive at the Museo Archeologico, worth a peek for its collection of antiquities from Etruscan to Medici times. Included in the number of Etruscan bronzes that make up most of the collection are the fifth-century BC *Chimera* and the later *Arringatore* (Orator), but the museum's much-envied showpiece is the French Vase (sixth century BC) discovered in an Etruscan tomb near Chiusi.

Continue along Via della Colonna and then south down Borgo Pinti to reach the **Convent di Santa Maria Maddalena dei Pazzi**, an old Cistercian convent given a new lease on life by Giuliano da Sangallo in 1492 and best known for Perugino's famous *Crucifixion* fresco (1493-96) that adorns the Chapter Room. From here, a left down Via dei Pilastri will take you to the Sant'Ambrogio market area, the second of the city's food halls and another spot for some delicious lunchtime bargains. Stop for a quick bite before heading into the square's church, the site of an Orcagna fresco of *The Madonna and Saints*, a Mino da Fiesole tabernacle and the tomb of Verrocchio (in a chapel along the left aisle).

THE SYNAGOGUE & JEWISH MUSEUM

As you wandered down Via dei Pilastri, you probably noticed the large green cupola to your left up Via L.C. Farini. This is Florence's Byzantine-style synagogue built at the end of the 19th century to replace the original synagogue destroyed during the construction of Piazza della Repubblica. You can read up on both the original building and Jewish history in Florence by popping into its museum (daily, 10 am-1 pm, 2-5 pm, closed Fri pm, free).

Continue along Via Pietrapiana and on your left is Vasari's Loggia del Pesce, which moved here from the Piazza Repubblica in the 19th century. It marks the site of a daily flea market on Piazza Ciompi. Continue along and you'll reach Via dei Pepi, where you should take a left to arrive on Piazza Santa Croce, the much-loved site of the Calcio Storico and another important port of call on the trail of Florentine churches.

CALCIO STORICO

Football meets rugby and wrestling at its most historical (and violent) on the Saint's Day of St John the Baptist (24th June; heats take place on various weekends leading up to the final). Preceded by a raucous procession in Renaissance costume, the two qualifying teams out of the original four – all resplendent in the most impractical of medieval garters and pantaloons (white for Santo Spirito, blue for Santa Croce, green for San Giovanni and red for Santa Maria Novella) – battle it out in a 50-minute scrum thought to date back to the *Arpasto*, played by Roman legionnaires. You'll be hard pressed to figure out the rules. For info, ☎ 055-2616052)

Chiesa di Santa Croce (Piazza Santa Croce, ☎ 055-244619, Mon-Fri, 9:30 am-5:30 pm, Sun, 1-5:30 pm, €3): This Franciscan basilica grew into its current size under the careful plans of Arnolfo di Cambio from the end of the 13th century, when the modest chapel that originally stood on its spot was enlarged into the glorious edifice you see today. It wasn't until the 19th century that the façade and campanile were added. Although neither the sides nor the back were completed, the stunning, although rather unconvincing, Neo-Gothic front gives a good idea of the intended effect. During the 15th century it was the final resting place of Florence's most distinguished residents and more than 250 tombstones line the floor of the church with grander monuments marking the spot of the more famous artists and writers buried here – Michelangelo (first chapel on the

Giotto, The Vision of Friar Augustine and Bishop Guido of Assisi

right with tomb designed by Vasari), Dante (farther along to the right, although not actually buried here), Galileo (opposite) and Machiavelli (the fourth chapel on the right and the most visited). You should also head into the Bardi and Peruzzi chapels to visit Giotto's radiant frescoes depicting *Scenes from the Life of St Francis* in the former and *Scenes from the Life of St John the Baptist* in the latter. The showpiece of the museum, to which your ticket also includes entry (☎/fax 055-2466105, same opening hours), is Cimabue's wooden crucifix. It still manages to retain its original splendor despite damage from the 1966 flood that ravaged the Santa Croce quarter. But there are also detached frescoes by Taddeo Gaddi (*The Last Supper* and the huge *Tree of the Cross*) and by Orcagna, as well as one of Brunelleschi's best but unfortunately uncompleted works, the Pazzi Chapel with terracotta décor by Luca della Robbia.

> **Stendhal Syndrome:** Moved to the point of collapse on visiting the Church of Santa Croce in 1817, Stendhal has given his name to a new type of sightseeing disorder. Coined by psychiatrists from the Santa Maria Nuova Hospital, "Stendhal Syndrome" affects Florence's most sensitive visitors who become charged with so much emotion in the contemplation of works of art that they feel mental and/or physical pain.

RAINY DAYS FOR ART FANS

Florence Art (Palazzo Antellesi 21/22, Piazza Santa Croce, ☎ 055-245354, www.florenceart.org) holds seven weekly lectures tracing how the intrigues of Florentine Renaissance history produced and influenced great artists such as Michelangelo, Botticelli, Masaccio and Giotto (from €12 to €30).

From the piazza, through the well-preserved medieval streets once frequented by Dante and Boccaccio, you should already have sighted the tower of your next port of call; the Bargello. For your quickest means of arrival, take Via dell'Anguillara and then a right up Via del Proconsolo.

Florence

Bartolomeo Ammanati,
Leda with the Swan

Museo Nazionale del Bargello (Via del Proconsolo 4, ☎ 055-2388606, fax 055-2388756, www.sbas.firenze.it/bargello, Tues-Sat, 8:15 am-1:50 pm, Sun, 8:15 am-5 pm, €4): With its austere fortress-like appearance, the Palazzo Bargello (formerly known as the Palazzo dei Priori) dates from 1255 when it was constructed to house the Capitano del Popolo (the commander of the local militia). It went on to become the seat of the podestà, (the city magistrate who replaced the previous aristocratic rule) and then of the Capitano di Giustizia (the town magistrate) or Bargello, from which it takes its present name. Since 1859, it has been the home of Florence's National Museum, important for its displays of Renaissance sculpture, which includes works by Ghiberti, Donatello (*Niccolò da Uzzano*, *Marzocco*, *Cupid*, *David*, *St. George*), Brunelleschi (including panels from the Baptistery doors), Verrocchio, Ammannati and Cellini (including his *Bust of Cosimo I*). You will also see works by Giambologna (such as *Florence Defeating Pisa* and the splendid bronze *Mercury*) and terracottas by the della Robbia brothers. Look out for Michelangelo's drunken *Bacchus* (his first major sculpture, created when he was 22), *Brutus*, *Tondo Pitti* and an unfinished *David* in bronze.

Almost directly in front of the Bargello is the **Badia Fiorentina** (Via del Proconsolo, ☎ 055-2344545, daily, 5-7 pm, Sun, 8.30-11:30 am, free), the city's oldest monastery. It was built for the Benedictines in 978 but completely restructured by Arnolfo di Cambio in 1285. Inside, it has a few artworks of note, including a striking marble tomb by Mino da Fiesole. Up in the Chiostro delle Aranci (to the right of the presbytery) is Filippino Lippi's *Apparition of the Virgin to Saint Bernard* (1485), while in the Chapel Pandolfini you'll find the spot where Boccaccio is said to have held the first public reading of Dante's *The Divine Comedy*.

LET'S GO TO DANTE'S

Just off Via D. Alighieri behind the Badia is a reconstruction of the former home of perhaps the greatest poet in the Italian language, Dante Alighieri. The museum is arranged on three floors, corresponding to phases in the poet's life; the first shows his early years up until his exile, the second traces his stays in the houses of the numerous lords where he wrote his masterpiece, *The Divine Comedy*; and the third depicts his influence on the writers and artists who followed him. (Casa Dante, Via S. Margherita, 1, ☎ 055-283962, 9:30 am-12:30 pm, 3:30-6:30 pm, closed Wed, €3)

■ The Oltrano

Piazza del Carmine – Piazza Santo Spirito – Palazzo Pitti – Piazzale Michelangelo – San Miniato al Monte

A picturesque neighborhood traditionally populated by craftsmen, restorers and antique dealers awaits you on the other side of the Arno. Originally the domain of those unable to offer themselves a palazzo on the north side of the river, the now trendy Oltrano first saw its fortune change with the construction of the Palazzo Pitti in the mid-15th century and since has gone from strength to strength. These days its windy, cobbled streets are both the site of the last vestiges of Florentine culture and the meeting place for Florence's globalized youth, a dichotomy also reflected in its much-frequented restaurants.

Start your tour on **Piazza del Carmine**, the heart of the San Frediano district and considered by many Florentines to be the only remaining location of the city's traditional sense of community. These days, the square is a rather bland car park which the fashionable caffè-bars (the Dolce Vita being one of the stars of the young nightlife scene) and the bleak exterior of the church of Santa Maria del Carmine only manage to exacerbate. Don't let this put you off; this church accommodates one of Italy's greatest fresco cycles in the Cappella Brancacci.

Cappella Brancacci (Brancacci Chapel, ☎ 055-2382195, daily, 10 am-5 pm, closed Sun am and Tues, €3.10): World-famous for its Renaissance fresco cycle depicting scenes from the Old Testament (from the *Original Sin* to the *Life of St Peter*) and a must-see for any serious art fan, the Cappella Brancacci was happily preserved from the 1771 fire that destroyed almost all the remainder of the 13th-century church (later reconstructed in its present Neo-Gothic style). The frescoes
were worked on by Masolino and his then-pupil Masaccio, then completed by Filippino Lippi after the death of the latter from the plague. But it is the frescoes by Masaccio that are the most celebrated, especially those of the *Expulsion from Paradise* (first panel left) and the episodes of *The Tribute Money* (top left). The work of Masolino can be seen in the lower tier to the right of the altar, while Filippino Lippi is responsible for most of the lower zone of the right wall.

The narrow Via S. Monica leads onto Via Sant'Agostino, where you'll find yourself in a much pleasanter tree-lined community square, **Piazza Santo Spirito**. Buzzing with gelato-eaters year-round, it is especially engaging during *Firenze Estate* (the city's summer festival, see page 66), when it sees live performances on an almost nightly basis. Its showpiece, apart from the bustling caffès and restaurants, is the Brunelleschi-designed church of Santo Spirito with its uncompleted, slightly dilapidated, yet somehow charming, façade.

Chiesa di Santo Spirito (☎ 055-210030, Mon-Fri, 8:30 am-noon, 4-6 pm, Sat-Sun, 4-6 pm, closed Wed pm, free): The last church designed by Brunelleschi, the Augustinian church of Santo Spirito is also said to be the one that fits most closely with his well-proportioned plans. Constructed in the shape of a Latin cross with three spacious naves and arches supported by 35 *pietra serena* Corinthian columns, the interior houses some great 15th-century works, including Filippo Lippi's *Madonna and Child with Saints* and Botticini's *St Monica and the Augustinian Nuns*. On the left of the church, the Cenacolo di Santo Spirito (☎ 055-287043, Tues-Sun, 9 am-2 pm, €2.10) occupies two cloisters. The refectory is also here, with its display of 14th-century frescoes (including the remainder of a *Last Supper* by Andrea Orcagna) and Romanesque sculptures.

Florence

THE FACE OF SANTO SPIRITO

The walls of Caffè Richi on Piazza Santo Spirito display the outcome of a recent competition to design a new façade for the church. It's worth an espresso or gelato break here to peruse the drawings on offer, which range from the traditional to the clichéd and the absurd (including one where the central window is transformed into a giant doorbell).

Make your way back towards the Ponte Vecchio along Via Santo Spirito (home to many of Florence's popular restaurants) before ducking down the palazzo-lined Via Maggio where, at no. 26, a beautiful *sgraffiti*-decorated façade adorns the house of Bianca Capello, the mistress of Ferdinando I. Take Strada dei Pitti through the Giardino di Boboli for the best approach to the Piazza and museum-packed palace of the same name. Or first continue down to the oft-ignored Piazza San Felice, home to an interesting 11th-century church with a crucifix linked to Giotto and a triptych from Botticelli's workshop. From here, Via dei Guicciardini will take you to Palazzo Pitti.

Palazzo Pitti: The regal Palazzo Pitti was actually commissioned to Brunelleschi by businessman-banker Luca Pitti in the mid-15th century in competition with the splendid palaces of his great rivals, the Medici. Ruined, the family ironically sold the building a century later to the wife of Cosimo I, Elenora di Toledo, who was eager to flee the sobriety of the Palazzo Vecchio, and the Grand-Dukes of Tuscany continued to inhabit and enlarge it for three centuries. With a 200-m/656-ft façade, this is by far the largest palace constructed in the Renaissance and built entirely of gigantic blocks. The work involved in quarrying, transporting and setting them in place is an indication of the pretensions of Luca Pitti and more than befits those of Cosimo I and the Medici who followed.

Museum Admission: You can buy a special ticket for the **Palazzo Pitti** which allows entrance to all of its sights (Galleria Palatina, Galleria d'Arte Moderna, Galleria del Costume, Museo degli Argenti, Giardino di Boboli and Museo delle Porcellane) for €10. The combined ticket, called Argenti-Boboli, covers Giardino di Boboli, Museo delle Porcellane and Museo degli Argenti and costs €4. Both are valid for three days from purchase.

Galleria Palatina & Appartamenti Reali (Palatina Gallery & Royal Apartments, Palazzo Pitti, ☎ 055-2388614, fax 055-2388613, www.sbas.firenze.it/palatina, Tues-Sun, 8:15 am-6:50 pm, closed Mon, €8.50): Housed in the Pitti's noblest rooms and considered by many to be Florence's most important art collection other than the Uffizi, this gallery displays many of the best works collected by the Medici and subsequent Lorraine dynasty. The gallery's showpieces are works by 16th-century artists spread over six main rooms: *Venus* (with masterpieces by Titian and Rubens), *Apollo* (with works by Titian, Pietro da Cortona, Rosso Fiorentino and Andrea del Sarto), *Mars* (Raphael, Rubens, Pietro da Cortona), *Jupiter* (Pietro da Cortona, Verrocchio, Bellini, Raphael, Andrea del Sarto, Fra Bartolomeo), *Saturn*

(Pietro da Cortona, Raphael, Perugino, Andrea del Sarto) and *Illiad* (Raphael and Andrea del Sarto). Annexed to the gallery are the royal apartments inhabited by King Vittore-Emmanuele for the short time when Florence was the capital of Italy between 1865 and 1871.

The Pitti's Other Museums: Just to prove Florentine art did continue after the Renaissance, the **Galleria d'Arte Moderna** (Gallery of Modern Art, ☎ 055-2388616, fax 055-2654520, www.sbas.firenze.it/gam, Tues-Sun, 8:15 am-1:50 pm, €5) conserves works from the 19th century on, especially those of the Macchiaioli (the Italian face of Impressionism). The **Galleria del Costume**, to which your ticket also allows entrance (Gallery of Medicean Clothing, ☎/fax 055-2388713, www.sbas.firenze.it/gam, same opening hours), displays the funeral wear of Cosimo I and Elenora di Toledo. The collection of treasures accumulated by the Medici and their successors, including some fine jewels, ivory and crystals, are displayed in the fresco-covered rooms now home to the **Museo degli Argenti** (☎ 055-2388709, fax 055-2388761, www.sbas.firenze.it/argenti, Tues-Sun, 8:30 am-1:50 pm, €2). The **Museo delle Porcellane** – (☎ 055-2388709, fax 055-2388310, www.sbas.firenze.it/argenti, daily, 8:30 am-1:30 pm) is worth your time only if you're a fan of antique tableware; what is on display here was used by the inhabitants of the Palazzo Pitti from the Medici on.

Giardino di Boboli (☎ 055-2651816, daily, summer, 8:15 am-6:30 pm, winter, 8:15 am-4:30 pm, €2): It was the wife of Cosimo I, Elenora di Toledo, who insisted the hilly area behind the Palazzo Pitti be turned into gardens. She commissioned Tribolo to transform it into what is now one of the most important remaining examples of Italian landscaping, with fountains, grottoes and some amazing sculptures. It's an opportunity to sit, relax and take in the great views over town from the summit. Don't miss the Isolotto, the small island in the center of the water garden, Buontalenti's grotto, the Kaffeehaus in its 18th-century Rococo pavilion, or the vast amphitheater where opera is said to have

Giambologna's Fontana dell' Oceano in the Boboli Gardens

been born. Recently reopened after five years of restorative work, the adjoining **Forte di Belvedere** – considered "Florence's balcony" for its far-reaching views – is also well worth a peek. The commission was given to Buontalenti at the end of the 16th century by Ferdinando I who wanted a Medici stronghold in case of uprisings in the city. Interestingly, it encapsulates an earlier Ammannati palace, which is itself said to have been built on the spot of a secret well guarding Medici treasures. Also home to the Belvedere dell'Arte exhibition (☎ 055-2001486, www.belvederedellarte.it, €8, conc. €6.50), the Forte is a great place to visit in summer when live music concerts are held and films are shown in an atmospheric open-air theater (see page 63-65).

Continue along Via dei Guicciardini to reach the **Church of Santa Felicita** (you'd already have had a sneaky look inside if you managed to get a ticket into the Corridoio Vasariano, see page 41). Its Brunelleschi-designed Chapel Capponi guards two works by Pontormo: the striking *Annunciation* (fresco on the right) and a canvas titled *Deposition,* showing Jesus being ripped from the Virgin's arms (1525-28), which is considered one of the great works of Florentine Mannerism.

From here it's an enjoyable hike up to the spectacular vantage points of San Miniato al Monte and Piazzale Michelangelo (take Bus #12 or #13 from the station if you don't want to walk). For the best and most scenic approach, take a right up Costa di San Giorgio up behind Forte Belvedere (and some magnificent views over the Giardino di Boboli), before heading left down Via di Belvedere (look out for sections of the old city walls) to arrive at the ancient city gate to San Miniato. From here a right up the winding Via del Monte alle Croci leads you to the foot of a large stairway. Once scaled, it brings you out in front of the celebrated church.

Chiesa di San Miniato al Monte (Via Monte alle Croci, ☎ 055-2342731, summer, 8 am-7:30 pm, winter, 8 am-12:30 pm, 2:30-7:30 pm, free): According to local legend, San Miniato, converted to Christianity and martyred in its name, walked decapitated up the hill before collapsing on the site of the present church, which was erected in his name in 1013. If you've made the short hike yourself, you'll probably find this a little difficult to believe, but you will find here one of the most serene churches in the city, a welcome change from the fume-enveloped sites of downtown. Known for the brilliant alternating white and green marble of the exterior (considered one of the finest examples of the Florentine Romanesque style), the façade is further embellished with a 13th-century gilded mosaic of Christ placed between the Virgin Mary and the martyred Saint. Inside, apart from the saintly remains, the main draw is the Renaissance Chapel with the crypt of Cardinale del Portogallo (carved by Rossellino), an Annunciation by Baldovinetti, a barrel-vaulted ceiling by Luca della Robbia and an altarpiece (original in the Uffizi) which is the work of Antonio and Piero del Pollaiolo. Luca della Robbia is also responsible for the careful decoration of Michelozzo's Crucifixion Chapel.

From outside the church, a staircase leads you back onto Viale G. Galilei and a short descent to **Piazzale Michelangelo**, the city's best-known viewpoint and easily-recognizable by the bronze replica of *David*, the souvenir sellers and, of course, the view. Built to the plans of Giuseppe Poggi in 1869, it offers a splendid panorama of the city best enjoyed in the early evening when the incessant tour buses decline a bit. From here, you can rejoin the city by following the steps down to Piazza G. Poggi and taking a left along Via di San Niccolò to arrive back at the Ponte Vecchio.

Lazy Touring: Hop on and off the daily **City Sightseeing Bus** (☎ 055-5650460, €20, ticket valid for 24 hours, every 30 minutes, 9:30 am-7 pm, every 60 minutes all other times, with commentary in English). It departs from the train station and skirts the historical center, stopping at the Duomo, San Marco, Santa Croce, Piazzale Michelangelo and the Palazzo Pitti among other places. ATAF city buses #12 and #13 offer a normal route up to Piazzale Michelangelo, without commentary, for the much cheaper single ticket of €1 (every 10-15 mins, 6-1 am).

Try a Guided Walking Tour

Join Florentine native Federica for walking, history and insider's information on her Florence Introduction Tour, the perfect choice for first-time visitors (book through **In Italy,** ☎ 055-2479880, www.initaly.com, two people, €135, three-six people, €221, seven-10 people, €263).

Mercurio Tours (☎ 055-266141, fax 055-283892, www.mercurio-italy. org), on the other hand, will take you on one-day walking tours through Florence's past and present (Mon-Sat) and on guided visits to the Uffizi (Tues-Sat), Accademia (Tues, Wed, Fri), Bargello (Mon), Palazzo Pitti (Thurs) and Medici Chapels (Mon). Tours cost from €26 to €55 and include museum entry.

Walking Tours of Florence (Piazza Santo Stefano 2, ☎ 055-2645033, www.artviva.com) offer a three-hour tour of Florence by day (Mon-Sat, €25, conc. €10) and a 1½-hour night tour (Mon-Sat, €25, children free), trips around the Uffizi (Tues-Sat, €37, conc. €15) and a performance tour of the Palazzo Pitti (Mon, Fri, Sat, €35, conc. €15).

Adventures

■ On Foot

Independent Hiking

Florence is well located for forays into the countryside with walking centers Chianti (see page 135), Mugello (see page 91) and the Montagna Pistoiese (see page 132) a short train, bus or car ride away. Closer still, the 20-minute bus ride to Fiesole will allow you to pick up routes onto **Monte Ceceri** that you can manage in an afternoon and longer itineraries north towards Borgo San Lorenzo and the Mugello (see page 88 for more information on adventures from Fiesole).

From Florence itself, you can pick up the steep, windy trail #7 beside the Villa Camerata Youth Hostel (take Bus #7 to Piazza T. A. Edison) up to **Fiesole** via the marked paths of Monte Ceceri and then down to **Settignano** on the looping panoramic #1 (return to Florence on Bus #10 from Settignano).

More central still, an unmarked trail leads from the Galleria degli Uffizi across the Ponte Vecchio and round the back of **Forte di Belvedere** along Costa di San Giorgio. If you follow this road up to Arcetri and on to the tiny village of **Pian de Giullari**, you can either continue into Chianti territory or return to the city via Monte alle Creci and Piazzale Michelangelo. For the exact route of the unmarked itinerary pick up KOMPASS map #660 Firenze-Chianti (1:50,000, www.kompass.at).

Although Florence's urban periphery may be somewhat less than attractive, it has plenty of starting points for pleasant afternoon strolls or multi-day hikes into the hills and countryside that surround them. From Sesto Fiorentino (Bus #28), trails #3 and #3B lead up **Monte Acuto**, from where you can return to Florence via Serpiolle (Bus #43 links back to the center) or continue north to the **Gualdo Alpine Refuge** (☎ 055-4481638). Shorter circuits are available from Scandicci

(Bus #27) and Signa, including the easy #2 around the **bird-watching** lakes of the **Parco dei Renai** (Signa, ☎ 3498852179). The park has a children's play area, three miles worth of bicycle tracks, rowboats for hire and, on summer evenings, a restaurant, bar and live music. Entry is free. Or you can try the longer #1 to the **Villa Medicea Artimino** (also known as "La Ferdinanda," see page 121). From Campi Bisenzio, northwest of Florence, you can explore the small **WWF Oasis Stagni di Focognano** (Via del Ronco, Bus #30). Or, from the southernmost point of the city, you can pick up the Firenze-Siena-Roma, 25-stage footpath, which takes you south to Siena and on as far as Rome.

> **TIP:** In 2004, Florence Tourist Board published *Renaissance Ring*, about the trekking and mountain biking route along trails and dirt roads, which has Brunelleschi's Cupola as its center and that passes through 13 nearby towns and villages. The booklet also includes a detailed map and a list of recommended accomodations and eateries. Request a copy from the tourist board on arrival.

FLORENTINE GREEN SPACES

The central Giardino di Boboli (see page 55) and the Parco delle Cascine (Bus #17C) may be the best known, but they're not the only parks of interest to strolling visitors; within easy reach of Florence is an extensive choice of trail-marked parks, many in the grounds of historic Medici villas.

The 14-acre **Parco del Ventaglio** can be discovered at the bottom of the hill up to Fiesole (Via Aldini 4, daylight hours, free, Bus #7). Adjacent to a 15th-century villa, these English-style gardens (remodeled in the 19th century by architect, Giuseppe Poggi) have a romantic little lake surrounded by copses of horse-chestnut trees, limes and elms, and a large holm-oak wood crisscrossed by trails.

North of Florence, you can find Giambologna's Grotta degli Animali (a manmade cave filled with animal sculptures) at **Parco Mediceo di Villa di Castello** (Via di Castello 47, ☎ 055-454791, 8:15 am-7 pm, closed second and third Mon. of the month, €2, Bus #28), as well as a lovely trail around the labyrinthine water gardens. Your ticket includes entrance to the nearby **Parco Mediceo di Villa la Petraia** (Via della Petraia 40, ☎ 055-452691, same opening hours), with its three-tiered and painstakingly geometrical Italian gardens. The villa occupies the third level and has some lovely 17th-century frescoes of note.

You can't enter the villa at **Parco Mediceo di Villa di Careggi** (Viale Pieraccini 17, ☎ 055-4279755, www.villamediceadicareggi.firenze.net, 9 am-6 pm, closed Sun and holidays, free, Bus #14), but you can freely enjoy the gardens and ancient woodlands with their hidden statues and central fountain.

There's a lovely nature trail at **Parco and Villa Demidoff** (Loc. Pratolino, Via Fiorentina 276, ☎ 055-409427, 10 am-8 pm, €3, Bus #25A), taking you past Giambologna's famous fountain statue, *Appennino* (a water-gushing shaggy mountain-man).

Hiking with the Locals

If you want to best appreciate the local countryside, join a trekking organization. Incredibly welcoming to fellow walkers and nature lovers whatever their nationality, most allow anyone to turn up and take part. Prices, if any, are much lower than with companies aiming their trips solely at tourists. Check with the organizations themselves for current itinerary information.

For the serious hiker, the national **Associazione Amici del Trekking e della Natura** has an office in Florence (Via dell'Oriuolo 17, ☎ 055-2341040, fax 055-2268207, www.trekkingfirenze.it) organizing day-long treks into the Tuscan countryside. They leave from various spots in the city most Suns and cost from as little as €6. Check out their website for the latest program and membership prices (currently €15.50, free for under 17s).

The Florence branch of the **CAI** (Club Alpino Italiano, ☎ 055-6120467, www.caifirenze.it) offers Sun treks to a range of Tuscan destinations, including the Alpuan Alps, for its large group of members (membership €45.50, conc. €16). You can take part in one or two treks without joining as a member.

All are welcome to join the treks organized by the cultural association **ARZACH**, based in Sesto Fiorentino (Via del Casato 18, ☎ 055-4490614, www.arzach.it), including Sun hikes of five to six hours into the Mugello and the Sienese Crete (from only €8).

Link up with **Ufficio Guide** (Libreria Stella Alpina, Via Corridoni 14b, ☎ 055-411688, fax 055-4360877, www.ufficioguide.it) on their Sat and Sun treks into the Florence area (including Chianti, the Parco Nazionale delle Foreste Casentinesi and around San Gimignano) from €8.

The bigger your group the better the deal with **Trekking & Ambiente** (Via Pandolfini 9, ☎/fax 055-2340238, trekamb@tin.it); their four-hour (€80 for groups of up to 20) and eight-hour (€140) excursions into the Florentine province include shorter trips to green spaces around Settignano and Fiesole or longer walks around Chianti, Medici Mugello and Collodi (where kids can visit the land of Pinocchio).

Group Hikes

If you like your walking tours as luxurious as possible, hate the idea of retracing your steps to get back to the car or waiting half an hour at the bus stop – or if you just want to hear more about the history and geography of the area you're walking – an all-inclusive tour may be the way to go. These offer half- and full-day guided tours in the area around Florence, with shuttle service, bilingual guide, all equipment and lunch included in the price.

To see the best of what's just outside the city, join **Mercurio Tours** (☎ 055-266141, fax 055-283892, www.mercurio-italy.org) on their half-day walking tour from Piazzale Michelangelo up little country roads to the hill of Arcetri, the antique village of Pian dei Giullari and beyond (pick up on Piazzale Michelangelo at 9 am, Fri only, €26).

You can accompany **The Accidental Tourist** (☎ 055-699376, fax 055-699048, www.accidentaltourist.com) on their full-day walking tour of the Chianti countryside, which includes wine and olive oil tasting for €68 (pick up at Piazza Demidoff, various dates).

Not just cycling tours, **I Bike Italy** (☎ 055-2342371, www.ibikeitaly.com) offers an easy five-mile, half-day outing to castles and villas in the Fiesole area (pick up at Ponte alle Grazie at 9:30 am; tour ends at 3:30 pm, €45).

On Rock

Guide Alpine Agai (Via Torre degli Agli 65, ☎ 055-431974), north of the Parco delle Cascine, organizes courses for all levels from expert climbing to five-day beginner excursions. Call for the latest expeditions and prices. You can also join **Ufficio Guide** (Libreria Stella Alpina, Via Corridoni 14b, ☎ 055-411688, fax 055-4360877, www.ufficioguide.it) on their monthly rock-climbing and ice-climbing excursions (from €180 for the three-day course).

■ On Wheels

Bicycling Around Town

Exploring Florence by bike can be an exhilarating but slightly frustrating experience. The cars and mopeds zooming by, the one-way streets (it's best to ignore the signs, as locals do) and the crowds in the car-free areas make a seamless ride impossible. That said, if you want to see as much in and out of the historical center as possible, renting a bike is the quickest way to get around the Oltrano, up to Piazzale Michelangelo and along the riverside. A favorite place for local joggers and cyclists, it's also worth taking a detour to the **Parco delle Cascine** (best avoided at night) for some lovely cycling down tree-lined avenues.

BIKE RENTAL

Mille e una Bici (rental points outside S.M.N., Campo Marte and Rifredi train stations). City bikes from €1.50 per hour, €8 per day, those with weekly train/bus passes €0.50 per hour, €1 per day.

Alinari (Via Guelfa 85r, ☎ 055-280500, fax 055-2717871, www.alinarirental.com). City bikes from €2.50 per hour, €12 per day, mountain bikes from €3 per hour, €18 per day, scooters from €12 per hour, €55 per day.

Florence by Bike (Via San Zanobi 91r, ☎/fax 055-488992, www.florencebybike.it). City bikes from €2.50 per hour, €12 per day, mountain bikes from €3.5 per hour, €18 per day, scooters from €30 per day.

For half-day guided bike tours taking you from the Sant'Ambrogio market area, through Santa Croce, across the Arno up to Piazzale Michelangelo and back via Forte Belvedere and Santo Spirito, contact **Best Tuscan Bike Tours** (☎ 339-7244446, BestBike2003@yahoo.com).

Bicycling Out of Town

Florence's periphery is layered with mountain bike routes. The most popular itinerary leaves from Coverciano in Florence's northeast and loops up through Fiesole before returning to the departure point via Settignano. From Fiesole itself (see page 89), you can pick up numerous trails heading north into the Mugello, while from Settignano, you can pick up a lovely route along some of the Arno's most scenic stretches to Pontassieve or south into the hills of Chianti.

From the Oltrano, a well-pedaled cycle route leads from the Ponte Vecchio, up Piazzale Michelangelo and south to Galluzzo Certosa. From there you can return to the city via Piazza Santo Spirito or continue south to Impruneta (see page 135). A track from Florence's southwest (pick up the trail by crossing over to the Oltrano from the Parco delle Cascine) leads west along the River Arno to Lastra a Signa and onto the Villa Medicea Artimino (also known as "La Ferdinanda," see page 121). All routes are manageable one-day outings. Take along KOMPASS map #660 Firenze-Chianti (1:50,000, www.kompass.at) to ensure you don't lose your way.

Group Cycling

Cycle tours differ dramatically between companies. While most include a shuttle service to the starting point, a bilingual guide, all equipment and lunch, some try to offer a smaller and more personal experience. I joined Dominick of **Best Tuscan Bike Tours** (☎ 339-7244446, BestBike2003@yahoo.com) on his one-day accompanied tour up to Fiesole. An expat who gave up his career in Wall Street to offer these tours, Dominick's aim is to tax your legs, improve your cycling style and ensure you leave with a better understanding of the Tuscan way of life. The tour includes a traditional lunch in a well-hidden family restaurant and talks on wine and olive oil production (with opportunity to buy). In addition to the Fiesole tour, Dominick also offers guided road bike tours for the more advanced cyclist. Tours depart from Florence center, 9 am-5 pm, by arrangement; €112 for two, €105 for three, €86 for four, €82 for five to eight and €79 for nine-10 riders.

I Bike Italy (☎ 055-2342371, www.ibikeitaly.com) will take you along the 15-mile uphill Florence-to-Fiesole route, unless you prefer the 30-mile (longer but flatter) itinerary around Chianti. There's also a two-day tour from Florence to Siena (three-star accommodation included). All tours pick up at Ponte alle Grazie at 9 am and return by 5 pm (single day from €52, two-day €210).

Bicycle Tuscany (☎ 055-222580, www.bicycletuscany.com) focuses on one-day tours of Chianti, but with an easier 29-km/18-mile route (pick-up at 10 am at Ponte Vespucci, return at 5 pm, €60).

The Accidental Tourist (☎ 055-699376, fax 055-699048, www.accidentaltourist.com) offers a similar tour of Chianti with an added wine-tasting incentive (pick-up at Piazza Demidoff, €74).

Also in the Chianti region, **Florence by Bike** (☎ 055-488992, www.florencebybike.it) guides you along a 35-km/22-mile tour at medium to difficult level (pick-up at the shop on Via San Zanobi at 9:30 am, return to Florence by 4:30 pm, €69.90).

Bike Florence Tuscany (☎ 055-2645033, www.bikeflorencetuscany.com) has perhaps the easiest route, taking you across the Ponte Vecchio, through town and into the Florentine countryside (daily, pick-up at Piazza Santo Stefano at 9 am, return by 2:30 pm, contact for price information).

■ On Water

Canoeing the Arno

Società Canottieri Firenze (Lungarno F. Ferrucci 4, ☎ 055-6812151, www.canottiericomunalifirenze.it) offers canoe courses and outings by arrangement under the Ponte Vecchio for groups of at least seven, dependent on river conditions (€55 per person, contact Alessandro at ☎ 349-4639519). In the Uffizi area, there's also canoe-rental just down the steps from Lungarno degli Archibusieri that operates on summer afternoons.

Hop on board an historic sand-collecting boat (moved using the traditional 8-m/26-ft punts) at Lungarno Diaz with **Associazione I Renaiolo** (c/o Società Canottieri Firenze, Lungarno F. Ferrucci 4, info@renaiolo.it). The one-hour boat trip runs from Ponte alle Grazie to Ponte alla Carrara and takes you under the Ponte Vecchio and Ponte Santa Trinità. Excursions run June to October, depending on weather conditions and participation of at least five passengers (€11 per person, contact Paolo at ☎ 3477982356).

CITY SUNBATHING

Florence has a range of glorious Olympic-size outdoor pools where you can swim, sunbathe, eat and drink in the summer heat:
Bellariva (Lungarno Colombo 6, ☎ 055-677521, Mon-Fri, 10 am-6 pm, Sat-Sun, 10 am-6:30 pm, €6.50, conc. €4.50).
Costoli (Viale P. Paoli, ☎ 055-6236027, daily, 10 am-6 pm, closed Mon am, €6.50, conc. €4.50).
Le Pavoniere (Parco delle Cascine, ☎ 055-3215644, daily, 10 am-6 pm, €7, conc. €5).
Piscina Comunale A. Franchi (Viale Maratona, ☎ 055-2616145).
Poggetto (Via M. Mercati 24, ☎ 055-484465, daily, 10 am-6:30 pm, €5)

■ On Horseback

 Serious horseback riders want to get themselves north into the Mugello (see page 91), south into Chianti (see page 134) or farther south into the Siena (see page 150) or Grosseto (see page 342) provinces to enjoy the best trails available. But if you are based in Florence, there are a few companies who will arrange to pick you up and take you to the saddle, as well as a few local riding schools offering lessons and treks.

Book online before you arrive for the six-hour riding tour into the Chianti countryside offered by **Popular Tours** (www.populartours.com, March-Dec, with pick-up at hotel, from €193).

In Florence's southwest periphery, the guided trek offered by **Scandicci Horse Riding Group** (Via Mosciano 34, Loc. Vingone, ☎ 055-740389, www.sportges.it) takes you into the green countryside of the Poggiona area with its views as far as the Duomo. Contact them for prices. More central still, the **Centro Ippico Toscano** (Via dei Vespucci 5a, ☎ 055-315621, fax 055-310213, www.centroippicotoscano.com) organize short horse and pony treks around the Parco delle Cascine.

Other riding schools in the periphery are **Bagno a Ripoli** (Centro Ippico L'Antellino, Via delle Torre 1, ☎ 055-621811, and Scuola Equitazione Fiorentina, Via Vicchio e Paterno 10, ☎ 055-632718), **Lastra a Signa** (Centro Ippico Lastra a Signa, Via Bracciatica 22, ☎ 055-8729223) and **Impruneta** (Centro Ippico Ugolino, Via dell'Oliveta 12, ☎ 055-2301289, and Club Ippico gli Olmi, Via Imprunetana per Tavarnuzze 43, ☎ 055-2011709).

The closest riding center outside the city is **Rendola Riding** in the Valdarno (Rendola Valdarno, Montevarchi, ☎ 055-9707045, http://go.supereva.it/rendolariding.freeweb), with one-hour rides from €15. Both lessons and treks (day, weekend and week-long excursions) are available in English with lessons specifically aimed at children and half-board accommodation available. The school will pick you up from Montevarchi train station. **Club Ippico Castello del Trebbio** near

Pontassieve (Via Montetrini 10, ☎ 055-8317371) is the best option for forays into the Montagna Fiorentina.

Entertainment & Events

■ Cinema

For any Italian-speaking movie fan, Florence has lots to offer, with films showing nightly in some great outdoor arenas over the summer, including **Forte Belvedere** (☎ 055-2001486), **Arena di Marte** (☎ 055-678841), **Villa Demidoff** (☎ 055-409155) and Fiesole's **Teatro Romano** (☎ 055-59187). Pick up a *Firenze Spettacolo* for the latest program information. Indoor cinemas reopen around September/October, although there still isn't much choice for original version viewing; cinemas here, with the exception of the following three, seem to prefer dubbing to subtitling. If you do arrive in season, you'll find up-to-date listings in *Leggo* and *City*, free publications available outside Florence S.M.N., in the local edition of *Le Nazione* (the national newspaper) or at the cinemas themselves.

Odeon Cinehall (Piazza Strozzi, Via Sassetti 1, ☎ 055-214068, www.cinehall.it, €7.20, conc. €5) is Florence's most central original-language cinema, with four showings every Mon, Tues and Thurs. Even if the film isn't much you'll be struck by the location of this stylish art-nouveau theater at the back of the elegant Palazzo Strozzino (built 1462).

Fulgor (Via Maso Finiguerra, ☎ 055-2381881, www.staseraalcinema.it/cinemafulgor, €7, conc. €5), near Piazza d'Ognissanti, shows the latest blockbusters in their original English format four times daily, on Thurs.

The British Institute of Florence (Palazzo Lanfredini, Lungarno Guicciardini 9, ☎ 055-26778270, www.britishinstitute.it, €7) stages older and generally British films (such as the recent Orson Welles retrospective) in English, followed by a brief discussion on Wed nights.

■ Theater

Florence has a great range of theaters offering anything and everything from the classics to the latest popular musical (in Italian). The summer **Firenze Estate** also adds some outdoor theater to the mix (see festival information, page 66 below); check local listings for the current program.

Teatro Comunale (Corso Italia 16, ☎ 055-213535, fax 055-287222) comes to the fore in the Maggio Musicale Fiorentino (see *Classical Music* below). More an auditorium than a theater, it also houses some great touring opera productions.

Performances at the **Teatro della Pergola** (Via della Pergola 12/32, ☎ 055-2264335, fax 055-245346, www.pergola.firenze.it, Sept-Apr, €21-€50) are mostly classical (Goldoni, Molière, Pirandello, Seneca), with some interesting contemporary dramas thrown in.

Teatro Puccini (Via delle Cascine 41, ☎ 055-362067, fax 055-331108, www.teatropuccini.it, Oct-Apr, from €34) offers a more risqué range of productions such as the X-rated version of the Marquis de Sade's *Philosophy in the Bedroom*. Book via the Box Office.

BOX OFFICE

The Box Office (www.boxoffice.it) takes reservations and makes advance ticket sales for most of Florence's theater shows, concerts, exhibitions and supporting events. There are three main city locations:
Via Alamanni 39, ☎ 055-210804, fax 055-213112
Via V. Emanuele II 303 (Teatro di Rifredi), ☎ 055-4220361
Viale D. Giannotti 13/15, ☎/fax 055-680362

If you're after something more mainstream, **Teatro Verdi** (Via Ghibellina 99, ☎ 055-212320, fax 055-288417, www.teatroverdifirenze.it, from €23) has popular dramas and musicals. All year; book via the Box Office.

A small theater with an interesting program of contemporary Italian drama, **Teatro di Rifredi** (Via V. Emanuele II 303, ☎ 055-4220361/4220362, fax 055-4221453, www.toscanateatro.it, €11.50, conc. €9.50) is located a bit north of the Fortezza da Basso. Book via the Box Office.

Original-language productions are scarce, the most frequent being offered at the **Limonaia di Villa Strozzi** (Via Pisana 77, ☎ 055-2625972, €12, conc. €8) by the Shakespeare at Stinson group (www.shakespeareatstinson.org).

ANNUAL FESTIVALS

These include the **Festival Nazionale sulla Drammaturgia Contemporanea delle Donne** (Teatro delle Donne, Piazza Santa Croce 19, ☎/fax 055-2347572, www.donne.toscana.it/centri/teatrodonne, Oct-Nov, €10, conc. €8) in celebration of contemporary female drama. There are also two **Florence Dance Festivals** (Borgo Stella 23r, ☎ 055-289276, www.florencedance.org, July/Nov-Dec).

It's also worth heading a little out of town to Sesto Fiorentino for the **Intercity Drama Festival** at the popular **Teatro della Limonaia** (Via Gramsci 426, ☎/fax 055-440852, www.teatro-limonaia.fi.it, 21 May-2 Aug) – there are also events scheduled in Florence itself if you don't want to make the trip out of town. Check the program for further information.

■ Classical Music

Probably Florence's most famous event, **Maggio Musicale Fiorentino** (Corso Italia 16, ☎ 055-213535, fax 055-287222, www.maggiofiorentino.com, Sept-Mar, €11-€70, conc. €8-€60) offers a wide choice of opera and ballet as well as classical performances by its in-house orchestra in a range of venues that includes the Teatro Comunale and the Teatro Verdi. Information and tickets are available from the sponsoring MPS banks (Monte dei Paschi di Siena, Banca Toscana, Banca Agricola Mantovana), from the Teatro Comunale or directly from the organization.

The **Amici della Musica** (Via Sirtori 49, ☎ 055-607440, fax 055-610141, www.amicimusica.fi.it, from €20) holds concerts throughout the year in the Teatro della Pergola, with a special emphasis on its Settembre Musica program (weekdays from 15 Sept-11 Oct).

Tuscany's regional orchestra, **Orchestra della Toscana** (Via Verdi 5, ☎ 055-2342722/2340710, fax 055-2008035, www.orchestradellatoscana.it, from €12) plays one or two concerts a month (Nov-July) at the Teatro Verdi (see details above).

Orchestra da Camera Fiorentina (Via E. Poggi 6, ☎/fax 055-783374, www.orcafi.it, €14, conc. €11) gives performances in Chiesa di Orsanmichele (Via Calzaiuoli, €12) and Palazzo Pitti in its busy summer season. Information and tickets from Via Luigi Alamanni 39, ☎ 055-210804, or an hour before the performance in the church.

The **Orchestre Giovanili** has a busy summer with the **International Festival of European Youth Orchestras** (information and tickets Accademia San Felice, ☎ 055-5978401, www.florenceyouthfestival.com) in the Chiesa di San Stefano al Ponte near Ponte Vecchio, and at other Italian venues. The equally youthful **Associazione Giovanile Musicale** (A.GI.MUS., Via della Piazzola 7r, ☎ 055-580996, www.agimusfirenze.it) holds year-round performances in the Teatro Puccini. Tickets from the Box Office.

Concerts of Italian music from the 14th to 17th centuries are performed by the **Associazione Culturale L'Homme Armé** in the Palazzo Medici Riccardi (Via Cavour 3, ☎ 055-695000, www.hommearme.it, Apr-July). Call for prices.

The summer **Il Suona dell'Anima** organizes three or four concerts a month (July-Sept) in the Chiesa di Orsanmichele on Via Calzaiuoli, ☎ 055-783874). Most are free.

Filarmonica G. Rossini (Piazza del Grano 29, ☎ 055-280236, www.filarmonicarossini.it) holds mostly free concerts once or twice a month throughout the year, the busiest months being June and September. There are a range of indoor and outdoor venues that include Piazza della Signoria, Piazzale Michelangelo, Palazzo Vecchio and Teatro della Pergola. **Orchestra Filarmonica Leopolda** (Via Panciatichi 38, ☎ 055-2352105, vincenzo.ruocco@inwind.it) conducts occasional performances at the same venues.

■ Live Popular Music

In the vicinity of Florence's airport, **Tenax** (Via Pratese 46r, ☎ 055-308160, www.tenax.org, from €13) is a popular club venue with live concerts and DJs. It's busiest on weekends. Take city Bus #29 or #30 from Firenze S.M.N.

Florence

For live jazz, be sure to visit the historic **Jazz Club** (Via Nuova de' Caccini 3, ☎ 5055-2479700, www.ejn.it/promo/jazzclub.htm) on the angle with Borgo Pinti in the Santa Croce/Duomo district. Closed summer; yearly membership €7.

The **Arena di Marte** (Palasport, Viale P. Paoli, ☎ 055-678841), up beside Campo di Marte stadium, hosts many of the biggest international touring acts. Tickets available from the Box Office. Take Bus #3 from the Duomo.

Saschall (Lungarno A. Moro 3, ☎ 055-6504112, fax 055-6503971, www.saschall.it), in the old Teatro Tenda, is the newest, and one of the largest, live music spaces in town and the venue for many touring big names. Located on the Arno east of the city; take Bus #14 from Firenze S.M.N. direction Varlungo.

Auditorium Flog (Via Mercati 24b, ☎ 055-4220300, fax 055-4223241, www.flog.it) a little out of the center in Il Romito, just north of the Fortessa da Basso, is a popular stopping point for touring Italian stars and more eclectic festivals such as the October **Musica dei Popoli** with its range of Angolan, Cuban, Romanian and Indonesian acts (also in the **Limonaia di Villa Strozzi**, from €10). Bus #4 from Piazza dell'Unità Italiana, just outside Firenze S.M.N., goes right past it.

October also brings the **Musicus Concentus** to Sala Vanni (Piazza del Carmine 14, ☎/fax 055-287347, www.musicusconcentus.com, €12) showcasing anything and everything from jazz and classical music to new experimental trends.

■ The Big Events

Scoppio del Carro

 Il Scoppio del Carro, or The Explosion of the Cart, is the first major folk event of the year, held Easter Sunday on Piazza del Duomo. For further information, see page 35.

La Festa del Grillo

The first Sun after Ascension Day sees the Parco delle Cascine come alive with eating, drinking and joviality. It also squeaks with the arrival of La Festa del Grillo, or the Cricket Festival. Although these days the live crickets have been mostly replaced by plastic imitations, hundreds of them are sold every year and released on the grass in a ritual that harks back to the days when crickets were placed on the doorsteps of loved ones to serenade them.

Festa di San Giovanni

In celebration of Florence's patron saint, the 24th of June sees much dressing up, dancing and singing followed by a candle-lit ceremonial procession from the Palazzo Vecchio and, in the early evening, a firework display up on Piazzale Michelangelo. For the most famous of its events, the Calcio Storico, see page 50.

La Rificolona

Piazza SS. Annunziata lights up every 7th September with La Rificolona, or the Festival of the Lanterns. Thought to be derived with the torch-laden influx of nearby country folk for celebrations of the Virgin's nativity (and the following day's market), these days it's the city's children that illuminate the streets and squares, while the river is lit up by a lovely parade-cum-competition of bright canoes.

Firenze Estate

As temperatures go up, bars shut and the nightlife moves outdoors with the arrival of the multifaceted Firenze Estate ("estate" means summer in Italian;

☎ 055-2625955, www.comune.firenze.it) and its equivalent in Fiesole (see below). Here are some of the best of their events and locations.

Jazz & Co. holds live performances on the beautiful loggia-covered Piazza SS. Annunziata (☎ 055-2645336, www.firenzejazz.it, Mar-July, mostly free) with restaurant and bar.

Impressive scenery at **Via di Fuga** in the courtyard of Le Murate (Via dell'Agnolo, ☎ 328-1767198, from 9:30 pm, July-Aug, mostly free), a building formerly used as a convent and then as a jail, with restaurant, bar and live DJ till 2 am after the concert or film.

Across the Arno, the slightly more cramped **Rime Rampanti** on Rampe di San Niccolò (Piazza Poggi, ☎ 055-2336712, July-Sept, free) fills its steps with dance, poetry and live music every night. Restaurant and bar.

Also in Oltrano, the **Notti d'Estate** in Piazza Santo Spirito (☎ 055-212911, from 9:30 pm, www.santospirito.firenze.it) sees free live performances on the square one or two nights a week throughout July.

Vola al Forte at Forte Belvedere (July-Oct) presents a range of art exhibitions (☎ 055-2001486, www.belvederedellarte.it), open-air films (☎ 055-293169, www.ateliergroup.it), music and poetry (☎ 055-5532962, www.musictrend.it) and live music at its bar and restaurant until 1 am (☎ 335-1037250, www.extrasrl.it). Events are free but entrance to the forte (via the Giardino di Boboli) costs €8, conc. €6.50.

Not just a political manifestation, the Communist-organized **Festa dell'Unità** at the Fortessa da Basso has become a well-loved local opportunity for mostly free live music and raucous outdoor drinking, with many of the bars that close over summer opened up here to supply the crowds. July 16-Aug 9, open till 2 am.

There's something for everyone at the Brazilian-themed **Stazione Leopolda** (Viale Fratelli Rosselli, ☎ 055-212622) between Porta al Prato and the Cascine Park. Open 6 pm-1:30 am from Feb 1 to 31 Aug. There is food and drink, as well as live concerts, short films, poetry recitals, fashion shows and exhibitions of Pop Art and photography. Free.

Estate Fiesolana (Teatro Romano di Fiesole, Via Portigiani 1, ☎ 055-59187, www.estatefiesolana.it, www.operafiesole.it) offers a great variety of outdoor films (5 July-7 Sept, €6), dance (July, €15, conc. €12), poetry (July, €7), prose (June, €7, conc. €4), music (7 June-2 Aug, €18, conc. €15) and opera (26 June-25 July, from €25). Take Bus #17 from Firenze S.M.N.

Shopping

 Coming from London, I must admit I've always found shopping in Florence a slightly frustrating experience, split as it is between the top-quality, high-priced fashion found around Via dei Tornabuoni and nearby Via della Vigna Nuova and the down-scale, low-priced, last-for-less-than-a-season clothing in the shopping center under Firenze S.M.N. The mid-range does exist, but it's a little harder to find; you should head to one of the town's department stores or into the high street shops that dot Via dei Cerretani and Borgo San Lorenzo. If it's **leather** you're after – and Florence is justifiably famous for its range of leather handbags, shoes and clothing – the shops around Santa Croce and the (usually cheaper) market stores by San Lorenzo all vie for your attention. Don't be afraid to barter to get the best deal. **Local crafts**, on the other hand (whether you're looking to buy or just want to stick your nose into the crafting skills of local artisans), can be found in the area around Santo Spirito and San Frediano with their small boutiques and craft workshops selling furnishings, handmade jewelry, lamps and gilded vases. The city's **antique shops** are mostly clustered around Via Maggio and Via dei Fossi.

■ High Fashion

The much-frequented **Armani** boutique is at Via dei Tornabuoni 48r (☎ 055-219041, www.giorgioarmani.com), while the younger, trendier and cheaper Armani lines are snapped up at **Emporio Armani** at Piazza Strozzi 16r (☎ 055-284315, www.emporioarmani.com).

Find the ultimate in designer jewelry on display at **Bulgari** (Via dei Tornabuoni 61r, ☎ 055-212469, www.bulgari.com), the major attraction after the traders on the Ponte Vecchio.

Adored by Hollywood stars, the glamour and flavor of **Dolce & Gabbana** is at Via della Vigna Nuova 27 (☎ 055-281003, www.dolcegabbana.it).

Bright colors are the trademarks of **Enrico Coveri** (Lungarno Guicciardini 19, ☎ 055-264411), a designer from just outside Florence whose unique fashion style has undergone something of a revival in recent years.

The huge flagship store of the shoemaker to the stars, **Ferragamo**, best known for his creations worn by screen sirens Audrey Hepburn and Sophia Loren, is found on Via dei Tornabuoni 14r (☎ 055-292123, www.salvatoreferrgamo.it). In addition to shoes for men and women, you'll also find women's clothing, handbags, ties and luggage on display.

One of the city's best-known trademarks, **Gucci**, on Via dei Tornabuoni 73r (☎ 055-264011, www.gucci.it) and Via Roma 38r (☎ 055-759221), has its roots in a luggage and saddlery company opened in Florence by Guccio Gucci in 1921.

Popular port of call for the independent woman, **Max Mara**, on Via dei Pecori 23r (☎ 055-287761) and Corso Italia 6 (☎ 055-280880), offers a great range of elegant and creative fashion.

There's plenty of chic clothing at **Prada** (Via dei Tornabuoni 53 and 67r, and Via Roma 8r, ☎ 055-294679, www.prada.it), a label best known for its sleek black dresses and famous handbags, both must-haves for serious fashion cognoscenti.

Legend has it that Marilyn Monroe was buried wearing **Pucci** (Via dei Tornabuoni 20r, ☎ 055-2658082, www.emiliopucci.com); its psychedelic prints were all the rage in the 60s when worn by stars such as Grace Kelly and Elizabeth Taylor.

Versace is at Via dei Tornabuoni 13r (☎ 055-2396167, www.gianniversace.com), with its younger, more street-wise, branch **Versus** on Via della Vigna Nuova 36-38b (☎ 055-217619).

SAVE MONEY AT THE MALL

Even those who can afford the international fashion labels and jewelry of the luxury district of the city can pick up Armani, Ferragamo, Gucci and Y.S.L. fashion at a much cheaper price if they catch a Sita bus to **The Mall** (Via Europa 8, Leccio Regello, ☎ 055-8657775, fax 055-8657801, Mon-Sat, 10 am-7 pm, Sun, 3 pm-7 pm). Buses depart from Via Santa Caterina da Siena (next to Florence S.M.N.) at 9 am and 12:30 pm, returning to Florence at noon or 5 pm (€5 round-trip). The journey takes one hour and two hours is more than enough to spend shopping at the outlet.

Prada fans should take a train to Montevarchi to visit the **Prada** and **Miu Miu factory outlet** (Loc. Levanella SS69, ☎ 055-91901, Mon-Sat, 9 am-7 pm, Sun, 3 pm-7 pm), only a short taxi trip from the train station. **Dolce & Gabbana** discount ware can be found at the outlet near Rignano Sull'Arno; the taxi from the station to the outlet (Loc. Santa Maria Maddalena 49, ☎ 055-8331300, fax 055-8331301, Mon-Sat, 9 am-7 pm, Sun, 3 pm-7 pm) takes about five minutes.

■ Affordable Fashion & Department Stores

Popular with locals, the department store **Coin** (Via dei Calzauioli 56r, ☎ 055-280531, www.coin.it), pronounced "co-en," is best for furnishings, shoes and men's clothing (ground floor). Women's clothing (1st floor) is worth a look, though you may find it to be a little on the formal side.

The large trendy **Diesel** store is at Via dei Lamberti 13r (☎ 055-2399963, www.diesel.com), a short walk from Piazza della Repubblica. Some of its women's wear is also on sale in La Rinascente, see below.

Department store **La Rinascente** (Piazza della Repubblica 1, ☎ 055-219113, www.rinascente.it) is your best bet for perfume and toiletries (ground floor), lingerie (basement) and male (1st floor) and female (2nd floor) clothing. There's also a tax-back service on the 5th floor for those that spend more than €100 in the store.

At prices considerably cheaper than elsewhere in Europe, **Miss Sixty** (Via Roma 20r, ☎ 055-2399549) is the first port of call for most fashion-conscious 20-somethings. Best for jeans and summer tops.

Another stylish brand aimed at the young and chic, **Replay** has three stores in Florence: Via dei Pecori 7r (☎ 055-293041), Via Por Santa Maria 27r (☎ 055-287950) and Piazza Goldoni 8 (☎ 055-2398833).

It's also worth checking out **Sisley** (Via Roma 11r or Via de' Cerretani 57-59, www.sisley.com) for stylish and affordable fashions.

If you're a **Benetton** fan, you won't be disappointed; Florence has three large stores (Via Por Santa Maria 68r, ☎ 055-287111, Piazza Stazione 16r, ☎ 055-281946, and Borgo San Lorenzo 15r, ☎ 055-2645643) with womens, mens and childrens clothing.

Crazy About Shoes: If your collection of shoes rivals that of Imelda Marcos, and the more expensive the better, you'll love the **Museo Salvatore Ferragamo** (Via dei Tornabuoni 2, ☎ 055-3360456, Mon/Wed/Fri, 9 am-1 pm, 2-6 pm, by appointment only) with its exhibits on the making of shoes, the shaping and the material used and its collection of the most original Ferragamo shoes for the die-hard fan.

■ Craft Workshops & Boutiques

BOTTEGHE

*They may be a dying breed but Florence does still have botteghe (artisan workshops) producing the ceramics, wooden furnishings, handmade paper and silverware that made Tuscany famous for shopping in the first place. If you want to find out more, the helpful **ARTEX** organization (Via S. Botticelli 9r, ☎ 055-570627, fax 055-572093, www.artex.firenze.it) is an invaluable source of information on the artisan industry all over Tuscany.*

Montelupo Fiorentina and Impruneta may be the best locations for ceramics but Florence has a justifiably famous workshop of its own in **Sbigoli Terracotte** (Via Sant'Egidio 4r, ☎ 055-2479713).

Woodcarving is well represented with **Bartolozzi e Maioli** (Via dello Sprone 20r, ☎ 055-282675), **Vanini** (Via M. del Popolo 44r), ☎/fax 055-2340800, www.handmadevannini.it), **Castorina** (Via Santo Spirito) and **Piero Borselli** (Via Ghibellina), who specializes in hand-decorated wooden frames.

One of the biggest glassworkers in the world, **Locchi Snc.** (Via Burchiello 10, ☎ 055-2298371) competes with the designers from Empoli and Colle Val d'Elsa.

One of the few locations keeping the city's handmade paper tradition alive, **Guilio Giannini e Figlio Snc.** (Piazza Pitti 37r, ☎ 055-212621) also boast one of Florence's best addresses.

There's famous silverware at **Brandimarte Srl** (Via L. Bartolini 18r, ☎ 055-239281), while you can pick up a little bit of everything through Francesca at tourist outlet **Solo a Firenze** (Borgo SS. Apostoli 37r, www.soloafirenze.firenze.net).

Not to be missed, **Bianco Bianchi & Figli** (Viale Europa 117, ☎ 055-8314509) is the only remaining company specializing in *scagliola*, a Renaissance technique in which carved marble is filled in with a colored paste.

Books

Books in English and a coffee shop with views over the piazza make the three-floor **Edison** (Piazza della Repubblica 27r, ☎ 055-213110) one of the most popular *librerie* in town.

The foreign-language branch of the Fetrinelli chain, **Fetrinelli International** (Via Cavour 12, ☎ 055-219524) has a good range of books in English on Florence and Tuscany (guidebooks and literature) as well as a large map section. It's a good place to purchase *Firenze Spettacolo* or look out for notices on the city's upcoming events.

The smaller **Libreria della Donne** (Via Fiesolana 2b, ☎ 055-240384), a short walk from the Duomo towards Sant'Ambrogio market, is your best bet for female literature, first- and second-hand.

For guidebooks and road maps, whether on Florence, Tuscany or Italy, visit **Libreria del Turista** (Viale S. Lavagnini 6r, ☎ 055-474192), between Fortezza da Basso and Piazza della Libertà.

Books can be exchanged or discounted for purchases of first- and second-hand books in English at the **Paperback Exchange** (Via Fiesolana 31r, ☎ 055-2478856) run by a friendly American couple; it's also a good place to pick up info on the latest events and entertainment.

If you turn up in Florence (or anywhere in Italy) during August, and especially the week of mid-August, you may be perplexed to find *Chiuso per ferie* signs on many of the city's shops and restaurants. Though less and less common in the immediate historical center, *ferragosto*, a holiday with its roots in the Roman *feriae Augusti*, has traditionally been the time for Italy's businesses and workers to shut shop and leave the city for a family break. It's a habit so well established in the Italian mentality, that even those who don't shut for the whole week (or in some cases, month), will take at least the first day off for a trip to the seaside.

■ Markets

Mercato Centrale di San Lorenzo, Piazza del Mercato Centrale (Mon-Sat, 7 am-2 pm; indoor market selling foodstuffs)

Mercato di San Lorenzo, Piazza San Lorenzo (daily, 9 am-7 pm, closed Mon in winter; outdoor market selling clothing and leather goods)

Mercato di Sant'Ambrogio, Piazza Sant'Ambrogio (Mon-Sat, 7 am-2 pm; market selling foodstuffs, flowers and clothing)

Mercato Delle Pulci o del Piccolo Antiquariato, Piazza dei Ciompi (last Sun of month, 9 am-6 pm; flea market with furniture, antiques, prints and jewelry)

Mercato del Porcellino, Loggiato del Porcellino, Via Porta Rossa (Tues-Sun, 9 am-7:30 pm; straw market now equally famous for leather goods)

Mercato delle Cascine, Viale Lincoln (Tues, 8 am-2 pm; the biggest of Florence's markets with clothing, shoes, household items, fruit and vegetables)

Arti e Mestieri d'Oltrano, Piazza Santo Spirito and Borgo Tegolaio (2nd Sun of month, 9 am-7 pm; crafts and traditional goods)

Mercato dell'Antiquariato, Piazza Indipendenza (3rd weekend of the month; antique market)

Fierucola di Santo Spirito, Piazza Santo Spirito (3rd Sun of the month except August; organic foods and products)

Where to Eat

It was with some trepidation that I showed a Florentine friend this list of recommended restaurants. For a start, it was through his insider's knowledge that I happened upon many of them in the first place, but more than this, I know only too well that he (like many of the city's residents) feel their once-favored locales are suffering from a severe dose of mounting prices and decreasing quality: "Twenty years ago, it was a Florentine institution to head out to a cheap, family-run restaurant on a Sunday to eat the

DINING PRICE CHART	
Price per person for an entrée, including house wine & cover.	
$	Under €20
$$	€21-€40
$$$	€41-€60
$$$$	Over €60

kind of traditional food your grandmother used to make. These days, those kinds of restaurants no longer exist in the center; either they've realized they can make a bigger buck if they replace *trippa alla Fiorentina* with hamburgers or they've

Florence

become so popular, they've raised their prices to the extent that we locals can no longer afford to eat there." Cynical his view may be, but you know that you won't get to taste the best of local cuisine (certainly not at the inexpensive to medium price range) if you're not prepared to venture out of the central Duomo area. You don't have to wander too far. Quality can still be found in spots around the churches of Santa Croce and Santa Maria Novella, and across the river in Oltrano, but for the best the city and its surroundings have to offer, follow locals farther out of the center to the places described in the last two sections, north and south of the center.

LOCAL FLAVORS

■ *Antipasti*
Affettati misti: Cold cuts of meat often served with wedges of bread.
Crostini di fegato: Chicken liver crostini.
Fettunta: Toasted bread with olive oil (often served with fagioli beans).

■ *Primi* (first courses)
Ribollita: Classic cabbage soup based on *fagioli* (white beans) and thickened with bread before re-boiling (hence the name).
Pappa al pomodoro: Tomato soup thickened with bread.
Pappardelle: Wide strips of pasta often served with a hare (*alla lepre*) or wild boar (*al cinghiale*) sauce.
Pasta e fagioli: Pasta with beans.
Sformato di patate e ricotta: A spongy mix of potato and ricotta served cone-shaped on a spicy tomato or *ragù* (spicy meat) sauce.

■ *Secondi* (second courses) tend to include a large choice of meats grilled *alla Fiorentina*.
The most famous is the *bistecca* (thick grilled T-bone steak served medium rare to rare), but there's usually also grilled pork (*bistecchine di maiale*), chicken (*pollo*), veal (*vitello*) and rabbit (*coniglio*).
Other local dishes of note include the *arista* (pork roasted with rosemary and garlic), *ossobuco* (braised veal shanks), *coniglio alla cacciatore* (rabbit braised hunter-style with vegetables, black olives and pine nuts) and *spezzatino* (a stew usually based on beef, pork or rabbit).
Those in search of a Tuscan offal experience, should try *trippa alla Fiorentina* (tripe stewed in a tomato sauce with parmesan to taste) and *lampredotto* (pork pancreas or intestines and often served in a sandwich).
Don't forget to order *contorni* (side dishes), generally a choice between *fagioli* (white beans either garnished with olive oil or a garlic-tomato sauce), *patate arrosto* (roasted potatoes), *spinaci* (spinach served in an oily garlic sauce) and a range of seasonal vegetables, often served fried in a light batter (*fritto misto*).

■ *Dolci* (desserts)
Try the *schiacciata alla Fiorentina* (light sponge cake), ravage the cheese board or settle your meal with *cantucci* (small, hard almond biscuits originating from Prato) dunked in *vin santo* (a fortified local desert wine).

■ Santa Croce

One of the best pizzerias/trattorias in and around the historical center is the family-run **Mastrociliegia** (Via Palmieri 34r, ☎ 055-293372, $), only a short walk from the Duomo in the direction of Teatro Verdi and Santa Croce. Its ongoing popularity with locals is a sure sign of its quality fare and charismatic welcome, with dishes of note including *Cappello mastrociliegia* (pasta with an asparagus, truffle and gorgonzola sauce), *straccetti di vitello all'aceto* (veal in a vinegar-based sauce), the classic *coniglio fritto* (fried rabbit) and some tasty wood-fired pizzas. Booking is recommended for the small terrace in summer.

One of my favorite spots for lunch around the Sant'Ambrogio market area, hectic **La Ghiotta** (Via Pietrapiana 7r, ☎ 055-241237, closed Mon, $) serves up some of the best priced dishes in town for those that care more about quality and less about décor. The menu is simple and traditional (roasted and grilled meats with a variety of *contorni*, pastas and pizzas in the evening) and so popular that the take-away part of the *rosticceria* is controlled by a ticket system in order to manage the lines.

Just a little farther along the same road, non-smoking **Trattoria il Giova** (Via Borgo la Croce 73r, ☎ 055-2480639, www.florence.ala.it/giova, closed Sun, $), with its small dining room of only seven tables, allows an intimate insight into the eating culture of the Florentines who crowd in. Condiments and conversations spill onto neighboring tables between mouthfuls of some innovative Tuscan dishes (gnocchi in a creamy truffle and zucchini flower sauce, Chianti pork with an onion and pear marmalade and some delicious homemade desserts). Booking recommended in summer.

For many, the best pizza in the city is at rustic **Il Pizzaiuolo** (Via dei Macci 113r, ☎ 055-241171, closed Sun, $$), with its lively Neapolitan mix of classic pizza toppings (such as the buffalo mozzarella, anchovies and capers that traditionally makes a Napolitana) and delicious fish and seafood *secondi* for those that want something different. Booking recommended for this popular but small locale.

Trattoria Baldovino (Via San Guiseppe 22r, ☎ 055-241773, www.baldovino.com, closed Mon, $$) offers some tasty pizza and pasta dishes, but I prefer **Enoteca Baldovino** (☎ 055-2347220) opposite the trattoria (the one with the small terrace), where the menu is a lot more innovative and where there is more ambiance. *Bruschetta* here are enormous, but it's the *carpaccio* (especially the tuna) presented on a bed of tangy wild rocket that gets the taste buds going. Reservations recommended for a terrace table.

Located in a small, cobble-stoned alleyway a short walk from the Duomo, **La Giostra** (Borgo Pinti 12r, ☎ 055-241341, www.ristorantelagiostra.com, $$) is best-known for its princely ownership. Portions are generous with a small range of antipasti offered free, while you make up your mind which of the dishes – *insalata di gamberoni*, *ravioli* and *spianata di Chianana* being the current specials – to plump for. A sommelier is on hand to suggest a matching wine.

The ever-popular **Acqua al 2** (Via della Vigna Vecchia 40r, ☎ 055-284170, www.acquaal2.it, evenings only, $$), just behind the Museo Nazionale del Bargello, offers a different insight into local cuisine. Piatti here are organised on a sample (*assaggio*) basis with up to five types of the same dish – five types of antipasti, five types of pasta, bistecca with various sauces, four different cheeses or desserts – served on the same plate. It's a perfect start for those who haven't a clue about Tuscan cuisine or just can't make up their minds.

Florence

Named after a classic Tuscan dish (chicken liver and egg stew), **Cibreo** is split between the restaurant on Via A. del Verrocchio (8r, ☎ 055-2341100, fax 055-244966, cibreo.fi@tin.it, closed Sun, $$$) and the equally tasty trattoria on Via dei Macci (112r, contacts as above, closed Sun, $$). Specialties include the *polenta alle erbe verdi* (a herby polenta), *sformato di patate e ricotta al ragù* (a cone-shaped mix of potato and ricotta cheese served with a spicy meat sauce), *calamari in inzimino* (stewed squid) and the *torta al cioccolato*; only the difference in décor explains the difference in price. Booking recommended.

Relatively new on the Florentine culinary scene, **Osteria del Caffé Italiano** (Via Isola delle Stinche 11/13r, ☎ 055-289368, fax 055-288950, www.caffeitaliano.it, closed Mon, $$$) is slowly building a reputation for quality food with an extensive wine list to match. The cuisine is predominantly Tuscan, with *zuppa di fagioli*, *bistecca* and *bistecchina di maiale alla Fiorentina* plus an extensive cheese board sure to tempt. While you can get equivalent quality at a lower price elsewhere, Caffè Italiano is a lovely locale in which to spend the evening.

Considered one of the world's top 10 restaurants is the **Enoteca Nazionale Pinchiorri** (Via Ghibellina 87r, ☎ 055-242757, fax 055-244983, www.pinchiorri.it, closed Mon, $$$$) – quality doesn't come cheap at Florence's best-known restaurant. But it is an experience all serious gourmands and oenophiles (it has one of the best-stocked wine cellars in the world) can't afford to miss. Centrally located in an imposing 16th-century palazzo, the emphasis here is on refined cuisine in a harmonious setting with the kind of hand-engraved silver cutlery, porcelain crockery and crystal glasses you're almost afraid to touch.

■ Santa Maria Novella

La Spada (Via della Spada 62r, ☎ 055-218757, $) offers a charming – if rather cramped – dining experience in its little restaurant of seven tables that backs up its take-away *rosticceria* counter. Jam-packed with locals and tourists unafraid of the scribbled blackboard menu, this is a great place to start your experience of simple but authentic Tuscan fare.

Intimate wine-bar turned osteria, **Belle Donne** (Via delle Belle Donne 16r, ☎ 055-2382609, closed Sun and Aug, $$) has exaggerated to an unbelievable degree its décor of dried fruit- and vegetable-covered walls, tiled tabletops and blackboard menu of daily specials. It has a small outdoor plant-covered terrace of three tables, but it's best to eat inside to experience the atmosphere of this dimly-lit spot.

A typical trattoria frequented by an international crowd, **Croce al Trebbio** (Via delle Belle Donne 47r, ☎/fax 055-287089, www.paginegialle.it/altrebbio, closed Tues, $$), with its attractive plant-filled terrace, offers a good range of primi pasta dishes and grilled and stewed meats, including a deliciously creamy veal. Booking recommended for the terrace. Aperitif offered on arrival.

Easy to spot by the huge queue that mills around its entrance, **Il Latini** (Via dei Palchetti 6r, ☎ 055-210916, fax 055-289794, closed Mon, $$) still manages to maintain the quality, especially of its almost mythical *bistecca*, that drew its fame in the first place. This is the place to come for a real Florentine culinary experience with everything – from the menu to the furnishings – recalling local tradition. Book in advance if you want to beat locals to the spot.

Reserve in advance or expect to wait for a table at the homely **Trattoria Marione** (Via della Spada 27r, ☎ 055-214756, closed Sun, $$), with its tables so squashed you may find yourself shouting to be heard over your neighbors' conversations. It's also the place to sample unfussy versions of local greats such as *ribollita*, *zuppa di fagioli* and *bolliti misti* (a range of boiled meats).

More upmarket, nearby **Buca Mario** in the atmospheric cellars of the Palazzo Niccolini (Piazza Ottraviani 16r, ☎ 055-214179, fax 055-2647336, www.bucamario.it, closed Wed, $$$) offers a similar range of typical Florentine dishes – *ribollita*, *pappardelle al cinghiale*, *ossobuco* and *bistecca* – in its large, trendy dining room. It's the perfect location for intimate, undisturbed dining.

One of the oldest restaurants in the city, **Buca Lapi** (Via Trebbio 1r, ☎ 055-213768, closed Sun, and Mon lunch, $$$) is another Florentine great with a unique wall décor of old faded posters. It occupies the basement of the Palazzo Antinori (*buca* meaning "hole"); if you haven't booked ahead, just wait in line. The freshly-made pasta and archetypal versions of *bistecca* or *coniglio fritto* (fried rabbit) more than make up for the wait.

It's friendly service and quality fare that you'll find at **Osteria N.1** (Via del Moro 22, ☎ 055-284897, fax 055-294318, closed Sun, $$$), a classy Tuscan restaurant where waiters hover attentively and you really do *mangiare bene*. Try the *ossobuco*, the *scaloppini di vitello tartufo*, the ubiquitous *bistecca* or the *lombatino di vitello* to get the best out of this popular culinary delight.

Nearby **Trattoria Garga** (Via del Moro 50/52r, ☎ 055-2398898, fax 055-211396, www.garga.it, closed Mon, $$$) isn't the cheapest place to eat this side of the center, but the quality of the food and careful décor (think romantic candlelit dinners) more than make up for that.

■ Oltrano

A cheap spot for a big lunch or an unfussy evening meal is **La Mangiatoia** (Piazza San Felice 8/10r, ☎ 055-224060, closed Mon, $). Although slightly frustrating for its chaotic service and sloppy décor, it offers a delicious range of pizzas, pastas and grilled meats, including a great *bistecca*. It's split onto two floors; you can dine at the counter if lunching or downstairs in the restaurant if you want to make a night of it.

A great spot for a light lunch, **Marino** (Via de' Serragli 19, $), just across Ponte alla Carraia, has only five small tables to serve its 1 pm rush. Thankfully, most are local workers who come for the takeout pastas, pannini and patisseries on display in the counter.

I've eaten some of the richest pasta in Florence in rustic **Borgo Antico** (Piazza Santo Spirito 6r, ☎ 055-210437, fax 055-214175, $$) and a delicious *insalata di polpa* (octopus salad with sundried tomatoes in a light lemon dressing). Book in advance for tables on the attractive terrace, especially during Firenze Estate when live bands perform in the square.

On the same piazza, **Osteria Santo Spirito** (Piazza Santo Spirito 16r, ☎ 055-2382383, $$) is a bustling place with an equally attractive terrace. Specialties here include *gnocchi gratinati al profumo di tartufo* (gnocchi in a cheesy truffle sauce), *tagliata di manzo con rucola e grana* (grilled beef on a rocket and parmesan salad) and *salsiccine di cinghiale con pecorino e pomodoro seche* (wild boar sausages with sheep cheese and sun-dried tomatoes). Reservations recommended for summer weekends.

Follow the Arno east to reach the large exposed brickwork and garlic and tomato vine-covered walls of busy **Angiolino** (Via di Santo Spirito 36r, ☎ 055-2398976, $$$). Ask for a spot in the main room where you get to see (and hear) the chefs chopping and frying the *bistecca* for which the restaurant is known. Be aware that the steak here is huge (no matter how small you request it to be) and it often makes sense to order one for two. Reservations recommended.

Along the same street, **Olio & Convivium** (Via di Santo Spirito 4, ☎ 055-2658198, www.conviviumfirenze.it, $$) is the second of two *olioteca* (the other is south of Florence at Viale Europa 4-6, ☎ 055-6811757) that are part-restaurant, part-fine food shop, wine cellar, bakery, delicatessen and olive oil vendor. As if that weren't enough, the 15th-century building that this version inhabits is made more irresistible by the fresh pasta dishes that overflow onto its counters.

Lovers of Tuscan cuisine can't seem to stop raving about **Il Cantinone** (Via di Santo Spirito 6r, ☎ 055-218898, closed Mon, $$) an *enoteca* specializing in Chianti Classico. Culinary specialties of note include the *zuppa di farro* (a wheat-based soup from the Garfagnana region), *pappardelle* (this time with a duck ragù) and *tagliata di manzo* (grilled beef), not to mention the extensive wine list and house desserts.

Between the Ponte Vecchio and the Palazzo Pitti, **Pitti Gola e Cantina** (Piazza Pitti 16, ☎ 055-212704, $$, closed Mon) is an inviting dimly-lit *enoteca* specializing in French and Italian wines, the perfect spot for an aperitif or a light meal of salami or *stuzzichini* on one of its four small tables, with views onto Piazza Pitti.

A chance to step way back in time, **Osteria del Cinghiale Bianco** (Borgo San Jacopo 43r, ☎/fax 055-215706, www.cinghialebianco.it, closed Wed, $$) serves some classic regional specialties in the medieval tower house it inhabits. The food and wine are more than fitting for the quality of the locale and the atmosphere – think candlelit tables and soft music – making it a great choice for romantic dining. Reservations recommended.

■ North of the Center

Just north of the Fortezza da Basso in the area known as Il Romito, **Fratelli Briganti** (Piazza Giorgini 12r, ☎ 055-475255, $) is so confident of its appeal that staff refuse to take reservations – if there are no free tables, you'll just have to wait in line. It's worth the wait; this relaxed and unaffected trattoria serves some of the cheapest, largest and most delicious helpings of pasta in town. If you've room for *secondi*, you'll also get to sample the kinds of local dishes rarely found elsewhere in their original form (*ossobuco*, *lombatina*, *trippa*, *tonno con fagioli*), hence the solely local crowd.

Also in Il Romito, the lively – if slightly pretentious – décor of the recently opened **Zero Zero** (Via Lorenzoni 8r, ☎ 055-495000, www.00pizzeria.com, $$) draws the crowds. The TVs in the window showing the chefs at work distract somewhat from the wait. There's no menu; the waiter will instead list for you that day's special *primi* (mostly seafood pasta dishes) and *secondi* (huge American-style pizzas with your choice of topping). Food quality and service are currently haphazard but give it a few more months and this could turn into one of Florence's most popular eateries.

If you're in the Campo di Marte stadium area around lunchtime, pop into one of the city's most famous sandwicheries, **Panineria Scheggi** (Viale dei Mille 1r, ☎ 055-588076, closed Tues, $) before finishing off, as is local tradition, with a gelato from nearby **Gelateria Badiani** (Viale dei Mille 20r, $).

Da Pepe (Via Antonio Pacinotti 5r, ☎ 055-574392, closed Mon, $), in the direction of Campo di Marte, was my local restaurant for my first three months in Florence and few places in town have managed to beat its ratio of quality to price. It serves a great *bistecca* (unlike many central restaurants you actually get to specify the weight, and therefore the price you're prepared to pay) and a generous range of wood-fired pizzas.

Also in the Campo di Marte area is **Café Godo** (Piazza Edison 3/4r, ☎ 055-583881, $$), an intriguing French-style bistro with cured meats and vines of garlic and tomato hanging from its ceiling. With very few tables, it makes the perfect place for a light, quiet evening meal (*carpacci, tapas*, grilled meats) or a delicious lunch baguette. Great wine list.

Serving typical Tuscan cuisine with an emphasis on grilled meats, **Perseus** (Viale Don Minzoni 10r, ☎ 055-588226, $$), just off Piazza della Libertà, is considered one of the best restaurants in Florence for *primi* such as *pappa al pomodoro* and *secondi* such as its delicious *bistecca*. Reservations recommended unless you're happy to wait in line. Terrace open in summer.

On the opposite side of the road, restaurant/pizzeria **Alfredo** (Viale Don Minzoni 3r, ☎ 055-578291, closed Mon, $$) is another local favorite with an emphasis on wood-fired pizzas and traditional piatti like *ravioli farciti di pappa al pomodoro con lamelle di tartufo bianco, tortelli di patate al ragù,* grilled meats and the not-to-be-missed homemade dessert, *sfoglia alla doppia crema di marroni*.

■ South of the Center

Well worth the drive out of town is osteria/pizzeria **La Paglietta** (Via San Lavagnini 14, San Polo in Chianti, ☎ 055-855444/3, closed Mon, $). It serves in abundance the traditional foods – roasted meats, *trippa alla Fiorentina* and a great range of grandmother-made desserts – that no longer exist at this price in central Florence. There's no English menu and no English is spoken, but just point at something on the daily specials and you can't go wrong. From Florence, head south through Bagno a Ripoli on the SS222 toward Grassina.

South of the Arno in the Gavinana district (east of Piazzale Michelangelo), the large terrace of **La Piazzetta** (Via di Ripoli 43r, on the angle with Viale Europa, ☎ 0556-800253, fax 0556-801898, www.lapiazzetta.com, $$) is at its best on warm summer nights. The menu ranges from tasty wood-fired pizzas to roasted meats, but it is the gargantuan *spiedi* (long skewers of grilled meats and vegetables) that are the biggest pull.

Alongside the nature reserve of the same name, the rustic **La Valle dell'Inferno** (Loc. Acquaborra, ☎ 055-9180031, fax 055-983372, www.frasca.it, closed Tues, $$) draws many locals into the Valdarno for its intimate riverside terrace dining (especially beautiful when lit in the evening), excellent wine list and fish-based menu. There's an onsite *agriturismo* ($$), a farm-stay cottage, if you don't want to drive back at night. Take the SS69 to Terranuova Bracciolini and follow signs to Levane.

On the SS2 from Florence to Siena, **La Trattoria del Pesce** (Via Cassia per Siena 132, Bargino, ☎ 055-8249045, $$$) comes highly recommended for its ever-changing menu of fishy delights and hearty welcome, no matter how good or bad your Italian. There's an extensive list of Italian whites to match. Just ask your waiter if you can't make head nor tail of the menu. Reservations recommended for larger groups.

COOKING LESSONS

From quick and easy local recipes to Cordon Bleu lessons in Michelin-starred restaurants, Florence has a cooking course to suit everyone's needs, abilities and spending power. Check out these websites to find the one that suits you.

Accademia Cordon Bleu (Via di Mezzo 5r, ☎/fax 055-234568, www.cordonbleu-it.com/pages/homeeng.html, various courses of four lessons, €360)

Accidental Tourist (various locations, ☎ 055-699376, fax 055-699048, www.accidentaltourist.com, day course, €78)

Apicius Cooking School (various, ☎ 055-287203, fax 055-2398920, www.apicius.it, day, week and month courses from €105 a day)

Centro Ponte Vecchio (Piazza della Signoria 4a, ☎ 055-294511, fax 055-2396887, www.cpv.it, five-day and one-week courses from €103 a day)

Divina Cucina (Via Taddea 31, ☎/fax 055-292578, www.divinacucina. com, one- to three-day courses from €315/day)

Enoteca de' Giraldi (various locations, ☎ 055-213881, fax 055-216949, www.vinaio.com, day and week courses from €55 a day)

Galilei (Don Chisciotte, ☎ 055-294680, fax 055-238481, www.galilei.it, week- or month-long courses from €2,200 a week)

Good Tastes of Tuscany (☎ 328-5694026, www.tuscany-cooking-class.com, one-day to three-day cooking classes in the Chianti countryside, from €140 a day)

Where to Stay

Hotel-wise, the decision in Florence is simple; it's all about price or location. If you're on a budget, you're looking at the station and San Lorenzo market area, a district whose hotels, while normally spotless inside, are brought down by their somewhat grotty location. If you only want to see the best of the city, plump instead for a hotel in the posh end of the historical center or around Piazza San Marco, but expect to pay a high price for the privilege. A few hotels in the Santa Croce, Oltrano and Ognissanti neighbourhoods offer a happy medium but, slightly removed from the center, you may feel you're missing out on the local atmosphere. If you arrive without a booking (it's best to reserve well in advance for the busy March-to-September season), ignore the touts who hang around outside and head into the official accommodation booking service in the train station (Informazioni Turistiche e Alberghiere, ☎ 055-282893, 283500, 288429, daily, 8:45 am-8 pm, charge applies).

HOTEL PRICE CHART

Rates are per room with private bath, based on double occupancy, including breakfast.

$	Under €40
$$	€41-€85
$$$	€86-€140
$$$$	€141-€210
$$$$$	Over €210

The Station & San Lorenzo Market Area

On the street that leads from the Fortezza da Basso to San Lorenzo, B&B **Il Ghiro** (Via Faenza 63, ☎ 055-282086, www.ilghiro.it, $$) offers one of the best deals in town. There are only five rooms so be sure to book well in advance. Kitchen for guests who really are on a budget.

Ask for a room with a balcony at the small B&B **Maison de Charme** (Largo F. Alinari 11, ☎ 055-292304, fax 055-281014, http://maisoncharme.hotelinfirenze.com, $$) for views over the church of Santa Maria Novella. With only six rooms, you're ensured a personal service including trip planning and museum reservations.

Just off Piazza Santa Maria Novella in the bustling restaurant area, **Hotel Balcony** ☆☆ (Via dei Banchi 3r, ☎ 055-283133, fax 055-289590, www.hotelbalcony.it, $$) has a great terrace with panoramic views over the Duomo. A great spot if you've come here with the intention to dine.

The budget choice east of the station, **Hotel Nazionale** ☆ (Via Nazionale 23, ☎ 055-2382203, fax 055-2381735, www.nazionalehotel.it, $$), midway towards Piazza della Indipendenza, may not be luxurious, but at least it is clean, comfortable and reasonably priced.

Nearby **Hotel Galileo** ☆☆☆ (Via Nazionale 22a, ☎ 055-496645, fax 055-496447, www.paginegialle.it/hgalileo, $$$) has one of the most genuinely warm welcomes in the city. Rooms, though simple, have been decorated with lovely wood furnishings. Trip-planning service available.

At the nicer end of Via Faenza (the end closest to San Lorenzo), you'll find **Palazzo Benci** ☆☆☆ (Via Faenza 6r, ☎ 055-213848, fax 055-288308, palazzobenci@iol.it, $$$) in a renovated 16th-century mansion belonging to the family of the same name. Ask for a room out front overlooking the Cappelle Medicee.

Hotel Albion ☆☆☆ (Via Il Prato 22r, ☎ 055-214171, fax 055-283391, www.hotelalbion.it, $$$) is in a quiet area northwest of Ognissanti. A bit of a walk from the historical center (despite website claims), its location in an interesting Neo-Gothic palazzo and the ratio of luxury to price ensure its ongoing appeal.

A short walk from the station, **Hotel Boccaccio** ☆☆☆ (Via della Scala 59, ☎ 055-282776, fax 055-268183, www.caporalehotels.com, $$$$) makes up in 18th-century history and authentic Florentine décor what it lacks in location. Rooms are soundproofed.

Run by the welcoming Bronzi family for the last century, **Hotel Principe** ☆☆☆☆ (Lungarno A. Vespucci 34, ☎ 055-284848, fax 055-283458, www.hotelprincipe.com, $$$$) boasts a great riverside location and caring service.

One of the oldest hotels in town is **Grand Hotel Baglioni** ☆☆☆☆ (Piazza della Unita'Italiana 6, ☎ 055-23580, fax 055-2358895, www.hotelbaglioni.it, $$$$). Though it sits in a slightly grotty square just outside the station, it occupies a 19th-century palazzo rich in history. Once the residence of the Carrega Bertolini princes, it has welcomed such illustrious guests as Puccini, Pirandello and Rodolfo Valentino. Be sure to check out the views from the rooftop bar.

The luxury choice in this area is the recently restored **Hotel Excelsior** ☆☆☆☆☆ (Piazza Ognissanti 3, ☎ 055-27151, fax 055-210278, www.westin.com/excelsiorflorence, $$$$$), which comes complete with the precious antique furnishings, tapestries and marble befitting its Renaissance history.

Florence

Historical Center:
From the Duomo to San Marco

On the road that leads from the Duomo to the Accademia, B&B **Il Campanile** (Via Ricasoli 10, ☎ 055-211688, fax 055-2675989, www.relaiscampanile.it, $$) possesses one of the best price-to-position deals in town. Rooms are simple but lovingly furnished with tiled floors and wrought-iron bed frames.

For a bit of musical history, try **Hotel Casci** ☆☆ (Via Cavour 13, ☎ 055-211686, fax 055-2396461, www.hotelcasci.com, $$$) in the frescoed 15th-century palazzo that once belonged to Rossini. Ever-attentive, the Lombardi family ensures that you leave with a great impression of Florentine hospitality.

For those in search of something exactly central, the family-run B&B **Soggiorno Battistero** (Piazza San Giovanni 1, ☎ 055-295143, fax 055-268189, www.soggiornobattistero.it, $$$) occupies a 13th-century palazzo slap bang beside the Battistero (ask for a room overlooking the piazza). On the ground floor can also be found the Museo di Bigallo and, right next door, the Loggia del Bigallo with its handsome 14th- and 15th-century frescoes and sculptures.

A short walk from Piazza San Marco, **Hotel Carolus** ☆☆☆ (Via XVII Aprile 3, ☎ 055-2645539, fax 055-2645550, www.carolushotel.com, $$$$) in its Neo-Classical palazzo offers an intriguing blend of history and refined accommodation. Staff are helpful with plenty of information on local sights and surroundings.

In one of Florence's oldest palazzos on the road from the Duomo to Palazzo Medici Riccardi, **Palazzo Ruspoli** ☆☆☆ (Via de' Martelli 5, ☎ 055-2670563, fax 055-2670525, www.palazzo-ruspoli.it, $$$$) has some singular views of the Duomo from its soft, spacious pastel-colored rooms. Book well in advance for the cupola vista.

In a beautifully restored 18th-century family house with fine views over Florence and the hills up to Fiesole, nearby **Hotel Cellai** ☆☆☆ (Via XVII Aprile 14, ☎ 055-489291, fax 055-470387, www.hotelcellai.it, $$$$) is a great choice for art fans; it organizes in-house (*arte in casa*) exhibitions of contemporary local artists.

On the other side of the Accademia inside a recently renovated Neo-Classical palazzo, **Hotel le Due Fontane** ☆☆☆ (Piazza SS Annunziata 14, ☎ 055-210185, fax 055-294461, www.leduefontane.it, $$$$) has some great balcony rooms for rent. Service is the key here, with a Jaguar on hand to escort you out on the town if you so desire.

On the same square, **Hotel Loggiato dei Serviti** ☆☆☆ (Piazza SS Annunziata 3, ☎ 055-289592, fax 055-289595, www.loggiatodeiservitihotel.it, $$$$), in the former home of the religious order Servi di Maria, has an elegant façade that mirrors the one constructed by Brunelleschi, a century earlier, on the opposite side of the square.

If it really is location-location-location you want, then go for **Hotel Duomo** ☆☆☆ (Piazza Duomo 1, ☎ 055-219922, fax 055-216410, www.eidinet.com/hotelduomo, $$$$) right outside the cathedral. Not exactly worth the price, it is nonetheless the perfect stopping point for lazy travelers.

Historical Center:
From Palazzo Strozzi to the Uffizi

Shoppers rejoice – conveniently located between Vuitton and Armani in a charismatic 14th-century building, **Hotel La Residenza** ☆☆☆ (Via dei Tornabuoni 8,

☎ 055-218684, fax 055-284197, $$$) offers the cheapest deal on this luxury shopping street, leaving you more to spend in its shops. The rooftop terrace has a great view of Piazza Santa Trinità.

One of the cheapest hotels off Piazza della Repubblica, **Hotel Medici** ☆☆ (Via de' Medici 6, ☎ 055-284818, fax 055-216202, $$$) with six floors, has a spectacular roof garden with fine views over the city. It's the perfect place to stay if you're prepared to sacrifice a bit of luxury to be in the midst of the action.

Located on the city's premier shopping street, **Hotel Beacci Tornabuoni** ☆☆☆ (Via dei Tornabuoni 3, ☎ 055-212645, fax 055-283594, www.Bthotel.it, $$$$) occupies the so-called "guest quarters" of Palazzo Strozzi with the antique Florentine furnishings and paintings that you would expect from such an illustrious location.

B&B **Residence del Proconsolo** (Via del Proconsolo 18, ☎ 055-2645657, fax 055-217501, www.proconsolo.com, $$$$) isn't the cheapest B&B in the city but this 15th-century mansion does have the kind of personal service that an albergo of few rooms affords and a great location just beside the Duomo.

With perhaps the best riverside location, the forward-facing rooms in **Hotel Berchielli** ☆☆☆☆ (Lungarno Acciaiuoli 14, ☎ 055-264061, fax 055-218636, www.berchielli.it, $$$$) have a spectacular vista of the Arno and the Ponte Vecchio, both seen at their best lit up in the early evening.

On the street connecting Palazzo Strozzi with the Piazza della Signoria, **Hotel Porta Rossa** ☆☆☆ (Via Porta Rossa 19, ☎ 055-287551, fax 055-282179, $$$$), in existence since the 14th century, is the oldest albergo in the city. This medieval palazzo with its antique furniture, chandeliers and wood-beamed ceilings was the chosen stopping point for both Stendhal and Balzac.

Right in the heart of the historical center, **Hotel Brunelleschi** ☆☆☆☆ (Piazza Santa Elizabetta 3, ☎ 055-27370, fax 055-219653, www.hotelbrunelleschi.it, $$$$$) offers some unique accomodations in the Byzantine tower and medieval church it has taken over. The private museum (guests only) displaying artifacts from their reconstruction is well worth a peek.

Just outside the church of Orsanmichele, **Hotel Pierre** ☆☆☆☆ (Via de' Lamberti 5, ☎ 055-216218, fax 055-2396573, www.remarhotels.com, $$$$$) sits behind a handsome 18th-century neo-medieval façade designed by Pietro Berti. It's a great location for forays onto Piazza della Signoria and into the Uffizi.

Want to splash out? Then the **Savoy** ☆☆☆☆☆ (Piazza della Repubblica 7, ☎ 055-27351, fax 055-2735888, www.roccofortehotels.com, $$$$), with its prime location on Piazza della Repubblica and its swish service, is the obvious choice.

The equally upper-class **Hotel Helvetia & Bristol** ☆☆☆☆☆ (Via dei Pescioni 3, ☎ 055-287814, fax 055-288353, www.charminghotels.it, $$$$$) provides a smaller, more intimate luxury experience a short hop from shop-stacked Via dei Tornabuoni. Ask for a "panoramic room" on the fifth floor for views over the Duomo.

Hotel Hermitage ☆☆☆ (Vicolo Marzio 1, ☎ 055-287216, fax 055-212208, www.hermitagehotel.com, $$$$$) is pretty expensive for a three-star hotel, but you have to bear in mind that this small, carefully-run hotel has some of the best décor, service (and views) in the city.

Florence

Santa Croce

Split onto three floors in a quiet area a short walk from the church of Santa Croce, the 14 rooms of **Hotel Dante** ☆☆☆ (Via di San Cristofano 2, ☎ 055-241772, fax 055-2345819, www.hoteldante.it, $$$) come complete with an eclectic range of stylish furnishings and, in some cases, a kitchen.

A little out of the center are the well-priced rooms and frescoed ceilings of **Hotel Villa Liana** ☆☆☆ (Via Vittorio Alfieri 18, ☎/fax 055-245303, $$$). The lovely 19th-century villa was, until 1960, the British Consulate.

On the banks of the Arno, looking up to Piazzale Michelangelo, the relaxed **Plaza Lucchesi** ☆☆☆☆ (Lungarno della Zecca Vecchia 38, ☎ 055-26236, fax 055-26236, www.plazalucchesi.it, $$$$) is one of the cheapest four-star choices in town. Ask for a room with views over the Arno.

On a quiet alley within five minutes of the Duomo, the 14th-century palazzo that houses **Hotel Monna Lisa** ☆☆☆☆ (Borgo Pinti 27, ☎ 055-2479751, fax 055-2479755, www.monnalisa.it, $$$$) comes complete with stucco walls, cotto fiorentino floors, wood-beamed ceilings and a glorious staircase in *pietra serena*.

For a complete B&B experience, try the **Le Stanze di Santa Croce** ☆☆☆☆ (Via delle Pinzochere 6, ☎ 055-2001366, fax 055-2008456, $$$$) just off Piazza Santa Croce. Its rooms are named after Florence's old city bells (Martinella, Trecca, Montanina, Squilla). Cooking courses and wine tasting available on request.

In a former convent, the rooms of **Hotel J&J** ☆☆☆☆ (Via di Mezzo 20, ☎ 055-26312, fax 055-240282, www.jandjhotel.com, $$$$$) have been artfully furnished with antiques and hand-woven fabrics to match the original frescoes, Renaissance cloisters and Doric columns which remain.

Oltrano

For the best deal just outside the historical center, B&B **Florence Old Bridge** (Via Guicciardini 22, ☎ 055-2654262, fax 055-2646693, www.florenceoldbridge.com, $$) is well-located between the Ponte Vecchio (300 feet away) and Palazzo Pitti. It offers some great services, including a two-hour guided tour of the city's main sights.

If it's a weekly rental you're after, choose from one of these two sister B&Bs (Via d'Ardiglione 28, ☎/fax 055-2382060, www.residenzailcarmine.com). **Residenza Il Carmine** ($$) is in a 17th-century palace in the residential and artisan San Frediano district, right next to the former home of Filippo Lippi. Or try the slightly more expensive **Residenza Santo Spirito** ($$$), set in part of the 16th-century Palazzo Guadagni, with fine views over Piazza Santo Spirito and its bustling caffès and restaurants.

The family-run **Hotel Boboli** ☆☆ (Via Romana 63, ☎ 055-2298645, fax 055-2336518, www.hotelboboli.com, $$$), a few meters from Porta Romana, has a warm welcome and some fine views over the gardens from which it takes its name.

On the road up to Piazzale Michelangelo, **Hotel David** ☆☆☆ (Viale Michelangelo 1, ☎ 055-6811695, fax 055-680602, www.davidhotel.com, $$$$) makes a good choice for a quieter break away from the bustle of the center. Its private garden has great views over the cityscape. A perfect choice for visitors arriving by car.

You enter the nearby **Villa Liberty** ☆☆☆ (Viale Michelangelo 40, ☎ 055-6810581, fax 055-6812595, www.hotelvillaliberty.it, $$$$), so-called for its period Liberty décor and Art Nouveau furnishings, through a lovely wrought-iron gate. Ask for one of the rooms with frescoed ceilings.

Palazzo Magnani Feroni ☆☆☆☆☆ (Borgo San Frediano 5, ☎ 055-239544, fax 055-2608908, www.florencepalace.it, $$$$$) dates back to the 1500s when it belonged to the aristocratic family from which it takes its name; its present look derives from the current owners who gave it an overhaul in the 18th century when their family took over.

Youth Hostels

You have to arrive early to get a room at the **Ostello Archi Rossi** (Via Faenza 94r, ☎ 055-290804, fax 055-2302601, $), found in the bustling station area near Fortezza da Basso. It's well known for its luxury breakfast, a rarity among hostels these days. Terrace and free Internet access.

A little out of town on the hill up to Fiesole and surrounded by a botanical garden, the huge 322-bed **Ostello della Gioventu' Villa Camerata** (Viale A. Righi 2/4, ☎ 055-601451, fax 055-610300, www.ostellionline.org/ostello.php?idostello=180, $) is well worth the 20 minutes by bus (#7) from the center if it's a more verdant break you're after.

Just behind the Uffizi, **Ostello Firenze Inn** (Via del Corno 3, ☎/fax 055-2399211, www.firenzeinn.com, $) has the best hostel location in town. Double and dormitory rooms are offered. Hostel-organized wine tasting, walking tours and pub crawls available (Bus #23 from the station).

Family-run **Ostello Gallo d'Oro** (Via Cavour 104, ☎/fax 055-5522964, $), between the Piazza San Marco and Piazza della Libertà, has seven dormitory rooms of 24 beds. Take Bus #1, #17 or #33 to the adjacent Via Lamarmora then walk.

The ancient 15th-century convent that houses the **Ostello Santa Monaca** (Via Santa Monica 6, ☎ 055-268338, fax 055-280155, www.ostello.it, $) is located in the Oltrano near Piazza del Carmine. No age limit applies nor is a YHA card compulsory, but the 1 am curfew may put many off (Bus #11, #36 or #37 from the station).

Also in the Oltrano, but a little farther away from it all to the west (15 minutes by Bus #12 from the station), is the **Youth Residence Florence 2000** (Viale R. Sanzio 16, ☎ 055-2335558, fax 055-2306392, www.florencegate.it/yo/emain.html, $). Rooms here have a maximum of four beds (minimum two) and many come with private bath. Paid parking.

A little out of the center, the **Ostello Sette Santi** (Viale dei Mille 11, ☎ 055-048452, fax 055-057085, 7santi@eidinet.com, $) occupies a converted convent next door to the Chiesa di Sette Santi (Campo di Marte area, Bus #17 from the station). Single, double and dormitory rooms available.

Camping

With a great position up near Piazzale Michelangelo looking over the Florentine cityscape, **Campeggio Italiani e Stranieri** (Viale Michelangelo 80, ☎ 055-6811977, fax 055-689348, www.ecvacanze.it/michelangelo/ingl.htm, $) offers one of the best tent views to be had in Italy. Camp shop, bar, Internet access and heated showers (Bus #12 or #13 from the station).

The campground of the youth hostel of the same name (see above), **Camping Villa Camerata** (Viale A. Righi 2/4, ☎ 055-601451, fax 055-610300, www.ostellionline.org/ostello.php?idostello=188, $) is shrouded in the greenery of the Fiesole hills and a great base if you're planning on doing some hiking. Take Bus #7 from the station.

Florence

Outside of Florence

In the heart of some of Tuscany's best-loved countryside – the Chianti hills to the south, the Medicean hotspot, the Mugello, to the north and the river valleys of the Arno and Elsa to the west – Florence isn't just about its Renaissance-colored city streets. Within easy reach are the smaller cities of Prato and Pistoia, with plenty of art treasures of their own, while just up the hill, Fiesole, Florence's older sister, offers a leisurely chance to soak it all in from its panoramic location.

THE REGION AT A GLANCE

Afternoon trips from Florence: Fiesole (page 84), Impruneta (page 135), La Certosa del Galluzzo (page 135), Vinci (page 106)
City breaks: Pistoia (page 122), Prato (page 111)
Rural retreats: Chianti (page 134), Mugello (page 91), Upper Valdarno (page 202), Val d'Elsa (page 160)
Spa towns: Montecatini Terme and Monsummano Terme (pages 128-29), Impruneta (page 135), Gambassi Terme (page 109)
Beach breaks: Versilia Coast (out of the region, page 249)

Fiesole

Best known for the commanding views over Florence that have drawn aristocratic Florentines and rich expats to build their country villas here since the Renaissance, hilltop Fiesole offers an easily accessible introduction to the area's rich Etruscan and Roman past. Although now subordinate to its larger neighbor, Fiesole was actually established first (by the Etruscans in the seventh century BC) and was considered the more important of the two cities up until the early 12th century. It was then that Florence took over, nearly destroying the town and surroundings by using it as a quarry for the growing city's architectural needs. These days it is little more than a village. The steep, winding roads that lead off from the bustling caffès and restaurants of the main Piazza Mino da Fiesole can be explored in a morning, the park of Monte Ceceri or the trails up into the Mugello occupying you for the remainder of your stay.

Fiesole is just six miles north of Florence. ATAF **Bus #7** departs from Firenze S.M.N. every 20 minutes (€1) dropping you off in Piazza Mino da Fiesole (for approaches on foot or mountain bike from Florence, see pages 88-89). If you're arriving by **car**, pick up the road through San Domenico from Piazza Edison in the north of Florence (Campo di Marte area). Once you're here, the town is small enough to navigate on foot, with Monte Ceceri a 10-minute walk to its south.

THE BUS & MUSEUM PASS

*If you plan to see absolutely everything, opt for the **ATAF Bus and Museum Pass** (€7, conc. €5 from Firenze S.M.N.), which gives entrance to Teatro Romano, Museo Bandini, Antiquarium Costantini and Chapel di San Jacopo, as well as return transport, for a saving of €2.*

Above: Chiesa di Santa Maria Novella in Florence (APT Florence)

low: The striking white marble of Florence's Chiesa di Santa Croce (APT Florence)

One of many sculptures decorating the Giardino di Boboli in Florence
(Tom Johnston / Emma Jones)

*Above: The Chiesa di San Miniato al Monte,
well worth the short hike up from Florence* (APT Florence)
Below: Florence's glove-makers show off their skills (Tom Johnston / Emma Jones)

Above: Donatello's Giuditta e Oloferne (detail), Sala dei Gigli, Palazzo Vecchio

Below: Florence's Ponte Vecchio

The **Ufficio Informazioni** (the Fiesole tourist office) is just up from the Teatro Romano (Via Portigiani 3-5, ☎ 055-5978373, fax 055-598822, www.comune.fiesole.fi.it). They have maps not just of the town, but also of all the walking and cycling routes to be enjoyed on Monte Ceceri.
[Map 2FT - Fiesole Town Map]

■ Sightseeing

 Nineteenth-century renovations explain the rather bare exterior of the **Cattedrale di San Romolo** (☎ 055-599566, daily, 7:30 am-noon, 3-6 pm, free), to your left as you arrive in Piazza Mino da Fiesole; it dates from the early 11th century, but only the 13th-century campanile has survived unscathed. The interior fares a little better, guarding its 15th-century polyptych *Maestà* by Bicci di Lorenzo and a marble altarpiece depicting *Madonna with Child and Saints* by Mino da Fiesole (Cappella Salutati) under its wood-beam ceiling. The other attraction on the main square is the 14th-century **Palazzo Pretorio**, right across the other side, and easily recognizable by the extensive range of coats of arms of town mayors from 1502 to 1808 that embellish its façade.

The steep Via San Francesco makes its winding path beside the **Palazzo Vescovile** (the Bishop's Palace), past the **Capella di San Jacopo** (☎ 055-59477, Sat only, 10 am-7 pm) with a great wall fresco by Bicci di Lorenzo (around 1440) – again both originally 11th century with heavy 19th-century restorations – up to the **Basilica di Sant'Alessandro** (☎ 055-59416). The 19th-century Neo-Classical façade here masks a church thought to have existed since at least the seventh century, itself built on the remains of former Roman and Etruscan temples. No longer in religious use, the basilica is now only open for shows and exhibitions. Try to make it inside whatever the event; it's well worth it to see the marvelous columns carved out of *marmo cipollino* (a marble named for its red onion-like swirls).

From here a well-worn staircase leads up to the **Convento e Chiesa di San Francesco** (☎ 055-59175, daily, 7:30 am-noon/3-7 pm, closed Sun am, free), the work of 14th-century Franciscan friars whose collection of Chinese bronzes can also be visited in the church's small museum, **Museo Etnografico della Missione Francescana** (Tues-Fri, 10 am-noon, 3-5 pm, closed Sat and Sun am, free). Also inside the church, you'll find an *Immaculate Conception* by Piero Cosimo (second altar on the right).

> **Check Out the Views:** You'll get some of the best views over Florence as you climb up to San Francesco. Watch for San Domenico amid the olive groves and cypress trees on the villa-lined route back to the city below. Fiesole's other celebrated viewpoint is among the peaks of Monte Ceceri along the panoramic "Terrace over Florence" trail.

Head back down into town though the adjoining public park (on the other side of the courtyard through a small iron gate), where a right on Via Duprè will lead you to the **Museo Bandini** (Via Duprè 1, ☎ 055-59477, daily, 9:30 am-7 pm, closed Tues and at 5 pm in winter, €6.50, conc. €4.50, ticket also includes entrance to the Teatro Romano and the Antiquarium Costantini). Its collection of 13th- to 15th-century Florentine art, the so-called Tuscan Primitives, includes a good range of Taddeo and Agnolo, Gardi, Naro di Cione and Lorenzo Monaco. You'll also spy a collection of 20 or so polychrome della Robbia terracottas of note.

Outside of Florence

Florence & Environs Key

FIESOLE
1. Cattedrale di San Romolo, Palazzo Pretorio, Palazzo Vescovile, Capella di San Jacopo, Basilica di Sant'Alessandro, Convento e Chiesa di San Francesco, Museo Etnografico della Missione Francescana, Museo Bandini, Teatro Romano, Antiquarium Costantini, Villa Medici, Convento e Chiesa di San Domenico, Badia Fiesolana
2. Monte Ceceri; Casa Careggi, Casa al Vento, Villa la Pergolata, Castello di Vincigliata

THE MUGELLO
3. Chiesa di San Romolo, Convento di Montesenario, Villa Demidoff
4. Villa di Cafaggiolo, Palazzo Pretorio, Castello dei Cattani, Badia di Santa Maria e Vigesimo, Chiesa di Sant'Andrea, Pieve di San Giovanni
5. Pieve di San Pietro, Fortezza di San Martino, Villa le Mozette, Castello del Trebbio, Convento di Bosca ai Frati
6. Il Torrino, Palazzo dei Vicari, Chiesa della Propositura dei SS Jacopo e Filippo, Museo di Arte Sacra, Artigiana e Contadina di Leprino, Centro Archeologico, Bottega di Coltellinaio, Museo dei Ferri Taglienti
7. Pieve di San Lorenzo, Museo Chini
8. Casa di Giotto; Monte Giovi
9. Abbazia di Mosheta (Badia di Mosheta), Museo del Paesaggio Storico dell'Appennino, Museo della Pietra Serena
10. Palazzo dei Capitani; Museo della Vita e del Lavoro delle Genti di Montagna

MONTE ALBANO & EMPOLESE VALDELSA
11. To Empolese Valdelsa: Museo della Collegiata, Collegiata di Sant'Andrea, Chiesa di San Michele, Convento e Chiesa di Santo Stefano degli Agostiniani (*Empoli*); Villa Medicea, Pieve di San Leonardo (*Cerreto Guidi*); Pieve di Sant'Ippolito e Biagio, Centro Comunale d'Arte, Museo di Arte Sacra, Chiesa di San Francesco (*Castelfiorentino*); Pieve di San Pietro in Mercato, Museo di Arte Sacra, Chiesa di San Martino e San Giusto (*Montespertoli*); Palazzo Pretorio, SS Tommaso e Prospero, Casa del Boccaccio, Chiesa di SS Jacopo e Filippo (*Certaldo*); Palazzo Pretorio, Chiesa di San Regolo, Sacro Monte di San Vivaldo, Santuario della Pietrina (*Montaione*); Gambassi Terme; San Gimignano; Colle di Val d'Elsa
12. Museo Archeologico e della Ceramica, Chiesa di San Jacopo a Puglignano, Chiesa di San Pietro, Abbazia di San Martino in Campo
13. Etruscan site (*Montereggi*); Villa Bibbiani, La Fornace Pasquinucci (*Capraia e Limite*)
14. Museo Ideale Leonardo da Vinci, Casa Natale di Leonardo
15. Basilica di Santa Maria delle Carceri, Castello dell'Imperatore, Chiesa di San Francesco, Palazzo Datini, Palazzo Pretorio, Palazzo Comunale, Museo del Tessuto, Cattedrale di San Stafano, Museo dell'Opera del Duomo, Museo di Pittura Murale, Chiesa di San Domenico, Centro per l'Arte Contemporanea Luigi Pecci, Monte Ferrato, Monti della Calvana, Monte Maggiore
16. Val di Bisenzio
17. Chiesa di SS Ippolito e Cassiano
18. Chiesa di Sant'Antonio Abate, Chiesa di San Giovanni Fuorcivitas, Chiesa e Convento di San Domenico, Chiesa San Paolo, Chiesa di Sant'Andrea, Museo Civico, Palazzo dei Vescovi, Museo Capitolare, Chiesa di San Bartolomeo in Pantano, Chiesa di Santa Maria delle Grazie, Ospedale del Ceppo, Chiesa e Conventa di San Francesco, Chiesa di Madonna dell'Umita, Giardino Puccini, Parco di Celle, Pistoia Zoo (*Pistoia*); Alto, Chiesa di San Pietro (*Montecatini Terme*); Svizzeria Pesciatina, Santa Maria Assunta, Chiesa di San Francesco, Oratorio di Sant'Antonio Abate, The Castelli, Il Parco di Pinocchio (*Pescia*)

MONTAGNA PISTOIESE
19. Abetone, Ski Resorts

CHIANTI
20. Basilica di Santa Maria
21. Villa di Vignamaggio (*Greve in Chianti*); Castello di Brolio (*Radda in Chianti*); Castelnuovo Berardenga, Castello di Montalto (*Gaiole in Chianti*)

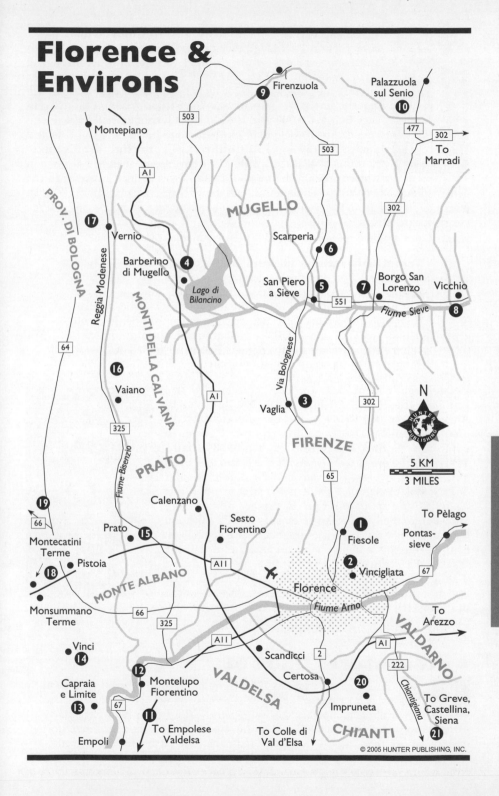

Florence & Environs

Montepiano

503

A1

PROV. DI BOLOGNA

17 Vernio

Reggia Modenese

64

Barberino di Mugello **4**

Lago di Bilancino

MONTI DELLA CALVANA

16 Vaiano

325

Fiume Bisenzio

PRATO

Calenzano

Prato **15**

Montecatini Terme

18 Pistoia

Monsummano Terme

19
66

66

325

MONTE ALBANO

A11

Vinci **14**

Capraia e Limite **13**

67

12 Montelupo Fiorentino

11 To Empolese Valdelsa

Empoli

9 Firenzuola

Palazzuola sul Senio **10**

503

MUGELLO

477

302

To Marradi

302

Scarperia

6

San Piero a Sieve **5**

Borgo San Lorenzo **7**

Vicchio

551

8

Fiume Sieve

Via Bolognese

Vaglia **3**

302

FIRENZE

N

5 KM
3 MILES

65

Sesto Fiorentino

A11

Fiesole **1**

2 Vincigliata

To Pèlago

Pontassieve

67

Florence

Fiume Arno

VALDARNO

To Arezzo

A1

Scandicci

2

Certosa

VALDELSA

To Colle di Val d'Elsa

222

Chiantigiana

20

Impruneta

CHIANTI

To Greve, Castellina, Siena

21

© 2005 HUNTER PUBLISHING, INC.

Just opposite, the entrance to the **Teatro Romano** unleashes a monumental archeological complex of ancient Etruscan, Roman and Lombard ruins within its eight acres of hillside. Stretching up to the remains of Etruscan walls at the back (so imposing that at one time superstitious locals believed them to be the work of giants), sites not to miss include the Etruscan temple (fourth century BC); the 3,000-seat Roman theater (home to an outdoor cinema during Fiesole Estate); the Roman baths; and the Lombard tombs. Nearby is the **Antiquarium Costantini** (Via Portigiani 1, ☎ 055-59477, daily, 9:30 am-7 pm, closed Tues and at 5 pm in winter, €6.50, conc. €4.50, ticket also includes entrance to the Teatro Romano and the Museo Bandini). It displays the area's prize findings, with pieces stretching from the Bronze Age to Lombard occupation and includes large *pietra serena* steles (from Etruscan tombstones), Roman ceramics, money and jewelry, and a whole host of Lombard funerary objects.

> **Tesori Ritrovati:** Re-discover Fiesole's treasures with the help of the local tourist office on Sundays in September when tour guides take you around the archeological findings of the Antiquarium Costantini before finishing up with a short classical music concert and Tuscan aperitif in the amphitheater itself at 6:30 pm. Tours start at 5:30 pm from outside the museum (museum entrance charge only applies). Tours in English can be arranged for large groups on reservation.

Heading south out of the town, Via V. Fiesolana escorts you past the Michelozzo-built **Villa Medici** (Via B. Angelico 2, ☎ 055-59164, visits by reservation only, Mon-Fri, 8 am-1 pm, €6) to the 15th century **Convento e Chiesa di San Domenico** (☎ 055-59230, daily, 7:30 am-12:30 pm, 2-6 pm, free). This is a cool and tranquil complex where you can enjoy a *Madonna and Saints* and *Crucifixion* painted by former prior Fra Angelico and a magnificent altarpiece illustrating scenes from his life. The bus stop outside will take you back to town or south to Florence, but before you hop on board, head up Via della Badia dei Rocettini to visit the **Badia Fiesolana**, right (☎ 055-59155, daily, 9 am-5 pm, closed Sat pm and Sun, free). Clad in white and green marble, this was Fiesole's cathedral from the ninth to 11th centuries and a particular favorite with Cosimo Il Vecchio, who had the interior transformed into the superb Renaissance structure you see today.

■ Adventures On Foot

According to local tradition, Leonardo da Vinci's famous attempt to fly took place on **Monte Ceceri**. True or not, today there's a marked trail in honor of his escapades, starting from the Regresso area where his assistant is thought to have crashed (next to the stop for Bus #7), and up along a former quarry service road into the wood-covered park. The path ends on Piazzale Leonardo, the center of the park and, according to the inscription on its pillar, the site from where Leonardo's flight took off. From here another trail along the Prato ai

Pini (a road built but never used by the Italian army in 1932 to haul anti-aircraft guns to the top of the hill) leads you to Via Corsica and back to Fiesole (catch Bus #45 or #47 if you don't want to walk).

A quicker and easier trail in the same park is the yellow-marked "Terrace over Florence" path which, departing from Piazza Mino, winds its way around the mountain, stopping at various viewpoints en route. Along its path you'll also see some gaping chasms left by the abandoned quarries of *pietra serena* (a blue and grey limestone) and *pietra morta* (a stone used for fireplaces and ovens). Indeed, so much of this mountain has been excavated, Fiesole's residents believe that up to half of its original mass has been incorporated into Florence's urban landscape!

From Fiesole, you can also pick up a number of marked **trails** offering hikes of various lengths both north and south of town. The marked footpath #1 offers a panoramic loop south through Settignano, touching the north of Florence before returning back, while #4 leads north around Monte Muscoli and up to the Olmo River and Mugello territory (see page 91). Leading off route #4 is the rolling #3, which takes you along Piano delle Tortore south to Compiobbi and the River Arno.

These trails and others are detailed in KOMPASS map #660 Firenze-Chianti (1:50,000, www.kompass.at). The tourist office also supplies the helpful *Itinerari Fiesolani*, a booklet and map (in Italian) detailing four looping walks and one longer loop split into two phases, which depart from Fiesole or nearby towns.

In spring and autumn, the local council organizes **guided tours** around the gardens of nine villas in the outskirts of Fiesole, including the villas Medici, Vincigliata and the vast Castel di Poggio with roots back as far as the third century (information and reservations on ☎ 800-414240). They also organize year-round tours to the Fonte Sottera, an artificial underground **cave** built for the collection of water in the heart of the Monte Ceceri Park.

■ Adventures on Wheels

There are two main **bike trails** to choose from in the Fiesole area; the first skirts the constructive footsteps of John Temple Leader while the second, longer itinerary, takes you through Pontassieve, Pelaago and Rufina before depositing you back in Fiesole's central square.

John Temple Leader

Part of a group of Anglo-Florentines who bought and restored many of the area's dilapidated villas in the 19th century, John Temple Leader went one step further. He purchased 700 acres of land between Fiesole and Settignano over 50 years and transformed it from its previous run-down and over-quarried appearance into a huge Italian garden of pines and cedars. The villas and hamlets he renovated are even today recognizable by his coat of arms.

The **Temple Leader trail** begins in Vincigliata, a three-mile bike ride from Fiesole (follow Via di Vincigliata), and takes you past four of his villas: the panoramic **Casa Careggi;** nearby **Casa al Vento; Villa la Pergolata** (with 16th-century oratory containing a Filippo Lippi fresco and sculptures by Giuliano e Benedetto da Maiano and Mino da Fiesole); and **Castello di Vincigliata** (guided visits by appointment only, ☎ 055-599556). The latter is the most famous of the Temple Leader villas, and the one he bought and rebuilt from the ground up in 1855 in the style of the original medieval fortress. Along the way, you'll not only catch some great views as far as Brunelleschi's Cupola but you'll also get to pass the quarry (Cave di Vincigliata) where the stone to construct its top part was sourced.

The five-hour itinerary through Pontassieve, Pelago and Rufina has its steep gradients but the rolling hills, and vine and olive groves you'll discover en route soon dull the pain. The route departs from Fiesole (although you can also pick it up from the northeast of Florence) looping around Monte Ceceri before dropping down to the Arno at Compiobbi and reaching **Pontassieve** via its opposite bank. From here, the trail climbs and drops through **Pelago** and **Rufina** with a pleasant ride alongside the Arno before climbing and descending to Fiesole along a road with some great views over Florence.

WHAT TO SEE

There's a small historical center at the otherwise unimpressive **Pontassieve**, with the remains of the city's ancient medieval fortifications and city gateways on display. Also worth a look if you fancy a break are the **Medicean Bridge** (built 1555 by order of Cosimo I and marked with his coat of arms), the **Palazzo Sansoni-Trombetta** and the **Filicaia Tower**.

Pelago makes a much better stopping point. This small town, built up around the old **Conti Guidi Castle**, is full of beautifully porticoed palazzi (such as Stupan, Ripi and Gerini) and has a lovely central piazza perfect for a quick coffee break.

In the territory of Chianti Rufina DOCG, **Rufina** makes a good stop for wine fans. First pop into the **Museo della Vita e del Vino** (Villa Poggio Reale, ☎ 055-8396529, Sun and holidays, 3-5 pm), before getting down to the serious business of wine tasting at one of the town *enoteche* or tasting rooms. If you want to go the whole hog and pick up the area's wine route, 15 of the area's producers offer visits by arrangement with **Consorzio Chianti Rufina** (Viale Belfiore 9, Firenze, ☎ 055-3245680, fax 055-3248252, www.chiantirufina.com).

■ Where to Eat

Most of Fiesole's restaurants sit around the touristy Piazza Mino. **Perseus** (☎ 055-59143, $$, closed Tues in winter) is the most popular of the terraces, but **Pizzeria Etrusca** next door (☎ 055-599484, $, closed Thurs in winter) is cheaper, with pizzas from €5. **L'Polpa** (☎ 055-59485, $$, 7-10 pm, closed Sun) is your best bet for authentic Tuscan cuisine. **Reggia degli Etruschi** (Via S. Francesco 18, ☎ 055-59385, www.lareggia.org, $$$, closed Tues) has the best views if you can manage the steep climb on an empty stomach. But many prefer to picnic in the public park below it – buy your provisions before 1 pm in the supermarket or in the *alimentari* on Via A. Gramsci.

■ Where to Stay

 Fiesole is close enough to Florence to allow you to travel to and fro on the same day, but consider basing yourself in this smaller town. **Hotel Villa Sorriso** (Via A. Gramsci 21, ☎ 055-59027, fax 055-5978075, $$) and **B&B Villa Le Scalette** (Via delle Cannelle 1, ☎ 055-5978484, fax 055-5979970, www.villascalette.it, $$$) are the cheapest central options, with **Villa Aurora** (Piazza Mino 39, ☎ 055-59100, fax 055-59587, www.logicad.net/aurora, $$$$) at the higher end of the price range. If you really want to treat yourself, opt for the **Villa San Michele** (Via Doccia 4, ☎ 055-5678200, fax 055-5678250, www.villasanmichele.orient-express.com, $$$$$, closed Dec to Mar), mid-way between Fiesole and Florence, which offers rooms in a converted monastery designed by Michelangelo with some great views over Florence from the terrace. You can stay in the **Convento di San Domenico** (Piazza San Domenico 3, ☎ 055-59230, vincap@tin.it, $) for much less if you're prepared to forgo an ensuite bathroom. The area's campground, **Camping Panoramico** (Via Peramonda 1, ☎ 055-599069, fax 055-59186, www.florencecamping.com, $, outdoor pool) is in woods one mile out of town (buses #47 and #49 take you some of the way) and is well placed for treks onto Monte Ceceri.

The Mugello

Many Florentines I've met have their summer homes in the Mugello, the territory of rolling hills, thick woodlands and mountain peaks that stretches north from Florence up to the border with Emilia-Romagna. They're not the first of the city residents to favor the spot. The Medici, who formally came from this area, blessed its hillsides with many of the beautiful villas and vast fortress complexes you see today. It is traditionally split into two sections, the lower **Mugello Valley** confined by the Apennines to the north, and the more northern **Alto Mugello** (also known as Tuscan Romagna), which claims the highest of the Mugello's rocks and peaks.

You really need a **car** to see the best of the Mugello, with four main routes of approach from Florence. The quickest (once you're on it – no mean feat by any standards in Florence) is the **A1**, which takes you up to the Barberino di Mugello toll-paying exit on the west of the region. More scenic approaches are offered by the Via Bolognese (**SS65**) through Vaglia to San Piero a Sieve and on; the quieter **SS302** direct to Borgo San Lorenzo; and the longer, winding **SS67** (from which you pick up the **SS551**), which also takes you to Borgo San Lorenzo but this time via Vicchio. It is off the latter that you will find the roads north into the Alto Mugello: **SS302** to Marradi and Palazzuolo sul Senio (change onto the **SS477**) and the **SS503** to Firenzuola.

Trains (☎ 848-888088, www.trenitalia.it) run from Florence to the Mugello Valley towns – Vaglia, San Piero a Sieve, Borgo San Lorenzo and Vicchio – and to the Alto Mugello town of Marradi. The **old Faentina railway line** (☎ 0558-459116, www.fs-on-line.com) also runs though the Mugello Valley with stops at Vaglia, San Piero a Sieve, Borgo San Lorenzo and Marradi.

CAP bus service (☎ 055-214637, www.capautolinee.it) links Florence to Vaglia, San Piero a Sieve, Borgo San Lorenzo and Palazzuolo sul Senio. **Sita** (☎ 800-373760, www.sita-on-line.it) will take you to Vaglia (#302, #303, #306 and

#307), Barberino di Mugello (#301 and #302), San Piero a Sieve (#302, #303 and #307), Scarperia (#302 and #303), Borgo San Lorenzo (#307, #308 and #310), Vicchio (#307 and #310) and Firenzuola (#303). Finally, **Florentia Bus** (Borgo San Lorenzo, ☎ 0558-490505, www.florentiabus.it) provide services to Vaglia, San Piero a Sieve, Borgo San Lorenzo and Vicchio.

■ Information Sources

? **Tourist Offices:** The **Ufficio Turistico Comprensoriale Mugello** (the main Mugello tourist office) is in **Borgo San Lorenzo** in the 14th-century Palazzo del Podestà (☎ 0558-45271, fax 0558-456288, http://turismo.mugello.toscana.it, Mon-Sat, 8:30 am-12:30 pm and 2:30-5:30 pm) with another office at Villa Pecori Giraldi (☎/fax 0558-456230, daily, 10 am-1 pm, 3-6 pm (closed Mon, Tues & Wed pm). The latter, along with the nearby **Communità Montana Mugello** (Via P. Togliatti 45, ☎ 0558-495346, www.cm-mugello.fi.it, Mon-Fri, 9 am-1 pm), offers considerable information on both sightseeing and sporting activities in the region.

Smaller offices are located in the **Villa Demidoff** (☎ 055-409784, 15 June-15 Sept, Thurs-Fri, 4-6 pm, Sat-Sun, 11 am-6 pm) en route to Vaglia; **Barberino di Mugello** (Via del Lago 33, Loc. I Boschi, ☎ 0558-420106, fax 0558-420946, daily, 10 am-7 pm, closes 1:30-2:30 pm on Wed and Thurs); **San Piero a Sieve** (Piazza Medici, ☎ 0558-487528, Mon-Sat, 9 am-1 pm); **Scarperia** (Piazza dei Vicari 1, ☎ 0588-468165, fax 0588-468862, prolocoscarperia@katamail.com, Wed-Fri, 9:30 am-12:30 pm, 3:30-5:30 pm, Sun and holidays, 10 am-1 pm, 3:30-7:30 pm); and **Vicchio** (Via Garibaldi 1, ☎ 0558-497023, fax 0558-844275, urp@comune.vicchio.fi.it, Mon-Sat, 8:30 am-12:30 pm).

Mugello Alto is well served by offices in **Firenzuola** (Palazzo Ex Pretura), Piazza Agnolo, ☎ 0558-199007, fax 0558-19366, June-Sept, Mon/Thurs, 10 am-noon, 3-7 pm, Sat-Sun, 10 am-noon); **Palazzuolo sul Senio** (Piazza E. Alpi 1, ☎ 0558-046125, fax 0558-046461, comunepalazzuolo@tin.it); and **Marradi** (Via Castelnaudary 1, ☎/fax 0558-045170, www.pro-marradi.it, June-Aug, Mon/Tues/Thurs-Sat, 2-6 pm, Sun July-Aug only, 9 am-noon, Sept-May, Mon-Sat, 9 am-noon).

Maps & Guides: The tourist office in association with the Communità Montana has put together the *Mugello, Alto Mugello e Val di Sieve* tourist and trail **map** (1:70,000), which provides detailed information on CAI and SOFT **trails** in the region. They also provide *Beyond the Gates of Florence*, a booklet with four itineraries laid out for **road bikes** in the Mugello Valley, with circular routes departing from Borgo San Lorenzo, Vicchio, Barberino di Mugello, and two in Mugello Alto (both departing from Firenzuola).

■ The Mugello Valley

Vaglia: Vaglia's major sights are a short drive or **hike** up the slopes of Monte Senario (2,600 feet/815 m). There is the Romanesque **Chiesa di San Romolo** (daily, 7 am-noon, 4:30-6 pm) with its wood-sculpted font decoration attributed to Michelozzo, Andrea della Robbia terracotta altarpiece and paintings by Pietro Annigoni at Bivigliano; and the **Convento di Montesenario** (daily, 7 am-12:30 pm, 3-7:30 pm, ☎ 055-46441, free), with fine views from its peak. The latter also offers a celebratory tipple of its homebrewed liqueur Gemma d'Abaete (available in the cloister drugstore) as well as an interesting itinerary around the caves and cells once inhabited by the friars of this Servite monastery established in 1241. (For information on Villa Demidoff, Vaglia's other main sight, see page 58.) **Hikers** can pick up the SOFT central ring at Bivigliano, with other CAI (Club Alpino Italiano) itineraries running from the outskirts of Vaglia to another SOFT stop the Badia Buonsollezzo (#20), north up Monte Gennaro (#8A then #00) and south up Monte Morello (#6). For **horseback riding**, contact **Club Ippico Corte Chiarese** (Loc. Bivigliano, ☎ 055-406404).

> **SOFT Trails:** Not an indication of an easy ride, the SOFT trails ("Florence Spring Trekking") that encircle the Mugello Valley are a network of paths suitable for both **trekking** and **horseback-riding,** offering a main 11-stage hike around the central ring and 22 secondary branches (each with a particular natural or historical theme).

Go by Train

The **Faentina Florence to Ravenna Transapennine railway** runs through the entire Mugello (☎ 0558-459116, www.fs-on-line.com) offering **hikers** and **mountain bikers** the opportunity to hop off, make their way to the next station and then hop back on as they please. Branches run from Firenze S.M.N to Borgo San Lorenzo (stopping in Vaglia and San Piero a Sieve), from Borgo San Lorenzo across the Tuscan border to Faenza (stopping in Ronta, Crespino sul Lamone, Marradi/Palazzuolo sul Senio) and from Borgo San Lorenzo to the Sieve Valley (stopping in Vicchio, Dicomano, Londa, Rufina and Pontassieve). Hikers will find well-marked CAI trails to greet them, while mountain bikers should pick up one of the established "Train and Bici" routes, the two shortest of which depart from Ronta (the 1½-hour Ronta to Borgo San Lorenzo or two-hour Ronta to Vicchio itineraries) and the two longest from Vicchio (the five-hour Vicchio to Crespino sul Lamone or the six-hour Vicchio to Marradi). You can also pick up **road bike** routes following nine miles of secondary roads from Ronta to Borgo San Lorenzo via Vicchio (or vice versa).

Barberino di Mugello: A Florentine border post founded in the early 14th century, Barberino di Mugello benefited from the work of Cosimo Il Vecchio's favored architect, Michelozzo, who converted the old fortress into the sumptuous **Villa di Cafaggiolo** (see below) and gave the main square its loggia. Today it's a pretty sleepy locale, but worth a leisurely stroll. Sights to look out for include the much-decorated **Palazzo Pretorio**, the ancient Pieve di San Silvestro, some beautiful aristocratic palaces and the remains of the ancient **Castello dei Cattani** at whose foot the medieval hamlet originally sprang up.

Forays into the town's surroundings will uncover the **Badia di Santa Maria e Vigesimo**, an early 17th-century Vollombrosan abbey, the elegant **Chiesa di Sant'Andrea** at Camoggiano (Sun, 10:30 am-noon, free) with classy 15th-century façade and portico, and the antique **Pieve di San Giovanni** in Petroio (1097). Longer **treks** will take you along one of the most panoramic of the SOFT secondary trails, up Monte Cuccoli and along the crest of the Apennine Ridge (SOFT #9).

Outside of Florence

There are also plenty of watersports to be enjoyed on **Lago Bilancino**, with **canoeing** (Canottieri Mugello, ☎ 055-8469864, polpergioco@hotmail.com and Planet Sport, Viale Gramsci 39, ☎/fax 0558-478049, www.planetmugello.com), both offering rental and courses), **sailing** (with Circolo Nautico Mugello, Via Montebello 22, www.mugello.net/cnm) and **windsurfing** (Windsurf Center Kia Orana, ☎ 53473541068, www.kiorana.it) on offer.

San Piero a Sieve: Best known for the Medicean fortresses, castles and villas (see below) that dot its surroundings, San Piero a Sieve is the starting point for many of the region's best **trails**. In addition to the Medicean itinerary that takes you to the Convento di Bosco ai Frati and the Castello di Trebbio, there's also a six-hour panoramic route around Monte Maggiore to Sieve Springs. Before you head out, visit the town's **Pieve di San Pietro** (☎ 0558-48161, daily, 8 am-noon, 4-5:30 pm), an 11th-century parish church guarding a prized Luca della Robbia baptismal font and a crucifix by Raffaello da Montelupo. **Cyclists** can pick up the tracks of the Medici through Villa di Cafaggiolo, Castello del Trebbio and back along a row of cypress trees to the main SS65 back to town.

IN THE FOOTSTEPS OF THE MEDICI

Lorenzo di Medici (Botticelli)

The Mugello was the Medici family's old stomping ground before it came to take over the reigns of Florence and, once firmly installed, they made sure that the family lands (concentrated in the area of San Piero a Sieve, Barberino di Mugello and Scaperia) reaped the rewards of their wealth and political power. By following SOFT trail #8 you can pick up some of the best routes, with the rest reachable by bicycle and car from the region's main towns:

There's a great walk and beautiful views to be enjoyed around the old walls of the 16th-century **Fortezza di San Martino** (☎ 0558-458793, under restoration at the time of writing), near San Piero a Sieve, a fortress built to plans of Buontalenti and Baldassare Lanci.

The Corsini-owned **Villa Le Mozette** just out of town (no public entry) houses the "cedro delle Mozzette," a cedar considered to be one of Italy's most beautiful trees, in its extensive gardens of age-old trees. The building itself dates from the 14th century, with later enlargements by the Medici.

Built on the ruins of a feudal tower by Michelozzo, nearby **Castello del Trebbio** (guided group visits by appointment, ☎ 0558-458793) has some delightful Italian gardens and a lovely 17th-century arbor.

Michelozzo is also to be thanked for the **Convento di Bosca ai Frati** (visits by appointment daily, ☎ 0558-484111), a secluded monastery up a rough three-mile track with a crucifix attributed to Donatello and 16th- and 17th-century art collection on view in its Museo d'Arte Sacra. The **Associazione Turismo e Ambiente** (☎ 0558-458793) organizes guided tours of the monastery in the busy summer season.

The favorite country home of Lorenzo Il Magnifico, Michelozzo's imposing **Villa di Cafaggiolo** (guided group visits by appointment,

☎ 0558-458793, www.castellodicafaggiolo.it, €5) sits amid dense wild forests near Barberino di Mugello. As with the castle in Trebbio, you can still see parts of the earlier structure it was built on.

Situated at the southeast corner of Scarperia's town walls, the 14th-century **Il Torrino** (guided group visits by appointment, ☎ 155-8458793) offers some fine views in addition to its interesting military history.

For the **Villa and Parco Demidoff** (near Vaglia) see page 58.

Scarperia: A 14th-century Florentine *terra nuova* (new land), there isn't really that much to see in Scarperia unless you're interested in its artisan knives – in which case you should try to get here for the town knife festival (Manifestazione del Diotto, ☎ 0558-43161, first three weeks of Sept). That said, the historical center is charming enough with its 14th-century **Palazzo dei Vicari,** decorated with the coats of arms of the different vicars of the Florentine Republic, and **Chiesa della Propositura dei SS Jacobo e Filippo** (daily, 8 am-noon, 4-6:30 pm), with a 15th-century marble *Madonna and Child* tondo by Benedetto da Maiano and a wooden crucifix attributed to a young Sansovino.

The most interesting of the area's sights can be found in the hamlet of **Sant'Agata**, whose church of limestone, sandstone and green serpentine marble, constitutes the most famous sacred structure in the Mugello (Sun, 9 am-noon, other times by appointment, ☎ 0558-406926). You'll also find quite a number of museums in this tiny hamlet. The **Museo di Arte Sacra** (☎ 0558-430671, 16 June-14 Sept, Sat/Sun and hols, 4-7 pm, 15 Sept-15 June, Sun and hols, 10 am-noon, 4-7 pm) is the pick of the bunch for its exhibition of altarpieces from the Florentine school, alongside a Bicci di Lorenzo shrine, polycrome della Robbia terracotta and *Madonna with Child* by Ghirlandaio. Kids will probably prefer the **Artigiana e Contadina di Leprino** (☎ 055-8406750, Sun and holidays, 3-6 pm), a display of moving characters depicting Mugellan craft scenes from 1920 to 1950 constructed by Faliero Lepri. There's also the **Centro Archeologico**, a small display of findings in the region (Archeological Center, ☎ 0558-430671, 16 June-14 Sept, Sat/Sun and holidays, 4-7 pm, 15 Sept-15 June, Sun and hols, 10 am-noon, 4-7 pm).

A Slice of Life

The tradition of knife making in Scarperia dates back at least five centuries, as a tour around the town's two museums will testify. The first, the historical **Bottega di Coltellinaio** (Cutler's Workshop, Via Solferino 19) reproduces the knife-makers' original working environment, while the second, the **Museo dei Ferri Taglienti**, takes you through its production history, evolution and big name producers (Metal Museum, ☎ 0558-468165, 16 June-14 Sept, Tues-Fri, 4-7 pm, Sat/Sun and holidays, 10 am-1 pm, 4-7 pm, 15 Sept-15 June, Sat/Sun and holidays, 10 am-1 pm, 3-6:30 pm). You can also pick up a few blades of your own at **Coltellerie Berti** (Via Roma 43, ☎ 0558-46585, info@coltellerieberti.it) or **Coltelleria Consigli** (Via Roma 8, ☎ 0558-430270, fax 0558-468014).

Scarperia is another good point of departure for **walkers**, with trails taking you up Monte Verruca (#38, five hours) from nearby Grezzano, up Monte Calvi from Sant'Agata (#42) and onto the GEA (Grande Escursione Appennina trails) and SOFT network at Passo del Giogo di Scarperia. If you don't want to do it on your own, local environmental trekking guide, **Michelangelo Marsili** (Via Matteo dei Neri 8, ☎ 0558-46709, www.marsilitrek.it) will tailor a walking tour to your ability and time requirements.

Borgo San Lorenzo: By far the most important town in the Mugello, Borgo San Lorenzo rose on the slopes of the Calvana Ridge under the Romans in the 12th century, settling quite happily under medieval counts the Ulbadini before the Florentine Republic took a fancy to the area in the 10th century. Centered around the striking brick campanile of the Romanesque **Pieve di San Lorenzo**, at right (☎ 0558-459295, Mon-Fri, 9 am-noon, 3-5 pm, Sat-Sun, 3-5 pm), with a Giotto *Madonna* and a *Maestà* attributed to Agnolo Gaddi, it's still a pretty rural setting with some pleasant park areas and medieval streets, if little else.

The biggest draw is for ceramics fans, with the **Museo Chini** in the restored Villa Pecori Giraldi displaying prolific family activity during the Liberty period (☎ 0558-456230, 16 June-14 Sept, Tues, 10 am-1 pm, Wed-Sat, 4-7 pm, Sun and holidays, 10 am-1 pm, 4-7 pm, rest of year times vary). If you've been inspired by the museum to buy them, the Chini-Pecchioli workshop (Cermaiche Franco Pecchioli, on the Borgo San Lorenzo ring road at the junction with the Via Faentina, ☎ 0558-459359) sells home furnishings and decorations in the traditional Chini colors. There's also a museum of peasant civilization at Grezzano (☎ 0558-457197, 16 June-14 Sept, Sat-Sun and holidays, 3-7 pm, rest of year times vary), although its main pull is an attractive one-hour **nature trail** through the surrounding countryside to a medieval water mill.

TRADITIONAL CRAFTS: WATER MILLS

Widespread since the Middle Ages when the local water sources fed the grindstone for wheat, maize, chestnuts and animal fodder, there are still a few Mugellan water mills in use:

Antico Mulino Margheri (Madonna dei Tre Fiumi, Ronta, ☎ 0558-403051, always open, shop selling milled produce)

Mulino di Grezzano (Grezzano, info and guided tours, ☎ 0558-457197)

Mulino Arrighetti (Via Stieto 1, Sala Cirignano, Barberino di Mugello, visits by appointment, ☎ 0558-417958, shop selling milled produce)

Mulino di Sant'Agata (Sant'Agata, always open)

Mulino dei Lotti (Via Cornacchiaia 91, Firenzuola, visits by appointment, ☎ 0558-149076, one of the most interesting, with the original grindstones, measures, lever scales and tools)

Mulino di Valtellere (San Pellegrino, Firenzuola, visits by appointment, ☎ 0558-19536)

You can also pick up a number of interesting **treks** in the area (SOFT #6, six hours through thick chestnut woods up Monte Giovi, probably the most attractive) and a range of **mountain bike** trails – east along the River Sieve to Vicchio, before looping back through Dicomano (2½ hours), or west in the shadow of the Apennines ridge to loop through Scarperia and Sant'Agata (2½ hours). It's also good territory for **road bikers**, with the "train and bici" itineraries providing two different paths between the stops, **Borgo San Lorenzo** and **Dicomano**.

> **Bike Rental:** Bikes can be rented from **Borgo San Lorenzo** tourist office, from **Mugello Bike** (Via B. Angelico 5, ☎ 0558-458713) or from **Il Ciclismo di Formigli Renzo** (Viale Pecori Giraldi 58/60, ☎/fax 0558-495422, www.formigli.com) in town.

Borgo San Lorenzo also has a **gliding** club that offers lessons, propelled flights and a May "Silent Flying Festival" with tourist flights on a first-come, first-served basis. (**Mugello Gliding Aeroclub**, Loc. Figliano, ☎ 0558-408665, fax 055-4215654, www.geoide.com/gliding, every Sat and Sun.)

The local **Associazione Turismo Ambiente** (Piazza Dante 29, Borgo San Lorenzo, ☎/fax 0558-458793, Mon/Wed/Fri, 9:30 am-12:30 pm, tea@terraditoscana.com) will guide you through many of the region's itineraries (nature walks, Medici properties, archeological tours and trips underground) for a minimal fee. **Cooperativa Ischetus** (Viale IV Novembre 14, 5003 Borgo San Lorenzo ☎/fax 0558-45-7056, www.ischetus.com) offers a similar service for those preferring to travel on two wheels.

Vicchio: Few places have vantages as supreme as Vicchio, on a plateau above the Sieve River between the slopes of Monte Giovi (992 m/3,254 feet) and those of the Tuscan-Emilian Apennines. Although it may be known as the birthplace of two of Italy's biggest artists, Fra Angelico and Giotto (just out of town in Vespignano), few traces remain of the first, born here in 1395. Even the museum dedicated to him doesn't conserve any of his works. Giotto fares only slightly better at house-museum **Casa di Giotto**, above (☎ 0558-448251, direction Borgo San Lorenzo, Tues/Thurs/Sat-Sun and holidays, 10 am-noon, 4-7 pm).

Luckily, the surrounding mountains don't disappoint: SOFT tracks take **hikers** up Monte Giovi (#5 and CAI#10) and Monte Campogianni (CAI#16), while mountain **bikers** get to enjoy one of the territory's most notorious ascents – the Salaiole climb up around Monte Senario (take Ponte a Vicchio across the River Sieve and over to Sagginale). **Horseback riders** can pick up the SOFT-loop or rest their horses at **Centro Ippico Il Forteto** (SS551, Loc. Caldeta, ☎ 0558-44-8183, fax 0558-38-7589 www.forteto.it).

Nearby, there are **canoeing** opportunities on the Sieve River and Lago di Montelleri; contact **Soggiono al Lago** (Via dei Pini, Vicchio, ☎ 055-8448638) for canoe courses on the latter. Vicchio also has a very helpful tourist sport center, **Centro Sportivo Le Sorgenti** (☎ 055-8448306), which organizes or provides information on **archery, fishing, canoeing, mountain biking, caving, rock-climbing** and other sporting activities in the region.

■ Alto Mugello

Firenzuola: Another of the Florentine Republic's *terre nuove* (new lands), Firenzuola still contains part of the medieval wall circuit that Sangallo Il Vecchio transformed into powerful perimeter defenses in the 15th century. Other than the ramparts, the main attraction is the nearby **Abbazia di Mosheta** (also known as the Badia di Mosheta), built by Giovanni Gualberto in 1034. It was one of the first Vallombrosan settlements in the country. Deconsecrated in 1744, it is has since been turned into a farm and outdoor activity center (with accommodation; see below). Its **Museo del Paesaggio Storico dell'Appennino** (Museum of the Historical Landscape of the Apennines, ☎ 0558-495346, 16 June-14 Sept, Thurs-Sat, 4-7 pm, Sun and holidays, 10 am-1 pm, 4-7 pm, rest of year hours vary) only distracts a few of the excursionists drawn here by the prime **walking** and **horseback riding** territory.

Common destinations in the area, such as **Monte Falterona**, the archeological park of the **Lago degli Idoli**, the **Aqua Cheta waterfall** (Dante's "hell valley," with ice-climbing routes during the frozen winter months), and summits of mountains **Acuto**, **Falco** and **Levante** are all well-signposted, with farm staff on standby offering tips and recommendations. Horseback riders should contact **Moscheta Horse Trekking** (Badia di Moscheta, ☎ 0558-144167, fax 0558-144167), **Il Cigno** (Badia di Susinana, ☎ 0558-046662) or the **Montefreddi Equestrian Centre** (Via Montefreddi 167, Loc. Pietramala, Firenzuola, ☎ 0558-136601, fax 0558-136921, www.cavalloweb.it).

There is also a three-hour **cross-country skiing** route that leads between the Badia di Moscheta and the Passo del Giogo near Scarperia along the ridge (pick up the GEA marked trail from the Passo del Giogo or from the abbey itself).

Adventurous **road bikers** are drawn here by the 86-mile **Tour of the Six Passes**, generally split into two- or three-day stages. Leaving from Firenzuola, it takes in the Paretaio Pass, the Sant'Ilario Pass, the Eremo Pass, the Peschiera Pass, the Muraglione Pass and the Giogio Pass, before arriving back in Firenzuola.

Before you head off, check out Firenzuola's **Museo della Pietra Serena** (Museum of Sandstone, Loc. La Rocca, ☎ 0558-199434, 16 June-14 Sept, Mon, Fri-Sat, 4-7 pm, Sun, 10 am-1 pm, 4-7 pm, rest of year times vary), a collection of stone objects, works of art and photographic history about the excavation and work of this highly-prized stone, so prevalent in this area that it has given birth to whole villages. Check out nearby hamlets **San Pellegrino** and **Tirli**, and you'll get the idea; from the paving on their streets to the chimneys on their houses, they're built entirely of the stone.

Palazzuolo sul Senio: A stronghold of the aristocratic Ulbadinis, who ruled the Mugello until the Medici took over in 1362, Palazzuolo sul Senio, is dominated by its **Palazzo dei Capitani** (c. 1300) and adjacent 14th-century bell tower. This evocative stone building also contains the town's main museum, **Museo della Vita e del Lavoro delle Genti di Montagna** (Museum of the Life & Work of the Mountain People, ☎ 0558-046114, fax 0558-046008, 16 June-14 Sept, Tues, 8-11 pm, Sat/Sun and holidays, 4-7 pm, 15 Sept-15 June, Sun and holidays, 3-6 pm, free), which is worth a visit.

Paths leave from town up towards the **Sambuca Pass** (CAI#505), up **Monte Gamberaldi** and over into Emilia-Romagna (CAI#519) and in a loop through **Badia di Susinana** (CAI#687). You can also pick up the SOFT main trail or follow CAI#519 along to the next destination, Marradi (four hours).

Eco-Friendly Breaks: Palazzuolo sul Senio's Green Energy Camp (Loc. Riaccio, ☎ 0558-046430) offers a range of environmentally responsible adventures in the wild hills of the Tuscan-Emilian Apennines. Adventures are suitable for both kids and adults and should be booked in advance.

Marradi: A Conti Guidi dominion of great wealth before being swallowed up by the Florentine Republic, the "chestnut town" of Marradi retains a remarkable historic center. Centered on Piazza delle Scalelle, its streets of *palazzi* provide a striking testimony of the noble families (such as the Fabbroni, Torrigiani and Cattani families) that once inhabited the town. Its other main attraction is the former house of poet Dino Campana (1885-1932), who has also inspired a range of **walks** in the surroundings. Pick up the tourist office's half-guide, half-literary tribute, *On Foot with Dino Campana*, to enjoy the routes so cherished by the poet, including the pilgrimage (here cut into three stages) he made at the age of 25 to La Verna (*Pellegrinaggio alla Verna*). Other **trails** take you up to the 11th-century hermitage of Gamogna (793 m/2,617 feet) through the Passo dell'Eremo, up Monte dell'Oro (#529) and onto the local stretch of GEA (Grande Escursione Appennina). From the latter, you can also access the mountain huts **Campigno** (Campigno, ☎ 0558-042273) and **Valnera** (Valnera, ☎ 0558-044277). Your best contact for **horseback riding** in the area is **La Casetta** (Via Borgo Casetta 11, ☎ 0558-045094, fax 0558-042175, diego.moffa@tin.it).

Outside of Florence

CHESTNUT TROVE

If you're in the area in October, you're just in time for the **Sagra delle Castagne**, the Chestnut Fair (www.sagradellecastagne.it, ☎ 0558-045005), with festivals organized all through the Mugello in celebration of this "albero del pane" (bread tree) that was at one time the stable diet of the mountain people. You can taste it at its best in the local *castagnaccio*, an oven-baked flat cake made from chestnut flour with raisins and walnuts.

■ Where to Eat

 Vaglia: You'll get typical Renaissance fare at L'Uovo di Colombo (Via Bolognese 39, ☎/fax 055-407539, closed Mon, $$) with long-standing dishes such as *maiale all'Artusi, bocconcini del pastore* (veal in a cognac sauce) and *zuppa alla Sorrentina* (a seafood and bean soup) dominating the menu.

Barberino di Mugello: For a light snack head to **Forno Fratelli Vivoli** (Via L. da Vinci, ☎ 0558-41152, $); they've been making the best local breads (the famous *schiacciata*),

DINING PRICE CHART	
Price per person for an entrée, including house wine & cover.	
$	Under €20
$$	€21-€40
$$$	€41-€60
$$$$	Over €60

biscuits and pastries in town for years. You'll get a hearty meal at nearby **Cosimo de' Medici** (Viale del Lago 19, ☎ 0558-420528, fax 0558-420370, closed Mon, $$), with Tuscan favorites *ribollita, papardelle al sugo di lepre* and *tortelli di patate alla mugellana* – just some of the traditional dishes on offer. Things get a little bit more inventive at **Girodibacco Osteria** (Via Nazionale 8/9, Loc. Cafaggiolo, ☎ 0558-418173, fax 0558-486865, $$), occupying the hotspot in front of the Medici Castello di Cafaggiolo, with *cenci alla perbacco* (sweet fritters) and *nastrini al tartufo* (pasta in truffle sauce) accompanying the usual range of soups and grilled meats.

LOCAL FLAVORS

■ *Primi*

Tortelli di patate mugellani: Pasta stuffed with potato

Tagliatelle sui funghi/sul cinghiale/sulla lepre: Flat and wide pasta served with a mushroom, wild boar or hare sauce

Tortellini fritti: Pasta stuffed and then fried

Farinata: Polenta (cornmeal) served with kale and *fagioli* (beans)

Ribollita con cavolo nero: A local take on this typical Tuscan bean soup, this time using black cabbage

Selvaggina: Porcini mushroom soup

Polenta al cinghiale: Wild boar with cornmeal

■ *Secondi*

Bistecca: Charcoal-grilled T-bone steak from the Mugello-bred cattle, "Le Muggellane"

Coniglio ripieno: Stuffed rabbit

Rosticciana: Roasted pork ribs

■ *Contorni*

Fagioli all'olio: Beans with an extra virgin olive oil dressing

■ *Dolci*

Schiacciata con l'uva: Flat cake made with grapes

Torta di marroni: Chestnut cake

Castagnaccio: Chestnut sponge made with raisins, walnuts and pine seeds

■ **Plus**: Pecorino, Chianti Rufina DOC and Pomino DOC wines from the Sieve Valley

San Piero a Sieve: Making the most of the local connection, **Taverna de' Medici** (Piazza Cambray Digny 5a, ☎ 0558-498404, closed Tues, $$), offers a hearty range of goulash and bourguignon, as well as some lovely chocolate deserts.

Borgo San Lorenzo: You'll get some delicious homemade pastas in the informal atmosphere of **Pub degli Artisti** (Piazza Romagnoli 1, ☎ 0558-457707, fax 0558-49032, closed Wed, $$). **Ristorante Feriolo** offers a more up-market blend of local game (Via Faentina 32, Loc. Polcanto, ☎ 0558-409928, $$) in its glorious 15th-century home. Be sure to try the p*appardelle al capriolo* (pasta with a venison sauce).

Vicchio: There's locally caught game on the menu at **La Casa di Caccia** (Loc. Molezzano, ☎ 0558-407629, fax 0558-407007, www.ristorantelacasadicaccia.com, May-Sept, $$), near Vicchio's Riserva Faunistica di Farneto (where you can still hunt). A former meeting place for hunters, it still serves traditional game-based dishes such as *tagliatelle al cinghiale, carni alla brace* (charcoal-broiled meats) and steaks of wild boar and venison.

Firenzuola: Trekkers should stop off at **Al Nuovo Postiglione** (Strada Provinciale per Bruscoli 168b, Passo della Futa, ☎ 0558-15222, $), a border post between Tuscany and Emilia Romagna, which enhances its magnificent view over the Mugello valley with a delicious range of homemade pastas (*tagliatelle ai funghi porcini, tortelli mugellani*). If you can't climb that high on an empty stomach, **I Cacciatori** (Piazza Agnolo 5, ☎ 0558-109009, closed Wed, $), in the center of town (rooms for rent, $), comes a close second with *ravioli mugellani* (ravioli stuffed with potatoes, pork and porcini mushrooms), grilled meats and some lovely homemade deserts.

Palazzuolo sul Senio: Things have gone a little back in time at **Locanda Senio** (Via Borgo dell'Ore 1, ☎ 0558-046019, fax 0558-046485, www.newnet.it/senio, $$), part of small six-room hotel ($) in Palazzuolo sul Senio, with a cuisine inspired by medieval recipes such as *zuppa con le erbe* (grass soup) and a menu *degustazione* (set tasting menu) if all sounds a bit too scary.

■ Where to Stay

Hotels

Vaglia: Closest of the Mugello towns to Florence, Vaglia offer a rural break within six miles of the city; try **Albergo Le Terazze** ☆ (Via Montorsoli 263-7, ☎ 055-401434, $$), a family-run hotel with a basic but tasty restaurant.

Barberino di Mugello: For stays in and around Barberino di Mugello, opt for the recently restored **Albergo Il Cavallo** ☆☆ (Viale della Repubblica 7, ☎ 05-8418144, fax 0558-418293, hotel.ilcavallo@tin.it, $$) occupying a former post-house for pilgrims crossing the Apennines. A small hotel with a well-reputed restaurant

HOTEL PRICE CHART	
Rates are per room with private bath, based on double occupancy, including breakfast.	
$	Under €40
$$	€41-€85
$$$	€86-€140
$$$$	€141-€210
$$$$$	Over €210

serving Mugellan specialties ($), the 10-room **Albergo Gualtieri** ☆☆ (Via S. Lucia 7, Fraz. S.Lucia, ☎ 0558-42163, fax 0558-423051, $$) sits in prime adventure territory north of the town on the approach to the Passo della Futa (and SOFT trails #11 and #12).

San Piero a Sieve: In the old center of San Piero a Sieve, the nearly 100-year-old **Albergo La Felicina** ☆☆ (Piazza Colonna 14, ☎ 0558-498181, fax 0558-498157, cristina19651@supereva.it, $$) also has a great in-house restaurant serving Tuscan soups and grilled meats (closed Fri, $).

Scarperia: In nearby Scarperia, your best choice is the lovely tree-shaded **B&B Villa Manini** (Via Ponzalla 57, ☎/fax 0558-492010, villamanini@hotmail.com, $$), a 19th-century manor house with only four rooms.

Borgo San Lorenzo: North of Borgo San Lorenzo, on the SS302 to Palazzuolo sul Senio (perfect for SOFT#17), you get some great views from the balconied rooms of **Parco dei Fiori** ☆☆☆ (Via Faentina 72, Ronta ☎ 0558-495713, fax 0558-403348, www.newnet.it/parcodeifiori, $$$). It overlooks a large park on the slopes of the Apennines.

Alto Mugello: The luxury choice is the lovely **Locanda Senio** ☆☆☆ (Via Borgo dell'Ore 1, ☎ 0558-046019, fax 0558-043949, www.locandasenio.it, $$$$) offering sauna and health club center, outdoor pool and cooking courses as well as tasty food in the restaurant.

Agriturismi

There are plenty of *agriturismi*, or farm-stay cottages, in the region.

Barberino di Mugello: Le Novelle ☆☆☆☆ (Via Pimonte 33, Loc. Le Novelle, ☎ 0558-48255, fax 0558-952935, www.lenovelle.it, $$$) is an old atmospheric stone farmhouse with open beamed ceilings and *pietra serena* fireplaces, swimming pool and access to trekking and mountain biking trails near Barberino di Mugello. It and nearby **Il Palazzacio** ☆☆☆ (Via Rezzano 9, Loc. Galliano, ☎/fax 0558-428110, www.villailpalazzacio.com, $$$$) and **Poggio di Sotto** (Via Galliano 17, Loc. Galliano, ☎ 0558-428447 fax 0558-428449, www.wel.it/poggiodisotto, $$) offer good adventure locations.

San Piero a Sieve: The first choice around San Piero a Sieve has to be the panoramic 15th-century farmhouses of **Castello Il Trebbio** ☆☆☆ (Via Trebbio 4, ☎ 0558-48088, fax 0558-498470, $$, Mar-Sept), in a small hamlet next to the castle, rather than in the castle itself.

Borgo San Lorenzo: Il Poggio Alle Ville ☆☆☆☆ (Loc. Le Ville, Mucciano ☎ 0558-408752, fax 055-599828, www.poggioalleville.it, $$) rents out seven independent farmhouses overlooking the Mugello Valley, with lovely terracotta floors as well as that all important outdoor pool.

Horseback riders and hikers should book into **Badia di Moscheta** (Loc. Moscheta, ☎/fax 0558-144015, www.badiadimoscheta.com, *agriturismo* $$, hostel $), a calm retreat between **Scarperia** and **Firenzuola** (near SOFT#15), where most of the region's trails depart.

Equally attractive is rustic **Rovignale** ☆☆☆ (Via Castro-Rovignale 492, Loc. Castro San Martino, ☎ 0558-149297, $), at the foot of the Passo di Futa. It has hunting opportunities (in season), horse-lodging facilities and a summer restaurant specializing in spit-roast meats.

Marradi: Al Volo del Nibbio ☆☆☆ near Marradi (Loc. Vonibbio, Popolano, ☎/fax 0558-044225, www.agrivonibbio.it, $$$) has extensive grounds with access to trekking, horseback riding and mountain biking trails, while the even more isolated **Monte di Sotto** ☆☆☆ (Viale A. Baccarini 22, ☎/fax 0558-045061, $$$), on the border at 345 m/1,000 feet, offers the same facilities but without a pool.

Affitacamere

Affitacamere are rooms for rent in private homes. Your best bets are **Affitacamere Linda** in **Barberino di Mugello** (Via S. Lucia 14, ☎/fax 055-423036, bracchilinda@libero.it, $), and **Casa Palmira** (Via Mulinaccio 4, Loc. Feriolo, ☎/fax 0558-409749, www.casapalmira.it, $) or **La Torretta** (Loc. Faltona 59, ☎ 0558-459862, fax 0558-403185, www.faltona.it) both near **Borgo San Lorenzo**.

"Pilgrims" can also rent rooms in the Convento di Montesenario near **Vaglia** (Bivigliano, ☎ 055-406441, fax 055-406554).

In the region of **Firenzuola,** opt for **Roberto Borgognini** (Fraz. Covigliano 55, ☎ 0558-12027, $) or **Crocetti** (Via Imolese 8, Fraz. Moraduccio, ☎ 0558-16010, $).

Camping

Unsurprisingly, the Mugello is a great area for campers with some prime locations up for grabs. Top picks in **Vaglia** include **Poggio degli Uccellini** ☆☆ (Via di Camping 38, Bivigliano, ☎/fax 055-406725, www.ccft.it, 76 pitches, $), in a lovely old chestnut wood at the foot of Convento di Montesenario, and an even more plush **Il Sergente** ☆☆☆ (Via S. Lucia 24, Monte di Fò, ☎ 0558-423018, fax 0558-423907 www.campingilsergente.it, $) over at **Barberino di Mugello**.

The campgrounds are also three-star at **San Piero a Sieve**, including **Mugello Verde** ☆☆☆ (Via Massorondinaio 39, ☎ 0558-48511, fax 0558-486910, www.florencecamping.com, 100 pitches, $) and **Vicchio** (Residence Park Val di Sieve ☆☆☆, Via Rossoio, Caldeta, ☎ 0558-44256, fax 0558-385749) with the town's second campground **Vecchio Ponte** ☆☆ (Via Costoli 16, ☎/fax 0558-448306, www.campingvecchioponte.it) well-placed next to the tourist sport center, Centro Sportivo Le Sorgenti.

Firenzuola has a nicely situated campground on the side of the Passo della Futa – **Lo Stale** ☆☆ (Via Provinciale per Bruscoli 169, Bruscoli ☎ 0558-15297, $). There's also a good campground near **Palazzuolo sul Senio – Visano** ☆☆ (Via della Faggiola 19, Visano, ☎/fax 0558-046106, $) if you're planning on hanging around Mugello Alto for a night or two.

Empolese Val d'Elsa

Southwest of Florence, local boy, Leonardo da Vinci, inspired the Valdarno's adopted tourist name; "Terre del Rinascimento" (Land of the Renaissance). It doesn't quite fit, the kind of fervent creativity the title suggests being long gone, but the charming hilltop towns and vineyard-covered hills that greet you more than make up for that. South of Empoli, the Elsa tributary flows south past a few notable hilltop towns en route to its more famous guardian at San Gimignano.

For information on the entire Empolese Val d'Elsa area, contact **Circondario Empolese Val d'Elsa** (Piazza della Vittoria 54, Empoli, ☎ 0571-980311, fax 0571-9803333, www.empolese-valdelsa.it). The Florence tourist offices can also provide plenty of information and maps.

■ Le Terre del Rinascimento

As for much of rural Tuscany, a **car** really is your best means of approach. Empoli and area is well served by the **A1** and the **SS67** (which takes you first through Montelupo Fiorentino and links with roads to Capraia e Limite). Once in Empoli, well-signposted and panoramic routes take you up to Vinci and Cerreto Guidi or west to Fucecchio. **Trains** (☎ 848-888088, www.trenitalia.it) run regularly from Florence to Empoli. From there, COPIT **buses** (☎ 800-277825) run hourly to Vinci (#8/49) and Cerruto Guidi (#52). Buy your tickets from the station or Bar Azzuro on Piazza della Vittoria, next to the bus stop. The slower REG or regional train service stops at Montelupo/Capraia en route. **Taxis** can be found outside Empoli FS or call ☎ 0571-73100.

For the most panoramic approach to Vinci from Empoli, ignore the road that passes through the Zona Industriale di Mercatale and turn off earlier at Sovigliana (direction Vitolini and Carmignano).

The office at Vinci (APT Terre del Rinascimento, Via della Torre 11, ☎ 0571-568012, fax 0571-567930, terredelrinascimento@comune.vinci.fi.it) is the main tourist board for the whole of the Terre del Rinascimento region, with smaller offices at Empoli (Via Guiseppe del Papa 98 ☎ 0571-76115) and Montelupo Fiorentino (Via Baccio Sinibaldi 74, ☎ 0571-518993, fax 0571-911421). Fucecchio is served by its own branch (Corso Matteotti 61, ☎ 0571-242717, fax 0571-21026, profucecchio@leonet.it).

Montelupo Fiorentino: A short hop along the Arno from Florence, the ancient borough of Montelupo Fiorentino is best known for its ceramic production. It's an occupation well documented in the **Museo Archeologico e della Ceramica** (Archeology and Ceramic Museum, ☎ 0571-51352, www.museomontelupo.it, Tues-Sun, 9 am-noon, 2:30-7 pm, closed Mon, €1.50), with its charming display of *Arlecchini* (harlequins), the decorative trend created in the 15th century that went on to epitomize the Montelupo style. Few visit the museum without wanting to take some of the local handiwork home. For the best and most interesting choices, try to time your visit with the **Festa Internazionale della Ceramica** (third week of June) or the town market (third Sun of the month). But, even if you miss both, you can see a great range for sale (produced according to stringent local tradition) at **Bartoloni** (Corso Garibaldi 34, ☎ 0571-51242).

Ceramics aside, there's not much else to entice you here save the Botticelli polyptych in the **Pieve di San Giovanni** (Sat-Sun, 4:30-7 pm) and the 13th-century fresco remains in the cypress-tree-encircled **Prioria di San Lorenzo** (Sat-Sun, 4:30-7 pm). Archeologists may find some interest in the Roman villa remains at Pulica (80-60 BC). Guided visits are by appointment through the Museo Archeologico e della Ceramica. The **Villa Medicea l'Ambrogiana** is just a short **cycle** on the other side of the Pisa River. While an interesting example of its type, built by Buontalenti and Ammannati at the request of Grand-Duke Ferdinando I toward the end of the 16th century, it can be seen only from the outside.

THE TERRE DEL RINASCIMENTO MUSEUM PASS

If you're planning on touring the area's major museums – the Museo Archeologico e della Ceramica in Montelupo Fiorentino, the Museo della Collegiata in Empoli and the Museo Leonardiano in Vinci – you should opt for the €6 cumulative ticket (available from any of the museum offices).

Capraia e Limite: Overlooking the right bank of the Arno, the former Pistoian strongholds of Capraia and Limite reached their peak in the early Middle Ages when they controlled the river traffic along this stretch. Since then, life has quietened down, with the towns only seeming to snap back to life during Limite's twice-yearly regattas. If you're in the area, it is worth seeing the Etruscan remains at **Montereggi** or heading up the slopes of Monte Albano to the mid-19th-century "romantic park" of **Villa Bibbiani** (summer only). Capraia's other main attraction is **La Fornace Pasquinucci**, an old terracotta kiln recently transformed into a showroom, which testifies to a ceramic production that at one time rivaled that of Montelupo Fiorentino.

Rowing Traditions

As befits the site of Italy's first boating club, Limite holds not one but two yearly regattas (a male and female race) in celebration of its rich river tradition. Both use the town's traditional *gozzi* (boats with eight oarsmen and one coxswain) decorated in the colors of the town's four districts, with the women racing first (Palio di San Lorenzo, third Sun of July), followed two months later by the men (Palio con la Montata, third Sun of September). The latter has an added challenge: a climber representing each team must race to the top of a rope suspended over the Arno after the oarsmen have done their job.

A range of pleasant **trails** depart from both Montelupo Fiorentino and Limite through woods and olive trees to some charming country churches, such as the 12th-century **Chiesa di San Jacopo a Pulignano** (Sat-Sun, 4:30-7 pm, #5), the **Romanesque Chiesa di San Pietro** (Sat, 10 am-7 pm, Sun, 2-7 pm) and the 12th-century **Abbazia di San Martino in Campo** (Sat-Sun, 4:30-7 pm), with its beautiful frescoes and stone altar and font. Capraia is also well placed on the **Sentiero Consorzio Montalbano** (Montalbano footpath), with trails over to Artimino and along the mountain ridge as far as Monsummano Alto and Serravalle Pistoiese.

Empoli: Traditionally one of the town's most important industries, glassmaking in its white, colored, crystal and traditional green forms is still going strong in Empoli. Pop into the showrooms at **Centro Vetro** (☎ 0571-72000, by appointment only) or **Nouva CEV Cristalleria** (Via Val d'Elsa 47/9, Ponte a Elsa, ☎ 0571-931593/4, fax 0571-931595, factory visits Mon-Fri, 9 am-noon) to find out (or buy) more.

The main sights sit around the quadrangular Piazza Farinata degli Uberti. Its all pretty laid-back, with the square's caffès occupying the porches of some fine palazzos (Palazzo Ghibelline and Palazzo Pretorio the most interesting). They have great views onto the white and green marble slabs of the town's main attraction, the **Collegiata di Sant'Andrea** (the sole example of the Florentine Romanesque style outside Florence). To its right, the **Museo della Collegiata** (☎ 0571-76284, Tues-Sun, 9 am-noon, 4-7 pm, €2, conc. €1), one of the oldest ecclesiastical collections in Tuscany, houses some of the best of its masterpieces. A baptismal font by Bernardo Rossellino, a frescoed *Pietà* by Masolino, sculptures by Mino da Fiesole and Tino di Camaino and, in the pinacoteca upstairs, two triptychs by Lorenzo Monaco and a small *Maestà* by Fillipo Lippi – the main reasons to pop in. There are also a couple of panels by local artist Jacopo Carrucci (known

Outside of Florence

as Il Pontormo, 1494-1556), but the best of him can really be seen in the **Chiesa di San Michele** in his birthplace **Pontorme** (a well-signposted bike ride away). There you can see a stunning *Life of St John the Evangelist* and *Archangel Michael* (around 1518). His house-museum, Casa Natale del Pontormo, is currently under restoration.

Back in Empoli, more Masolino frescoes (and preparatory *sinopie*) are conserved in the **Convento e Chiesa di Santo Stefano degli Agostiniani**, an Augustine church erected in 1367, while a marble *Annunciation* by Rossellino (around 1447) constitutes the main reason to visit the 14th-century **Chiesa di Santo Stefano** (Sat-Sun, 4:30-7 pm).

Angel from Annunciation (Pontormo, 1527, Santa Felicita, Florence)

Vinci: Amid the vineyards and olive groves of Monte Albano, the area's main attraction is, of course, Vinci and its native son, Leonardo. His *casa natale* (birthplace) is actually a short walk out of town in the hamlet of **Anchiano** (☎ 0571-56055, Mar-Oct, daily, 9:30 am-7 pm, Nov-Feb, daily, 9:30 am-6:30 pm), but you will get more of an insight into his life by visiting the recently re-launched **Museo Ideale Leonardo da Vinci**, which takes you on a tour of his sketches and drawings, such as the one of *Leda* above, 3D models of his designs, the tools he used and a multimedia section that traces the creation of his some of his funkiest machines for moving through air, water and earth. (☎/fax 0571-56296, www.museoleonardo.it, daily, 10 am-1 pm, 2-7 pm, €3.50, conc. €2, tickets include audio guide.)

LOCAL WINES GIVE YOU WINGS

An interesting take on local harvest festivals occurs every year on the last Wed in July when Vinci recreates the miraculous escape of Cecco di Santi, a captain of the Vinci army, who, sentenced to be thrown from the tower for his treasonous love of a woman from an enemy town, flew off to safety after a glass of the local wine. You can sample a glass of the local produce by popping into **Cantine Leonardo** (Via P. di Mercatale 291, ☎ 0571-902444, fax 0571-509960, visits by appointment only).

The town is also a great location for **trails** into the 45,000 acres of **Monte Albano**, with treks taking you to Leonardo da Vinci's birth home in Archiano (#14, one-hour round-trip), up to Faltognano with its panoramic views over Vinci (and a sacred 300-year-old holm oak) and into the remains of the **Barco Reale**

Mediceo, a vast area transformed by the Medici into a hunting reserve. **Cyclists** arriving from Empoli on the strada bianca #12, should also stop off at the **Pieve di San Giovanni Battista** in Sant'Ansano (Sat, 10 am-7 pm, Sun, 2-7 pm), an ancient parish church with a Giotto altarpiece and an *Apparition of the Angel to Pope Alexander I* (1625) attributed to Manetti.

> **Sun Stroll:** The main Vinci tourist office offers guided **tours** and **bike rides** around Le Terre del Rinascimento one or two Sundays a month. Common treks include itineraries departing from Capraia and Limite up the slopes of Montalbano and walks into the hills of Vinci in the footsteps of Leonardo (finishing with a guided tour of the museum). Participation is free, but must be booked in advance.

Cerreto Guidi: A panoramic **bike ride** takes you from Vinci through rolling hills to Cerreto Guidi, a former fief of the aristocratic Guidi. Their original fortress was replaced in 1564 by the austere **Villa Medicea** (daily, 9 am-7 pm), a creation best known for the pair of bulky staircases in unplastered brick and stone (known as the "ponti Medicei," the Medici bridges), which were later added by Buontalenti. The town **Pieve di San Leonardo** is also worth a look. Here you'll find a beautiful glazed terracotta font attributed to Giovanni della Robbia (1511) and a wooden crucifix by Giambologna. The town is also the location of the area's main **horseback-riding** center, **Podere San Pietro** (Via di Strognano 6a, ☎ 0571-959021, fax 0571-559444 www.spietro.com).

Fucecchio: Although out of the "Terre del Rinascimento" *per se,* Fucecchio and its marsh (the **Padule di Fucecchio**, ☎ 057-384540) can be found only a short drive west. The marsh (which stretches as far north as Monsummano Terme) makes an interesting diversion for naturalists and **bird-watchers** – 150 species have been noted here, including nesting herons and migratory birds such as the stilt-plover, crane and black stork (right). There are also nine **walking** itineraries to enjoy, many taking you past some of the marsh's collection of endangered plant species, such as beautiful yellow-flowered water lilies otherwise rare in Italy. If you're interested, sign yourself up for one of the three guided itineraries led by the **Centro di Ricerca, Documentazione e Promozione** (Via Castelmarini 125a, Larciano Pistoia, ☎/fax 0573-84540, www.zoneumidetoscane.it), signposted off the SS436 north of Fucecchio. They are also the people to contact if you are interested in **canoeing** along one of the reserve's canals.

> **Flying Visits:** The Padule's research center leads guided **bird-watching** visits to the reserve in English every July (Sat, 9 am-noon) on a tour that takes in the impressive heronry and some of the 150 bird species sighted here. There are also occasional evening visits (7:30-10:30 pm), which allow you to watch the sunset with the sounds and calls of the reserve's birds and animals. Book in advance through the center (€5 per person).

Where to Eat

Many Florentines head out of the city to the restaurants in and around **Montelupo Fiorentino**. Those well worth a stop include the rustic **La Fornace di Sammontana** (Via del Colle 5, Fraz. Sammontana,

☎ 0571-994071, $$), best visited during the autumn hunting season when the menu features a delicious range of locally caught hare, duck and rabbit. Also try the microbiotic and vegetarian menu of **San Vito in Fior di Selva** (Via San Vito 32, ☎ 0571-51411, www.san-vito.com, $$), with its lovely outdoor veranda.

A local I met on the train to **Empoli** recommended the *casalinga* (housewife) cuisine of **Il Cantuccio** (Via Piave 2, ☎ 0571-944533, closed Mon, $$), slightly out of town in the direction of the hospital, while the more central **Café de l'Academia** (Via del Gelsomino 28, ☎ 0571-72185, closed Sun, $$) – between Piazza F. degli Uberti and Piazza dell Vittoria – is the best bet if you're not a driver. Both serve fresh pastas and grilled meats.

If you plan to dine in **Vinci**, **La Torretta** (Via della Torre 19, ☎ 0571-56100, closed Mon, $) in the historical center offers a superb *bistecca*. Both the **Caffè del Castello** (Via della Torre 10, ☎ 0571-568149, $) and **Enoteca** (Piazza L. da Vinci, ☎ 0571-568041, $) are delightful spots for a light lunch or aperitif.

Where to Stay

Your best hotel choices can be found at **Montelupo Fiorentino** (**Baccio da Montelupo** ☆☆☆, Via Don Minzoni 3, ☎ 0571-51215, $$$) and just outside **Vinci** (**Gina** ☆☆☆, Via Lamporecchiana 27-9, ☎ 0571-56266, fax 0571-567913, www.hotelgina.it, $$$).

The bulk of accommodation consists of *agriturismi* or farmhouses. Try **Petrognano** ☆☆☆☆☆ (Via Bottinaccio 116, ☎ 0571-913795, fax 0571-913796, www.petrognano.it, $$$$) for the added incentive of ceramic courses near **Montelupo Fiorentino**. Or there's the lovely farmhouse accommodation on the DOCG wine and olive oil-producing 500-acre **Tenuta Cantagello** (Via Valicarda 35, ☎ 0571-91078, fax 0571-583399, www.enricopierazzuoli.com, $$$) near **Capraia e Limite**. Your best bet at **Vinci** is **Il Vincio** ☆☆☆☆ (Via San Pantaleo 24, Loc. San Pantaleo, ☎/fax 0571-56009, www.ilvincio.it, $$). **La Gioconda** ☆☆☆ (Loc. S. Lucia ☎ 0571-909002, fax 0571-909043, $$$) has the best view in Anchiano, situated as it is above Leonardo's birthplace.

The **camping** choices aren't quite as extensive. **Village San Giusto**, in a pine and oak wood near **Capraia e Limite** (Via Castra 71, ☎ 055-8712304, fax 055-8711856 www.campingsangiusto.it, Mar-Oct, $) and **Camping Barco Reale** (Via Nardini 11, St Baronto ☎/fax 057-388332, $) are your only real options.

■ Val d'Elsa

From Empoli, the **S429** follows the Elsa River south to Certaldo, with the **SS2** offering an alternative route to Montespertoli and Certaldo through the Chianti hills south of Florence. **Trains** (☎ 848-888088, www.trenitalia.it) on the Empoli-Siena line stop at Castelfiorentino and Certaldo. Sita **buses** (☎ 800-373760, www.sita-on-line.it) link Empoli with Castelfiorentino, Gambassi Terme, Certaldo and Montespertoli. From Certaldo train station, two stone-flagged paths (Costa Alberti and Costa Vecchia) make the steep ascent to Certaldo Alto (the upper town).

The main tourist offices in the area is at **Castelfiorentino** (in the station, ☎/fax 0571-629049, Apr-Oct), **Certaldo** (Via Cavour 32, ☎/fax 0571-664953, Apr-Dec), **Gambassi Terme** (Piazza Roma 8, ☎ 0571-639192, fax 0571-638925, Apr-Oct), **Montaione** (Museo Civico, ☎ 0571-699255, fax 0571-699256) and

Montespertoli (Via Sonnino 21, ☎/fax 0571-609412), with the larger Florence offices serving the region out of season.

Sightseeing & Adventures in the Val d'Elsa

Castelfiorentino: Dominated by the 13th-century **Pieve di Sant'Ippolito e Biagio** (a steep street away from the main Piazza del Popolo), tourist traffic in the *alto* (the upper historical center) of Castelfiorentino tends first to make a beeline for the **Centro Comunale d'Arte** (Tues, Thurs, Sat, 4-7 pm, Sun 10 am-noon, 4-7 pm), with its two important (but flood-damaged) fresco cycles illustrating the *Life of the Virgin* by Benozzo Gozzoli (1484). Down in the newer town, the large Baroque **Santuario di Santa Verdiana** (Sat-Sun, 4:30-7 pm), itself decorated by interesting frescoes from the life of the saint, introduces the second of the town's museums, the **Museo di Arte Sacra** (Sat, 4-7 pm, Sun and public holidays, 10 am-noon, 4-7 pm). It contains polyptychs from the 13th to 16th centuries taken from nearby churches, including a *Madonna and Child* attributed to Cimabue and works by Taddeo di Bottolo, Taddeo Gaddi and Francesco Granacci. The nearby brick **Chiesa di San Francesco** has managed somehow to keep hold of some of its art; check out the frescoes of the *Life of Saint Francis* in the nave.

Montaione: Before checking out the sights, take in the stunning view over the Elsa Valley from the small square off Montaione's Via Cavour (known by locals as "Il Monumento" due to its war memorial). The town itself has been heavily reconstructed after damage in WWII; the 14th-century **Palazzo Pretorio** (home to the Museo Civico) and the 17th-century **Chiesa di San Regolo** (with an impressive 18th-century bell tower) are some of the few buildings to have come through unscathed.

Hiking and mountain biking trails abound in the Montaione area's thick forests. The most popular takes you up to "Tuscany's Jerusalem" at **Sacro Monte di San Vivaldo** (☎ 0571-680114, Sat-Sun, 10 am-7 pm) where a complex of religious buildings (on the site where San Vivaldo was found dead in the trunk of a chestnut tree) reproduces in miniature the layout of Palestine's sacred sites. You'll need to book in advance for a tour of the 16th-century chapels (only 17 remaining of the original 33) but it's well worth it for the decorative terracotta statues enacting the *Life and Passion of Christ*.

An agreeable **bike trip** will take you on from here to the **Santuario della Pietrina**, whose location (on top of a sheer cliff top) offers a breathtaking panorama of the Era Valley with Volterra visible in the distance. Public transport is a little haphazard. Renieri buses from Montaione will take you as far as San Vivaldo if you don't want to walk (between two and four daily trips, no service on Sun or holidays), but from there you're on your own.

Gambassi Terme: An historical resting point on the medieval road networks of Via Francigena and Via Volterrana, Gambassi Terme remains a well-favored retreat. The light tourist traffic splits between the salty thermal waters of the **Sorgente Salsa** (Via Volterrana 31, ☎ 0571-638401) and its shops selling glass products. If you're interested, a permanent exhibition displays the town's glassmaking past at a set of recently-excavated medieval kilns.

Certaldo: Hilltop Certaldo is a stunning sight from afar; its redbrick tower-houses jutting up within a well-preserved ring of medieval walls. Once inside, the center is marked by the **Palazzo Pretorio** (summer, daily, 10 am-1 pm, 2-7:30 pm, winter, Tues-Sun, 10 am-12:30 pm, 3-7:30 pm). It's easily recognizable by its façade of terracotta coats of arms left by the governors of the town after the replacement of original rulers, the Alberti. The interior, decorated with more coats of arms and frescoes (some attributed to Gozzoli), leads on to the ex-church of **SS. Tommaso e Prospero**, home to a another Gozzoli fresco, the *Tabernacle of Justice*, which is shown detached opposite its *sinopia* or preliminary drawing.

The footsteps of *Decameron* author Boccaccio (1312-1375) can be traced in the home where he spent the last 12 years of his life: **Casa del Boccaccio** (daily, 10:30 am-12:30 pm, 3:30-6:30 pm, free). In the nearby 13th-century **Chiesa di SS. Jacopo e Filippo** (Via Boccaccio, daily, 10 am-7 pm) a cenotaph marks the spot of his destroyed grave. The town also has the best of the local **horseback riding** centers. Try **Centro Ippico P. Luigi Ballerini**, ☎ 0571-668813.

Monterspertoli: Heading back north, the *città del vino* (city of wine) of Monterspertoli is the proud home of two DOCG wines: Chianti Montespertoli and Chianti Colli Fiorentini. Apart from its annual wine exhibition, the main attraction is the **Museo di Arte Sacra** (Pieve di San Pietro in Mercato), which contains a precious *Madonna and Child* by Filippo Lippi. A **bike** ride away in Lucardo, there's also a polyptych by Raffaello Botticini worth visiting in the Chiesa di San Martino e San Giusto.

The Local Trail Networks

The network of trails running through the towns of Certaldo, Castelfiorentino, San Gimignano, Gambassi Terme, Volterra and Montespertoli is outlined in *Dolce Campagna, Antiche Mura* (available in English from Certaldo's tourist office). The paths are suitable for **trekking, horseback riding** and **mountain biking** with a main "TR" (trail ring) and 24 shorter secondary itineraries branching off from it.
Montaione Commune (☎ 0571-699254, fax 0571-699256, comune.montaione@mbr.it) also publishes its own booklet of trails suitable for walking, biking and horseback riding – *Montaione Il Paese del Turismo Verde* (Montaione the Town of Green Tourism) – which includes the loops up to San Vivaldo and Pietrina mentioned earlier.
You can also join locals from **Montespertoli** on their weekend treks and bike rides by contacting **Montagna Nuova** (☎ 0571-671858, www.montagnanuova.it).

Where to Eat

 Along the SS429 between Certaldo and Poggibonsi, the **Osteria di Vico** (Loc. Vico d'Elsa, ☎ 055-8073222, closed Wed, $) is a wonderfully atmospheric faux medieval locale with a Tuscan menu of high seasonal quality.
Carpe Diem (Viale V. da Filicaia 67, ☎ 0571-697888, $$) is a great restaurant and three-star hotel ($$), its menu a delicious mix of in-house pastas and grilled meats, including Chianina steak.
The tasty dishes and extensive wine list of **Lo Staccio** (☎ 0571-608405, $$) definitely make it the pick of the bunch and well worth the drive to Montespertoli.

Where to Stay

 Your best option in Castelfiorentino is **La Pieve** ☆☆☆ (Via V.O. Bacci 2, ☎ 0571-62203, fax 0571-64045, $$), along the road to Montespertoli. **Il Castello** ☆☆☆ (Certaldo Alto, Via della Rena 6 ☎ 0571-668250, $$) also has a great restaurant for local cuisine. In Montaione, there is the pricey **Palazzo Manniaoli** ☆☆☆☆ (Via Marconi 2, ☎ 0571-698300, $$$$). **Antica Posta** ☆☆☆☆ (Piazza Zannoni 1/3, ☎ 055-822313, $$$) is in San Casciano Val di Pesa if you're stopping here for the night before exploring Chianti.

As usual, *agriturismi* or farmstay options abound, with the following among the best.

Cabbiavoli ☆ (Castelfiorentino, Via del Vallone 42/49, ☎ 055-59122, fax 055-599405, www.cabbiavoli.it, $$$$) has a pool. **Casa Mori** ☆☆☆☆ (Certaldo, Via Bagnano 32, Fraz. Sciano, ☎ 0571-665500, casamori@inwind.it, $$$) is a good site for trekking enthusiasts; and **Castello di Tavolese** ☆☆☆☆ (Via Tavolese 71, ☎ 0571-660232, fax 0571-660213, www.tavolese.it, $$$$$) are good, if pricey, choices (both have pools).

Horseback riders should opt for **Pistolese Ranch** ☆☆☆ (Montaione, Via Saniminiatese-Mura 117, ☎/fax 0571-69196, http://pistoleseranch.it, $$).

Camping is pretty scarce, with the only decent choice the **Toscana Colliverdi** (Via Marcialla 108a, Loc. Marcialla, ☎ 0571-669334, $) a short distance from **Certaldo** in the direction of the Chianti hills. **Hostellers** have a much better time of it with options in **Castelfiorentino** (**Ostello Castelfiorentino**, Viale Roosevelt 26, ☎/fax 0571-64002, $), **Montaione** (**Peter Pan**, Via Marconi 25/27, ☎ 0571-628251, fax 0571-629176, $) and between **Barberino Val d'Elsa** and Tavernelle Val di Pesa (**Ostello del Chianti**, Viale 1 Maggio 98, ☎ 055-8077009, $).

Prato

Prato has been one of Italy's biggest textile centers since the Middle Ages and it's an industry that still flourishes in the town suburbs. Inside the hexagonal circuit of gray stone walls that delineate its small historical center, it's a different story; the city castle, museums and churches – not to mention the Filippo Lippi frescoed walls of the cathedral – all show there's more to the town than the industrial hub most expect. In its surroundings, you'll also find the thickly wooded Bisenzio Valley to its northeast and the fertile hills of wine-producing Carmignano to the south.

Prato is relatively easy to reach by public transport. **Trains** (☎ 848-888088, www.trenitalia.it) from Firenze S.M.N. depart every 15-30 minutes between the two cities (Florence to Viareggio line); while **buses** by **CAP** (☎ 055-214637, www.capautolinee.it) and **Lazzi** (☎ 055-351061, www.lazzi.it) run equally frequent bus services that drop you off at Prato's Piazza del Duomo. **Taxis** are available outside Prato station and on Piazza del Duomo (Radiotaxi, ☎ 0574-5656).

If you're arriving by **car**, the city is only 10 or so miles from Florence, with exits off both the A1 and A11. Cars can be rented in Prato from **Avis** (c/o Art Hotel, Viale della Republica 289, ☎ 0574-596619), **Hertz** (Viale Montegrappa 208, ☎ 0574-527774), **Dream Car** (Via Ristori 40, ☎/fax 0574-22610) and **Maggiore** (Via di Ponzano 24, ☎ 0574-536000) for ventures into the surrounding countryside.

Outside of Florence

APT Ufficio Informazioni (Prato tourist office) is on Piazza Santa Maria delle Carcerias as you enter town (☎/fax 0574-24112, www.prato.turismo.toscana.it, Mon-Sat, 9 am-7 pm, Sun, 10 am-1 pm, 2-6:30 pm) and is your best source of information for the city and its province.
[Map 2PC - Prato City Map]

■ Sightseeing ~ The Historical Center

With such a small historical center, it's easy enough to take in Prato during a long morning, leaving plenty of time to explore the surrounding countryside before you head back to Florence. Arriving from the train station, you'll see the walls' entrance announced by a Henry Moore white marble sculpture (*Square Form with Cut*). From there a choice of two cobbled streets (Via G. Mazzini is the more picturesque) take you to Piazza Santa Maria delle Carceri and the start of the town's major sights.

Basilica di Santa Maria delle Carceri (☎ 0574-27933, daily, 7 am-noon, 4-7:30 pm, free): According to local folklore, this basilica takes its interesting name (St Mary of the Dungeons) from a miraculous talking image of a *Madonna and Child* that appeared on the outside walls of the prison that originally stood here. In celebration, Giuliano da Sangallo constructed the current edifice on its ruins in the late 15th century. The inside, which takes the form of a Greek cross, features a small dome with blue and white terracotta medallions (Andrea della Robbia) and bright stained glass windows added by Ghirlandaio.

Castello dell'Imperatore (The Emperor's Castle) (☎ 0574-38207, 9 am-1 pm, 4-7 pm, closed Tues and pm from Oct to Mar, castle entry only €2, combined ticket €5, conc. €3): This imposing albarese-stone castle is empty but for July and August when it becomes an atmospheric open-air cinema during Prato's summer festivities (☎ 0574-37150, 1 July-31 Aug, from 9 pm, €5, conc. €4, Italian showings only). Although heavily reconstructed, it originally sprung up in 1239 when Swabian Emperor Frederick II nominated Prato as the best spot for his imperial base. The result is the only example of Swabian architecture in Northern Italy (watch for the lions sculpted over the entrance). The Florentines later modified it in the mid-14th century when they established a garrison here after buying title to the town from its former Neapolitan rulers. They also built the recently restored **Cassero** (Viale Piave, ☎ 0574-36693, daily, 9 am-1 pm, 4-7 pm, closed Tues), a two-layered keep, which offered them safe passage from the Florentine Gate, at the walls of the city, into the castle.

> **Museum Entry:** You can buy a combined ticket for entry to the Castello dell'Imperatore, the Museo di Pittura Murale and the Museo dell'Opera del Duomo for €5, conc. €3 at any of the three ticket offices.

A narrow passageway facing the entrance to the castle takes you directly to the typical two-tone (white alberese and green marble) façade of the 13th-century **Chiesa di San Francesco** (☎ 0574-31555, daily, 8 am-noon, 4-7 pm, free). Inside, you'll find Rossellino's tomb of Gemignano Inghirami (on the left of the single aisle), Marco Datini's tomb (in the floor near the high altar), and in the cloister (1439-40) the Cappella Migliatori with frescoes by the early 15th-century Florentine painter Niccolò di Pietro Gerini (*Crucifixion* and *Life of St Mathew* on the right and *Stories of St Anthony the Abbot* on the left).

MARCO DATINI

Prato's textile industry flourished in the 14th century thanks to Datini's commercial know-how. A genius at finance, shown in a fresco portrait at left, he invented the letter of credit for bank payments and set the ball rolling for many of the accounting methods still in use today. One of the richest men in Europe, he certainly wasn't a scrooge; he left his entire fortune to the "poor folk of Prato" on his death. You can find out more about his life at his former home, **Palazzo Datini** (Via Mazzei 33, ☎ 0574-21391, Mon-Sat, 9 am-noon, 4-6 pm, free), which is frescoed both inside and out with scenes from his life.

The 13th-century Piazza del Comune, the heart of the old town, is a quick hop up Via Ricosoli. It is home to two impressive medieval palazzi. The **Palazzo Pretorio**, which houses the **Museo Civico** (Civic Museum), is under restoration now and due to re-open in 2005. Its paintings are currently on display in the Museo di Pittura Murale. The city's town hall is also here, the **Palazzo Comunale,** which houses the original Bacchus fountain by Ferdinando Tacca (the fountain in Piazza del Comune is a copy). The Palazzo Comunale is also the temporary home of the **Museo del Tessuto** (Textile Museum, ☎ 0574-611503, www.po-net.prato.it/tessuto, daily, 10:30 am-6:30 pm, closed Tues and at 2:30 pm on Sat, €4, conc. €3), with its display of over 5,000 textile samples and an historical overview dating back to the fifth century.

From here, the half-Romanesque, half-Gothic **Duomo**, shown at left (Cattedrale di San Stefano, ☎ 0574-26234, Mon-Fri, 7 am-12:30 pm, 3:30-7 pm, Sun and holidays, 7 am-noon, 3:30-8 pm, free) is up Via Firenzuola. An unusual pulpit in the right corner of the façade introduces both it and the city's most famous religious festivity. It was decorated by Donatello (original reliefs now shown in the Museo dell'Opera del Duomo) for the periodic displays of the Virgin's Sacred Girdle (see below). If you miss one of these, you can see the relic inside the Chapel of the Sacred Girdle; the history of its arrival in Prato is depicted in the chapel's fresco cycle by Agnolo Gaddi. Other cathedral chapels conserve Paolo Uccello's *Stories of the Virgin and St Stephen* (1433-34, Cappella dell'Assunta), frescoes by local-born Franchi (1872-76, Vinaccesi Chapel) and the famous fresco cycle by Filippo Lippi (1452-66, Cappella Maggiore), which is still hidden by ongoing restoration work (see below).

Outside of Florence

THE VIRGIN'S SACRED GIRDLE

Make it to Prato on September 8th and you're in for a treat. Not only is the sacred girdle exhibited, it's also accompanied by an historical procession with much dressing up and medieval tomfoolery to be enjoyed as the relic makes its way from the Castello dell'Imperatore to the Piazza del Duomo. The girdle itself is said to have been handed to the Apostle Thomas at the Assumption by a priest, one of whose descendants married a local boy, who brought the relic, and centuries of pilgrims, back here in the 12th century. You'll get a good insight into its supposed journey by checking out Gaddi's famous fresco *The Legend of the Holy Girdle* (1392-95) in the Chapel of the Sacred Girdle (immediately left of the Duomo entrance).

Filippo Lippi at the peak of his fame is responsible for the fresco cycle depicting the *Lives of St Stephen and St John the Baptist* (detail at left), now hidden behind scaffolding along the wall of the cathedral's main chapel. Completed over a period of 14 years (1452-66), it seems to be taking just as long to be restored, a wait allayed somewhat by the opportunity to tour the cycle guided by its restorers, Restauro Filippo Lippi. The one-hour tour along the maintenance scaffolding, suspended 32 feet above the choir, offers a not-to-be-missed occasion to see the bright colors of a 15th-century masterpiece up-close. (www.restaurofilippolippi.it; book through the tourist office, min. six, max. 12, €8.)

The neighboring **Museo dell'Opera del Duomo** (Museum of Cathedral Works, ☎ 0574-29339, 9:30 am-12:30, 3-6:30 pm, closed Tues and Sun pm, €5, conc. €3) occupies the Palazzo Vescovile's beautiful Romanesque cloister with its paintings and sculptures (including the seven panels of dancing angels designed by Donatello that originally decorated the pulpit). Maso di Bartolomeno, Paolo Uccello and Filippo and Filippino Lippi provide the museum's other works of note.

Prato's second-most important museum, the **Museo di Pittura Murale** (☎ 0574-440501, daily, 10 am-6 pm, closed Tues and Sun pm, €5, conc. €3) is in a wing of the Gothic **Chiesa di San Domenico** (☎ 0574-30013, Mon-Fri, 6:30-11:30 am, 4-7 pm, Sat and Sun, 7:30 am-noon, 4-7 pm), a short walk up Via L. Muzzi (turn right onto Via Cesare Guasti). It displays a collection of 14th- to 17th-century detached frescoes, *sinopie* and *sgraffiti* (preliminary sketches) by artists as prestigious as Niccolò Gerini, Agnolo Gaddi, Paolo Uccello and Il Volterrano. Thanks to its temporary "Treasures of the City" exhibition, you can also check out a rich collection of works that have been moved here from the Museo Civico – watch for altarpieces by Filippo Lippi and son Filippino, and a polyptych by Bernardo Gaddi. Filippino's precious *Tabernacle del Mercatale* (1489) has been temporarily installed in the **Antiche Stanze di Santa Caterina** (Via Dolce dei Mazzamuti 1, ☎ 0574-33240, visits by appointment).

If all this Renaissance art is a little bit much, finish off your tour of Prato with a visit out of town to the **Centro per l'Arte Contemporanea Luigi Pecci** (Viale della Repubblica 277, ☎ 0574-5317, www.centropecci.it, 10 am-7 pm, closed Tues, €5, conc. €3). Its vast park offers the opportunity for a relaxing stroll among sculptures by major artists of the last 30 years or so.

■ Adventures on Foot

Prato lies in rich **hiking** territory, with the Acquerino-Cantagallo Nature Reserve and Val di Bisenzio to its north and Monte Albano and the wine hills of Carmignano to its south. From the city itself, you can strike out onto the western face of the 12,600-acre protected area of **Monteferrato** (the famous quarry where the green serpentine marble seen in church façades all over Tuscany was sourced) and west onto the slopes of the massive karst formation of **Monti della Calvana**. Both are detailed below.

Some of Monteferrato's best trails leave from Montemurlo. The CAI#70 offers one of the best walks; it takes you along the original stone paving of the Via Francigena to the town Rocca. Galceti (CAI#12), Bagnolo di Sopra (CAI#12b), Figline di Prato (CAI#12b) and various other hamlets along the SS325 (La Foresta and La Briglia being the closest to Prato) are equally well served with trails into the park.

For trips up the Monti della Calvana, pick up paths from Filettole and Carteano in the northwest of the city. The first boasts the panoramic trail known as "Il sentiero della Cementizia," a pleasant hike that leads up past a lonely waterfall to Rio Buti before looping back to Carteano or continuing along the Calvana ridge.

Out of Town with Locals

Prato and surroundings have a number of trekking and environmental organizations that organize cultural and naturalistic excursions into the province's rich countryside. Contact them to find out about any programs coinciding with your visit.

Cooperativa Alta Via Trekking (Via del Serraglio 90, ☎ 0574-606453, fax 0574-467973, altaviatrekking@mbox.comune.prato.it) Sunday excursions only.

CAI Prato (Via dell'Altopascio 8, ☎ 0574-22004, fax 0574-484450, www.comune.prato.it/associa/cai/home.htm) has an Alpine school, Guido Rossa, which organizes mountaineering and rock climbing courses.

Polisportiva Aurora (Via Cantagallo 250, Figline di Prato, ☎ 0574-460405, www.comune.prato.it/associa/aurora) runs Sunday treks into the Val di Luce.

Gruppo Trekking Storia Camminata (c/o Biblioteca Comunale B. della Fonte, Via Toscanini 1, Montemurlo, ☎ 0574-558301). Treks on Fri, Sat and Sun, especially to Apennine destinations.

La Querce (Via Filippo Mazzei, ☎ 0574-595967). Sunday only. History and nature walks from the Molino della Sega in Casciana to the faggione di Lougomano.

If you have some experience, check out the movements of Prato's three **orienteering** organizations: **Team Prato Orient** (Via Rossini 26a, ☎ 0574-603491), **Orienteering Prato** (Via Orvieto 7, ☎ 0574-35282) and **IKP Prato** (Via del Cilanuzzo, ☎ 0574-463420).

Outside of Florence

■ Adventures on Wheels

 Monte Ferrato and the Monti della Calvana also offer rich **cycling** territory. One of the best trails takes you up to **Monte Maggiore** (850 m/2,788 feet), the highest point of the Calvana, by first following the SS325 to Faltugnano, where you can pick up the road through the Roman village of Fabio to Savignano. From here CAI#46b takes you onto the saddle of the Passo della Croce (754 m/2,473 feet) and up around the peak. Head back to Prato by dropping down through the Crocicchio Meadow (#20) to Carteano and then Filettole.

Prato is quiet enough outside the peak tourist season to allow trouble-free exploration by bike. If you want to combine cycling with some interesting historical tidbits, join **Tandem** (c/o Circolo La Macine, Via Firenze 253, Prato, Alessio ☎ 348-5102029, fax 0574-34069, www.comune.prato.it/associa/tandem). They offer bicycle tours every Tues at 9 pm as part of an effort to promote cyclotourism in the city.

Bikes can be rented in advance at **Pedala** (Viale Galilei 4, ☎ 339-3840910, closed Mon) or **Obrii** (Via Arcanfeli 75, ☎ 0574-35609).

■ Adventures on Horseback

 The main riding centers can be found north in the Bisenzio Valley (see page 118) or south in Carmignano (see page 121), but **Riding Center la Querce** (Via la Querce, 41, ☎ 0574-682138, fax 0574-799409), in nearby Montemurlo, organizes weekend excursions for those based in the city.

■ Shopping

You'll find much of Prato's shopping on **Via Garibaldi** (adjacent to Piazza del Duomo) and on the streets fanning out from the **Piazza del Comune**. Plenty of clothes and knickknacks can be found, but it is actually the region's food produce that proves the biggest draw, especially the city's *biscotti* (the hard almond biscuits also known as *cantucci*), *mortadella* (bright-colored spicy sausage) and wines (Bagnolo Pinot Nero, Carmignano Rosso DOCG, Carmignano Vin Santo DOC and Carmignano Vin Ruspo DOC are the best known).

The place in Prato to buy *biscotti* is **Antonio Mattei** (Via Bettino Ricasoli, 20, ☎ 0574-25756). They've been making the biscuits since 1858. It's also worth picking up a pack of the superb *brutti ma bonni* (ugly but good), biscuits so called because they are more pleasing to the palate than to the eye.

Picnic fodder (bread, cheese, wine, mortadella, etc) can be picked up at **Chigurni** (Via S. Trinità 15, ☎ 0574-25665), **Migrana** (Via Firenzuola 63/65, ☎ 0574-31419) or **La Fattoressa** (Via della Sirena 3/5, ☎ 0574-27606), right next to Piazza del Duomo.

Textiles (especially knitwear and cashmere) overflow from outlets such as **Osvaldo Bruni** (Via Galcianese 67/69, ☎ 0574-607591, Mon, 4-8 pm, Tues-Fri, 9 am-1 pm, 3:30-7:30 pm, Sat, 10 am-1 pm) and **Maglifico Denny** (Via Zarini 261, ☎ 0574-592191, Mon-Fri, 9 am-1 pm, 3-7:30 pm).

■ Where to Eat

To sample Pratese fare in and around the center, check out the old-fashioned cuisine of **La Vecchia Cucina di Soldano** (Via Simintendi 1, ☎ 0574-34665, closed Sun, $), a great choice for *sedani ripieni alla pratese, ribollita* (reboiled cabbage and bread soup) and *taglierini* (chops, often served with white beans).

Osteria Cibbe (Piazza Mercatale 49, ☎ 0574-607509, closed Sun, $$) comes heartily recommended in porcini mushroom season when they do a great fresh mushroom soup.

DINING PRICE CHART	
Price per person for an entrée, including house wine & cover.	
$	Under €20
$$	€21-€40
$$$	€41-€60
$$$$	Over €60

LOCAL FLAVORS

Crostini di fegato: Chicken liver crostini.

Pappa al pomodoro: Tomato soup thickened with local dry bread.

Sedani ripieni: Celery stuffed with minced veal or *alla pratese* (with mortadella).

Tagliatelle sui funghi: Pasta with porcini mushrooms from the Val di Bisenzio.

Fagioli all'uccelletto: White beans with sausages.

Cantucci e *vin santo* (dessert biscuits dunked in wine, a practice that many consider sacrilegious to the wine's quality!)

Pesche: Peach-shaped pastry.

Other local restaurant landmarks include **Osvaldi Baroncelli** (Via Fra'Bartolomeo 13, ☎ 0574-23810, closed Sat lunch and Sun, $$) and **La Grotta di Bacco** (Piazza S. Domenico 16, ☎ 0574-440094, closed Wed, $$). **La Cucina di Paola** (Via Banchelli 14, ☎ 0574-24353, closed Mon, $$), with its artfully presented range of grilled meats and fish, is a little more off the beaten track.

Non meat-eaters should opt for the fish at **Il Pirana** (Via Valentini 110, ☎ 0574-25746, closed Sat lunch and Sun, $$) or the vegetarian cuisine of **Salomè** (Via Cairoli 3, ☎ 0574-33521, evenings only, closed Sun, $), the terrace-restaurant of the historical Hotel Flora, which not only does a great *pappa al pomodoro* but also has an extensive range of local cheeses and tasty organic wines.

All in the Name

Every sommelier has a different version of the history behind the name of *vin santo* (or holy wine), but the commonly accepted theory leads back to 15th-century Florence when a group of visiting Greek Orthodox bishops compared the taste of an old bottle of wine made from dried grapes to the wine from Xantho, a similar sounding word to the Italian *santo*.

Outside of Florence

■ Where to Stay

The best budget hotel options within Prato's walls are **La Toscana** ☆☆ (Piazza G. Ciardi 3, ☎ 0574-28096, $$) and **Il Giglio** ☆☆ (Piazza S. Marco 14, ☎ 0574-37049, $$), with the historical **Flora** ☆☆☆ (Via B. Cairoli 31, ☎ 0574-33521, www.prathotels.it, $$$) representing the best choice in the three-star range. Just outside the walls, **Art Hotel Milano** ☆☆☆ (Via Tiziano 15, ☎ 0574-23371, www.arthotel,it, $$$$) and **President** ☆☆☆☆ (Via A. Simintendi 20, ☎ 0574-30251, www.hotel-president.net, $$$$) offer the best in the higher price bracket.

HOTEL PRICE CHART	
Rates are per room with private bath, based on double occupancy, including breakfast.	
$	Under €40
$$	€41-€85
$$$	€86-€140
$$$$	€141-€210
$$$$$	Over €210

If you want to stay somewhere in the surrounding countryside, **Hermitage** ☆☆☆ (Via Ginepraia 112, Loc. Bonistallo, ☎ 055-877244, fax 055-8797057, www.hotelhermitageprato.it, $$$) down near **Poggio a Caiano** is a great spot. Nearby, **Paggeria Medicea** ☆☆☆☆ (Via Papa Giovanni XXIII 3, ☎ 055-875141, fax 055-8751470, www.artimino.com, $$$$) is a fine choice if you intend to explore Artimino's archeological sites and Medici villas.

Although there are no campgrounds near town, there is a decent enough **youth hostel** at Galceti on the edge of the Monteferrato Protected Area (**Ostello Villa Fiorelli**, Via di Galceti, 64, Loc. Galceti, ☎ 0574-697611, fax 0574-6976256, www.hostels-aig.org, $, single and triple rooms). You must be a cardholder to get a room.

■ Excursions from Prato

Val di Bisenzio

On the western slopes of the Monti della Calvana, Val di Bisenzio is a charming backwater territory of little towns that are as traditionally tied to the textile industry as Prato. Though its sights may be few, hikers, horseback riders and mountain bikers will love exploring the mountain paths, which take you through rich vegetation, shallow brooks and creeks, lovely views and on easy climbs.

From Prato, you'll need a **car** if you want to explore the Bisenzio Valley without too much frustration (take the SS325 north). There are fairly frequent CAP **buses** from Prato to Vaiano and Vernio (both of which are also on the Firenze-Bologna **train** line), but the stops are far from many of the trekking trails.

Tourist Offices: Prato's tourist office is also your best bet for information on the Prato province as a whole. If you do want to contact smaller *Pro Locos* (small tourist offices) in the Val di Bisenzio area, ask the Prato office to phone in advance for you first (most are simply helpful residents without fixed opening hours). For trekking information, it's also worth popping into the **Comunità Montane Val di Bisenzio** (Via V. di Bisenzio 351, Mercatale di Vernio, ☎ 0574-957018).

Mountain bikers will find the region's **MTB clubs** helpful for information on the current state of trails, some even inviting tourists along on their weekend forays: try **Club MTB Schignano** (c/o Circolo Schignano, Via Cantagallo 16, Schignano, ☎ 0574-983074) or **Val Bisenzio Team Bike** (c/o Cicli Santoni, Via G. Braga 328, Vaiano, ☎/fax 0574-987153).

Maps & Guides: The *Appennino Bolognese, Pistoiese e Pratese* (Carta dei Sentieri e Rifugi, 1:25,000, Edizioni Multigraphic Firenze) shows CAI and other established trails in the area north of Prato (Monteferrato, Acquerino-Cantagallo Nature Reserve and Val di Bisenzio). The Tourist Office's free *Val di Bisenzo Carta degli Itinerari Turistici* is just as good, and well-marked with accommodation and horseback-riding centers, as well as churches, windmills, museums and other points of interest. Unfortunately, neither includes the trails of the Monti della Calvana.

Cultural Association **FareArte** (☎ 0574-562076, May-Sept) organizes journeys north into the Bizenzio Valley, with tours around its towns and villas and tastings of local gastronomic fare. Contact the Prato tourist office for the latest program information.

Vaiano: The first important town you'll meet along the SS325 is Vaiano. It took its current form in the Middle Ages when it grew up around the 11th-century Benedictine **Badia di San Salvatore**, at left, which – announced by its green and white marble fortified campanile – still marks the center of town. There's a small collection of little interest in its adjacent **Museo di Arte Sacra** (Museum of Sacred Art, Piazza A. Firenzuola 1, ☎ 0574-989022, Sat, 4-7 pm, Sun and holidays, 9 am-noon, 4-7 pm, other times by appointment, free).

Vaiano is a great center for walkers; you can pick up **hikes** and **mountain bike** itineraries southwest through the stunning, wide field of Parco di Vallupaia to Monte Javello (CAI#14). There's also a gorgeous tabernacle-studded route (the so-called "Trail of the Rogazioni"), which leaves from nearby Badia di Vaiano.

The strada bianca to Sofignano links you to trails that lead up the left flank of the Monti della Calvana. From there you can continue east into the Mugello (see page 91), south to Monte Maggiore or north along the Bisenzio River.

THE STRADA BIANCA

Literally "white street," this is the name for a specific type of country road found in many areas of Tuscany and Umbria, particularly in the Chianti countryside, where the unpaved roads take their distinctive color from the powdery chalk of the landscape.

Itineraries also depart from nearby Migliana and Cantagallo into the **Acquerino-Cantagallo Nature Reserve** (entrance at the Mollino della Sega, with trails also departing from the center car park) or north to Luicciana, itself an important trekking center with an interesting outdoor sculpture gallery of note (**Museo all'Aperto**, Loc. Luicciana).

Horseback riding can be organized with **Club Ippico Little Western Stable** (Loc. Del Bello, ☎ 0574-988977) and **Club Ippico Casa Nuova** (Loc. Casa Nuova

Outside of Florence

di Savignano, ☎ 0574-988546), both on the outskirts of Vaiano, or from **Club Ippico Selvapiana** (Loc. Selvapiana, Luicciana, ☎ 0574-956045).

For a guided tour of the Acquerino-Cantagallo Nature Reserve, including a visit to the cave called Faggione di Luogomano; contact Il Laboratorio Ambientale di Cave (☎ 0574-989296).

MOUNTAIN REFUGES

CAI Rifugio L. Pacini (Pian della Rasa, Loc. Cantagallo, ☎ 0574-956030, $).

Rifugi Alpino Poggio di Petto (Via Alpi di Cavarzano, Loc. Poggio di Petto, **Vernio** ☎ 335-5618593, www.poggiodipetto.it, $).

Vernio: Although little more than a market town, Vernio (a short drive up the SS325) is actually the largest town in the valley. Its main sights are the Romanesque **Chiesa di SS Ippolito e Cassiano** and the old fortress, **Rocca di Vernio** (just north of San Quirico). The latter, reached from Vernio along a pleasant medieval mule track, is also a hot spot for **trails** up the Calvana ridge. It's also prime **horseback riding** territory, with centers **Club Ippico Corboli** (Loc. I Corboli, ☎ 0574-938126), **Club Ippico Mocali Paolo** (Loc. Il Gallo, ☎ 0574-938036) and **Club Ippico Poggio di Petto** (Loc. Poggio di Petto, ☎ 0574-984038) organizing short excursions.

One of the best **walks** in the valley is to its far north in the outskirts of **Montepiano** (#23 and #25). Both trails take you past the 1,000-year-old *badia*, which shields an important cycle of frescoes from the mid-13th century depicting the life of hermit Fra Pietro.

Monte Albano

South of Prato, on the vineyards and olive orchard-covered slopes of the Monte Albano, lie the towns of Poggio a Caiano and Carmignano. Producers of fine DOC and DOCG wines and extra virgin olive oil, the towns also offer easy access for excursions into the province.

DOC & DOCG WINES

DOC stands for Denominazione di Origine Controllata (Wine from a Controlled Area), while DOCG means Denominazione di Origine Controllata e Garantita (Wine from a Controlled and Guaranteed Area). Both mean that the wine must come from a specific area, be produced according to specific techniques and be of a set quality. The DOCG regions, however, are subject to more stringent rules about production and quality.

Monte Albano is best approached by **car**. The SS66 takes you south from Prato with **Cap buses** running to Carmignano and Poggio a Caiano if you do have to go the public transport route. **Copit** (☎ 800-277825, www.copitspa.it) also runs services from Prato to Monte Albano and Poggio a Caiano.

Both **Carmignano** (Piazza V. Emanuele II, ☎ 055-8712468, fax 055-8711455, www.comune.prato.it/associa/carmignano, Tues-Fri, 9 am-noon, 3-5:30 pm, Sat-Sun, 9 am-noon) and **Poggio a Caiano** (Via L. Il Magnifico, ☎ 055-8798779, Tues-Sun, 3-6:30 pm) have helpful offices.

 Sightseeing & Adventures: Your first port of call, **Poggio a Caiano**, drew its first breaths as a river port in the 13th century, growing in power with the arrival of Lorenzo Il Magnifico, who commissioned Giuliano da Sangallo to build a rural palace here. The finished product, though only in part created under his direction, **Villa Ambra**, right, is arguably the most sumptuous of the Medici villas especially in its Salone di Leone X,

which Lorenzo had frescoed by Pontormo and Andrea del Sarto. (Via Pistoiese; ☎ 055-877012, daily with hourly visits, Mar-Oct, 8:30 am-6:30 pm, Nov-Feb, 8:30 am-3:30 pm, €2, conc. €1.)

There are rich Etruscan legacies to be discovered in the south at **Comeana**, an area inhabited since the seventh century BC as the surrounding excavations bear witness. Get an insight into the ancient civilization by visiting the **tomb of Montefortini** (☎ 055-871974, 9 am-2 pm, closed Sun and holidays, free). It measures 12 m (39 feet) high and 70 m (230 feet) wide. Also of interest are the smaller **tomb of Boschetti** (☎ 055-8719741, Mon-Sat, 9 am-2 pm, free) and the **necropolis of Prato di Rosello** (Loc. Poggio alla Malva, ☎ 055-8719741, Sat, 10 am-1 pm). Tours for the latter depart from Montefortini and reservations are required.

From Comeana, it's only a short hike through thick woods to the well-preserved medieval village of **Artimino**. The town's biggest draw, the **Villa Medicea dell'Artimino**, also known as "La Ferdinanda" (after Grand Duke Ferdinando I) and the "Villa of the Hundred Chimneys" (for obvious reasons), was built as a grandiose 16th-century hunting lodge. Its location dominates the horizon of the Barco Reale hunting reserve that encircles it. (☎ 055-8792030/8718081, visits by appointment on Thurs, 9:30 am-12:30 pm, free.)

The town also offers a fitting finale to the Etruscan trail in its **Museo Archelogico** (Archeology Museum, ☎ 055-8718124, 9 am-12:30 pm, closed Wed, €4, conc. €2).

West of Poggio a Caiano (and easily accessed along trail #1), little remains of the original **fortress** at **Carmignano** save for the watchtower, Il Campano, and part of the Rocca (Via di Castello, Carmignano, ☎ 055-8712468, Thurs, Sat-Sun, 3-7 pm, free). The rest was destroyed during the Middle Ages when the area served as a battlefield in disputes between Florence and Pistoia. This hasn't seemed to spoil the town's tourism, with a steady stream of visitors lured here by wine (and figs), at the **wine museum** (Palazzo Pretorio, ☎ 055-8712468, Tues-Sun, 9 am-noon, 3-7 pm, €1) and a precious *Visitation* (1536) by Pontormo up a footpath in the heavily reconstructed **Pieve di SS. Francesco e Michele** (☎ 055-8712046, 7:30 am-6 pm).

Other trails can be picked up through centuries-old woodland to the peak of Monte Pietramarina (586 m/1,922 feet, #2) or south to Artimino (#300). Local **horseback riding** is offered by the **Associazione Equitazione Montalgeto** (Via Montalgeto 3, ☎ 055-8719988) and **Azienda Agricola Montalbano** (Via Montalbano 1, ☎ 055-8799053).

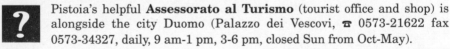

TREKKING WITH LOCALS

*Participation is free and open to all with **Gruppo Escursionistico La Traccia** in Poggio a Caiano and **Gruppo Escursionistico Montalbano** in Carmignano (c/o Circolo Arci, Piazza V. Emanuele II, Carmignano, ☎ 055-8712274). These are two branches of the same organization. Contact the head office above for information on upcoming routes.*

Pistoia

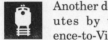

One of the richest art cities in Tuscany with a fascinating cathedral square often missed on Tuscany's well trampled tourist circuit, Pistoia's town center makes one of the most pleasant day-trips from Florence. And the surrounding province will fill all your rural hankerings with plenty of hot springs, mountain trekking and hilltop villages to be explored.

■ Getting Here & Around

Another destination easily-reached from Florence, Pistoia is just 35 minutes by **train** (☎ 848-888088, www.trenitalia.it) on the Florence-to-Viareggio line. **Lazzi** (☎ 055-215155, www.lazzi.it) and **Copit** (☎ 800-277825, www.copitspa.it) offer frequent **bus** routes.

By **car**, take the exit along the A1 or follow SS435 from Prato, before parking in one of the Copit-maintained car parks. Copit also runs the city buses, including the free park-and-ride service, from its car parks. One of the few places for car rental, **Sedoni** (Via Montessori 100, ☎ 0573-534438, fax0573-536219, www.sedoni.it) is also the pick-up point for Hertz rentals (follow Via E. Fermi east out of the city walls). **Taxis** can be found outside the station (**Pistoia Taxi**, ☎ 0573-27763/24331/24291/21237).

■ Information Sources

Pistoia's helpful **Assessorato al Turismo** (tourist office and shop) is alongside the city Duomo (Palazzo dei Vescovi, ☎ 0573-21622 fax 0573-34327, daily, 9 am-1 pm, 3-6 pm, closed Sun from Oct-May).

The best map for the territory is the *CAI Appennino Pistoiese* (Carta Escursionistica e Turistica, SELCA Firenze), 1:50,000, with the *Appennino Bolognese, Pistoiese e Pratese* (Carta dei Sentieri e Rifugi, 1:25,000, Edizioni Multigraphic Firenze), showing CAI trails to the east of Pistoia only.

[Map 2PPC - Pistoia City Map]

■ Sightseeing in the Historical Center

A small and well-delineated historical center makes the main sights of Pistoia easy to explore in a long afternoon. The city street plan follows the ripples of the town's three sets of city walls. The first two, although barely visible, contain the main sights - the first (seventh and eighth century) delineating the Piazza del Duomo north of Via Cavour, and the second (12th century) giving form to the Corso Gramsci. The third set of walls, added by the Medici in the 16th century, is still very visible as you approach from the train station.

Chiesa di Sant'Antonio Abate (7 am-noon, 4:30-6 pm): The first church you meet as you take a right on Corso Gramsci is the 14th-century Sant'Antonio Abate (also known as del Tau from the saint's T-shaped staff). It conserves the city's longest fresco cycle, a work showing stories from the Old and New Testaments and the life of the saint by the Florentine Niccolò di Tommaso and the Pistoian Antonio Vite (1372). The ex-convent also houses the **Centro di Documentazione e Fondazione Marino Marini** (Marino Marini Museum, ☎ 0573-30285, Tues-Sat, 10 am-6 pm, Sun and holidays, 9 am-1 pm), with a selection of sculptures and paintings by Pistoia's most famous modern son.

The heavily restored **Chiesa e Convento di San Domenico** (same hours), across the square, has little other than the Rosellino brothers' tomb of Filippo Lazzari (1468) to recommend it. **Chiesa di San Paolo** (same hours), farther along on the corner, offers the more attractive option with a stunning Gothic-style entrance portal and bright façade of dark green and white inlays topped by a statue of St James.

Chiesa di San Giovanni Fuorcivitas (7 am-noon, 4:30-6 pm): Follow the road up alongside San Paolo and take a left on Via Cavour to reach a church that is considered the masterpiece of Romanesque Pistoian architecture. Its style, characterized by the lively contrast of green and white, as well as light and dark, took off during the city's heyday in the 12th and 13th centuries. The church also contains one of Pistoia's trio of pulpits (see callout), as well as a polyptych by Taddeo Gaddi (1354), a glazed terracotta *Visitation* (1445, on the left wall) by one of the della Robbia brothers and, Gruamonte's *Last Supper* bas-relief (on the architrave of the door before you enter).

THE PULPIT TRIO

State-of-the-art 13th-century Tuscan pulpit sculpture can be witnessed in three of Pistoia's churches:

The earliest (although least intact) is at **San Bartolomeo** (see page 125). It is a comparatively simple yet stunning rectangular box with roots still plainly visible in the earlier Romanesque style. The pulpit is decorated with four boxed sections showing episodes from the life of Christ by Guido Bigarelli of Como (completed 1250).

Resting atop fierce lions, the more sophisticated three-lectern pulpit of **San Giovanni Fuorcivitas**, above, depicts scenes from Christ's infancy and the Passion cycle on its parapet (attributed to Fra Guglielmo of Pisa, completed 1270).

The magnificent hexagonal pulpit of **Sant'Andrea** (see page 126) is the first ever such work by Giovanni Pisano (completed 1303). He went on to reach new heights of splendor with the pulpit of **Pisa Cathedral**, the third and most impressive of the trio. Its panels depict stories from the life of Christ (*Nativity, The Adoration of the Magi, the Massacre of the Innocents, Crucifixion* and *The Last Judgement*).

Opposite San Giovanni Fuorcivitas, a whole host of lovely narrow streets lead up to the vibrant market square, **Piazza della Sala** (morning market till 2 pm). Here, the centerpiece well is topped with a *Marzocco fiorentino* (the heraldic lion, symbol of Florence) gifted to the city by Cosimo I. From here, a choice of narrow restaurant- and antique shop-lined streets lead to the quadrangular **Piazza del Duomo**, which, vast and well preserved, offers a stunning introduction to the city's two great symbols of civic and religious power; the Palazzo Comunale and the Duomo.

Bear Joust

Giostro dell'Orso, July 25, 9:30 am-12:30 pm, Piazza del Duomo (€5 tickets from the tourist office). is a two-by-two race to hit some pretty convincing cardboard cut-out bears, the Giostro dell'Orso sees 12 colorful horsemen, in faux-medieval attire, unite on the piazza under the heraldic emblems of the city's four historical districts (lion, white stag, griffon and dragon). Held on the feast day of the city's patron saint, St James, and announced by a raucous procession of standard bearers, trumpeters and drummers, the joust forms the centerpiece of the **Luglio Pistoiese** (Pistoia July) festival season. The season also includes the popular **Blues Festival** (www.pistoiablues.com, first week of July), which has welcomed musicians such as BB King and Bob Dylan in the past.

Duomo (Cattedrale di San Zeno) (7 am-noon, 2:30-6 pm): With a striking façade of striped black and white marble, broken up by delicate tiers of arches and topped by two 18th-century statues of St Zeno and St James, it is the Duomo, at the bottom of the gently sloping square, that is the first of the square's monuments to draw the eye. The slightly ponderous 70-m (230-foot) campanile to its side (essentially still a Lombard watchtower of plain sandstone) distracts from the effect somewhat, although attempts were made to include it in the party, as the top three levels of Romanesque-Gothic green and white marble show. Works by Andrea della Robbia brighten your approach – colorful terracotta tiles in the Gothic portico and a serene *Mother with Child and Angels* in the lunette above the door. Inside, Andrea da Fiesole's baptismal font (1498-99) is the first work to grab your attention before the silver altar dedicated to St Jacopo attracts you into the Cappella del Giudizio with its shimmer. Its delicate design conceals what was really a laborious work (weighing almost a ton and populated with 628 figures) that occupied Tuscany's finest Gothic silversmiths between the late-13th and mid-15th centuries.

Cellino di Nese (also responsible for the Duomo's monument to Cino da Pistoia) laid the finishing touches to Giovanni Pisano's octagonal **Battistero di San Giovanni in Corte** when he swathed it in green and white striped marble in the mid-14th century. Also watch for the Pisano brothers' *St John the Baptist* and *St Peter* flanking sculptures of the *Madonna and Child* above the main portal.

The arcaded façade of the Duomo appears even more fragile in contrast to the towering bulk of the Gothic **Palazzo Comunale**, right, created in *pietra serena*, built from 1294 to house the city podestà or magistrate. Inside the five even arches that support its ground floor, the palace opens out onto an elegant courtyard, which links onto the Sala Maggiore (with a frescoed *Virgin* from the Giotto school); the **Centro di Documentazione Michelucci** (dedicated to one of Italy's most important of architects); and its main attraction, the **Museo Civico** (☎ 0573-371296, Tues-Sat, 10 am-6 pm, Sun and holidays, 9 am-12:30 pm). The latter occupies the top floor with a collection of paintings, ceramics, porcelain and glasswork that covers the whole of Pistoia's artistic history from the Romanesque *Pala di San Francesco* (13th century) to the city's great 15th-century altarpieces, alongside works by Lorenzo di Credi, Ghirlandaio and Gerino Gerini.

Also on the Piazza del Duomo, the **Palazzo Pretorio** (façade under restoration at time of writing) conserves its mid-14th-century entrance hall, elegant courtyard and monumental stone bench of justice, though it no longer dispenses the justice it was built for. Just behind the Duomo (head past the tourist office and take a left), the **Palazzo dei Vescovi** houses a run-of-the-mill archeological collection (with Etruscan findings from the sixth to fifth centuries BC) and a more interesting collection of sacred art in the **Museo Capitolare** (including works taken from the Duomo and the Chiesa di San Jacopo).

The earliest of Pistoia's three pulpits can be found behind the Romanesque façade of the **Chiesa di San Bartolomeo in Pantano**. From here, Via del Ceppo will take you back to the center past the modest Michelozzo-constructed **Chiesa di Santa Maria delle Grazie** (Piazza San Lorenzo) and the more richly decorated exterior of the **Ospedale del Ceppo**, left. The bright polychrome terracotta frieze (the work of Giovanni della Robbia and Santi Buglioni), which decorates the colonnaded porch of the latter, is one of the most precious of its type, not only for its dimensions and state of preservation but also for the endearingly realistic depiction of Renaissance pilgrims, prisoners, the sick and the dying it displays.

While You're in the Area...

Pop into **Confetteria Corsini** (Piazza San Francesco 42, ☎ 0573-2038) to stock up on the *confetti di Pistoia*. These sugarcoated almond "confetti" balls are one of the city's most famous snacks, and were originally thrown during the weddings of the city's 16th-century nobility.

Outside of Florence

Via delle Pappe will take you from here to the mid-12th-century **Chiesa di Sant'Andrea**, site of the third and most important of the Pistoia pulpits. It also has a second piece attributed to its artist Giovanni Pisano – the Crucifix mounted on the wall of the right aisle.

You'll find two more churches of interest on your route back to the central square; the Gothic **Chiesa e Convento di San Francesco** (Piazza San Francesco d'Assisi), worth a look for its fresco cycle (Cappella Maggiore); and the **Chiesa di Madonna dell'Umita** (closed for restoration at the time of writing) which, built to the designs of Giovanni da Sangallo, was almost destroyed when succeeding architect Vasari tried to load too heavy a dome on its walls.

PISTOIAN GREEN SPACES

While there's a pleasant enough park alongside the Fortezza di Santa Barbara, it is far outclassed by the superb green areas in the vicinity: **Giardino Puccini** (Puccini Park & Villa, Via Dalmazia 356, Scornio, ☎ 0573-904604, free) was created – along with the Villa di Scornio – in the first half of the 19th century in typical "romantic park" style. Today it serves as a popular green space for the inhabitants of Pistoia, just outside the city walls.

Parco di Celle (Fattoria di Celle, Santomato, ☎ 0573-479907, goricoll@tin.it, free visits on advanced written request from Miranda MacPhail) is a 56-acre garden of sculptures, lakes, fountains and water games that constitutes one of the most extensive outdoor museums in Tuscany. It includes works by international greats such as Fausto Melotti, Robert Morris (who designed the vast labyrinth) and Polish artist Magdalena Abakanowick, who did its 33 totem poles.

One for the kids, the 210,000-acre **Pistoia Zoo** (Via Pieve a Celle 160, 0573-911219, www.zoodipistoia.it, daily, Apr-Sept, 9 am-7 pm, Oct-Mar, 7 am-5 pm, €8, conc. €6) is immersed in green hills just out of the center. There are over 600 animals, including the rare Madagascar lemur catta, white bears, elephants, hippos, flamingos and stalks.

■ Adventures

Pistoia is well placed for **trekking** and **mountain biking** with prime territory to the north in the trail-lined **Montagna Pistoiese** (see page 132), south on the slopes of **Monte Albano** and west in the **Svizzera Pesciatina** (see page 130). From Pistoia itself, CAI#208 "Pungitori" leaves from the northwest of the city near Burgianco up Monte Cattai (and the MPT – Montagna Pistoiese Trekking – network). En route you can also pick up the #210 "Merlo" and the #212 to Castagno Casale. The #204 "Picchio Verde" leaves from Candeglia in the northeast looping back to Pistoia at Ponte Nuovo (five miles out of town).

Horseback-riding centers can be found in town (**Centro Equitazione Groppoli**, Via Groppoli 8, ☎ 0573-572347) or south of the city on the slopes of Monte Albano (**Club Ippico Bavigliano**, Via Bavigliano 11, Quarrata, ☎ 0573-775769). **Skiers** should head north to Abetone (see page 132).

■ Where to Eat

 Some of the nicest (and most convenient) spots for a tasty lunch can be found on and around the market square Piazza della Sala. Pizzeria **La Sala da Ale** (Via S. Anastasio 4, ☎ 0573-24108, closed Thurs, $); the terraces of **Lo Storno** (Via del Lastrone 8, ☎ 0573-26193, $$); and the more elegant redbrick arches of **La Bottegaia** (Via del Lastrone 17, ☎ 0573-365602, closed Mon, $), with adjacent wine shop, constitute three of the nicest.

There's also **San Jacopo** (Via Crispi 15, ☎ 0573-27786, closed Mon and Tues lunch, $$) on the road alongside San Giovanni Fuorcivitas if you want something a little more formal. Or, on the other side of Piazza del Duomo, **La Tavernetta di Jack** (Via del Presto 9, ☎ 0573-20491, closed Tues, $) offers a considerably less touristy and deliciously informal opportunity to try the local cuisine.

LOCAL FLAVORS

Spring cheeses: Pecorino from the Montagna Pistoiese bought *fresco* (younger than 20 days) or *abrucciato* (35-40 days). Plus the soft cheese, *ravaggiolo*, and fresh ricotta served in the local *necci* (pancakes cooked between two stone or iron disks).

Hot soups: *Zuppa di farro* (soup made of the farro grain), *cionci* (a stew made from ox muzzle) and *zuppa di fagioli di Sorana* (soup with beans from Sorana).

Sweet desserts: *Brigidini* from Lamporecchio and *cialde* (sweet ground almonds sandwiched between two paper-thin wafers) from Montecatini Terme.

■ Where to Stay

 Pistoia's nearest **campground** is at **Montecatini Alto** (**Belsito**, Via delle Vigne 1a, ☎ 0572-67373, $) with others located north in the Montagana Pistoiese at **Cutigliano** (**Le Betulle**, Via Cantamaggio 6, Loc. Ponte Sestaione, ☎ 0573-68004, $; **Neve Solo**, Viale di Rivoreta 30, ☎ 0573-629279, $; and **Il Pinguino**, Via Pian di Novello, ☎ 0573-673008, $) and **Maresca** (**Foresta del Teso**, Via del Teso, ☎ 0573-64175, $). The area's **youth hostel** is also found here (**Abetone**, Via Brennero 157, ☎ 0573-60117).

■ Excursions from Pistoia

Valdinievole

You're entering some of Italy's prime spa territory as you head west into Valdinievole, the "Valley of the Mist."

Trains on the Florence-to-Viareggio line stop at Montecatini Terme (get off at "Montecatini Centro") after passing through Pistoia. From here Lazzi buses depart from the train station every 15 minutes to Monsumanno Terme (which can also be reached on **Copit buses** directly from Pistoia). The towns are also reached by **car** from the Montecatini exit of the A1. You can also reach Monsummano **on foot** by picking up the Sentiero Consorzio Montalbano over the hill from Serravalle Pistoiese (a stop earlier on the train).

Tourist Offices: The biggest of the region's tourist offices is at **Montecatini Terme** (Viale G. Verdi 66, ☎ 0572-772244, Mon-Sat, 9 am-12:30 pm, 3-6 pm, and in summer, Sun, 9 am-noon), with smaller offices at **Monsummano Terme** (☎ 0572-959227, fax 0572-522283, www.comune.monsummano.pt.it) and **Lamporecchio** (Piazza Fra G. Giraldi 10, ☎ 0573-856008).

Montecatini Terme: An elegant thermal town marked by its Art Nouveau architecture and leafy boulevards, Montecatini is one of the most famous (and consequently most expensive) spa towns in Italy. Although there may be little to bring you to the downtown area if you're not a spa enthusiast (except perhaps the Modern Accadamia d'Arte, Mon-Sat, 3-6 pm, free), the medieval **Alto** or upper town perched 100 m (328 feet) above it, a funicular ride from 10 am, spring and summer only, or a two-mile drive, makes a pleasant diversion. The medieval **Chiesa di San Pietro** (a short climb from the main square) houses most of the Alto's artistic treasures, including a 15th-century *Madonna* fresco by Perugino school, an *Ascension* by Santi di Tito (1595) plus the relics of the town's patron saint, St Barbara.

Liberty Lanes

Characteristic of *Stile Liberty* (the Italian term for Art Nouveau), Montecatini's Viale Verdi and offshoots house some of the town's most richly decorated buildings. In addition to the Tettuccio, Tamerici, Leopoldine and Excelsior spas, structures to look out for include the Locanda Maggiore and the Gambrinus portico (built by Giulio Bernardini in 1913), Teatro Politeama (today the Cinema Imperiale, built 1926), the Palazzo Comunale (with Chini-frescoed ceiling), Cinema Excelsior and the Hotel Grande Bretagne on Via Don Minzoni. If you want to find out more, contact Veronica Ferretti (☎ 0572-72151, veronicaferetti@supereva.it). She gives guided tours of the town's Liberty fronts in English.

Cyclists should head north to the superb views found in medieval hilltop towns like **Massa** (with an ancient church housing a lovely della Robbia *Madonna*) and **Cozzile** (check out the view from the "Porta di Mezzogiorno"). An ancient Roman road network unites the two. Alternatively, you can go into the Buggiano Valley and see the stucco and gilded ornamental façade of the Bellavista Villa (midway between Borgo a Buggiano and Chiesina Uzzanese).

Walkers should pick up the trails south around **Monsummano Terme** or north at **Marliana**, which is a stop on the VT (Valleriana Trekking) network. It's also worth making your way to the hilltop town of **Buggiano Castello**, whose vermillion-hued façades shield gardens ranging in size and style from miniature secret gardens too small to sit in, to the more formal Baroque garden of the 17th-century Villa Sermolle (garden tours can be arranged through the Associazione Culturale Buggiano Castello, ☎ 0572-32191).

If you're carless but still want to explore the surrounding area, the Montecatini Tourist Office organizes various half-day trips to the surroundings' less accessible sights (June-Oct, Mon/ Wed/Fri, 2:30 pm).

The Spas

With traditional hydro-cures, fango mud baths and plenty of beauty and health treatments, Montecatini Terme has nine classic baths to visit. Each is named after the salt-sulphur-alkaline springs they control and all are found in the **Parco delle Terme** (10 minutes walk from the train station, Viale Verdi 41 ☎ 0572-7781, fax 0572-778444, www.termemontecatini.it). They are open May-Oct (except for the Excelsior, which is open year-round). Restructured in the 18th century after a visit by Grand Duke Leopardo, the best-known include the Neo-Renaissance **Excelsior,** built in 1915 to a plan by Bernardini; the mock-medieval **Torretta**; the mud baths of **Leopoldine**, built to plans by Giovannozzi; and the Neo-classical **Tettuccio**, a kind of thermal village with pavilions, streets and rest areas. Note the Belle Époque furnishings and ceramics, and the Moroni frescoes in the Sala della Scrittura.

At Monsummano Terme, the spas (or rather steam caves) can be found on the eastern outskirts at **Grotta Giusti** (Via Grotta Giusti 171, ☎ 0572-51008, fax 0572-9077200, www.grottagiustispa.com, Apr-Oct) and north at the **Grotta Parlanti** (Via Francesco Nord 41d, ☎ 0572-953029, fax 0572-953881).

Spa Diving: The underground lake beneath the **Grotta Giusti Terme** offers a unique diving experience in its clear 36°C/92°F waters. Although devoid of animal life (no animal can survive in such a warm and chemically-saturated environment), there are plenty of stalagmites, stalactites, tunnels and ravines to be explored. The one-hour dive is guided by the spa with two theory lessons included in the price. To book, contact MeDit (www.meditonline.it).

Monsummano Terme: A few miles to the southeast, Monsummano Terme's biggest draw apart from the sauna-type cures of its steam caves is the spectacular view from the old town of Monsummano Alto. Two miles from the center, up a lovely steep and narrow road, it is also the starting point of many **hiking** trails. Choose from routes heading north to the ancient Pistoian stronghold of **Serravalle Pistoiese** (#30 then #00) or south to the **Monte Albano** (#00) or **Montevettolini** (the "geological" #30).

The Padule di Fucecchio is just a **bike ride** away with trails taking you along the manmade Terzo and Capannone Canals. As are Vinci and Cerreto Guidi – stop off in **Lamporecchio** en route to stock up on some of the town's distinctive *brigidini* (crunchy biscuits with a light aniseed taste) or to follow trekking trail (#18) up to the 12th-century **Chiesa di San Baronto** (on the mountain summit). The Padule can also be reached on Copit bus from Montecatini, the head office (Conzorzio Bonifica Padule, Ponte Buggianese, ☎ 0572-93221, cbpadule@italway.it) organizing **canoe** tours for groups of two to three people.

Chocfest: The antithesis to Monsummano Terme's other health-giving treatments, the third weekend of January sees the arrival of **Cioccolosità** (www.cioccolosita.it), a three-day event that occupies Piazza Giusti and surrounding streets with some mouthwatering chocolate-covered stalls. Don't despair if you miss the event. The Slitti family (Via Francesca Sud 1268, ☎ 0572-640240) offer a year-round selection of sweets so delicately crafted, it almost seems a shame to eat them.

Outside of Florence

Pescia & the Svizzera Pesciatina

Pescia is just west of Montecatini Terme with the Svizzeria Pesciatina easily accessible by car to its north.

The main tourist board is at Collodi (Via B. Pasquinelli 54, ☎ 0583-978205).

Sightseeing & Adventures

 The ascent towards the Svizzeria Pesciatina (a name coined by the exiled Swiss historian Sismondi di Geneva in the 19th century) begins once you cross the Pescia River from Montecatini Terme. You'll get a good idea of the landscape, which extends up to 1,000 m (3,280 feet) crests northwest of Pietrabuona, from **Uzzano** (said to be the site of Puccini's inspiration for the second and third acts of *La Bohème*) perched as it is on hills of olive groves and cypress trees over the Pescia Valley. Other than Pescia, the area's major manmade charm is provided by the 10 medieval villages (*castelli*) which, stacked on the northern hillside, are joined together by the Valleriana **trekking** network (VT).

The Castelli

Today a tiny chestnut-wooded village, **Medicina** has ancient defensive fortifications and the remains of an underground passage still visible.

Historically the battlefield of the Florentines and Lucchesi, **Fibbialla** offers some of the region's best views.

Perhaps the most stunning of the 10, the medieval stone houses of **Aramo** are perched on a precipice over the Pescia River valley with wine vaults and underground passages – ancient escape routes – dug into the rock.

At one time Pescia's most important fortified settlement, **Vellano** still preserves the town outline, part of the walls and a 10th-century church.

Worth a visit for the *pietra serena* altar, font and pulpit of Chiesa di San Pietro, **Sorana** is a pleasant hike from Vellano.

On a natural terrace, the hexagonal watchtower of **San Quirico** dominates the valley to the south.

Famous for its 12th-century Pieve di San Tommaso – the best-known monument in the area with its two-part façade – **Castelvecchio** is one of the most popular Pescian hideaways.

A steep climb up the northern slope of Mount Battifolle, **Stiappa**, at 627 m (2,057 feet), is one of the highest of the 10.

Surrounded by characteristic fan-shaped mounds, **Pontito** is the site of two of the well-preserved sister citadels.

If you don't want to go it alone, hiking tours of the castelli can be arranged through the **Montagnardi Association** (☎ 0572-476471, montagnardi@hotmail.com).

The river that cuts through the Pescia Valley also divides Pescia in two (linked since ancient times by the cathedral bridge). The left side (the so-called "religious quarter") cradles the parish church, which is now the cathedral, and the right side (the "civic" or "commercial" district), the castle, market and feudal court. It is also the site of the majority of the houses – four of the town's five districts (or *quinti*) are built in long rows parallel to the river in an urban form thought to date back over a thousand years.

Blooming Marvelous: Pescia may only be a small city but it still manages to box thousands of lilies, carnations and gladioli a day at the height of the season (which explains the miles of nurseries in the nearby valley). You'll get the idea by a visit to the vast morning market, but even this pales in comparison to the September **Biennale del Fiore** (biannual flower shower, even-numbered years, www.bienaledelfiore.it), a 36,000-square-yard feast of technicolor blooms.

Flowers aside, the town has a pretty interesting cathedral in the Baroque-overhauled **Santa Maria Assunta** (only the campanile remains of the original 14th-century building), its main attractions a della Robbia terracotta triptych (Cappella del Vescovado) and the 15th-century Sienese and Florentine works in the Biblioteca Capitolare. But it is justifiably the nearby **Chiesa di San Francesco** (Via Battisti) that draws the crowds. Its precious *Scenes from the Life of St Francis* (at left, 1235) by Bonaventura Berlinghieri is considered the oldest and most faithful representation of the saint, and is just one of the marvelous images on exhibit. Check out Puccio Capanna's *Crucifixion* in the sacristy and Bicci di Lorenzo's *Life of the Virgin*. Another work by the latter (*Life of St Anthony,* interesting for its ancient representation of the town) is found in the **Oratorio di Sant'Antonio Abate** (Sun, 10 am-1 pm, 4-7 pm), along with an outstanding wooden *Deposition* popularly called the *Santi Brutti*.

If you've walked around town and still hanker for more, the so-called **"fairytale road"** (Via della Fiaba) offers a pleasant five-mile diversion west from Pescia to **Collodi** (where it joins onto Valleriana Trekking), a beautiful hillside town best known as the home of Pinocchio. But before you head into the theme park dedicated to the long-nosed hero, take in the grandiose Villa Garzoni (where Collodi is said to have written the masterpiece in the first place) with its famous Baroque gardens of circular fountains, topiary animals, patterned flowerbeds, water staircase and zigzagging steps and terraces (☎ 0572-429590, 9 am-sunset). Collodi's father was the once the estate manager here.

THERE WAS ONCE UPON A TIME A PIECE OF WOOD...

Created in the 1950s in homage to Carlo Lorenzini's (pen name Carlo Collodi) most famous tale, **Il Parco di Pinocchio** (☎ 0572-429342, summer, daily, 8 am-8 pm, winter, 7 am-5:30 pm) offers the kind of cultural journey that puts to shame the Disney theme parks most children now grown up on. Split into two sections, the oldest (created in 1956) displays character statues by Emilio Greco and Venturino Venturi, while the newer "Toy Land" walks you through the plot of the story with the help of 21 statues by Pietro Consagra. There's also an inn planned by Giovanni Michelucci (architect of Florence's train station and prestigious churches), a summer palace designed by Diodati and, for young kids, a year-round glove puppet show.

The Montagna Pistoiese

Delineated by the Apennines, the Montagna Pistoiese fans out north of Pistoia in a V-shape (one branch leading up to Abetone, the other to Sambuca Pistoiese), offering a rich choice of skiing, trekking, horse-riding, mountain biking, canoeing and climbing opportunities.

North of Pistoia, the SS66 (the Regia Modenese) forks off to the left side of the Montagna Pistoiese, the right side reached along the panoramic SS64 "Porrettana" (also linked by the Porrettana tourist railway). Both are served by **Copit buses** although you'll find that most head towards Abetone (the line allows for the transportation of bicycles), especially during the winter ski season.

There are tourist offices at **Abetone** (Piazzale Piramidi, ☎ 0573-60231, fax 0573-60232), **Cutigliano** (Piazza Catilina 22, ☎ 0573-68029, fax 0573-68200) and **San Marcello Pistoiese** (Via V. Vittoria 129a, ☎ 0573-775252, fax 0573-622120), next door to the **Comunità Montane Appennino Pistoiese** (Via V. Vittoria 129b, ☎ 0573-622462).

Adventures on Foot: Well-detailed by the vast MPT (Montagna Pistoiese Trekking) and GEA (Grande Escursione Apennina) networks and enhanced by AT (Abetone Trekking), PT (Porrettana Trekking, parallel to the train line) and Via Verdi d'Europa (an Italy-long network that stretches up from its southernmost tip in Puglia), there are plenty of routes in the Montagna Pistoiese to enjoy. Some of the best depart from **Abetone** (the six-mile "Rhododendron Itinerary" up the peaks of Monte Libro Aperto and the six-mile "Deep Blue Kale Itinerary" through the icy lakes and majestic ridges of the Val di Luce), **Cutigliana** (the CAI#6 north to La Doganaccia), **San Marcello Pistoiese** (with a stunning path over a narrow hanging bridge (220 m/722 feet long and 40 m/131 feet high) built in 1922 to connect the two banks of the River Lima) and, over to the east, **Sambuca Pistoiese**. If you're in the Abetone area and don't know where to start, contact **Gruppo Trekking Val Sestaione** (☎ 0573-630145). They lead group hikes for free upon payment of a mandatory insurance fee.

ALPINE REFUGES

Rifugio Alpino La Selletta (Via Brennero 249, Abetone, ☎ 0573-60171)

Rifugio CAI Portafranca (San Marcello Pistoiese, ☎ 0573-490338)

Two major routes dedicated to **orienteering** can be found in the Montagna Pistoiese, one at Cutigliano, the other at the biogenetic nature reserve of Piano degli Ontani, near Abetone. There are also some fascinating **nature walks** offered by the nature reserve of **Macchia Antonini**, the 5,600-acre forest of **Maresca** and **Abetone** (the Abetone nature trail taking you around the beech, silver fits, maples and birch trees and sandstone rock plants that live in it) and, with the permission of the Forester, the nature reserve at **Campolino.**

The Pistoiese Mountain Eco-Museums

For a spot of local history when you're in the area, pick up one of the five historic itineraries that introduce you to the area's ice-producing past (including ruined ice houses and a restored ice-making factory near the village of Le Piastre), iron-working trades (including the Sabatini works that processed iron from the mines of Elba), sacred art and folk

Above: Fiesole, in the hills above Florence
Below: Donatello's pulpit in Prato Cathedral

Above: Prato's Castello dell'Imperatore and Basilica di Santa Maria delle Carc
(APT Prato)

Below: Detail of Filippo Lippi's Convito di Erode in Prato *(APT Prato)*

Detail of Filippo Lippi's Convito di Erode in Prato (APT Prato)

Duccio's Crevole Madonna (1283-84), Museo dell'Opera del Duomo, Siena

religion (with trails following sacred tabernacles or Verginine), farming and natural history (including some lovely walks through the woods of the villages of Maresca, Popiglio and Cutigliano). For more information on the trails and traditions of the area, contact Pistoia Tourist Office.

Adventures on Wheels: The best mountain biking trails can be picked up from Abetone, with various marked routes starting from the Copit bus stop and heading down into the nature reserve (a beautiful beech wood forest) of Pian degli Ontani.

Adventures on Horseback: The route most suitable to horseback riders is covered by the **Via Verdi d'Europa**, which can be picked up at Piteglio or Abetone. Contact the **Associazione Ippica Montagna Pistoiese** (☎ 0573-622261) to organize excursions along its paths.

Adventures on Water: Vertigo-sufferers should take in the hanging bridge of Mammiano – the world's longest pedestrian suspension bridge – from below. Popular canoe tours leave from just under it down the River Lima to Ponte di Lucchio (three miles) and Ponte Maggio (four miles). Contact the San Marcello Pistoiese tourist office to book a trip.

Adventures on Snow: The most important of the Apennine ski resorts and the one closest to Florence, **Abetone** (1,400 m/4,592 feet) covers over 50 km (31 miles) of fir-tree flanked piste in the Sestaione, Lima, Scoltenna and Luce valleys, with all-ability runs, including night skiing, tree skiing and off-piste slopes. Other smaller resorts can be found north of Cutigliano (Doganaccia and Pian di Novello) and San Marcello Pistoiese (Casetta Pulledrari). **Doganaccia** is the best choice for downhill beginners and cross-country skiers – it is linked to the Pian di Novello by a 15-mile cross-country ring.

The Low Down: Skiing in Abetone

When to go: Best between January and March; the ski season officially runs from Dec to April.

What to take: Ski wear (the only ski accessory you cannot rent in the resort).

Access: Valid for one day, the Abetone Multipass (Via Brennero 429, ☎ 0573-60556, Mon-Fri, €22.50 ($28.35), Sat-Sun, €26.60 ($33.52)) allows unlimited use of the slopes at all four valleys.

What if I can't ski? Book on arrival with one of Abetone's five ski schools: Le Regine (Via Brennero, Loc. Le Regine, ☎ 0573-60322), Monte Gimito (Via Brennero 1, ☎ 0573-60392), Val di Luce (Loc. Val di Luce 1, ☎ 0573-609020), Zeno Colò (Via Brennero 203, ☎ 0573-60032) or Colò (Via Brennero 489, ☎ 0573-607077).

Adventures in the Air: The truly adventurous should book a course with Filippo Lo Giudice, Tuscany's **paragliding** expert, found in Lizziano (a 15-minute drive from Cutigliano on the Copit bus route). Classes range from one to three days and include a tandem jump at 442 m/1,450 feet (☎ 340-3369516, www.nonsolovolo.it).

Chianti

For all its dramatic hills, dusty views, isolated castles and olive groves, the Chianti region is above all known for one thing: wine. And, as clichéd and over-visited as it may be, no trip to Tuscany is complete without a tipsy jaunt – whether by bike, horse or on foot – along the *strade bianche* that link its medieval villages, winding streets, Gothic churches and monasteries.

■ Getting Here & Around

The best approaches to the Chianti region, which lies south of Florence and northeast of Siena, are the old Florence-to-Siena Road (SS2) along the western edge and the SS222 Chiantigiana from Siena into its heartland. Cycling, horseback riding and walking are all good here, with smooth roads, beautiful scenery, challenging climbs, long downhill runs and historical sites and vineyards on almost every route.

If you are constrained by public transport, **Sita Bus** #345 (☎ 800-373760, www.sita-on-line.it) runs roughly twice a day from Florence to Radda in Chianti (1 hour 35 minutes, €3.40 one-way), Castellina (1 hour 35 minutes, €3.20 one-way) and Gaiole (1 hour 55 minutes, €3.80 one-way). **Tra-In** (☎ 0577-204111, www.trainspa.it) offers a similar service from Siena to Castelnuovo Berardenga (#134, 25 minutes, €2), Castellina (#125, €2), Gaiole (#127, €2), Radda (#125, €2.70).

■ Information Sources

Tourist Offices: As the chief town in the Gallo Nero region, **Greve** is equipped with a vineyard-oriented tourist office in **La Torre** (Via Luca Cini, ☎ 055-8545243, Mon-Sat, 10 am-1 pm, 2-5 pm, closed Thurs, and Via G. da Verrazzano 33, ☎/fax 055-8546287). You can find smaller offices at **Castellina** (Piazza del Comune 1, ☎ 0577-742311), **Radda** (Piazza Ferrucci 1, ☎ 0577-738494, fax 0577-739384, proradda@chiantinet.it, Mar-Oct, 10 am-1 pm, 3:30-6:30 pm), **Gaiole** (Via Antonio Casabianca, ☎/fax 0577-749411, Apr-Oct, Mon-Sat, 9 am-12:30 pm, 3:30-7:30 pm), also the base for the **Associazione Parco Ciclistico del Chianti** (c/o Tourist Office) and **Castelnuovo Berardenga** (Via del Chianti 61, ☎/fax 0577-355500, www.berardenga.it, 10 am-1 pm, 3-6 pm).

Maps & Guides: Associazione Parco Ciclistico del Chinati and the Siena Tourist Office provide *Biking Through Siena's Countryside* (Fabio Masotti, Nuova Immagine Editrice), with details and maps of 20 cycling itineraries around Castellina, Castelnuovo Berardenga, Gaiole, Greve and Radda. You can also get information and print it out before you go by visiting www.terresienainbici.it.

Toscana in Mountain Bike, Volume II: Preappennino-parte prima (S. Grillo and C. Pezzani, Ediciclo Editore, in Italian only) features 31 mountain-bike itineraries departing from Siena, including routes through Chianti.

Chianti e Colline Senesi (Carta Turistica Stradale, 1:50,000, Edizioni Multigraphic Firenze) and *Siena-Chianti-Colline Senesi* (Carta Turistica Stradale 661, Kompass, 1:50,000) are the best maps for drivers and road bikers (though they do show CAI trails and mountain bike itineraries), while the more detailed *Chianti Classico, Val di Pesa and Val d'Elsa* (Carta Turistica e dei

Sentieri, IGM, 1:25,000) is a good choice for mountain bike and CAI trails. *Monti del Chianti* (Carta dei Sentieri e Rifugi, Edizioni Multigraphic Firenze, 1:25,000) is the better option for longer hikes.

■ Sightseeing & Adventures

 Your route down from Florence offers two pleasant detours in the pre-Chianti attractions of the **Certosa di Galluzzo** and the market town of **Impruneta** (both just a short drive south of the city). The first, a Carthusian monastery founded in the 14th century by Florentine banker Niccolo Acciaioli, is home to a fresco cycle by Pontormo (*Scene della Passione*, 1525, in the Pinacoteca) and terracotta *tondi* by Andrea and Giovanni della Robbia (Chiostro Grande). Open summer, Tues-Sun, 9 am-noon, 3-6 pm, winter, Tues-Sat, 9 am-noon, 3-5 pm, Sun, 9 am-noon, 3-6 pm, free). Impruneta, the sleepy beige-colored center of the local terracotta industry, is also home to a raucous October wine festival, which sees the town's main square covered with a gargantuan wine barrel (unfortunately empty). Inside the terracotta-decorated **Basilica di Santa Maria** (daily, 9:30-11:30 am, 3:30-7 pm), which overlooks the square, two chapels attributed to Michelozzo house more terracotta decorations by Luca della Robbia, while the attached museum guards the miraculous image of the *Madonna* that prompted the 11th-century construction of church in the first place.

Greve

Both above attractions easily link onto the SS222 and a short drive along it takes you to the capital of the Chianti Classico Gallo Nero region, Greve. Its triangular Piazza Matteoti with beautifully porticoed arcades, bustling at the best of times, reaches its pinnacle during the September **Festa del Vino** when tasting stalls of the local Chianti Classico inebriate visitors in time for the Sat night climax at the Castello di Montefioralle. If you do manage to drag yourself away from the bottles, the **Chiesa di Santa Croce**, at the top of a square, has a beautiful triptych by Bicci di Lorenzo.

In addition to the pleasant walk up to Montefioralle, nearby trails take you through olive groves to the Romanesque **Pieve di San Cresci** (Fri, 9:30-12:30, 4-7 pm) or east onto the Pian della Canonica, which loops back to Greve through Uzzano. Otherwise you'll need to get to the Castello di Lamole – a short **bike** ride away – where the huge 15th-century **Villa di Vignamaggio**, left (where the Mona Lisa of da Vinci's portrait is thought to have been born) marks the start of trails up to the peak of the highest point in the region, **Monte San Michele** (#28 and #30).

Road cyclists can also follow the SS222 south to pick up the Old Chiantigiana as far as Panzano. The **Pieve di San Leolino** here (☎ 055-852041, Tues, 09:30-12:30, 4-7 pm, Thurs, 4-7 pm, other times by appointment) is one of the region's oldest churches, and offers a delightful view of the circle of hills known as the Conca d'Orco (Golden Hollow). If you want to explore the area on **horseback**, contact the area's riding club (**Club Ippico Cintoia**, Loc. Strada in Chianti, Via

Outside of Florence

Cintoia Bassa 5, ☎ 055-8547973); for those based in nearby Impruneta (see page 135).

Designed to promote cyclo-tourism in the Chianti hills, the **Associazione Parco Ciclistico del Chianti** (www.parcociclisticodelchianti.it) doesn't just dole out advice; they also organize guided bike tours on a relaxed turn-up-and-join-in basis. Contact the office (c/o the tourist board) for information on the latest events.

Castellina, Radda & Gaiole in Chianti

The first of the traditional Lega di Chianti triad (which also includes Radda and Gaiole), Castellina in Chianti offers some great views from the turrets of the medieval *castello* that once defended Florence's borderline from territorial rival Siena, not to mention some of the biggest of the region's *enoteche*. You'll find Radda in Chianti a manageable trek away to the east (CAI#88). Its historical center, sloping around Piazza Ferrucci with its frescoed and shield-covered 15th-century town hall, is considered the capital of the Chianti region (a title actually held by Castello di Brolio to its south).

From Radda, **trails** include one of the regions' most popular routes (#52, also suitable for mountain **bikes**), which passes through five miles of vineyards to reach the hillside hamlet of **Volpaia**, best known for the Castello di Volpaia wine estate. Other routes take you south to the tiny Chiesa di San Giusto and onto Ama (#68, also suitable for mountain bikes), which is home to another of Chianti's first-rank wine estates, Castello di Ama (closed to visitors in August). Another pleasant **cycle** route takes you south to Gaiole in Chianti, passing first through Badia a Coltibuono (you can pick up CAI trails in the oak and pine woods surrounding it), now also a wine estate. Gaiole itself offers an interesting and (well signposted) itinerary in the Strada dei Castelli, which takes you past a half-dozen ruined fortresses in the area before depositing you back in the brisk market square.

Pedal Back in Time

 Things go antique in the final weekend of September, when riders wobble out of Gaiole's town center on vintage bicycles – spare tubes around their necks and vintage jerseys on their backs – for a race over 100 km/62 miles of unpaved road. Few make it back smoothly to the finishing line. For information on both watching and participating in the **Eroica Bicycle Race**, contact Parco Ciclistico del Chianti, c/o the Tourist Office. But remember, modern bicycles are not permitted!

Castello di Brolio

Reached on **foot** from both Radda and Gaiole (CAI#56), the rose-colored Castello di Brolio provides Chianti's most potent symbol. It was here that vinicultural pioneer Baron Bettino Ricasoli, Unified Italy's second Prime Minister, revamped the recipe of what was previously a mediocre table wine into the superb Chianti you taste today. Tours of his apartments (☎ 057-77301, summer, Mon-Sat, 8 am-noon, 1-7 pm, shorter hours at other times) understandably play second fiddle to the tasting that goes on in the estate's salesrooms.

Castelnuovo Berardenga

Here, you can get a different view of the 14th-century Sienese bastion of Castelnuovo Berardenga by booking a trip with the local **balloon** club (☎ 0577-363232). Back on ground level, a panoramic **bike trip** takes you along a trail (SC#2) past abbeys and monasteries up to the Castello di Montalto, with other itineraries taking you to the 18th-century Villa Chigi-Saracini and the Certosa di Pontignano with its important frescoes by the Florentine, Bernardino Poccetti. This also offers the best of the territory's **horseback riding**, with day treks and weeklong trips bookable from **Centro Ippico della Berardenga** (Podere S. Margherita, Castelnuovo Berardenga, ☎/fax 0577-355071, www.chiantiriding.it, spring to autumn, min. four riders, from €65).

■ Where to Eat

Standards aren't that great on **Greve's** restaurant-covered Piazza Matteoti. **Nerbone di Greve** (Piazza Matteoti 22, ☎ 055-853308, closed Tues, $$) is the best of an inconstant lot for its menu of traditional local dishes like *trippa* (tripe), *bollito* (braised meat), *ribollita* (reboiled cabbage and bread soup) and *tagliatelle al cinghiale* (flat strips of pasta served in a wild boar sauce).

Quality perks up considerably just out of town with the rustic **Borgo Antico** (Via Case Sparse 115, Loc. Lucolena, ☎ 055-851024, closed Tues, $$) and the innovative **Le Cernacchie** (Via Cintoia Alta 11, Loc. La Panca, ☎ 055-8547968, closed Mon, $$). It's well worth the drive. Think sweet and soar wild boar, lemon rabbit and other such originalities.

DINING PRICE CHART	
Price per person for an entrée, including house wine & cover.	
$	Under €20
$$	€21-€40
$$$	€41-€60
$$$$	Over €60

If you just want a light snack with your wine, you can't go wrong with **Le Cantine** (Piazza delle Cantine 2, ☎ 055-8546404, fax 055-8544521, www.lecantine.it), the largest of the Chianti Classico *enoteche* with 120 wines to choose from. Try **Enoteca Fuoripiazza** (Via 1 Maggio 2, Greve in Chianti, ☎ 055-8546313), near Greve's central piazza, which serves Tuscan specialties and wine by the glass.

For great views over the Sienese hills, book a table on the terrace of **L'Albergaccio** (Via Fiorentina 63, ☎ 0577-741042, fax 0577-741250, www.albergacciocast.com , closed Sun, $$$) in **Castellina in Chianti**.

Radda in Chianti is well served by **Le Vigne** (Podere le Vigne, ☎ 0577-738640, $$$) – try the Mancini, a local handmade pasta – and **Il Vignale** (Via XX Settembre 23, ☎/fax 0577-738094, www.vignale.it, $$$, closed Thurs), a part-restaurant, part-winebar, part-fattoria, part-hotel that occupies an old mill.

Outside of Florence

The most atmospheric pick is near **Giaole**, where **Castello di Spaltenna** (Loc. Spaltenna, ☎ 0577-749483, fax 0577-749269, www.spaltenna.it, closed Mon, $$) has a seasonal menu with a list of 250 wines. It's inside an old fortified monastery (booking recommended).

Osteria del Laghetto (Loc. Quornia, ☎ 0577-743125, closed Mon, $$) and **La Bottega del Trenta** (Via S. Caterina 2, Loc. Villa a Sesta, ☎ 0577-359226, evenings only, closed Tues, $$$) offer the best of local fare in the vicinity of **Castelnuovo Berardenga**.

■ Where to Stay

 Hotels: Colle Etrusco **Salivolpi** ☆☆☆ (Via Fiorentina 89, ☎ 0577-740484, fax 0577-740998, www.hotelsalivolpi.com, $$$, 19 rooms) offers traditional farm-style accommodation just outside **Castellina** in an old country house surrounded by vineyards, olive groves and cypress trees. Rooms are furnished in rustic Tuscan style with wrought-iron beds and wooden beams. Large garden with swimming pool. Parking.

The inviting **Albergo Girasole** ☆☆☆ (Via Trento e Trieste 45, **Castellina,** ☎/fax 0577-741327, www.girasole.it, $$$, 12 rooms) is plush in its old-fashioned modernity. The service is friendly, with lots of advice on nearby attractions for first-timers in the region.

HOTEL PRICE CHART	
Rates are per room with private bath, based on double occupancy, including breakfast.	
$	Under €40
$$	€41-€85
$$$	€86-€140
$$$$	€141-€210
$$$$$	Over €210

The views from the swimming pool are enough to warrant a night in the **Relais Vignale** ☆☆☆☆ (Via Pianigiani 8, ☎ 0577-738300, fax 0577-738592, www.vignale.it, $$$$$, 25 rooms), near **Radda**. The converted manor house of a large wine estate has an outdoor pool.

The delightful **Residence San Sano** ☆☆☆ (Loc. San Sano, ☎ 0577-746130, fax 0577-746156, www.sansanohotel.it, $$$, 14 rooms), with its tasty in-house restaurant near **Gaiole**, offers a comfy and friendly introduction to the Chianti region, as well as the chance to stay in a restored defensive structure with 13th-century foundations. Outdoor pool.

The luxury **Villa la Grotta** ☆☆☆☆ (Loc. Brolio, ☎ 0577-747125, fax 0577-747145, www.hotelvillalagrotta.it, $$$$$, three rooms + nine apartments) sits on the slopes of Pratomagno (follow signs to San Guistino Valdarno) in a restored 19th-century villa and adjacent farmhouse. Indoor pool and spa facilities.

Occupying a 16th-century villa, **Villa Curina** (Loc. Curina, ☎ 0577-355630, fax 0577-355610, www.villacurina.it, $$$, seven rooms) near **Castelnuovo Berardenga**, offers a romantic break with its four-poster beds, large tree-lined garden to wander through and small chapel decorated with a fresco by Arcangelo Salimbeni. Outdoor pool.

Four miles from **Castelnuovo Berardenga**, the prestigious **Relais Borgo San Felice** ☆☆☆☆ (Loc. San Felice 4, ☎ 0577-3964, fax 0577-359089, www.borgosanfelice.com, $$$$$, 43 rooms) sits in a restored medieval hamlet with rooms in the main palazzo or in the medieval stone homes. Outdoor pool and leisure facilities.

Agriturismi: Two miles from **Radda**, **Agriturismo Poggerino** ☆☆ (Via Poggerino 6, ☎ 0577-738958, fax 0577-738051, www.poggerino.com, $$, five apartments, min. week stay, Apr-Oct) has semi-isolated apartments for two or four guests, attached to a 12th-century church, deep in the Chianti countryside and perfect for a romantic or rural break. Outdoor pool.

Around **Castellina**, your best choices are the **Castello di Fonterutoli** ☆☆☆ (Via Oltone III 5, Loc. Fonterutoli, ☎ 0577-73571, fax 0577-735757, www.fonterutoli.it, $$$, four apartments), **Querceto** ☆☆☆☆ (Loc. Querceto, ☎ 0577-733590, fax 0577-733636, www.querceto.com, $$$, nine apartments) or **Relais Riserva di Fizzano** ☆☆☆ (Loc. Fizzano, ☎ 0577-7371, fax 0577-743163, www.roccadellemacie.com, $$$$, 19 apartments), the latter run by the Rocca delle Macie vineyard.

How many times do you get the chance to stay in a castle? **Castello Meleto** (Loc. Castello Meleto, ☎ 0577-79217, fax 0577-749762, www.castellomeleto.it, $$$$, six apartments, min. week stay) near **Gaiole** offers you the chance to do just that. Well almost; the apartments are attached to the walls of the fortress, which was added by the Ricasoli family in the 15th century.

Near **Castelnuovo Berardenga, Canonica a Cerreto** ☆☆☆ (Loc. Canonica a Cerreto, ☎/fax 0577-363261, www.canonicacerreto.it, $$$, three apartments, min. week stay, Apr-Oct) occupies a medieval monastery and former summer villa of the Archbishop of Siena. It's now part of a wine- and olive oil-producing estate with three self-sufficient apartments and outdoor pool.

Camping & Hostel: The area's main campgrounds are found in the surroundings of Florence (see page 83) and Siena (see page 158), but there is a good youth hostel in Greve in Chianti (**Villa San Michele**, Loc. San Michele, Via Casole 42, ☎ 055-851034, fax 055-851034, Apr-Nov, $).

Outside of Florence

Siena

N HUNTER PUBLISHING

- San Gimignano **4**
- Fiume Elsa
- Castellina in Chianti
- Arezzo
- Poggibonsi
- Radda in Chianti
- Colle di Val d'Elsa
- Castiglion Fiorentino
- **3**
- Monteriggione **2**
- Castelnuovo Berardenga
- Fiume Arbia
- SIENA **1**
- Cásole d'Elsa **11**
- Sovicille
- Taverne d'Arbia
- Fiume Ombrone
- Rapolano Terme
- VAL DI CHIANA
- Rosia
- 78
- A1
- Asciano
- Chiusdino
- **6**
- Fiume Merse
- **5**
- Sinalunga
- 78
- Monticiano
- Buon-convento
- **10**
- Montepulciano
- Bagni di Petriolo
- Pienza
- Montalcino **7**
- **8**
- Chianciano Terme
- Chiusi
- S. Quírico d'Órcia
- **9**
- Sarteano
- THE MAREMMA
- Fiume Órcia
- Fiume Órcia
- A1
- Badia San Filippo
- Sasso d'Ombrone
- Castel del Piano
- 80
- 78
- Arcidosso
- Abbadia San Salvatore
- Casciano dei Bagni
- Fiume Ombrone

NOT TO SCALE

1. SIENA: Piazza del Campo, Duomo, Pinacoteca Nazionale, Museo Storia Naturale Accademia dei Fisiocritica, Basilica di San Francesco, Oratorio di San Bernardino, Basilica di Santa Maria di Provenzano, Santuario di Santa Caterina da Siena, Fortezza Medicea, Centro d'Arte Contemporanea, Torre del Mangia
2. The Montagnola
3. Montriggione: Abbadia Isola, Chiesa dei Santi Salvatore e Cirino, Eremo di San Leonardo al Lago, Monte Maggio
4. San Gimignano & The Valdelsa: Chiesa di San Francesco, Torre della Rognosa, Collegiata Santa Maria Assunta, Museo d'Arte Sacra, Rocca di Montestaffoli, Chiesa di Sant'Agostino, Museo Archeologico, Galleria d'Arte Moderna e Contemporanea, Museo Criminale Medioevale
5. The Crete: Valdarbia Trails, Museo della Grancia, Collegiata di Sant'Agata, Museo Civico Archeologico e d'Arte Sacra, Museo Cassioli, Abbazia di Monte Oliveto Maggiore, Museo della Mezzadria Senese

6. Val di Merse: Alto Merse, Basso Merse & Tucchí Nature Reserves
7. Montalcino: Chiesa di Sant'Egidio, Chiesa di Sant'Agostino, Musei Civico e Diocesano, Duomo, Abbazia di Sant'Antimo
8. Pienza: Palazzo Borgia, Duomo, Museo Diocesano, Chiesa di San Francesco, Riserva Naturale di Lucciobella
9. The Valdorcia: San Quírico d'Órcia, Collegiata dei Santi Quírico e Giulitta, Palazzo Chigi, Parco dei Mulini, Horti Leonini, Castiglione d'Órcia, Rocca d'Órcia
10. Montepulciano & Val di Chiana – Duomo, Chiesa di Sant'Agnese, Palazzo Avignonensi, Fattoria di Pulciano, Palazzo Buccelli, Torre del Pulcinella, Arco della Cavina, Teatro Poliziano, Museo Civico Pinacoteca Crociani; Chiusi – Museo Archeologico Nazionale, Duomo, Museo della Cattedrale, Labirinto Etrusco, Catacombe, Riserve Naturale di Lago di Chiusi, Monte Cetona, Parco del Bianchetto
11. Colline Metallifere

Siena & its Surroundings

Most visitors arriving from the hustle and crowds of busy Florence cannot help but fall under the charm of Siena's gracefully winding (and pedestrianized) medieval streets. Laid out on the slopes of three steep hills (the historical terzi or "thirds" of the city), the center of town, geographically and emotionally, is the fan-shaped and gently sloping, redbrick Piazza del Campo, a wonderfully preserved monument to Siena's medieval heyday when merchants, bankers and artists flocked here and some of the city's greatest monuments were

constructed. Overlooked by the Palazzo Pubblico and the Torre del Mangia, it is also the site of the famous bareback horserace, Il Palio and a fitting starting point for the exploration of Siena's other major sights.

NOT TO BE MISSED

- **Piazza del Campo**: Square of medieval delights (see page 143).
- **Duomo**: Glorious monument to Sienese wealth and pretensions (see page 146).
- **The *Bottini***: The underground aqueducts that feed Siena's fountains (see page 144).
- **Santa Maria della Scala**: One of Europe's first hospitals with glorious "this is your life" fresco (see page 148).
- **The views**: Climb to the top of Torre del Mangia (see page 145) or the uncompleted *facciatone* (see page 147) for a bird's-eye view of the city and province.
- **The museums**: Pinacoteca Nazionale (Sienese art at its grandest, Museo Civico (startling pre-Renaissance frescoes), Museo dell'Opera del Duomo (Duccio's unforgettable *Maestà* and much more).

Getting Here

By Air: Most visitors arrive via Pisa's **Aeroporto Galileo Galilei** (☎ 050-849111, www.pisa-airport.com) from where hourly trains run to Empoli, which links with services to Siena. Tickets can be purchased inside the airport Arrivals Hall. From Florence's **Aeroporto Amerigo Vespucci** (☎ 055-3061700, www.safnet.it) to the northwest of the city, **Sita/Ataf** (☎ 800-424500, www.ataf.net, ☎ 800-373760 www.sita-on-line.it) run a "vola in bus" (air bus) service to Firenze S.M.N. (€4 one-way, buy on board) from where you can catch a train or coach to Siena.

Siena

The small airport near Sovicille (Loc. Ampugnano, ☎ 0577-392226/7438990, www.siena-airport.it) outside Siena is currently served only by **Air Alps** (www.airalps.at) with flights from Vienna.

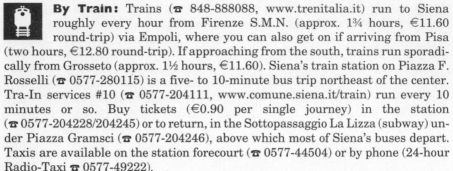

By Train: Trains (☎ 848-888088, www.trenitalia.it) run to Siena roughly every hour from Firenze S.M.N. (approx. 1¾ hours, €11.60 round-trip) via Empoli, where you can also get on if arriving from Pisa (two hours, €12.80 round-trip). If approaching from the south, trains run sporadically from Grosseto (approx. 1½ hours, €11.60). Siena's train station on Piazza F. Rosselli (☎ 0577-280115) is a five- to 10-minute bus trip northeast of the center. Tra-In services #10 (☎ 0577-204111, www.comune.siena.it/train) run every 10 minutes or so. Buy tickets (€0.90 per single journey) in the station (☎ 0577-204228/204245) or to return, in the Sottopassaggio La Lizza (subway) under Piazza Gramsci (☎ 0577-204246), above which most of Siena's buses depart. Taxis are available on the station forecourt (☎ 0577-44504) or by phone (24-hour Radio-Taxi ☎ 0577-49222).

By Bus: SITA coaches (☎ 800-373760, www.sita-on-line.it) run around four times an hour from Florence bus station via Poggibonsi and Colle Val d'Elsa (1½ hour, 1¼ hour if non-stop) €6.50 one-way (€13 round-trip); validate your tickets on the bus. **Sena** (☎ 0577-283203/247934, www.sena.it) runs services to and from Rome and **Tra-In** to and from Grosseto and Arezzo (☎ 0577-204111, www.trainspa.it). **Rama** (☎ 0564-475111, www.griforama.it) #18 runs between Florence and Grosseto, stopping just outside Siena's Porta Camollia every hour.

By Car: From Florence and the north, Siena is reached on the **SS2 Cassia**, which continues into the southeast of the province (if arriving via the A1, take the "Firenze-Certosa" exit and follow signs to the SS2). From Grosseto and the south, you can reach the city on the **SS223** (if arriving from the south on the A1, take the "Val di Chiana-Sinalunga" and follow signs to the SS223).

Tip: The Italian Autostrade Company (www.autostrade.it) has an online route planner in English.

Your best chance for **parking** is up by the Fortezza Medici, where there are three large parking bays on Viale XXV Aprile, Viale V. Veneto and Viale R. Franci, as well as the car park by the nearby stadium. If arriving from the south or west, opt instead for the car parks just outside Porta Fontebranda and just inside Porta Romana. For further information, contact Siena Parcheggi (☎ 0577-288711 www.sienaparcheggi.com).

Car Rental: Cars can be rented from **Avis** (Via Simone Martini 36, ☎ 0577-270305, www.avisautonoleggio.it), **Hertz** (Viale Sardegna 37, ☎ 0577-45085, www.hertz.it), **Alessandro De Romanis** (Via Duccio di Buoninsegna 10, ☎ 0577-226974), and **General Car** (Viale Toselli 20/26, ☎ 0577-40518, fax 0577-47984). For car rental from Pisa and Florence airports, see page 32.

Information Sources

Tourist Offices: APT Siena (Siena tourist office) is on the central Piazza del Campo (☎ 0577-280551, fax 0577-281041, www.terresiena.it, Mon-Sat, 8:30 am-7:30 pm, Sun and public holidays, 9 am-3 pm). They have maps of the town and an information booklet on cycling in the province (*Biking Through Siena's Countryside*) with detailed itineraries on artistic and historic themes. For more information on the province's natural parks, contact **Riserve Naturali** (Nature Reserves, Via delle Sperandie 47, ☎ 0577-241416, fax 0577-241419, www.riservenaturali.provincia.siena.it, Mon-Fri, 8 am-2 pm, and Tues and Thurs, 3-5:30 pm).

Guides & Maps: *Toscana in Mountain Bike, Volume II: Preappennino-parte prima* (S. Grillo and C. Pezzani, Ediciclo Editore) features 31 mountain bike itineraries of choice through the Chianti, Montagnola, Crete Senesi, Colline Metallifere, Val d'Orcia and Monte Amiata. V*iaggio sul Treno Natura* (Stefano Maggi and APT Siena, Nuova Immagine) sets out the itineraries of CAI treks along the routes of the Treno Natura (see page 150, 171).

Carta Stradale Provinciale, scale 1:100,000 (Provincial Road Map, Edizione Multigraphic Firenze) and *La Via Francigena in provincia di Siena,* scale 1:175,000 Touring Map, Touring Club Italiano) are the best maps for drivers, with *Itinerari nella Montagnola Senese,* scale: 1:25,000 (Touring and Trail map, CAI and Edizioni Multigraphic Firenze) your best bet for hiking and mountain bike routes.

Siena

■ Sightseeing

Piazza del Campo: With curved palazzi, brick arches, bustling caffè-terraces and a vast redbrick sloping square that leads the eye and the feet down to the Palazzo Pubblico (the town hall), prepare to be enamored by Siena's Piazza del Campo. For those lucky enough to arrive in season, 2nd July and 16th August (plus four days of pre-race trials) see the outer perimeter of the square fenced off and covered with sand for the famous Palio bareback horserace, a dazzling spectacle of local culture in which 10 of Siena's 17 *contrade* (neighborhoods) compete to the cries of their impassioned supporters.

> **Something Different:** For the unusual sight of eagles and falcons flying above Siena's towers, head to the falconry shows on Vallata di Porta Guistizia, just a short distance from Piazza del Campo (☎ 333-4499345, Mar-Nov, shows at 12, 2:30 and 5:30 pm, €8, conc. €6.50, children under six, free).

Il Palio

Age-old *contrade* or neighborhood rivalries come to the fore in Siena's twice-yearly bareback horserace, a competition that still provokes tears and more than the occasional fight. The race itself, three hectic laps around Piazza del Campo, lasts just over a minute (not counting the numerous false starts) and the prize (the

Siena

banner from which the event takes its name) is given to the winning horse, whether its jockey has managed to hang on or not. Opened by parades in historical costume and some impressive flag throwing, the event is thought to have its roots in the victory celebrations after the Battle of Monteaperti but was more than likely instigated as a means of giving a harmless outlet to antagonism between rival *contrade*.

You have two options when it comes to viewing Il Palio: squash yourself in with the majority of spectators on the Piazza del Campo (inside the race track) or buy a seat in the grandstands or at a window of one of the private residences overlooking the piazza. Both take some organisation. To find a place on the square you should arrive around 2 pm, but if you don't want to wait all day in the sun, the latest you can enter is around 6 pm (follow the crowds through Via Giovanni Duprè to the Piazza del Mercato behind the Palazzo Pubblico). Be prepared to push and be pushed as you enter. Tickets should be purchased up to six months in advance of the race from Palio Viaggi (Piazza Gramsci 7, ☎ 0577-280828) or directly from local shops and buildings (contact the Tourist Board for a list of current outlets). If you arrive out of Palio season, the Cinema Moderno on Piazza Tolomei shows a 20-minute history of the event (nine daily showings in English, Apr-Oct, Mon-Sat, 9:30 am-6 pm), which does an impressive job of conveying its atmosphere and traditions. (Information, ☎ 0577-280551, www.ilpaliodisiena.com.)

Fonte Gaia: The piazza's centerpiece is the marble Fonte Gaia (Fountain of Joy), a copy of the original Jacopo della Quercia monument (1409-19), a 15th-century sculptural masterpiece considered "Queen of Sienese Fountains" and almost destroyed by centuries of exposure (remains can be seen in the loggia of the Palazzo Pubblico). The water that rushes inside comes from hills situated 16 miles away along an aqueduct that has served the city since the 14th century.

Going Deeper Underground

Built on top of three hills a considerable distance away from the region's main waterways, Siena saw much medieval head scratching when it came to the important question of watering the growing city. Building on existing veins that had survived since Roman and even Etruscan eras, local workmen completed a 16-mile network of underground tunnels and cavities known as the *bottini*, "little barrels," a vast underground aqueduct that to this day serves the Fonte Gaia and all other city fountains. It takes some forward planning, but it's well worth contacting Associazione La Diana (www.comune.siena.it/diana, ☎ 0577-41110) for a guided visit to the *bottini* (spring and autumn only when water levels permit, written request by fax to 0577-292346 indicating your contact details and number of participants). Be aware that the current waiting time is over six months.

Palazzo Pubblico: Built of local red brick and stone between 1284 and 1305 to serve as the headquarters of the Government of the Nine (hence the nine sections on the Piazza del Campo), this huge Gothic palazzo today houses the head office of the City Council. You can take a tour around the Museo Civico (www.comune.siena.it/museocivico, Mar-Oct, 10 am-7 pm, Nov-Feb, 10 am-5:30 pm, €6.50 conc. €4), its walls covered in pre-Renaissance frescoes including Simone Martini's *Maestà* (1312) and *Equestrian Portrait of Guidoriccio da Folgiano* (1328, both Sala del Mappamondo) and Ambrogio Lorenzetti's famous *Allegories of Good and Bad Government* (1337, Sala della Pace, the Room of Peace), a huge cycle depicting Siena's bustling streets, local gentry and rural workers in action in the 14th century.

THE GOVERNMENT OF THE NINE

In a history otherwise characterized by internal and external conflict, Siena enjoyed a relatively trouble-free period of wealth, urban development and artistic boom under the so-called Government of the Nine (1287-1355). Civic monuments such as the Piazza del Campo and Palazzo Pubblico were constructed, the main streets were paved with stone or brick, and an attempt to build the largest cathedral in Christendom was initiated. The arrival of the Plague in 1348 soon put an end to this stint of growth, decimating three-fifths of the city's population and, along with another bout of political infighting, left the city open for archenemy Florence to make its move.

The strenuous climb to the top of the slender 14th-century **Torre del Mangia** (erected 1338-45, Mar-Oct, 10 am-7 pm, Nov-Feb, 10 am-4 pm, €5.50), the 88-m (289-foot) bell tower of the Palazzo Pubblico is well worth the effort. At the top of the 412 steps you have wonderful views over Piazza del Campo, the Duomo and the winding cobbled streets that lead into the city.

A right out of the piazza will take you to the first of the two 15th-century Piccolomini palazzi (**Palazzo Piccolomini**, Via Banchi di Sotto 52, Mon/Fri, 8 am-2 pm, Sat, 8 am-1:45 pm, Tues-Thurs, 8 am-5:30 pm, closed Sun and holidays, free) designed for the Renaissance humanist Enea Silvio Piccolomini (whose career as Pope Pius II is detailed in the Duomo Libreria) who also commissioned its architect, Bernardo Rossellino, to redesign an ideal city for his hometown of Pienza. Today, other than the State Archive, it houses the *Biccherne*, a collection of 103 wooden account book covers painted by the best of Sienese artists between the 13th and 18th centuries. Before heading in, check out the grandiose Logge del Papa, opposite to your left, another of Piccolomini's Renaissance commissions, this time to sculptor and architect Antonio Federighi in 1462.

Siena

Follow Via di Banchi around the Piazza del Campo to arrive on Via di Città and the second Piccolomini palazzo, **Palazzo delle Papesse** (the Palace of the She-Popes), built 1460-1495 for Caterina Piccolomini, sister of Pope Pius II and now home to the **Centro di Arte Contemporanea** (Center of Contemporary Art, www.papesse.org, Tues-Sun, 12 am-7 pm, €5 conc. €3.50).

En route, look for the impressive **Palazzo Chigi-Saracini** (Via di Città 89). Built by the Marescotti family in the 12th century – check out their eagle coat of arms above the mullioned windows – it passed first to the Saracini family before being restored by Count Guido Chigi Saracini to house the musical foundation he started, Accademia Musicale Chigiana (☎ 0577-22091, fax 0577-288124, www.chigiana.it).

Via di Città will also lead you to **Piazza Postierla**, or the "Quattro Cantoni" (the four corners) as it known to locals, an important crossroads, which marks the center of the Contrada dell'Aquila (the Eagle) – their motifs decorate the tiny central fountain – with the cathedral to the north (up Via del Capitano) and the city art gallery to the south.

The Contrade

Siena's 17 *contrade* (neighborhoods) play a central role in their residents' social life, not least in the twice-yearly Palio (see page 143). Each has its own church for weddings (the fervor of members is such that even today it isn't considered a good idea to marry into another *contrada*), its own fountain for baptisms with its heraldic logo (usually an animal) on display, its own museum depicting its unique history and Palio trophies. Just wandering the streets, you can see the colors, flags and emblems hanging from the windows of the various *contrade*. *Contrade* museums can be visited by arrangement with the tourist office (try to arrange a visit at least a week in advance if you're arriving at Palio time).

Duomo (Cathedral, Piazza del Duomo, Mar-Oct, 7:30 am-7:30 pm, Nov-Feb, 7:30 am-5 pm, free): Constructed from 1136 to a design by Giovanni di Pisano, Siena's cathedral was meant to be the biggest church in the Christian world until the plague, rising costs and technical difficulties all combined to put a spanner in the works. But, incomplete though it may be, it remains one of the most spectacular cathedrals in Italy for its black

and white marble façade, a mix of Romanesque and Gothic styles, and equally decorative interior. On entering you'll be immediately struck by the magnificent marble floors. Designed by Beccafumi (who is also to be thanked for the angel-decorated pillars), it took over 40 artists almost 200 years to complete the 52 biblical accounts it includes. Other works of importance include Donatello's bronze *St John the Baptist* (left transept) and the stunning marble pulpit decorated with statues of the Saints and Virgin and Child carved by Nicola Pisano in 1265. There are also two of his later works, *Mary Magdalen* and *St Jerome*, in the Bernini-designed Cappella Pontificia (on the right), along with the 13th-century *Madonna del Voto* in front of which the citizens of Siena delivered the "l'atto di votazione" on the eve of the famous battle of Monteaperti. From the cathedral interior you can also reach the Libreria Piccolomini (Mar-Oct, Mon-Sat, 9 am-7:30 pm, Sun and holidays, 1:30-7:30 pm, Nov-Feb, 10 am-1 pm, 2-5 pm, €1.50). Its fresh-looking frescoes were painted in 1502-07 by Pinturicchio to illustrate the life of Pope Pius II.

THE BATTLE OF MONTEAPERTI

Sienese history is wrought by economic rivalry and territorial conflict with neighboring Florence – the Guelph, or anti-imperial adversary to Siena's pro-imperial, or Ghibelline, stance. The two groups were at each other's throats throughout the Middle Ages. The clash reached its pinnacle on September 4, 1260 when the Sienese crushed the Florentines at the Battle of Monteaperti. Success was short-lived, with Florence having its definitive revenge just nine years later.

Museo dell'Opera del Duomo (Museum of the Cathedral, Piazza Jacopo della Quercia, ☎ 0577-283048, fax 0577-280626, www.operaduomo.it, Mar-Sept, 9 am-7:30 pm, Oct, 9 am-6 pm, Nov-Feb, 9 am-1:30 pm, €5.50): Occupying part of the unfinished nave, one of this museum's biggest draws has to be the exceptional views from the parapet on top of the *facciatone* (part of the uncompleted façade – the wall you see to your right as you approach the museum). Up here you'll also get to envision just how big the cathedral was supposed to be. But that's not all. Its ground floor displays carvings from the original façade, including Pisano's marble life-size figures (1284-90), and Duccio's famous *Maestà* (*Madonna and Child Enthroned,* 1308-11, Sala di Duccio, first floor), detail shown above, the largest piece of art to come out of the Middle Ages. Opposite it are the *Scenes of the Passion*, which were originally created on its back. There's also a *Virgin and Child* by the artist and a triptych *Nativity of the Virgin* by Pietro Lorenzetti in the room.

Battistero di San Giovanni (Baptistry, Piazza San Giovanni, Mar-Sept, 9 am-7:30 pm, Oct, 9 am-6 pm, Nov-Feb, 9 am-1 pm, 2-5 pm, €2.50): The steps leading down from the right side of the cathedral bring you to the unfinished marble façade of the Gothic Battistero (built between 1316 and 1325). It is the home of Jacopo della Quercia's superb marble font (1411-30) decorated with bronze reliefs by Ghiberti (*Baptism of Christ*, 1424-27) and Donatello (*Feast of Herod, Faith* and *Hope*).

Sala del Pellegrinaio, Santa Maria della Scala

Santa Maria della Scala (Piazza del Duomo, ☎ 0577-224811, fax 0577-224829, www.santamaria.comune.siena.it, 16 Mar-Oct, 10 am-6 pm, Nov-15 Mar, 10:30 am-4:30 pm, €5.20 conc. €3.10): Just opposite the entrance to the Duomo, this was one of Europe's first hospitals, set up by the canons of the Cathedral to offer pilgrims of the Via Francigena hospitality. Its history is portrayed in the frescoes that decorate its Sala del Pellegrinaio (The Pilgrims' Ward). Realized by Dominico Bartolo, with the collaboration of other painters, including Vecchietta, in 1440, it provides a lively insight into both the history of the hospital and the society of the time. Other rooms of interest include the Sagrestia Vecchia (the Old Sacristy), the Cappella delle Reliquie (with lunette by Domenico Beccafumi), the Cappella della Madonna and the Chiesa della SS. Annunziata. The Marcacci, Novaro and Stretta rooms host the **Museo Archeologico** (same opening hours), which exhibits Etruscan and Toman remains taken mainly from the Siena and Chiusi areas.

Return to the Piazza Postierla to pick up Via San Pietro to the **Pinacoteca Nazionale** (the National Painting Gallery, Palazzo Buonsignori, Via San Pietro 29, ☎ 0577-281161, fax 0577-286143, Mon, 8:30 am-1 pm, Tues-Sat, 8:15 am-7:15 pm, Sun and holidays, 8:15 am-1:15 pm, €4.30, conc. €2), a must visit for its collection of Sienese art from the 12th to the mid-17th century. It features works by masters Simone Martini (*Madonna col Bambino*), Ambrogio (*Annunciation*) and Pietro Lorenzetti (*Risen Christ*), Giovanni di Paolo (*Madonna dell'Umiltà*) and Duccio di Buoninsegna (*Madonna dei Francescani*).

South from the Pinacoteca, you'll come to the vast **Chiesa di Sant'Agostino** (Via P. A. Mattioli, 10:30 am-1:30 pm, 3-5:30 pm, €2, conc. €1.50), its original 13th-century shell heavily renovated in the 18th century after fire damage. It's worth a diversion for the early 17th-century treasures that include a *Crucifixion* by Perugino, the only known frescoes by Francesco di Giorgio (in Chapel Bichi) and a *Maestà* fresco by Ambrogio Lorenzetti (in the Chapel Piccolomini). Retrace your steps and take a left on Via Pendola past **Cappella delle Carceri di Sant'Ansano**. Siena's first martyr, and later patron saint, Sant'Ansano was undeterred by his jail fetters as he continued to baptize the townsfolk from the tower's little window. Proceed to the Carmelite **San Niccolò al Carmine** on Piano dei Mantellini (from *mantelli*, the Carmelite capes). Among its art works on display is the second *St Michael* by Mannerist Domenico Beccafumi, his first attempt (housed in the Pinacoteca) considered far too rude for the prudish occupants.

SOMETHING FOR THE KIDS

There's a little bit of everything from the Sienese province in the **Museo di Storia Naturale Accademia dei Fisiocritici** (Natural History Museum, Prato di S. Agostino 5, ☎ 0577-47002, www.accademiafisiocritici.it, Mon-Fri, 9 am-1 pm, 3-6 pm, free), including some small fossils found on Amiata and a display entirely devoted to funghi, mushrooms.

Head back to Piazza del Campo and turn north along Via Banchi di Sopra to the Terzo di Camollia, the city "third" that encloses some of its most important churches. You'll encounter the first along Via dei Rossi, a vast aircraft hanger of a church – the late 13th-century **Basilica di San Francesco**. Its construction, according to local legend, was funded by donations from Siena's conscience-stricken lowlife underworld, anxious to save their souls. A fire destroyed most of the original works of art in the early 17th century, but the fragments of frescoes by brothers Pietro and Ambrogio Lorenzetti are still well worth a look.

Also overlooking the Piazza San Francisco, the **Oratorio di San Bernardino**, with enclosed **Museo Diocesano di Arte Sacra** (Museum of Sacred Art, Piazza San Francesco 9, Mar-Oct, 10:30 am-1:30 pm/3-5:30 pm, €2.50), was built during the 1400s on the site of the Saint's former preaching ground. Its interior features some splendid Mannerist frescoes by Domenico Beccafumi and Sodoma (a huge cycle depicting the *Life of the Virgin*), a *Madonna del Latte* by Pietro Lorenzetti and other works by Ventura Salimbeni, Raffaello Vanni and Rutilio Manetti spread out over its two floors. The lofty **Basilica di Santa Maria di Provenzano** is on Piazza Provenzano; it sprang up in 1595 to house a "miraculous" image of the Madonna (the one commemorated by the July Palio), which was partly destroyed by the wayward bullet of a Spanish soldier in 1552.

Back on Banchi di Sopra, take a right through Vicolo della Torre and you'll reach **Santuario di Santa Caterina da Siena** (entrance on Costa di Sant'Antonio, 9 am-12:30 pm, 3-6 pm, free). Watch for the seven arches of the Via della Galluzza off to your right en route. The Portico dei Comuni d'Italia provides a pretty solemn introduction to what was once the home of the Patron Saint of Italy. She was the Doctor of the Church most responsible for mediating between the papal and anti-papal claims of the Great Schism. The stone pillow in Oratorio della Camera (her bedroom) gives a pretty good indication of her altruistic approach to life. The sanctuary's other main sight is the 12th-century wooden crucifix in the chapel where she received the Stigmata.

Saint Catherine of Siena, Neroccio di Bartolomeo Landi, 1447-1500

Down at the Porta Fontebranda and a steep climb up Vicolo di Camporegio (a former dirt path known as the Costa del Serpe after the snakes once scurrying in its wild undergrowth) brings you to the site of St. Catherine's remains (and not much else), the 13th-century **Basilica di San Domenico**. Just to its left, there's a great view over the roofs and streets of the elegant San Prospero neighborhood (easily recognized by its Art Nouveau villas) to the city cathedral.

From here it's just a short stroll to the **Fortezza Medicea** (also known as the Forte di Santa Barbara) with the Enoteca Italiana wine bar (Fortezza Medicea 1, Siena, ☎ 0577-288497, fax 0577-270717, www.enoteca-italiana.it, closed Sun and Mon), making a perfect end to the walk. Before you head inside, take a quick jaunt around the 16th-century walls, now also home to **Siena Jazz** (one of the most important jazz schools in Europe), for some magnificent city views.

Siena

Join a Walking Tour

AGT Siena (Piazza Madre Teresa di Calcutta 5, ☎ 0577-43273, fax 0577-279717, www.guidesiena.it, various prices dependent on number of participants) organizes tours of Siena in English, including walks for younger and older visitors and more unusual passages into Siena's heritage of wine and gastronomy.

The nationwide **Legambiente** runs a variety of urban tours (☎ 055-6810330, fax 055-6811620, www.legambiente.com), including treks around the historical center, a walking tour of the city's artisan and artistic heritage and a culinary tour with *degustazione* of ancient Sienese recipes (day tour €48 per person).

You're guaranteed a personal tour with local **Roberto Becchi** (c/o Patricia Becchi, Via del F. Vecchio 14, Serre di Rapolano, ☎ 0577-704789, www.toursbyroberto.com), who offers anything and everything from half-day tours of Siena to painting, wine-tasting, cooking and craft tutorials (from €65 per person dependent on number in group, maximum eight).

If the thought of following an umbrella around town fills you with shame or dread, opt instead for the Siena Tourist Board's **self-guided audio tour** (full day €15.95).

■ Adventures

Siena sits in prime hiking, bike riding and horseback riding territory with Chianti on one side, Val d'Elsa on the other and the Val d'Orcia, the Val di Chiana and Monte Amiata farther to the southeast. From the town itself you can easily strike out into the Montagnola Sienese, while the trails around the Val di Merse are a little farther south (both are detailed in this section). Do bear in mind that hiking in this region takes a little planning. Most of the marked trails run through, rather than loop, the countryside, meaning you often have to retrace your steps or pick up public transport to return to your starting point (join a local trekking group or opt for an all-inclusive deal if you want to avoid the fuss). Cyclists have an easier time of it, with plenty of nearly deserted back roads and *strade bianche* to enjoy.

On Foot

If you're departing from Siena itself, you can follow up steps of Sienese foot soldiers en route to the battlefields of Monteaperti north of the city (marked by a commemorative stone), a 13-mile trail (provincial trail #2, Siena-Montalcino-Amiata) that first takes you past the 94° baths of the Terme di Aqua Borra. If you don't want to walk the 13 miles, you can pick up a five-mile trail to the same spot from Taverne d'Arbia (eight miles away on the Tra-In bus route). You can also pick up the next stage of the Firenze-Siena-Roma, 25-stage footpath, which takes you north in the direction of Florence or south to Monte Amiata and over into the Grosseto province.

Hop aboard the **Treno Natura** (Piazza Rosselli 5, ☎ 0577-207413, ☎ 0577-207343, www.ferrovieturistiche.it, 10 daily services) into the Arbia and Ombrone valleys (Siena-Buonconvento-Monte Antico), where at each stop CAI trails either lead you back round in a loop or take you to the next station where you can hop back onboard the train to Siena.

Organized Tours

You can join the Siena branch of the **CAI** (Viale Mazzini 95, ☎/fax 0577-270666, caisiena@libero.it) on their Sun treks into the province without joining as a member. The group is a great source of information, having marked most of the territory's trails.

The nationwide **Legambiente** organizes a variety of treks in the outskirts of Siena (☎ 055-6810330, fax 055-6811620, www.legambiente.com), leaving from the city. One is a walking tour of the Crete (see page 169) with an opportunity to sample typical products and visits by coach to towns such as Buonconvento and San Giovanni d'Asso; day tours cost €48 per person.

Tours by **Roberto Becchi** (c/o Patricia Becchi, Via del F. Vecchio 14, Serre di Rapolano, ☎ 0577-704789, www.toursbyroberto.com) offer an interesting truffle hunting tour (in season), guided visits into the Val d'Elsa and Chianti, treks around Etruscan tombs in Montagnola and two-day tours to the Maremma and Val d'Elsa (from €65 per person depending on number in group, maximum eight).

All Around Siena (Banchi di Sopra 31, ☎ 0577-40919, fax 0577-217844, www.allaroundsiena.com, Mon-Fri 9 am-1 pm, 2-6 pm) offers a variety of guided walks into the surrounding countryside, including a one-day tour around Siena (from Porta Romana south to Vico d'Arbia) and trips into all the regions featured in this chapter.

Into the Montagnola

Montagnola is the group of hills to the west of Siena, peaking just south of Monteriggioni. It's a great area for hikers and riders with plenty of Roman and Etruscan archeological sites, and pretty little villages to explore. Most itineraries can be picked up in **Sovicille** and **Rosia**, easily within cycling distance of the city on the SS73 (Bus #106) or from Santa Colomba to the west (Bus #37).

The local unit of CAI maintains a network of trails departing from Santa Colomba (CAI#102 to Monteriggioni, CAI#106 to Abbadia Isola, and CAI#114 through Tegoia to Molino d'Elsa), Rosia (CAI#118 to Tonni, CAI#119 to Tegoia) and Sovicille (CAI#122 to Santa Colomba). There are only two circular trails, CAI#123 (Lecceto – San Leonardo al Lago – Pastine – Pianali – Toiano – Lecceto) and CAI#125 (Valli – Le Piagge – Valli).

From Sovicille, there's also a 12-mile circuit taking you past the Etruscan necropolis of Malignano, the medieval village of Torri and across the River Merse to Orgia and the Museo Etnografico del Bosco.

At the **Museo Etnografico del Bosco** (Orgia, ☎ 0577-582323) there's a pleasant three-mile guided nature walk to be enjoyed along a well-laid out network of paths tracing traditional rural activity such as chestnut cultivation, woodcutting and charcoal burning. In late spring and late summer, there's also an actual charcoal furnace that charts the various stages of its conversion. Kids will love the folk stories of rural tradition provided by the guides.

Into the Val di Merse

Farther to the south, the Val di Merse is a local hotspot for **fishing**, **canoeing** and **hiking**, rife with local fauna (roebucks, wild boars, fallow deer and birds of prey). The zone itself runs from Colline Metallifere (the Metal Hills) just north of Chiusdino and across the valley to join the Ombrone River near Murlo and includes three nature reserves, the sulfuric waters of Petriolo and one of Tuscany's most-visited abbeys.

Siena

The best of the Val di Merse routes depart from the thousand-year-old village of **Chiusdino** (Bus #122). If you have time for only one, opt for the 11-mile circular trek along *strade bianche,* past the Montagne Rosse (Red Mountains) to the **Abbazia di San Galgano** and the **Chiesa di Montesiepi**.

Religious Remains

 Surrounded by trees and gentle fields, the abandoned 13th-century **Abbazia di San Galgano** more than lives up to its picturesque reputation as the "abbey without a roof." The skeleton that remains (with grass floor and sky roof) is a fascinating example of Cistercian Gothic architecture, best visited in the early morning or late afternoon when its pointed arches and shapely windows create an atmospheric shadow. If you're here around 25 July-20 August, you're in for a treat; the Festival di Chiusdino (information ☎ 0577-756738) includes prose, classical music, opera and dance performances in the abbey.

Arthurian legends are reversed with the "sword in the stone" taken from the abbey and displayed at the nearby Romanesque **Chiesa di Montesiepi**. Rather than St. Galgano pulling the sword from the stone, he plunged it in, creating with the hilt the shape of the Cross. While you're here, there are also some lovely Andrea Lorenzetti frescoes to enjoy.

Chiusdino and **Monticiano** are also in the region's three **nature reserves** (Alto Merse, Tocchi and Basso Merse), all of which have trails suitable for strolls. For information on the monthly openings of trails, contact Refettorio dell'Abbazia di San Galgano (☎ 0577-756738, www.riservenaturali.provincia.siena.it, June-Sept, 10:30 am-6:30 pm, Oct-May, 10:30 am-3 pm). Of the three, Alto Merse is the closest to Siena, with trails from Brenna (Bus #106) leading into it past the wild castle at Castiglion che Dio Sol Sa (literally "that God only knows"), Stigliano and Poggio di Siena Vecchia to Torri (Bus #106).

Farther to the east, **Murlo** (Bus #110 and #111 to Vescovado) is deep in some haunting forests around the Crevole River. An easy four-mile trail from here leads to the old mining village Miniere di Murlo (abandoned after WWII) from where another eight-mile trail departs along the ancient train line used by the miners. You can also walk to the area's important Etruscan remains at Vescovado, a trail best finished off with a visit to the town's archeological museum (Antiquarium di Poggio Civitate, Piazza della Cattedrale, Murlo, ☎ 0577-814099, museoetrusco@comune.murlo.siena.it).

Nearby **Bagni di Petriolo**, the preferred bathing spot of Pope Pius II, is the only example of a fortified spa in the Tuscan province (☎ 0577-757104, fax 0577-757092, www.termesaluteambiente.com, Apr-Nov); it can be reached on CAI #32, which stretches all the way down from Siena.

On Wheels

 Whether you're a cyclotourist heading to your next stop or just want to spend a day or a few hours discovering the countryside before returning to the city, you'll find the Siena province a great place to bike. For the latest recommendations, contact the enthusiastic **Gli Amici della Bicicletta** cycling association (Via Campansi 32, ☎/fax 0577-45159, www.comune.siena.it/adb, Thurs, 6 am-7:30 pm). They freely recommend routes in Siena and its countryside and also organize day-long bicycle trips on which all are welcome to join (check their online newsletter *Il Ciclone* for events).

BIKE RENTAL IN SIENA

CentroBici (Viale Toselli 106, ☎ *0577-282550, www.sienabiking.com, €16 a day, €155 a week); DF Bike (Via Massetana Romana 54,* ☎/fax *0577-271905, dfbike@biemmepro.it); Ginanneschi Antonio (Via E S Piccolomini 35,* ☎ *0577-283930); Ricci Autonoleggi (Piazza Maestri del Lavoro 12,* ☎ *0577-226068); and, just out of the city, Berti Guiliana-Rent Bike (c/o Bar Sport, Via Campo a Paolo, Casciano di Murlo,* ☎ *0577-818058).*

A number of loop trails take you out and back from Siena, including routes to **Monteriggioni** (23 miles), the 18th-century wheat *grancia* (grain storehouse) at **Cuna** (22 miles), **Monteaperti** and **Chianti** (21 miles), and **Radda** and **Castellina in Chianti** (37 miles).

Cyclotourists should consider making their next destination **San Gimignano**. There's an enjoyable 25-mile cycle through Monteriggioni and Colle di Val d'Elsa before the hard final climb up to San Gimignano. Other options are Chianti (following the SS222 Chiantigiana), the **Crete** (Asciano, Chisure, Monte Oliveto Maggiore and Buonconvento along the legendary Lauretana SS438 racing bike road) or **Montepulciano** (44 miles along deserted local roads).

Guides

In such prime cycling territory it's no surprise to find an equally extensive range of companies offering guided tours. But while many international tour adventure operators offer a complete package, it makes sense to go with a smaller Siena-based company to get the most out of the countryside, its history and fine foods.

All Around Siena (Banchi di Sopra 31, ☎ 0577-40919, fax 0577-217844, www.allaroundsiena.com) offers a variety of guided bike excursions into the surrounding countryside, including a one-day tour around Siena (from Porta Romana south to Vico d'Arbia) and trips into all the regions featured in this chapter.

Welcome (Via Simone Martini, 18, ☎ 0577-282810, fax 0577-220248, www.welcomesiena.com) offers bike rides both in the surrounding countryside and through the streets and bike roads of Siena.

Cinghiale Cycling tours (www.cinghiale.com) was founded by retired professional cyclist Andy Hampsten (the only American cyclist to win the prestigious Giro d'Italia).

Heading down to Soviciille, you can pick up rides into the **Montagnola** and from Montagnola into the quieter **Val di Merse** (print out itineraries from www.terresienainbici.it before you travel). The non-profit **Gruppo Ciclistico Val di Merse** (Via del Borgo 21, Rosia, ☎ 0577-344001, www.rosiabike.it) will also help you out; they promote cycle culture in the Val di Merse, with monthly cycle

Siena

events (races, tours, nature, art and gastronomic routes) as well as invaluable advice. You can also identify your routes of interest by popping into **Orso on Bike** (Montalcino, ☎ 0577-835532, fax 0577-835545, www.bikemontalcino.it).

Trails that first grab the attention take you along *strade bianche* from Chiusdino to the Abbazia di San Galgano (an easy 11 miler, 13 miles if picking it up at Monticiano), from Monticiano into the eerie landscape of the Colline Metallifere (a more challenging 30 miles), and the rolling 16-mile journey between the Val di Merse and Crete, also picked up from Monticiano.

On Horseback

The main **Club Ippico Senese** is based in Il Ceppo (Loc. Pian del Lago, ☎ 0577-318426/0577-318316, fax 0577-318267, pipporamirez@hotmail. com) near Monteriggioni. There are three centers based in nearby Sovicille, **La Casella Cavalgiocare** (Loc. Casella, Sovicille, ☎ 0577-314323, www.cavalgiocare.it), **Giovanni Gamberini** (Loc. Casella, Sovicille, ☎ 0577-314323) and **Giovanni Regoli** (Loc. Viteccio, Sovicille, ☎ 0577-393476), one in nearby Lecceto (**Il Cannuccio**, ☎ 0577-317069) and another at Monteroni d'Arbia (**Centro Ippico Casa Bassa**, Sparse Ville di Corsano 87).

Farther south near Murlo, you'll find the **Casini Riding Center** (Loc. Ginepreto, Casciano di Murlo, ☎ 347-1475494, fax 0577-818018, www.ginepreto.com). They organize one- to seven-day treks into the Val di Merse with visits to Montalcino, Etruscan Murlo, San Gimignano and Monteriggioni (from €75 for a one-day trek). Other nearby riding centers include **Casabianca** (Casciano di Murlo, ☎ 0577-811033, fax 0577-811037), **Viamaggio** (Murlo, ☎ 0577-811127, fax 0577-814935) and **Tenuta della Selva** (Casciano di Murlo, ☎ 0577-817588).

Or you can opt for an all-inclusive deal with **All Around Siena** (Banchi di Sopra 31, ☎ 0577-40919, fax 0577-217844, www.allaroundsiena.com, half- , full- and multi-day excursions from €75) or **Welcome** (Via Simone Martini, 18, ☎ 0577-282810, fax 0577-220248, www.welcomesiena.com, half- or full-day rides through Sienese woods and vineyards from €100). Both will pick you up in Siena.

On Water

The rivers Merse (and tributary Farma) and Ombrone, south of Siena, offer some of the best canoeing possibilities, with many outfitters basing themselves on the river between Brenna and Macereto or farther south in Bagni a Petriolo. **All Around Siena** (Banchi di Sopra 31, ☎ 0577-40919, fax 0577-217844, www.allaroundsiena.com) offers four- to five-mile canoe excursions on the River Merse whether you are a beginner or a seasoned waterbabe.

SOMETHING FOR THE KIDS

The **75esima Aventura** sports club (Via Santa Croce 29, Loc. Belforte, Radicondoli, ☎/fax 0566-997649, www.75avventura.it) has a wide range of programs – trekking, mountain biking, horseback riding, canoeing, archery, birdwatching – aimed at children and young adults (prices start from €18).

Centro Studi Etologici (Convento dell'Osservanza, Radicondoli, ☎ 0577-790738, www.centrostudietologici.it) does research into ethology and ecology and offers historical and nature walks on these themes to children (and adults) in the Corbaiola Ethological Park.

In the Air

 All Around Siena (Banchi di Sopra 31, ☎ 0577-40919, fax 0577-217844, www.allaroundsiena.com) organizes hot-air balloon excursions into the Siena province, as do **Welcome** (Via Simone Martini, 18, ☎ 0577-282810, fax 0577-220248, www.welcomesiena.com), the **Chianti Balloon Club** (Podere il Porto, Pianella, ☎ 0577-363232) and **Ballooning in Tuscany** (Podere La Fratta, Montisi, San Giovanni d'Asso, fax 0577-845211, www.ballooningintuscany.com). Prices start at €250 per person.

■ Shopping

Picnic fare can be purchased at the **market** (Piazza del Mercato, south of Piazza del Campo), but if it's something a little more classy you're after, try **Morbidi** (Via Banchi di Sopra 75, ☎ 0577-280268), a famous local delicatessen selling Tuscan salamis, local cheese and various pâtés and take-out pasta dishes, or **Manganelli** (Via di Città 63, ☎ 0577-280268), a member of the Slow Food Movement (www.slowfood.it) and seller of cured meats, cheese, olive oil, panforte and ricciarelli.

A TASTE FOR KIDS

 Every June, July, September and October, the Slow Food Movement organizes events in Siena dedicated to instruct kids from six to 14 through games on the use of the senses, with visits to estates and farms, and guided tastings of typical Sienese products (information and booking via the tourist board on ☎ 0577-283004, fax 0577-270676, incoming@terresiena.it).

If you want to stock up on regional produce, visit **Consorzio Agrario Siena** (Via Piangiani 9, ☎ 0577-222368), along your route into town from the Sita bus stop, where you can purchase regional wine, cured meats, cakes and jams directly from the local farmers.

Siena's artisan heritage is kept alive at **SienArtefice** on Via Fontebranda, the area of Siena that has been from the Middle Ages the home to craftsmen (weavers, jewelers, glassmakers, potters and printers) and their workshops. It's worth a trip to see the old-fashioned techniques, even if you're not intending to buy.

■ Where to Eat

 Behind the Palazzo Pubblico, on the slightly dilapidated Piazza del Mercato, don't be put off by the equally dilapidated terrace (overhung by local washing lines) of **Antica Trattoria Papei** (Piazza del Mercato 6, ☎ 0577-280894, closed Mon, $), inside the bustling modern interior, you'll find a delicious and well-priced menu of *pici alla Cardinale, trippa Senese, pappardelle al cinghiale* and *vitella al forno*.

DINING PRICE CHART	
Price per person for an entrée, including house wine & cover.	
$	Under €20
$$	€21-€40
$$$	€41-€60
$$$$	Over €60

Siena

LOCAL FLAVORS

Antipasti: *Salumi di Cinta senese.*
Primi: The local *ribollita, panzanella* (a cold summer bread soup of basil, onion, oil, vinegar and salt), *pici* (spaghetti rolled by hand and seasoned with ragù or garlic).
Secondi: *Frittata con gli zoccoli* (omelette with lardons), grilled Chianina steak.
Dolci: The famous *panforte* (spiced sticky cake), *cavallucci* and *ricciarelli* (oval-shaped almond biscuits) that have existed in this area since the Middle Ages. For a quick coffee and cake head to **Caffé Nannini** (Via Massetana Romana, 56, ☎ 0577-287545, $), one of a chain of three, which includes the gelaterie next door and the Pasticceria Nannini on Banchi di Sopra. It is the most famous location to sample the delicious ricciarelli or panforte that Siena is known for.

Dimmed lights and wall graffiti make **Osteria Castelvecchio** (Via Castelvecchio, 65, ☎ 0577-49586, www.osteriacastelvecchio.com, closed Tues in winter only, $$) an interesting spot for a quick lunch or classic evening meal. It is also one of a few local restaurants to consciously offer a good vegetarian choice. Opt for the *degutazione* with a little bit of everything if you can't make up your mind.

Try to book a table on the terrace at **Il Biondo** (Vicolo del Rustichetto 10, ☎ 0577-280739, www.ristoratori.it/ilbiondo, closed Wed, $$) down a tiny medieval side street with views onto a small piazza.

Family-run **Medioevo** (Via dei Rossi 40, ☎ 0577-280315, www.medioevosiena.com, closed Thurs, $$) occupies a 13th-century townhouse right in the heart of Siena with all the ceiling vaults, banners, coats of arms and antiques that you would expect from such a historic location. Booking recommended.

Just outside the northern Porta Camollia, **Pizzeria Ezio** (Viale V. Emanuelle II 32, ☎ 0577-48094, closed Thurs, $$) is worth a detour out of the historical center for its range of pizza, grilled meats and fish. There's also a seasonal *degustazione* and homemade desserts to enjoy. Good international wine list.

South of the Duomo near the Pinacoteca Nazionale, atmospheric family-run **Osteria da Cice** (Via San Pietro 32, ☎ 0577-288026, closed Sun, $$) offers a mixed local menu with all the old favorites; *pici al funghi, ravioli burro e salva* and *cinghiale al cacciatore* are some of the best you'll find.

Close to the Duomo, **Osteria da Divo** (Via Franciosa 25, ☎ 0577-286054, closed Sun, $$) occupies some of the most intimate and atmospheric rooms in the city, with candlelit underground grotto dining, romantic half-hidden niches and exposed brickwork. The menu is local and delicious.

You'll be surprised by the quality of food at **Al Mangia** (Piazza del Campo 42-6, ☎ 0577-281121, www.almangia.it, closed Mon, $$$), right in the midst of prime sightseeing territory. It has been run by the Senni family for four generations and its recipes hark back almost as far. Booking recommended.

Just outside the town walls, **Antica Trattoria Botteganova** (Via Chiantigiana 29, ☎ 0577-284230, www.anticatrattoriabotteganova.it, closed Mon, $$$) offers a great *degustazione* of the daily dishes (fresh pasta, grilled meats and fish) inside its elegant terracotta walls.

Things are a little more formal at **Al Marsili** (Via del Castoro 3, ☎ 0577-47154, www.ristorantealmarsili.it, closed Mon, $$$), more than fitting for the charismatic medieval building it inhabits. Along with an extensive wine list, the menu features some classic Tuscan dishes. Booking recommended.

■ Where to Stay

Hotels

Uphill 800 m/2,000 feet from Porta Pispini, **Il Giardino** ☆☆ (Via B. Peruzzi 33, ☎ 0577-285290, fax 0577-221197, www.hotelilgiardino.it, $$) sits in a centuries-old garden of olive trees. The spacious rooms, outdoor pool and leisure facilities make this good value in an expensive city like Siena, plus there are discounts if you book well in advance. Parking. Shuttle service.

HOTEL PRICE CHART	
Rates are per room with private bath, based on double occupancy, including breakfast.	
$	Under €40
$$	€41-€85
$$$	€86-€140
$$$$	€141-€210
$$$$$	Over €210

Just outside Porta Ovile, **Moderno** ☆☆☆ (Via B. Peruzzi 19, ☎ 0577-288453, fax 0577-270596, www.sienanet.it/moderno, $$) far exceeds what you might expect from its name with some gorgeously decorated superior rooms and a peaceful garden. Good restaurant. Parking.

Reasonably priced for such a central location, the atmospheric **Antica Torre** ☆☆☆ (Via di Fieravecchia 7, ☎/fax 0577-222255, www.anticatorresiena.it, $$$) is in a 16th-century medieval tower down a quiet street close to the Piazza del Campo. Rooms in the top of the tower have great views over Siena.

There are beautiful high ceilings, parquet floors and panoramic balconies in **Chiusarelli** ☆☆☆ (Viale Curtatone 15, ☎ 0577-280562, fax 0577-271177, www.chiusarelli.com, $$$) near the Fortezza Medici. Bike rental. Parking.

In a converted Renaissance palace, the central **Palazzo Ravizza** ☆☆☆ (Pian dei Mantellini 34, ☎ 0577-280462, fax 0577-221597, www.palazzoravizza.it, $$$) has been owned by the same family since it was transformed into a pensione in the 1920s. Rooms, salons, bar and restaurant are elegantly decorated with original terracotta floors, frescoed ceilings, carved wooden doorframes and antique 17th-to 19th-century furnishings. Parking.

A short drive outside Porta Romana, cozy **Piccolo Hotel Oliveta** ☆☆☆ (Via E.S. Piccolomini 35, ☎ 0577-283930, fax 0577-270009, www.oliveta.com, $$$) occupies a converted 18th-century farmhouse with original features – beamed ceilings, terracotta tiles, exposed brickwork – still intact. Panoramic terrace. Chianti wine-tasting tours and cooking courses available on request. Shuttle service. Parking.

On the same road even closer to the Porta Romana, the converted 18th-century villa that now houses **Santa Caterina** ☆☆☆ (Via E.S. Piccolomini 7, ☎ 0577-221105, fax 0577-271087, www.hscsiena.it, $$$) is furnished to traditional Tuscan tastes. Al fresco breakfast dining is accompanied by some splendid Sienese vistas.

Just outside the city walls, **Villa Scacciapensieri** ☆☆☆☆ (Via Scacciapensieri 10, ☎ 0577-41441, fax 0577-270854, www.villascacciapensieri.it, $$$$), in a hilltop 19th-century villa, offers panoramic views over Siena and Chianti from its

Siena

well-tended gardens (with outdoor pool) and wood-beamed rooms. Bicycle available for use. Tennis courts. Bus #8 from center or #3 from station. Parking.

If you book into one of the 17 rooms at **Certosa di Maggiano** ☆☆☆☆ (Via Certosa 82, ☎ 0577-288180, fax 0577-288189, www.certosadimaggiano.com, $$$$$) you'll actually be staying in a converted monastic cell. The hotel occupies an ancient monastery dating from 1314, just outside the Porta Romana Gate. Outdoor pool and leisure facilities. Garage, shuttle service.

Just a few steps from Piazza del Campo , the luxurious **Grand Hotel Continental** ☆☆☆☆☆ (Via Banchi di Sopra 85, ☎ 0577-56011, fax 0577-5601555, www.ghcs.it, $$$$$) offers one of the best city locations, inside a former aristocratic home with restored original décor, coffered wooden beams, terracotta floors and a magnificent 15th-century fresco in the San Cristoforo suite. Garage.

B&Bs

A good value B&B just 200 m/500 feet from the Piazza del Campo, is the 18th-century **Palazzo Bruchi di Masignani** (Via Pantaneto 105, ☎/fax 0577-287342, www.palazzobruchi.it, $$). Rooms have frescoed ceilings and eclectic period furnishings. Good views over a garden courtyard and the old town walls.

Affittacamere

In a great location at a very reasonable price, the rooms of **Soggiorno Sabrina** (Via Calzoleria 16, ☎ 0577-47237, fax 0577-394108, www.dormisiena.it, $$, discounts for longer stays) are just off the Piazza del Campo. Book early if arriving in peak season.

Just outside the town walls, 100 m/280 feet from the station, newly refurbished **Soggiorno Lo Stellino** (Via Fiorentina 95, ☎ 0577-51987, fax 0577-588926, www.sienaholidays.com, $$) offers modern and spacious rooms at inviting prices. Buses to the town center every 20 minutes.

Agriturismi

Two miles northeast of Siena, **Residence Le Tolfe** (Strada delle Tolfe 14, ☎ 0577-255111, fax 0577-44591, www.letolfe.it, $$, min. three-day rental), with its five converted farmhouses, sits atop a hill covered in vineyards and olive groves. Best for those with a car (the nearest bus stop is 30 minutes walk), the farm also produces wine, oil and grappa. Outdoor pool.

Only three miles from Siena in the direction of Massa Marittima (SS73) and bordering an eighth-century monastery, **La Prodaia** (Strada di Monastero 49, Loc. Castafabbri, ☎ 0577-394193, fax 0577-391991, www.laprodaia.com, $$$, min. two-day rental) has horseback riding, tennis and golf facilities near its two self-sufficient apartments.

Past acres of vineyards, olive trees and red poppy fields, **B&B Frances' Lodge** (Strada di Valdipugna 2, Loc. Santa Regina, ☎ 0577-281061, fax 0577-222224, www.franceslodge.it, $$$$, min. two-day rental) commands a spectacular view over Siena. Owner Frances gives guided tours of the elegant garden and patient explanations of the Tuscan dishes on offer. Outdoor pool, use of mountain bikes and nearby horseback riding and golf facilities.

Camping

 Two miles from the center is **Colleverde** ☆☆☆ (Strada degli Scacciapensieri 47, ☎ 0577-80044, fax 0577-333298, campingsiena@terresiena.it, $, 200 sites, 21 Mar-10 Nov). This is Siena's nearest campground (Bus #8, signposted from town center) with great views of the city and surrounding countryside from its hilltop location. Outdoor pool, bar, restaurant and shop.

If that's full, try **Luxor** ☆☆ (Loc. Trasqua, Monteriggioni, ☎/fax 0577-743047, www.luxorcamping.com, $, 100 sites, 17 Mar-7 Nov). It's a 10-minute drive north of Siena in the direction of Poggibonsi (bus to Lilliano then 10-minute walk) and an equally good base for travels into Chianti. Outdoor pool, bar and restaurant.

For stays in the **Montagnola**, your two options are **Le Soline** ☆☆☆ (Loc. Casciano di Murlo, ☎ 0577-817410, fax 0577-817415, www.lesoline.it, $, 100 sites), with outdoor pool, bar and restaurant, and **La Montagnola** ☆☆ (Via Cava del Siciliano, Sovicille, ☎/fax 0577-314473, www.montagnola.it, $, 66 sites, Apr-Sept).

Youth Hostels

Hostel Guidoriccio ☆☆☆ (Via Fiorentina 85, ☎ 0577-52212, fax 0577-50277, siena.aighostel@virgilio.it, $) is a short drive northwest of Siena center (Bus #4, #10 or #15) in a quiet residential area with garden, caffè and small restaurant. Booking recommended for double and family rooms (reception open 7-10 am, 3-11:30 pm). You must be a Hostelling International Member (www.ostellionline.org) to book. **Ecoturismo Casa Gialla** ☆☆☆ (Loc. Cetine, ☎ 0577-799063, fax 0577-799105, www.cetine.com, $$), on the other hand, offers hostel-type accommodation in the **Val di Merse** that is open to all.

■ Entertainment & Events

Organized by the Accademia Musicale Chigiana and the Monte dei Paschi bank, the **Settimane Musicali Senesi** (☎ 0577-22091, www.chigiana.it, 5 July-27 Aug, most events are free) are "musical weeks" of classical orchestral and soloist concerts held in various churches, courtyards and piazzas in Siena, Chiusdino, Asciano and Montalcino.

With such a prestigious jazz school it should come as no surprise to find an equally important festival. **Siena Jazz** (Fortezza Medicea, ☎ 0577-271401, www.sienajazz.it, 23 July-7 Aug, most events are free) sees performances, courses and master-classes every year in Piazza del Campo, the Enoteca Italiana and Piazza Jacopo della Quercia.

Also part of *Siena Estate,* **La Città Aromatica** (☎ 0577-292230, fax 0577-292409, www.comune.siena.it, 26-29 Aug, most events are free) holds live jam sessions on Piazza del Campo and Piazza Jacopo della Quercia.

For the best in Sienese theater, watch for productions (a mix of drama, music and dance) in the **Teatro dei Rinnovati** (Piazza del Campo, ☎ 0577-292265, Nov-Mar, tickets from €7, conc. €5, closed for restoration at the time of writing) and the **Teatro dei Rozzi** (Piazza Indipendenza 15, ☎ 0577-46960, Nov-Apr, tickets from €7, conc. €5).

Siena

Outside of Siena

For many, the province of Siena offers the enduring image of rural Tuscany with the medieval city of Siena at its heart, the rolling hills of Chianti to its north, the white clay hills of the Crete to its east, the abbeys and castles of the Val d'Orcia and the thermal springs of Val di Chiana on the border of Umbria to the south and the medieval hill-top villages of Val d'Elsa to the west. It contains some of Tuscany's most visited attractions: the towers of San Gimignano, the Renaissance city of Pienza, the wine-producing areas of Montepulciano, Montalcino and San Gimignano and the Etruscan city of Chiusi. And its capital Siena has plenty of medieval architecture, classic canvases and well-preserved traditions to drag you away from its great rival, Florence.

REGION AT A GLANCE

- **Main city:** Siena
- **Afternoon trips from Siena:** Abbazia di San Galgano (page 152), Monteriggioni (page 176).
- **Town breaks:** Montepulciano (page 188), Pienza (page 174), San Gimignano (page 160), Volterra (out of province, page 308).
- **Rural retreats:** Chianti (page 134), the Crete (page 169), Montagnola Sienese (page 151), Monte Amiata (page 182), Val di Chiana (page 188), Val d'Elsa (page 160), Val d'Orcia (page 180).
- **Spa towns:** Bagno Vignoni, Bagni San Filippo (page 182), Chianciano Terme (page 193), Montepulciano Terme, Petriolo (page 193), Rapolano Terme (page 173), and San Casciano dei Bagni.

San Gimignano & the Val d'Elsa

The sunflower-filled Elsa Valley is an area of frontier fortress towns and military outposts that attest to the fierce territorial rivalry between Volterra and Florence, of Kodak-colored red-brick towers that jut up in a show of its medieval wealth, and an adventure-rich territory of forests, pleasing country walks, vineyards and farmhouses.

■ Getting Here & Around

 By Bus: The best approach into the Val d'Elsa from Siena is by bus; regular **Tra-In** services (☎ 0577-204111, www.trainspa.it) run to San Gimignano (#130), Colle Val d'Elsa (#124), Monteriggioni (#126), Poggibonsi (#130 and #136) and Casole d'Elsa (#126). From Florence, **SITA** coach #350 (☎ 800-373760, www.sita-on-line.it) runs to Poggibonsi (roughly twice an hour), where you can change for the services to San Gimignano and Colle Val d'Elsa.

By Train: Poggibonsi has a train station on the Florence-to-Siena line served by roughly one train an hour (☎ 848-888088, www.trenitalia.it). The same line stops less frequently at Castellina Scalo, just north of Monteriggioni, from where buses will link you to town.

 By Car: Drivers will have a much easier time of it; from both Siena and Florence the **SS2** leads through Poggibonsi and Monteriggioni, with turn off to San Gimignano, Colle and Casole Val d'Elsa en route.

By Bike: For the approach from Siena by bike, see page 152. Once you're here, bikes can be rented in Colle di Val d'Elsa (**Mario Antichi**, Via Livini 1/3, ☎/fax 0577-923366), Poggibonsi (**Ciclosport di Porciatti**, Via Trento 82, ☎ 0577-938507, fax 0577-996732; **Cicliofficina di Bettini**, Via Redipuglia 17/19, ☎/fax 0577-936881 and Jolly, Via Fugnano 10, ☎ 0577-940575).

■ Information Sources

Tourist Offices: Your best source of information for the region (other than the Siena Tourist Office) is the *pro loco* (local tourist office) in **San Gimignano** (Piazza del Duomo 1, ☎ 0577-940008, fax 0577-940903, www.sangimignano.com, Mar-Oct, 9 am-1 pm, 3-7 pm, Nov-Feb, 9 am-1 pm, 4-6 pm), with other offices in **Casole Val d'Elsa** (Piazza della Libertà 1, ☎ 0577-948705, fax 0577-948118), **Colle Val d'Elsa** (Via Campana 43, ☎ 0577-922791, fax 0577-922621), **Monteriggioni** (Largo Fontebranda 5, Castello di Monteriggioni, ☎/fax 0577-304810) and **Poggibonsi** (Via Borgaccio 23, ☎ 0577-987017, fax 0577-992775, tourists@valdelsa.net).

Guides & Maps: Both *Chianti Classico, Val di Pesa and Val d'Elsa,* 1:25,000 (Carta Turistica e dei Sentieri, Instituto Geog Militare, Firenze) and *San Gimignano and Volterra* 1:25,000 (Carta Turistica e dei Sentieri, Instituto Geog Militare, Firenze) cover CAI trails and mountain bike routes in their respective zones.

■ Sightseeing

 The Route to San Gimignano: **Monteriggioni**, right, your first turreted medieval hilltop, appears on the horizon not far out of Siena, its 550 m (1,804 feet) of well-preserved town walls (so famous they were cited in Dante's *Divine Comedy*) making a detour impossible to resist. Constructed in 1213 and fortified by Siena a century later (they added the 14 quadrangular towers), the town's military formation is best visited via the external footpath that links the main door to the second entrance. Once inside, the town is tiny, with the population reviving somewhat after dropping to only 30 inhabitants in 1900.

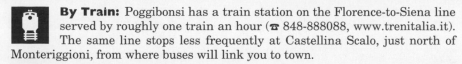

Bike and foot excursions from the town will take you along remains of the old Via Francigena to **Abbadia Isola** (Island Abbey), a small town named after its breathtaking 11th-century Benedictine abbey (on a one-time flood plain). Unsurprisingly, its sights are mainly religious: the Romanesque **Chiesa dei Santi Salvatore e Cirino**

guarding a grand 14th-century *Maestà* by an unknown local artist; and the 14th-century **Eremo di San Leonardo al Lago** (☎ 0577-317021, Tues-Sun, 9:30 am-3:30 pm, free guided visit) retaining a large cycle of frescos by Lippo Vanni and a fresco *Crucifixion* (regarded as one of the pinnacles of 15th-century Sienese art) by Giovanni di Paolo.

In addition, there's an easy seven-mile foot excursion through thick maquis to the top of **Monte Maggio** (671 m/2,200 feet) and two **bike rides** of interest. The first, a difficult 14-mile loop along CAI trails (Monteriggioni-Abbadia Isola-Riciano-Fioreta-Mandorlo-Monteriggioni) and the second an easier but longer 24-mile journey part-trail and part-road (Monteriggioni-Abbadia Isola-Strove-Scorgiano-Ceppo-Monteriggioni). It takes you past the local **horseback-riding** center, **Club Ippico Senese** (Loc. Pian del Lago, Il Ceppo, ☎ 0577-318426, fax 0577-318267, pipporamirez@hotmail.com).

From the train station at Castellina Scalo, a **footpath** (take the paved road on the left across the railway line, turn right then right again to reach the unpaved path, 2¼ hours) leads you from the station car park to Monteriggioni, passing first through the vineyards and olive groves that overlook the Staggia River.

Monteriggioni also makes a good stopping off point if you're in the area during **Festa Monteriggioni** (4-6 and 10-13 July, ☎ 0577-304810), two weekends of medieval festivities – music and fringe theater, street artists, jugglers and acrobats – that liven up the town's tiny central square.

VIA FRANCIGENA

Local towns such as Abbadia Isola, San Gimignano and Siena were first built along the ancient **Via Francigena** (roughly parallel to today's SS2 Cassia) to cater to the stream of medieval pilgrims making their way from Canterbury to Rome (later also used by merchant traders and maneuvering armies). At that time the most important communication artery in the peninsula, the Via Francigena (or Francisca) entered Tuscany over the Apennine Cisa pass, traversing the province of Lucca before reaching the Val d'Elsa and continuing down to Rome, leaving impressive religious and civic constructions in its wake.

Italian crystal capital **Colle di Val d'Elsa** (split into the *Alta*, the medieval hilltop part, the *Bassa*, the new town at its base and the *Piana*, the glass production area) is a pretty quiet warren of narrow streets, steeped alleys and historic churches often missed en route to the more tourist-crowded San Gimignano. That's not to say there isn't much to visit. The top sights are: the **Torre di Arnolfo** designed by local-born Arnolfo di Cambio (the architect who designed Florence's Palazzo Vecchio); 17th-century **Duomo**; **Palazzo dei Priori** (seat of the **Museo Archeologico**, ☎ 0577-922954, summer, 10 am-noon, 3:30-6:30 pm, winter, 3:30-5:30 pm, closed Mon, €1.55); and **Palazzo Pretorio** (seat of the **Museo Civico d'Arte Sacre**, ☎ 0577-923888, Apr-Oct, Tues-Sun, 10 am-noon, 4-7 pm, Nov-Mar, Sat-Sun, 10 am-noon, 3:30-6:30 pm, €3, conc. €2). The latter has a *Maestà* taken from Abbadia Isola and a 13th-century wooden crucifix of note. It's also worth a stroll around town to check out the great views of the surrounding countryside, which suddenly become visible between the medieval houses, towers and churches.

Down in Colle Bassa, the town's other main site, the **Chiesa di Sant'Agostino**, was renovated to its present look in the 16th century by Antonio da Sangallo il

Vecchio. It houses a *Madonna and Child* by Sienese painter Taddeo di Bartolo and a precious marble work by Baccio da Montelupo. In the outskirts, the **Badia di Santa Maria** at Còneo warrants a wander for its well-preserved Sienese-Romanesque architecture (first quarter of the 12th century).

Those attracted here by the crystal production (at its peak during late-August and early-September exhibition), should make a beeline to the **Museo del Cristallo** (Via dei Fossi 8a, ☎ 0577-912260, Oct-Apr, Tues-Fri, 3-6 pm, Sat-Sun, 10 am-noon, 3-6 pm, May-Sept, 10 am-noon, 3-6 pm, €3). It makes a good introduction to any intended purchases with its display of crystal work from over the centuries.

Although these days the least interesting of the area's towns (its major monuments having been destroyed in the last war), **Poggibonsi** was, during the 12th century at least, its most important. The former medieval *Alto* or upper town of Poggiobonizio sprang up at an important crossroads along the Via Francigena and was destroyed by the Florentines in 1270 (only the restored Fonte alla Fate, the "Fountain of the Fairies" halfway up the hill remains).

Today it is the starting points for many of the region's **trails,** which take you to more attractive sights like the fortified town of Staggia, the Castle of Strozzavolpe, the Franciscan Basilica di San Lucchese (with Taddeo Gaddi, Cennino Cennini and Bartolo di Fredi frescoes) and the La Magione di San Giovanni al Ponte (the enforested seat of the *Spedale Gerosolimitano*, a medieval hospital). The map for the town's six looping trails can be printed out from www.comune.poggibonsi.si.it before you leave, or picked up at the tourist office on arrival (routes are also suitable for mountain **bikers**).

Organized Tours from Poggibonsi

The nationwide **Legambiente** organizes a variety of treks in the Val d'Elsa (☎ 055-6810330, fax 055-6811620, www.legambiente.com), including trails along the ancient Via Francigena from Poggibonsi through San Gimignano, Colle Val d'Elsa and Monteriggioni (day tour €48 per person).

Two of Poggibonsi's **cycling** associations are worth contacting for local events: **Guide Ambientali Excursionistiche** (c/o Maria Zuddas, Via Fiume 22, ☎/fax 0577-982923) and **Associazione Grandama** (☎ 338-9706898), the latter having put together the six hiking routes that leave from the town periphery.

Walking San Gimignano: One of the best-preserved medieval towns in Tuscany, with a stunning skyline of jutting towers and narrow streets that slope around the hill contour, San Gimignano, the magic "city of towers" is the kind of destination Toscanaphiles dream of (as the tour buses testify all too well). Easily viewed in a day, you'll enjoy it a lot more if you avoid the August crowds, or at least the midday rush, which sees the main street almost grind to a halt with tourists clutching their prized bottles of Vernaccia.

The bus drops you off on Piazzale Martiri di Monte Maggio just outside Porta San Giovanni, from where Via San Giovanni leads past the Pisan-Romanesque black and white striped marble of **Chiesa di San Francesco** (now a wine cellar) through the Arco dei Becci (the gates of the original city walls) and onto the gently sloping Piazza della Cisterna and adjoining Piazza del Duomo. The former, watched over by the colossal **Torre della Rognosa** and surrounded by striking palazzi, towers and medieval family houses, is the liveliest spot in town, while the latter is the venue of many of the city's main sights.

BRISTLING SKYLINES

In a medieval version of keeping up with the Joneses, 12th- and 13th-century San Gimignano saw a tower-building frenzy that resulted in the construction of 76 increasingly giant defensive tower-houses, 14 of which remain today. The situation got so out of hand that city edicts forbade anyone build a tower taller than Torre della Rognosa, the 50-m (165-foot) tower of the town hall. They later broke their own rule with the construction of the new town hall tower, La Torre Grossa (the "big tower") built in 1310 (see below for entrance information).

Collegiata Santa Maria Assunta (Piazza del Duomo, Apr-Oct, 9:30 am-7:30 pm, Nov-Mar, 9:30 am-5 pm, open Jan-Feb for religious services only, entrance to the Cappella di Santa Fina, €3, conc. €1.50): In its three naves, the town's 12th-century Romanesque Collegiata (the former cathedral) has some of the most frescoed walls in Italy. Two are entirely covered by a spectacular three-level, 26-scene display of stories from the Old and New Testament by Bartolo di Fredi, with a mesmerizing *Last Judgment* at the back by Taddeo di Bartolo (detail at right), and frescoed scenes by Simone Martini and Lippo Memmi. Then there is Dominico Ghirlandaio's *Stories of St. Fina* (1475) in the Cappella di Santa Fina (to the right). Benedetto da Maiano (also responsible for the marble altarpiece) erected the latter to the plans of his brother Giuliano, who enlarged the cathedral, in 1468.

The **Museo d'Arte Sacra** (Museum of Sacred Art, ☎ 0577-942226, same opening hours, €3, conc. €1.50, or combined ticket with the Cappella di Santa Fina for €5.50, conc. €2.50) holds the treasures of the Collegiate Church plus a variety of religious artifacts pulled from the former churches and monasteries in the surrounding countryside.

A staircase leads up behind the cathedral to the remains of the **Rocca di Montestaffoli**. Summer evenings offer the best views, the Rocca (plus the Piazza del Duomo, Piazza delle Erbe, Badia a Elmi, Castel San Gimignano and Santa Lucia) enlivened with open-air opera, classical concerts and film screenings (information ☎ 0577-940008, from €6, conc. €5).

Palazzo del Popolo, Museo Civico & Torre Grossa (☎ 0577-990312, Mar-Nov, 9:30 am-7:30 pm, Dec-Feb, 10 am-5:50 pm, €5, conc. €4): To the left of the Collegiata and heralded by its 54-m (177-foot) Torre Grossa, the Palazzo del Popolo (the new town hall) is the seat of the Museo Civico, with a collection of Sienese and Renaissance paintings. Taddeo di Bartolo's *Virgin and Child* is in the courtyard and works by artists such as Filippino Lippi, Pinturicchio, Benozzo Gozzoli and Lippo Memmi, including his spectacular *Maestà*, are inside. There is a 12th-century painted crucifix and several Gothic altarpieces (*Scenes from the Life of St Gimignano, Madonna with Sts Gregory and Benedict* by Pinturicchio) to take in before climbing up for some spectacular views. This is the only town tower admitting visitors.

Museum Entry: Die-hard museum fans should purchase San Gimignano's combined museum ticket with entry to the Museo Civico and Torre Grossa, the Museo Archeologico, the Speziera di Santa Fina, the Galleria d'Arte Moderna e Contemporanea and the Museo Ornitologico for €7.50, conc. €6.50.

Out of the Piazza del Duomo, the scenic Via San Matteo leads you past the best of the art galleries, jewelers and artisans, toward the 13th-century Porta San Matteo. Here, a right up Via Cellolese will take you to the 13th-century **Chiesa di Sant'Agostino**, its Romanesque-Gothic exterior contrasting somewhat with the Rococo interior. Inside, Piero del Pollaiolo's *Coronation of the Virgin* (1483), above the main altar, and Benedetto da Maiano's elaborate marble altar to St Bartolo (1494) are just two of the works that pave the way for the choir-covered 14th-century fresco cycle, *Life of St Augustine* (Benozzo Gozzoli, 1465), San Gimignano's most famous work of art. Benedetto da Maiano's **Chapel of St. Bartolo** is also worth a look. It has a terracotta floor carved by Andrea della Robbia and a great altar decorated with Antonio del Pollaiolo's *Coronation of Madonna and Saints* (1483).

The former Conservatorio di Santa Chiara is now the home of the **Museo Archeologico** and the **Galleria d'Arte Moderna e Contemporanea** (Via Folgore da San Gimignano, ☎ 0577-940348, Fri-Mon, 11 am-6 pm, €3.50, conc. €2.50). But it is the nearby **Speziera dello Spedale di Santa Fina** that pulls most of the tourists with its tour through the ancient pharmaceutical techniques that characterized the medieval hospital once found just below the hilltop town (one of the oldest in the world).

From here, a right takes you to the wool-washer's fountain outside the Porta dei Fonti, a large well house of 10 arches (a mix of 12th-century round and 14th-century pointed arches) and an impressive series of tubs originally used for public washing. Then Via delle Romite takes you back to the center via the grisly collection of medieval torture instruments in the **Museo Criminale Medioevale** (Via del Castello 1, ☎ 0577-942243, Mon-Fri, 10 am-1 pm, 2-7 pm, Sat-Sun, 11 am-1 pm, 2-6 pm, €7, conc. €3).

Vernaccia

The gluttons stuck in Purgatory in Dante's *Divine Comedy* liked to glug it down, the table of Lorenzo Il Magnifico was never without a bottle of it and even a pope or two was said to have been a bit partial to its taste. The history of this white wine goes back almost as far as the town. You can find out more by following the wine road established by **Strada del Vino Vernaccia di San Gimignano** (Via della Rocca, ☎ 0577-940008, fax 0577-955084, stradavinovernaccia@sangimignano.com), which stretches from San Gimignano Libbiano, Pancone Santa Andrea and Bibbiano to Castel San Gimignano, with numerous producers offering taste-it and buy-it *degustazione*.

■ Adventures on Foot & on Wheels

Attempting a walk out of San Gimignano can be a little daunting (you'll spend your whole trek with the knowledge that a steep hike awaits when you return to town), but the nearby countryside holds enough sites of interest to make it worth your while. Most trails depart from San Donato (downhill from the San Giovanni Gate) with routes taking you into the **Castelvecchio Nature Reserve** and the two miles to **Pieve di Céllole**, a pretty Romanesque parish church with a beautiful, and quite surprising, view back to San Gimignano.

A pleasant bike ride south will take you to **Casole D'Elsa**, a typical walled military outpost that grew up on the frontline between Volterra and Florence. The main sight in its picturesque streets of medieval townhouses is the towering **Collegiata di Santa Maria** (with **Museo Archeologico e di Arte Sacra**, Archeological and Sacred Art Museum, ☎ 0577-948705, Mar-Oct, 10 am-noon, 4-7 pm, Nov-Feb, 3-6 pm, closed Mon, €3, conc. €2), which has some interesting 14th- to 17th-century Sienese and Florentine canvases.

You can also pick up trails from town into the **Foreste del Berignone Nature Reserve** and the little-frequented Castello dei Vescovi in its solitary and panoramic position outside town. There's also a grueling 31-mile bike loop through Monteguidi, Montecastelli (and the stunning Colline Metallifere) and round to Radicondoli. But, as challenging as it may be, the number-one local bike itinerary has to be the 19-mile route from San Gimignano to Volterra, taking you down to Castel San Gimignano and along the SS68 to Volterra – save some strength for the last punishing two-mile climb!

RADICONDOLI

*Near Radicondoli, there are the **Bagni delle Gallerie**, a thermal spa (Loc. Le Gallerie, ☎ 0577-793151, fax 0577-792821, www.termesaluteambiente.com, May-Oct). On the perimeter of three nature reserves, there are flora and fauna to discover here as well as the recuperative properties of the hot spring itself. Trekking and guided tours can be arranged on request.*

■ Where to Eat

> ### BUYING LOCAL
>
> San Gimignano's famous products – Vernaccia (one of Italy's finest white wines), *prosciutto di cinghiale* (wild boar ham), the local *panforte* and saffron, which bolstered the town's economy in the Middle Ages – garnish most of the main street's shops. For gastronomic gifts from some of the best-known, try **Antico Latteria** (Via San Matteo 19, ☎ 0577-941952) for savories, **Nuova Bristot** (Via Martiri di Citerna 35, ☎ 0577-940506) for panforte and **Bazar di Sapori** (Via San Giovanni 8, ☎ 0577-942021) for saffron and other local specialties.

 One of the best of San Gimignano's medieval-styled restaurants is family-run **Il Pino** (Via San Matteo 102, ☎ 0577-942225, closed Thurs, $$), right in the historical center. It offers a good mix of local dishes at some of the most competitive prices. Booking recommended for evenings. The small **La Grotta Ghiotta** (Via Santo Stefano 10, ☎ 0577-942074, closed Thurs, $$) is the other low-priced higher-quality option in town.

You're paying for location at **Le Terrazze** (Piazza della Cisterna 24, ☎ 0577-940328, www.hotelcisterna.it, $$$), the restaurant of Hostel Cisterna ($$$) in the old Palazzo Braccieri overlooking the bustling square. Not that the menu particularly disappoints in an over-visited city like San Gimignano. The same applies to **Bel Soggiorno** (Via San Giovanni 41, ☎ 0577-940375, www.hotelbelsoggiorno.it, closed Wed, $$), probably the best located of the city restaurants set as it is in the town walls (booking recommended for the tables with countryside views). The charming **Le Vecchie Mura** (Via Piandornella 15, ☎ 50577-940270, www.vecchiemura.it, closed Tues, $$$) is also within the town walls, but this time in the old stables.

Out of town, your best options are a follows. **Vecchio Granaio** (Vicolo degli Innocenti 21, ☎ 0577-941919, www.dulcisinfundo.net, closed Wed, $) is more an *enoteca* or wine bar than a restaurant, offering a range of light dishes (salami, salads, cheeses) and a small wine museum. **Da Pode** (Loc. Sovestro, ☎ 0577-943153, fax 0577-943089, failli_sergio@libero.it, $$) has a panoramic summer terrace. And, just a short hop from San Gimignano, **Enoteca da Niso** (Loc. Sovestro 32, ☎ 0577-941029, info@danisio.com, closed Tues, $$$), offers a flavorsome range of Tuscan cuisine to accompany the local Vernaccia.

Top picks in the Val d'Elsa are mostly centered around **Monteriggioni** – try **Il Pozzo** (Piazza Roma, ☎ 0577-304127, $$, closed Mon), **La Bottega di Lornano** (Loc. Lornano, ☎ 0577-309146, $$, closed Mon) or **La Leggenda dei Frati** (Loc. Abbadia Isola, ☎ 0577-301222, $$, closed Mon).

Your best choice in **Colle di Val d'Elsa** is **Arnolfo** (Via XX Settembre 50, ☎ 0577-920549, closed Tues, $$$), with **Casole d'Elsa** well served by **Il Colombaio** (Loc. Colombaio, ☎ 0577-949002, closed Mon, $$).

■ Where to Stay

San Gimignano

 Very reasonably priced for the quality it provides, **Vecchio Asilo** ☆ (Via delle Torri 4, Loc. Ulignano, ☎ 0577-950032, fax 0577-950280, www.vecchioasilo.it, $$), a few miles out of San Gimignano, has some lovely elegant rooms with timbered ceilings and tiled floors.

Well-positioned on San Gimignano's central piazza in a 16th-century nobleman's palace is **Leon Bianco** ☆☆☆ (Piazza della Cisterna 13, ☎ 0577-941294, fax 0577-942123, www.leonbianco.com, $$$). Its rooms have some lovely original timbered and arched ceilings, which perhaps explains why you need to book so far in advance to secure a room.

Another popular venue with a great location in the center of town is **L'Antico Pozzo** ☆☆☆ (Via S. Matteo 87, ☎ 0577-942014, fax 0577-942117, www.anticopozzo.com, $$$$), which has done a good job of preserving the medieval character of the 15th-century restored townhouse it occupies.

In a former Franciscan convent surrounded by a park of cypress trees, the stunning redbrick **La Collegiata** ☆☆☆☆ (Loc. Strada 27, ☎ 0577-943201, fax 0577-940566, www.lacollegiata.it, $$$$$), overlooking the towers of San Gimignano, has to be your first choice for luxury accomodation out of town. Outdoor pool.

Picturesque and reasonably priced *agriturismi* are abundant in the vicinity of San Gimignano. Of those closest, try **Podere Santa Croce** ☆☆☆☆ (Loc. Santa Croce, ☎/fax 0577-943073, www.alfapi.com/santacroce, $$, Mar-Jan) or the spacious **Fattoria Voltrona** ☆☆☆ (Loc. Montauto 50, ☎ 0577-943152, fax 0577-906077, www.voltrona.com, $$, 15 Mar-15 Oct) with outdoor pool, lake for swimming and fishing, hiking, cycling and horseback riding facilities, plus wine and olive oil for sale.

There's an equally large choice in *affitacamere*. For the best central location, first try **Sangirooms** (Via Berignano 24, ☎ 333-2953891, fax 055-8075862, www.sangirooms.com, $$). It is one of the most luxurious options for the price, with terracotta flooring, open-beamed ceilings and some great views over the towers. Nearby **La Casa di Giovanna** (Via S. Giovanni 58, ☎ 0577-940419, http://casagiovanna.cjb.net, $$, three rooms) isn't quite as classically decorated, but it does have equally good views from its spacious modern rooms.

Campers should head to the popular **Il Boschetto di Piemma** ☆ (Loc. Santa Lucia, ☎ 0577-940352, fax 0577-941982, bpiemma@tiscalnet.it, $, 63 pitches, 27 Apr-15 Oct), only a short distance south of the town, with bar and restaurant and outdoor pool. Book early to avoid disappointment. The area's **youth hostel** can also be found in San Gimignano (Via delle Fonte 1, ☎ 0577-941991, fax 055-8050104, $).

Val d'Elsa

Midway between **Monteriggioni** and Colle Val d'Elsa, **Casalta** ☆☆☆ (Via G. Matteotti 22, Loc. Strove, ☎/fax 0577-301002, casalta@chiantiturismo.it, $$$), occupying one of Strove's famous fortress houses, is one of the area's cheapest options. **Monteriggioni** ☆☆☆☆ (Via I Maggio 4, Castello, ☎ 0577-305009, fax 0577-305011, www.hotelmonteriggioni.net, $$$$$), within the medieval walls of the town, is the best located but most expensive. Both have outdoor pools.

In **Colle Val d'Elsa** on a budget, your cheapest option is **Il Nazionale** ☆☆ (Via Garibaldi 20, ☎ 0577-749483, fax 0577-920168, $$), but if you have a car and plan on staying a few days, it's worth the drive to **La Fornace** (Loc. La Fornace, ☎/fax 0577-922677, $$, three rooms) for an even cheaper deal.

If you're traveling out of season, be sure to check for last-minute deals with **Villa Belvedere** ☆☆☆ (Via Senese, Loc. Belvedere, ☎ 0577-920966, fax 0577-924128, www.villabelvedere.com, $$$), a lovely yellow-washed 17th-century villa with outdoor pool, tennis facilities and cooking courses.

The former home of Cardinal Giuliano della Rovere, later to become Pope Giulio II, the charming Renaissance **Relais della Rovere** ☆☆☆☆ (Via Piemonte 10, Loc. La Badia, ☎ 0577-924696, fax 0577-924489, dellarovere@chiantiturismo.it, $$$$$) has some beautiful views over Colle Bassa and Colle Alta. Outdoor pool.

In **Relais La Suvera** ☆☆☆☆☆ (Loc. Pievescola, ☎ 0577-960300, fax 0577-960220, www.lasuvera.it, $$$$$), **Casole d'Elsa** has one of Tuscany's most luxurious hotels, a former medieval castle gifted to Pope Giulio II and now owned by the family of the Marquis Ricci, whose collection of antiques is on show to guests. For those on a more normal budget, **Colombaio** (Loc. Scorgiano 19, ☎/fax 0577-301242, www.scorgiano.it, $$) offers nightly and weekly stays on its 1,200-acre working farm.

If you're planning on hanging around the region for a little longer, there are plenty of *agriturismi* to choose from near **Colle Val d'Elsa**; try **Fattoria Belvedere** ☆☆☆ (Loc. Belvedere, ☎ 0577-920009, fax 0577-923500, www.fattoriabelvedere.com, $$, Mar-Oct), **Tenuta di Mensanello** (Loc. Mensanello 34, ☎/fax 0577-971080, $$$) or **Residence Tana de' Lepri** (Loc. Il Colombaio 7, ☎/fax 0577-958961, www.tanadelepri.com, $$$, Mar-Oct), all with outdoor pool and outdoor activities within close range.

The Crete

The Crete (meaning the "Clay"), which rolls southeast of Siena, takes its name from the unusual clay *biancane* (domelike mounds free of vegetation) and *calanchi* (sheer cliffs carved by the whipping rain and wind) that characterize it. Bare of the hilltop fortifications, ruined castles and lush vegetation that typically dot Siena's province, the milk-gray clay of the Crete instead offers travertine-marble quarries, tiny medieval villages, isolated abbeys and lonely clumps of cypress trees on its sweeping horizons.

■ Getting Here & Around

 By Bus: The best approach from Siena is by bus. Regular **Tra-In** services (☎ 0577-204111, www.trainspa.it) run to Monteroni d'Arbia (#105 and #111), Asciano (#105 and #109), San Giovanni d'Asso (#109 and #119), Buonconvento (#112 and #114) and Serre (#105). **Rama** (☎ 0564-475111, www.griforama.it) also runs service #9 through Monteroni d'Arbia and Buonconvento en route to the Orcia Valley towns.

 By Train: Trains (☎ 848-888088, www.trenitalia.it) on the Siena-to-Chiusi/Chianciano Terme line also stop approximately every hour at Asciano and Rapolano Terme. Both Monteroni d'Arbia and Buonconvento are on the Siena-to-Grosseto line (about one train every two hours).

By Car: Drivers can reach Monteroni d'Arbia and Buonconvento on the **SS2 Cassia**, Asciano on the **SS438** and Rapolano Terme on the **SS73** from Siena. Monte Oliveto Maggiore and San Giovanni d'Asso are a short drive from Asciano or Buonconvento on the SS451.

You can arrange **bike rental** from Asciano (**Real**, Via Roma 46/50, ☎ 0577-719138) and Buonconvento (**Rossi Mirko**, Via Roma 36/38).

■ Information Sources

Tourist Offices: The main tourist office for the Crete is found in **Monte Oliveto Maggiore** (☎ 0577-707262) with others at **Monteroni d'Arbia** (Piazzetta del Mulino 3r, ☎ 0577-372104, www.comune.monteronidarbia. si.it), **Asciano** (Corso Matteotti 18, ☎ 0577-719510, fax 0577-719517, May-Oct), **San Giovanni d'Asso** (Piazza Gramsci 1, ☎ 0577-803101, fax 0577-803203), **Buonconvento** (Museo di Arte Sacra della Val d'Arbia, Via Soccini 18, ☎/fax 0577-807181, Sat-Sun only Nov-Feb) and **Rapolano Terme** (Piazza Matteotti 9, ☎ 0577-724079, fax 0577-726591, inforapolano@inwind.it).

Guides & Maps: *Crete Senesi 1 – Val d'Arbia*, scale: 1:25,000 (Tourist and Trail map, Edizioni Multigraphic Firenze) is your best bet for routes in the region.

■ Sightseeing & Adventures

THE VALDARBIA TRAILS

A well-trodden path system taking you through the unpolluted countryside of the Sienese Crete, the **Valdarbia Trails**, a mix of dirt roads, country trails and wood path suitable for **trekking**, **mountain biking** and **horseback riding**, departs from the towns of Monteroni d'Arbia, Asciano, San Giovanni d'Asso, Buonconvento, Rapolano Terme and Trequanda. The "Via Francigena Trail," the "Grance del Santa Maria della Scala Trail," and the "Etruscan itinerary of the Valle dell'Ombrone" are just some of the 67 artistic, natural and historic trails on offer. Contact the Valdarbia tourist offices to pick up detailed itineraries.

 Heading out of Siena on the SS2 Cassia, the first hamlet you'll meet is **Monteroni d'Arbia**, an agricultural center, crossed by the Via Francigena, whose bustling market square was fortified at the start of the 14th century. Its most interesting monuments are found out of town; the terracotta *Grancia* (grain storehouse) at the military-style farm in **Cuna** (the former domain of Siena's powerful Santa Maria della Scala) and the fortified village of **Lucignano d'Arbia** with its 16th-century frescoes by Arcangelo Salimbeni in the Romanesque **Pieve di San Giovanni Battista**. From here you can pick up the 30-mile **bike** ride to Asciano (through Mucigliani and Torre a Castello) and the shorter 18-mile itinerary, which just loops as far as Mucigliani but this time through San Martino.

Local Grancia

 A common medieval sight in Siena's wheat-producing hinterland, generally abbey- or church-owned, are the fortified granaries (Grancia di Cuna shown at left). You can visit Serre di Rapolano's **Museo della Grancia** (Via dell'Antica Grancia 11, ☎ 0577-705055, fax 0577-705682, summer, 9 am-1 pm, 3:30-6:30 pm, to 5 pm in winter, €3, conc. €2) with its display on the history and function of this massive agricultural construction at one time owned by Siena's Spedale di Santa Maria della Scala.

Asciano is the welcoming little "commercial capital" of the Crete, still enclosed by its late medieval fortifications. Here, the heart of town is dominated by the 12th-century **Collegiata di Sant'Agata** with unusual octagonal cupola and interior architectural details still obviously influenced by earlier Lombard designs. There is a *Madonna and Child* by Signorelli and a *Deposition* by Sodoma, but its most notable works, along with others taken from the surrounding country churches, can be found in the **Museo Civico Archeologico e di Arte Sacra** (Palazzo Corboli, Corso Matteotti, ☎ 0577-71441). It has works by Ambrogio Lorenzetti and Taddeo di Bartolo, along with a basic collection of Etruscan vases, money and funerary urns taken from the nearby necropolis of Poggio Pinci (fifth century BC) and the tomb at Molinello (seventh century BC).

If you want something a little more modern, there's a gallery of paintings by Asciano-born Purist Amos Cassioli (1832-91) and son Giuseppe (1865-1942) in the **Museo Cassioli** (Via Mameli, ☎ 0577-71441, Tues-Sun, 10 am-12:30 pm, and 4:30-6:30 pm, June-Sept, €4). Nearby on Via del Canto, you can see a polychrome mosaic pavement, which marks the remains of a large spa.

TREKKING TRAINS

Get off, trek and get back on the ancient **Asciano-Monte Antico train line** (Treno Natura Ferrovia Val d'Orcia, Piazza Rosselli 5, ☎ 0577-207413, 0577-207343, www.ferrovieturistiche.it) with CAI-marked foot and mountain bike trails leading you from the train stations into the Crete, Asso and Orcia valleys (Asciano to Castelnuovo Berardenga Scalo; Asciano to San Giovanni d'Asso; and San Giovanni d'Asso to Buonconvento).

You can also pick up trails from Asciano that lead you northwest to Siena or east over La Bandita to Trequanda (#4). From Trequanda, you can follow further itineraries south towards Monte Amiata (see page 182). **Horseback riders** can also head to Trequanda (Scuderia Le Vigne, Via delle Trove 10, Castelmuzio – Trequanda, ☎ 0577-665032, fax 0577-665093, www.scuderielevigne.com).

There are some pretty breathtaking roads for **bikers** leading out of Asciano. For road bikers, the historical **Lauretana** runs to Asciano from Siena before continuing south past Chisure and the Abbazia di Monte Oliveto Maggiore. Mountain bikers can use the 19-mile unpaved loop from Asciano to Monte Sante Marie along the River Ombrone and the CAI-marked circle, which runs through Rapolano, Serre di Rapolano and San Giovanni d'Asso.

The most important and impressive of Siena's monasteries is the redbrick **Abbazia di Monte Oliveto Maggiore** (summer, 9:15-noon, 3:15-6 pm, to 5 pm in winter, free). It was the first of the Olivetan branch of the Benedictine faith, founded in 1313 when Giovanni Tolomei (the Fra Bernardo under whom the offshoot went on to obtain papal recognition) abandoned his worldly goods to dedicate himself to a life of poverty and solitude inside the patch of wild and secular cypress forest where the monastery still stands. The approach is pretty stunning itself, with some of the Crete's most spectacular *calanchi* intro-ducing the dark woodlands, which sheild the complex from the outside world. Only the glazed terracotta entrance gate-tower (the work of Andrea della Robbia) indicates that there is a building here at all.

Following the woodland **trails** inside (park in the car park opposite the entrance gate), the complex appears surprisingly large, its center formed by the impressive **Chiostro Grande**, with its famed 36-scened fresco cycle *Stories of St Benedict*, initiated by Luca Signorelli (the west side, 1497-98) and finished off by Sodoma (the 27 scenes on the opposite side, 1505). To the latter artist is also attributed the *Christ Bearing the Cross* in the corridor that leads to the early 15th-century church (the Gothic portal and the Romanesque-Gothic campanile dating from the first phase of construction). Its main interior sight is the wooden inlaid choir by Fra Giovanni da Verona, which occupies practically the whole nave (1503-05).

Further spectacular *calanchi* (sheer cliffs carved by rain and wind) lead you to nearby **San Giovanni d'Asso**, the white truffle capital of Italy with a popular fes-tival during the second and third weeks of November. The town otherwise merits a quick look for its imposing Gothic castle, Romanesque Chiesa di San Giovanni Battista, and late 11th-century half-terracotta Chiesa di San Pietro in Villore located in the lower part of town.

Back on the SS2 Cassia, the Crete opens out at **Buonconvento** (another of the Via Francigena progeny), the sunny stretch leading south along the lush Arbia and Ombrone rivers belying an otherwise gruesome history of contest and conflict. Inside the ancient redbrick city walls, everything is medieval in layout with some charming *chiassi* (alleyways) leading off from the central Palazzo Pretorio (the one covered with the crests of the town's former *podestà*), although many of the buildings underwent something of a facelift in the 18th century.

Religious art gathered from the Valdarbia churches is displayed in the town's **Museo di Arte Sacra** (Via Soccini 18, ☎ 0577-807181, Tues-Sun, 10:30 am-1 pm, 3-7 pm, €3, conc. €2), its 100 paintings and sculptures including impressive pieces by Duccio di Buoninsegna, Pietro Lorenzetti, Sano di Pietro and Brescianino. That done, you should head into the surroundings to the lovely forti-fied **Pieve di Sant'Innocenza a Piana** (11th century), built almost entirely out of terracotta and conserving some fabulous 13th-century frescoes.

One of the region's best **bike** rides departs from Buonconvento (the 24-mile Buonconvento-Chiusure-Monte Oliveto-S.Giovanni d'Asso-Buonconvento itiner-ary), a mix of *strade bianche* and unpaved road. You can also pick up a range of **horseback riding** itineraries; contact **Club Ippico Valdarbia** (Loc. Pian delle Noci, Buonconvento, ☎ 348-4125561) to organize a tour.

Local Events: If you're around the third Sunday in July, get yourself to Buonconvento for the *Trebbiatura sotto le mura*, an old-time grain thrashing re-enactment complete with dinner and dancing in the town square.

Step back into the region's agricultural past with the **Museo della Mezzadria Senese** (Sienese Share-Cropping Museum, Tinaia del Taja, ☎ 0577-809075), a celebration of the region's share-cropping past (the medieval practice of tenants paying the landowner rent with half their crop rather than cash). The museum offers a presentation of key players such as the landowner, the worker, the housewife and the machinery.

The Crete meets the Val di Chiana and the Chianti woodlands at **Rapolano Terme**, a border town whose famous views over the hamlets, churches, farms and winding dirt roads of the Crete stretch as far as Siena's towers (just a 15-minute drive away). The approach into town is equally stunning. The roadside is characterized by the brightness of the gaping white travertine quarries, which fed the town's architecture (everything from the city walls to the castle and Romanesque Chiesa di San Bartolomeo is constructed with the stone). The same is true of Siena (the Torre del Mangia and the Palazzo Piccolomini), Montepulciano (the Chiesa di San Biagio) and Pienza (the façade and campanile of the cathedral).

> **Rapolano Spas:** The **Antica Querciolaia di Rapolano** (Via Trieste 22, ☎ 0577-724091, fax 0577-725470, www.termeaq.it, winter, 10 am-6 pm, to 11 pm on Sat, summer, 10 am-7 pm, to noon Fri and Sat) and **Terme di San Giovanni** (Via Terme San Giovanni 52, ☎ 0577-724030, fax 0577-724053, www.termesangiovanni.it, May-Oct, 9:30 am-7:30 pm, one mile southwest) have been frequented since the Etruscans first took a dip in their sulphuric-bicarbonate-calcium waters in the fourth century BC. If you don't want to pay for the privilege of a dip, you can visit the **Rapolano Cascades** (southeast of Terme di San Giovanni) without having to spend a cent.

Foot **trails** out of Rapolano Terme take you to the Terme di San Giovanni, past the Pieve di San Vittore and along the Ombrone River (five miles), across to Serre di Rapolano and past the necropolis of Poggio Pinci toward Asciano (#4) and up Poggio Capanne (629 m/2,063 feet). The best **bike** rides, on the other hand, loop the 19 miles through Rigomagno, Calcione and back along the SS438 Lauretana, or take you a panoramic 12 miles through travertine quarries to Serre di Rapolano and Asciano. There's also **horseback riding** to enjoy; contact **Villa dei Boschi** (Fraz. San Gimignanello 50, Rapolano Terme, ☎ 0577-704394, fax 0577-704082) to book yourself a trip.

SOMETHING FOR THE KIDS

KID FRIENDLY At Petroio near Trequanda, kids will love the **Museo della Terracotta** (Terracotta Museum, Via Valgelata 10, Petroio, ☎ 0577-662114, fax 0577-665188, www.comune.trequanda.siena.it), which displays the history and evolution of terracotta production in the area. It also organizes hands-on sessions with craftsmen on the third Friday of every month (participation must be booked in advance).

■ Where to Eat

 Considered by locals to be the best pizzeria in the area, family-run **Pizzeria San Rocco** (Via San Rocco 32, Serre di Rapolano, ☎ 0577-70422, closed Mon, $), three miles from Rapolano Terme, has an attractive garden for summer dining. Booking recommended for Sat evenings, when it's generally full.

Booking is also recommended for the small **Trattoria La Patria** (Via Sobborgo Garibaldi 12, ☎ 0577-724464, Rapolano Terme, closed Sat, $), one of the best examples of a "classic Tuscan trattoria" you will find in such a touristy region. Though not chic by any means, the atmosphere is welcoming, while its home cooking is top quality and low-priced.

A tiny trattoria close to the Terme Antica Querciolia, **Albergo Ristorante Trento** (Via Provinciale Nord 48, ☎ 0577-724071, closed Mon, $) serves the kind of Tuscan cooking found in homes all over the province. Booking recommended; it's crammed with locals every evening. There's also a small hotel serving the budget market ($).

About four miles from Terme di San Giovanni, **Ristorante Da Ottirino** (Loc. S. Marie 114, ☎ 0577-718770, closed Mon, $$) not only offers tasty and top-quality local dishes but the owners also sell beautiful terracotta ceramics and antique furnishings. It's worth visiting the adjacent exposition even if you're not intending to buy.

The elegant and well-reputed **Ristorante La Sosta** (Loc. Crocevie, near Serre di Rapolano, ☎ 0577-704177, www.hotelserre.it, closed Mon, $$), is in the four-star Grand Hotel Serre ($$$) on the Siena-Bettolle road (about three miles from Rapolano Terme). It serves classic versions of typical Tuscan dishes.

In a stunning medieval structure, exclusive hotel and restaurant **Casabianca** (Loc. Casabianca, ☎ 0577-704362, www.casabianca.it, $$$) is your best choice if you're looking to splash out in the Asciano area. It also has a well-furnished wine cellar.

Pienza, the Val d'Orcia & Monte Amiata

This area is instantly recognizable to anyone who has watched *The English Patient*. The film's director, Anthony Minghella, was so struck by the local landscape, he set scenes in Pienza and the monastery at Sant'Anna in Camprena. The Val d'Orcia (comprising the towns of Castiglione d'Orcia, Montalcino, Pienza, Radicofani and San Quirico d'Orcia) offers an extraordinary landscape of country roads lined by cypress trees, sleepy vineyards and geometrically cultivated fields en route to its main attractions. These are the Renaissance town of Pienza, the mystical abbey of Sant'Antimo, the main square in Bagno Vignoni and the wine cellars of Montalcino. Sightseeing done, there are plenty of adventures to be had on the slopes of Monte Amiata.

■ Getting Here & Around

 Two approaches by **bus** are possible. The first takes you south from Siena (Tra-In #144 to Montalcino, Rama #9 to San Quirico d'Orcia, Bagni San Filippo, Bagno Vignoni, Castiglione d'Orcia, Vivo d'Orcia, Amiata FS, Castel del Piano, Abbadia San Salvatore, Piancastagnaio and Santa Fiora), the second departs from Chiusi via Chiancianco Terme Station (three or four **train** services an hour from Firenze S.M.N.) with LFI (☎ 0578-31174, www.lfi.it) services to Bagni San Filippo, Abaddia San Salvatore and the Amiata area. Monte Amiata is also served by the Treno Natura (see page 150, 171). If you're arriving by **car**, the same SS2 Cassia, will take you into the valley with wellposted turns off to Montalcino and Abbadia San Salvatore. **Bikes** can be hired at Pienza (Cicloposse, Via I Maggio 27, ☎ 0578-749983, fax 0578-749983, www.cicloposse.com, from €16 a day).

■ Information Sources

Tourist Offices: There are *pro locos* dotted all over the Val d'Orcia or Orcia Valley, with the bigger centers at **Pienza** (Piazza Pio II, ☎/fax 0578-749071, www.comunedipienza.it, Mon-Sat, 9:30 am-1 pm, 3-6:30 pm), **Montalcino** (Costa del Municipio 1, ☎/fax 0577-849331, www.prolocomontalcino.it, Tues-Sun, 10 am-1 pm, 2-5:30 pm) and **Abbadia San Salvatore** (Via Adua 25, ☎ 0577-775811, fax 0577-775877, www.amiataturismo.it, Mon-Sat, 9 am-1 pm, 4-6 pm, Sun and public holidays, 9 am-1 pm). Otherwise you can pick up plenty of information at **Castiglione d'Orcia** (Viale Marconi 13, ☎ 0577-887363), **Radicofani Informazioni** (Via R. Magi 31, ☎ 0578-55684), **San Quirico d'Orcia** (Via Dante Alighieri 33, ☎ 0577-897211, www.parcodellavaldorcia.com, Apr-Oct, 10 am-1 pm, 3:30-6:30 pm) and over in the Grosseto province at **Piancastagnaio** (Viale Gramsci 1, ☎ 0577-784134). The **Communità Montana Amiata Senese** (Sienese Amiata Mountain Community, Via Grossetana 209, Piancastagnaio, ☎ 0577-787186) is also a good contact for information on adventures on Monte Amiata.

Guides & Maps: The region is served by the *Pienza-Montalcino-Monte Amiata*, scale 1:50,000 (Touring and Cycling Map n.653, Kompass, www.kompass.at) and the *Val d'Orcia*, scale 1:25,000 (Trail Map, Edizioni Multigraphic).

■ Sightseeing ~ Montalcino

Worth a trip just for the local vine, Montalcino has the added bonus of being one of the best-preserved hilltop towns in the region. Dominating the horizon from its 500-m (1,640-foot) crest, fortified by the Sienese in 1361, you'll have plenty of time to take it in as you wind up through the 8,400-acres of Brunello-producing vineyards in the Orcia and Ombrone valleys.

Built to mark the passage of Montalcino to Siena's dominion, the **Rocca** (Piazzale della Fortezza, Tues-Sun, 10 am-6 pm, to 8 pm from Apr to Oct, €3, conc. €2) marks the southern and highest point of the town, an excellent example of early Renaissance military architecture, shown at right. The Sienese were presumably very glad architect Mino Foresi did such a good job when they sought refuge here in 1555, although even this, their ultimate stronghold, eventually fell to Florence and the advancing

Spanish army. Today, it marks the social heart of town with the year-round Brunello "enoteca-temple" at its most vibrant during the summer festivities when it becomes the site of the towns' theatrical and cultural events.

LOCAL EVENTS

Montalcino's famous **Jazz and Wine Festival** (☎ 0577-84011, info@banfi.it, 10-20 July) occupies the inner courtyard of the Rocca with its well-known Italian and international stars and glasses (albeit plastic) of local booze. Expect to find sponsoring vineyard, Banfi, on the menu.

Further festivities are shared between Cetona, Radicofani and Pienza in the **Incontri in Terra di Siena** (Meetings of the Siena Land, ☎ 0578-69101, 19-27 July). Founded by the daughter of Anglo-Italian writer Iris Origo, the chamber music concerts are all organized from the writer's villa at Foce.

The geographical center of town is down the hill (past the Gothic-Romanesque **Chiesa di Sant'Egidio**) on the atmospheric Piazza del Popolo. The slender tower of its rather odd-looking 14th-century **Palazzo dei Priori** provides the town's other main symbol. No less of an attraction, the wonderful turn-of-the-century décor of the **Caffè Fiaschetteria**, on the right-hand side of the piazza, provides the perfect spot for a coffee break.

From here, the route takes you down to the **Chiesa di Sant'Agostino** on Via Ricasoli. Its beautifully decorated marble doorway offers a stunning introduction to a nave decorated with frescoes by Bartolo di Fredi and others. More of his work can be accessed from the church cloister in the **Musei Civico e Diocesano** (☎ 0577-846014, Tues-Sun, 10 am-6 pm, €4.50, conc. €3), one of the most important medieval art museums in the province with

works from Sienese artists such as Simone Martini and Ambrogio Lorenzetti, Giovanni di Paolo, Sano di Pietro and Il Vecchietta. Top picks from its interesting anthology of works from the Middle Ages to the 16th century are the noteworthy collection of 14th-century wooden sculptures, a 12th-century painted cross taken from Sant'Antimo, a glazed della Robbia terracotta and an early Renaissance *Madonna with Child and Saints* by Ambrogio Lorenzetti.

Though not quite competing with the views from the Rocca (which stretch south to Monte Amiata and north over the town as far as Siena), there are other beautiful views from Piazza del Duomo (the square's main attraction, the **Duomo**, is a disappointing reconstruction from the 1820s) and from Porta al Corniolo. Pop into the **Chiesa della Madonna del Soccorso** on your way down to the latter; it has some exquisite Baroque altarpieces behind its modern façade.

Tip: You can buy a combined museum ticket for entrance to the Rocca and the Musei Civico e Diocesano for €5, conc. €4.

■ Adventures ~ Montalcino

Leaving Montalcino, a scenic seven-mile **bike ride** or **hike** leads you along provincial #2 to the **Abbazia di Sant'Antimo** (☎ 0577-835659, 10:30 am-12:30 pm, 3-6:30 pm, free), one of Italy's most stunning examples of Romanesque architecture, particularly in the early morning or late afternoon when the travertine façade takes on a golden hue. A Benedictine monastery, it was extremely powerful up until the late 13th century, when, too big for their britches, the land-owning abbots fell out with the ruling Sienese. Although it's quiet these days, at 12:45 and 2:45 pm the monks start their 10-minute chant. It makes for an evocative ending to the trip and puts you in the mood for the further nine-mile route up the hill to the medieval village of Castelnuovo dell'Abate and back to Montalcino.

From nearby Torrenieri, you can pick up **footpaths** that follow the ancient Cassia Way through Cosona into the Crete and its *calanchi* (cliffs) to the Olivetan Monastero di Sant'Anna in Caprena.

Mountain **bikers** can pick up council trail #2 south through Castelnuovo dell'Abate to Castiglione d'Orcia, before looping back via San Quirico d'Orcia (a 20-mile round trip) or continuing onto Pienza. There's plenty of opportunity to take in the Brunello vines with an 18-mile route that first descends from Montalcino (follow signs to Sant'Angelo in Colle) and then climbs back to town, passing first the castles of Castelgiocondo and Tavernelle, the latter home to the prestigious Banfi vineyard.

The Granfondo del Brunello

If you think wine and bikes do not mix, the locals of Montalcino will prove you wrong. Every year, they take part in the **Granfondo del Brunello,** a 34-mile (with a shorter 20-mile "mini Brunello") road-bike route, starting and finishing at the Rocca di Montalcino. It takes in the best of the region's vineyards. For some a race, for others an opportunity to taste the local wine, anyone and everyone is welcome to take part. Book your place through **Orso on Bike** (☎ 0577-835532, fax 0577-835545, info@bikemontalcino.it). Participation in the three-day event (17-19 Sept) costs €25.

Get a little closer to the local tipple by following the **wine trail** from Montalcino's Porta Brunelli through the local vineyards to Colombaio and Torrenieri. Guided tours to the region and visits to the wine-producing *poderi* (farms) can be arranged with the **Val d'Orcia Artistic, Natural and Cultural Park** (☎ 0577-898303, www.parcodellavaldorcia.com).

THE WINE LIST

Invented by Feruccio Biondi Santi in the 19th century and now considered one of the best wines in the world, it was the color of **Brunello** that gave it its name: "little brown." Unlike other Tuscan wines, it takes a long time to age and often uses grapes from vines that are at least 10 years old. It is generally aged for a minimum of five years (six years for Reserve), two of which must take place in oak casks. It was one of the first Italian wines to be awarded DOC (Denominazione di Origine Controllata) appellation in 1966 and DOCG (Denominazione di Origine Controllata e Garantita) in 1980.

The town's other well-known brand, the **Rosso di Montalcino** is ready after only one year of aging. Montalcino also produces the lesser-known reds and whites of the Moscadello di Montalcino and Sant'Antimo, and there are reds, whites and dessert wines to be sampled in the Orcia DOC. The latter are ready after three years of aging. To find more about visiting Brunello producers, pop into the **Consorzio Vino Brunello** (Costa del Municipo 1, Montalcino, ☎ 0577-848246, fax 0577-849425). You can also arrange visits to the Orcia vineyards through **Consorzio del Vino DOC Orcia** (Via D. Alighieri 33, La Galleria, San Quirico d'Orcia, ☎/fax 0577-898141, www.orciadoc.it).

■ Sightseeing ~ Pienza

 If you've arrived in peak season and San Gimignano is heaving, the small picturesque city of Pienza, on the sinuous decline into the Orcia Valley, is a less-visited destination (the added driving time and the complications of public transport make a world of difference to the tourist numbers). Rather than the "perfect" medieval town, here you'll find a complete Renaissance city, built from the ground up under the direction of Enea Silvio Piccolomini (Pope Pius II), who had his moment of vision when refuging himself in his father's birthplace, the Castello di Corsignano (on which the city was built) after being chased out of Siena during its fights over civil power.

Piccolomini got Florentine architect Bernardo Gamberelli (known as Il Rossellino) on the case. Fresh from collaborations with his mentor and former teacher Leon Battista Alberti, he did an impressive job designing and building the town in just three years (1459-62). The measured trapezoid Piazza Pio II marks the center of town (its central well also the work of Rossellino), around which are constructed all of Pienza's major monuments – Palazzo Piccolomini, the Duomo, Palazzo Borgia and Palazzo Comunale.

 **Palazzo Piccolomini** (Piccolomini Palace, Piazza Pio II 2, ☎ 0578-748503, 10 am-12:30 pm, 3-6 pm, €3, conc. €2): Alberti's influence is clear in the imposing Piccolomini family residence (note the resemblance to Florence's Palazzo Rucellai). The building is now a museum, where you can visit the ancient hall of arms, Pius II's study, bedchambers, as well as the art and sculpture collection he built from the 15th century on. But before you head inside, check out the fabulous panorama from the palazzo loggia. On a clear day, you can see over the Val d'Orcia as far as the wooded slopes of Monte Amiata. The Palazzo is shown above, to the right of the Duomo.

Duomo (Cathedral, free): Flanking the palace, the cathedral's Gothic travertine façade (also of distinct Albertian flavor) and octagonal campanile mask a Germanic, hall-like, interior. Its luminous two-aisled nave is itself home to works by major Sienese artists such as Giovanni di Paolo, Matteo di Giovanni, Sano di Pietro and Il Vecchietta. The light is admitted through the vast stained-glass windows designed at the request of Pius II; he wanted a *domus vitrea* (literally "a house of glass") to symbolize the spirit of intellectual enlightenment of the Humanist Age. While you're in the Duomo's east end, take a look at the cracks in the walls and floors, they're a worrying sign of the subsidence that is sure to close the cathedral off from visitors sometime in the near future while a solution is sought.

Palazzo Borgia (Borgia Palace): The Palazzo Borgia (or Palazzo Vescovile), to the left of the cathedral, was built by Rodrigo Borgia, the future Pope Alexander VI. It's the current seat of the **Museo Diocesano** (Corso Rossellino 30, ☎ 0578-749905, Mar-Nov, 10 am-1 pm, 3-6:30 pm, closed Tues, other times to 6 pm, €4/US45, conc. €3). An 11-room gallery of Renaissance Sienese art (the best offered by Pietro Lorenzetti and Luca Signorelli), Flemish tapestries and nearby Etruscan and Roman finds.

Opposite the cathedral, the other main palazzo in the square is the travertine **Palazzo Comunale**. It was started 1463 but heavily restored in 1900, its open colonnaded ground-floor loggia providing the most interesting architectural element.

After the main square, a wander behind the Palazzo Piccolomini will bring you to the **Chiesa di San Francesco**, built in the 13th century. It is one of the oldest Franciscan structures in the country. Sadly, all that remains of the original frescoes that once spread over all its walls are some 14th-century pictorial depictions.

■ Adventures ~ Pienza

Heading out of town, you can pick up a variety of **foot** and **mountain bike trails**. These take you to the **Eremo** (Hermitage), a collection of cells excavated by hermit monks in the local sandstone, which includes a small chapel and a few evocative halls added from the 11th century on. There is also the austere **Pieve di Corsignano** (Via delle Fonti, visit by appointment with the tourist office), where Pius II was baptized. Another site to visit is **Sant'Anna in Camprena**, an Olivetan monastery built on top of a primitive Lombard construction. It is especially popular thanks to its use in *The English Patient*. Look for the beautiful fresco cycle by Giovanni Antonio Bazzi (Il Sodoma) in its Refectory. Finally, there is the **Castello di Spedaletto** (midway along the Via Francigena to Bagno Vignoni), which was erected in the 12th century as a hospice for pilgrims, and later became a *grancia* (grain storehouse) of the Spedale di Santa Maria della Scala in Siena.

From the Castello di Spedaletto, you can also pick up a well-trod itinerary looping through Monticchiello and south toward Bagno Vignoni along the remains of the medieval Via Francigena. There's also an interesting nature walk to pick up at the 2,400-acre **Riserva Naturale di Lucciolabella**, whose *calanchi* or steep cliffs and wooded copses (home to wild roses, porcupines, wolves and boars) descend south as far as Monte Amiata.

Monticchiello & the "Poor Man's Theater"

Heading east out of Pienza (on the *strada bianca* to Montepulciano), you'll reach the medieval town of Monticchiello. Alhough worth a visit for its well-preserved fortress walls and 13th-century **Chiesa di SS Leonardo e Cristoforo** (with fascinating, if damaged, frescoes), it is best known for the theatrical performances of its **Teatro Povero** (☎ 0578-55118, www.teatropovero.it, Jan-Apr, performances at 9:30 pm, 5:30 pm on Sun, €11, conc. €6), which traditionally focus on original village legends. The adjacent theater museum tracks the performances' growth from a festival of local culture to an event of international importance.

Five or so well-established **mountain bike** trails depart from Pienza. One of the nicest (but most challenging) leads southwest through **Bagno Vignoni**, **Ripa d'Orcia** and **Castiglione d'Orcia** before dropping you back in town (15 miles). One of the easiest takes you northeast to **Montepulciano** through Monticchello before looping back (19 miles). Maps for these two itineraries (plus three routes along the Orcia River) can be printed out from www.portalepienza.com.

You can also book a guided ride through the local cycling organization, **Becero Bike Pienza** (Luca, ☎ 380-3552674) but it makes more sense just to turn up at one of their frequent Sunday jaunts (generally to the Amiata or Montalcino areas; book your place with Luca in advance). **Ciclioposse** (Via I Maggio 27, ☎/fax 0578-749983, www.cicloposse.com) offers a similar guided bike ride through the Orcia Valley for the slightly higher price of €100.

■ Sightseeing & Adventures ~ The Val d'Orcia

Midway between Pienza and Montalcino, the Orcia Valley winds north from Monte Amiata through the territories of San Quirico d'Orcia, Castiglione d'Orcia and Radicofani. It's a well-marked territory thanks to the newly-formed **Parco Artistico Naturale e Culturale della Val d'Orcia** (The Artistic, Natural & Cultural Park of the Val d'Orcia, Via D. Alighieri 33, San Quirico d'Orcia, ☎ 0577-898303, www.parcodellavaldorcia.com). They have set up a comprehensive trail network that takes you along paved roads, winding trails and dirt tracks through the best of the valley's vineyards, panoramic country streets, abbeys, parish churches and castles.

San Quirico d'Orcia: South from Buonconvento on the SS2 and midway between Pienza and Montalcino on the SS146, San Quirico d'Orcia still conserves its original medieval street plan from back in the days when it was

San Quirico d'Orcia, town gate

known as the Via Francigena town of *Osenna*. In the heart of its turreted walls is the splendid travertine **Collegiata dei Santi Quirico e Giulitta** (12th to 13th century), its Romanesque entrance door guarded by two lion sculptures. Inside, there's a 15th-century triptych by Sano di Pietro (*Madonna with Child and Saints*) and a wooden crown by Antonio Barili.

Siena's late 13th-century Basilica di San Francesco

Above: Siena's Duomo

Below: Interior of the Duomo

A cypress-lined avenue leading from Montepulciano to Pienza
(Tom Johnston/Emma Jones)

Other than the splendid terracotta pavestones that line the streets, the only other sights that merit a look are the recently restored **Palazzo Chigi** (a 17th-century building designed by Carlo Fontana for Cardinal Flavio Chigi with a rich collection of Romanesque art) and the **Horti Leonini**, beautiful 16th-century gardens designed in *giardini all'italiana*-style by Diomede Leoni and hemmed in by parts of the city walls.

There are plenty of **hiking** and **mountain bike trails** to choose from, with the most popular taking you eight miles along a dirt track through farmland and oak woods to **Bagno Vignoni**. Further itineraries take you to the **Parco dei Mulini** (the park of watermills), where traditional mills, constructed of the local travertine marble, are at work, and through Bagno Vignoni to Ripa d'Orcia. The latter has a 12th-century reconstructed fortress that once belonged to the Salimbeni and Piccolomini families.

BAGNO VIGNONI

*Although you can no longer take a dip in the vast thermal swimming pool that constitutes the very impressive main square of Bagno Vignoni (as Lorenzo Il Magnifico, St Catherine, Pope Pius II and many of the Via Francigena's pilgrims once could), you can plunge into the 87°F waters at the **Stabilimento Termale di Bagno Vignoni** (Piazza del Moretto 32, ☎ 0577-887365, fax 0577-887365, bagnovignoniterme@tin.it, June-Oct, 8 am-1 pm, 4-7 pm). The town's other main sight is the **Chiesa di San Giovanni Battista** (at the corner of the town's rectangula hot water pool), which has a fresco fragment of note attributed to Ventura Salimbeni.*

For **mountain bikers,** there's also an easy 20-mile route, which takes you from San Quirico through Celamonti and the Monastero di Sant'Anna in Camprena to Pienza.

Castiglione d'Orcia: Before arriving at Castiglione d'Orcia, you'll pass through the picturesque village of **Rocca d'Orcia**. This medieval military stronghold and one-time home of St Catherine of Siena (Italy's patron saint) is dominated by the ruined tower (summer, daily, 10 am-1 pm, 3-6 pm, winter, Sat-Sun, 10 am-1 pm, 2:30-4:30 pm, €2) from which it takes its name. If you're stopping, there's also a 13th-century Pieve di San Simeone and Chiesa di Madonna del Palazzo (now a house) of note.

Lofty Castiglione d'Orcia also has a picturesque medieval center, marked by a main square dedicated to the painter and sculptor Lorenzo di Pietro (Il Vecchietta). The **Palazzo Comunale** here contains a frescoed *Madonna and Child with two Saints* taken from the nearby Rocca d'Orcia and it overlooks a well in travertine marble dating to 1618. There are also two images of the *Madonna and Child* in the **Chiesa dei Santi Stefano e Degna** (one by Pietro Lorenzetti, the other by Simone Martini).

Some of the best **foot** and **mountain bike** itineraries depart from here, taking you though chestnut forests (home to the rare green woodpecker), past the ancient Eremo at Vivo d'Orcia (now replaced by a 16th-century palazzo attributed to

Sangallo Il Giovanne), and alongside waterfalls and caves up to the slopes of the extinct volcano of Monte Amiata.

A mighty 70-km (44 mile) mountain bike itinerary, which departs from Castiglione d'Orcia, takes you back north through Bagno Vignoni, then south on the SS438 to Radicofani and **Bagni San Filippo**, before returning to Castiglione through Campiglia d'Orcia. Campiglia d'Orcia is also the location of the area's main **horseback riding** facilities; contact **Centro Ippico Val d'Orcia** (Podere La Martina 18, www.digitamiata.com) to book an excursion onto Monte Amiata.

Monte Amiata: Swathed from its foothills to its peak by a huge beechwood forest, misty Monte Amiata is so atmospheric, even the local mountain residents call it "the damned and the beloved." An ancient dormant volcano, which marks the border between the tidy agriculture of the Val d'Orcia and the wild hills of Grosseto, it is a popular nature destination for walkers, cyclists and horseback riders alike, with six different routes to the top, 10 different nature reserves and a whole host of dirt roads and trail paths to be enjoyed.

If you don't want to do it alone, **Trekking and Bike Amiata** (☎ 333-9402001, www.trekkingbike.it) offers guided bike rides and hikes to the peak (from €10 for half a day).

Bagni San Filippo

A calcium-rich waterfall runs out of the Amiata slopes at 132°F at Bagni San Filippo forming the curious icycle-like calcerous rock formations that are known as the *Fosso Bianco* (the "white whale"). It constitutes the most popular of the town's "wild" springs – all found along a barely-marked dirt path that heads into the woods from town. If you're not happy dumping your clothes on a local rock or prefer a mirror in which to do your hair, opt instead for the town's spa establishment, **Terme San Filippo** (Loc. San Filippo 23, ☎ 0577-872982, fax 0577-872684, www.termesanfilippo.it, Mar-Oct, thermal pool open all year, 8:30 am-7 pm).

Radicofani: An impressive fortress at the southern border of the Val d'Orcia, Radicofani has for centuries regulated passage between the Grand Duchy of Tuscany and the Latium Papal territories. The importance of commerce and travel along the Via Francigena explains some of the power wielded by both Radicofani and its bandit-baron Ghino di Tacco, mentioned by Dante in his *Divine Comedy*. Later the fort became the possession of the Republic of Siena and finally, in 1559, of Cosimo I Grand Duke of Tuscany. Built sometime before the year 1000 and then repeatedly remodeled in the 16th and 19th centuries, its Rocca tower-museum (☎ 0578-55700, daily, 10 am-6 pm, €3, conc. €2) is a 20-minute walk up  from Radicofani. At 37 m (47 feet), it offers great views over Val d'Orcia, Monte Amiata, the Apennines, Lake Trasimeno and Lake Bolsena.

Back in town, the main sights are the churches of **San Pietro** and **Sant'Agata** (both have a considerable collection of della Robbia terracotta and wooden sculptures); the forbidding **Palazzo Pretorio** (the Town Hall); and the old **Palazzo della Posta** (a Medici villa first transformed into a customs house and then into a hotel).

Abbadia San Salvatore: From a distance, Abbadia San Salvatore looks like a pretty modern town. You get yourself ready for the disappointment and then suddenly, as you reach the historical center, things change. For a start, you arrive at the abbey from where the town gets its name. Once the richest abbey in Tuscany, it was founded as a Benedectine monastery in 743, although the present two-towered church (or rather 1½-towered) dates from the mid-11th century. Inside its single-aisled interior, the raised presbytery has a 12th-century wooden cross and 15th-century choir of note. It also houses the **Museo di Oggetti Sacri** (Museum of Sacred Objects, ☎ 0577-778083, fax 0577-773901, July-Aug, 10 am-noon, 4-7 pm, other times by appointment with Monaci Cirstercensi, free).

The town's other main attraction is the **Parco Museo Mineraio** (Area Mineraia, ☎ 0577-778324, fax 0577-775221, daily, 9 am-1 pm, 3-7 pm, €3, conc. €2), a mineral-themed museum-park, which sprang up on the slopes of Monte Amiata after the closure of the area's mercury mines.

Hiking: Marked footpaths to the 1,700-m (5,576-foot) peak of **Monte Amiata** depart from Vivo d'Orcia, Abbadia San Salvatore, Piancastagnaio, and over in the Grosseto province, the towns of Castel del Piano, Arcidosso and Santa Fiora. Whichever route you pick up, you will join up with the "anello della Montagna" (the mountain ring), a magnificent itinerary of 28 km (17 miles) that loops around the volcano. The route can be split into three sections: Laghetto Verde to Fonte delle Monache (six km/four miles, three hours), Fonte delle Monache to Madonna del Camicione (10 km/six miles, five hours) and Madonna del Camicione back to Laghetto Verde (14 km/nine miles, seven hours).

Other footpaths link Piancastagnio to Santa Fiora (in the province of Grosseto), and Monte Amiata to Monte Civitella and Castell'Azzara (again in the province of Grosseto) along the footpaths of the Riserve Naturali del Pigelleto e del Monte Penna (the Pigelleto and Mt Penna nature reserves, see below).

From Monte Amiata, you can also pick up longer footpaths into both provinces, with trails taking you into the province of Siena as far as Montalcino, Pienza, Montepulciano, Chiusi and even Siena (along the Firenze-Siena-Roma, 25-stage footpath). And trails into the Grosseto province take you as far as Pitigliano, Saturnia, Scansano and Monte Argentario on the coast.

Into the Province of Grosseto

If you follow the Amiata footpaths into the province of Grosseto, there are a few sights to keep you amused before you head back:

Jutting on a rocky outcrop above the Fiora Valley, the attractive medieval town of **Santa Fiora** has some fine Andrea della Robbia terracottas in its Romanesque Chiesa di Santa Fiora. It also has the interesting 17th-century **Palazzo Cesarini-Sforza** (recognizable by its military-style clock tower) and **Museo delle Miniere**, which traces the mining past of the Amiata region (Piazza Garibaldi 25, Fri, 5:30-7:30 pm, Sat, 10:30 am-12:30 pm, 5:30-7:30 pm, Sun, 10:30 am-12:30 pm, €2, conc. €1).

Arcidosso has an historic Rocca Aldobrandesca.

Castel del Piano has a Museo della Vite e del Vino to celebrate its position on the DOC Montecucco wine road. To its north, near Seggiano, the 42-acre **Giardino di Daniel Spoerri** is a sculpture park and nature reserve that was initiated in 1991 by the Swiss Artist, Daniel Spoerri.

Nature Walks: You can spy plenty of fauna and flora at the 5,600-acre **Riserva Naturale del Pigelleto** (Pigelleto Nature Reserve, Vicolo del Castello 12, Piancastagnaio, ☎ 0577-788004, info@abiesalba.com). Its well-marked paths take you through woods that are home to protected species like the harrier eagle, the honey buzzard, the sparrow hawk, and nocturnal creatures like the barn owl, the white owl and the tawny owl. There are also deer, wild boar, porcupines and wild cats on the prowl, and red lilies, cyclamens, wood anemones, violets and the rare belladonna plant providing seasonal color.

Footpaths from this reserve lead south into the Grosseto province and the 2,940-acre **Riserva Naturale Monte Penna**, near Castell'Azzara. Its peak is the 1,177-m (3,860-foot) Monte Civitella, a calcerous mass with many underground caves. Paths lead into woods of black pine and over the Mediterranean scrub, which is typical of the Grosseto province. The reserve also includes the 22-acre maple woods of Fonte Penna.

Over to the east, the 420-acre **Riserva Naturale Pescinello** is on the left valley slope of the Albegna River near Roccalbegna. It is particularly interesting for its geological rock formations and extraordinary flora. Higher up the same valley, the 1,038 acres of the **Riserva Naturale Rocconi** are incorporated in the **WWF Bosco Rocconi**. This is the place to come for colorful wild orchids, with 28 species to be seen along the four-km (2½-mile) reserve footpath.

Santa Fiora also has a wooded nature reserve of interest in the 45-acre **Riserva Naturale bosco della SS Trinità**. It has some of the most interesting mixes of wood vegetation in Italy (lime, beech, maple) in among the white fir trees that dominate the area.

The **Parco Faunistico dell'Amiata** (Monte Amiata fauna park) is to the north on the slopes of Monte Labbro at **Arcidosso** (in the province of Grosseto). Its footpaths are the places to come for a peak at the roe and fallow deer that roam wild in the protected area.

Also near Arcidosso, the 1,800-acre **Riserva Naturale Monte Labbro** spreads over the southwesterly slopes of Monte Amiata, offering a spectacular view of the Maremma and the Tyrhenian Coast. Apart from the occasional chestnut tree copse, it is a scarsely vegetated reserve, most interesting for its Etruscan remains and wild animals (wild cat, polecat, badger, hawk, etc).

Underground: Potholing enthusiasts should head to the caves of Sassocolato or Bacheca inside the **Riserva Naturale del Monte Penna**. Trips are limited due to a colony of pipistrelle bats and should be organized in advance with the Gruppo Speleologico l'Orso di Castell'Azzara (through the Tourist Office).

On Horseback: All the Monte Amiata footpaths and some nature reserve paths are suitable for horseback riding. As a result most local *agriturismi* offer "menage" (guided trekking). For two- or three-day forays along the mountain's ancient tracks, contact **Toscana Trips** (Via Dante 23, Poggibonsi, ☎/fax 0577-939307, www.toscanatrips.com).

Mountain Biking: There are six main mountain bike itineraries to the peak of Monte Amiata: the easiest depart from Abbadia San Salvatore and Arcidosso (both are nine miles on a steady uphill gradient) with more difficult approaches form Castel del Piano (nine miles on a steady uphill gradient for the first six miles only), Piancastagnaio (8½ miles with a few challenging parts), Santa Fiora (a shorter and steeper climb of seven miles) and Seggiano (11 miles with a challenging first four miles).

Other routes of interest include the 60-km (37-mile) paved loop around the mountain, which takes in (and can be picked up from) Abbadia San Salvatore, Vivo d'Orcia, Santa Fiora, Piancastagnaio, Castel del Piano, Arcidosso and Seggiano. There's also an historical 23-km (14-mile) route from the **Riserva Naturale del Pigelleto** (it can also be started from Piancastagnaio), which takes in the fortifications of Monte Amiata via Castell'Azzara and Monte Penna.

Radicofani has two mountain bike itineraries of note. The first takes you north through Contignano and returns to town via the Romanesque Pieve di San Piero in Campo; the second leaves from the Rocca, and takes you west to **San Casciano Terme**.

For more information, contact the **Le Macinaie-Amiata Mountain Bike Cycling Association** (Loc. Prato delle Macinaie, Castel del Piano, ☎/fax 0564-959001, www.lemacinaie.it).

Road Biking: Many of Monte Amiata's bike routes are "tuttoterreno" (all bike types) with classic paved cycle routes taking you onto Monte Amiata and around into the Maremma or the Val d'Orcia. The only area road to avoid is the Via Cassia, which attracts the worst of the traffic.

The best of the road bike itineraries depart from **Abbadia San Salvatore**, including an easy 16-km (10-mile) paved route into the surrounding woodland; a more difficult 28-km (17-mile) paved route to the hot springs of Bagni San Filippo and back; a spectacular (and difficult) 60-km (37-mile) paved loop to Radicofani; and a 36-km (22-mile) circular route around Monte Amiata with possible stopoffs at Piancastagnaio, Santa Fiora and Arcidosso.

On Snow: Amiata's winter sports activity is centered on **Abbadia San Salvatore** and, across the border in the Grosseto province, at **Castel del Piano**. Both have facilities for downhill and cross-country skiing. To book yourself a lesson, contact the **Scuola di Sci Monte Amiata** (Loc. Pianello (Vetta Amiata), Abbadia San Salvatore, ☎ 0573-789740).

■ Where to Eat

Local Flavors

Beyond just the local wines, this is also a region of tasty gastronomy, with exquisite olive oil, honey, cheeses and cold meats (particularly from the lean *cinta Senese* – a pig first bred here by the Etruscans) provided by the Val d'Orcia and world-renowned pecorino (sheep cheese) from Pienza. Devotees of the latter should visit the Pienza Fiera del Cacio (cheese festival) held on the first Sunday in Sept.

■ *Antipasti & primi*

Acquacotta con spinaci e ricotta: "Water soup" with spinach and ricotta

Capriolo in bianco con funghi porcini: Venison with a porcini mushroom sauce

Crostini coi fegatini: Chicken liver pâté on toasted bread

Maccheroni alla cacciagione: Pasta with a game sauce

Maccheroni con ceci: Pasta with chickpeas

Minestra di pane: Bread soup

Pappa di pane con il pomodoro: Bread and tomato soup

Pappardelle al cinghiale: Flat strips of pasta in a wild boar sauce

Ravioli di coniglio con le noci: Pasta stuffed with rabbit and nuts

Tagliatini con i ceci: Small chop with chickpeas

Zuppa di cipolle: Onion soup

■ *Secondi*

Arista di maiale al finocchio con cime di asparagi: Roast pork with fennel and asparagus

Capriolo con pinoli: Venison with pinenuts.

Cinghiale alla maremmana con olive nere: Wild boar with black olives (Maremma style)

Cinghiale in umido con prugne: Wild boar steamed with plums

Collo di gallo ripieno all'acciugata: Chicken neck stuffed with anchiovies

Fegatelli di maiale: Pork liver

Spezzatino di maiale con patate: Medaillons of pork with potatoes

Zampa di maiale con fagioli: Pork trotter with beans

■ *Dolci*

Ricotta con caramello e mandorle: Ricotta with caramel and almonds

Crostata di noci: Toasted nut tart

Pandolce di castagne: Soft chestnut bread

Montalcino: Montalcino and its surroundings have plenty of tasty restaurants in which to sample the local cuisine (and, more importantly, its wine). Try **Taverna dei Barbi** (Loc. Podernovi, ☎ 0577-849357, closed Wed, $$), **Trattoria Sciame** (Via Ricasoli, ☎ 0577-848017, closed Tues, $$) and **Osteria del Vecchi o Castello** (Loc. Pieve di San Gimignano, ☎ 0577-816026, $$) at the lower end of the price scale, with **Osteria Porta al Cassero** (Viale della Libertà 9,

DINING PRICE CHART	
Price per person for an entrée, including house wine & cover.	
$	Under €20
$$	€21-€40
$$$	€41-€60
$$$$	Over €60

☎ 0577-847196, closed Wed, $$$) boasting the best location under the Rocca.

For a lighter lunch or evening meal, **Enoteca Osteria Osticcio** (Via Matteotti 23, ☎/fax 0577-848271, www.osticcio.com, closed Sun, $$$) has some splendid views over the Crete and the Val d'Orcia to accompany its range of Brunello and Italian wines.

In the fortress itself, **Enoteca La Fortezza** (Piazzale della Fortezza, ☎/fax 0577-849211, www.enotecadellafortezza.com, $$$) offers light dishes of salumi (cuts of pork preserved in salt) and cheese to accompany its large glasses of Brunello.

Pienza: Both **Il Falco** (Piazza D. Alighieri 7, ☎ 0578-748551, closed Fri, $$) and **Taverna di Moranda** (Via di Mezzo 17, ☎ 0578-755050, closed Mon, $$) come heavily recommended for their reasonably priced local fare.

Val d'Orcia: The best of the Val d'Orcia restaurants can be found in the region's spa towns. Try **Osteria del Leone** (Piazza del Moretto, ☎ 0577-887300, closed Mon, $$) in Bagno Vignoni, and **Osteria Lo Spugnone** (☎ 0577-872030, closed Tues, $) in the center of scenic Bagni San Filippo. The latter is a particularly cosy and welcoming spot with a menu of traditional Monte Amiata fare – *pici con le briciole* (long thick pasta in breadcrumbs), *acquacotta* and *fagioli con le cotiche* (pork and beans) are just some of the top picks.

■ Where to Stay

Montalcino: Montalcino has two reasonably priced hotels: **Il Giardino** ☆☆ (Via Cavour 4, ☎/fax 0577-848257, $$) and **Il Giglio** ☆☆☆ (Via S. Saloni 5, ☎/fax 0577-848167, $$, hotelgiglio@tin.it). **Fattoria dei Barbi** (Loc. Podernuovi, ☎ 0577-841111, www. fattoriadeibarbi.it, $$$), **La Crociona** (Loc. La Croce, ☎ 0577-848007, www.lacrociona. com, $$$) and **Piombaia** (Loc. La Crocina 1, ☎ 0577-847197, www.piombaia.it, $$$) are some of the best *agriturismi*.

HOTEL PRICE CHART	
Rates are per room with private bath, based on double occupancy, including breakfast.	
$	Under €40
$$	€41-€85
$$$	€86-€140
$$$$	€141-€210
$$$$$	Over €210

Pienza: For hotels, your top choices are **Corsignano** ☆☆☆ (Via della Madonnina 11, ☎ 0578-748501, fax 0578-748166, www.corsignano.it, $$$) and **Albergo Rutiliano** ☆☆ (☎ 0578-749408, fax 0578-749409, www.albergorutiliano.it, $$$). For a farmstay, there is **Agriturismo Cretaiole di Luciano Moricciani** (Via S. Gregorio 14, ☎/fax 0578-748378, www.cretaiole.it, $$).

Val d'Orcia: The best hotels are **Palazzuolo** ☆☆☆ (Via S. Caterina 43, ☎ 0577-897080, fax 0577-898264, www.hotelpalazzuolo.it, $$) in San Quirico d'Orcia and **Osteria dell'Orcia** ☆☆☆☆ (☎ 0577-887111, fax 0577-8889111, www.cretedisiena.com/hotel_dell_orcia, $$$) in Castiglione d'Orcia.

If you're looking to stay in a spa hotel, try **Albergo Le Terme** ☆☆☆ (Via Sorgenti 13, ☎ 0577-887150, fax 0577-887497, www.albergoleterme.it, $$$) in Bagno Vignoni or **Terme San Filippo** ☆☆☆ (Via San Filippo 23, ☎ 0577-872982, fax 0577-872684, termesfilippo@tin.it, closed Feb, $$$) in Bagni San Filippo.

Agriturismi can be found at Castiglione d'Orcia with **Aiole** (SP della Grossola, ☎/fax 0577-887454, www.agriturismo-aiole.com, closed 16 Jan to 28 Feb, $) and **San Marcello** (SS 2 Cassia, ☎ 0577-887101, fax 0577-888342, www.agriturismosanmarcello.com, $$$) representing the top options.

Monte Amiata: A good bet in Abbadia San Salvatore is **Hotel Parco Rosa** ☆☆☆ (Via Remedi 108, ☎/fax 0577-779735, www.parcoerosa.it, $$$), while over in Arcidosso, **Aiuole** ☆☆☆ (Loc. Auiole, ☎ 0564-967300, $$) and **Luce Sorgente** ☆☆☆ (☎ 0564-967049, $$$) provide equally good hotel options. In Castel del Piano the cheapest option is **Amiata** ☆ (Via D. Alighieri 10c,

☎ 0564-955407, $), but there's also **Contessa** ☆☆☆ (☎ 0564-959000, $$) and **Lo Scoiattolo** ☆☆ (☎ 0564-959003, $$) if you're happy to spend a little bit more.

Out of local *agriturismi*, the farmhouse **Podere Casano** (☎/fax 0578-52107, www.poderecasano.it, week bookings only, $$) at Radicofani is one of your top options. With an outdoor pool, they also offer bike rental, fishing and hiking.

The region's campground, **Amiata** ☆☆☆ (Via Roma 15, Loc. Montoto, ☎ 0564-955107, $) is near Castel del Piano.

There's also a mountain hut south of Monte Amiata near Piancastagnaio (**La Direzione**, Loc. La Direzione 2, Saragiolo, ☎ 0557-788004, fax 0577-7880214, www.abiesalba.com, $). It's the perfect spot for exploring both Monte Amiata and the Riserve Naturale del Pigelleto to its south.

Montepulciano & the Val di Chiana

To the west of Pienza, you'll find Montepulciano towering from its hilltop position over the surrounding woods and vineyards. It introduces the Val di Chiana, a territory that has been a first-rate agricultural area since its land was fully reclaimed by Tuscan Grand Dukes, and is today famous not only for its Chianina cattle, which gives the region its T-bone steak, and also for its cheese, grain, olive oil and wine. Its main hubs of tourist interest, Montepulciano apart, are the spa town of Chianciano Terme and the Etruscan city of Chiusi, with its fascinating catacombs and mysterious underground *Labirinto di Porsenna* (Porsenna's labyrinth). Adventurers will find their terrain at Cetona and its mountain peaks, and at the lakes of Chiusi and Montepulciano (both important birding sites).

■ Getting Here & Around

By Train: The Val di Chiana is the easiest part of the Siena province to navigate both by car and public transport. Regional trains (☎ 848-888088, www.trenitalia.it) run to the Chiusi/Chianciano Terme station, stopping at Montepulciano, roughly every hour from both Siena and Firenze SMN.

By Bus: From the stations, both a little way out of town, regular **bus** services provide an easy link. **SITA** (☎ 800-373760, www.sita-on-line.it), **Sena** (☎ 0577-283203/247934, www.sena.it) and **Tra-In** (☎ 0577-204111, www.trainspa.com) provide coach services. The local **LFI** bus service (☎ 0578-31174, www.lfi.it) links Montepulciano with Chianciano Terme (ST#3,ST#7) and Chiusi (T#2, T#4 and T#5).

By Car: The region is easy to access by car. It is crossed by the Florence-to-Rome section of the A1 highway (take the toll exit at Val di Chiana for Montepulciano and at Chiusi for Chiusi and the Val di Chiana). If arriving from Siena, take the SS326 to join the SS327 through Torrita di Siena to Montepuliciano and the Val di Chiana. Cars can be rented at Chiusi (AVIS, Piazza Dante 22, ☎ 0578-227993, essedue1@libero.it).

By Bike: For bike routes from Siena see page 152; for routes from Pienza see page 179. Bikes can be rented at **Montepulciano** (Bici Cicloposse, Via Matteotti 45, ☎ 0578-716392, biketuscany@bccmp.com) and **Sarteano: Il Pedale** (Via del Turismo 5, ☎ 0578-267300).

■ Information Sources

Tourist Offices: The main office of **APT Val di Chiana** (Val di Chiana tourist office) is at **Chianciano Terme** (Piazza Italia 67, ☎ 0578-671122/23, fax 0578-63277, www.valdichiana.it, Apr-Oct, Mon-Sat, 8 am-2 pm, 4-7 pm, Sun and public hols, 9 am-noon, Nov-Mar, Mon-Sat, 8 am-2 pm, 3:30-6:30 pm).

There are smaller branches at **Cetona** (Piazza Garibaldi 63, ☎/fax 0578-239143, June-Sept, Tues-Sun, 10:30 am-noon, 5-7 pm), **Chiusi** (Piazza Duomo 1, ☎/fax 0578-227667, www.evols.it/chiusi, Apr-Sept, Mon-Sat, 9 am-12:30 pm, 3:30-7 pm, shorter hours at other times), **Montepulciano** (Via Gracciano nel Corso, ☎/fax 0578-757341, www.comune.montepulciano.si.it, Mon-Sat, 9:30 am-12:30 pm, 3-8 pm, shorter hours at other times), **Sarteano** (Corso Garibaldi 1, ☎/fax 0578-265312, Mar-Dec, 10 am-noon, 5-6 pm) and **Torrita di Siena** (Piazza Matteotti, ☎ 0577-685452, fax 0577-685620, May-Oct, Wed-Sun and public holidays, 10:30 am-12:30 pm, 4:30-6:30 pm, shorter hours at other times).

Adventure Information: You can get information on adventures on Monte Cetona by contacting **Communità Montagna Monte Cetona** (Corso Garibaldi 10, Sarteano, ☎ 0578-268081).

Guides & Maps: The best map for cyclists is the *Toscana in biciletta tra la Val di Chiana e la Val d'Orcia* (Luigi Pagnotta, APT Chianciano Terme), a cycling guide with 12 itineraries of varying difficulty with historical and cultural information, available from APT Chianciano Terme. These and CAI walking trials are also depicted on *Lago Trasimeno* (Kompass Guide #662, www.kompass.at).

■ Sightseeing ~ Montepulciano

At 600 m (1,968 feet), Montepulciano is one of Tuscany's highest hilltop towns. Fortified along a narrow limestone ridge that dominates the Val di Chiana, the town is best known for its exquisite Nobile wine and goat cheese, and the glorious Renaissance churches and palazzi, which gave rise to its nickname, "Pearl of the 1600s." Easily visited in a day, its one main road (the "Corso"), winds through the town up to the Duomo on Piazza Grande, the town's highest point.

The bus drops you just outside the walls on Piazza Don Minzoni (also the location of the town's main car parks), where the **Chiesa di Sant'Agnese** warrants a quick look for its Simone Martini fresco before following the walls round to the entrance at the 12th-century Porto al Prato. The Corso starts here, taking you first to Piazza Savonarola, with its column decorated with the *Marzocco* (lion with shield), the symbol of Florence, which replaced the original Sienese *Lupa* (she wolf), during their brief period of rule.

CHANGING HANDS

Montepulciano spent most of the Middle Ages yo-yoing between Sienese and Florentine rule. Fortunes went briefly in the favor of Siena in 1232 and again in 1495, but the land definitively transferred to Medici rule in 1511. It was they who dispatched Antonio da Sangallo Il Vecchio here, one of the greatest architects of the period, to shore up the walls Siena had razed under their rule in 1232. But Florentine interest wasn't just strategic or territorial. Montepulciano was the hometown of poet Angelo Ambrogini (better known as *Il Poliziano*). A friend of Lorenzo Il Magnifico and the educator of his sons (one of whom went on to become Pope Leo X), it was his fame that ensured most of the town's structures were rebuilt in the 16th century.

Piazza Savonarola is also the home of two elegant palazzi: the **Palazzo Avignonesi** (the palazzo with the two lion heads flanking the entrance) and the **Palazzo Tusci**. **Fattoria di Pulcino** (free) occupies the bottom floors of the latter. It's worth looking in; the self-guided tour of its cellars takes you down into a labyrinth of tunnels complete with casks of wine, medieval weapons and torture implements on display in the empty Etruscan tombs.

VINO NOBILE - "THE KING OF ALL WINES"

CROCIANI

2000

Rosso di Montepulciano

DENOMINAZIONE DI ORIGINE CONTROLLATA

13% Vol · 750 ml e

If you've come to Montepulciano to sample the local specialty, look into **Informazioni Strada del Vino Nobile** (Information on the Vino Nobile Wine Road, Piazza Grande 7, ☎ 0578-717484, fax 0578-752749, www.stradavinonobile.it, Mon-Sat, 10 am-1 pm, 3-7 pm, Sun and public hols, 10 am-1 pm). They can give you information both on the local producers offering *degustazione* (wine tasting and purchasing) and the production of the wine, which uses Prugnolo Gentile, a clone of the red Sangiovese Grosso (50-70%), Canaiolo Nero (10-20%), Malvasia del Chianti and Trebbiano Toscano (10-20%), as well as limited quantities of Pulcinculo (Grechetto Bianco) and Mammolo (5%). The wine must be aged for at least two years (three years for Riserve quality) in oak or chestnut wood barrels before bottling.

Farther along the Corso, **Palazzo Buccelli** (Via di Gracciano nel Corso 73) stands out for its extraordinary exterior. A range of antique sculptures were added to the façade by Pietro Buccelli in the early 1700s (including fragments from Etruscan funerary urns and frieze plaques).

From here it's a short hop to the Michelozzo-designed **Chiesa di Sant'Agostino** (Piazza Michelozzo). He constructed the church in 1427 before adding the elaborately carved portal, showing the *Virgin and Child between St Jean and St Augustin* – justifiably famous. Inside, you'll find Cesare Nebbia da Orvieto's *Ascension,* Barroccio's *Madonna della Cintola,* and a *Crucifixion* that Vasari attributes to Donatello.

As you exit the church, watch for the **Torre della Pulcinella** opposite. This 15th-century tower, shown at left, has a statue of Pulcinella, donated by a Neapolitan, that strikes the hour with his stick.

Continuing up the Corso, you'll pass through the **Arco della Cavina**, a set of gates that have survived from an earlier set of city walls. It leads onto the graceful **Palazzo Cervini** (Via di Voltaia nel Corso 21), the former home of Cardinal Marcello Cervini, who reigned for only a few days as Pope Marcello II in 1555. **Chiesa del Gesù** is the next sight. It may look simple on the outside, but inside the décor is sumptuously Baroque with trompe l'oeil statues, cornices and columns for which the artist, Andrea Pozzo, is famous. He created the frescoed architectural ornaments on the walls.

There are more of his Baroque stucco works along the Corso at the Gothic **Santa Maria dei Servi**, as well as the *Madonna with Child* attributed to Duccio di Buoninsegna. But most come to visit the church, or at least its adjacent bar, for the wine served out of its medieval cellar.

Before you head straight there, look into the **Casa Natale di Poliziano** (the birthplace of *Il Poliziano*), the next stop on your left. It contains a brief insight into the life of poet Angelo Ambrogini, who, after fleeing the town following the assassination of his father, went on to become friend and advisor of Duke Lorenzo Il Magnifico.

Past the **Fortezza**, Via San Donato takes you to Piazza Grande. In addition to the town's major sights – the Duomo, Palazzo Comunale, Palazzo Contucci, Palazzo Nobili-Terugi, and the wells Pozzo dei Grifi and Pozzo dei Leoni – the streets around the Piazza Grande are home to a great range of restaurants, caffès and antique shops, making it the perfect place to stop for a bite of lunch (see page 197 for restaurant recommendations).

The **Duomo** replaced the square's former occupant, the Pieve di Santa Maria (the campanile still survives from the original parish church) following Montepulciano's elevation to bishop by Pope Pious IV in 1561. Construction on the Ippolito Scalza design began in 1586 and continued until 1630 when it was finished, except for the marble façade.

Inside its three sober-looking naves, top picks include the triptych of the *Assumption* by Taddeo di Bartolo (1401, note the image of Montepulciano in the hand of St Antilia on the right-hand panel), the *Madonna with Child* by Benedetto da Maiano, and the tomb of Archpriest Bartolomeo Aragazzi. The latter is all that remains of an elaborate funerary monument designed by Michelozzo, which was broken up and sold in the 18th century. Two of its original decorative angels even made it as far as London's Victoria and Albert Museum.

Michelozzo added the tower and façade to the Gothic **Palazzo Comunale** (town hall) in the 15th century. Reminiscent of Florence's Palazzo Vecchio in style, it's worth heading inside; the summit offers some great views over the Val di Chiana countryside.

Construction of the nearby **Palazzo Contucci** began in 1518 under the direction of Antonio da Sangallo and continued until after his death in 1534 (his contribu-

tion stops where the bricks begin). The great hall on the ground floor has more frescos by Andrea Pozzo (visits by request only).

Antonio da Sangallo is also said to be responsible for the **Palazzo Nobili-Tarugi**, at left. He also designed the elegant wall to its side, a skilful pairing of the symbolic griffons and lions that represent Florence and Montepulciano.

Local Events

To the right of Palazzo Cantucci, Via del Teatro leads to the **Teatro Poliziano**, a beautiful 18th-century theater now used for, among other things, the **Cantiere Internazionale d'Arte** (International Art Workshop), a dance, drama, music and performance art festival that takes place every summer.

Other events of note include the "Bruscello," an ancient form of street theater performed on Piazza del Duomo during the Feast of the Assumption (Aug 15).

Montepulciano's medieval history is relived in the "Bravio delle Botti," a festival on the last Sunday of August recalling the rivalry that has existed since 1337 between the town's eight *contrade* (neighborhoods). Each team competes for a painted cloth banner by rolling barrels of 176 lbs in an uphill 1,800-m (1,904-foot) race that starts at 7 pm from the Marzocco column and finishes at the town's highest point on Piazza Grande. Each team has two *spingatori* (pushers) and a team of supporters that introduce the race with a ceremonial branding of the barrels, a colorful procession and much impressive flag throwing. For details, www.paliodeisomari.it.

Back on Piazza Grande, Via Ricci takes you down past Palazzo Ricci to the **Museo Civico Pinacoteca Crociani** (Via Ricci, ☎ 0578-715322, Mar-Dec, Tues-Sun, 10 am-1 pm, 3-6 pm, Jan-Mar, shorter hours, €4, conc. €3), which occupies the Gothic Palazzo Neri Orselli and its collection of Sienese and Florentine paintings from the 13th to 18th centuries. Its main attractions are Andrea and Luca della Robbia terracotta pieces, Duccio's *Madonna col Bambino e Due Angeli*, and works by Filippino Lippi.

Finish your tour with the two-km (1.2-mile) walk down the cypress-lined Via dei Grassi to the travertine **Tempio di Madonna di San Biagio** (Via di San Biagio 14), a serene and harmonious church that is considered the peak of Antonio da Sangallo's architectural brilliance. He worked on the honey- and cream-colored building from 1518 until his death in 1534 (try and visit in the late afternoon when the ochre brick becomes golden). The building also incorporates a small chapel with an image of the *Madonna* whose miracles had at one time attracted pilgrims from all over Christendom.

■ Adventures on Foot

In addition to the short walk to the Tempio di Madonna di San Biagio, there's an enjoyable short walk (or cycle) to Sant'Albino, home of the local spa – **Terme di Montepulciano** (Via delle Terme 46, ☎ 0578-7911, fax 0578-799149, www.termemontepulciano.it, open all year).

Longer itineraries take you along quiet dirt roads to the medieval hill town of Monticchiello and onto Pienza (11 miles, see page 178), and past the Tempio di Madonna di San Biagio and up to **Montefollonico** (seven miles).

Birdwatchers should head to the **LIPU Oasis Lago di Montepulciano** (Loc. Tre Berte, ☎ 0578-767518, www.riservenaturali.provincia.siena.it, Wed-Sun, 9 am-1 pm, 3-7 pm). Two marked trails departing from the Visitor Center take you past hides where you can view more than 130 species of birds, including nesting species such as the purple heron and little bittern, and residents like the great crested grebe, water rail, Cetti's warbler, fan-tailed warbler and sedge warbler.

> **Team Nobil Bike** (Via Roma 7, Montepulicano Station, ☎ 348-5160175, www.nobilbike.it) guides and advises hikers, cyclists and watersport enthusiasts in the region.

■ Adventures on Wheels

From Montepulciano, a road bike route takes you along the SS146 north to Torrita di Siena, east to Chianciano Terme and Chiusi or west to Pienza, depending on your next intended stop. You can make it into a 46-km (29-mile) roundtrip by taking the SS146 from Montepulciano toward Chianciano, picking up signs to (and leaving the road at) Monticchiello and La Foce, onto Chianciano and then Montallese (Chianciano station), Lago di Montepulciano, and back to Montepulciano along the SS326 through Salcheto and then Acquaviva.

■ Sightseeing ~ Chianciano Terme

There's little to recommend Chianciano but its spas and a semi-interesting archeological museum, which traces their history back to the King of Porsenna – **Museo Civico Archeologico delle Acque** (Water Archeological Museum, Via Dante, ☎/fax 0578-30471, Apr-Oct, Tues-Sun, 10 am-7 pm, Nov-Mar, Sun, 10 am-1 pm, 3-7 pm, other times by appointment, €4, conc. €3). There's also a Romanesque **Collegiata** up in the historical center (*centro storico*) with **Museo della Collegiata di San Giovanni Battista** worth your attention (Collegiate Church Museum, Via Solferino 38, ☎ 0578-30378, Apr-Oct, Tues-Sat, 10 am-noon, 4-7 pm, by appointment at other times, €2). It displays works taken from nearby churches (including a crucifix by Segna di Bonaventura, a *Madonna* by Nicola Pisano and a *Madonna and Saints* by Maestro di Chianciano). Otherwise, the town is really only worth visiting if you're planning on a dunk.

Spas in Chianciano Terme

Chianciano (Via delle Rose, ☎ 0578-68111, fax 0578-60622, www.termechianciano.it)

Stabilimento Acqua Santa (Piazza Martiri Perugini, open all year)

Parco Fucoli (Via G. Baccelli, Apr-Oct)
Stabilimento Sillene (Piazza G. Marconi, open all year)
Sorgente Sant'Elena Spa (Viale della Libertà 112, ☎ 0578-31141,
fax 0578-31369, www.termesantelena.it, Apr-Nov)

■ Adventures On Foot in Chianciano Terme

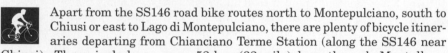

The town's main footpaths depart from Piazza Italia, with #1 taking you the five kilometers (three miles) into the the Astrone Valley to Fucoli, and #2 taking you the seven kilometers (four miles) into the Monti di Chianciano. You can also do a short walking itinerary north of the town, which takes you past Convento de Cappuccini and up the Monti di Sopra.

Chianciano Terme is also a good destination for nature walks. Footpaths head into the **Riserva Naturale di Pietrapiana**, with itineraries over Poggio di Pietraporciana, south towards Sarteano or west (over La Foce) into the **Riserva Naturale Lucciola Bella**.

■ Adventures on Wheels in Chianciano Terme

Apart from the SS146 road bike routes north to Montepulciano, south to Chiusi or east to Lago di Montepulciano, there are plenty of bicycle itineraries departing from Chianciano Terme Station (along the SS146 near Chiusi). These include an easy 52-km (32-mile) loop through Montallese, Salcheto, Chianacce, Fornace and Acquaviva, and a more difficult 38-km (24-mile) route through Cetona, Sarteano and back to Chianciano Terme. From the center of town itself, you can pick up a 57-km (35-mile) itinerary past Montepulciano train station to Abbadia, Torrita di Siena and back, a shorter 49-km (30-mile) loop through Pienza, Val d'Orcia and La Foce, and a very long and difficult 116-km (72-mile) ride through Salcheto, Pozzuolo, Castiglione del Lago, Monte del Lago, Passignano and back to town.

■ Adventures on Horseback in the Val di Chiana

Chianciano Terme also has the region's horseback-riding center, with **Associazione Equestre I Tre Laghi** (Chianciano Terme, ☎ 338-8586475) the people to contact no matter where you are staying.

■ Sightseeing ~ Chiusi

An important Etruscan city that crowns a maze of layered tunnels (the famous Porsenna's Labyrinth), Chiusi is set in a countryside dotted with Etruscan necropoli. Its lake (Lago di Chiusi) lies past the tombs at the end of a pleasantly winding road three or four miles north of town.

Before you set off, look into the **Museo Archeologico Nazionale** (National Archeological Museum, Via Porsenna 93, ☎ 0578-20177, daily, 9 am-7:30 pm, €4, conc. €2), which has a collection of sarcophagi and Etruscan funerary objects

Tomba della Pellegrina

taken from the surrounding countryside. Your ticket includes entry to the outlying tombs: **Tomba della Pellegrina e del Leone** (same opening hours) and **Tomba della Scimmia** (guided tours only, Mar-Sept, 11 am-noon, 4-5 pm, Oct-Feb, Tues, Thurs and Sat, 11 am-noon, 2:30-3:30 pm).

The town **Duomo** (Piazza Duomo) should be your next stop. Built of Etruscan and Roman blocks, the interior of the Romanesque cathedral is decorated with a mosaic-like painting (1887) by Arturo Viligiardi. In its cloister, the **Museo della Cattedrale** (Cathedral Museum, ☎ 0578-226490, June-Oct, daily, 9:30 am-12:45 pm, 3:30-6:30 pm, Nov-May, am only, €2, combined ticket, €4) presents a range of Roman, Lombard and medieval sculptures. More importantly, this is the place to organize trips to

the **Labirinto Etrusco** (Etruscan Labyrinth, 10 am-12:30 pm, entry included with the combined museum ticket, Labyrinth only, €3), an intricate maze of subterranean passages believed to house the mythical tomb of King Porsenna, and the **Catacombe**, part of the Etruscan tunnels transformed in the fifth century into Christian catacombs (guided tours only, June-Oct, daily, 11 am-4 pm, Nov-Apr, 11 pm only, entry included with the combined museum ticket, catacombs only, €3).

If you have time for only one, opt for the Labyrinth. It takes you through a network of paths

Etruscan tomb

and branches that originally functioned as an aqueduct, past rooms packed with Etruscan funerary urns, to an underground lake originally used as a reservoir and at one time linked by Leonardo da Vinci to the Lago di Chiusi.

SOMETHING FOR THE KIDS

KID FRIENDLY

In **Archeology Week**, the first week in July, the museums of Sarteano, Cetona and Chianciano Terme open their excavations to children on the weekends, led by archeologists. Among the attractions:

The **Museo Civico per la Preistoria del Monte Cetona** (Museum of Prehistory of Mt Cetona, Via Roma 37, Cetona, ☎ 0578-237632, June-Sept, Tues-Sun, 9 am-1 pm, 5-7 pm, Oct-May, Sun, 9:30 am-12:30 pm, normally €2, conc. €1.50) takes kids on a visit of the principal prehistoric sights of the **Parco Archeologico Naturalistico del Monte Cetona** (Archeological and Natural Park of Monte Cetona, Loc. Belvedere, ☎ 0578-227667, July-Sept, 9 am-1 pm, 4-7 pm, other times by request, free).

The **Museo Archeologico delle Acque** (Via Dante, Chianciano Terme ☎/fax 0578-30471, Apr-Oct, Tues-Sun, 10 am-7 pm, Nov-Mar, Sun, 10 am-1 pm, 3-7 pm).

The **Museo Civico Archeologico** (Archeological Museum, Via Roma 24, Sarteano, ☎ 0578-269261, museo@comune.sarteano.siena.it, June-Sept, Tues-Sun, 10:30 am-12:30 pm, 4-7 pm, on request at other times, normally €2.50, conc. €2).

■ Adventures on Foot in Chiusi

 From Chiusi, an 11-km (seven-mile) loop takes you from the historical center (*centro storico*) to Lago di Chiusi, passing the Etruscan tombs of Scimmia and Pellegrina, and returning past the two medieval towers, *Beccati Questo* (Take This) and *Beccati Quello* (Take That).

The **Riserve Naturale di Lago di Chiusi** also offers some pleasant nature walks, with one itinerary taking you from the lake through the reserve and up to the Lago di Montepulciano.

■ Adventures on Wheels in Chiusi

 One of the best road bike itineraries in the region leaves from Chiusi following 46.5 km (29 miles) of paved road past both the lakes of Chiusi and Montepulciano, with other routes taking you south to Monte Cetona and over to Lago Trasimeno in Umbria (see page 373). There's also a 46-km (29-mile) loop through Salcheto, Pozzuolo, Binami, Mugnanese, Gioiella, Valiano and back to Chiusi. Stop off in Valiano and you can visit the **UISP Lega Ciclismo Val di Chiana Cycling Association** (Via Laurentana Nord 1, ☎/fax 0578-724242), a mine of information on cycling in the territory.

■ Adventures on Water in Chiusi

 Known as "Il Chiaro" (its Etruscan name), Lago di Chiusi is swathed in mystery. Legends tell of a St Mustiola, one of the first Christian martyrs, who was said to have glided over the lake on her own cloak, and traditions recount the "Chiana weddings," when locals would celebrate nuptials by throwing silver rings into its still waters.

You can check out any shimmering, as well as the lake's rich vegetation and birdlife, by booking yourself a canoe trip or renting a row boat from **Pesce d'Oro** (Via Sbarchino 36, ☎ 0578-21403).

■ Adventures on Foot on Monte Cetona

 Trekking itineraries up Monte Cetona can be picked up from Cetona and Sarteano. Some of the best include the half-day walk from Centona into the Parco del Biancheto on the side of Monte Cetona (site of some of its best prehistoric caves).

Post-Trek Treats

After a hard slog in the Chiana countryside, head to the tiny village of Casciano dei Bagni, south of Monte Cetona. Unlike many of the commercial spas, the 42 thermomineral springs that erupt out of the ground around the village are mainly left to run free. You can visit the town spa complex (Centro Termale Fonteverde, Loc. Terme 1, ☎ 0577-58023, fax 0577-58023, www.termedisancascianobagni.it, daily 9 am-7 pm) or hunt out hot springs in the countryside, where you can soak in a natural pool or river. The easiest to find, just below the *centro storico*, is a hot spring that flows into open stone baths.

■ Adventures on Wheels on Monte Cetona

The mountain's best mountain bike itineraries can also be picked up from either Cetona or Sarteano. If you can only choose one, opt for the 30-km (19-mile) loop that follows the contours of the mountain from Sarteano to San Casciano dei Bagni and back via the Abbazia di Spineto (built in 1085).

■ Where to Eat

LOCAL FLAVORS

This is an area best known for its Vino Nobile and Chianina steak (try it accompanied by *ciaccia*, a flat bread dunked in oil), but there are also simple country recipes to tempt you. Some of the tastiest include the *pici* (handmade spaghetti-like pasta), *panzanella* (bread salad), *ribollita* (refried bread and cabbage soup), *rivoltolo* (flour dough cooked in oil), *ravaggiolo* (local soft sheep cheese), *porchetta* (pork roasted with garlic and rosemary), game (such as pheasant and rabbit) and *pansanto* (bread with boiled cauliflour vinegar and oil).

Fine views and some local history make the **Art-Deco Antico Caffé Poliziano** (Via di Voltaia nel Corso 27/29, 0578758615, www.montepulciano.com/caffepoliziano) a must-visit in Montepulciano. It has been the stopping point for many a famous face (Carducci, Pirandello, Prezzolini among others) and is now divided into a caffè (perfect for a coffee and cake break, $) and restaurant ($$$) with panoramic terrace.

Out of the many restaurants on Piazza Grande, **Enoteca Incontri Nobili** ("meet the wines") is your best choice. In addition to the local vine, there's a range of cold meats (salami from Cinta Senese) and cheese to tempt.

If you make the trek to Tempio di Biagio in the early evening, finish up with a meal at **La Grotta** (Loc. San Biagio, ☎ 0578-757607, $$). You'll get some tasty local fare at a much cheaper price than can be found in town.

There are also a couple of good restaurants to the south of the city; try **Santa Chiara** (Piazza Santa Chiara 30, ☎ 0578-265412, $$) in Sarteano, or **La Frateria di Padre Eligio** (Convento di San Francesco, ☎ 0578-238261, $$$) in Cetona.

■ Where to Stay

Montepulciano: The cheapest option is to rent one of the six doubles from **Meublé Evoé** (Via di Cagnano 13, ☎/fax 0578-758757, www.meuble-evoe.it, $$), just off the Piazza Grande. Its *affiticamere* are color-themed around flowers; ask for the orchid room (the only one with a balcony and views over the main Corso).

Just out of town is the tranquil **Albergo Sangallo** ☆☆ (Via dei Fiori 30, Loc. Sant'Albino, ☎ 0578-798005, www.albergosangallo.it, $$), named after the architect who designed it. The hotel is on the road to Chianciano and a good choice for trekkers and mountain bikers and provides a guide to 12 itineraries in the region.

In the heart of the old town, overlooking the old city walls, **Il Borghetto** ☆☆☆ (Borgo Buio 7, ☎ 0578-57535, fax 0578-77354, www.ilborghetto.it, $$$) offers a magnificent panorama over Val di Chiana's three lakes from its 15 rooms decorated in the style of the 16th-century building they occupy.

In the lower part of the town center, **Il Marzocco** ☆☆☆ (Piazza Savonarola 18, ☎ 0578-757262, fax 0578-757530, www.cretedisiena.com/albergoilmarzocco, $$$) has lovely panoramic terraces off its 16th-century rooms.

The surrounding countryside is jam-packed with *agriturismi*. At the cheaper end of the scale is **Nobile** ☆☆☆ (Loc. San Benedetto, ☎ 0578-757398, fax 0578-716602, www.agriturismonobile.it $$) and **Le Due Chiarine** ☆☆☆ (Via Pozzolese 61, Fraz. Acquaviva, ☎/fax 0578-767282, www.leducchiarine.com $$). **Casa delle Querce** ☆☆☆ (Loc. Cevognano, ☎ 0578-767789, fax 0578-767798, www.casadellequerce.it $$$$) and nearby **Borgo delle More** (Loc. Cevognano, ☎/fax 0578-768166, www.borgodellemore.com $$$$) are the best choices at the higher end of the price range.

Chianciano Terme: The town is jam-packed with hotels serving the clients who flock to its spas, making it worth avoiding unless you're here for a spa treatment. If you do wish to hang around, you're best off booking a room in or near the spa of your choice. Try **Sole** ☆☆☆ (Via dele Rose 40, ☎ 0578-60194, fax 0578-60196, $$) near Chianciano Spa; **President** ☆☆☆ (Viale Baccelli 260, ☎ 0578-64131, fax 0578-62122, $$); **Le Sorgenti** ☆☆☆ (Viale G. Baccelli 42, ☎/fax 0578-64056, albergolesorgenti@tiscalinet.it, $$) near Parco Fucoli; or the more expensive **Centro Benessere Spa'Deus** ☆☆☆☆ (Via delle Piane 35, ☎ 0578-63232, fax 0578-64329, www.spadeus.it, $$$$$), which offers everything in-house.

Chiusi: To base yourself in town, **La Sfinge** ☆ (Via G. Maconi 2, ☎/fax 0578-21057, www.albergolasfinge.com, $$) is surprisingly luxurious for its star rating, with rooms whitewashed to bring out the lovely wood-beamed ceilings.

The rural hotel-restaurant **La Fattoria** ☆☆☆ (Loc. Paccianese, Lago di Chiusi, ☎ 0578-21407, fax 0578-20644, lafattoria@ftbcc.it, $$$) has the best lakeside views. **Residenza Santa Chiara** ☆☆☆ (Piazza Santa Chiara, Sarteano, ☎ 0578-265412, fax 0578-266849, www.conventosantachiara.it, $$$), six miles out of Chiusi, has to be the top pick for the picturesque moss-covered walls of the restored 16th-century convent it inhabits. It offers walking tours, cooking courses and live jazz every Friday.

Quality *agriturismi* can be found in the lovely old stone cottage at **La Bruciata** (Loc. Caselle Basse 26, ☎ 0578-798330, fax 0578-799917, http://web.tiscali.it/labruciata, $$$); at the cypress-tree-lined **La Sovanna** ☆☆☆☆ (Via di Chiusi 37, Loc. Sovana, ☎/fax 0578-274086, www.lasovana.com $$$$), with a large outdoor pool and fishing lake; and at the gorgeously isolated **Il Pulito** ☆☆ (Via Provinciale 142, Loc. Le Piazze, ☎/fax 0578-244088, www.ilpulito.it $$$), a complex of three restored farmhouses with rustic furnishings, wooden beams and great views over Monte Cetona.

If you want to spend time exploring Monte Cetona, make your base at the **Casa Vecchia** ☆☆☆ (SS321, ☎ 0578-238383, www.agriturismocasavecchia.it, $$$$) at the foot of the mountain. It has an amazing tree-lined entrance and a vast pool overlooking the countryside.

There are plenty of **campgrounds** in the area of Lago di Chiusi. Your first choice should be **Camping La Fattoria** ☆ (on the grounds of the hotel, see above, $, 29 spaces, May-Nov). If this is full, the slightly dishevelled **Pesce d'Oro** down by the lakeside (Via Sbarchino 36, ☎ 0578-21403, $, 27 spaces) really is for emergencies only. It was particularly unattractive when I visited last September, though may have improved since.

More luxurious options can be found near Sarteano (**Delle Piscine** ☆☆☆☆, Via Campo dei Fiori 31, ☎ 0578-26971, fax 0578-265889, www.bagnosanto.it, $, 418 spaces, Apr-Oct) and just outside of Cetona (**Sovana** ☆☆☆, SS321, Loc. Sovanna, ☎ 349-2334359, www.campingcetona.cjb.net, $$$, six spaces).

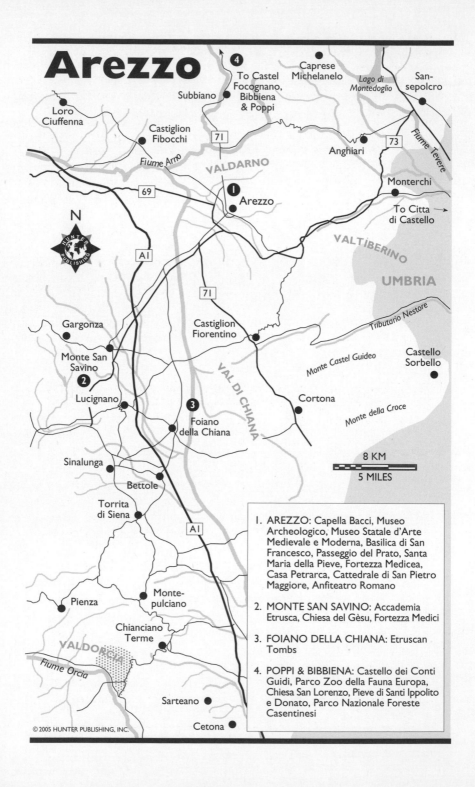

Arezzo

4 To Castel Focognano, Bibbiena & Poppi

Caprese Michelanelo

Lago di Montedoglio

Sansepolcro

Subbiano

Loro Ciuffenna

Castiglion Fibocchi

71

Anghiari

73

Fiume Tevere

Fiume Arno

VALDARNO

Monterchi

69

1 Arezzo

To Citta di Castello

N

A1

VALTIBERINO

UMBRIA

71

Tributario Nestore

Gargonza

Castiglion Fiorentino

Monte Castel Guideo

Castello Sorbello

Monte San Savino

2

VAL DI CHIANA

Cortona

Lucignano

Monte della Croce

3

Foiano della Chiana

8 KM

5 MILES

Sinalunga

Bettole

Torrita di Siena

A1

Pienza

Montepulciano

Chianciano Terme

VALDORCIA

Fiume Orcia

Sarteano

Cetona

1. **AREZZO:** Capella Bacci, Museo Archeologico, Museo Statale d'Arte Medievale e Moderna, Basilica di San Francesco, Passeggio del Prato, Santa Maria della Pieve, Fortezza Medicea, Casa Petrarca, Cattedrale di San Pietro Maggiore, Anfiteatro Romano

2. **MONTE SAN SAVINO:** Accademia Etrusca, Chiesa del Gèsu, Fortezza Medici

3. **FOIANO DELLA CHIANA:** Etruscan Tombs

4. **POPPI & BIBBIENA:** Castello dei Conti Guidi, Parco Zoo della Fauna Europa, Chiesa San Lorenzo, Pieve di Santi Ippolito e Donato, Parco Nazionale Foreste Casentinesi

Arezzo & Its Surroundings

Hanging onto a steep hillside first inhabited by the Etruscans; Arezzo is one of the most peaceful of the Tuscan cities, with a pleasant pedestrianized historical center that is a pleasure to walk around. The Aretines (inhabitants of Arezzo) are a pretty proud lot (the Florentines like to call them "snobby"). Their important commercial and military history has generated a local character so distinct from that of their Tuscan neighbors that the province is often referred to as the "anticamera dell'Umbria" (Umbria's lobby). The city's cultural and artistic heyday came at the end of the 12th century when it was established as an autonomous comune under Bishop Guido Tarlati (under whose rule were built its most beautiful monuments). Adhesion

Arezzo

with the Ghibellines saw the start of violent skirmishes with the Florentine Guelphs. The Florentine victory at Campaldino brought Arezzo's under the control of Florence and later of the Medici (their only real addition to the city being the Fortezza behind the Duomo).

NOT TO BE MISSED

- **Basilica di San Francesco:** Don't let the grumpy entrance guards put you off enjoying the *Legend of the True Cross* (see page 206).
- **Passeggio del Prato:** Peaceful park at the top of the city with stunning views over the Val di Chiana (see page 208).
- **Duomo:** Imposing Gothic mass flanked by the steps of *Life is Beautiful* fame (see page 230).
- **Coffee breaks Renaissance-style:** Pull up a chair in Vasari's celebrated loggia for views over the gently sloping Piazza Grande (see page 212).
- **Creative streets:** Take a wander up Via Borgunto to see the artisans at work (see page 211).
- **Santa Maria della Pieve:** Check out the church's funky tower (see page 207).
- **Antique central:** Back to the future with Arezzo's renowned antiques market (see page 211).
- **Cool tunnels:** Escape the summer heat in the Fortezza Medicea (see page 333).
- **Chiesa di San Domenico:** Barren church with a gilded treasure (see page 209).

Getting Here & Around

By Train: Frequent train (☎ 848-888088, www.trenitalia.it) services to Arezzo run from Florence, Perugia and Rome, with the slower **REG** services first stopping in the Valdarno towns of Figline and San Giovanni Valdarno, Montevarchi, Bucine and Laterina (between Florence and Arezzo). Catch the **IC** service if you don't want to be slowed town by stops in these towns.

By Bus: Sita (☎ 800-373760, www.sita-on-line.it) connects Florence with Arezzo through the Valdarno (#330 Florence-San Giovanni Valdarno-Peregrine Valdarno-Arezzo; #380 Florence-Montevarchi-Arezzo; #338 Arezzo-Peregrine Valdarno-San Giovanni Valdarno; #342 Florence-San Giovanni Valdarno-Montevarchi), change at Montevarchi for services to Terranuova Bracciolini (#331) and Bucine (#332 and #333).

By Car: Three main road approaches take you to Arezzo from Florence: the **A1** highway, which continues down to Rome; the **SS69**, which takes in Pontassieve before running more or less alongside the A1 into the city; and the longer **SS70**, which approaches the city from the other side of the Pratomagno mountain range via Poppi, Bibbiena and the Foreste Casentinesi. In the western valley of the Pratomagno you can also approach the city via the traces of the old Etruscan road that once united Fiesole and Arezzo (known as the **SP1**, *Setteponti*, for its seven bridges), but be prepared to take your time, since it's a pretty tortuous drive.

Information Sources

Tourist Offices: The very helpful **APT Arezzo** (Arezzo tourist office) is to your right as you exit the train station (Piazza della Repubblica 28, ☎/fax 0575-20839, www.apt.arezzo.it). It and the Florence tourist offices (see page 32) are your best bet for information on the Valdarno, although there are smaller offices at **Castelfrano di Sopra** (Via A. de Gasperi 1, ☎ 055-148055, fax 055-9149096, June-Sept), **Cavriglia** (Via Chiantigiana, ☎ 055-966421, fax 055-9668849, Apr-Sept), **Figline Valdarno** (Piazza Salvo Acquisto 58, ☎ 055-951569, fax 055-953112), **Loro Ciuffenna** (Piazza Matteotti 7, ☎ 055-9170139, fax 055-9172279) and **San Giovanni Valdarno** (Piazza Cavour 3, ☎ 055-943748, fax 055-9121123).

Adventure Information: For further information on adventures in the Pratomagno mountain area, contact the **Comunità Montane del Pratomagno** (Pratomagno Mountain Community) in Loro Ciuffenna (Via Genova 1, ☎ 055-9172277).

Maps & Guides : The Pratomagno is best served by *Massiccio del Pratomagno (Multigraphic 1:25,000)*.

Arezzo

■ Sightseeing in the Upper Valdarno

While it may not be the most attractive area of Florence's rural hinterland, this stretch of the Valdarno does tend to get an overly bad press. There is a fair amount of light industry and an extensive road network, but the less attractive valley towns do actually hide some pretty little hilltop villages. Especially on the slopes of the Pratomagno, rolling greenery, much of it belonging to locally born shoe-magnate Ferragamo, can only really be explored by ambling along the SP1 Setteponti.

A worthwhile first diversion north off the SP1 will take you to the splendid **Riserva Biogenetica Naturale di Vallombrosa** (Biogenetic Nature Reserve of Vallombrosa, ☎ 055-862029) with, at its heart, the stark white monastery founded by Florentine St Giovanni Gualberto in 1036 (the present building dates from the 16th century), which gave birth to the whole Vallombrosan order. It's a winding drive up to the monastery, but you are rewarded by some stunning views through the beech, fir and chestnut-forested woods that shield it from the outside world and there are plenty of trekking **trails** to explore (routes depart from Saltino and the abbey itself). Just north of the reserve, the **Passo della Consuma** (Consuma Pass, 1,050 m/3,444 feet) will take you over toward **Poppi** (the lovely rustic bar, **Chalet Il Valico**, on the pass itself, serves some tasty homemade cakes to its mostly truck-driving clientele). The main 20-km (12-mile) itinerary, which can also be followed on **cross-country skis**, takes you from the Passo della Consuma through the centuries-old forests of the Riserva Biogenetica Naturale di Vallombrosa along CAI #00 (pick up the red and white signs on the right of the SS70). You can also pick up another foot trail to the abbey suitable for cross-country skiing starts at Bagno di Cetica (23 km/14 miles).

Of the Romanesque churches built alongside the Setteponti, the olive oil-producing hamlet of **Reggello** has some of its best: the 12th-century **Pieve di San Pietro in Cascia** (take a right after you pass through the town) whose **Museo Masaccio d'Arte Sacra** has somehow managed to keep hold of its *Triptych of St. Giovenale* (the first noted work by the artist Masaccio, shown at left); the 12th-century **Pieve di Sant'Agata** in Arfoli (with two marble angels attributed to Mino da Fiesolo), and the **Chiesa di San Clemente in Sociana** (with marble bas-relief, the work of Antonio Rossellino). There are also plenty of Pratomagno-bound hiking trails departing from the town, including #18 over the Poggio Mazza Nera to Vallombrosa.

Arnolfo di Cambio is credited for the town plan of **Castelfranco di Sopra** (the town walls and gates once formed a checkered effect around the main square). The main attraction, just out of town, is the **Badia di Soffena** (Via Pian di Badia 2, ☎ 055-9149551, Mon-Sat, 9 am-1 pm), a 14th-century church, cloister and convent complex built here by Vallombrosian monks. The church, in Greek cross form, built on the cusp between the Romanesque and Gothic styles, has some fresco remains, mostly Bicci di Lorenzo and Masaccio's younger brother, Giovanni di Ser Giovanni (known as Lo Scheggia). There's a dig going on next door, with some medieval and Renaissance tombs currently being uncovered.

Arezzo

Loro Ciuffenna takes its unusual name from the river flowing through it, the river itself thought to have been christened by the town's original Etruscan inhabitants. In among the medieval houses stacked up parallel to the river, the **Chiesa di Santa Maria Assunta** houses a Lorenzo di Bicci triptych (15th-century) and the **Museo Venturino Venturi** (Piazza Matteotti 7, ☎ 055-9170163, Sat-Sun, 10:30 am-12:30 pm, 4:30-7:30 pm, €1.50, conc. €1), a collection of works by the artist born here in 1918. You'll also want to visit the **Pieve di San Pietro in Gropina** (☎ 055-9172103, 8 am-noon, 3-7 pm, till 5 pm in winter), one of the oldest Romanesque churches in Tuscany (originally eighth-century, the current building dates from the 11th), with a beautifully carved bas-relief showing some unusual iconography from the Old and New Testaments.

If you decide instead to venture along the SS69, what you'll find is a sleepy little backwater dotted with *terre murate* (fortified villages) that the Guelph Florentines built in the 13th century to guard against attacks

from the Ghibelline Aretine Republic. One of the most typical is **Incisa** (the birthplace of Petrarch) at **Figline Valdarno** (there's a terracotta-covered Palazzo Pretorio of interest if you do look inside). The most important is a little farther along at **San Giovanni Valdarno**, a dozy little hamlet gathered around **Palazzo Pretorio**, right, its stately town hall – the work of Arnolfo di Cambio (although it has been altered many times). The Palazzo is still striking with its terracotta and stone coats of arms covering the façade. The town also has a nice church in the 15th-century **Basilica di Santa Maria delle Grazie** (Piazza Masaccio, 7 am-noon, 4-7 pm, closed Mon), the Beato Angelico *Annunciation* (1430-32) now moved to the attached church museum (☎ 055-9122445, 10 am-12:30 pm, 3:30-6:30 pm, closed Wed, €2.50, conc. €1.50). It contains works by Domenico di Michelino and native son Masaccio, who is also honored with a **Museo Casa** (Corso Italia 83, ☎ 055-9121471, Tues-Sat, 4-7 pm, Sun and holidays, 10 am-noon, 4-7 pm).

On the slopes of the Monti del Chianti (the Chianti Hills), just south of San Giovanni Valdarno, the town of **Cavrgilia** offers the region's best **nature itineraries**, its 1,500-acre park (www.parcocavriglia.com) crisscrossed with **footpaths** (including the CAI Florence-Siena), **mountain bike** trails (bicycle rental Apr-Oct, ☎ 055-967422) and **horseback-riding** routes (trekking and guided excursions all year, ☎ 055-967544). It's also the site of some of the region's best **campgrounds**: **Del Lago** ☆☆ (Via Diga, Loc. S. Cipriano, ☎ 335-7226845, Apr-Sept, $) and, inside the park, **Piano Orlando** ☆☆ (Loc. Cafaggiolo 170, ☎ 055-967422, fax 055-967546, www.parcocavriglia.com, Apr-Sept, $) and **youth hostels**. Among the hostels are **Ostello del Campo Solare** (Loc. Cafaggiolo 168, ☎ 055-967544, fax 055-967546, www.parcocavriglia.com, $) and **Ostello del Parco** (Loc. Cafaggiolo 169, ☎ 055-967418, $). Arezzo's other nearest camping opportunity is at the Valdarno town of **Bucine** (**La Chiocciola** ☆☆☆, Via Guilio Cesare 14, Loc. Capannole, ☎/fax 055-995776, Mar-Oct, $).

■ The Montagna Fiorentina

Those that make the approach to Arezzo along the SS67 via the Foreste Casentinesi will be passing first through the area known as the Montagna Fiorentina, a picturesque wander along the vineyard-covered Sieve River Valley (home to the Chianti Rufina DOC) and up toward the 1,000-m (3,280-foot) heights of the chestnut-forested Pratomagno.

 Getting There: Trains from Florence run into the Montagna Fiorentina towns of Pontassieve, Rufina, Londa and Dicomano. Sita **bus** services #310 and #311 follow the same route, with an additional stop at San Godenzo. To arrive by **car**, pick up the SS67 (the "Muraglione") north from Pontassieve.

 Information Sources: The **Communità Montana Montagna Fiorentina** (Mountain Community of the Florentine Mountains, Via XXV Aprile 10, Rufina, ☎ 055-839661, fax 055-8396634, www.provincia.fi.it/cm) is your best information on adventures in the territory, but there are also small tourist boards of some help at **Dicomano** (Piazza della Repubblica 3, ☎ 055-838541, fax 055-8385423) and **San Godenzo** (Via G. Matteotti 3, ☎ 055-8374267, July-Aug).

The best **maps** for the adventures is the *Parco Nazionale Foreste Casentinesi, M. Falterona e Campigna* (Multigraphic, 1:50,000).

What to See: Passing first through **Rufina**, the main sight, the Museo della Vite e del Vino in the 15th-century Villa Poggio Reale is also home to the consortium enoteca (Tues-Sat, 2-7 pm). You'll next come to **Dicomano**. It has two noteworthy churches, a rare example of Neoclassical architecture in the 18th-century porticoes of the **Oratorio di Sant'Onofrio** (Via Pinzani, ☎ 055-838050, Sat, 9 am-noon, 5.30-7 pm, Sun and holidays, 5:30-7 pm) just outside town, and the more commonplace Romanesque style of the **Pieve di Santa Maria** (Loc. La Pieve, ☎ 055-838050, Sat, 4-5 pm, Sun and hols, 10 am-12:30 pm). It overlooks the town, with a run-of-the-mill collection of 16th- and 17th-century art inside. There are interesting digs going on in the surrounding countryside at **Frascole** (☎ 055-838541, Easter-Oct, Sun and public holidays, 10 am-noon, 3-6 pm), which have uncovered the foundations of a Romanesque church and the walls of a third-century BC Etruscan building.

The location of the famous 1302 meeting between the Florentine Ghibellines and White Guelphs attended by Dante, **San Godenzo**, right, developed around its Benedictine abbey (☎ 055-8374061, daily, 8:30 am-noon, 3-5 pm) at the turn of the last millennium. It is definitely worth a look for Baccio da Montelupo's muddy *St Sebastian* (1506) and the Bernardo Daddi *Madonna and Saints* (1333) altarpiece.

Adventures: From San Godenzo, foot **trail #6** leads to **Castagno d'Andrea,** birthplace of artist Andrea del Castagno, on the slopes of Monte Falterona, and then on to the Parco Nazionale delle Foreste Casentinesi, Monte Falterona e Campigna (GEA/SOFT #1 taking you from Castagno d'Andrea into the park).

From Castagno d'Andrea, one of the most popular routes (especially in winter when you can **snowshoe** it) follows GEA routes up over to the neighboring province of Emilia Romagna via the summits of Monte Falterona (marked by a wooden cross, 1,654 m/5,425 feet) and Monte Falco (1,658 m/5,438 feet). The latter also has a ski lift for **downhill skiing** in season.

Arezzo

CHIANTI RÙFINA E POMINO

*Though often overlooked in favor of their more famous relatives in the hills south of Florence, the wines of Chianti Rùfina e Pomino from the slopes of the Valdisieve, actually were the basis for the first wine road in Tuscany. You can visit one of the region's 24 producers or follow one of its four trails by contacting the **Chianti Rufina Consortium** (www.chiantirufina.it).*

■ Sightseeing in Arezzo

From the city train station (the best place to leave your car), two main approaches take you into its heart – the wider, modern shop-lined Via Guido Monaco, which has the benefit of taking you past a statue of the city's famous son, Via Guido Monaco (better known as Guido d'Arezzo) and the more atmospheric, cobbled Via della Madonna del Prato, which brings you up alongside the unfinished stone façade of Basilica di San Francesco, the first main sight.

ALL IN ONE

The combined museum ticket includes entrance to the Cappella Bacci, the Museo Archeologico, the Museo Statale d'Arte Medievale e Moderna and Casa Vasari for the price of €10. Tickets can be purchased from any of the museum ticket offices.

Basilica di San Francesco (Piazza San Francesco, 8:30 am-noon, 2-7 pm, entrance to the church is free, ☎ 0575-20630, www.pierodellafrancesca.it): A commentary board at the entrance to the church introduces one of Italy's most important Renaissance fresco cycles: Piero della Francesca's *Legend of the True Cross*, detail at right, in the Cappella Bacci behind the choir (tickets available from the gift shop adjacent to the church, ☎ 0575-24001, 9 am-7 pm, till 6 pm in winter, reservations required, €4, conc. €3 including audio commentary). It was begun by Bacci di Lorenzo in 1447 but, on his death in 1452, only the four *Evangelists* in the cross-vaulted choir ceiling, the *Last Judgment* on the front wall of the arch and the two

Doctors of the Church inside the arch had been completed. Local boy, Piero della Francesca took over in 1453, completing the cycle 13 years later. It is currently seen at its brightest after 15 years of restoration.

The fresco was inspired by Jacopo da Varagine's 13th-century *Golden Legend*, and you really do need the audio guide to help you follow the narrative, jumping about as it does from scene to scene. Many believe that scene five (*The Annunciation*) should actually be placed last, partly because it doesn't appear in Varagine's original story.

An interesting cross with *St Francis* above the main altar (1270, unknown Umbrian artist) and a circular stained glass window by Guillaume de Marcillat (*St Francis and Pope Onirio III*, 1524) will keep you occupied in the church's ample interior while you wait to enter.

A right along the antique-shop lined Via Cavour and Corso Italia will take you up past the deliciously crumbling **Santa Maria della Pieve** (☎ 0575-22629, undergoing restoration at the time of writing), known to locals as "La Pieve." One of the largest Romanesque buildings in Tuscany (and one of Arezzo's emblems), the interior of this mid-12th-century Pisan-Romanesque gem (built with a stone façade rather than the traditional marble) houses a marvelous polyptych by Pietro Lorenzetti (*Madonna with Child and Four Saints, Annunciation, Assunta and Twelve Saints*) painted in 1320 for the then Bishop Guido Tarlati. To its left, sits the dramatic "tower of a hundred holes" (so-called for the five layers of mullioned windows on each side).

A stunning approach from here to Arezzo's slanted main square, Piazza Grande, is provided by the **Logge Vasariane.** It was erected by homegrown talent, Giorgio Vasari, in the second half of the 15th century, and its vast porticoes are today the suggestive home to some of the city's most tourist-frequented caffès and restaurants. It's hardly surprising: they have great views over the glorious jumble of building shapes, heights, colors and styles, from the Romanesque to the Gothic and the Renaissance to the Baroque, that line the sloping square. It's a mix epitomized by the 14th- to 16th-century Palazzo della Fraternita dei Laici (the one with the clock), a characteristic Renaissance tower built on top of a pre-existing Gothic palazzo structure.

> **Giorgio Vasari:** Learn more about this artist, writer and favored architect of Cosimo I de' Medici by visiting **Casa Vasari** (Via XX Settembre 55, ☎ 0575-409040, 9 am-7 pm, closed Tues, free), the house-museum of the great man born in Arezzo in 1511.

The Giostra del Saracino (Joust of the Saracen)

(Piazza Grande, ☎ 0575-377262, www.giostradelsaracino. arezzo.it, third Sun of June and first Sun of Sept, night joust on the 2nd Sun in Sept, seat up to €25, standing room €5.)

Every self-respecting Tuscan city has a medieval folkloric celebration of note, and this chivalrous joust is Arezzo's. Comprising a colorful horseback charge (no mean feat itself given the size and slope of the square), jousters represent the four historical quarters. Red and green are for Porta Crucifera; yellow and cream, Porta del Foro; white and green, Porta Sant'Andrea; and yellow and blue, Santo Spirito. They attempt to hit a "dartboard" on the

Saracen's torso. Those that may consider the festivity's premise a little politically uncorrect will be relieved to see that the wooden dummy gets its revenge by swinging around and attempting to clobber them back with his cat-of-three-tails. Points from one to four are allocated, depending on the proximity to the bull's eye, with the winning quarter awarded the much-prized "Lancia d'Oro" (the Golden Lance).

Although traced back to Christian military training for combat in the Crusades, the joust these days represents a well-used opportunity for the enthusiastic rival *contrade* to battle their traditional rivals (you may not understand the songs or cries, but you'll probably get their meaning from the hand signals). The fun gets off to a solemn start in the morning, when the town herald reads out the challenge, inviting participants to meet in front of the cathedral for the benediction.

Tip: To see the best of the ceremonial cortege and flag-waving, get yourself a spot in the caffè or on nearby park benches on Passaggio del Prato around 2 pm, where the musicians and knights unite before parading to the cathedral. If you haven't got a ticket for the joust, you can purchase a standing-room place up to five minutes before it begins by following the crowds to the outlet on Via Bicchieraia.

Piazza Grande, Arezzo

From Piazza Grande you can join the vast **Passaggio del Prato** – the "field" between the knolls on which the cathedral and **Fortezza Medici** stand (7 am-8 pm, till 6 pm in winter, free) – by following the steps up through the Logge Vasariana. With a stupendous panorama of the city over one side and that of the Val di Chiana on the other, it comes as no surprise that this is *the* place in Arezzo for that post-dinner gelato stroll. The statue in the center commemorates another local great, Francesco Petrarch, born in the province in 1304. You can find out more about his life and works by visiting his Aretine museum-home (**Casa Petrarca**, Via dell'Orto 28, ☎ 0575-24700, fax 0575-298846, www.accademiapetrarca.it, Mon-Sat, 10 am-noon, 3-5 pm, free).

The old city walls bring you around the Passaggio del Prato to Piazza del Duomo, where you will find the imposing **Cattedrale di San Pietro Maggiore** (☎ 0575-23991, 6:30 am-12:30 pm, 3-7 pm, free), Arezzo's boldest and most sober religious edifice. The church was built in various phases from the end of the 13th to the beginning of the 16th century (when its Gothic imprint was finally completed), with the Neo-Gothic façade added over

Casa Petrarca

three centuries later to replace an incomplete 15th-century predecessor. Inside, Giullaume de Marcillat's 16th-century stained glass windows keep the three naves pleasantly light. Note the *Arca di San Donato*, a rich urn of decorated white marble (15th-century, presbytery), an interesting *Trinity* by Andrea della Robbia (Cappella della Madonna del Conforto, off the left nave) and, just behind the 14th-century sculpted cenotaph of Bishop Guido Tarlati, a fresco of *Mary Magdalen* by Piero della Francesco (around 1460, entrance door to the sacristy).

LIFE IS BEAUTIFUL

If the Duomo steps bring back memories of dark rainy nights, rolls of red fabric tumbling down the stairs and a cushion-topped umbrella, then you've probably seen Roberto Benigni's Oscar-winning *Life is Beautiful* (*La Vita è Bella*, 1988) once or twice. You can follow in the footsteps of Guido and his *principessa* thanks to the tourist office's *Life is Beautiful* tour, which takes you around eight key locations from the film, starting from Piazza della Libertà (in front of the cathedral) and including Piazza San Francesco (the three-on-a-bike scene that decorates the film poster) and Teatro Petrarca (where Guido spends the entire production watching his future wife Dora rather than the drama itself). Pick up an itinerary from the tourist office beside the train station on arrival.

Heading past the Palazzo Comunale (these days home to the **Galleria Comunale d'Arte Contemporanea**, Gallery of Contemporary Art, ☎ 0575-377671, closed at the time of writing), Via Sassoverde will take you up to **Chiesa di San Domenico** (☎ 0575-22906, fax 0575-300940, 8:30 am-7 pm, closed 1-3:30 pm in winter, free), a pretty barren church, built in 1275 according to the guidelines of Bishop Guido Tarlati. In contrast to the church's sparse interior, the recently restored 13th-century *Crucifix* designed by a young Cimabue (left, 1260-65) – particularly interesting for its Byzantine iconography – seems all the more splendid. You can learn more of its history and design by visiting the church's permanent exhibition: *Cimabue ad Arezzo. Il Crocifisso Restaurato* (☎ 0575-24001, Tues-Sat, 9:30 am-7 pm, Sun and holidays, 9:30-11 am, 12:30-7 pm, €4, con. €3), which traces the work of the artist in Arezzo and the four years it took to restore his work.

At the nearby **Museo Statale d'Arte Medioevale e Moderna** (State Museum of Medieval & Modern Art, Via San Lorentino 8, ☎ 0575-409050, 8:30 am-7:30 pm, €4, conc. €2), you'll find a pleasant enough collection of works by some of the city's artists (Margaritone, Spinello, Bartolomeo della Gatta, Luca Signorelli and Vasari being the best-known), as well as its centerpiece: the 13th-century *Margarito d'Arezzo* by Piero della Francesco. Via Cavour takes you from here past **Badia SS Flora e Lucilla** (Piazza di Badia, ☎ 0575-56612, 8 am-noon, 4-7 pm, free) back to Piazza San Francesco.

The town's next attraction is to the south on Via Margaritone. Next to the **Anfiteatro Romano** (Roman Amphitheater, ☎/fax 0575-20882, daily, 8:30 am-5 pm, free), the **Museo Archeologico** (Archeological Museum, 8:30 am-7:30 pm, €4, conc. €2) is worth a visit. It has some Greek and Etruscan pottery, bronzes and an ample collection of *coralline* vases, the locally produced red vases much vaunted in the Roman world. Corso Italia, the main street, takes you back from here to the train station through the Bastioni di Santo Spirito.

From here, Arezzo's remaining sight is a few miles out of town. The **Chiesa di Santa Maria delle Grazie** (Via Santa Maria 1, ☎ 0575-323140, www.abd.it/santamaria, 8 am-7 pm) is the location of what is considered the earliest porticoed square in the Renaissance – built by Benedetto da Maiano in the 15th century – it is also the proud home of a beautiful marble and terracotta pulpit by Andrea della Robbia.

■ Adventures

 Arezzo's prime **hiking** territory is in its northeast at the **Parco Nazionale delle Foreste Casentinesi** and north in the **Pratomagno**. There are a few itineraries you can pick up outside of the town, including the following nature reserves, parks and ANPIL sites:

The **Riserva Naturale Ponte Buriano e Penna** (Nature Reserve of Ponte Buriano and Penna, ☎ 0575-3161, parchi@provincia.arezzo.it), stretches 2,000 acres west of Ponte a Buriano to the Valdarno town of Laterina and south to Civitella in Val di Chiana.

The 900 acres of the reforested **Parco di Lignano** (Lignano Park, Loc. Rigutino, ☎ 0575-979446, www.parcodilignano.it) can be found on the slopes of the 837-m (2,745-foot) Mount Lignano to the south of Arezzo.

The 30 acres of **ANPIL Bosco di Sargiano** (Sargiano Woodland **Bird-watching** Site, ☎ 0575-3161, parchi@provincia.arezzo.it) are enclosed within the walls of the Convent of Sargiano. The well-preserved oak woodland is home to nocturnal predators such as the screech-owl and the tawny owl.

To arrange **horseback riding** in the area, contact **Club Ippico Aretino** (Loc. Sant'Anastasio 49, ☎ 0575-99204, fax 0575-949899, www.cfsarezzo.com).

■ Entertainment & Events

 Teatro Petrarca (Via Guido Monaco 8/14, ☎ 0575-23975, www.arezzoteatro.com, Nov-Mar, from €11, conc. €9) is the city's main theater set in a building renowned for its acoustics. It offers a mix of theater, opera, ballet and classical music, which includes the **Guido d'Arezzo**, one's of Europe's largest polyphonic competitions (☎ 0575-23952, second two weeks of Aug).

The city's most important folkloric event is, of course, the **Giostro del Saraceno**, but there is also the July rock festival, **Arezzo Wave** (☎ 0575-23952, www.arezzowave.com, five days usually starting the Wed after the first Sun, free). It's a "love festival" that attracts over 150,000 spectators a year to the Passeggio del Prato and Fortezza Medicea.

■ Where to Shop

One of Italy's leading antique fairs, the **Fiera Antiquaria** swamps Arezzo's streets the first Sun and last Sat of the month with its 600 dealers (and 20,000 browsers) of 19th-century furniture, 17th- to 19th-century glassware and wood-carved antiques (7:30 am-7 pm, till 3 pm in winter). If you want to find out more, you can visit the museum house of its founder, **Casa Museo di Ivan Bruschi** (Corso Italia 14, ☎ 0575-900404, www.fondazionebruschi.it, Tues-Sun, 10 am-1 pm, 2-6 pm, €3, conc. €2).

If you miss the market, stop by one of Arezzo's many antique shops; the best-known are found off Piazza San Francesco and Piazza Grande. Try **La Nuova Chimera** (Via San Francesco 18, ☎ 0575-350155) for furnishings, **La Belle Epoque** (Piazza San Francesco 18, ☎ 0575-355495) for antique laces and embroidered linens or **Grace Gallery** (Via Cavour 30, ☎ 0575-354963) for painting and sculpture.

A bustling ceramic store is **Da Arete** (Piazza Grande 38, ☎ 0575-352803), with local terracotta arts and crafts, but a wander up nearby Via Borgunto (leading east of Piazza Grande) will uncover many more, including the workshops of the city's surviving artisans.

For gastronomy – and there's Aretine honey, artisan cakes, patisseries and chocolate, as well as the usual oil, pasta and wines to purchase here – make your way to shops such as **Canto de' Bacci** (Corso Italia 65, ☎ 0575-355804, www.cantodebacci.com), **Pasticceria Dé Cenci** (Via dé Cenci 17, ☎ 0575-23102) and, for incredibly tasty artisan chocolate, **Vestri** (Via Romana 161a, ☎ 0575-907315, www.cioccolateriavestri.com) and **La Chicca** (Via di Beccheria 3b, ☎ 0575-354714). Wine purchases are served by **Enoteca Cristallo** (Piazza San Jacopo, ☎/fax 0575-27202, www.enotecacristallo.it) with personalized wine tastings and organized wine shipping. For those wanting to stock up on a bit of everything, there's also a big outlet of "Tuscan products" just outside of town at **Collina Toscana** (Viale Europa, loc. Ponte d'Arno, Castel San Niccolò, ☎ 0575-560688, www.collinatoscana.com).

■ Where to Eat

LOCAL FLAVORS

Bringoli: Flat spaghetti made of wheat flour served with various game and truffle sauces (both from the Valtiberina).

Stufato alla sangiovannese: A meat stew originating from San Giovanni Valdarno.

Pollo del Valdarno: Chicken cooked in tomato sauce (a Valdarno specialty).

Bistecca: Charcoal-grilled steak from Chianina cattle.

Gatto: A chocolate cake of French origin introduced to Arezzo in the Napoleonic era.

Historical Center

An old literary caffè opposite the Chiesa di San Francesco, **Caffè dei Costanti** (☎ 0575-371403, $) and neighboring **Caffè Vita Bella** ($) are your best bets for a quick sandwich or coffee and cake on one of the terraces pictured in the background of Benigni's film. Ice cream needs are satisfied at nearby gelateria **Cremi** (Corso Italia, $), which heaps an impressive amount of ice cream on even its smallest cones.

More an old-fashioned delicatessen than a restaurant, the **Antica Fiaschetteria de Redi** (Via de' Redi 10, ☎ 0575-355012, closed Mon, $) has an outdoor terrace with only one table! It's a great choice for a light lunch and a large glass of wine (check out the wine-making equipment along with more tables inside), with a tasty menu of pastas, meats and Tuscan cheeses to tempt.

DINING PRICE CHART	
Price per person for an entrée, including house wine & cover.	
$	Under €20
$$	€21-€40
$$$	€41-€60
$$$$	Over €60

The checked tablecloths of small family-run **Osteria Agania** (Via G. Mazzini 10, ☎ 0575-295381, fax 0575-295381, www.osteriagania.it, closed Mon, $) justly indicate that this serves traditional Aretine fare. You won't be disappointed: the range of homemade pastas, *grifi, trippa, bistecca* and roast meats are finished off with the *torta della nonna*.

A good *bistecca* can be had at non-smoking **Da Guido** (Via Madonna del Prato, $), a small restaurant of only seven tables, a handwritten daily menu and a fine wine list.

A couple of small wooden tables make enoteca **Vinodivino** (Corso Italia 53, ☎ 0575-299598, closed Mon, $$), a relaxed choice for a light evening meal. The menu of cured meats, creamy pastas and local cheeses goes well with the local wines sampled by the glass.

The large terrace at the back of **Bruschetta Toscana** (Via Tolletta 20, ☎ 0575-299860, fax 0575-3102948, tratt.brusch.toscana@virgilio.it, closed Tues, $$) make this trattoria a great summer choice. Specialties include *bistecca chianina*, Valtiberina game, charcuterie (pork products) and homemade desserts.

There's intimate dining to be had at **Le Tastevin** (Via de' Cenci 9, ☎ 0575-28304, closed Mon and second week in Aug, $$), whether you book a table on the small terrace or inside its dimly lit walls. Traditional Tuscan dishes crop up once again, this time *minestra di farro*, the house *risotto, acquacotta* and *bistecca chianina* accompanying the extensive wine list. The adjacent piano bar has live acts.

Known for its stews, *fegatelli* (pork liver sausages), roasts and steaks, **Trattoria Il Saraceno** (Via G. Mazzini 6, ☎ 0575-27644, www.ilsaraceno.com, closed Wed and last two weeks in July, $$) is located up a cobbled street off the main Corso Italia. It makes a friendly rustic choice.

You almost feel as if you are eating in somebody's garden on the terrace of **Osteria del Borghiccolo** (Corso Italia 35, ☎ 0575-24488, fax 0575-54555, james@ats.it, closed Tues, $$ with set menus for €16/$20). It's up a narrow street in a square of townhouses, their balconies overhung with flowers and laundry.

Booking is recommended at the ever-popular **Buca di San Francesco** (Via di San Francesco 1, ☎/fax 0575-23271, www.bucadisanfrancesco.it, closed Mon pm and Tues, plus two weeks in July, $$$) in the basement of a 14th-century building next to the church from which it takes its name. Dishes include homemade pasta, saporita and some great cakes.

For the best location, try the terrace of **Ristorante Logge Vasari** (Piazza Grande, ☎/fax 0575-300333, www.loggevasari.it, closed Tues and Jan, $$$). The menu features modern takes on the local traditions like handmade *pici al sugo di* *nana* (goose sauce), *filetto al brunello* (fillet steak in Brunello), and great desserts like *sfogliatina fragole e chantilly* (strawberries in puff pastry with chantilly cream).

Out of Town

Two miles out of town en route to the Casentino, restaurant-pizzeria **Il Coccio** (Case Nuove di Ceciliano 84a, ☎ 0575-320269, ilcoccio@libero.it, closed Mon, $) comes alive on weekends with a piano bar on Fridays and salsa music on Saturdays. Throughout the week you can sample its local cuisine – mostly home-made pastas, steaks, and pizzas. Take the SS71 and follow the signs.

Midway to Castiglion Fibocchi, **La Doccia** (Via Setteponti 24, Loc. Rondine, ☎ 0575-364222, fax 0575-364426, doccia@tin.it, closed Tues and first three weeks of Aug, $$).

Found on the SS71 toward Cortona, is a typical Tuscan setting and typical Tuscan cuisine (*carne alla brace,* fresh fish from June-Sept) of **Osteria del Gallo** (Via Romana 44, Rigutino Arezzo, ☎/fax 0575-97288, www.osteriadelgallo.com, closed Tues and Nov, $$).

Six miles from Arezzo, rustic **Il Mulino** (Strada Provinciale della Libbia 75, Arezzo Chiassa Superiore, ☎ 0575-361878, www.il-mulino.com, closed Tues, $$$) is the place to go if you want to splash out but stay traditional. Try the *pappardelle al germano* (wild duck sauce), *ribollita, tagliata* or *fegatelli* (pork liver sausages).

■ Where to Stay

 Arezzo's central budget hotel accommodation is offered by **Cecco** ☆☆ (Corso Italia 215, ☎ 0575-20986, fax 0575-356730, www.hotelcecco.com, $$). Other options are **Europa** ☆☆☆ (Via Spinello 43, ☎ 0575-357701, fax 0575-403501, www.cittadiarezzo.com, $$), **B&B La Terrazza** (Via Guido Monaco 25, ☎ 0575-28387, fax 0575-523292, http://web.tiscali.it/la-terrazza, $$) and the slightly more expensive **Casa Volpi** ☆☆☆ (Loc. Le Pietre 2, ☎ 0575-354364, fax 0575-355971, www.casavolpi.it, $$$). All should be booked well in advance during the peak season.

HOTEL PRICE CHART	
Rates are per room with private bath, based on double occupancy, including breakfast.	
$	Under €40
$$	€41-€85
$$$	€86-€140
$$$$	€141-€210
$$$$$	Over €210

With one foot in the historical center and one close to the train station, the recently refurbished **Cavaliere Palace** ☆☆☆☆ (Madonna del Prato 83, ☎ 0575-26836, fax 0575-21925, www.cavalierehotels.com, $$$) is well placed for those planing day-trips into the province. It's on a street with some of Arezzo's less-touristy restaurants.

Well-positioned near the Chiesa di San Francesco, **Il Patio** ☆☆☆☆ (Via Cavour 23, ☎ 0575-401962, fax 0575-27418, www.arezzoresorts.it, $$$$) has four rooms and three luxury suites modeled after places visited by celebrated travel writer Bruce Chatwin (India, China, Australia, etc.) in its converted 18th-century town-house. Downstairs, there's an atmospheric bistro with 1930s-style American Bar.

Book well in advance if you plan to stay during the antiques fair; the hotel has a great vantage point and fills quickly.

Most visitors head farther into one of the four valleys for *agriturismi*, but if you do want to stay within striking distance of the city, your best choice is **Il Palazzo** ☆☆☆☆ (Libbia di Tregozzano, Tregozzano, ☎/fax 0575-315016, www.ilpalazzo.toscana.it, $$$). They also organize horseback riding. Another option is **Lo Spicchio Casa Vittoria** ☆☆☆ (Loc. Lo Spicchio, Fraz. Cincelli 36, ☎/fax 0575-965090, www.chiantionline.com/casavittoria, $$), on the region's trekking route.

Basic but friendly hostel accomodation is offered by **Ostello Villa Severi** (Via F. Redi 13, ☎ 0575-299057, www.peterpan.it/ostello.htm, $), a 30-minute walk north of Arezzo in a converted 16th-century villa surrounded by lovely gardens (take Bus #4 to Via F. Redi from Piazza Giudo Marco). The nearest **campgrounds** are in the Valdarno, on the outskirts of the Parco Nazionale delle Foreste Casentinesi or in the Valtiberina.

Outside of Arezzo

Right on the Tuscan border, the Arezzo province may be the *anticamera dell'Umbria* (Umbria's lobby), but it also includes some of Tuscany's richest cultural and natural sights. This is a land of illustrious sons, with Masaccio, Piero della Francesca, Michelangelo and Giorgio Vasari just some of the best known. It's known for gastronomy, spiritual retreats, well-preserved medieval hilltop towns (including the classic townscape of Cortona), and forest adventures.

REGION AT A GLANCE

- **Main city:** Arezzo.
- **Afternoon trips from Arezzo:** Caprese Michelangelo (see page 225), Sansepolcro (see page 224).
- **Town breaks:** Cortona (see page 228).
- **Rural retreats:** Foreste Casentinesi (see page 220), Montagna Fiorentina (see page 204), Val di Chiana (see page 232), Valtiberina (see page 224).
- **Spiritual centers:** Eremo di Camaldoli (see page 215), Santuario della Verna (see page 216).

The Casentino

The Casentino is the name given to the green upper valley of the Arno in the northeast of Arezzo. It is an area dominated by the 100,000-acre Parco Nazionale Foreste Casentinesi and Monte Falterona e Campigna (Casentinesi Forest, Mt Falterona and Campigna National Park) – half of which belongs to the neighboring province of Emilia Romagna – with its wide choice of walking, trekking, mountain biking and horseback-riding routes. Considered the best-pre-served woodland in Italy, the immense forest of chestnuts, beeches, oaks and firs that form the park's heart conceals structures of religious and historical interest, such as the Monastero and Eremo (Hermitage) di Camaldoli and the Sanctuario della Verna.

■ Getting Here & Around

By Bus: Your best approach to the region is by bus. From Florence, **Sita** (☎ 800-373760, www.sita-on-line.it) runs services #320 (Bibbiena-Poppi-Pratovecchio-Stia), #310 and #311 (Londa-San Godenzo). And from Arezzo, **LFI** (☎ 0578-31174, www.lfi.it) provides H#1 (Pratovecchio-Stia), H#2-#4 (Poppi-Bibbiena), H#11 (Bibbiena-Chiusi), H#12 (Bibbiena-La Verna) and LH#2 (Rassina-Salutio-Talla).

By Car: The Florence-to-Arezzo SS70/1 enters the park at the Passo della Consuma (Florence end) and exits at the Passo della Giova (Arezzo end), passing first through Poppi and Bibbiena with turn-offs to the other towns.

■ Information Sources

Tourist Offices: The Parco Nazionale Foreste Casentinesi, Monte Falterona e Campigna has its Head Office at **Pratovecchio** (Via G. Brocchi 7, ☎ 0575-50301, fax 0575-504497, www.parcoforestecasentinesi.it) with further information offices at **Chiusi della Verna** (Parco I Maggio, ☎/fax 0575-532098, Mar-Jan), **Londa** (Loc. Parco del Lago, ☎ 055-8351202, Apr-Oct), **Serravalle** (Via Coselschi, ☎ 0575-539174, Apr-Sept), **Stia** (Via Montegrappa 2, ☎/fax 0575-504596, Mar-Sept), **Badia Prataglia** (Via Nazionale 14A, ☎/fax0575-559477, all year) and **Castagno d'Andrea** (Via della Rota 8, ☎/fax 055-8375125, Apr-Oct). They are the best sources of information for sightseeing and adventure activities in the park. Alternatively, you can contact the **Communità Montana del Casentino** (Casentino Mountain Community, Via Roma 203, Ponte a Poppi, ☎ 0575-5071, fax 0575-507230, www.casentino.toscana.it) for further information, particularly on trekking excursions.

Guides & Maps: The Parco Nazionale Foreste Casentinesi, Monte Falterona e Campigna has its own high-quality guide and map, *Trekking nel Parco,* available from park information points. You can also pick up CAI routes and mountain bike trails through *Parco Nazionale Foreste Casentinesi, Monte Falterona e Campigna* (1:50,000, Multigraphic).

■ Sightseeing ~ North into the Foreste Casentinesi

A narrow winding road leads you north from Arezzo as far as Bibbiena, where the countryside suddenly flattens out into a bowl between the ridge of Pratomagno to the west and that of Falterona to the east. There are a few little towns to look out for on the way. **Socana**, whose recently excavated **Pieve di Sant'Antonino** (☎ 0575-592561, summer, 8 am-1 pm, 3:30-7 pm, winter, 8:30 am-12:30 pm, 3-5:30 pm, free) houses a large sacrificial altar. It belonged to the fifth-century BC Etruscan temple that originally stood in its place. Then there is **Talla**, the birthplace of Guido Monaco (see below); and **Castel Focognano**, whose watchtower is occupied by the Centro di Documentazione della Cultura Rurale del Casentino (Torre di Ronda, ☎ 0575-592020, by appointment only, €1.50, conc. €1), with exhibits on the history of agriculture and farming in the territory. Otherwise, the sights start once you hit Bibbiena.

> **Musical Pilgrimages:** In among the thick chestnut woods of Pratomagno, you'll find the birthplace of Guido Monaco: **Museo della Musica "Guido d'Arezzo"** (Loc. Castellaccia, Talla, ☎ 0575-597512, fax 0575-597693, June-Sept, Thurs, Sat-Sun, 4:30-7 pm, Oct-July, Sat-Sun, 2:30-5 pm, €3, conc. €2). It has a display on the history of musical innovations and traditions, as far back as the revolutionary musical notation system developed by medieval monks. The house-museum also organizes concerts of Gregorian chants in August.

The most important town in the Casentino, **Bibbiena**, grew on the roots of the Etruscan center of Vipena. The heart of the old town (a short drive uphill from the far less attractive new town below) is marked by the Renaissance **Chiesa di San Lorenzo**, which took its present form (apart from the cloister, added in the first half of the 17th century) when it was enlarged to house Franciscan friars in the

15th century. It is best known for its two noteworthy della Robbia terracottas – a *Nativity* by Andrea della Robbia on the right, and a *Deposition* opposite. The Romanesque **Pieve di Santi Ippolito e Donato** (Via Rosa Scoti 41, ☎ 0575-593079, fax 0575-569820, 7:30 am-7 pm) contains the town's most important work: a triptych *Maestà* by Bicci di Lorenzo. Another piece of his (a fresco of *Madonna del Sasso*) is just out of town, en route to La Verna, at the **Basilica di Santa Maria del Sasso** (Loc. Santa Maria del Sasso, ☎ 0575-593266, fax 0575-569813, Apr-Oct, 7 am-noon, 3-7:30 pm, Nov-Mar, 7 am-noon, 2:30-6 pm, free). It also has a beautiful 15th-century cloister designed by Giuliano da Maiano. Before you head out, check out Bibbiena's range of historical palazzi. The most important is the late 15th-century **Palazzo Dovizi**, with rusticated façade evidently inspired by Florentine palazzi. There's also the 17th-century **Palazzo Niccolini** and, next door, the **Palazzo Marcucci**, with its striking façade and delicately frescoed rooms.

Maiolica della Natività, Andrea Della Robbia

The well-signposted SS208 takes you from Bibbiena to **Chiusi della Verna**. Found on the slopes of the 1,120-m (3,674-foot) Monte Penna in the midst of thick beech and fir woods, it is the gateway to one of Italy's most important Christian centers: the **Santuario della Verna** (Via Convento 45, ☎ 0575-5341, fax 0575-599320, summer, 6:30 am-9 pm, winter, 6:30-7:30 pm, free). The Verna sanctuary, a quiet and majestic monastery on the *Sacro Monte* (Sacred Mountain), has been a site of pilgrimage since San Francesco d'Assisi received his stigmate in a nearby cave in 1224 (he had established the monastery 11 years earlier). The event is re-enacted every September. The oldest part of the complex is the Chiesa di Santa Maria degli Angeli, which houses the first three (*Annunciation, Nativity, Pietà*) of a fine 16-strong collection of glazed della Robbia terracottas (see above) – the remaining works can be seen in the Basilica Maggiore, the Cappella delle Reliquie and the Cappella delle Stimmate, where Andrea della Robbia's grandiose *Crucifixion* marks the spot where St Francis is said to have received the stigmate. Included in the area of the Parco Nazionale Foreste Casentinesi, Monte Falterona e Campigna (Casentinesi, Mt Falterona and Campigna National Park), the sanctuary is also well known for its stunning natural surroundings. The buildings look out onto a 300-m (984-foot) precipice, and the site includes the famous **Sasso Spicco**, a giant mass that seems suspended in the void below.

Just past Bibbiena, a right on the SS71 will take you into the Parco Nazionale Foreste Casentinesi, Monte Falterona e Campigna, but this time at **Serravalle**, a picturesque hillcrest-town (777 m/2,549 feet) built around the ruins of an ancient castle, which marks the beginning of a two-mile scenic stretch of road to Camaldoli. If you want to stop off en route, **Partina** has a permanent exhibition on the region's Etruscan roots (**Casentino Archeologico dalla Preistoria al Periodo Romano**, Piazza Dante 29, ☎ 0575-593791, fax 0575-595312, www.elledi.it/enti/bibliobibbiena, Sat, 9 am-noon, 4-7 pm, Sun, 10 am-noon, 4-7 pm, free).

Along the *sentiero natura* into splendid fir forest, the Monastero and Eremo di Camaldoli comprise the second of the important centers of spirituality in the region. It is split into sections, with the more isolated Eremo (hermitage, 1,111 m/3,644 feet), a two-mile walk along a mystical old monk path from the 16th-century monastery complex (814 m/2,670 feet). The 16th-century **Monastero di Camaldoli** (Loc. Camaldoli 1a, ☎ 0575-556012, fax 0575-556079, www.camaldoli.it, daily, 8:30 am-12:30 pm, 2:30-6:30 pm, free), is reached first. It includes a fascinating 15th-century Farmacia (Pharmacy, ☎ 0575-556143, June-Oct, 9 am-12:30 pm, 2:30-6 pm, Nov-May shorter hours, closed Wed, free). The **Eremo di Camaldoli** (☎ 0575-556021, daily, 9 am-11 pm, 3-6 pm, free) comprises 20 isolated cells. Only one of these is accessible to the public, that of San Romualdo, the founder of the Eremo and its faith in 1012.

Back on the SS71, the next stop before the Emilia Romagna border is **Badia Prataglia**. It stands tall at 843 m (2,765 feet) on a thickly wooded Apennine ridge. A popular starting point for many of the park's most popular trails, is the nearby **Museo Ornitologico Forestale Carlo Simeoni** (Via Nazionale 14, ☎/fax 0575-559155, cfspostofissobadia@interfree.it, guided visits by appointment, free). An *arboreto* of exotic trees, it was built to study the progress of the trees being reintroduced to the region in 1835 under the watchful eye of Carlo Simeoni (Karl Siemon).

SOMETHING FOR THE KIDS

The **Centro Visita di Badia Prataglia** (☎ 0575–559477, fax 0575–559447, cvbadiaprataglia@interfree.it) organizes monthly activities (nature games, guided visits, orienteering, product-tasting and so on) for children and young adults from July to September.

Asqua (Serravalle, ☎/fax 0575–539173, www.asqua.it) organizes L'Educagioco (Mon-Fri, 1-5:30 pm, €5), a summer babysitting center for kids aged seven to 12 with games and lessons about the local environment.

Dominated by the profile of the late 13th-century Castello dei Conti Guidi, **Poppi** (back on the SS70) is a medieval jewel on a hill, which dominates the entire Casentino. La Costa (a medieval path) takes you up from the new town to the walls of the historical center and onto its main church square. The recently restored **Castello dei Conti Guidi** (Piazza Repubblica 1, ☎/fax 0575-520516, castellodipoppi@libero.it, daily, 10 am-6 pm, €4, conc. €3), a grand testimony to the wealth and pomp of the Guidi counts, lies on its left. Its elegant courtyard leads you to the castle stairs, which in turn lead to the first floor with its Biblioteca Tilliana and chapel decorated with 14th-century frescoes by Taddeo Gaddi (*Stories of Jesus* and *St John the Baptist*).

The Guidi Castles

The castle in Poppi is the most important of the Guidi Counts' chain of medieval defenses in the Casentino – a land, which, due to its location at the northeastern edge of Tuscany, has seen much in the way of feudal conflict. The Guidi were lords of the land, and their castles can be found crowning the area's most strategic locations: Romena, Porciano, Urbech, Castelleone, Castel San Niccolò, Borgo alla Collina, Montemignaio and Fronzola. Of these, the most interesting is the fortification in **Castel San Niccolò** (Loc. Strada in Casentino, Fraz. Castello, ☎ 0575-570072, by appointment only, free). It once belonged to the Contessa Matilde di Toscana and has a church-museum covering the history of the castle, castle society and castles in the region. Another is the **Castello di Romena**, an imposing construction with 14 towers encircled by the remains of three rings of walls.

The main rivals of the Guidi were the Tarlati and Ubertini families from Arezzo, who owned the lands on the Arezzo side, but most of their castles were destroyed in the conflict between the Guelphs and the Ghibellines at the crucial Battle of Campaldino (1289), which marked the victory of the Guelphs – a battle also famous for the participation of Dante Alighieri. Following the defeat of the Conti Guidi in the Battle of Anghiari (1440), the Casentino became part of the Florentine Republic, subsequently passing under the control of the Medici and then, the Grand Duchy of Tuscany.

Leaving the castle, you meet the Baroque **Oratorio della Madonna del Morbo** (Piazza Amerighi, ☎ 0575-529136, Sun and holidays, 8 am-noon, 3-7 pm, free). It's an elegant, circular late 17th-century oratory adjoining the late 12th-century **Chiesa di San Fedele** (Via Cavour, ☎ 0575-529136, Sun and holidays, 10 am-noon, 3-6 pm, free). The latter has a Guidi mausoleum and a beautiful 14th-century crucifix by the Giotto school.

SOMETHING FOR THE KIDS

KID FRIENDLY The **Parco Zoo della Fauna Europea** in Poppi (Via Parco Zoo 16, ☎ 0575-504541, fax 0575-504174, www.parcozoopoppi.it, 9 am to one hour before sunset, €5, conc. €4.50) was opened in 1972. It exhibits a whole host of specifically European fauna (deer, fawns, wolves, bears, birds of prey and species in danger of extinction such as the Asinara donkey) in its 140 acres of pines, chestnuts and secular oaks. Botanical garden, pony rides and children's play area.

Take the SS310 from Poppi and you'll reach **Pratovecchio**, a town that announces its presence by the cypress-lined remains of the 12th- to 14th-century Castello di Romena, onetime home of Dante. You can find out more about the castle's illustrious history at the **Associazione Culturale Museo Archeologico e delle Armi Castello di Romena** (Loc. Romena, ☎ 0575-582520, fax 0575-504526, Sat-Sun, 10 am-noon, 3-6 pm, €3). From the castle, a narrow road leads directly to the **Pieve di San Pietro di Romena** (Loc. Romena 1, ☎/fax 0575-582060, 9 am-noon, 3-6 pm, free), a mid-12th-century creation that is by far the most important Romanesque building in the Casentino for its three-apse design, beautifully decorated chapels and sandstone columns decorated with intricate and mysterious symbols. In Pratovecchio itself (a two-hour trek from the castle along #26), the sloping **Piazza Paolo Uccello**, named after the great Renaissance painter born here in 1397, marks the heart of town. It is overlooked by the **Propositura**, with a collection of 17th-century paintings and not much else. Other sights include the **Monastero Camaldolese di San Giovanni Evangelista** (Convent of the Camaldoli Nuns, Piazza Landino 20, ☎ 0575-58376, camaldolesipratovecchio@interfree.it, May 1-Oct 15, 10 am-noon, 3-6 pm, free), founded by the Guidi in the 12th century, and the **Monastero Monache Domenicane Santa Maria della Neve** (Monastery of the Dominican Nuns of Santa Maria della Neve, Piazza Landino 26, ☎ 0575-583774, www.casentino.net.monasterodomenicane, daily, 8 am-noon, 3-6 pm, free). Its adjoining church is equally uninspiring.

Castello di Porciano

The bridge across the Staggia River leads to the historical center of **Stia**. The last town in the Casentino zone, it is renowned for its arcaded main square, medieval architecture and the remodeled façade of the 12th-century Romanesque **Pieve di Santa Maria Assunta** (Piazza Tanucci 11, ☎ 0575-583722, daily, 7:30 am-7 pm), whose sober interior contains an Andrea della Robbia, *Madonna col Bambino*, and some beautifully-decorated columns and capitals. A few miles from Stia, a hilly road leads to the 11th-century **Castello di Porciano** (Loc. Porciano, ☎ 0575-583533, 15 May-15 Oct, Sun and holidays, 10 am-noon, 4-7 pm, 15 Oct-15 May, same hours, daily, free). One of the first Conti Guidi castles, this was also once the home of Dante (he wrote the letters to Emperor Arrigo VI here). Although only the tower and some remains of the walls are left, part of the castle today houses a small museum with displays on local history and traditions.

■ Adventures on Foot

The **Parco Nazionale Foreste Casentinesi, Monte Falterona e Campigna** has over 530 miles worth of trails, all signposted with the red and white of the territory. Routes depart from both the Tuscan and Emilia Romagna sides. The following nine are marked by the park itself. They are the so-called *Sentieri Natura* (nature trails) and tend to offer between two and three hours of walking. You can pick up a detailed itinerary and map of these routes from any of the park offices (Italian only).

1. The Chestnut Trail: A three-km/two-mile trail departing from Castagno d'Andrea that follows in the footsteps of the chestnut, from its growth to its use in local recipes.

2. The Beechwood Trail: This two-km/1.2-mile trail links Badia Prataglia with the Eremo di Camaldoli, taking you through the heart of the Camaldoli forest and along the charming valley of the Archiano d'Isola.

3. The Tree & Wood Trail: A two-km/1.2-mile trail departing from Camaldoli that takes you through woods around the Monastero di Camaldoli, the famous spiritual center founded by San Romualdo.

4. The Nature, History & Spirituality Trail: This 2.5-km/1.6-mile trail departing from Chiusi della Verna climbs up Monte Penna (1,283 m/4,208 feet) to the Santuario della Verna, an area of much spiritual and naturalistic interest. Also suitable for cross-country skiing, it follows the Via Francigena through the splendid secular forest the monks have been managing since the sanctuary was first established, and on to the summit of the "sacred mountain," where a little chapel built in 1570 once welcomed pilgrims.

5. The Silver Fir Trail: A 2.5-km/1.6-mile trail that departs from Campigna, just over the border in Emilia Romagna. The trailhead can be reached by following the road from Pratovecchio to Santa Sofia.

6. The Dante's Valley & Waterfall Trail: Also just over the border (but this time in the far north of the park), this 4.5-km/2.8-mile itinerary takes you from San Benedetto in Alpe along the valley to the waterfall made famous by Dante in the *Divine Comedy*:

> *Like as that stream, whose separate waters glide*
> *By their own channel from Mount Vesulo,*
> *Eastward above the Apennines' left side,*
> *On high call'd Acquacheta, ere the flow*
> *Precipitant has reach'd its lowly bed,*
> *No more at Forlì then that name to know;*
> *Above San Benedetto, from her head*
> *Sounds thundering headlong to a base, just where*
> *Full many, in truth, might well be hous'd and fed;*
> *So from the summit of the craggy stair*
> *Such found we that ensanguin'd water's roar,*
> *As in a little space no ears could bear.*
> (Inferno, Canto XVI)

7. The Footsteps of Man Trail: A two-km/1.2-mile route departing from Fiumicello in Emilia Romagna that traces the nearly extinct population of the Apennines and their works, which have shaped the landscape.

8. The Stone Traces Trail: Departing from Ridracoli, again on the Emilia Romagna side, this 2.5-km/1.6-mile route takes you up to the Rifugio Cà di Sopra along a panoramic trail rich in wild fauna. Of the walks departing from Emilia Romagna, it is most difficult to reach from the Tuscan side; the only road is the slow, winding route from Badia Prataglia.

9. The Nature & Shape Trail: This 3.5-km/2.2-mile route departs from Tredozio and leads through one of the wildest areas of the park to the Lago di Ponte. Again in Emilia Romagna, it can be reached easily from San Godenzo.

There are further walks on offer, such as the **trails of the Resistance** (with itineraries running between Castagno d'Andrea to Biserno near Santo Sofia on the Emilia-Romagna side) or classic itineraries like the **GEA**. There are 160 numbered paths on the GEA#00. Each is suitable for **mountain bikes** as well.

Another long-distance path links Vallucciole and Chiusi della Verna (50 km/31 miles, two days) but it is most suitable as a **horseback-riding trail**.

There's also a pleasant nine-km (5.6-mile) nature trail departing from Campigna and heading into the Riserva di Sasso Fratino (Sasso Fratino Nature Reserve).

If you want to book a guide contact **Le Guide del Parco** (Loc. Gaviserri 1, Pratovecchio, ☎/fax 0575-509066, guide.pnfc@comunic.it).

■ Adventures on Wheels

Badia Prataglia is a great location for mountain bike forays into the Parco Nazionale Foreste Casentinesi, with seven itineraries:

■ The seven-hour Badia Prataglia – Serravalle – Camaldoli – Badia Prataglia (#40, #66, #70 then #21 to Camaldoli, then #68, Sentiero Italia 1991 and GEA along Archiano d'Isola back); some steep sections.

■ The six-hour Badia Prataglia – Poggio Tre Confini – Serravalle – Badia Prataglia (#60, #66, GEA#68, #70 and SS71 back); one steep climb followed by a steep descent.

■ The five-hour Badia Prataglia – Passo della Crocina – Monte Penna – Badia Prataglia (#64, #00, #445, #00 and then GEA back); steep climb then descent.

■ The 5½-hour Badia Prataglia – Passo dei Mandrioli – Passo Lupatti – Passo dei Cerrini – Badia Prataglia (GEA, SS71, #00 then #62 back); rolling route.

■ The 4½-hour, Badia Prataglia/Serravalle – Prato alla Penna – Giogo Seccheta – Passo Porcareccio – Poggio Scali (GEA): rolling route.

■ The seven-hour Badia Prataglia – Passo della Crocina – La Lama – Fangacci – Badia Prataglia (#64, #457, #45, #453, #64, #45, GEA back); one climb and one descent.

■ The five-hour Badia Prataglia – Passo della Crocina – Passo dei Cerrini – Scaviccioli – Badia Prataglia (#64, #00, #62 and #71 back); one sharp climb.

You can rent mountain bikes from **Mountain Bike Casentino** (www.mountainbike.toscana.it, ☎/fax 0575-560747) from €20 for a day and €100 for a week); they also organize two- and three-day excursions in the Casentino (from €135).

■ Adventures on Horseback

Horseback riding can be organized via any of the region's hotels or *agriturismi*. If you are here for a day, your best bets are **Equi Trekking** (Loc. Le Casine 17, ☎ 055-8375128) and **Le Amazzoni Riding School** (based in the Fattoria di Marena, Bibbiena, ☎ 0575-593655, fax 0575-569773, www.fattoria-marena.it). Both offer one-hour lessons from €16 and treks by arrangement.

Environmental guides, **Welcome in Casentino** (Via Roma 35, Castel San Niccolò, ☎ 0575-570303, www.welcomecasentino.it), are the ones to contact for horseback riding, mountain biking, kayaking and parasailing in the region (from €110 for a group of 20).

ADVENTURES IN EMIGLIA ROMAGNA

Nature walks: You can choose among three woodland trails (with botanical signposts) in the **Giardino Botanico Valbonella** (Loc. Corniolo, ☎ 0543-971297, Tues-Fri pm, Sat am, Sun all day).
Canoeing: Portico and **San Benedetto** are the places to check out for watersports such as canoeing.
Skiing: There are cross-country skiing and downhill skiing facilities at **Santa Sofia**. Lessons are offered by Scuola Italiana di Sci Campigna (☎ 0543-980054).

■ Adventures on Snow

From **Campigna**, you can pick up one of the finest cross-country skiing routes in the **Tosco-Emiliano Apennines**. The 20-km (12-mile) itinerary departs from Passo della Calla and loops back via the Eremo di Camaldoli. There are two shorter cross-country itineraries in the area: one between **Badia Prataglia** and the **Eremo di Camaldoli** and the other, from the **Eremo di Camaldoli** to the **Monastero di Camaldoli** (nine km/5½ miles along #12). A 2½-km/1.6-mile route leads from **Chiusi della Verna** to the **Santuario della Verna**, and the 21½-km (13-mile) GEA #00 goes from the **Passo del Muraglione** (near San Godenzo on the SS67) to the **Eremo di Santa Maria** near the Acquacheta waterfalls.

The snow is generally at its best between December and March. For downhill skiing and lessons around Campigna, contact **Scuola Italiana di Sci Campigna** (☎ 0543-980054).

■ Where to Eat

Casentino Honey: Get your honey from **Apicoltura Casentinese** (Via dell'Artigiano 10/12, Loc. Ferrantina, Bibbiena, ☎ 0575-536494, fax 0575-536029, www.apicolturacasentinese.com).

Just out of **Partina Bibbiena** on the road to Badia Prataglia, **La Pergolina** (Via Santa Rita 54/58, Partina Bibbiena, ☎ 0575-561954, fax 0575-561721, www.lapergolina.it, closed Mon and Nov, $$$) offers local favorites *acquacotta, filetto al Chianti* (fillet in Chianti wine) and a variety of wild game in a traditional setting. Booking recommended.

In the center of **Chiusi della Verna**, **Letizia** (Via Roma 26, ☎ 0575-599020, www.hotel-letizia.net, closed Wed and winter, $) serves simple but tasty rustic cuisine, including some great *tortelli di patate*.

Nine miles out of town on the SS208, you'll get typical Tuscan cuisine like homemade pasta, *arrosti girati* (spit roasts), *capriolo* (venison) and wild boar at **Corazzesi** (Via Nazionale 13, Loc. Corezzo, ☎ 0575-518012, closed Tues, $).

In a 15th-century hall in **Poppi**, complete with vaulted roof, **Campaldino** (Via Roma 97, Ponte a Poppi, ☎ 0575-529008, fax 0575-529032, priccica@virgilio.it, closed Wed and July, $$) serves typical Tuscan cuisine especially *primi con funghi* (pasta with mushrooms), *cinghiale al barolo* (wild boar in barolo), steak and roasts. In Poppi's central square overlooked by the castle, **Casentino** (Piazza della Repubblica 6, ☎ 0575-529197, fax 0575-529067, www.albergocasentino.it, closed Tues and Nov, $$) serves generous portions of homemade pasta and grilled meats.

Things go rustic near Poppi at **La Foresta** (Via di Camaldoli 5, Loc. Camaldoli, ☎ 0575-556015, closed Wed, $$), a beautiful setting accentuated by the tasty dishes (*cinghiale alla cacciatore, polenta,* grilled meats and homemade pasta).

Along the SS71 near the historic center of **Pratovecchio**, **Caffè Toscana Twist** (Via della Libertà 3, ☎ 50575-582120, www.toscanatwist.ar.it, closed Sun and Mon and one week in Jan and Nov, $$) may be a modern enoteca but it serves traditional cuisine like *tortelli alla lastra, ravioli di farina di castagne* (chestnut flour ravioli) and *scottiglia*.

Just under a mile out of **Stia** (direction Farli), **Da Loris** (Loc. Papuano, ☎ 0575-583680, www.casentinonline.it/loris, closed Tues and pm Oct-May, and first two weeks of July, $$) dishes out more *tortelli di patate, scottiglia* and *acquacotta*.

In **Subbiano**, a good place to stop off en route to the Casentino from Arezzo, is **Chenno** (Via D.L. Faschi 31, ☎ 0575-488002, fax 0575-421982, www.teta.it/chenno, closed Sat and Aug, $), right in the historical center. Farther up the SS71, things are more traditional at **Torre Santa Flora** (Loc. Il Palazzo 169, ☎ 0575-421045, fax 0575-489607, www.santaflora.it, closed Jan, $$) with typical local cuisine such as *tortelli di patate, suprema di faraona* (guinea hen), *piccione ripierno* (stuffed pigeon).

■ Where to Stay

 It makes more sense to stay in an *agriturismo* if you want to stay over in this rural zone. There are plenty of options around Bibbiena, Chiusi della Verna, Poppi and Stia, and many offer horseback riding and trekking facilities.

Around **Bibbiena,** check out **Agricola Casentinese** ☆☆☆☆ (Loc. Casanova 63, ☎ 0575-594806, fax 0575-539826, $$), along the SS209 toward La Verna, which has horseback riding and trekking. You can even pick up a trail through the forest to the Monastero di Camaldoli from **Casale Camalda** ☆☆☆☆ (Loc. Castagnoli 33, Serravalle di Bibbiena, ☎/fax 0575-519104, www.agriturismocamalda.it, $$$), a "biological" *agriturismo* and excursion center.

There's camping and trekking at **La Motta** ☆☆☆ (Via Motta 53, Loc. Motta, ☎/fax 0575-518089, closed 15 Jan-15 Feb, $$$) near **Chiusi della Verna.**

Top picks in **Poppi** (especially if you want to spend a day trekking or horseback riding in the zone) are **L'Emera** ☆☆☆ (Loc. Filetto 17, ☎/fax 0575-550538, www.emera.it, $$) and **Belvedere** ☆☆☆ (Via del Corniolo, Loc. Belvedere, ☎ 0575-509231, fax 0575-536493, www.fattoriadibelvedere.com, $$$).

Also check out **Borgo Tramonte** ☆☆☆ (Via Borgo Tramonte 18, Loc. Papiano, ☎/fax 0575-581404, www.borgotramonte.it, $$) near **Stia** and **Le Greti** ☆☆☆ (Via Le Greti 128, Loc. Santa Maria, ☎/fax 0575-487090, www.legrettuscany.it, $$$) near **Subbiano**.

The region is well served with **campgrounds**. In the area around **Camaldoli**, try **Camaldoli** ☆ (Loc. Camaldoli, ☎/fax 0575-556157, www.campingcamaldoli.com, 90 spaces, June-Sept, $), **Camaldoli Pucini** ☆ (Loc. Camaldoli, ☎ 0575-556006, fax 0575-556157, www.campingcamaldoli.com, 25 spaces, June-Sept, $) or **La Pineta** ☆☆ (Loc. Le Farnie, Fraz. Avena, Camaldoli, ☎ 0575-529082, fax 0575-529712, www.casentino.it, 80 spaces, May-Sept, $).

There's also **Falterona** ☆☆ (Loc. Montalto, Fraz. Papiano, www.campingfalterona.com, 15 June-15 Sept, $) near **Stia**, **La Verna** ☆ (Loc. Vezzano 31, ☎ 0575-532121, fax 0575-532041, www.campinglaverna.it, Apr-Sept, $) near **Chiusi della Verna** (with pool) and **Capanno** ☆ (Via Fangacci, Loc. Capanno, ☎ 0575-518015, 20 May-20 Sept, $) near **Badia Prataglia**.

For **youth hostels**, try **Casanuova** (☎ 0575-559320, fax 0575-299047, www.peterpan.it, June-Sept, $) in **Badia Prataglia**. Another option is **Il Vignale** (Via Acquacheta, ☎ 0543-965279, fax 0543-951289, ostello.vignale@iol.it, all year, $) near the famed waterfalls in San Benedetto in Alpe. Or **Di Casalino** (Loc. Casalino 80a, ☎ 0575-558122, www.ostellocasalino.it, all year, $) in **Pratovecchio**.

The region's main **mountain hut** accommodation is at **Camaldoli – Asqua, Centro di Educazione e Formazione Ambientale** (☎ 0575-520462, fax 0575-520463, www.asqua.it, all year, $).

Sansepolcro & the Valtiberina

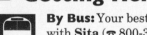

The Valtiberina (or Upper Tiber Valley) occupies the easternmost edge of Tuscany, on the border with Umbria, Emilia-Romagna and Mare. Much fought over between papal Rome and imperial Florence, this countryside is peppered with castles and monasteries. It is the homeland of Michelangelo (Caprese) and Piero della Francesca (Sansepolcro), plus hilltop medieval villages like Anghiari, Badia Tedalda and Monterchi, river centers like Pieve Santo Stefano, and abbeys, convents and sanctuaries.

■ Getting Here

By Bus: Your best route of approach is via bus from Arezzo or Florence, with **Sita** (☎ 800-373760, www.sita-on-line.it) running services. If arriving from Florence, you can also reach the area via **Sita** #380 (Anghiari, Sansepolcro, Pievo Santo Stefano). From Bibbiena and Chiusi della Verna in the Casentino, you can reach Pievo Santo Stefano with **LFI** (☎ 0578-31174, www.lfi.it).

By Car: Pick up the SS73 from Arezzo to Sansepolcro (turnoffs to Anghiari and Caprese Michelangelo), with other roads linking the area to nearby Casentino and Emilia-Romagna.

■ Information Sources

?

Tourist Offices: There are two main tourist offices in the region, one in **Anghiari** (Corso Matteotti 103, ☎ 0575-749279) and the other in **Badia Tedalda** (Piazza dei Tedaldi 1, ☎ 0575-714014).

Adventure Information: Trekkers should contact the **Comunità Montane Alto Tevere** (High Tiber Mountain Community, Loc. Daga, Pieve Santo Stefano, ☎ 0575-799097).

■ Sightseeing

From Arezzo, the SS221 (toward Città di Castello in Umbria) leads you first to the hilltop village of **Monterchi**. This is the hometown of Piero della Francesca's mother, which perhaps explains why it also contains one of his finest works; the 1465 fresco of the *Madonna del Parto*, now detached from the small chapel in which it was painted and on display in the **Museo Madonna del Parto** (Via della Reglia 1, ☎ 0575-70713, Apr-Oct, 9 am-1 pm, 2-7 pm, Nov-Mar, 9 am-1 pm, 2-6 pm, €3.10, conc. €2).

A turnoff onto the SS73 will take you in the direction of **Anghiari**, a well-preserved medieval hilltop town built on a steep gradient with an interesting square of noble palazzi added outside the city walls in the 16th century. There are a few churches of interest: the medieval **Chiesa di Sant'Agostino** and the sixth-century **Chiesa di Santo Stefano** (one of the oldest in the region) at the foot of the hill. But the most important attraction is the **Centro Documentazione della Battaglia di Anghiari** (Piazza Mameli 1, ☎ 0575-787023, www.anghiari.it, Apr-Oct, Tues-Sun, 9 am-1 pm, 3-7 pm, Nov-Mar, Fri-Sat, 8:30 am-7 pm, Sun, 9 am-1 pm, 3-6 pm, €2, conc. €1). This is a documentation center about the Anghiari battle which, immortalized by Leonardo da Vinci, took place between the Milanese and the Florentine armies in 1440.

The hilltop citadel of **Caprese Michelangelo** lies to the north. Its famous son is celebrated in the **Museo Michelangiolesco** (Via Capoluogo 1, ☎ 0575-793776, fax 0575-793589, June 16-Oct, daily, 9:30 am-6:30 pm, Nov-June 15, daily, 10 am-5 pm, €2.50, conc. €2).

THE PALIO DELLA BALESTRA

The second Sunday of September Sansepolcro's Piazza Torre di Berta travels back in time when its crossbow competition with archrival Gubbio takes place. In May, Gubbio hosts a similar tournament.

To the east is the birthplace of Piero della Francesca, **Sansepolcro**. Four of his paintings dedicated to this town – *Resurrection*, shown at right, plus the two small frescoes of *St Julian* and *St Ludovic* in Room One, and the polyptych of the *Misericordia* in Room Two – are on display in the **Museo Civico** (Via Aggiunti 65, ☎ 0575-32218, fax 0575-736824, June-Sept, 9 am-1:30 pm, 2:30-5:30 pm, Oct-May, 9:30 am-1 pm, 2:30-6 pm, €6.20, conc. €4.50). Other important buildings include the Romanesque **Cattedrale** (Via Giacomo Matteotti 4, ☎/fax 0575-742129, 8 am-noon, 3-7 pm, free), the 16th-century Loggia delle Laudi, and the **Collegiata di**

Santo Stefano (Piazza S. Stefano 6, ☎ 0575-799050, daily, 8 am-7 pm, free), which has a *Deposition* by Rosso Fiorentino.

Mountainous **Badia Tedalda** grew up around an old abbey. Its main sights are the della Robbia panels in the **Chiesa di San Michele Arcangelo** (Via Castello, ☎ 0575-714225, 10 am-6 pm, free).

■ Adventures on Foot

One of the main footpaths, also suitable for winter cross-country skiing, leads from **Caprese Michelangelo** to the **Eremo (Hermitage) della Casella**. A panoramic route, the 11-km (seven-mile) itinerary (#039) takes you along a forest road that climbs to the ridge of the Alpe di Catenaia. Another itinerary to the Eremo along the Catenaia ridge, again also suitable for cross-country skiing, departs from Falciano, this time 19 km/12 miles (#03 then #50).

■ Adventures on Horseback

Sansepolcro is the place to go to organize horseback treks. Contact the **Centro Ippico Violino** (Loc. Gricignano 99, ☎/fax 0575-720174, www.podereviolino.it) to find out more.

■ Where to Eat

Just under a mile out of Anghiari, **Locanda al Castello di Sorci** (Loc. San Lorenzo 25, ☎ 0575-789066, fax 0575-788022, www.italyone.com/castellodisorci, closed Mon, $) is the area's best-priced option with a menu of homemade pastas and grilled meats. Also in Anghiari, *ristorante-enoteca* **Cantina del Granduca** (Piazza Mameli 13, ☎ 0575-788275, closed Tues and winter, $$) offers a range of hearty Tuscan fare in classic peasant dishes such as *spaghetti di farro con il lardo di colonnata* (spaghetti made with farro, a light brown grain, and colonnata lard). In the historical center of Anghiari, **Da Alighiero** (Via Garibaldi 8, ☎ 0575-788040, fax 0575-788517, www.daalighiero.it, closed Tues and Feb, $$) is a good choice for homemade pasta or whole-roasted duck (*petto di anatra porchettato*).

DINING PRICE CHART	
Price per person for an entrée, including house wine & cover.	
$	Under €20
$$	€21-€40
$$$	€41-€60
$$$$	Over €60

On the road to Arezzo, **Vecchia Osteria la Pergola** (SP11, Loc. Tavernelle, ☎/fax 0575-723010, www.osterialapergola.it, closed Mon, $$) specializes in duck; try the *tagliolini all'anatra* (taglioni in a duck sauce) or *anatra in porchetto* (whole-roasted duck). There's also *agnella in umido* (stewed lamb), *piccione in salmi* (jugged pigeon) and homemade pasta.

If you're in the area of Badia Tedalda, **Il Sottobosco** (Via Svolta del Podere 145, ☎ 0575-714240, fax 0575-714427, closed Wed, Jan and second week of June, $), on the SR258, and **Bardeschi** (Fraz. Pratieghi, ☎ 0575-713027, fax 0575-713035, $) are two top rustic locales with a heavy emphasis on wild game.

The place to eat in Caprese Michelangelo is **Buca di Michelangelo** (Via Roma 51, ☎ 0575-793921, fax 0575-793941, closed Thurs, $$). It occupies an old stone house just a brief stroll away from the house where Michelangelo was born. Four miles from town, **Fonte della Galletta** (Loc. Alpe Faggeta, ☎ 0575-793925, fax 0575-793652, closed Mon and Tues, $$) makes a much quieter choice, with some tasty game, roasts and homemade pastas.

In Pieve Santo Stefano, fish fans should make a date with **Locanda Bellavista** (Via Bellavista 6, ☎ 0575-795024, closed Wed and Nov, $). We're talking all the old favorites, but with a modern twist – *linguine all'astice ed ai gamberoni* (linguine in a lobster and crawfish sauce), *penne della locanda,* and *astice alla catalana* (lobster Catalan style).

In Sansepolcro, **Oroscopo** (Via P. Togliatti 68, ☎/fax 0575-734875, closed Sun and one week in Jan and July, www.relaisoroscopo.com, $$) is located in the hotel of the same name. It's earning a good reputation for its mix of rural and modern cooking traditions, with dishes such as *tortino di verdura in crema di basilica* (vegetable quiche in basil cream), *bringoli al ragù di anatra* (duck sauce), *piccione disossato* (boneless pigeon). A 200-yearold restaurant in the town center, **Fiorentino** (Via L. Pacioli 60, ☎ 0575-742033, closed Wed and second half of July, $$) specializes in Tuscan food from the Renaissance! Try if you dare: *lombo e salsicce sott'olio* (homemade chin and sausages in oil), *pappardelle con sughi di caccia in bianco* (pappardelle in white game sauce), *piccione con le olive* (pigeon with olives), *girello con uvetta e pinoli* (rump with raisons and pine kernels), *raviggiolo* and *lattaiolo.* The recently refurbished **L'Osteria in Aboca** (Fraz. Aboca 11, ☎ 0575-749125, fax 0575-749124, www.losteriainaboca.it, closed Mon and second half of Sept, $$) is along the SR258, five miles out of Sansepolcro.

■ Where to Stay

There are a few good hotels in and around Anghiari. **Oliver** ☆☆☆ (Via della Battaglia 16, Anghiari, ☎ 0575-789933, fax 0575-789944, www.oliverhotel.it, $$) is one of the best-priced. On the outskirts, **B&B Relais la Commenda** (Loc. Commenda 6, ☎ 0575-723356, fax 0575-723921, www.relaislacommenda.com, $$$$) is the most picturesque. It occupies a former monastery surrounded by cypress, oak, beech and olive woods, and organizes cookery courses, sailing and windsurfing. Outdoor pool.

HOTEL PRICE CHART	
Rates are per room with private bath, based on double occupancy, including breakfast.	
$	Under €40
$$	€41-€85
$$$	€86-€140
$$$$	€141-€210
$$$$$	Over €210

Cafaggio ☆☆☆ (Loc. Toppole 42, ☎ 0575-749025, www.cafaggio.it, $$$) is one of the best *agriturismi* choices if you're planning on some horseback riding. Trekkers should opt instead for **Il Sasso** ☆☆☆ (Loc. San Lorenzo 38, ☎/fax 0575-787078, www.agriturismoilsasso.it, $$$).

Caprese Michelangelo also has one or two good *agriturismi.* Try **Priello** ☆☆☆☆, Loc. Priello 244, ☎/fax 0575-791218, www.priello.com, $$; **Borgo Tozzetto** ☆☆☆, Via Tozzetto 247, ☎ 0575-793853, fax 0575-79354, www.borgotozzetto.it, $$$; or **Selvadonica** ☆☆☆, Loc. Selvadonica, ☎/fax 0575-791051, www.selvadonica.it, $$$. It is also the best choice for camping, with **Michelangelo** ☆☆ (Loc. Zenzano, ☎ 0575-793886, fax 0575-791183, Apr-Oct, $) just outside of town. There's also a popular youth hostel – **Michelangelo** (Loc. Fragaiolo, ☎ 0575-792092, fax 0575-793994, May-Sept, $).

For the best choice among Sansepolcro's centrally located hotels, opt for **La Balestra** ☆☆☆☆ (Via dei Montefeltro 29, ☎ 0575-735151, fax 0575-740282, www.labalestra.it, $$), **Fiorentino** ☆☆☆ (Via Luca Pacioli 60, ☎ 0575-740350, fax 0575-740370, www.albergofiorentino.com, $$) or **Borgo** ☆☆☆☆ (Via Senese Aretina 80, ☎ 0575-736050, fax 0575-740341, www.borgopalace.it, $$$). Just out of town, **Relais Palais di Luglio** ☆☆☆☆ (Fraz. Cignano 35, ☎ 0575-750026, fax 0575-759892, www.relaispalaisdiluglio.com, $$$$$) is the place to splash out in, if you feel like spoiling yourself.

There are plenty of *agriturismi* outside Sansepolcro. **Centro Ippico Violino** ☆☆☆☆ (Loc. Gricignano 99, ☎/fax 0575-720174, www.podereviolino.it, $$) and **La Conca** ☆☆☆☆ (Fraz. Paradiso 16, ☎/fax 0575-733301, www.laconca.it, $$$$) both have horseback-riding facilities. **Valcinaia sul Lago** ☆☆☆ (Via F. Redi 23, Loc. Montedoglio, ☎/fax 0575-742777, www.wel.it/calcinaia, $$$) and **Il Giardino** ☆☆☆ (Loc. Rio II, ☎/fax 0575-734370, www.il-giardino.it, $$$) are both well placed for trekking. All four have outdoor pools.

Cortona & the Val di Chiana

Cortona boomed as a tourist destination after the publication of Frances Mayes' *Under the Tuscan Sun* and with a recent film adaptation inspiring a new generation of visitors to the medieval hilltop town, things aren't likely to change for a while. The Etruscans dwelt in the region for centuries, leaving remarkable signs of their presence in the surrounding necropoli. The Romans came next, turning Cortona into a significant trading center until the Goths came along and destroyed the whole lot. It re-grew as a free *comune* in the 11th century before being sold by the King of Naples to the Florentine Republic but, apart from a few Renaissance palazzi, the town is truly medieval at heart.

From its position on a spur of the 600-m (1,968-foot) Monte Sant'Egidio, Cortona dominates the Val di Chiana, an agricultural plain (producer of the highly-prized beef known as the Chianina) that spreads as far as the Siena mountains to the north and Lake Trasimeno to the east. It has been a zone of agriculture since the third century BC, when Hannibal stopped over here to feed his entire army before crossing over to Trasimeno and defeating the Romans. But it's also a zone of great artists: Luca Signorelli (Cortona, 15th century), Pietro Berrettini, also known as Pietra da Cortona (Cortona, 16th century), Andrea Cantucci, also known as Il Sansovino (Monte San Savino) were all born near here, while Beato Angelico, chose to spend much of his life in Cortona's Dominican monastery.

■ Getting Here

By Train: If approaching from Arezzo or Florence, the **Cortona-Camucia** station (☎ 848-888088, www.trenitalia.it) is your best option. It is linked to the town by a 10-minute shuttle bus (€1, tickets available in the station *tabacchi*). From Umbria or the South, the same shuttle departs from **Terontola** station (☎ 0575-67027), this time taking 30 minutes, and stopping in Cortona-Camucia station en route. The shuttle runs every half-hour or so (once an hour between 9 am and 1 pm) with taxis available outside both stations

The Valdichiana seen through the walls of Montepulciano
(Tom Johnston / Emma Jones)

In Montepulciano

Above: Via del Fosso, Lucca

Below: Lucca's Duomo

Above: *Pisa's San Michele in Borgo*

Below: *Monte Argentario Peninsula*

if you don't want to wait. Call the tourist board at ☎ 0575-630352 for the latest timetable. REG or regional trains stop first at Castiglion Fiorentino from Arezzo and the North.

 By Bus: LFI (☎ 0578–31174, www.lfi.it) runs twice an hour between Arezzo and Cortona, stopping at Castiglion Fiorentino and arriving on Piazzale Garibaldi at the entrance of Cortona.

 By Car: Cortona can be reached from Florence on the **A1** (Val di Chiana exit), from Arezzo through Castiglion Fiorentino on the **SS71** and along the **SS75bis** from Perugia and Umbria. Once you arrive in Cortona, you'll find the free parking spaces just outside the walls on Viale Cesare Battisti, Piazzale del Mercato and Piazza Mazzini, or inside the walls, on Piazza del Duomo and Piazzale di Santa Margherita right at the top. The paying car parks on Piazza Franciolini, Piazza Signorelli, Piazzale Garibaldi and Largo Beato Angelico generally have spaces if the free car parks are full.

Car Rental: There are a few rental places close to Camucia train station – **Boninsegni Auto** (Via Gramsci 66/68, ☎ 0575-605052) and **Lancia Cuculi & Taucci** (Via Carducci 25, ☎ 0575-630495).

Bike Rental: Bikes and mopeds can be rented at Cortona's **Axofidis** (Piazza Signorelli 26, ☎ 0575-604244).

■ Information Sources

 APT Cortona can be a little hit and miss with tourist information but it's still worth popping in (at Via Nazionale 42, ☎ 0575-630352) to pick up a brochure. You can also purchase bus and train tickets here, but with the small booking charge added – you may as well just get them from the train station. **Castiglion Fiorentino** also has a small office (Corso Italia 111, ☎ 0575-658278).

■ Sightseeing ~ Walking Cortona

From the shuttle-bus drop-off point on Piazza Garibaldi, the main Via Nazionale – known locally as *Ruga Piana* (the flat walk) because it is the only level street in town – leads to the two main caffè-filled squares, Piazza della Repubblica and Piazza Signorelli. The former has the 13th-century **Palazzo Comunale** (town hall), the tower and steps added much later in the early 16th century, while the latter slopes up past the **Teatro Signorelli** (☎ 0575-601882, theater and cinema), **Palazzo Fierli** and the **Museo dell'Accademia Etrusca** (Palazzo Casali, ☎ 0575-630415, fax 0575-637248, www.academia-etrusca.net, Apr-Oct, 10 am-7 pm, Nov-Mar, 10 am-5 pm, closed Mon, €4.20, conc. €2.50). It offers an unmissable insight into the area's Etruscan past with displays of artifacts like the fourth-century BC bronze chandelier known as the "lamp of Cortona." There are also funeral items and jewelry from the Melone del Sodo II (see below) – but there are also important Egyptian works dating back to 2000 BC, paintings by Luca Signorelli, Pinturicchio, Bartolomeo della Gatta and Pietro Berrettini, and a room dedicated to Gino Severini, which houses his *La Maternità* (1916).

BURIAL SITES

It's worth making your way out of Cortona in the direction of Foiano della Chiano to visit the two sixth-century BC *Meloni* (Etruscan tombs) recently discovered here. If you have to opt for one, Melone del Sodo II is the most impressive, with its terraced altar and stone sculptured steps.

In the direction of Arezzo, there's also the third century BC Tanella di Pitagora, which, according to local legend, guards the remains of Pitagora, while in Camucia town center, a seventh-century hypogeum with two main chambers, atrium and corridors is open to exploration.

All visits by appointment with the Museo dell'Accademia Etrusca: **Melone del Sodo I** and **Tanella di Pitagora** (Apr-Oct, closed Mon, €5.20 (€10.50 with guided tour), conc. €2.50); **Melone del Sodo II** and **Tumulo di Camucia** (closed Mon, free).

The **Cathedrale** (Piazza del Duomo, ☎ 0575-62830, summer, 7:30 am-12:30 pm, 3-6:30 pm, winter, 8 am-noon, 3-5:30 pm, free) lies at the top of Via Casali. Although the exterior isn't that attractive (it was built over a Romanesque base in the 16th century), the interior, designed by Giuliano da Sangallo, has a lot more charm. It also includes a stunning *Annunciation* by Andrea del Sarto.

GIOSTRA DELL'ARCHIDADO

Cortona's biggest historical event takes place every year on June 8 to commemorate the 1397 marriage between two noble Cortona families. It is the Giostra dell'Archidado (the Joust of the Archidado), a crossbow competition, which draws representatives resplendent in period costume from Cortona's ancient quarters to Piazza Signorelli. A true battle of skill and speed, the competition is quick and hard to follow, but the ending is flamboyantly topped off with the presentation of the *verretta d'oro* (the golden dart).

Opposite the cathedral, the **Chiesa del Gesù** is the deconsecrated home to the **Museo Diocesano** (Piazza del Duomo, ☎ 0575-62830, Apr-Sept, 9:30 am-1 pm, 3:30-7 pm, Nov-Mar, 10 am-1 pm, 3-5 pm, closed Mon, €5, conc. €3). Their collection includes works by local boy, Luca Signorelli (including a *Deposition* and the *Comunione degli Apostoli*), Pietro Lorenzetti, Bartolomeo della Gatta, Beato Angelico (with an elegant *Annunciation* he painted during his stay at the Monastery of San Domenico) and some important Roman finds.

Pop behind the museum to see one of Cortona's most characteristic streets: the medieval overhanging houses of Vicolo Janelli are some of the oldest that have survived in Italy.

The steep Via G. Maffei will take you from here to the crumbling **Chiesa di San Francesco** (Via Berrettini, ☎ 0575-603205). It has been much altered over the years but, if you look carefully, you can still see some of the 13th-century Gothic architecture of its original design. The arcaded building next to it is the city **Ospedale**. Take the road alongside it to join the steep panoramic Via Santa Maria at **San Marco**, a taxing climb in hot weather, but one that affords beautiful views over Val di Chiana and Lake Trasimeno on its way up to the 19th-century mock-Romanesque **Basilica di Santa Margherita** (Piazzale S. Margherita 1, ☎ 0575-603116, fax 0575-603116, summer, 7:30 am-noon, 3-7 pm, winter, 8 am-noon, 3-6 pm, free). Along the walk you will see the 15 Stations of the Cross, with mosaic illustrations by Gino Severini and, opposite San Marco, the ancient **Porta Berada**. According to legend, the St Margaret whose remains are guarded in the basilica, entered Cortona for the first time through this gate.

An even steeper climb takes you from the basilica up through the gardens to the **Fortezza Medici** (also known as Fortezza del Girifalco, ☎ 0575-603793, 10 am-6 pm, closed Mon, €3, conc. €1.50) built in the second half of the 16th century for Cosimo I de Medici.

Steps lead back via **Chiesa di San Cristoforo** and then, to the right, the 15th-century **Chiesa di San Niccolò,** with coffered ceiling by Luca Signorelli (Via San Niccolò, ☎ 0575-604591, closed for restoration at the time of writing), which itself takes you back to Via G. Maffei. From there a stepped alley leads to Via Nazionale.

■ Adventures on Foot

Just outside the town walls, the **Chiesa di San Domenico** (Largo Beato Angelico, ☎ 0575-603041, Apr-Oct, 9 am-noon, 3-7 pm, Nov-Mar, 9 am-noon, 3-5 pm, free) is a short stroll away. It is a late 14th-century Gothic church with an elegant 15th-century polyptych by Lorenzo di Niccolò Gerini and a 16th-century altarpiece depicting *Madonna and Child with Saints* by Luca Signorelli.

From here you can continue to the Renaissance **Santuario di Santa Maria delle Grazie** (Loc. Calcinaio, ☎ 0575-62537, fax 0575-604830, summer, 4-8 pm, winter, 3-7 pm, free), built to the Latin-cross design of Francesco di Giorgio Martini. Under its octagonal dome, there's a stained glass window by Marcillat and a *Madonna and Child* fresco of note.

■ Adventures on Wheels

There are plenty of road bike routes in the vicinity of Cortona. One of the best takes you north to the **Convento delle Celle** (Loc. Le Celle 73, ☎ 0575-603362). Founded by St Francis in a hollow of Monte Sant'Egidio, it is thought to have been his favored resting place on many of his travels.

Another worthy diversion is the **Abbazia di Farneta** (Loc. Farneta 1, ☎ 0575-610010, 9 am-7 pm, free), a Benedictine abbey founded between the ninth and 10th centuries. While you're there, it's also worth going into the **Museo Archeologico e Paleontologico** (Archeology and Paleontology Museum, Loc. Farneta 1, ☎ 0575-610010, www.bccmp.com/valdichiana/valdich/farneta/farneta.htm, dawn to dusk, free).

■ Adventures on Horseback

There are quite a few riding centers in the plain around Cortona: **Associazione Ippica Farnetese** (Loc. Farneta, ☎ 0575-610052), **Azienda Ippoturistica** (Loc. Farneta, ☎ 0575-610048), **Centro Ippico Cortonese** (Loc. Piazzanella, ☎ 0575-601214), **Centro Ippico Saltafossi** (Loc.

Tecognano, ☎ 0575-638130) and **Il Molino** (Loc. Santa Maria Nuova, ☎ 335-7771771).

■ Adventures in the Val di Chiana

On the SS71 between Arezzo and Cortona, the interesting town of **Castiglion Fiorentino** sits inside a lovely medieval girdle of walls in the shade of the **Cassero** museum-fortress. Its main sights are the Gothic **Chiesa di San Francesco** (Piazza San Francesco, ☎ 0575-658278, Mon-Sat, 10:30 am-12:30 pm, free), the **Collegiata di San Giuliano** (Piazza della Collegiata, ☎/fax 0575-658080, May-Oct, 8:30 am-6 pm, Nov-Apr, 8:30 am-5 pm, free) and the nearby **Chiesa del Gèsu** (☎/fax 0575-658080, June-Sept, 9:30 am-noon, until 12:30 pm on Sun).

Walkers and **bike riders** should cover the short distance to the Renaissance **Chiesa Madonna della Consolazione** (☎ 0575-658278, Mon-Sat, 10:30 am-12:30 pm). It has an interesting octagonal frame. Then continue on to the medieval castle of Montecchio (Loc. Montecchio Vesponi), although it is currently closed while its unstable tower is being restored.

A **cycle** ride from Cortona, Foiano della Chiana makes a pleasant first stop before arriving at **Lucignano**, a hilltop town renowned for its elliptical layout. There is a grid of streets – named *via povera* (the poor street; Via Roma with its simple medieval buildings) and *via ricca* (the rich street; Via Marconi with its Renaissance palaces) – converging at the town's highest point, the **Collegiata San Michele Arcangelo** (Via San Giuseppe 1, ☎/fax 0575-836122, 10 am-noon, 4-6 pm, free).

Lucignano's art and history is documented on the walls of the nearby **Museo Comunale** (Piazza del Tribunale 22, ☎ 0575-838001, fax 0575-838026, summer, 10 am-1 pm, 2:30-6 pm, winter, Tues, 10 am-1 pm, Thurs, 10 am-12:30 pm, Fri, 3-5 pm, Sat, 10 am-1 pm, Sun, 4-5 pm, €3, conc. €2). It houses a collection of 13th- to 16th-century paintings (including works by Bartolo di Fredi, Lippo Vanni, Luca Signorelli) and a grand gold and silver tree-shaped reliquary known as the *Golden Tree of Lucignano*, the crowning glory of 14th- to 15th-century Sienese and Florentine goldsmiths. Next door, the Gothic **Chiesa di San Francesco** (Piazza San Francesco, ☎ 0575-836122, 10 am-noon, 4-5 pm, free) has some delightful 14th-century frescoes by Taddeo di Bartolo and Bartolo di Fredi.

Continue north to reach the elegant stone architecture of the Renaissance town of **Monte San Savino**. Built high on a hill to guard the agricultural plain below, the town was first inhabited by the Etruscans. It was the birthplace of Pope Giulio II and of the sculptor Andrea Contucci (Il Sansovino). Entered through the small stone gate of Porta Fiorentina (or Porta Romana), the main street, Corso Sangallo takes you past some fine Renaissance palazzi (Palazzo Comunale, Palazzo Pretorio) to the 12th-century **Chiesa dei SS Egidio e Savino** (Piazza di Monte 6, ☎/fax 0575-844030, 8 am-noon, 3-6 pm, free).

Your next stops should be the **Rocca del Cassero** and museum (Piazza Gamurrini, ☎ 0575-843098, www.citymonte.it, Apr-Oct, 9 am-noon, 3-6 pm, Nov-Mar, 9 am-noon, 3-6 pm, closed Mon, €1.55), before moving onto the ceramics museum in the 14th-century tower of the **Palazzo Pretorio** (Corso Sangallo, www.citymonte.it, Wed, Sat, Sun, 9 am-noon, 3-6 pm, €1), the **Santuario delle Vertighe** (Via delle Vertighe 563, ☎/fax 0575-849326, Apr-Sept, 9 am-noon, 3:30-5:30 pm, Oct-Mar, 9 am-noon, 3-4:30 pm, closed Sun, free) and the 14th-century **Chiesa di Sant'Agostino**, which contains a fresco cycle by Spinello Aretino and an *Annunciation* by Vasari.

■ Where to Shop

Cortona's best-known shopping attraction is **Cortonantiquaria**, the oldest antique fair in Italy. It takes over the 18th-century halls of Palazzo Casali and Palazzo Vagnotti every 23 Aug-7 Sept with its antique stalls of paintings, sculptures, ceramics, prints, tapestry and arms. If you miss the event, head to the open-air market held on Piazza Repubblica every Sat morning.

Top pick for handmade Tuscan arts and crafts is the "Etruscan gift shop" of **Il Girasole** (Via Casali 2/4, ☎ 0575-601616, www.il-girasole.com), with its range of ceramics, bronzes, jewelry and local crafts. There are more ceramics – especially the yellow sunflower designs of the locally-produced terracotta – at **Il Cocciaio** (Via Nazionale 54, ☎ 0575-604405, www.toscumbria.com/cocciaio).

■ Where to Eat

 A good spot for lunch in Cortona, **Taverna Pane e Vino** (Piazza Signorelli 27, ☎ 0575-631010, www.pane-vino.it, closed Mon and Jan, $) offers a light menu of cold meats and sausages, cheese, salads, soups and cakes in a traditional setting.

Also in Cortona, there's budget but quality fare at central **Trattoria Dardano** (Via Dardano 24, ☎ 0575-601944, closed Wed and Jan and Feb, $) with its handmade pasta (especially a tasty *pici alla contadino)* and grilled and roasted meats. **La Bucaccia** (Via Ghibellina 17, ☎/fax 0575-606039, www.labucaccia.it, closed Mon from Jan-Apr, $) offers medieval Tuscan cuisine in a rustic building dating back to 1242.

For a real farm dining experience, **Farneta** (Via Farneta 3, Fraz Farneta, ☎/fax 0575-610241, www.farneta.it, $) is your best bet. Follow directions for Abbazia di Farneta and opt for the house speciality: *tagliatelle alla farnetese.*

The menu is as traditional at **Il Cacciatore** (Via Roma 9, ☎/fax 0575-630552, closed Jan, $$) with dishes such as *soufflè di ricotta* and *pappardelle al cinghiale*, while the menu of **La Locanda nel Loggiato** (Piazza Pescheria 3, ☎ 0575-630575, closed Wed, $$) cannot help but play second fiddle to the beautiful medieval lodge terrace it occupies. Booking is recommended in high season.

You can't go wrong with the recently-moved **Osteria del Teatro** (Via Maffei 2, ☎ 0575-630556, www.osteria-del-teatro.it, closed Wed and two weeks in Nov, $$), though you'll have to book in advance during the hot summer months.

There's some fish in the monastic dining hall of **Le Contesse** (Via delle Contesse 1, ☎ 0575-630354, fax 0575-630477, www.hoteloasi.org, closed mid-Nov to mid-Apr, $$), including a tasty *spiggola alla citta* (sea bass with green apple salad, celery, ginger, lemon and pecorino).

If you want a bloody steak, get yourself to rustic **La Grotta** (Piazzetta Baldelli 3, ☎ 0575-630271, www.pdq.it/lagrotta.htm, closed Tues and Jan, $$) or, on the outskirts of town, **Agrisalotto** (Loc. C.S. Burcinella 88, ☎ 0575-617417, www.agrisalotto.it, closed Mon and Nov, $$$). Both serve a tasty Chianina.

Heading out of town, things start to get a bit pricier at **Il Falconiere** (Loc. San Martino a Bocena, ☎ 0575-612679, fax 0575-612927, www.ilfalconiere.com, closed Mon and Tues lunch, $$$$), but it is worth it; this old country hotel has frescoed walls and original antique furniture. Choose from the elegant period dining room, wrought-iron and glass conservatory or outdoor terrace, with a view over the Val di Chiana. The wine list concentrates on the local Baracchi estate (www.baracchiwinery.com). Booking advisable in high season.

In the historical center of Castiglion Fiorentino, your two best options are the traditional fare of **Da Muzzicone** (Piazza San Francesco 7, ☎ 0575-658403, fax 0575-658813, www.muzzicone.it, closed Tues, $$) and the pizzas, pastas and *fegatelli* (pork liver sausages) of the nearby ristorante-pizzeria **Roggi** (Via Tinaia 9, ☎ 0575-657081, www.residence-roggi.it, closed Mon and Sept, $).

In the center of Civitella in Val di Chiana, **L'Antico Borgo** (Via di Mezzo 35, ☎ 0577-448160, closed Mon and Tues and Nov, $$) does a fine *pici all'anatra* (pasta and breadcrumbs with a duck sauce).

Head a few miles out of **Lucignano** and you will reach **I Girasoli** (Loc. Selve di Sotto 89c, ☎ 0575-819020, fax 0575-837350, www.ilgirasoli.ar.it, $), a fine spot for *tegamaccio, pici* and *ribollita*. Booking recommended.

In the town itself, **Osteria Totò** (Piazza del Tribunale 6, ☎ 0575-836763, fax 0575-836988, www.tuscanycooking.com, closed Tues, Jan and Feb, $$) serves its "peasant fare" in a rustic atmosphere right in front of the Collegiata.

If you go through Marciano della Chiana, it's worth stopping at the **Osteria La Vecchia Rota** (Via XX Settembre, ☎ 0575-845362, www.osterialavecchiarota.it, closed Mon and Tues, $$) in the village's main square.

On to Monte San Savino. **La Terrasse** (Via g. di Vittorio 2/4, ☎ 0575-844111, www.ristorantelaterrasse.it, closed Wed and first two weeks in Nov, $$) sits alongside Porta Fiorentina, the entrance to the medieval center of town. Out the other side of town, **La Torre di Gargonza** (Loc. Gorgonza, ☎ 0575-847065, fax 0575-847054, www.gorgonza.it, closed Tues and Nov and Jan, $$) has the area's best traditional menu by far: *pici al cinghiale* (hand-rolled pasta in wild boar sauce), *malfatti con fonduto al tartufo nero* (vegetable dumplings in black truffle fondu, *tagliata al rosmarine* (lamb chps with rosemary), *agnella marinato alla brace* (grilled marinated lamb).

Also out of town, **Pizzeria Tavola Calda Il Poggetto** (Via Badicorte, Loc. Badicorte, ☎ 0575-845033, closed Mon and June, $$) has local food without an English menu in sight. Six miles from Monte San Savino, the 18th-century stone walls of **La Scuderia** (Via Senese Aretina 14a, Loc. Palazzuolo, ☎ 0575-847014, fax 0575-360546, lascuderia@libero.it, closed Mon and two weeks in Nov and Jan, $$) serves grilled meats and game (try the tasty *cinghiale alla cacciatore,* wild boar served hunter style, with a vegetable and black olive sauce).

■ Where to Stay

For budget hotel accommodation, you need to book well in advance to get a room in a touristy town like Cortona. Try **Sabrina** ☆☆☆ (Via Roma 37, ☎ 0575-630387, $$), **Athens** ☆ (Via San Antonio 12, ☎ 0575-630508, $$), **Oasi** ☆☆☆ (Via delle Contesse 1, ☎ 0575-630354, fax 0575-630477, www.hoteloasi.org, $$$) or even **San Luca** ☆☆☆☆ (Piazza Garibaldi 2, ☎ 0575-630460, fax 0575-630105, www.sanlucacortona.com, $$$), where prices drop considerably during the quiet winter period.

There's also well-priced accommodation at **Italia** ☆☆☆ (Via Ghibellina 5, ☎ 0575-630254, fax 0575-605763, http://emmeti.it/hitalia.it.html, $$$), a traditional palace dating from the 1600s a few steps from Cortona's main square. The large roof terrace offers panoramic views and there's a tasty restaurant downstairs (**Il Ghibellino**, ☎ 0575-630564, $$$).

San Michele ☆☆☆☆ (Via Guelfa 15, ☎ 0575-604248, fax 0575-630147, www.hotelsanmichele.net, $$$$) sits in a Renaissance palace in the center of the ancient town. The rooms are newly modernized but the elegant lounge area and terrace give a good idea of the building's roots.

There are also a few *affitacamere*: **Casa Betania** (Via G. Severini 50, ☎ 0575-604299, fax 0575-605499, $) and **Rugapiana Vacanze** (Via Nazionale 63, ☎ 0575-630364, fax 0575-630447, www.tuscanytravel.net, $$) the best placed.

The city youth hostel, **Ostello San Marco** (Via Maffei 57, ☎/fax 0575-601392, www.cortonahostel.com, 15 Mar-15 Oct, $) has a great location opposite Chiesa di San Marco. Unfortunately, you must be a member of YHA to stay here.

There are some great *agriturismi* in the Val di Chiana. **Castiglion Fiorentino** offers **Il Moro** ☆☆☆ (Via Montecchio 301b, Loc. Pievuccia, ☎/fax 0575-651370, www.ilmoro.toscana.it, $$), a great location for trekking and with horseback-riding facilities, **La Pievuccia** ☆☆☆☆ (Via Santa Lucia 118, Loc. Pievuccia, ☎/fax 0575-651007, www.lapievuccia.it, $$$), which has a pool, and **Le Capanne** ☆☆☆ (Loc. Pieve di Chio 106, ☎ 339-1668363, www.lecapanne.com, $$$), which has all three (horseback riding, trekking and pool).

There's also horseback riding, trekking and pool at **Camperchi** ☆☆☆☆ (Via del Burrone 38, ☎ 0575-843184, fax 0575-844354, www.camperchi.com, $$$$) in Civitella in Val di Chiana, while Monte San Savino is well served by **Foresteria Il Giardino di Fontarronco** ☆☆☆☆ (Loc. Chiana 255, ☎ 0575-846044, fax 0575-846045, www.foresteria.it, $$) and **Montemaggiore** ☆☆☆ (Loc. Palazzuolo Vecchio, Fraz. Capraie, ☎/fax 0575-847083, www.marengo.it, $$$). Again these all have horseback riding, trekking and pool.

Lucca & Pisa

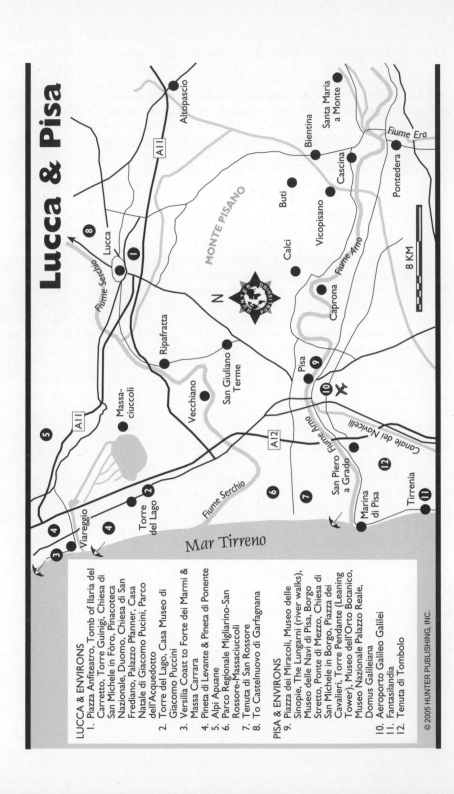

MONTE PISANO

Mar Tirreno

Altopascio
A11
Lucca
Fiume Serchio
Ripafratta
Massa-ciuccoli
A11
Vecchiano
San Giuliano Terme
Fiume Serchio
Viareggio
Torre del Lago
Fiume Serchio
Bientina
Santa Maria a Monte
Cascina
Fiume Era
Pontedera
Buti
Vicopisano
Fiume Arno
Calci
Caprona
Pisa
Fiume Arno
San Piero a Grado
Canale dei Navicelli
A12
Marina di Pisa
Tirrenia

8 KM

LUCCA & ENVIRONS
1. Piazza Anfiteatro, Tomb of Ilaria del Carretto, Torre Guinigi, Chiesa di San Michele in Fòro, Pinacoteca Nazionale, Duomo, Chiesa di San Frediano, Palazzo Pfanner, Casa Natale di Giacomo Pucini, Parco dell'Acquedotto
2. Torre del Lago, Casa Museo di Giacomo Puccini
3. Versilia Coast to Forte dei Marmi & Massa Carrara
4. Pineta di Levante & Pineta di Ponente
5. Alpi Apuane
6. Parco Regionale Migliarino-San Rossore-Massaciuccoli
7. Tenuta di San Rossore
8. To Castelnuovo di Garfagnana

PISA & ENVIRONS
9. Piazza dei Miracoli, Museo delle Sinopie, The Lungarni (river walks), Museo delle Navi di Pisa, Borgo Stretto, Ponte di Mezzo, Chiesa di San Michele in Borgo, Piazza dei Cavalieri, Torre Pendante (Leaning Tower), Museo dell'Orto Botanico, Museo Nazionale Palazzo Reale, Domus Galileiana
10. Aeroporto Galileo Galilei
11. Fantasilandia
12. Tenuta di Tombolo

Lucca

Situated in a fertile plain between the Apennines and Monte Pisano, Lucca is a delightful city to explore. Inside its four-kilometer (2½-mile) stretch of city walls, narrow streets lead onto irregularly shaped squares revealing pleasant gardens, 16th-century palazzi, jutting medieval tower-houses and half-hidden churches. Its layout (especially the stunning amphitheater) was created by the Romans, who transformed what was previously a swamp town (*luk* meaning "swamp" in Ligurian) into the important center it was to remain.

Emperor Federico Barbarossa kicked off what was to be a heady accumulation of medieval wealth from the wool, silk and banking trades when he made the city a free *comune* in the 12th century. It was this wealth that produced the beautiful Duomo. A later boom under the 14th-century *signorie,* first under Uguccione della Faggiuola and then Castruccio Castracani degli Antelminelli, led to a happy four years of Republic rule before it was eventually toppled by the arrival of the French in the 17th century. The Bourbons replaced the government of Felice and Elisa Baciocchi (Napoleon's sister), and created one of Lucca's most popular attractions when they transformed the city walls into the lovely tree-lined public walkway you see today.

NOT TO BE MISSED

- **Piazza Anfiteatro:** Extraordinary mix of the Roman and the medieval (see page 242).
- **The *Volto Santo*:** A large wooden crucifix said to imitate the true effigy of Christ (see page 240).
- **The city walls:** Fine views from a walking, jogging and cycling track that was once used by the Bourbons for car races (see page 239).
- **The Tomb of Ilaria del Carretto:** A beautiful sculptural masterpiece (see page 241).
- **Torre Gunigi:** The culmination of Lucca's 14th-century craze for tower building (see page 241).
- **San Michele in Fòro:** Renaissance church topped with a statue said to be wearing a diamond ring that can be seen glittering at night.

Getting Here

By Air: The closest international airport is Pisa's **Aeroporto Galileo Galilei** (☎ 050-849202, www.pisa-airport.com), which is 20 km (12 miles) from Lucca on the SS12. Two daily services run from the airport to Lucca, with more frequent hourly services from Pisa Central (take the first train to the main station and change). Visitors arriving via Florence's **Aeroporto Amerigo Vespucci** (☎ 055-3061700, www.safnet.it), 75 km (47 miles) away, should get onto the A11 (and leave at the Lucca toll-paying exit) or catch a train or bus from the town center. For car rental from Pisa and Florence airports, see page 32.

 By Rail: Hourly trains (☎ 848-888088, www.trenitalia.it) run between Pisa and Lucca (30-minute travel time) and Florence and Lucca (65 minutes). Lucca station is on Piazza Ricasoli, a short walk south of the city walls.

 By Bus: Lazzi (☎ 0583-584876) buses run to Lucca from Florence (24 daily, 1¼ hours) and Pisa (22 daily, 40 minutes), dropping you off in Piazzale Verdi (just inside the western walls). **CLAP** (☎ 0583-587897) services link the city with the Versilia Coast.

 By Car: Lucca is well placed on the Tuscan highway system with the **A11** (Florence to the coast) and the A12 (and adjacent SS1 "Aurelia," which skirts the Tuscan coast up to La Spezia and Liguria) passing nearby.

Getting Around Town

 By Car: It's best to avoid Lucca's one-way system and explore the town on foot or by bicycle (see below). There are 10 paying **car parks** within the walls and another two just outside; of the 12, the easiest and most convenient place to leave your car is by the tourist office on Piazzale Verdi or just behind it by Piazza S. Donato. If these are full, there's a large car park just outside along Viale C. del Prete.

Car Rental: ACI-Hertz (Via Catalani 59, ☎ 0583-53535, fax 0583-418058, www.hertz.it), **Autonoleggio Giglio** (Via Orzali 391, ☎ 0583-492698, fax 0583-490958), **Avis** (Via Luporini, ☎ 0583-513614, www.avisautonoleggio.it), **Europcar** (☎ 0583-464590, fax 0583-463542, www.europcar.it) and **Nolo Auto Pittore** (Piazza Santa Maria, ☎ 0583-467960).

 By Taxi: There are ranks outside the train station, and on the central Piazza Napoleone, on Piazzale Verdi at the west entrance and along the north walls by the car park on Piazza Santa Maria. Otherwise **Radiotaxi** (☎ 0583-333434) and **Taxi Lucca** (☎ 0583-955200) both offer a swift service.

By Bicycle: Lucca is a great city to explore by bike. Not only is the historical center well suited for cyclists, but it is the best way to explore the full charms of the *passegiate delle mura urbane* (the city walkway).

The **tourist information gift shop** on Piazzale Verdi rents bicycles (€2.50 per hour), tandems (€6 per hour) and inline skates (€2.50 per hour). If their bikes are all out, head to **Barbetti Cicli** (Via Anfiteatro 23; ☎ 0583-954444), **Cicli Bizzarri** (Piazza Santa Maria 32; ☎ 0583-496031) or **Poli Antonio Biciclette** (Piazza Santa Maria 42, ☎/fax 0583-493787). You can also rent bikes from most hotels.

Information Sources

Tourist Offices: For general tourist information, contact the largest tourism office in the city, **APT Lucca** (Lucca Tourist Office, Piazzale Verdi, ☎ 0583-91991, fax 0583-490766, www.luccaturismo.it), while all mountain-related queries are better served at the **Communità Montana Area Lucchese** (Lucca Area Mountain Community, Via della Cavallerizza 11, ☎ 0583-492151/493124, fax 0583-490882) or the very helpful **CAI** (☎ 0583-582669, Mon-Fri, 7-8 pm). It can be found with the smaller of Lucca's tourist offices (☎ 0583-919941) in the Cortile Carrara of the Palazzo Ducale just off Piazza Napoleone.

Sightseeing & Adventures

■ Walking Lucca

The nearest entrance to the city walls from the train station is Porta San Pietro, itself just a short hop to the leafy **Piazza Napoleone** (also known as Piazza Grande) along Via V. Veneto. Those arriving by bus can reach the square by taking Via V. Emanelle II just in front of the bus station. To the left of the square is the **Palazzo Ducale**, site of the first of Lucca's three tourist information points, a vast edifice built by Bourbon rulers in the early 19th century as an attempt to give some "air" to the tight medieval structure of the town at that time. They also created the *passegiata delle mura* along the city walls (see below), reworked the streets around the amphitheater and established the **Orto Botanico** along the eastern walls (Botanical Gardens, Via San Micheletto, ☎ 0583-442160, fax 0583-442161, summer, Mon-Fri, 9:30 am-12:30 pm, Sun and public hols, 11 am-5 pm, winter, closed Sun) .

THE CITY WALLS

Whether you walk, jog or cycle, you can't come to Lucca and not take a tour around the wide 40-foot-high boulevard lined with plane, lime, ilex and chestnut that tops the four-km (2½-mile) stretch of city walls. Known as Lucca's balcony, there are 11 bastions, caffès and plenty of green space to take a breather while you soak up exceptional views over the city and surrounding countryside.

Continue along Via V. Veneto to arrive on **Piazza San Michele**, the old Roman forum and, for the Lucchese at least, the very heart of town. You can't miss the magnificent white calcareous stone façade of the **Chiesa di San Michele in Fòro** that occupies it, right. Heralded as one of the best examples of the architectural style known as Pisano-Lucchese, its construction started in the 11th century but wasn't completed for over a century. The result is a Romanesque lower level (marked by the blind arcades and Pisan-style apse) topped off by a sheer vertical Gothic design that surges above the church roof. It is crowned with a colossal statue of Archangel St Michael, which accentuates the height even more. Inside, the Romanesque chapels guard some precious Andrea della Robbia terracotta altarpieces, Filippo Lippi's *SS Jerome, Sebastian, Roch and Helena* (right-hand nave) and a 13th-century crucifix by the Lucchese school.

City Audio Tour

The Tourist Information gift shop on Piazzale Verdi rents out *My Guide*, an audio tour of Lucca's most important attractions (€9, conc. €7). It takes you on a one-kilometer (0.6-mile) walk around the city's main sights and is full of interesting historical tidbits and insights into some of the city's lesser-known spots. There is background on Lucca's silk weaving history (when the breaking of strict rules about production and counterfeiting was punishable by death), and meandering asides past some traditional Lucchese shops (like the typical T-shaped shop at number 13 Via Santa Luccia) and into hidden courtyards. One of these is the Corte delle Uova, so-called after a former egg market that used to stand here; it also has the city's last remaining wooden balcony, once seen everywhere in the city.

Just behind the church, Chiasso Barletti will take you to the **Torre delle Ore** (Via Fillungo; ☎ 336-203221, 10 am-7 pm Mar-Sept, 9 am-5 pm, Sept-Feb, €3.50, conc. €2). This is one of the city's three remaining towers and the city's clock since 1471 (hence the name).

> **Museum Admission:** You can purchase a joint ticket for the Palazzo Manzi and Villa Guinigi at €6.50, conc. €3.25, or a joint ticket for the Torre Guinigi and Torre delle Ore at €5, conc. €3 from any of the individual ticket offices.

A right turn at Torre delle Ore, down Via Cenami, will take you into what could be considered the city's religious nucleus – a network of three interlinking piazzas that house the old and new cathedrals. The first you'll meet is the old cathedral, **Chiesa di San Giovanni e Reparata,** which held that role until 715. It preserves a lion-flanked carved Romanesque portal and inside, archeological remains which include some first-century Roman villa mosaics.

Duomo (Cattedrale di San Martino, Piazza del Duomo, daily, summer, 7 am-7 pm, winter, 7 am-5 pm, free): Swathed in polychrome marble, Lucca's elegant and richly-decorated cathedral, dedicated to San Martino, is the elegant fruit of Anselmo da Baggio's desire for a religious center befitting Lucca's important position on the Via Francigena (he went on to consecrate it in 1070 as Pope Alessandro II). In its construction, which took 300 years, you can see the passage from the Romanesque (the porticoes; the three airy loggias) to the Gothic (the three interior naves with transepts and semicircular apses). Backed by a robust Lombard watchtower, it manages to function despite the mismatch of the styles.

The city's religious centerpiece is inside – the Volto Santo, a wooden crucifix of an impressive size por-

Tomba di Ilaria del Carretto (died 1405) in the Duomo

trayed with its eyes open according to the iconography of Christus Triumphanus (the "true effigy" of Christ carved by Nicodemus). It is displayed in a gold-decorated tabernacle added to the left nave by local architect Matteo Civitali (1484). Nearby lies the city's artistic pride and joy, the tomb of Ilaria del Carretto (cathedral sacristy, Mon-Fri, 9:30 am-5:45 pm, Sat, 9:30 am-6:45 pm, Sun, 1-4:45 pm, i2, conc. i1.50, combined ticket with the Museo della Cattedrale). She was the young wife of Paolo Guinigi. The tomb is rightly considered the masterpiece of Sienese sculptor, Jacopo della Quercia, who manages to portray less an image of death and more an idea of calm repose. Indeed, the statue is so beautiful, the English writer Ruskin claimed to have fallen in love with it. Other works to look out for include the statue of St Martin on Horseback with the Beggar (west wall), Madonna and Child between Saints by Domenico Ghirlandaio, and, on the bas-reliefs that decorate the exterior, the works by Nicola Pisano around the left-hand door (Deposition, Annunciation, Adoration of the Magi) and Guidetto da Como (Life of St Martin). Complete your visit with a trip to the adjacent Museo della Cattedrale (Cathedral Museum, Piazza Antelminelli 5, %/fax 0583-490530, Mar-Nov, daily, 10 am-6 pm, Nov-Mar, Mon-Fri, Sat-Sun, 10 am-5 pm, i3.50, conc. i2). It displays paintings and sculptures taken from both the new and old cathedrals.

THE DEVIL'S STONE

Through Piazza Antelminelli and past the fountain Nottolini built to crown the completion of the aqueduct (1832-35), a road leads to **Palazzo Bernardini**. It is here that you can spy the so-called "devil's stone," a warped stone that, despite numerous replacements and even the use of metal bars, hampered the building's 18th-century construction. Although the stone's propensity to distort in this particular spot (to the right of the entrance) has never been explained, locals believe it is because a religious image was removed that same location.

A 160-foot-high tower announces your next stop, the **Palazzo Guinigi**, former home of the richest and most powerful of Lucca's silk-weaving and banking families and the city *signori* between 1400 and 1430. Built entirely of red bricks, its crowning tower is the **Torre Gunigi** (Via Sant'Andrea, ☎ 336-203221, Mar-Apr, 9 am-7:30 pm, May-Sept, 9 am-midnight, Oct-Feb, 9 am-7 pm, €3.50, conc. €2). The Torre represents the culmination of Lucca's 14th-century tower building, which at one time peppered Lucca's skyline with over 100 towers of varying heights. This one, situated in the midst of the historical center, offers a 360-degree panorama of the city from the top of its 230 steps.

Lucca's major art museum, the **Museo Nazionale** (National Museum, ☎/fax 0583-496033, Tues-Sun, 8:30 am-7 pm, 8:30 am-1 pm, €4, conc. €2) is across the *fosso* (the ditch that separates the quarter of San Francesco from the rest of the city, and which marks the boundary of the original medieval city walls) on Via della Quarquonia. It occupies the 14th-century Guingi Villa, which was built by the family to supplement the medieval townhouse you've just visited. Inside, there is a diverse collection of painting and sculpture tracing not only the artistic heritage of the Lucchese area (including works by della Quercia, Matteo Civitali, Fra Bartolomeo, Passignano and Pietro da Cortona), but also its history, with artifacts dating back to Ligurian and Etruscan times as well as a large number of relics from Roman rule.

Lucca

The best of Roman rule can be found north of Torre Guinigi on the remarkable **Piazza Anfiteatro**, left. Although these days its design appears medieval, the towering townhouses with their haphazard mix of shapes, heights and colors are actually built on the foundations of a classical Roman amphitheater – hence the oval shape. Interestingly, this was a slum area before the Bourbons cleared it up, removing the buildings that once occupied the oval's center, to make a market square (hence its other name "Piazza del Mercato"). Unfortunately, they were a little too late to save many of its original features, most having been carried off for the construction of city churches and homes, but you can still see some of the original second-century arches and columns on the exterior at the north side.

The piazza is flanked by one of the city's most beautiful streets, **Via Fillungo**. It is the heart of the pedestrian quarter and often considered the "city living room" for its fashionable shops, lovely 14th-century buildings, Liberty-style fronts and elegant caffès – including the prestigious Caffè di Simo, formerly known as Caffè Casalli and once frequented by poets, painters and musicians such as Puccini and Soffici.

Before you head down Via Fillungo, first take a detour across it, to the imposing Chiesa San Frediano and, just off it, Palazzo Pfanner.

Chiesa di San Frediano (8:30 am-noon, 3-5 pm, free): Watched over by its towering campanile – itself a testimony to the church's history with its white marble Roman base – San Frediano, left, is one of the oldest churches in Lucca. Its present layout was fashioned in the 12th century when the concurrent construction of the second ring of walls obliged the architects to reverse its original form. The beautiful *Ascension* mosaic, which crowns the otherwise sober Romanesque façade, was added just a century later. The Chiesa is vast and

dimly lit inside. Three naves with bare columns (most probably taken from the amphitheater you just visited) lead to the church's main sights. These include the 12th-century marble pavement, which lies alongside the beautifully crafted Fonte Lustrale (a 12th-century baptismal font); and the Gothic marble polypytch by Jacopo Della Quercia showing *Madonna & Child With Saints* (1422) in the Cappella Trenta. You should also watch for the urn conserving the remains of St. Zita (traditionally an object of great devotion to the Lucchese); and the 16th-century frescoes by Amico Aspetini charting the *Miracle of San Frediano* and the *Arrival of the Volto Santo*.

Flower Power: Commemorated on April 27 by a flower market outside the church, the story of the much-cherished St. Zita (who died 1278) started in serfdom. According to legend, she was working for a rich Lucchese family when the master caught her sneaking out scraps of bread to feed the poor. When he asked what she had in her apron, she replied "roses and flowers" – to which the scraps were duly transformed.

Palazzo Pfanner (Via degli Asili 33, daily, 10 am-6 pm, closed Nov-Feb, €4, conc. €1): In a huddle of important palazzi, the 17th-century Palazzo Pfanner stands out above the rest for its beautiful Italian garden (open to the public). Its flamboyant design appears all the more luxurious in contrast to its austere exterior. You can get a quick look before entering by climbing up onto the walls.

Return to Piazza San Michele down Via Fillungo, only this time taking Via di Poggio west out of the square to pass the house of Lucca's most famous son, **Casa Natale di Giacomo Puccini** (1858-1924), now a music school and small museum conserving documents and objects from his life (Via di Poggio 9, ☎ 0583-584028, 10 am-1 pm, 3-6 pm, till 7 pm July-Aug, €3, conc. €2). The street arrives at the 17th-century Palazzo Mansi, site of the **Pinacoteca Nazionale** (Via Galli Tassi 43, ☎ 0583-55570, fax 0583-312221, Tues-Sun, 8:30 am-7 pm, 8:30 am-1 pm on public hols, €4, conc. €2). It contains works by Tuscan masters such as Andrea del Sarto, Beccafumi, Bronzino and Pontormo. A partly frescoed room houses an exhibition on Lucca's textile industry.

Church Crawling

Lucca has many more churches worth a look.

Sant'Alessandro – An 11th- to 12th-century church with a grey and white marble façade touted as the best example of the initiative phase of the Romanesque-Lucchese style.

San Cristofano – A 12th- to 13th-century construction with a recently-decorated architrave.

Santa Maria Fuorisportam – This church was begun in the 12th century and finished in the 16th.

San Pier Somaldi – It has a façade created between the 12th and 13th centuries.

Chiesa di San Romano – This church was built in the 13th century over an oratory that has existed since 792. Its single-nave interior with transept is one of the most important examples of the Baroque style in Lucca, thanks to the transformations by Giovanni Buonvisi and the Lucchese architect Vincenzo Buonamici.

San Paolino – Baccio da Montelupo added the marble façade to this Renaissance church in the 16th century. Inside, you'll find a 14th-century *Coronation of the Virgin*, which shows the city as it was then.

■ Adventures on Foot

There is no shortage of hills for hiking in and around Lucca – the Apennines and the Alpuan Alps are a short drive or train ride to the north, and Monti Pisani is an even shorter distance to the south. But, if you've strolled the *passeggiata delle mura* one time too many, and don't want to go far from town, the **Parco dell'Acquedotto Monumentale** may be the answer. It is a trekking and cycling route along the old Roman aqueduct that can picked up south of the train station.

There's more trekking, mountain biking and horseback riding over to the east near Montecarlo. Contact **Ai Comunali** (Montechiari, ☎ 0583-22971) for details.

■ Adventures on Wheels

One of Lucca's best cycling itineraries takes you on a tour of the bourgeois villas that dot the predominantly agricultural landscape surrounding Lucca. These summer residences, built between the 15th and 19th centuries, are said to number 300. Those reachable by bicycle from the city center include the following:

- Seven-km (4.3 miles) north of Lucca is **Villa Oliva** (San Pancrazio, ☎ 0583-406462, fax 0583-406771, villaoliva@villelucchesi.net, 15 Mar-5 Nov, 9:30 am-12:30 pm, 2-6 pm, by appointment at all other times). It was designed by Matteo Civitali around 1500. Pretty plain in design, it does have an attractive 14-acre garden with an ilex-tree amphitheater and a *grottesco* of water and marble statues.

- Nearby, you'll find **Villa Grabau** (San Pancrazio, ☎/fax 0583-406098, villagrabau@villelucchesi.net, 15 Mar-1 Nov, 10 am-1 pm, 3-7 pm, closed Mon and Tues am, Nov-14 Mar, Sun only). Built in the 16th century by the Diodati over the ruins of a medieval village, it also has a stupendous 25-acre park, with a 16th century English garden and *Limonaia* (lemon-garden with over 100 lemon trees).

- From here it's only a short cycle to **Villa Reale** (Marlia, ☎/fax 0583-30009, villareale@villelucchesi.net, Mar-Nov, Tues-Sun, guided visits on the hour 10 am-6 pm, Dec-Feb by appointment only). It lies six km (four miles) from the center of Lucca. Built on the site of a 14th-century fortress, it was restyled in 1806 into its present Neoclassical look under the direction of Napoleon's sister, Elisa Baciocchi during her reign as Grand Duchess of Tuscany. It's worth stopping by, if only to explore the English garden with huge ornamental lake, splendid Teatro di Verzura, "Viale delle Camelie" and, hidden in woods, the Grotto of Pan, an elaborate two-story hideaway with mosaic floor.

- Continue to **Villa Mansi** (☎ 0583-920234, fax 0583-928114, villamansi@villelucchesi.net, Apr-Sept, 10 am-1 pm, 3-6 pm, Oct-Mar, 10 am-1 pm, 3-5 pm) in Segromigno, 10 km (six miles) from Lucca. Originally a plain 16th-century country house, it was enlarged in 1635 by Muzio Oddi and expanded many times in later centuries after the silk-merchant Mansi family purchased it in the 17th century. The late Renaissance façade is impressive, adorned with much statuary. The park – part-English, part-Italian style – was reorganized by Filippo Juvarra and is famous for its beautiful gardens and elegant architectural lines.

- Less than a mile away in Camigliano, the façade of **Villa Torrigiani** is said to be the best example of Baroque architecture in Tuscany (☎/fax 0583-928041, villatorrigiani@villelucchesi.net, Mar-Nov, 10 am-noon, 3-7 pm). Ten km (six miles) from Lucca, its approach is a magnificent one-km (0.6-mile) avenue of cypress trees and the villa is mirrored in the waters of the large fountain in front. Originally built for the Buonvisi family in the 16th century, the gardens were transformed almost entirely by Alfonso Torrigiani two centuries later into the then-prevalent English style. These days, it is mostly famous for the remains of the Giardino di Flora water games (*giochi d'acqua*) intended to drench unsuspecting visitors.

- Another villa worth a mention (and the closest to the city) is two miles south of Lucca in Vicopelago. It is the Renaissance **Villa Bernardini**, which was built by Bernardino Bernardini in 1615 (☎/fax 0583-370327, villabernardini@ villalucchesi.net, Apr-Oct, 9:30 am-noon, 5-7:30 pm, closed Mon mornings, Nov-Mar, 10 am-noon, 2:30-5:30 pm).

- Northeast of Lucca, a panoramic road leads to **Villa Basilica**. Just on the border with the Pistoia province, it has a magnificent Romanesque parish church and the restored Palazzo Pievanale with 17th-century Flemish paintings and Antonio Franchi's masterpiece, the *Madonna del Carmine*.

Oenophiles should also consider picking up the **wine route**, the *Strada del Vino*, which passes through verdant hills, centuries-old olive groves and vines to arrive at the best-known estates for wine tasting. You can find out more by contacting the head office of the Strada Del Vino directly (Via Barsanti E Matteucci, ☎ 0583-417514, fax 0583-417502, www.luccanet.it/stradadelvino). If you follow the route to its end at the panoramic town of **Montecarlo**, you'll find the ancient fortress-home of the Montecarlo DOC, Fortezza di Cerruglio. While here, make a point to see the late 14th-century fresco of *Madonna del Soccorso* in **Santuario Maria Santissima del Soccorso** (☎ 0583-22888).

■ Adventures on Horseback

Lucca's nearest riding centers are at **Club Ippico Lucchese** (Sant'Anna, Via della Scogliera 887, ☎ 0573-467054), **Anna Equitazione** (Marlia, Via C. Ceccotti 24, ☎ 0573-407262) and **Centro Equestre** (Pescaglia, Loc. Consani 1, ☎ 0583-38010).

Ecoadventure (☎ 0347-6781127, alexpicchi@tin.it) organizes horseback-riding tours in the Lucchese countryside, taking you around the Lucchese villas, along the wine route and into the Garfagnana.

Events & Entertainment

Lucca and its province is a great spot for entertainment – especially musical events – with the **Puccini Festival** at Torre del Lago (see page 251), the **Barga Jazz Festival** (see page 266) and **Viareggio Carnival** (see page 251) always ensuring a good turn out.

Lucca Estate (☎ 0584-46477, www.summer-festival.com, July-Aug) is one of Tuscany's most popular pop and rock festivals, with international big names performing on both Piazza Napoleone and Piazza Anfiteatro.

More high-brow music is supplied by the Associazione Musicale **"Clima della Bella Epoque"** (Atmosphere of the Belle Epoque, San Micheletto, Via A. Custode 6, ☎ 0583-491548, f.lucii@tin.it, July-Sept, free). Over the winter season, there are drama, dance and classical music performances held in the 19th-century **Teatro del Giglio** (☎ 0583-467531, Piazza del Giglio, www.teatrodelgiglio.it, Sept-Mar, €25, conc. €12).

Where to Eat

LOCAL FLAVORS

Zuppa di farro della Lucchesia: Thick soup made from spelt grain.
Biroldo di Garfagnana: Spicy salami.
Tordelli Lucchesi: Meat-stuffed egg pasta.
Red beans: Local kidney-shaped beans served in traditional dishes like pasta and beans, or steak and beans.
Capretto: Roast mountain goat.
There's also slow-cooked rabbit stew, eel from the Serchio river *in zimino* (cooked with herbs), and *dolci* such as *buccellato*, a large round cake made of wheat flour, sugar, vanilla and aniseed.
Accompany these flavors with DOC wines from Montecarlo and the Colline Lucchesi, and digestives such as China Lucchese Massagli (an elixir produced as a cure for malaria).

 Try a spot of lunch at the famous **Caffè di Simo** (Via Fillungo 58, $) or a light evening meal from enoteca **La Corte dei Vini** (Corte Campana 6, ☎/fax 0583-55364, www.lacortedeivini.it, $), which serves Italian cheese and salami to accompany its extensive range of wine.

Otherwise, your best budget choices are **Buatino** (Via del Borgo Giannotti 508, ☎ 0583-343207, $) and **Gli Orti di Via Elisa** (Via Elisa 1, ☎ 0583-491241, $).

Lucca's finest and oldest eatery, **Buca di Sant'Antonio** (Via della Cervia 1, ☎ 0583-55881, closed Sun pm and Mon, $$) is also one of its most popular, with a menu of predominantly Lucchese cuisine, which includes grilled and roasted meats, homemade pastas and some tasty vegetarian dishes. Booking recommended for evening meals.

> **The Taste Train:** The *Treno dei Sapori* is designed for gourmets looking to discover delicious local dishes as they travel on the Apuan Range. Depending on the time of year, stops offer the chance to sample wild chicory cakes, *biroldo* (black pudding to the British, blood sausage to everyone else), serchio trout, honey, chestnut pancakes, maize bread and many other local specialties. Run in association with the local Slow Food office, the Taste Train departs from Lucca, Viareggio and Massa stations into the mountains and valleys of the Apuan Range at intermittent dates throughout the year. To see if any trips coincide with your stay, contact Slow Food (c/o Enzo Pedreschi, Loc. Buggina, Castelnuovo Garfagnana, ☎ 0583-62192, www.ilvecchiomulino.com).

There's more tasty fare in the $$ price range at **All'Olivo** (Piazza San Quirico 1, ☎ 0583-496264), **Da Guilio in Pelleria** (Via della Conce 45, ☎ 0583-55948), **Giglio** (Piazza Puccini 2, ☎ 0583-494058), **Puccini** (Corte San Lorenzo 1, ☎ 0583-316116) and, out of town, in **Alla Taverna di Mario** (Piazza Carrara 12, Montecarlo, ☎ 0583-22588) and **Butterfly** (Loc. Ponte alla Posta, Capannori, ☎ 0583-962801).

One of Lucca's most famous restaurants for its location within the historic city walls is **Antico Caffè delle Mura** (Piazzale V. Emanuele, ☎ 0583-467962, closed Tues, $$$). There is a candlelit indoor dining room and tables set up in summer under the pillars in front of the restaurant. Try the home-cooked *tortelli*. Booking recommended for tables on the terrace. If the restaurant is full, try **Antica Locanda dell'Angelo** (Via Peschiera 21, ☎ 0583-47711, $$$).

A Tavola Con l'Olio d'Oliva

Every November, Lucca hosts "At the table with Olive Oil" to celebrate its local produce, considered some of the best in Tuscany, with local restaurants serving fixed-price menus on the same theme. For further information, contact **CCIAA di Lucca** (Corte Campana 10, ☎ 0583-9765, www.lu.camcom.it).

Where to Stay

Close to Chiesa di San Michele is **Puccini** ☆☆☆ (Via di Poggio 9, ☎ 0583-55421, fax 0583-53487, www.hotelpuccini.com, $$), a small, friendly hotel in the very heart of Lucca. The rooms, although small, are low-priced, especially considering the location, and fill quickly, so book ahead.

Well-sited near the cathedral, **Albergo San Martino** ☆☆☆ (Via della Dogana 7/9, ☎ 0583-469181, fax 0583-490513, www.albergosanmartino.it, $$$) has comfortably furnished rooms with all the modern conveniences. Upon request, an English speaker pops into the hotel at 6 pm every evening to give guests a talk on what to see and do in Lucca. Bicycle rentals are available.

Pleasant alternatives include **Diana** ☆☆ (Via del Molinetto 1, ☎ 50583-492202, fax 0583-467795, www.albergodiana.com, $$), **Celide** ☆☆☆☆ (Viale Giusti 25, ☎ 0583-954106, fax 0583-954304, www.albergocelide.it, $$$) and **Rex** ☆☆☆ (Piazza Ricasoli 19, ☎ 0583-955443, fax 0583-954348, www.hotelrexlucca.com, $$$).

Outside the walls, **Grand Hotel Guinigi** ☆☆☆☆ (Via Romana 1247, ☎ 0583-4991, fax 0583-499800, www.grandhotelguinigi.it, $$$$) and **Locanda L'Elisa** ☆☆☆☆☆ (Via Nuova per Pisa 1952, Massa Pisana, ☎ 0583-379737, fax 0583-379019, www.locandalelisa.com, $$$$) are the favorites, located in attractive mountainous surroundings within easy reach of town. The latter occupies a converted 18th-century villa thought to have been built under instructions from Napoleon's sister, Elisa Baciocchi.

A five-minute drive northwest of Lucca on the SP24 brings you to **B&B Vigna Ilaria** (Via Per Pieve S.Stefano 967c, Loc. Sant'Alessio, ☎ 0583-332091, www.locandavignailaria.it, $$), home to one of the area's best restaurants. Although the outside looks old, the rooms are modern and recently decorated with bright tiling or carpets, pastel walls and wood-beamed ceilings. Vigna Ilaria lies on Lucca's *Strada del Vino* (wine road), so it comes as no surprise to find that the restaurant has a list of over 300 wines. Booking recommended.

The vine-covered **Villa la Principessa** (Via Nuova per Pisa 1616, Massa Pisana, ☎ 0583-370037, fax 0583-379136, www.hotelprincipessa.com, $$$$$), two miles south of Lucca toward Pisa, is the former home and court of Castruccio Castracani, the Lord and Duke of Lucca, famed as the inspiration for Machiavelli's *The Prince*.

Opt for *affitacamere* at **La Torre** (Via della Colombaia 14, ☎ 0583-311079, fax 0583-957044, www.paginegialle.it/latorreaffittacamere, $$), **Casa Alba** (Via Fillungo 142, ☎/fax 0583-312800, www.casa-alba.com, $$), **Villa Romantica** (Via Barbaranti 246, ☎ 0583-496872, fax 0583-957600, www.villaromantica.it, $$), near Piazza del Carmine, or **Da Elisa alle Sette Arti** (Via Elisa 25, ☎/fax 0583-494539, www.daelisa.com, $$). The latter offers rooms in a 19th-century building decorated with chandelier ceilings and patterned floor tiles. All arrange bicycle rentals.

The nearest campground is at Torre del Lago or along the Versilia Coast, see page 258). There are two youth hostels: **Ostello San Frediano** (Via della Cavallerizza 12, ☎ 0583-469957, fax 0583-461007, ostello.san.frediano@virgilio.it, $) and, two miles out of town (Bus #6 or #7), **Ostello Il Serchio** (Via del Brennero 673, ☎ 0583-341811, Mar-Nov, $).

Outside of Lucca

REGION AT A GLANCE

- **Main city:** Lucca.
- **Afternoon trips from Lucca:** Torre del Lago (see page 250), Villa Basilica (see page 245).
- **City breaks:** Massa (see page 272), Carrara (see page 273).
- **Rural retreats:** The Apuan Alps (Alpi Apuane, see page 258), Garfagnana (see page 263), Lunigiana (see page 276).
- **Spa towns:** Bagni di Lucca (see page 265), San Giuliano Terme (see page 265), Equi Terme (see page 279).
- **Beach breaks:** Viareggio (see page 251), Forte dei Marmi (see page 255) and the Versilia Coast (see page 249), the Apuan Riviera (see page 271).

Lucca is well-placed for both sightseeing and exploring. With the Versilia Coast, the Lucca province has one of the most popular stretches of beach in the country; the Garfagnana is one of its plushest valleys; and the white peaks of the Apuan Alps and the high ridge of the Apennines await discovery.

The Versilia Coast

Twelve miles of uninterrupted sandy shores stretch from Torre del Lago Puccini up to Vittoria Apuana, at the border of Massa Carrara province. What would otherwise be a run-of-the-mill stretch of beach is made extraordinary by the white peaks of the Apuan Alps, which rise like snow (it's actually the glow of marble) in the distance. Viareggio Carnival (see page 251) breaks up the quiet of the winter months before summer arrives and the nightlife heats up (Lido di Camaiore and Forte dei Marmi are the most vibrant). This province is also a hub of more classical culture. Giacomo Puccini spent much of his life in his villa at Torre del Lago (hence the town's adopted name), which he chose for its proximity to the Migilarino-San Rossore-Massaciuccoli Regional Park.

■ Getting Here & Around

 By Train: Hourly trains (☎ 848-888088, www.trenitalia.it) run to Viareggio from Lucca on the Florence-to-Viareggio line, stopping first in Massarossa. For Forte dei Marmi (Querceta station), Pietrasanta and Torre del Lago, change trains in Pisa or Viareggio.

 By Bus: **Lazzi** (☎ 0583-584876) and **CLAP** (☎ 0583-587897) services link Lucca's Piazzale G. Verdi with the Versilia Coast.

 By Car: From Lucca, the **A11 Firenze-Mare** (Florence-Sea) connects to Viareggio and Lido di Camaiore via Massrossa. Just before Viareggio, you can turn onto the **A12**, which heads north to Forte dei Marmi or south through the Migilarino-San Rossore-Massaciuccoli Regional Park into the province of Pisa.

Viareggio has car rental outlets for **Avis** (Via Aurelia Nord 101, ☎ 0584-45620, www.avisautonoleggio.it), **Europcar** (Piazza Dante 1, ☎ 0584-430506, www.europcar.it), **Hertz** (Viale Marconi 107a, ☎ 0584-564499, www.hertz.it), and **Montaresi** (Via S. Martino 91, ☎ 0584-32333, fax 0584-30248). You can also rent cars at Lido di Camaiore from **Matteucci Automobili** (Via S. Andrea 10, ☎ 0584-745737).

 By Taxi: Viareggio has ranks on Piazza D. Alighieri, Piazza d'Azeglio, Piazza Puccini, and outside the train station. While Torre del Lago has cabs on Piazza del Popolo, Forte dei Marmi on Piazza Garibaldi and Via Matteotti, and Lido di Camaiore on Piazza Lemmetti, Piazza Matteotti and Piazza Castracani.

 Bicycle Rental: Bicycles can be rented in Viareggio from **Stand Cicli** (Viale Capponi ☎ 033-87759895), in Torre del Lago from **Pieri Stefano** (Viale Marconi 236, ☎ 0584-359584), and in Forte dei Marmi from **Guigi Isauro** (Via Stagio Stagi 56, ☎ 0584-80994), **Maggi Claudio** (Viale Morin 85, ☎ 0584-89529), **Maggi-Coppa** (Via A. Franceschi 4d, ☎ 0584-83258) and **Tonetti Aladino** (Via Provincale 146, ☎ 0584-89834). Farther along, in Lido di Camaiore, bicycles are available from **Paolinelli** (Viale Colombo 324, ☎ 0584-914168), from **Bertilotti Alberto** (Viale Colombo 274, ☎ 0584-617534) and from **Belli Alberto** (Via del Fortino 9, ☎ 0584-67010). In Marina di Pietrasanta they can be rented from **Bacci Renzo** (Via Tremaiola 76, Tonfano, ☎/fax 0584-745626), **Neri Mario** (Via Versilia 137, Tonfano, ☎ 0584-21021) or **Tognetti Gino** (Via Carducci 213, Tonfano, ☎ 0584-20086).

By Boat: You can pick up boats on **Viareggio Wharf** (☎ 0584-32033); see page 252 for information on boat rental.

■ Information Sources

Tourist Offices: The main **APT Versilia** (tourist office for the Versilia region) is at **Viareggio** (Piazza Mazzini 22, ☎ 0584-48881, fax 0584-48406, www.versilia.turismo.toscana.it) with smaller offices at **Massarossa** (Via Sarzanese 157, ☎ 0584-937284, fax 0584-937288), **Torre del Lago Puccini** (Viale Kennedy 1, ☎/fax 0584-359893), and along the coast in **Forte dei Marmi** (Via Franceschi 8d, ☎ 0584-80091, fax 0584-83214), **Marina di Pietrasanta** (Via Donizetti 14, Loc. Tonfano, ☎ 0584-20331, fax 0584-24555) and **Lido di Camaiore** (Piazza Umberto, ☎ 0584-617397, fax 0584-618696).

The **Migilarino-San Rossore-Massaciuccoli Regional Park** has a tourist office (Via Aurelia Nord 4, ☎ 050-525500, fax 050-533650, http://comunic.it/PARKS/Indice/ParcReg/PRMS/PRMS.htm).

Maps & Guides: *Migilarino San Rossore Massaciuccoli* (IGM, 1:25,000) covers Torre del Lago and the Versilia Coast down to the Marina di Pisa.

BATHING FEES

Anyone who's anyone in Florence owns or rents a summer retreat on the Versilia Coast, which perhaps explains why the prices are so high even to lie on its beaches. Many visitors who arrive with no knowledge of Italian bathing customs are perplexed at the practice, which generally involves forking out a minimum of €20 for a day on a sun-lounger at one of the *stabilimenti* (beach establishments). Free beaches do exist, but they tend to be either at the grimy edges of town, and are therefore small, crowded and dirty, or a car trip away along the less-developed areas of the coast. The nicest stretch of free beach (*spiaggia pubblica)* is set in pine forests, a 20-minute cycle ride south of Viareggio.

■ Sightseeing & Adventures

Torre del Lago

It was in Torre del Lago that Puccini found the inspiration to compose the majority of his operatic works, from *La Bohème* to *Turandot*, and his beautiful lakeside house is open for visits, not least during the Festival Puccinaio (see below). Set back from the shore and surrounded by bars, trees and high iron railings, the **Casa Museo di Giacomo Puccini** (Giacomo Puccini Villa-Museum) can be visited as part of a 30-minute guided tour (Piazzale Belvedere, ☎ 0584-341445, summer, 10 am-noon, 3-7 pm, winter, 10 am-noon, 2-4:30 pm, closed Mon). The tours explore not only his artistic works, but also the flora and fauna in the seaside scrub that drew him here in 1891.

Giacomo Puccini

FESTIVAL PUCCINAIO

*At two paces from Villa Puccini, the **Festival Puccinaio** (Puccini Festival, ☎ 0584-359322, www.puccinifestival.it, July-Aug, €29-€96), Torre del Lago's outdoor opera festival, draws 40,000 spectators every year to its four performances of Puccini classics. It generally features the four he wrote here: La Bohème. Tosca, Turandot and Madame Butterfly.*

Puccini spoke of this area as "Gaudio supremo, Eden empireo" (supreme joy, empyrean paradise) and it's not hard to see why: his house sits on **Lago di Massaciuccoli** (Lake Massaciuccoli), a marshy lake with a maximum depth of five feet. At 2,200 acres, the lake is equal in size to the city of Pisa.

Making up part of the Migilarino-San Rossore-Massaciuccoli Regional Park, the lake is also a protected bird sanctuary. **Bird-watching** can be organized with the managing organization, **LIPU** (Italian Society of Bird Protection, Massarosa, Via Porto 6 ☎ 0584-975567; wwwalgol.Sirius.pisa.it/lipupisa/index.htm). Their guided tours give ample opportunity to explore the *Phragmites communis* (the tallest species of grass in Italy) and to check out the 260 different bird species recorded here. Depending on the time of year, you may see grebes and cormorants, nesting swamp hawks, purple herons, little bitterns, black-winged stilts, collared pratincoles, marsh harriers, warblers, terns and gulls.

Your other alternative for visiting the area is by guided **boat** trip from the dock next to the Villa Puccini with **Eco Idea** (Piazzale Belvedere Puccini, ☎ 0360-342005, fax 0584-250252). But if you want something a little more active, there are plenty of opportunities to paddle: try **Canoa Kayak** (Via di Montramito, Loc. San Rocchino, ☎ 0584-941708) or **Kayak Airone** (Via di Montramito, Loc. San Rocchino, ☎ 056-529018). They are also the people to contact for information on the basin's regular sailing races, as well as for sailing and surfing lessons.

A long, straight tree-lined avenue leads from Torre del Lago to the coast, and it is this road that marks the boundaries with the province of Pisa (which contains the remainder of the Migilarino-San Rossore-Massaciuccoli Regional Park, see page 11, 258) to the south. North of the divide is the area known as the **Macchia Lucchese**, which stretches up from the Marina di Tore del Lago to Viareggio and contains the best of the area's free beaches (as well as most of its campgrounds). It is closed to cars, but there is a more than pleasant **nature trail** suitable for **walking** (pick it up from the Viale dei Tigli between Torre del Lago and Viareggio), **cycling** and **horseback riding.** The latter can be organized at Massarosa through **Horse Country Club** (Via Cala Grande 1, ☎ 0584-997326) or **Amici della Marcia** (Via Roma, ☎ 092-1757448).

Viareggio

Viareggio has been the most popular resort town on the Versilia Coast since the mid-19th century, but the crowds don't just come for the gorgeous climate or the wide stretches of beach. There's also the colorful winter carnival, the Liberty architecture, the seafront promenade and a picturesque harbor at the mouth of Canale Burlamacca.

Viareggio Carnival: This was envisioned in 1873 by some well-to-do youths chatting in Viareggio's Caffè del Casino, and the first parade of floats has since grown into a huge three-week procession of allegorical *carri* (wooden floats) and satirical papier-mâché caricatures. Dealing especially with current politics and customs that inspire the artisans who create them, the floats seen in procession along the seafront every February can take up to a year to perfect. They can be visited during the preparatory stages (in huge sheds) by arrangement with the carnival headquarters (Piazza Mazzini 22, ☎ 0584-962568, www.ilcarnevale.com).

The town itself straddles the Burlamacca Canal, with two pine forests (Pineta di Levante to the south and Pineta di Ponente to the north) linked by a two-mile seafront promenade, Passeggiata Regina Margherita. On this (just a 10-minute stroll from the train station) you'll find the best of the town's Art-Deco Liberty architecture, not to mention the *stabilimenti*, beachfront establishments that charge for access to the sand, monopolizing the best areas of the beach.

PROMENADE HOTSPOTS

Viareggio's history is reflected in its seafront promenade of historic bars and Liberty-style coffee houses:

The Neoclassical **Cinema Savoia** was built to a design by Alfredo Belluomini and decorated by Galileo Chini. It has all the Belle Époque stuccoes, lamps and decorations that epitomize the work of Chini, the famous majolica artist, who made his mark here.

The architecture takes an Art Nouveau twist at the **Duilio 48** department store.

The nearby **Galleria del Libro** began as a fashion house in 1929 before it was remodeled into its present Art-Deco style.

Unmistakable for its cupola, the Art-Deco **Gran Caffè Margherita**, the exclusive meeting point of Puccini and his crew, still dominates Viareggio's Viale Regina Margherita. It is the most famous of the Belluomini-Chini collaborations.

The two are also to be thanked for the grandiose façade and triumphal arch of the **Bagno Balena** with their ornate curves, rosettes and glazed roundels. The twin domed pavilions of **Bagni Martinelli** and **Bertuccelli** sit happily under multicolored overlapping tiles.

The town's harbor shelters a characteristic blend of old wooden ships, fishing boats and an impressive contingent of luxury yachts, but it also sees its share of bird life, with cormorants and herons making a trip on the *Burlamacca* motorboat (**Ecotour**, Largo Risorgimento, ☎/fax 0584-48449), along the canal to the Lago di Massaciuccoli, a worthwhile choice for any **birdwatcher**. If you prefer a more leisurely pace, contact **Polisportiva Canoa-Kayak** (Via Galvini 4, ☎ 0584-46197) to arrange **canoe** or **kayak** rental.

For those interested in sea animals (especially dolphins and whales), the cetaceous sanctuary, 10 miles out to sea, makes a great alternative. The **boat trip** with **CE.TU.S** (Darsena Europa, Via Coppino, ☎ 0335-6564469, fax 0584-389675) will also take you within sight of the Tuscan Archipelago.

Boat Charters

There are plenty of opportunities to get out into the Tyrrhenian Sea from Viareggio, with boat trips departing from the wharf throughout the summer season. If you prefer doing it yourself, you can charter a boat from any of the following organizations:

Agenzia Marittima Aliboni (Via Coppino 433, ☎ 0584-384394, fax 0584-387652, cirillo.francesco@tiscalinet.it).

Alta Marea (Via Coppino 50, ☎ 0584-34383, fax 0584-388480, nauticaltamarea@tin.it).

Captian Broker (Via Coppino 207, ☎ 0584-384222, fax 0584-396255, capitanbrokers@tiscalinet.it).

Gruppo Nautico Italiano (Via P. Savi 347, ☎/fax 0584-976216, info@gnicharter.it).

International Mackenzie (Via Coppino 433, ☎ 0584-38422, fax 0584-387951, mackenzievg@caen.it).

Marcuzzo Antonella (Via Coppino 333a, ☎/fax 0584-384595, www.marcuzzo.it).

Mediterranea (Via dei Pescatori 11, ☎/fax 0584-388362, medit.nautica@tiscalinet.it).

Time Charter (Via Coppino 333, ☎ 0584-395198, fax 0584-388075, timecharter@caen.it).

UFAN Sagramoni (Via Garibaldi 11, ☎ 0584-961012, fax 0584-962631, sagramoni@iol.it).

Viareggio Yacht Broker (Via Coppino 433, ☎/fax 0584-387402, info@viareggioyachtbroker.it).

Finally for **horseback riders**, there are many companies offering excursions into the surrounding pinewoods. In Viareggio itself, try **Associazione Ippica Burlamacco** (Via Comparini 212, ☎ 0584-387553), **Società Ippica Viareggina Maneggio Pineta di Levante** (Via Comparini 8, ☎ 0584-391176/4389028) or **Ophelia Equitazione** (Via dell'Oleificio 3, ☎ 0584-393063).

A **cycle path** runs the length of the coast, from the Migilarino-San Rossore-Massaciuccoli Regional Park to Cinquale.

Treno nei Parchi

Take the train and hike with the "park train," which links CAI trails with the Viareggio-to-Massa and Viareggio-to-Minucciano routes (in the Valdiserchio). Trains run four times daily with stop-offs at Borgo a Mozzano, Bagni di Lucca, Ghivizzano, Fornaci, Barga, Castelnuovo Garfagnana and Piazza al Serchio (€5 round-trip). For further information, contact the Centro Visite Parco Alpi Apuane (Piazza delle Erbe 1, Castelnuovo di Garfagnana, ☎ 0583-65169, fax 0583-648435, www.garfagnanavacanze.it, www.garfprod.it) or the Valle del Serchio Tourist Office (Via Vallisneri, Castelnuovo di Garfagnana, ☎ 0583-641007, fax 0583-644354, www.corrierdigarfagnana.com).

Join the Locals: In August, the local tourist boards and nature-loving organizations get together to offer guided cycling and walking excursions into the Apuan Alps departing from **Forte dei Marmi** (☎ 0584-80091, in Italian only), cycling races for non-professionals, such as the **Florence-Viareggio** (☎ 0584-966819) and amateur mountain races from **Pietrasanta** (☎ 0584-795570).

Camiore

A few miles north of Viareggio, backed by pine forest and a game park, **Lido di Camaiore** is as popular for its nightlife as it is for its beaches. It is the beach resort of inland Camaiore, a small picturesque town of Roman origin, set amid olive trees. It is noteworthy for its Romanesque **Collegiata** (Piazza di San Bernardino) with an imposing 14th-century Campanile, and 11th-century **Chiesa di San Michele** with the **Museo d'Arte Sacra** (Museum of Sacred Art, Via IV Novembre, ☎ 0584-980551) next door in the Confraternita del SS Sacramento.

The 11th-century Benedictine **Badia di San Pietro** (one km/0.6 mile) offers a worthwhile **cycle** out of town from Camaiore. From here, you can continue onto the Romanesque **Pieve SS Giovanni e Stefano** (three km/two miles), with a mullion-windowed bell tower built in 810, and up the slopes of Monte Magno (six kilometers/four miles of quite heavy climbs). From the top, you can continue along the road to Lucca (18 km/11 miles), or follow the branch off towards Monte Pitoro and Massarosa (three kilometers/two miles).

A pleasant three-hour **hike** in the foothills of the Apuan Alps starts from Lombrici (just under two miles from Camaiore), where a muletrack (#104) leads through woods to the foot of Monte Prana (1,220 m/4,002 feet) and up to Campo all'Orzo. From here a ridge leads over Monte Ciuraglia (850 m/2,778 feet) and back down the north side of Monte Prana. You can return around the mountain or extend your walk up Monte Piglione (1,232 m/4,041 feet).

Pietrasanta

Continuing along the coast from Lido di Camaiore, you'll arrive at the small but important bathing center of **Marina di Pietrasanta**. It is known as the "four sister beach" due to the four adjacent areas of Fiumetto, Tonfano, Motrone and Focette, which make up its five-kilometer (three-mile) stretch of beach.

To the north of town, the 224 acres of the public Parco della Versiliana is a great area for short bursts of walking, cycling and horseback riding. It is part of the remains of the pine forest that once covered the Tyrrhenian Coast north of the Arno, and its cluster and stone pines, Mediterranean scrub and picturesque canals are well dotted with marked trails. To arrange **horseback riding** in the park, contact **Maneggio La Versiliana** (Parco della Versiliana, ☎ 0584-24280), **Maneggio La Torretta** (Via Torretta, ☎ 0584-23337) or **Associazione Ippica-Club Riviera della Versilia** (c/o Luciano Borzonasca, Via Carducci 4, ☎ 0584-745733).

By **bicycle**, follow the track through the park to reach Via Nizza, and you can continue on through Forte dei Marmi to Vittoria Apuana (12 km/seven miles). Return through Fiumetto to pass **Villa la Versiliana**, where the poet Gabriele D'Annunzio once lived. The natural theater to its left is the summer venue for the town's drama, ballet and music festivities. You can continue south along the cycle path to Viareggio (22 km/14 miles).

Another bicycle route goes from Tonfano (the center of Marina di Pietrasanta) inland to **Pietrasanta** (seven km/four miles) along a long and straight tree-lined avenue. The town is the ancient capital of the Medici-run *Capitanato*, which was founded in 1255 by Guiscardo da Pietrasanta, Lucca's *podestà*, and its Piazza del Duomo is the site of much of the area's most luxurious architecture: the tripartite marble façade and large central rose window of the 14th-century **Cattedrale di**

San Martino; the **Battistero**; the arched **Chiesa di Sant'Agostino** with its adjoining frescoed cloister; **Palazzo Moroni**; and the **clock tower**. It's all over-looked by the **Rocchetta Arrighina** (a small Lombard fort rebuilt in 1487) at the top of the hill. If you arrive in summer, enjoy the marble exhibitions held by local art studios.

You can **hike** along traces of the Via Francigena from Pietrasanta to Camaiore. The five-hour route (picked up near Pietrasanta cemetery) takes you past the vil-lage of Valdicastello, where poet Giosué Carducci was born.

MARBLE IN PIETRASANTA

With the marble mountains of the Apuan Alps on its doorstep, Pietrasanta quickly rose to prominence in the marble industry. Impor-tant local sculptors made their mark on the town architecture: the bap-tismal font in the cathedral by Bonuccio Pardini (1389), the *logetta* of the Chiesa di Sant'Agostino by Leonardo Riccomanno (1431) and the decoration of the cathedral chancel (1502-07) by Lorenzo Stagi, with son Stagio later adding the two holy water fonts and 16th-century can-delabra. Find out about their inspiration in the **Museo dei Bozzetti** (Museum of Sculptor's Models, Via Sant'Agostino 1, ☎ 0584-791122). **CAMP** (Viale Marconi, ☎ 0584-733363) has a permanent exhibition on local craftsmanship.

Pietrasanta stands at the foot of the hills that link the plain to the Apuan Alps and as such is well placed for **hikes** into the mountains. Most start from nearby Stazzema (see page 259) and Cardoso (see page 260-61).

Boat rental can be arranged with **Versilia Nautica** (Viale Roma 94, Marina di Pietrasanta, ☎ 0584-745366).

Forte dei Marmi

Immersed in the green of the Mediterranean *macchia*, Forte dei Marmi, the youn-gest *comune* in Versilia, is famed for its exclusive hotels, stupendous villas and luxury beach chalets. The town's 100-m (328-foot) jetty was erected in the 16th century for loading the quarried marble that came from the marble mountains backing the beach. This stone and the **Forte** (built 1782) gave the town its name (fort of marble).

In the 1930s, the Fiat-founding Agnelli family made the town famous by buying a summer residence here, and the holiday home trade hasn't stopped since. The maze of tree-lined streets that lead off Roma Imperiale, to the south of the historic center, hold the plushest villas and celebrity hotspots: Giorgio Armani and Miuccia Prada both own houses here and Naomi Campbell is a regular – her ex-boyfriend owns Twiga, one of the town's most expensive beach clubs.

Just out of town, the **spa** areas of **Terme della Versilia** and **Centro Termale del Benessere** are set in a 6.2-acre tree-filled park.

> **Tip:** Every July and September Forte dei Marmi sees the arrival of the **International Festival of Satire**. If you arrive out of season, take in the year-round **Museo per la Satira e la Caricatura** (Center for Collection & Study of Satire & Carica-ture, Fortino di Leopoldo 1, Piazza Garibaldi 1, ☎ 0584-86277).

A **cycle** path links the town to Marina di Pietrasanta (four km/three miles), from where you can pick up many of the area's best trails (see above). However, there are also routes heading north, such as the 11-km/seven-mile route through **Strettoia** (the center of Versilia's wine production) to the **Lombard Castello Aghinolfi** (c. 600), left, where a magnificent view of the Versilia coast awaits.

Another 11-km/seven-mile route takes you through olive groves to **Valdicastello**, the birthplace of the poet Giosué Carducci (1835-1907; house open Tues, Wed, Fri-Sat, 4-7 pm, Thurs, 9 am-noon, 4-7 pm). Along the way, watch for the Romanesque **Pieve di SS Giovanni e Felicita**, the oldest and most famous religious monument in the region. Its façade is decorated with a wonderful early-14th century rose window.

A shorter road bike route leads to **Seravezza** (8½ km/five miles) and first takes you along Via Provinciale toward Vallecchia, a road that was originally marked out by Michelangelo when arranging the transportation of marble in the 11th and 12th centuries (see page 260).

The best **hiking** trails from the vicinity depart into the Apuan Alps from Levigliani and Arni (see page 261).

Vittoria Apuana

The long beach of Vittoria Apuana joins Forte dei Marmi with Marina di Massa. It has one of the most bountiful stretches of free beach thanks to the 20 acres of the WWF Oasis Dune Forte dei Marmi, which protects one of Tuscany's last strips of sand dunes and wild flora. It also includes a **nature walk** and a botanical garden.

Where to Eat

LOCAL FLAVORS

Cacciucco alla Viareggina – Locally caught fish flavored with tomato, garlic and hot peppers.
Castagnaccio – Chestnut cake.
Farro con il pesce – Spelt with fish.
Focaccia del calvatore – Quarryman's bread.
Sparnocchi con fagioli – Prawns and beans.
Triglie con fave, pomodori e basilico – Mullet with broad beans, tomato and basil.
Zuppa alla frantoiana – Ham, bean, potato, carrot and celery soup dressed with newly-pressed oil.

In a region famed for its seafood, you can't really go wrong when choosing a daily special from the board at **Angelo** (Viale Europa 20, ☎ 0584-341668, $$$) in Torre Del Lago. The same applies in Lago di Massaciuccoli at **Da Cecco** (Belvedere Puccini, ☎ 0584-341022, $$), although many are drawn here by the local history as much as for the food.

In Viareggio, there are almost as many restaurants as there are hotels. Popular choices include **Cabreo** (Via Firenze 14, ☎ 0584-54643, $$), **Il Garibaldino** (Via Fratti 66, ☎ 0584-961337, $$), **Il Patriarca** (Viale Carducci 79, ☎ 0584-53126, $$$) and **L'Oca Bianca** (Via Coppino 409, ☎ 0584-84030, $$). Opt for the seasonal fish dishes.

Ariston Mare (Viale Colombo 660, ☎ 0584-904747, $$) and **Emilio e Bona** (Loc. Lombrici 22, ☎ 0584-989289, $$) are the best of the bunch in Lido di Camaiore and Camaiore respectively. Again, both are well known for their fish dishes, but Emilio e Bona just takes the edge for its creative approach to local catches.

In Pietrasanta, **Enoteca Marucci** (Via Garibaldi 40, ☎ 0584-791962, $$) provides a simple but tasty menu to accompany its vast range of local wines.

In Forte dei Marmi, the Michelin-starred **Lorenzo** (Via Carducci 61, ☎ 0584-84030, $$$) takes top billing. **Bistrot** (Viale Franceschini 14, ☎ 0584-89879, $$$) and **Gilda** (Via Arenile 85, ☎ 0584-880397, $$) are also worth trying if you're staying in town for a few days.

Where to Stay

 Versilia has more than 600 hotels on its 12-mile stretch of beach, with 100 one-star options in Viareggio alone. Here are some of the best:

Villa Rosy ☆ (Viale Marconi 315, ☎ 0584-341350, fax 0584-354141, viallarosy@viareggio.it, $$) in Torre del Lago.

In Viareggio, the majority of one-star hotels are on the roads between the train station and the sea front. For something a little more upmarket, try **Lib - erty** ☆☆☆ (Viale Manin 18, ☎ 0584-46247, fax 0584-4249, hotelliberty@viareggio.it, $$$) or **Astor** ☆☆☆☆ (Lungomare Carducci 54, ☎ 0584-50301, fax 0584-55181, www.astorviareggio.com, $$$$) on Viareggio's promenade with splendid views over the sea, indoor heated pool and renowned fish restaurant La Conchiglia.

At the Marina di Pietrasanta, your best options are **Aqua Marina** ☆☆☆ (Via Bellini 5, ☎ 0584-23768, $$$$), **Ermione** ☆☆☆☆ (Viale Roma 183, ☎ 0584-745852, $$$$) or **Lombardi** ☆☆☆☆ (Viale Roma 27, ☎ 0584-745848, $$$$). The best cheaper places are inland at Pietrasanta itself. Try **Stipino** ☆☆ (Via Traversagna 3/5, ☎ 0584-790031, vitalianove@hotmail.com, $) or **Da Piero** ☆☆ (Via Provinciale 50, ☎ 0584-71448, fax 0584-72421, stipino@tiscalinet.it, $).

At glitzy Forte dei Marmi, the best-placed budget options include **Villa Elena** ☆☆ (Viale Morin 36, ☎ 0584-787532, $$), **Le Pleiadi** ☆☆☆ (Via M. Civitali 51, ☎ 0584-881188, fax 0584-881653, lepleiadi@versilia.toscana.it, $$$) and **Marsiliana** ☆☆☆ (Via N. Sauro 19, Forte dei Marmi, ☎ 0584-787151, www.marsiliana.it, $$$), all around five minutes from the beach.

Bigger spenders should opt instead for the celeb haunts of **Augustus** ☆☆☆☆☆ (Viale Morin 169, ☎ 0584-787200, fax 0584-787102, augustus@versilia.toscana.it, $$$$$) and **Byron** ☆☆☆☆☆ (Viale Morin 46, ☎ 0584-787052, fax 0584-787152, byron@versilia.net, $$$$$).

Lucca

You can book into the guest rooms of the **Migilarino-San Rossore-Massaciuccoli Regional Park** through the park head office (Via Aurelia Nord 4, ☎ 050-525500, fax 050-533650), with the option of renting rooms in buildings of historical and artistic interest, such as the Medici Villa of Coltano or the Sterpaia of San Rossore.

The few *agriturismi* are near Camiore and Massarossa. Only one has a pool: **Fattoria di Campo Romano** near Massarossa (Loc. Piano del Quercione, ☎/fax 0584-92231, $$$$).

There are plenty of campgrounds in the pinewoods stretching between Torre del Lago Puccini and Forte dei Marmi:

Bosco Verde ☆ (Viale Kennedy 5, Loc. Cordone ☎ 0584-359343, fax 0584-341891, www.boscoverde.com, $), **Europa** ☆ (Viale dei Tigli, ☎ 0584-350707, fax 0584-342592, www.europacamp.it, $) and **Burlamacco** ☆ (Viale Marconi 142, ☎ 0584-359544, $) are all near Torre del Lago. **La Pineta** ☆☆ (Via dei Lecci, ☎/fax 0584-383397, $), **Paradiso** ☆☆ (Viale dei Tigli, ☎ 0584-392005, $) and **Viareggio** ☆ (Via Comparini 1, ☎ 0584-391012, fax 0584-395462, campingviareggio@tin.it, $) are all a pleasant cycle out of town from Viareggio. **Camaiore** has **Versilia Mare** ☆☆ (Via Trieste 175, ☎ 0584-619862, fax 0584-618691, versiliamare@tiscalinet.it, $). Farther up the coast, there's the **Internazionale Versilia** inland from **Forte dei Marmi** (Via V. Apuana 33, Fraz. Querceta, ☎ 0584-880764, fax 0584-752118, campingversilia@tiscalinet.it, $).

The Apuan Alps

This dramatic mountain chain runs parallel to the north Tuscan coast for 40 km/25 miles. It is a striking mix of rugged summits and enclosed valleys, chestnut woods and charming villages, green plateaus and streams cascading into waterfalls, natural caves (including the largest in Italy at Monte Corchia) and marble quarries. All are united in the 168,000-acre **Parco Naturale delle Alpi Apuane** (the Apuan Alps Nature Park) and equally divided between the two provinces of Lucca and Massa Carrara. Rising up to 1,947 m (6,386 feet), the park constitutes one of the largest limestone massifs in the world, with the best of the walks concentrated in the peaks east of Forte dei Marmi and Pietrasanta, around Pania della Croce (1,859 m/6,098 feet) and Monte Forato (1,223 m/4,011 feet). But it's not just about great walking. There's also rock climbing, caving, hang-gliding, mountain biking and horseback riding to be enjoyed.

■ Getting Here & Around

By Car: To take in the park at its best, you really have to travel by car. The park is easily reached from the north or south along the **A12 Genoa-Livorno** highway (take Versilia, Massa or Carrara exits). From Versilia, take the **SS1** through Pietrasanta to Seravezza and on; from Massa, take the **Provinciale 4** for Antona and the Passo del Vestito; from Carrara, take the **Provinciale 446** towards Equi Terme.

By Bus: Lazzi (☎ 0583-584876) and **CLAP** (☎ 0583-587897) run fairly frequent bus routes from Lucca, Massa Carrara, Pietrasanta, Castelnuovo di Garfagnana, Forte dei Marmi and Pietrasanta to the Alps. Those from Pietrasanta are the most useful, with services regularly departing into the mountains from the central Piazza Matteotti. Change at Serravezza for

Stazzema and Levigliani. Forte dei Marmi also has good links to Seravezza, Levigliani, Stazzema and Farnocchia.

■ Information Sources

Tourist Offices: The main information center for the Apuan Alps is the **Centro Accoglienza Visitatori del Parco** (Park Welcome Center) at **Castenuovo Garfagnana** (Piazza Erbe 1, ☎/fax 0583-315300, www.parcapuane.toscana.it) and Via C. del Greco 11, ☎/fax 0584-756144, with a smaller information office at **Equi Terme** (☎ 0585-97445). The tourist information at **Seravezza** (Via Corrado del Greco 11, ☎/fax 0584-756144) is also the headquarters of the **Communità Montana Alta Versilia** (High Versilia Mountain Community, Via Delatre 69, ☎ 0583-756275).

Guides & Maps: The best hiking map is the *Alpi Apuane, Carta dei Sentieri e dei rifugi* 1:25,000 (Edizioni Multigraphic, Firenze), but there are also three naturalist guides of note: *I fiori delle Apuane, le guide del Parco n.1* (Flowers of the Apuan Alps), *I funghi delle Apuane, le guide del Parco n.2* (Mushrooms of the Apuan Alps) and *Le orchidee delle Apuane, le guide del Parco n.3* (Orchids of the Apuan Alps). All published by Baroni editore, Viareggio, 1994.

■ Sightseeing

Seravezza, a little town at the foot of the Apuan Alps, is delimited by the two rivers from which it takes its name (Serra and Vezza). In a mountainous territory characterized by marble quarries, it is unsurprisingly one of the biggest working centers for marble in the region. Michelangelo came here in person to choose the raw materials for his work. It was also an important summer resort.

Ammanati designed a **Palazzo Mediceo** here in 1555 as a seasonal residence for Cosimo I, although he never inhabited it. Today it contains the **Museo del Lavoro e delle Tradizioni Popolari** (Museum of Work and Folklore Traditions, ☎ 0584-756100). The town's other main attraction is inside the 16th-century **Duomo**. It houses the precious polychrome marble baptismal font created by Stagi from Pietrasanta.

Continue on for a couple of miles and you arrive at **Stazzema**. It is a hiking hot spot, well-placed as it is on the slopes of Monte Matanna, surrounded by the peaks of the Pania della Croce and Monte Corchia. It's also within reach of the caves of Antro del Corchia, the karst Marmitte dei Giganti, the peat bogs of Fociomboli, the alpine grasslands of Mosceta and the massifs of Monte Procinto and Monte Forato.

The **Museo Storico della Resistanza** in nearby Sant'Anna (Historical Museum of the Resistance, Piazza Don Lazzeri, ☎ 0584-772025) remembers the 561 inhabitants killed by retreating Nazis in World War II.

■ Adventures on Foot

The Apuan Alps are not short of hiking routes and, quite unusually, for the country, they are all well-marked according to the conventional red and white international route-marking system (the blue markers, without numbers, indicate shortcuts to the mountain summits). Long-distance paths include the three-day **Piglione Trekking Route** (pick it up from Metato, near Camaiore) and the eight-day **Apuane Trekking Path**, which follows the ridge from north to south (marked by "AT").

Shorter routes can be joined in and around Seravezza, Stazzema, Cardoso, Levigliani, Arni, Lago di Vagli, Resceto and Seranaia, the best of these are outlined below.

The most worn route from **Seravezza** takes you between the dizzy mountain heights and green woods of Pania della Croce to Monte Altissimo (1,589 m/5,212 feet). Start the route from Azzano, and you can also approach the mountain on the *vie di Lizza* (the zigzagging marble roads) once used by quarrymen to transport the blocks downhill. From Azzano, you can also pick up the route to the quarries of Cervaiole, Monte Cavalla (where Michelangelo lived between 1518 and 1520) and the Galleria del Cipollaio.

MICHELANGELO'S ROAD

Local marble provided Michelangelo with the material for masterpieces such as *David*, but with prices so high and transportation so difficult and dangerous, he decided to take matters into his own hands. The result was a new road, built to transport the huge blocks to the sea. But the road was thought lost until traces of it were discovered several years ago in the most overgrown part of the Apuan Alps: the Valley of Monte Carchio. It can be started from Serravezza by following the road alongside the Serra River , where a barrier marks the start of the trail to Monte Altissimo. After crossing a stream (not much of the bridge remains so be prepared to jump from one stone to the next), Michelangelo's Road is easily recognizable by its three-foot-long paving stones squared to perfection and fitted together with symmetrical precision.

From **Stazzema**, you can easily reach the spectacular *via ferrata* (climbing walls) of Procinto, one of the region's most challenging rock climbs, along #5. Other trails (#5 then #121 or #126) take you into the southern group of the Apuan Alps whether you choose the short two-hour trek up **Monte Matanna** (1,317 m/4,320 feet), or prefer to base yourself at the Rifugio Alpe della Grotta (CAI Forte dei Marmi, ☎ 0584-777051, daily, mid-June-mid-Dec, Sats and public holidays for the rest of the year, sleeps 52). This is a good starting point for treks up **Monte Nona** (1,291 m/4,234 feet), Monte Forato (1,223 m/4,011 feet) and Pania Secca (1,711 m/5,612 feet), where a second *rifugio* awaits – Rifugio Enrico Rossi (CAI Lucca, ☎ 0583-710386, daily, July-Aug, public holidays for the rest of the year, sleeps 20).

The amazing natural arch of **Monte Forato** (26 m/85 feet high by 32 m/105 feet wide) can be reached via mule tracks from **Cardoso.** The main routes are #8 and #12, the latter being the shortest and also the steepest (three hours through a thick chestnut forest). Looking through the arch you can see the towns of Pruno and Cardoso and, in the other direction, the Versilian Coast.

Mount Cyclops: The natural arch of Monte Forato lies between Stazzema and Vergèmoli. The vast *finestra* (window) cut into the mountain crest is often compared to the eye of a Cyclops and, according to local legend, there is one moment every year when the setting sun shines through the hole and casts a sunny beam on the darkened villages to the east.

Another route from Cardoso takes you the difficult but rewarding four hours to the Grotta del Vento (#6, see page 263 for entrance information).

Easier itineraries can be picked up from **Retignano** (including an easy CAI-marked trail into the alpine grasslands of Campiglia and Gordici), **Terrinca** (including a mule track through ancient chestnut woods), **Pruno** (including the trail to the Acqua Pendante waterfalls) and from Monte Pasquillo to Monte Folgorito (along the Gothic Line). South of Stazzema at **Farnocchia**, you can take a path down to the war memorial at **Sant'Anna**; another itinerary goes up to **Monte Gabberi** (1,108 m/3,634 feet), where there are lovely views over the coastline.

The north group of peaks can be reached from **Levigliani**. The five-hour Levigliani-to-Pania della Croce (#9 then #126) takes you past the Rifugio Giuseppe del Freo (CAI Viareggio, ☎ 0584-778007, daily, mid-June to mid-Sept, Sats and public holidays for the rest of the year, sleeps 32) up to the panoramic peak of **Pania della Croce** (1,859 m/6,098 feet).

The five-hour **Passo-di-Croce-to-Mosceta** route (#11, #9 and #129) passes the Rifugio Giuseppe del Freo en route to Monte Corchia, and the six-hour **Arni-to-Monte-Fiocca** route (#3, #31 and #144) takes you around the 1,437-m (4,713-foot) Monte Fiocca and over the Passo di Fiocca (1,560 m/5,117 feet) for an impressive view of the marble mountains.

From **Lago di Vagli**, you can reach the highest ridges of the Apuan Alps. Some of the best walks head southwest into the Tambura Valley before picking up #35 to Monte Facoletta (1,620 m/5,314 feet) or #144 to the peak of Monte Sumbra (1,765 m/5,789 feet). Route #177 climbs up to the **Passo della Focolaccia** (1,642 m/5,386 feet) with views to the Alps' highest point, Monte Pisanino (1,946 m/6,383 feet) and #179 that takes you to the top of **Monte Grondilice** (1,805 m/5,920 feet) and into Massa Carrara territory.

Lucca

GHOST TOWN

Created after World War II, the artificial **Lago di Vagli** (Vagli Lake) covers the town of Fabbriche di Carèggine, which reappears every 10 years when the electricity company, ENEL, empties the lake for maintenance (the next showing is in 2014). As it drains, the ghostly village reappears: first church steeple, then campanile, stone house, bridge and finally the dilapidated paving stones, which you are allowed to walk upon. If you arrive out of drainage season, you can rent boats at **Vagli Sotto**, which come with instructions on how to row to the church tower, which is always visible above the water.

You can reach the rock walls from nearby **Seranaia** (four hours), which also sits within reach of the mountain huts (Rifugio Aronte, Rifugio Garnerone and Rifugio Monte Grondilice). Many routes depart from the huts into Massa Carrara (see page 270).

Nature Walks: Established in a much older geological era than the Apennines, the steep forms of the Apuan Alps contrast sharply with the gentle hills of

Garfagnana from which they arise. Their calcareous rock faces have interested naturalists from at least the 17th century on, when Galileo, Andrea Cesalpino, and Silvio Bocconi, the botanist of the Grand Duke of Tuscany (who was seeking herbal plants and remedies), among others, came here to classify the plants, flowers, and animals. Among their discoveries was a rare alpine plant, which still lives here and dates back to the last Ice Age.

There are walking and bird-watching opportunities at the **LIPU Oasi di Campocatino** (Campocatino Bird Sanctuary, Vagli Sotto, ☎ 0583-664103, daily in summer, Sun only in winter). Walks (along *strada bianca* suitable for mountain bikers) take you around the Lago di Vagli and along to the Eremo di San Viviano. There's an educational footpath up through the glacial basin to Monte Volsi.

Flora & Fauna

With beech, black alder, bay oak, cluster-pine, chestnut woods, holm oaks and alpine-like grasslands, the Apuan Alps offer an interesting mix of vegetation and an equally diverse range of fauna. Two thirds of Italy's known species grow here, and in late spring the upland meadows are carpeted with flowers. There are ferns, butcher brooms, sorrels, maidenhair and saxifrages in the underwood; wild boar, marten, mice and deer in the shrub; and coral choughs (the park symbol), woodpeckers, red-legged partridges (above), sand-martins and golden eagles in the air. There are also peregrine falcons, kestrels and buzzards; short-eared owls, barn owls, little owls and tawny owls; ravens, alpine accentors, black redstarts and migrants such as wry-necks, cuckoos and wall-creepers to be seen.

 Rock Climbing: The Apuan Alps have plenty of rock faces and *vie ferrate* for free climbing, with challenging climbs such as the Pizzo d'Uccello, Procinto, Penna di Sumbra and Monte Nona. The most impressive is the 200-m (650-foot) isolated rock tower called **Procinto** (mentioned in Dante's *Divine Comedy*), whose rock walls, along with those of Pizzo d'Uccello to the north, are the finest of the many climbing areas in the zone.

For information on climbing in the mountains, contact the local branch of the CAI: **Lucca** (☎ 0583-710386), **Barga** (Piazza Angelio 5, Fri, ☎ 0583-724125, 9-11 pm) or **Castelnuovo di Garfagnana** (Via V Emanuele 5, ☎ 0583-74352).

 Caving: There are more than 1,300 caves in the Alps, but most can be visited only with a cave tour-guide or require a high level of expertise. Still, walkways, steps and lighting have been installed in part of the Antro del Corchia, the Grotta del Vento and the Grotta d'Equi Terme to make them easier for novices to tour.

The 1,200-m (3,936-foot) deep **Antro del Corchia** occupies part of the underbelly of Monte Corchia (near Stazzema), one of the largest known karst systems in Italy and one of the deepest caverns in the world. Its network of grottoes, canyons, large chambers, "waterfalls" of stalactites, galleries and branching passageways extends for 60 km (37 miles).

You can visit the 1,978-m (6,488-foot) cavern gallery of the Antro del Corchia, the largest in the park. It is divided into three branches via two entrances: one at Buca d'Eolo (1,100 m/3,608 feet) and the other at Buca del Serpente (200 m/656 feet). The itinerary takes you past the Galleria delle Stalatatti (Stalactite Gallery), the Galleria degli Inglese (English Gallery) before reaching the *ramo del fiume* (river branch) and the Laghetto del Venerdi (Friday Lake).

Getting There: From Forte dei Marmi (the nearest train station), CLAP buses run to Levigliani, from where a free shuttle bus takes you to the cave. Tickets should be reserved in advance from Foresteria del Parco Regionale delle Alpi Apuane (Via IV Novembre 70, Levigliani, ☎/fax 0584-778405, www.antrocorchia.it, Apr-Nov, 1:30-7:30 pm, €10.50, conc. €8).

The Real Thing

Those who prefer to go caving and potholing in the Apuan Alps on their own should contact the local branches of **CAI Gruppo Speleologico** (the caving division of the Club Alpino Italiano) at Lucca (☎ 0583-710386), **Barga** (Piazza Angelio 5, Fri, ☎ 0583-724125, 9-11 pm) or **Castelnuovo di Garfagnana** (Via V Emanuele 5, ☎ 0583-74352). The head office is in Florence (CAI Gruppo Speleologico, Via del Proconsolo 10).

You can find yellow signs marking easy potholes on the road from Arni to Castelnuovo di Garfagnana (down below Tre Fiumi).

The nearby **Grotta del Vento** (Fornolasco, Vergemoli, ☎ 0583-722024, fax 0583-722053, www.grottadelvento.com), "the wind cave," is considered Tuscany's best. It has an extraordinary variety of feautres such as vibrant stalactites and stalagmites, polychrome earth-flows, curtains of alabaster, crystal-encrusted lakes, subterranean streams and bizarre forms of erosion. The main attractions are the Sala del Ciondolo (Pendant Room), the Camino Rosa (Pink Chimney), the Sala dei Monumenti (Room of the Monuments), the Galleria dei Drappeggi (Curtained Gallery), the Baratro dei Giganti (Giants' Abyss), the Salone dell'Infinito (Room of Infinity), a mysterious subterranean river whose passage has polished the cliff sides, vertical crevices and a small bridge suspended over an abyss plunging down 24 m (79 feet).

Getting There: **CLAP** buses run from Forte dei Marmi station to the Grotta d'Equi Terme (near Fivizzano, see page 279).

■ Adventures on Snow

 There is a ski resort near Carèggine (☎ 0583-661061, fax 0583-661062) with slopes at Formica, Vianova (with ski school) and Monte la Cima (the longest piste is three kilometers/two miles).

There are also excellent snow climbs in the Alpi Apuane, especially on the **Pania delle Croce** (north) and the crests of **Pisanino**. Contact CAI branches for further information.

La Garfagnana & the Valle del Serchio

Over the wild and rocky Apuan Alps, the green valley of the Garfagnana offers a pleasant reprieve before the slopes rise again to the heights of the Apennines. It is an area well-signposted and mapped with the best walks found to the east of the Serchio Valley around Bagni di Lucca and in the mountains of the Parco Naturale dell'Orecchiella in the far north. Although higher than the Apuans, these mountains are tamer, more accessible and thickly wooded.

■ Getting Here & Around

 By Train: From Lucca hourly trains (☎ 848-888088, www.trenitalia.it) running the length of the Serchio Valley to Aulla stop at Borgo a Mozzano, Bagni di Lucca, Barga, Castelnuovo di Garfagnana and Piazza al Serchio. There are added services in the summer when the **Treno Estate** (summer train, ☎ 0583-641007, www.corrieredigarfagnana.com, €5, free for under eights) runs between Viareggio and Municciano. It stops at Lucca, Borgo a Mozzano, Bagni di Lucca, Ghivizzano, Barga and Castelnuovo di Garfagnana.

 By Bus: CLAP (☎ 0583-587897) bus routes link Lucca to local villages Bagni di Lucca, Barga, Borgo a Mozzano, Camiore, Capannori, Castiglione di Garfagnana, Cinquale, Fabbriche di Vallico, Isola Santa, Pietrasanta and Serravezza.

 By Car: From Lucca, the parallel **SS12** and **SP2** run to Borgo a Mozzano. From there the SS12 turns east to Bagni di Lucca, and the SS445 joins the SP2 as it winds through the length of the Garfagnana Valley to Aulla. The Garfagnana can also be approached via the panoramic SS13 over the Apuan Alps from Massa Carrara.

 By Bicycle: Bicycles can be rented at Castelnuovo di Garfagnana (Cicli Maggi 2, Via N Fabrizi 40, ☎/fax 0583-639166).

■ Information Sources

 Tourist Offices: The main office for the Valle del Serchio is in **Castelnuovo di Garfagnana** (Via Vallisneri, ☎ 0583-641007, fax 0583-644354, www.corrierdigarfagnana.com), with smaller offices at Borgo a Mozzano (Via Umberto 2, ☎ 0583-888881 and **Barga** (Piazza Angelico 3 ☎ 0583-723499).

Adventure Information: For information on hiking and other activities in the zone, it's also worth popping into one of the two **Communità Montane**, Media Valle del Serchio in Borgo a Mozzano (Via Umberto 100, ☎ 0583-88346), on the road from Lucca just before Bagni di Lucca, and Garfagnana in Castelnuovo di Garfagnana (Via V. Emanuele 9, ☎ 0583-644911). The **Centro Visite Parco Alpi Apuan**e can also be found at Castelnuovo di Garfagnana (Piazza delle Erbe 1, ☎ 0583-65169, fax 0583-648435, www.garfagnanavacanze.it, www.garfprod.it), while that for the **Parco Naturale dell'Orecchiella** is at Corfino (☎ 0583-619098).

Maps: The best hiking maps are the widely available 1:25,000 Multigraphics.

■ Valle del Serchio

Sightseeing

 Borgo a Mozzano: The Serchio Valley begins with one of the area's most photographed attractions: the **Ponte del Diavolo** (also known as the Ponte della Maddalena) at Borgo a Mozzano. This unusual 13th-century construction – a wide bridge whose five arches of differing sizes and heights peak drastically in the center – is the valley's symbol and source of much history and intrigue. It has been attributed to Matilde di Canossa (around 1100),

Ponte del Diavolo

Natale Santi (about 500 years later), the famous Lucchese *condottiere* Castruccio Castracani and even to the Devil (hence the name). A local legend tells that the Devil aided in its construction in return for the soul of the first to cross it. Fortunately, St Giuliano, who made the deal, out-maneuvered the Devil by sending across a dog.

From **Fabbriche di Vàlico**, to the west, **trails** lead along the Tùrrite River, north to Vergèmoli and the Grotta del Vento, or west to the Pania Secca crest (1,711 m/5,612 feet).

Bagni di Lucca: Farther along the SS12, the spa town of Bagni di Lucca spreads out in the lower valley of the Lima River. The buildings that house its 19 **thermal springs** (Complesso Termale di Casa Boccella e Jean Varraud, Piazza San Martino 11, ☎ 0583-87221, www.termebagnidilucca.it, Mar-Nov, treatments from €16), grew up in the early 19th century when Elisa Baciocchi made the town fashionable among Europe's elite, ensuring the patronage of English poets Byron, Shelley, Robert and Elisabeth Browning, as well as Heine, Dumas, Strauss and Liszt.

Beyond Bagni di Lucca looms the **Orrido di Botri**, an imposing and spectacular calcareous-stone gorge whose sheer vertical walls have been dug into the heart of the mountain by the waters of the Marianna and Ribellino rivers. The steep walls – some of which rise to a height of 200 m (656 feet) – have been incorporated into a nature reserve. Access to the reserve's 12 **nature walks** is permitted only with a guide authorized by the Corpo Forestale dello Stato di Lucca (☎ 0583-955525). The reception center is at the entrance at Ponte Gaio. It's worth your time to hike here: the canyon is quiet and eerie, with color and atmosphere provided by the butterworts, columbines and rural primroses that grow at the foot of its walls, and the kestrels, sparrow hawks, buzzards, honey-buzzards and peregrine falcons that fly overhead.

Coreglia Antelminelli: From Orrido, the road descends to Coreglia Antelminelli, an ancient fortress of the Rolandinghi family (medieval lords of southern Garfagnana), which was later fortified by the Antelminelli of Ghivazzano. In a stunning position in the Valle dell'Ania, the historical center still partially preserves its medieval fortress appearance. Its industry has revolved around the artisan manufacture of plaster statues since the 16th century and it merits a visit if only to admire the statues drying in the factory grounds or displayed in the **Museo della Figurina dei Gesso** (Museum of Plaster of Paris Figurines, Palazzo Vanni, ☎ 0583-78082, summer, Mon-Fri, 8 am-1 pm, Sat-Sun, 10 am-1 pm, 4-7 pm, winter, Mon-Fri, 8 am-1 pm, €3, conc. €2).

Barga: Second of the two important towns in the Valle del Serchio, Barga has conserved intact the narrow winding streets of its medieval town plan. The steep Via del Pretorio, dotted with pretty piazzette of Renaissance palaces, leads to the hilltop **Duomo**, built of the honey-blond stone known as *albarese di Barga* and fronted by a terrace with a panorama of the town's rooftops, the surrounding mountains and the villa-dotted hills. Originally dated pre-1000, this cathedral is the fruit of almost continuous renovations between the 11th and 14th centuries (with further restoration after earthquake damage in 1920). Above the side-door is the most famous frieze, known as *Agape*, which is attributed to Biduino, and inside, a 13th-century marble pulpit by Guido Bigarelli and mid-12th-century polychrome wooden statue of *St Christopher,* as well as various terracottas from the della Robbia workshop. The **Museo Civico del Territorio di Barga** (Palazzo

Lucca

Pretorio, Arringo del Duomo, ☎ 0583-711100, €3, conc. €2) contains a collection of geological exhibits.

Barga Jazz Festival

Established in 1986, this international event (☎ 0583-723352, last week in August) sees an orchestral jazz competition held in the town's Teatro dei Differenti, on its Piazza Angelio (and neighboring streets), in Lucca's Palazzo Ducale and in Castelnuovo di Garfagnana's Piazza Umberto. If you arrive out of season, visit **Osteria Angelio** (Piazza Angelio, ☎ 0583-724547, closed Mon from Dec-Mar, $$), in the heart of old Barga, owned by charismatic jazz buff and fluent English speaker Gian-Marco. It's the only music he plays and all he talks about, and he warns potential guests not to come (or at least not to voice their opinion) if they don't like jazz.

■ The Garfagnana

The Garfagnana takes over from the Valle del Serchio at Ponte di Campia and extends up through the Parco Naturale dell'Orecchiella to the Passo di Pradarena, which reaches over the Apennines to Emilia-Romagna.

Sightseeing & Adventures

Gallicano: The first main stop is Gallicano, a town of medieval origin along the Tùrrite River. Its most important building is the **Pieve di San Jacopo**, which dates to the year 1000 and preserves many della Robbia terracottas. From town, an educational **footpath** leads through chestnut woods to the *metari* (huts for drying chestnuts), and another takes you onto the **Eremo di Calomini** (☎ 0583-767003). This 11th-century hermitage (the present building dates from the 17th century) nestles in the sheer rock face of a calcareous wall; the sacristy is literally dug out of the rock.

ADOPT A CHESTNUT TREE

Garfagnana is a land of chestnut trees and, to help it remain so, you can adopt one of the 150 trees of the ancient Cerasa woods around Pieve a Fosciana. For €75 a year, you can take part in the gathering of chestnuts, their drying in the traditional metati and milling in the old mills. You'll also receive 44 lbs of fresh chestnuts, 11 lbs of dried chestnuts, 11 lbs of sweet flour and the typical chestnut gathering apron as part of the deal. See www.adottauncastagno.it to find out more.

From Gallicano you can **walk** to fortified **Vergèmoli,** a site of great naturalistic interest, not least for its vicinity to the natural caves of the **Grotta del Vento** (see page 263). From Vergèmoli, you can head up to the slopes of Pania delle Croce (1,858 m/6,094 feet), known as the "Queen of the Apuan Alps" and on to the natural arch of Monte Forato (see page 260).

One of the Apuan Alps' classic walking routes departs just past Vergèmoli at the **Cappella Monte Piglionico**. The five-hour walk (#7, #126, #139 then #127), famed for its unusual karst geology and breathtaking views, takes you up past

Rifugio Rossi to the saddle of Pania Secca and Pania della Croce before returning to your starting point at the chapel.

The nearest **rock climbing** facilities are at **Molazzana** (on the training face "Le Rochette"), which is also the gateway to the Fortezza di Cascio, built in 1615 by Alfonso III to defend this land much fought over between Lucca and the Estensi family.

Castelnuovo di Garfagnana: The capital of these northern slopes, Castelnuovo di Garfagnana, is farther up the panoramic SS324. It sits at an important crossroads between the Apennine and Apuan mountain ranges, which formed part of the Via Francigena, the pilgrim road between Rome and northern Europe.

Lucca conquered the town in 1248, and Castruccio Castracani fortified and ruled the territory until it passed to the Este family in 1430. The **Rocca Ariostesca** (☎ 0583-6448315, 10 am-noon, 3-6 pm), which dominates the town from on high, remains the most significant architectural mark of the Este family's dominion in Garfagnana. It was commissioned in its vast dimensions by Alfondo II d'Este during the second half of the 16th century and should be your first port of call before heading down to the town **Duomo**. Although 10th-century in origin, the Duomo has both Renaissance and Baroque modifications. Inside is a 15th-century wooden sculpture known as the "Black Christ," a glazed terracotta della Robbia altarpiece and a marble font created by the Civitali school.

Rocca Ariostesca

Castelnuovo is the obvious base for adventures both into the Apuan Alps and the Orecchiella, with **hiking**, **mountain biking** and **climbing** (contact CAI, ☎ 0583-74352) all within easy reach. A circular 10-stage walk known as **Garfagnana Trekking** (GT) departs from town, passing through the Alps and the Orecchiella before circling back to town. Pick up a map from the Centro Accoglienza Visitatori del Parco (Piazza Erbe 1, ☎/fax 0583-315300, www.parcapuane.toscana.it).

Mountain bikers should follow the path from **Castelnuovo to Massa**, which runs along the tree-lined Tùrrite Valley near the SS13 and offers views over the vast crags of the Pania delle Croce.

Castiglione di Garfagnana

Castiglione di Garfagnana: Take the SS72 and you'll find yourself heading up the steep slopes of the Apennines to the Passo delle Radici (1,529 m/5,015 feet). It passes first through the ancient town of **Pieve Fosciana** (the meeting place of the two major roads to the Apennine ridge, Via Vandelli and the Strada delle Radici) before an abrupt ascent to Castiglione di Garfagnana. Within this fortified medieval village, one of the most beautiful in the province of Lucca, the defensive bastions of the 12th-century **Rocca** (Fortress, ☎ 0583-68543, 10 am-noon, 3-6 pm) are still joined to the 750-m (2,460-foot) stretch of town walls. The 13th-century **Chiesa di San**

Michele conserves a precious façade and some stunning art, including a 1389 *Maestà* by Giuliano di Simone da Lucca.

> **Via Vandelli:** One of the most daring Italian road constructions, the Via Vandelli was designed by Abbot Domenico Vandelli during the first half of the 18th century (1738-51) to connect Modena with Massa. It is most impressive at the Passo del Tambura (on the Massa side), where it clings to the calcareous stone above a 1,100-m (3,608-foot) drop. The route was so difficult and rough, it became impossible to travel just a few years after its inauguration. Fortunately, much of it can now be walked (CAI#35).

San Pellegrino in Alpe: The steep and winding Via Vandelli takes you to Passo delle Radici and the border at San Pellegrino in Alpe. Its main attraction, apart from the amazing natural location, is the **Museo della Campagna** (Museum of Garfagnana Peasant Traditions, Via del Voltone 14, June-Sept, Tues-Sun, 9:30 am-1 pm, 2:30-7 pm, Oct-May, Tues-Sun, 9 am-noon, 2-5 pm), which contains a collection of some 4,000 objects historically used in local peasant activities. It's really only worth a visit if you can tear yourself away from the amazing town panorama.

Trails depart from town into the Garfagnana, Orecchiella and Lower Serchio Valley. The most famous include the *trifoglio*, the three marked circular walks pioneered in the 1980s by *Airone* (an Italian history magazine): the first (five hours) takes in the craggy limestone and nature reserve (see below) of **Pania di Corfino** (1,603 m/5,258 feet); the second (four hours) is a more manageable trail through forests of oak and beech; and the third (two days) is the longest and most taxing itinerary.

There are **ski** opportunities around San Pellegrino in Alpe: **Casone di Profecchia** on the road from Castiglione di Garfagnana (1,314 m/4,310 feet, ☎ 0583-649028, fax 0583-649048, three pistes) and **Passo delle Radici**, just after the mountain pass itself (☎ 0583-649071, fax 0583-649079, three pistes). There are also plenty of **cross-country** routes in the Orecchiella.

Parco Naturale dell'Orecchiella: The small town of Corfino is the access gate to the Parco Naturale dell'Orecchiella, which occupies the calcareous massif of Pania di Corfino and Monte Prado, which at 2,054 m (6,734 feet) represents the highest peak in Tuscany. Noted for its flora and fauna (including peregrine falcons), it is one of the region's most popular destinations for both treks and **nature walks**, with the latter mainly confined to the **Orto Botanico Pania di Corfino** (Botanical Gardens, Villa Collemandina, ☎ 0583-644911, open all year).

GEA (Grande Escursione Apenninica) trails also run through the Orecchiella Natural Park, offering the opportunity to see up-close colorful flora (violets, alpine anemones, alpine primroses) and fauna (wild boar, roe deer, wolves).

■ Where to Eat

LOCAL FLAVORS

Castagnaccio – Chestnut cake.
Farinata – Half-polenta and half-minestrone soup from the Valle del Serchio.

Necci – Chestnut flour crêpes served with ricotta.
Torta coi becchi – Chestnut tart.
Zuppa di farro – Spelt soup from the Serchio Valley (flavored with beans, sage, garlic and pork).
Garfagnana is also known for its mushrooms (including the rare *Prugnoli primaverili*) and its roasted meats. Barga is famous for its black and white truffles.

 Local specialties can be sampled at small family-run *trattorie* throughout the region. Some of the most charming are in Barga. The Castelvecchi family has been running hotel-restaurant **Alpino** (Via Pascoli 41, ☎ 0583-723336, www.bargaholiday.com, $$) for over 100 years. Part-restaurant, part-*enoteca*, the Alpino is noted for its excellent wine list and tasy local dishes. Try the *tortelloni barghigiania alla crema di parmigiano* (Barghi tortelloni with parmesan) as a first course, the *filetto di maiale in agrodolce* (sweet and sour pork fillet) as a second, and the *crêpes di castagne con miele d'acacia e ricotta locale* (chestnut flour crêpes with local honey and ricotta cheese) to finish.

Another top choice in the area is **Osteria Vecchio Mulino** (Via V Emanuele 12, ☎ 0583-62192, www.ilvecchiomulino.com, $$) in Castelnuovo di Garfagnana. In addition to its famous chestnut-flavored coffee (*caffè al vetro con il miele di castagno*), it also serves an extensive range of local meats and cheeses.

In the heart of the Garfagnana, **Villa delle Rose** (Piazza Tellini 2, ☎ 0583-68992, fax 0583-699042, villarose@tin.it, closed Tuesday, $), on the main square at Villa Collamandina, draws the crowds. The emphasis is on tradition, with dishes such as *lasagnetta su ragù di coniglio* (lasagne with rabbit meat sauce) and *semifreddo con castagne e biscotti di neccio* (semifreddo ice cream – literally, half-frozen – with chestnuts and biscuits).

■ Where to Stay

 There are quality hotels around Bagni di Lucca. Try **Albergo Corona** ☆☆☆ (Via Serraglia 78, Loc. Ponte a Serraglio, ☎ 0583-805134, www.coronaregina.it, $$) or **Pensione Serena** ☆☆☆ (Via Paretaio 1, Loc. Ponte a Serraglio, ☎ 0583-87455, $$) just out of town on the road from Borgo a Mozzano.

At Barga, **Il Ciocco** ☆☆☆☆ (Via C. Pascoli, ☎ 0583-7171, fax 0583-723197, www.ciocco.it, $$$) offers the best deal, with lower priced luxury at **Da Carlino** ☆☆☆ (Via Garibaldi 15, ☎ 0583-644270, fax 0583-62616, www.dacarlino.it, $) and **Ludovico Ariosto** ☆☆☆ (Via F. Azzi 26, ☎ 0583-62369, fax 0583-65654, www.hoteludovicoariosto.com, $$) in Castelnuovo di Garfagnana.

To place yourself in the heart of the Orecchiella, opt instead for a room around Villa Collemandina. Hotels here such as **Panoramico** ☆☆☆ (Via F. la Terra 9, Loc. Corfino, ☎ 0583-660161, fax 0583-660159, www.hotelpanoramico.com, $$$), **Linda** ☆☆ (Loc. Sassorosso, ☎ 0583-68178, fax 0583-68673, $$) and **Albergo La Torre** ☆ (Via San Leonardo 15, Loc. Corfino, ☎ 0583-660098, www.hotellatorre.net, $) are all within easy reach of the area's many trekking trails.

The best of the *agriturismi* can similarly be found around Borgo a Mozzano (**Borgo Giusto** ☆☆☆, Via Soccolognora 6, Loc. Partigliano, ☎ 0583-835568, fax 0583-835970, www.borgogiusto.it, $$$), **Barga** (**La Rocca** ☆☆☆, Via Pegnana

Lucca

Alta, ☎/fax 0583-723362, www.aziendaagrituristicalarocca.com, $$$) and Castelnuovo di Garfagnana (**La Palazzina** ☆☆☆☆, Loc. La Palazzina, ☎/fax 0583-62631, www.agriturismolapalazzina.com, $$$; and **La Piastra** ☆☆, Loc. La Piastra, ☎/fax 0583-62491, www.agriturismolapiastra.com, $$). But, there's also the beautifully located **Il Tendaio** ☆☆☆ (Loc. Tendaio, ☎/fax 0583-649103, www.agriturismoiltendaio.com, $$) near San Pellegrino in Alpe.

Backpackers should opt instead for the pilgrim rooms of the **Eremo di Calomini** (☎ 0583-767020, fax 0583-747983, eremocal@tin.it, $) or a space in one of the area's campgrounds. Choose from camps at Coreglia Antelminelli (**Pian d'Amora** ☆, Fraz. d'Amora, ☎/fax 0583-78426, $), Camporigiano (**Il Prato**, Loc. Prato al Molino, ☎ 0583-618163, www.ristoranteilprato.com, $), Giuncugnano in the far north (**Argegna** ☆☆, ☎ 0583-611154, fax 0583-611500, www.biancospinocoop.it, $) and Minucciano to the west (**Lago Paradiso** ☆☆, Via della Piana, Fraz. Gorfigliano, ☎ 0583-610662, Fraz. 0583-610106, www.campeggiolagoparadiso.it, $).

There's a youth hostel at San Romano in Garfagnana north of Villa Collamandina (Via Roma 22, ☎ 0583-613426, www.aicanipai.it, $), not to mention the many mountain refuges:

- **Rifugio La Maestà** (Via Vallisneri 30, Loc. Trassilico, Gallicano, ☎ 0583-711108, $).

- **Rifugio Alpino CAI Enrico Rossi** (Molazzana, ☎ 0583-710386, $).

- **Rifugio Alpe di Sant'Antonio** (Loc. Alpe di Sant'Antonio, ☎ 0583-65169, fax 0583-648435, www.garfaganavacanze.it, $).

- **Rifugio Isera** (Loc. Isera 4, Villa Collamandina, ☎ 0583-660203, $).

- **CAI Donegani** (Loc. Orto di Donna, Minucciano, ☎ 0583-610085, $).

- **La Foce** (Fraz. Metello, Silano, ☎ 335-7726321, fax 0586-828840, $).

Massa Carrara

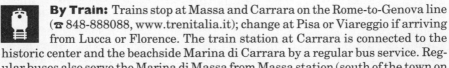

Linked politically and administratively since the 15th century, the neighboring cities of Massa and Carrara, at the far edge of the Tuscan border, are completely different in character and structure. Traditionally antagonistic, they are united only by the local marble, which supplies the industry in the cities, the sculptures to decorate their main squares and the dust on their streets. Both towns are backed by the Apuan Alps (themselves more dramatic behind Carrara, and less scenic but more approachable from Massa) and fronted by the pine forests and beaches of the Apuan Riviera.

■ Getting Here & Around

By Train: Trains stop at Massa and Carrara on the Rome-to-Genova line (☎ 848-888088, www.trenitalia.it); change at Pisa or Viareggio if arriving from Lucca or Florence. The train station at Carrara is connected to the historic center and the beachside Marina di Carrara by a regular bus service. Regular buses also serve the Marina di Massa from Massa station (south of the town on Piazza IV Novembre).

By Bus: If approaching from Viareggio and the Versilia Coast, it's best to take a **Lazzi** service (☎ 0583-584876). Buses run up and down the coast every two hours (every hour in July and August), stopping in Marina di

Massa and Marina di Carrara. Massa and Carrara themselves are served by bus from Lucca. Buses drop you in Massa at the terminal on Piazza della Liberazione and in Carrara at the terminal on Giovanni Minzoni.

 By Car: If arriving by car, join the **A12** at Viareggio and head north along the coast (direction La Spezia). You can rent cars at **Massa** (ACI, Via Aureli Ovest 193, ☎ 0585-831941, fax 0585-831944; Aviotti Giampietro, Via Patriota, ☎ 0585-41221/44230), **Carrara** (Agenzia Lunezia, Viale da Verrazzano, ☎ 0585-788200), **Marina di Massa** (Pellizzari Sergio, Viale Roma 354, ☎ 0585-241360) and **Marina di Carrara** (Volpi, Via Venezia 5, ☎ 0585-630112).

 Taxis are available in **Massa** at the train station and on Piazza della Liberazione; in **Marina di Massa** by the bus stops on Piazza Betti; in **Carrara** on Piazza Farini; and in the **Marina di Carrara** on Piazza Menconi.

 Bicycles can be rented at **Marina di Massa** (Giorgeri, Viale Roma 286, ☎ 0585-245479); **Marina di Carrara** (Ciclo '94, Via San Leonardo 214, ☎ 0585-250062); and **Ronchi** (Maggi, Via Verdi 39a, ☎ 0585-24448).

■ Information Sources

 Tourist Offices: APT Massa (Massa Tourist Office) is in the Marina di Massa (Viale Vespucci 24, ☎ 0585-240063, fax 0585-869015); and **APT Carrara** (Carrara Tourist Office) is in the Marina di Carrara (Piazza G. Menconi 6b, ☎ 0585-632519). There's also a small office near **Montignoso** (loc. Cinquale, Via del Freo, ☎ 0585-808751). The nearest **Centro Accoglienza Visitatori del Parco** (Park Welcome Center) for the Apuan Alps is north of Massa at Forno (Via Biforco 1, ☎ 0583-644242).

Adventure Information: There are some useful **trekking organizations** in the area: **Le Prade** (Monte Brugiana, ☎ 0585-42676/540840) near Massa; and the **CAI** in Massa (☎ 0585-488081) and Carrara (☎ 0585-776782) are useful sources of information. **Mountain** and **road bikers** will get their questions answered at the local branch of the **Federazione Ciclistica Italiana** (Italian Cycling Federation, Via Cucchiari, 6, Carrara ☎ 0585-74493).

Maps: The best hiking maps are the widely available 1:25,000 Multigraphics (#101 and #102).

■ Sightseeing & Adventures

Apuan Riviera: The Versilia Coast becomes the Apuan Riviera at **Cinquale** (really Marina di Montignoso), with the best sunbathing opportunities found in the early stretch up to the Marina di Massa (things start getting a little bit too industrial at Marina di Carrara). Sheltered by the Apuan Alps, this part of the coast is also the preferred destination of **surfers**, with some of the biggest waves in the Mediterranean hitting the shores during spring and autumn. You can book lessons and rent boards alongside Marina di Ronchi's long beach at the **Time Out Shop** and **Scuola di Surf** (Via Ronchi, ☎ 0585-243262).

Sailing on the Apuan Riviera

Marina di Massa: **Circolo della Vela** (Viale Vespucci 84, ☎ 0585-240900 and Lungomare di Ponente, ☎ 0585-241633)
Marina di Carrara: **Club Nautico** (Via Colombo 2, ☎ 0585-785364).
Cinquale: **Circolo Velico** (Viale IV Novembre, ☎ 0585-308032).

The seafront promenade, which started earlier on the Versilia Coast, continues on from Cinquale, with **cycle** paths reaching the border with Liguria.

THE VIEW FROM ABOVE

The small airport you'll find signposted between Cinquale and Ronchi is the **Aeroclub Marina di Massa** (Via Intercomunale 12b, Ronchi, ☎ 0585-309088). During the summer season it offers tourist flights over the beaches and Apuan Alps.

Spa Breaks: You can find the **Terme della Versilia** (Versilia Spa, Villa Undulna, Viale Marina, ☎ 0585-807788, fax 0585-807791, www.villaundulna.com) at Cinquale and the **Terme San Carlo** (Via dei Colli 81, Loc. San Carlo Terme, ☎ 0585-47703, fax 0585-47704, www.acquasancarlo.it) near Massa.

Montignoso: Nature lovers should follow directions inland to Montignoso. The **Lago di Porta** is all that remains of the old swamp that once connected up to Massaciuccoli. Its widespread cane thicket has a great many nesting birds (such as the penduline, sedge-warbler, reed warbler, wagtail and chiffchaff). They can be seen in association with ANPIL, who protect the area (arrangements should be made through Parco Didattico WWF di Ronchi, Via Donizetti, Marina di Carrara, ☎ 0585-348502).

Montignoso itself lies in a narrow valley at the point where the Apuan Alps meet the coast. **Castello Aghinolfi** dominates it from above (☎ 0585-82711, winter, Sun, 3-5 pm, summer, Tues-Sun, 10 am-noon, 5-8 pm, €3, conc. €1.50). This medieval manor of Lombard origin represents the southernmost gateway to the Lunigiana.

■ Massa

Massa became capital of the small Duchy of Cybo-Malaspina in the 16th century, and two of its major monuments hail from those days. One dominates the historical center: the imperial Rocca (shown at left, also known as **Castello Malaspina**, ☎ 0585-44774, winter, Sat, 9 am-noon, Sun, 3:30-6 pm, summer, Tues-Sun, 9 am-noon, 4-8 pm, €5, conc. €3). It was transformed into a splendid Renaissance palace (with verandas, porticoes and loggias) when the Cybo-Malaspina took over

the defensive castle, which had originally been built here by the Obertenghi in the 12th century. The second, the residential **Palazzo Cybo-Malaspina**, commonly known as the Palazzo Rosso (the red palace), is on the town's lower level on Piazza degli Aranci. This is the heart of the ducal city in every sense and was itself re-designed in the mid-16th century to fit the needs of the *signori,* the Cybo-Malaspina.

The imprint of Cybo-Malaspina can also be seen in the nearby **Duomo** (Piazza del Duomo) in which a subterranean chapel serves as their mausoleum. But the cathedral is more commonly visited for its Chapel of SS. Sacramento, which houses fragments of a *Madonna* fresco by Pinturicchio; the triptych from the school of Filippo Lippi; and the **Museo d'Arte Sacra** (closed for restoration at the time of writing, ☎ 0585-810704).

Massa is within easy reach of the Apuan Alps, a paradise for **rock-climbers**, **hikers**, **horseback riders** and even drivers, since the views are so beautiful. To pick up the trails and mule tracks, take the winding road to Castelnuovo di Garfagnana. It's a beautiful drive that loops around the entire valley from Altagnana to finally arrive at Antona on the opposite side. From here, you can not only look back on the earlier town, but also over the entire coast. Just past Antona, pick up the first of the **CAI walking trails** (#41 and #188 up Monte Altissimo, 1,589 m/5,212 feet).

The road toward Monte Altissimo also takes you to the Pian della Fioba. This is where you'll find the **Orto Botanico delle Alpi Apuane Pellegrini** (Pellegrini Botanical Garden, ☎ 0585-4920259, office 9 am-noon, 3-6 pm, gardens always open), one of the most unusual of the region's botanical gardens, one that leaves the plants in their natural mountainside locations. **Nature walks** are taken accompanied by a guide who points out interesting plants – saxifrage, *Contorti ramnus* (a type of natural bonsai), *Cerastium apanum* (a large plant with white flowers) and *Globularia incanescens* (with purple blooms not found in any other part of the world) – and explains their characteristics.

A must for **bikers** is the road from Massa to the **Passo del Vestito**, which, after going beyond the valley of the same name, loops through Arni, the Galleria del Cipollaio and Seravezza.

■ Carrara

Half a million tons of marble pass through Carrara each year, so it should come as no surprise to learn its nickname is the "city of marble." The city is completely tied up in its production, with all churches, monuments, squares, palazzi and fountains bearing the mark of the calcareous rock, which brought artists such as Michelangelo here to choose their own. Writers and poets such as Dickens and Tolstoy, d'Annunzio and Pirandello also came to check out the source that provided the material for some of the most beautiful monuments in the world.

Duomo

The rock itself can be seen in town at its brightest on the grey and white marble façade of the 11th-century **Duomo** (☎ 0585-71942, daily, 7 am-noon, 3:30-7 pm, holidays till 8 pm), the city's most important monument and, along with the marble, its symbol. The design is a mix of Romanesque and Gothic, with the latter added primarily to the upper part from the 13th century on. The intricate rose window was added in the 14th, as were Bergamini's five marble statues of the *Annunciation*. The polychrome marble pulpit arrived in the 15th century.

A fragile and often difficult material to sculpt with, the local marble can be seen mid-design at the **Fontana del Gigante** (known locally as *Il*

Gigante – the Giant), an incomplete sculpture by Bandinelli. Or you can see it at its most elegant in the extraordinary pavement of the **Piazza Alberica**, the venue for the annual *Scolpire all'Aperto* (Sculpture Outside, late July-early Oct), which sees sculptors from around the world given a block of marble and left to work in the middle of the square. It is held concurrent with a display of *lizzatura* (the old technique used to transport large blocks of marble down the hillside).

Fontana del Gigante

And, if you still haven't had enough of the local rock, Carrara has dedicated a museum to its most prized possession. The **Museo Civico del Marmo** is a few kilometers outside the center (Marble Museum, Viale XX Settembre, Loc. Stadio, ☎/fax 0585-845746, http://giove.cnuce. cnr.it/museo.html, June-Sept, 10 am-8 pm, May and Oct, 10 am-5 pm, Nov-Apr, 8:30 am-1:30 pm, closed Sun, €3, conc. €1.50). The collection – a mix of antique and modern marble sculptures and exhibitions of the original machines used to extract marble – is of greatest interest to the specialist.

Also on Piazza Alberica can is the house where Michelangelo stayed while checking out his marble supplies. On nearby Via Santa Maria, Casa Repetti marks the spot of Petrarch's former home. It makes a pleasant diversion on the way to the **Palazzo Cybo-Malaspina**, now the Academia di Belle Arti (Piazza Gramsci, ☎ 0585-71658, visits by appointment, closed Monday, free).

Checking Out the Marble Quarries

The Carrara section of the Apuan Alps has huge quarries of marble dug into the mountain. Yellow signposts lead from town to the three main quarrying valleys, Colonnata, Fantiscritti and Ravaccione, each of which you can visit.

The quarries of **Colonnata** are the most important of the three and offer beautiful views over the *ravaneti* (heaps of white marble detritus), which lie on the sides of Monte Maggiore and Monte Spallone. The view is best taken in from the ancient village of Colonnata, which is perched 532 m (1,745 feet) on the side of the mountain. Local tradition says that the Romans founded it as a rest camp for slaves working in the quarry.

The quarries of **Fantiscritti** were named after the Roman bas-relief housed in Carrara's Accademia di Belle Arti, but the settlements are only 19th-century in origin. They were created during the building of the Marmifera railway, which was used for transporting the marble.

The quarries of **Ravaccione** start in the area of Piastra. You can get an exceptional view of the basin from the lookout on Campo Cecina (1,350 m/4,428 feet), on the slopes of Monte Sagro (1,748 m) and from the small town of Vinca, at the foot of the Pizzo d'Uccello to the north.

Getting There: If you don't have your own transport, the quarries of Colonnata are the easiest to visit. An hourly CAT **bus** covers the eight kilometers (five miles) from Carrara's Via Don G. Minzoni (just behind the main terminus on Piazza Matteotti). Get off at the *Visita Cave* signs by the mine. If **driving**, follow the yellow *Cava di Marmo* signs from the town up the twisting road.

Above Carrara, the tiny town of **Colonnata** is not just about marble or the famous lard which takes its name (see below); it is also Carrara's closest entrance point for **hikes** into the Apuan Alps. CAI#38 leads from behind the village to a dense network of paths. Some take you up the lower **Monte Brugiana** (974 m/3,195 feet), while others bring you close to **Monte Grondice** (1,805 m/5,920 feet) on the border with the Lucca section of the Alps.

> **Colonnata Lard:** This is a region that produces a special kind of lard. They cover it with salt and pepper, rosemary, sage, cinnamon, cloves and coriander, then leave it to mature in marble urns, turning periodically, before reopening after 10 months of "curing," to find it white as snow. It is best enjoyed thinly sliced on toasted bread or hot focaccia.

Other, gentler **trails** depart from **Campo Cecina** (18km/11 miles north of Carrara), particularly around the Rifugio Carrara, and **Resceto,** where you can pick up the historic tracks of the Via Vandelli to Vagli di Sopra in the province of Lucca (#170, #166, then #35, six hours). It will take you past the so-called *Finestra Vandelli* (Vandelli window), which is cut into the crest at 1,450 m (4,756 feet). Both Campo Cecina and Resceto are actually part of a hiking circuit, which takes in Passo Tambura, Passo Focolacia, Equi Terme and Vinca. They can be reached from Massa on the regular **CAT bus** service (☎ 0585-41930).

Mountain bikers will also find some pleasant itineraries. One of the most popular climbs from Carrara to Campo Cecina and then down to Equi Terme in Lunigiana (see page 279).

■ Where to Eat

LOCAL FLAVORS

Cacciucchi (spicy fish soup from Marina di Massa), grilled squid, prawns, sea bass, sea spiders (a type of large crab) and pasta and risotto dishes (especially *tordelli,* a local type of ravioli). Meals should be accompanied by the DOC Candia dei Colli Apuani, a light white wine produced from the vines of the hills between Carrara and Massa, which is perfect for fish and seafood.

There are plenty of pleasant caffès and *gelaterie* in Massa and Carrara, but neither town is the type of city location where you really feel like staying for an evening meal. It makes much more sense to head to the coast for fish, or into the fresh air of the Apuan Alps to taste some mountain cuisine in a local restaurant.

Il Muraglione (Via Fivizzano 13, ☎ 0585-52337, $$$) is a short drive from Carrara in Avenza; **La Peniche** (Lungomare di Ponente, ☎ 0585-241070, $$$) and **Da Riccà** (Lungomare di Ponente, ☎ 0585-241070, $$$) lie near the coast at Marina di Massa; and **Il Bottaccio 1**, ☎ 0585-34031, $$$) is equally pricey in Montignoso. If you are stuck in Massa for the night, your tastiest options are **Ninan** (Via Lorenzo Bartolini 3, ☎ 0585-74741, $$) or **Ruota** (Strada della Brugiana, ☎ 0585-42030, $$).

Lucca

■ Where to Stay

I wouldn't recommend staying the night in either Massa or Carrara. They have a very different feel from the rest of Tuscany, and you're much better off returning to the Versilia Coast or heading inland to the Apuan Alps of the Garfagnana to make the most of your time here. There are a few **campgrounds** – one at **Marina di Carrara** (**Carrara Camping**, Via C. Fabbricotti, ☎ 0585-785260, $); another at the much nicer **Marina di Massa** (**Apuano**, Via Silcia 26, ☎ 0585-869288, $); and the best across the border at **Luni** (**Luni**, Via Luni 12, ☎ 0585-869278, $). There's also a **youth hostel** at Marina di Massa (**Ostello Apuano**, Viale delle Pinete, Partaccia 237, ☎ 0585-780034, fax 0585-774266, ostelloapuano@hotmail. com, $).

Things look a lot better for **mountain huts** with **Rifugio Carrara** (Loc. Campo Cecina, ☎ 0585-841972), **Rifugio Capanna Garnerone** (Loc. Fonte della Vacchericcia, ☎ 0585-776782) and **Rifugio Massa** (CAI Nello Conti, Loc. Campaniletti della Tambura, ☎ 0585-793059) all providing beds for weary walkers.

Lunigiana

Confined by the borders of Emilia-Romagna and Liguria, the rocky, forest landscape of the Lunigiana Valley is Tuscany's most extreme limb and, consequently, one of its least visited areas. Known as the "Land of the Hundred Castles," this insular boundary location has left an extraordinary landscape of military architecture, as would-be rulers built castles to defend their land and to exact tolls from those passing along the Via Francigena.

■ Getting Here & Around

By Train: Equi Terme and Aulla, the valley's main towns, are on the Lucca-to-Aulla train line (☎ 848-888088, www.trenitalia.it) with 10 services running daily. Change at Aulla to reach Villafranca, Filattiera and Pontremoli.

By Car: Aulla and Pontremoli have toll-paying exits on the **A15**, and can also be reached on the **SS62** from Massa. From Lucca, the **SS445** traverses the Garfagnana into Lunigiana (where it becomes the SS63) and onto Aulla where it joins with the SS62 north. You can rent cars in Aulla (Lupi Giglio e Figli, Viale Resistenza, 1, ☎ 0187-420190) and Pontremoli (Antonini Fabrizio, Loc. Careola, ☎ 0187-835040).

■ Information Sources

Tourist Offices: The main tourist information center for the region is in **Pontremoli** (Consorzio Lunigiana Turistica, Piazza della Repubblica 6, ☎ 0187-833701, fax 0187-832480, www.lunigianaturistica.com), which also is home to local trekking organization, **Postitappa Trekking Lunigiana**.

There are small offices in **Aulla** (Piazza A. Gramsci 23, ☎ 0187-421439), **Bagnone** (Via V. Veneto 2, ☎ 0187-429773), **Equi Terme** (Via N. Verde 1, ☎ 0585-97544), **Fivizzano** (Via Roma, ☎ 0585-926925), **Villafranca in**

Above: Fontana Maggiore in Perugia's Piazza Grande *(ENIT New York)*

Below: Spoleto's Cathedral contains important frescos by Pinturicchio and Filippo Lippi *(IAT Spoleto)*

Duomo, Spoleto (IAT Spoleto)

Above: Vicolo Sant'Angelo, one of Spoleto's medieval streets (IAT Spoleto)

Below: San Gimignano, Piazza Duomo

Street in Spoleto's old town (IAT Spoleto)

Lunigiana (Via Nazionale, ☎ 0187-493568) and **Zeri** (Loc. Coloretta, ☎ 0187-447608).

Adventure Information: Lunigiana's **Communità Montane**, the mountain region administration, has offices in Fivizzano (Piazza della Libertà 1, ☎ 0585-942011), Pontremoli (Via Mazzini, ☎ 0187-830075, fax 0187-833045) and Fosdinovo (Piazza Garibaldi, ☎ 0585-926922, fax 0585-948080). There are **CAI** branches at Pontremoli (Via Mazzini 17, ☎ 0187-830714) and Fivizzano (Via Vigna di Sotto, ☎ 0585-92519).

■ Sightseeing & Adventures

Luni: Although Luni (just across the Tuscan border from Carrara) now belongs to the territory of La Spezia, its history, not to mention its name, is indelibly linked to that of Lunigiana. Founded by the Luni tribe at the mouth of River Maga, it was eventually taken over by the Romans in 177 BC. It then grew in importance as a military port as the vast remains from the time of Augustus testify.

This growth tailed off in the fourth century, leaving the town almost deserted, until Lorenzo Il Magnifico and his Renaissance crew rediscovered it as a model of classicism. These days, you can visit the *capitolium*, the nearby **Casa degli affreschi** (House of Frescoes) and the second-century stone and marble **amphitheater**, which at one time was capable of holding 5,000 spectators.

Fosdinovo: North of Carrara, the SS446 takes you to Fosdinovo. The town was seriously damaged in World War II, but it does conserve what is probably the most impressive – and definitely the most photographed – of the castles erected by the Malaspina in Lunigiana in the 14th century. **Castello Malaspina** (☎ 0187-68891, daily, 10-11 am, 4-6 pm, till 5 pm on Sun, closed Tues, €5, conc. €3) was the refuge for an exiled Dante in 1306. The castle's solid, quadrangular walls with their high cylindrical towers sit majestically on a spur 500 m (1,640 feet) high, overlooking steep, wooded valleys. It should be your first stop before heading to the 14th-century **Chiesa di San Remigio**, which conserves the much-venerated marble sepulchre of Galeotto Malaspina.

THE MALASPINA

A feudal family of Lombard origin, the Malaspina once ruled Sardinia, the Ligurian Levante River and the valley of the Lunigiana, before fragmenting into the Guelph "Spino Fiorito" and the Ghibelline "Spino Secco" divisions of the family. Fierce adversaries of the Vescovo family of Luni, the Malaspina reached their peak of power when Spinetta Il Grande conquered the Vescovile capital of Sarzana (1334-43). He went on to create the Marquise of Fosdinovo, which itself gave origin to the Duchy of Massa and Carrara before its annexation to the Kingdom of Italy in 1859.

The Malaspina ruled their lands and road networks through complete domination, building the defensive castles that dot the land from Massa to Piagnaro, above the ancient hamlet of Pontremoli.

Fosdinovo lies on a **hiking** and **mountain bike** loop, which runs northwest to Aulla and northeast to Equi Terme and Casola in Lunigiana.

Trekking in Lunigiana

A circular trail network suitable for **trekking** and **mountain biking** runs through the Lunigiana. It is traditionally divided into 13 stages, starting and finishing at Aulla:

1a. Bagni di Podenzana to Villa di Tresana (five hours; 15 km/nine miles) through Podenzana, Novegigola, Foce Monte Piaggia and Castello.

1b. Villa di Tresana to Montereggio (three hours; 4½ km/three miles) passing through Villecchia, Parana and Ponte San Giuseppe.

2. Montereggio to Coloretta di Zeri (five hours; 13 km/eight miles) through Foce Fiscala, Foce Orsaro, Chiesa di Rossano and Foce Crosa.

3. Coloretta di Zeri to Cervara (six hours; 15 km/nine miles) through Torrente Gordana, Formentara, Lago Peloso and Barca.

4. Cervara to Groppoli di Valdantena (six hours; 17 km/10½ miles) through Grondola, Polina, Montelungo and Cavezzana.

5. Groppoli di Valdantena to Serravalle (six hours; 16 km/10 miles) passing through Casalina, Topelecca, La Crocetta, Arzenigo and Amuzzolo.

6. Serravalle to Treschietto (six hours; 16 km/10 miles) through Rocca Sigillina, Vignolo, Passo Coletta, Ponte di Valle, Valle and Vico.

7. Teschietto to Tavernelle (five hours; 13 km/eight miles) through Jera, Compione, Foce Monte Colla and Apella.

8. Tavernelle to Comano (four hours; 13 km/eight miles) passing through Catognano, Monte Nueto, Sommocomano and Castello di Comano.

9. Comano to Sassalbo (six hours; 15 km/nine miles) through Castello di Comano, Prati di Monte Fiascone, Torsana, Camporaghena. You can also continue the walk to Orto Botanico dei Frignoli (30 minutes; 2½ km/1½ miles).

10. Sassalbo to Casola in Lunigiana (seven hours; 19 km/12 miles) passing through Passo Giogo di Vendaso, Costa Miserino, Castello di Regnano, Castiglioncello and Vigneta.

11. Casola in Lunigiana to Monzone (five hours; 13 km/eight miles) passing through Argigliano, Ugliancaldo, Equi Terme, Aiola, Ponte di Monzone and Monzone Alto.

12. Monzone to Fosdinovo (six hours; 18 km/11 miles) through Vezzanello, Viano, Posteria and Pulica.

13. Fosdinovo to Aulla (six hours; 15 km/nine miles) through Passo del Cucco, Le Prade, Ponzanello, Canale del Torchio, Vecchietto and Bibola.

A scenic **bike trip** departs from Fivizzano, passing through Maesta' del Monte, Reusa, Casola di Lunigiana and Codiponte en route to Equi Terme (32 km/20 miles).

Casola in Lunigiana: If arriving from the Garfagnana, you'll enter Lunigiana along the SS445 at Casola in Lunigiana. It's a stunning approach to a town where narrow streets lead to intricately decorated *palazzi*, jutting medieval towers and, the major reason for a visit, one of the most interesting Romanesque parish churches in the region: the 12th-century **Pieve di Codiponte**.

A **hiking** and **mountain bike** trail runs south from Casola in Lunigiana to Equi Terme or west to Gragnola and the majestic Castel dell'Aquila. Other shorter trails take you up Monte Spiaggone (636 m/207 feet) and over into the province of Lucca.

Equi Terme: The small thermal station of nearby Equi Terme has been visited since Roman times for its sulphuric waters (**Terme di Equi**, Via Noceverde 20, ☎/fax 0585-949300, June-Sept). The small village also boasts a beautiful natural location, placed as it is amid a scenic backdrop of crags and knife-edge peaks, at the foot of the towering canyon known as Il Solio. This is one of Italy's richest cave zones, and the two-km route underground offered by the **Grotte di Equi** offers the third of this region's caving draws (☎ 0585-942122, Mon-Fri, 2:30-6 pm, Sat-Sun, 10 am-12:30 pm, 2:30-6 pm, €3, conc. €1.50). You can take tours of pre-historic **La Buca** (daily, 3 pm), a cave once inhabited by Neolithic man, and the archeological site called **Grotta della Tecchia**, where examples of man's early stone industry and ceramic crockery have been discovered.

A **hiking** and **mountain bike** trail leads out of town north through Ugliancaldo to Casola in Lunigiana and east through Aiola and Posterla to Fosdinovo. There's also a pleasant short walk up Monte Grande (692 m/2,270 feet).

There's a scenic **biking** road that departs from Equi Terme, passes through Ponte di Monzone, Marciaso, Pulica, Fosdinovo, Le Prade, Ponzanello and Bibola to arrive at Aulla (46 km/29 miles).

Fivizzano: To the north, along the SS63, the massive Medicean ramparts of Fivizzano enclose what was once the Lunigianese seat of the Florentine government. They were built in 1540 by Cosimo Il Vecchio, and offer the most evolved example of defensive walls in the region. Inside, you'll find a handful of Renaissance palaces gathered around the Piazza Medicea. Cosimo II erected the central fountain in 1683.

The Malaspina, who once ruled here, left the 14th-century **Chiesa di SS. Jacopo e Antonio**, although its façade underwent something of a facelift in the 16th century. The **Palazzo Comunale** was once the residence of the Malaspina, and the nearby **Castello della Verrucola** (☎ 0585-92466, Fri, 2-5:30 pm, free) was built by the most forward-thinking of the rulers, Spinetta Malaspina Il Grande, in 1300. It was he who finally engineered peace with the Vescovo of Luni. But much of the town's ancient appearance was otherwise destroyed in the last war.

There are some great **nature trails** farther along the SS63 at **Foresteria dell'Orto Botanico dei Frignoli** (Frignoli Botanical Garden, ☎ 0187-422598/0585-949688, 5 June-30 Sept). A **hiking** and **mountain bike** trail also runs through the garden and south to **Pieve San Paolo**, a Romanesque parish church in Vendaso and south to Casola in Lunigiana.

TERRE E DI CORTE

Every second Saturday and Sunday in July sees the arrival in Fivizzano of the archers of the "Terre e di Corte." This ancient contest, dating back to the year 1572, is held between the archers of the Terre (the urban nucleus of the town) and the Corte (the court or surrounding villages). It begins on the Saturday afternoon with a presentation of the teams' weapons and is introduced on the Sunday with a grandiose Renaissance parade. The whole point is to hit the bull's eye from a distance of 30 m (98 feet), but the use of old-fashioned bows complicates things somewhat. (Information from Fivizzano tourist office, ☎ 0585-92217.)

Lucca

Aulla: Medieval Aulla was the access gate to Lunigiana Alta (Upper Lunigiana). It grew up along the Via Francigena on the confluence of the Aulella and Magra rivers. Unfortunately, much of its original look and feel was destroyed in the last war, and only the 16th-century Malaspina **Fortezza della Brunella** survives of its main sights. The castle, a square mass with heavy triangular bastions built to plans by Antonio da Sangallo Il Vecchio, is encircled by a pleasant botanical garden. It is today the seat of the **Museo di Storia Naturale della Lunigiana** (Lunigiana Natural History Museum, ☎ 0187-400252, fax 0187-420727, winter, 9 am-noon, 3-6 pm, summer, 9 am-noon, 3-7 pm, closed Mon, €3.50, conc. €2).

The local **trekking** and **mountain bike** network takes you to the unusual spiral structure of **Bibola**, where the winding main road terminates at the remains of a huge 12th-century castle; **Podenzana**, which conserves one of the most famous religious sanctuaries in the valley; and **Caprigliola**, a medieval walled village on the Magra River with the ruins of a magnificent 12th-century cylindrical tower.

There's a pleasant **biking** road between Aulla and Pontremoli (30 km/18 miles; follow signs for the "tourist cycle way" through Barbarsaco, Lusuolo and Borgo Castelvoli). Lusuolo is worth a visit for its unusual design: it grew up along a road cut into the mountain ridge and is supported by a series of wide-vaulted buttresses, which dominate the Magra Valley below.

For **horseback riding** in the region, contact **Associazione Cavalli** (Loc. Albiano Magra, ☎ 0187-415149).

Licciana Nardi: The SS655 takes you northeast to the elaborately decorated hamlet of Licciana Nardi. It extends along a main road of intricate portals to the town's **Castello Malaspina**, the first of three nearby castles. There is also the 14th-century castle at **Monti** (occasional tours, ☎ 0187-474014); while you're in Monti, check out the 1,000-year-old **Abbazia di Venelia**. Then, there is the 15th-century castle at **Bastia** (privately owned).

The heavily crenellated castle, which you would have seen before the turnoff, is that of **Terrarossa**. The 16th-century construction is expected to open to visitors soon (☎ 0187-474016 for the latest info).

The local **hiking** and **mountain bike** network (see callout) can be picked up along the SS663 at Tavernelle or Comano.

Villafranca in Lunigiana: North past Terrarossa on the SS62 is Villafranca in Lunigiana. This small town has been inhabited since prehistoric times, as the statue-stele found in the zones of Malgrate and Fornoli testify. You can find out more at the **Museo Ethnologico della Apuane** in the ancient 15th-century mill (Via dei Mulini, ☎ 0187-493417, Tues-Sun, 9 am-noon, 4:30-7 pm, €3, conc. €1), although the main stele museum is to the north in Pontremoli.

The town **Castello Malaspina** is within sight of the 14th-century **Castello di Malgrate** (closed for restoration at the time of writing, ☎ 0187-494400), a rectangular castle transformed into an elegant and stately palazzo in the 15th century and dominated by a tall cylindrical tower crowned with corbels – one of the highest and most elegant Italian medieval towers. Nearby, there's also **Castiglione del Terziere** (daily, ☎ 0187-429010/429100, free), the 11th-century Florentine castle-seat renovated by Loris Jacopo Bonomi.

Bagnone: This pretty little hamlet is northeast of Villafranca di Lunigiana on a rocky outcrop. It is divided into two parts: the **Castello Malaspina** high up on the promontory (only the characteristic round tower remains of the original 14th-century castle), and the village below. The main sight in the village is a 16th-century portico along the town road.

At nearby **Traschietto**, the ruins of a castle erected on a cliff mark the start of the territory's **hiking** and **mountain bike** network. You can pick up the loop north alongside Pontremoli to the very edge of Tuscany or south through Comano to the Orto Botanico dei Frignoli. Shorter walks lead up Monte Cimarola (1,140 m/3,739 feet), Monte Cornela (1,324 m/4,343 feet), Monte Tre Castelli (934 m/3,064 feet) and Monte Colla (909 m/2,982 feet), among others.

Road bike routes depart from Bagnone, following an 18-mile (30-km) track through Castiglione del Terziere, Licciana Nardi, Agnino and Posara to Fivizzano.

Filattiera: Next stop east of the Magra River, the ancient Ligurian-Apuan settlement of Filattiera was once the capital of Byzantine Lunigiana. In the Middle Ages, it became the capital of the *Spino Fiorito* line of the Malaspina family, who left many important religious constructions in the territory. One of the most important is the Romanesque **Chiesa di San Giorgio**, which conserves the *Lapide di Leodegar,* a 13th-century Evangelical epigraph that records their mission. The other is the 11th-century **Pieve di Sorano** at the bottom of town, shown at left – the territory's most famous monument and a splendid example of Romanesque architecture, despite later renovations.

Walks from town take you to **Ponticello**, a quaint little village of tower-houses and fortified residences left by noble local family, the Rocca Sigillina; and into the valley of the Caprio River. The local **hiking** and **mountain bike** network can be picked up north of Filattiera at Serravalle. There are also walks from here up Monte Bosto (863 m/2,831 feet) and Monte Logarghena (1,279 m/4,195 feet).

Mulazzo: On the opposite side of the river and road, Mulazzo is the ancient Byzantine settlement that became the capital of the *Spino Secco* line of the Malaspina family in the Middle Ages. The only remains of the 15th-century **Castello Malaspina** are the towering octagonal tower – known as "Dante's Tower" after he stayed here as a guest of the Malaspina – and the massive arches of the aqueduct, which once supplied its water.

The 16th-century **Palazzo Malaspina** is in better condition. It contains a museum dedicated to the navigator Alessandro Malaspina. Born here in the 18th century, he went on to circumnavigate the globe in 18th century.

The town lies in prime **trekking** territory, with routes taking you to the 16th-century castle and eighth-century **Chiesa di San Martino** in Gavedo; the chestnut wood-surrounded hamlet of **Montereggio** (itself a stop on the Lunigiana trekking network); the medieval monastery at **Madonna del Monte**, with its great views over Lunigiana; and **Campoli**, where a statue-stele guards the village church.

The local **hiking** and **mountain bike** network can be picked up past Mulazzo at Montereggio.

Pontremoli: Fosdinovo may introduce Lunigiana, but its capital is most definitely Pontremoli. The northernmost town in Tuscany, Pontremoli grew up to control the end of the Apennine stretch of the Via Francigena. It underwent a second renaissance when it was annexed to the Grand Duchy of Tuscany in 1650 and most of its architectural sights – the palazzi, the bridges over the Magra and

Verde rivers, the **Cattedrale di Santa Maria** (beneath its 19th-century Neo-Classical façade) and the Rococo **Oratorio della Madonna del Ponte** (a rare example of its type in Tuscany) – were added from this time on.

There is some of its earlier architecture to be seen in the **Torre del Campanone** (or dell'Orolgio), now the cathedral campanile, which is all that remains of a 1322 fortification built by Lucca's *signore*, Castruccio Castracani, to control a town vacillating between Guelph and Ghibelline rule. There's also the **Chiesa di San Pietro**, which has a stone carved with an early pilgrim's maze; the severe architecture and impressive carved wood vestry of the **Chiesa di SS. Annunziata** (1471), which was built to celebrate an appearance of the Virgin, and the medieval **Castello del Piagnaro**, now home to the **Museo delle Statue Stele Linigianesi** (Museum of Statue-Menhirs, ☎ 0187-831439, winter, 9 am-noon, 2-5 pm, summer, 9 am-noon, 3-6 pm, closed Mon (except for July and Aug), €3, conc. €1.50).

THE LUNIGIANA STATUE-STELE

Pontremoli's **Museo delle Statue Stele Linigianesi** preserves a vast collection of the carved statue-stones created in the Lunigiana area by the indigenous populations that existed here in prehistoric times. These mysterious male and female figures carved out of sandstone – which so inspired Henry Moore – have been found in various parts of Europe, but the ones found here in the Val di Magra represent the most numerous. They are split into three distinct periods:

Group A (second millennium BC): These are the oldest of the statues; they have a *cippus* shape with a head joined directly to the body and a virile symbol (a dagger for the men and stylized breasts for the women).

Group B (second-first millennium BC): The statue head is more distinctly separated from the body with a circular strip, the face is in a U-shape, the males carry axes and daggers; the female figures are more human.

Group C (seventh to fifth century BC): The statues have completely rounded figures and show an evident Etruscan influence in their inscriptions and a Celtic touch in the weapons portrayed. Christians who came here intending to destroy all forms of idolatry decapitated those displayed in the museum without heads.

You can pick up the Lunigiana **trekking** and **mountain bike network** east of town at Arzengio or north along the SS62 at the spa town of Montelungo. West from the latter you'll arrive at Cervara, where Lago Verde is said to cover frightening stone faces constructed in ancient times to keep away evil spirits.

The Cerrara to Montelungo section of the trek network follows the footsteps of the old Via Francigena, and at Montelungo you can choose to continue along Lunigiana Trekking (to Groppoli and south) or to follow the Via Francigena north to the Passo della Cisa and into Emilia Romagna. At the pass, you can also pick up the GEA "Sentiero Italia" trail, which unities Liguria to Umbria along the Apennine ridge.

From Pontremoli, an eight-mile (13-km) **bike road** follows the SS63 to Pieve di Sorano and on through Filatto to Bagnone.

ADVENTURES ON SNOW

*Winter brings enough snow to the northernmost corner of Lunigiana to allow for downhill skiing. The major resort in the area is **Zum Zeri** (☎ 0187-4447422) along the ancient Via Francigena, but there are also cross-country skiing opportunities at **Passo di Cerreto** (1,261 m/4,136 feet) on the Emilia-Romagna border.*

■ Where to Stay & Eat

LOCAL FLAVORS

Focaccette di Aulla – A type of round flatbread cooked in terracotta pots and delicious dunked in olive oil.
Panigacci – Chestnut bread cooked in *testi* (cast-iron pans used in the area for thousands of years).
Spalla cotta di Filattiera – Salted shoulder of pork (a ham specialty of Filattiera).
Testaroli – Thin flat cakes of wheat flour briefly boiled and eaten with olive oil or pesto and sheep's cheese.

Many of the valley's best restaurants also offer accommodation. Try **Ca del Moro** (Loc. Casa Corvi, ☎/fax 0187-830588, www.cadelmoro.it, restaurant closed Sunday evening and Monday, hotel $$, restaurant $) just three km (two miles) outside Pontremoli. Deep in an ancient chestnut grove, this romantic country inn has five rooms and an excellent menu with accompanying wine list.

Pontremoli itself, **Caveau del Teatro** (Piazzetta S Cristina, ☎ 0187-833328, www.caveaudelteatro.it, restaurant closed Monday, hotel and restaurant closed January, hotel $$$, restaurant $$) has been serving fine traditional food in town since 1990. Try the *gnocchi di farina di grano e di castagno* (potato pasta with chestnut flour) or one of their house tarts that come *di erbe* (with herbs), *di riso e cipolle* (with rice and onion) or *di patate* (with potato). The small but elegant rooms and apartments are located in the ancient tower-house above the restaurant.

Over in Aulla, **Demy** (Via Salucci, ☎ 0187-408370, hotel $$, restaurant $$) has 43 bedrooms and a popular restaurant serving homemade pastas, meats grilled on terracotta by the fire and delicious homemade desserts such as the *meringa al cioccolato* (chocolate meringue).

Family-run **Da Pasquino** (☎ 0187-420509, hotel $$, restaurant $$), also in Aulla, has just 10 rooms. The restaurant is also a more intimate affair with a tasty range of local dishes including polenta with thinly-sliced grilled meats, *focaccette di aula*, and plenty of homemade cakes to follow.

Lucca

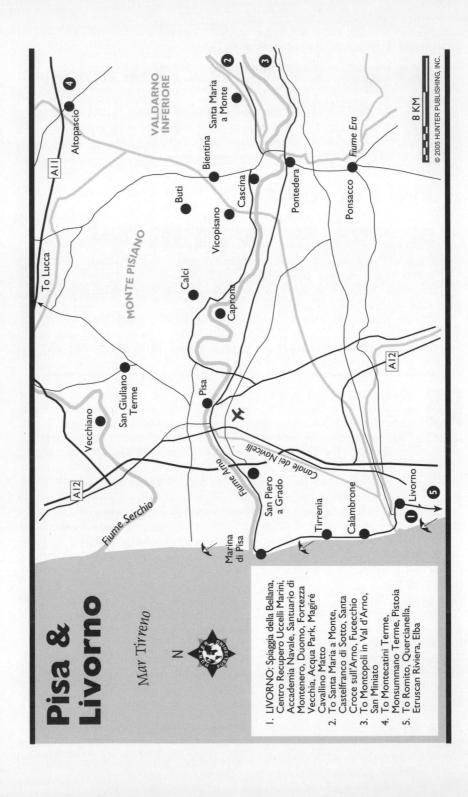

Pisa & Livorno

Mar Tirreno

N

Mar Tirreno

MONTE PISIANO

VALDARNO INFERIORE

To Lucca

Fiume Serchio

Fiume Arno

Canale dei Navicelli

Fiume Era

A11

A12

A12

8 KM

Vecchiano

San Giuliano Terme

Pisa

Marina di Pisa

San Piero a Grado

Tirrenia

Calambrone

Livorno

Calci

Caprona

Vicopisano

Buti

Cascina

Bientina

Santa Maria a Monte

Altopascio

Pontedera

Ponsacco

① ② ③ ④ ⑤

1. LIVORNO: Spiaggia della Bellana, Centro Recupero Uccelli Marini, Accademia Navale, Santuario di Montenero, Duomo, Fortezza Vecchia, Acqua Park, Magiré Cavallino Matto
2. To Santa Maria a Monte, Castelfranco di Sotto, Santa Croce sull'Arno, Fucecchio
3. To Montopoli in Val d'Arno, San Miniato
4. To Montecatini Terme, Monsummano Terme, Pistoia
5. To Romito, Quercianella, Etruscan Riviera, Elba

Pisa

A fascinating city of art and culture, Pisa isn't just about its leaning campanile. It is the city of the *lungarni* (the "sides of the River Arno"), and it was this winding river path that dictated the city's development and fortunes. Both peaked under the grand rule of the Pisan Maritime Republic during the 10th to 13th centuries, when the historical center, with its unbeatable heritage of medieval monuments and artwork, was formed.

NOT TO BE MISSED

- **Piazza dei Miracoli:** Site of the Duomo, Battistero, Camposanto and Leaning Tower (page 286).
- **Museo delle Sinopie:** What's going on behind those frescoes (page 289).
- **The Lungarni:** Take it all in with a riverside stroll (pages 299-300).
- **Museo delle Navi Antiche di Pisa:** The port's Roman remains on show (page 291).
- **Borgo Stretto:** The best of Pisa's shops (page #).
- **Basilica di San Piero a Grado:** The frescoed site of St Peter's landing spot (page 298).
- **Sloping views:** Get up the Leaning Tower before it leans too far (page 288).

Getting Here & Around

By Air: The city is easily reached from the international **Aeroporto Galileo Galilei** (☎ 050-849202, www.pisa-airport.com), where regular buses and trains connect to the main Pisa Centrale station, south of the city.

By Train: Trains (☎ 848-888088, www.trenitalia.it) from elsewhere in Italy drop you off at the same spot, with buses and coaches depositing passengers on the nearby Piazza V. Emanuele II. From Pisa Centrale train station, the main sights are a pleasant 20-minute walk (along Corsa Italia), but you can catch Bus #1 from outside the station or hail a station taxi (☎ 050-41252) if you don't want to walk it.

By Car: Those arriving by car (follow turnoffs from the **A11** or **A12**) will find five car parks within walking distance of town – the largest (and best situated) is outside Porta Nuova near Piazza dei Miracoli. Cars are best rented at the airport (see page 32), and you can pick up scooters and bicycles in the city at **Bike Rental** (Via Santa Maria 129, ☎ 329-0825861).

Information Sources

Tourist Offices: The main **APT Pisa** (Pisa tourist office) is in the eastern section of the city in the San Michele district (Via Pietro Nenni 24, ☎ 050-929777, fax 050-929764, www.pisa.turismo.toscana.it), but there are smaller offices at the train station and behind the Leaning Tower. There are also private companies offering tourist services: **Guide Turistiche Pisane** (Via C. P. Maffi 24, ☎ 050-555085, fax 050-561794) and **Consorzio Turistico dell'Area Pisana** (Via C. S. Cammeo 2, ☎ 050-830253), mostly organizing a range of guided tours.

The head office of the **Migilarino-San Rossore-Massaciuccoli Regional Park** is inside the park along Via Aurelia Nord 4, ☎ 050-525211, fax 050-533650, www.parks.it/parco.migliarino.san.rossore/index.html). There are smaller visitor centers at the Villa Medicea in Coltano (Via Palazzi 21, ☎ 050-989084) and the Ostello Sterpaia (Viale delle Cascine, ☎ 050-523019). The **Tenuta di San Rossore** (one of the estates that makes up the Regional Park) has its own estate office (Via delle Cascine Vecchie, ☎/fax 050-530101, www.parcosanrossore.it).

Maps: The best map choice is the *Monti Pisani e Colline Livornesi* (Edizioni Multigraphic, 1:25000).

Sightseeing

■ Walking the Historical Center

Midway along the Arno River, the **Ponte di Mezzo** marks the southern boundary of Pisa's main historical district. The arcaded Borgo Stretto stretches in front of you, its range of increasingly classy shops representing the city's commercial heart. As you head up it, look on your right for the 14th-century façade of the **Chiesa di San Michele in Borgo**, right. Built in 990 and successively amplified, it documents magnificently the passage from the Romanesque to Gothic styles. Inside, you'll find a 13th-century marble crucifix, sculpted for the portal of the Camposanto by Nino Pisano and moved here in the 18th century.

A left along Via Dini takes you to **Piazza dei Cavalieri**, the medieval heart of the city. Before Vasari adapted it to the current Renaissance look, it was known as the Piazza delle Sette Vie (the Square of the Seven Roads). He remodeled it to honor the Knights of Santo Stefano, an order founded by Cosimo I in 1561 to defend Pisa's coast from scavenging pirates. You can visit the **Chiesa di San Stefano dei Cavalieri** (☎ 050-580814, Mon-Sat, summer, 10 am-7 pm, winter, 11 am-4:30 pm, €1.50), with works by Vasari and Bronzino and spoils from the knights' victorious sea battles, as well as their former headquarters, the *sgraffiti*-decorated Palazzo della Carovana (1562-64). The latter went on to became the seat of the prestigious Scuola Normale Superiore, while the tower to its right (the Torre della Muda) is said to have been the medieval prison where Count Ugolino della Gherardesca died of hunger in 1289.

THE CANNIBAL COUNT

Condemned in Dante's *Inferno* to an eternity of skull gnawing, it seems that Cannibal Count, Ugolino della Gherardesca, wasn't as blood-thirsty as was previously thought. Gherardesca was found guilty of treason and left to die of hunger with his children and grandchildren in the Torre della Muda in the late 1280s, where according to legend, he staved off the inevitable by eating his relatives. However, DNA tests of bones found in the family crypt in 2002 disproved the theory: "We should bear in mind that Ugolino was by then almost 80 years old," commented excavating Professor Mallegni. "He presumably had very few teeth and there were no dentures in the 13th century. Even if he had wanted to gobble his sons, he would have only been able to suck on them a little."

From the political heart to the religious heart: a short walk along Via Santa Maria takes you to the Piazza del Duomo, better known as the **Piazza dei Miracoli** (the Square of Miracles). It is the well known and impressively spacious home of the city cathedral, campanile (better known as the Leaning Tower), baptistery and monumental cemetery. It's a remarkable collection, not just in terms of craftsman-ship – the buildings are considered *the* best representations of the architectural style known as Pisan-Romanesque – but also in the uniformity of their style. They were built during the 11th to 13th centuries, the grandest years of the Marine Republic, which saw the city blossom in art and architecture.

Pisa

Did You Know? Traditional Tuscan urban planning usually sees the Duomo – and all the city's most expensive constructions – placed right in the heart of the town center, yet in Pisa the Ca-thedral is up at the extreme northeast of the old town city walls. Why? Apart from ensuring that the buildings have remained in such a remarkably intact state, it would seem it was so planned in order to dishearten potential enemies; after all, a city with such wealth on its periphery could represent only a foolhardy ob-ject for attack.

Architect Buscheto started the work, and Rainaldo took over, following Buscheto's style. But, although the square's major sights were finished by the end of the 13th century, its current look and feel is actually from the late 1800s, when buildings of lesser impor-tance were moved to liberate the space around the main monuments.

Duomo (Cattedrale di San Giovanni, daily, summer, 10 am-8 pm, spring/autumn, 9 am-5:30 pm, winter, 9 am-5 pm, €2): Considered the epitome of Pisan-Romanesque craftsmanship and imitated in various forms all over Tuscany, the Duomo, at left, occupies the heart of the square. Buscheto laid the first brick in 1064 after the victorious crusade of

Palermo in the previous year, and it was completed and consecrated relatively quickly in 1118. Rainaldo extended the cathedral and finished the façade a century later, but much of his work suffered from serious fire damage at the close of the 16th century. The Medici restored the façade and nave, and Luigi Cambrai-Digny had another crack in the 1800s. He replaced much of its sculptural decoration with replicas (originals in Museo dell'Opera del Duomo).

Of the four doors originally created by Bonanno Pisano, only one remains from the 1596 fire (the others were created in the 19th century as replacements). Celebrated for its bronze depictions of the *Life of Jesus*, the door, known as San Ranieri after the city's patron saint, is on the side that opens to the Leaning Tower.

Once inside, it is Giovanni Pisano's superb marble pulpit (1302-1311), right, considered by many to be the peak of Italian Gothic sculpture, which takes pride of place. But the 14th-century tomb of Emperor Arrigo VII by Tino di Camaino, the Baroque chapel di San Ranieri, the famous light chandelier (said to be by Galileo), a canvas *Sant'Agnese* by Andrea del Sarto, and the 13th-century *Jesus between Giovanni Evangelista and the Madonna*, to which Cimabue is thought to have contributed, all deserve your attention.

Torre Pendante (Leaning Tower, Piazza del Duomo, ☎ 050-560547, fax 050-560505, www.opopisa.it, 8:30 am-8:30 pm, guided tours of 35-40 minutes. €15, tickets can also be reserved online for €17 more than 15 days in advance, no access to children under the age of eight): In Dec 2001, after almost 12 years of structural work, Pisa's most famous sightseeing attraction (and probably the best known Italian monument in the world) was finally reopened to the public. A spiral staircase leads up the marble tower's 294 stairs to the panoramic terrace above the last floor.

Tower Facts

- The height of the building is 60 m (197 feet).
- The ring-shaped foundation has an external diameter of 19.6 m (64 feet).
- Galileo made his experiments on gravity from the top-floor belfry.
- The tower is estimated to weigh 14,500 tons.
- The tower inclines five degrees and 31 inches toward the south; this means that the seventh cornice protrudes 2½ m (8.2 feet) over the first.
- It isn't the only tower in Pisa to tilt; both the campaniles of Chiesa di San Nicola and Chiesa di San Michele degli Scalzi incline through ground subsidence, as does the Duomo.

The first stone of the campanile was laid in 1173, attributed variously to Bonanno Pisano, Gherardo, Rainaldo and Guglielmo (the truth is we just don't know), and construction was halted after only three levels on the appearance of the first lean in 1185. Giovanni di Simone limited the leaning effects and work restarted, but in 1278, it was interrupted again after the three stories he added made the tower tilt in the opposite direction. By the time Tommazo Pisano fitted the bell cubicle on the belfry (the seventh and last tier) two years after the first stone had been laid, the tower had subsided vertically by as much as 2.8 m (nine feet).

> **Moonlit Viewing:** If you're in Pisa in July or August, book yourself an evening ticket at the Leaning Tower for a not-to-be-missed opportunity to see the town nightscape from up high. Groups of up to 30 participants can take the climb between 8:30 and 11:50 pm; ticket cost and contact details as per day visit.

Battistero (Baptistry, ☎ 050-560547, daily, summer, 10 am-8 pm, spring/autumn, 9 am-5:30 pm, winter, 9 am-5 pm, €5): Mirroring the style of the Duomo façade and topped by an octagonal cupola in pyramidal form, Pisa's large and circular baptistry is one of the most vibrant examples of the Pisan-Romanesque style. Architect Diotisalvi started the work in 1152, but it was Nicola Pisano who finished it off in the following century – hence the Gothic style of the upper loggia. Inside, it contains a range of sculptures from the workshop of Nicola and Giovanni Pisano, including a valuable altarpiece from 1260, and a remarkable baptismal font (1246) by Guido da Como.

Camposanto Monumentale (also known as Camposanto Vecchio, Monumental Cemetery, ☎ 050-560547/561820, daily, summer, 10 am-8 pm, spring/autumn, 9 am-5:30 pm, winter, 9 am-5 pm, €5): The Camposanto Monumentale is the last and by far the largest monument in the quadrille. It was built from 1278 to a design by Giovanni di Simone, and was finished in the second half of the 15th century in late-Gothic form by Lupo di Francesco; although Giovanni Pisano and Tino da Camaino also put in their two pennies' worth somewhere in between.

The Triumph of Death, detail

Its walls house the best existing complex of medieval frescoes in the world with works by Francesco Traini and Buonamico Buffalmacco (*The Triumph of Death* cycle that so inspired Franz Liszt), Taddeo Gaddi, Spinello Aretino, Andrea di Bonaiuto, Antonio Veneziano and 15th-century additions by Benozzo Gozzoli making up 26 large squares with stories from the Old and New Testaments. Seriously damaged in the last war, the frescoes underwent a long series of restorations, and can now be seen detached from their original *sinopie* (now in the Museo delle Sinopie, see below).

The Triumph of Death, detail

The City Walls: The Piazza dei Miracoli is the best vantage point for the remaining four-mile stretch of what was once a complete circuit of city walls. Constructed in the mid-12th century by consul Cocco Griffi, they border the piazza on the north and west sides, split only by the 13th-century Porta dei Leoni (Gate of Lions – note the fierce marble lion in its corner).

Museo delle Sinopie (*Sinopie* Museum, ☎ 050-560547/561820, daily, summer, 10 am-8 pm, spring/autumn, 9 am-5:30 pm, winter, 9 am-5 pm, €5): For those interested in completed frescoes and in their conceptualization, this museum, the

Pisa

only one of its type in the world, offers the key to their art. It displays the *sinopie* (the original sketches onto which the frescoes are painted) of the cycle, which decorate the huge complex of the Camposanto, and which were brought to light during repairs after World War II.

> **Did you know?** *Sinopie* take their name from the red earth coloring with which many of them were painted. The paint came from Sinope on the Black Sea.

Located in the 13th-century Spedale di Santa Maria Chiara on the southern side of the square, the collection includes the original sketches, basic layouts and studies behind the creation of *The Triumph of Death, The Last Judgment, Stories of the Anchorites* and Benozzo Gozzoli's *Biblical Stories*, among others. It also offers a not-to-be-missed opportunity to see the *spedale* itself – the old hospital built here in 1258 to designs by Giovanni di Simone, as a gesture of penitence and obedience to Pope Alessandro IV.

Museo dell'Opera del Duomo, ☎ 050-560547/561820, daily, summer, 10 am-8 pm, spring/autumn, 9 am-5:30 pm, winter, 9 am-5 pm, €5): The museum is in the Palazzo dei Canonici del Duomo (the former seat of the canons of the cathedral) east of the cathedral square. Moved here in 1986, the important collection of 12th- to 14th-century sculpture includes the original works taken from the monumental buildings in the square and include: the busts by Nicola and Giovanni Pisano taken from the Baptistery (*Madonna and Child, The Four Evangelists, Moses* and *David*); the bas-reliefs by Giovanni Pisano that once ran around the Duomo; an altarpiece by Tino di Camaino; and the funerary monuments to Archbishop Giovanni Scherlatti by Nino Pisano.

Via Santa Maria takes you south from the Museo dell'Opera del Duomo into town. The significant role the street played from medieval Pisa on – an all-important link between the cathedral square and the Arno River – is reflected in the grandeur of its buildings, many of which were modernized under the Medici and Lorraine dynasties. The result is a charming blend of medieval tower-houses and noble Renaissance palazzi.

On your right, you'll pick up the side-street entrance to the **Museo dell'Orto Botanico** (Botanical Gardens and Museum, Via Luca Ghini 5, ☎ 050-911350/374, fax 050-551345, www.dsb.unipt.it, closed Sat pm and Sun, free). Seat of the University of Pisa's Botanical Institute, these are the oldest university botanical gardens in Europe, and were founded by Luca Ghini as "Giardino dei Simplici" while he was Chair of Medicine and Botany in 1543. Moved to their present location in 1951 (they were originally sited on the Lungarno Simonelli), the eight-acre grounds include the stunning 16th-century *Fonderia*, its façade decorated with assorted shells and stones.

Back on Via Santa Maria the road leads you to the banks of the Arno and the **Museo Nazionale Palazzo Reale** (Museum of the Royal Palace, ☎ 050-2201384, Mon-Fri, 9 am-2:30 pm, Sat, 9 am-1:30 pm, €3, conc. €1.50). The palace was constructed between 1583 and 1587 to a design by Buontalenti, and incorporated an earlier 13th-century tower, known as the Torre della Verga d'Oro (it can be seen on

Via Santa Maria), which is where Galileo is thought to have shown Grand Duke Francesco I the satellites of Jupiter through his telescope. Transformed into a museum in 1989, the collection includes historical armaments from the *Gioco del Ponte* (see page 299) and artifacts from the court and traditions of Pisa from the 16th century to the present day.

Galileo Galilei: At no. 26 Via Santa Maria, you'll find the **Domus Galileana** (his house, visits by appointment, ☎ 050-23726), which was set up in 1942 as a center for research into the studies of mathematician, astronomer and physicist, Galileo (1564-1642).

Two large archways out the back link the museum to the **Chiesa di San Nicola**. Founded in the 12th century, it has a uniquely shaped 13th-century campanile that starts as a cylindrical form and concludes with a hexagonal cell. You can access its interior staircase from the church, which, like the famous tower, is slightly inclined. It is thought to have been the inspiration for the stairs of the Pozzo di San Patrizio in Orvieto (see page 383).

A pleasant stroll takes you right along Lungarno Simonelli to the Arsenali Medicei and the **Museo delle Navi Antiche di Pisa** (Museum of Ancient Pisan Ships, Lungarno Simonelli, ☎ 050-21441/055-3215446, Tues-Sun, 10 am-1 pm, 2-6 pm, €3, conc. €2.50). Occupying a 16th-century Medici storehouse along the Arno, the museum displays 12 Roman ships, which were discovered and excavated when digging to extend the Pisa-San Rossore railway station in 1988. At least one of the ships dates back to the first century BC. Many of the their contents are also on display, including clay vases, skeletons and even vials containing wine and olives some 20 centuries old. From the top of the nearby **Torre Guelfa**, you can enjoy a beautiful view of the city.

Pisa

Rise & Fall

Having served as an important seaport under Imperial Rome, Pisa really grew in military and economic power after its fleet inflicted a heavy defeat on the Saracens in 828. It became a free *comune* in the 11th century, dominating the Mediterranean as far as Sardinia and Corsica. Its rising status as a powerful maritime republic was accompanied by a fertile period of demographic and urban growth, which saw the construction of its major monuments as the town grew rich due to its strategic position in the middle of a maritime, fluvial and road network, aided by a fertile hinterland rich in timber and stone.

The city began to decline in the late 13th century, a result of internal strife and bullying by long-term rival Florence, who annihilated the Pisan fleet in 1284, and went on to take the city in 1509. Under Medici rule, Pisa began to pick itself up again as the Medici freed the city from its water problems and malaria, installed land reclamation processes and built the Canale dei Navicelli to connect Pisa to the new city of Livorno.

Take the Ponte della Cittadella over the Arno and turn left up Lungarno S. Sidney, which leads to the **Chiesa di San Paolo Ripa d'Arno**, a ninth-century church rebuilt during the 11th and 12th centuries, and heavily restored again after air-raid damage in 1943. It is often referred to as the *Duomo Vecchio* (old cathedral), as it was here that the archbishop would celebrate Mass when the current cathedral was being built.

The river walkway becomes Lungarno Gambacorti at **Chiesa di Santa Maria della Spina**. This church was named "spina" after a thorn from Christ's crown, which it claims to conserve. It was originally just a riverside oratory until it was expanded to its current size between 1323 and 1360 to honor the relic – its former extent is indicated on the north wall by a small tabernacle of Stagio Stagi. Repeated flood damage led to the church being dismantled piece-by-piece and moved to its current location on slightly higher ground in 1871. Before you head inside, look for the sculpture of *Madonna and Child with Saints* attributed to Giovanni Pisano on the two-color marble façade.

Follow the bend around the Arno and you'll pass a variety of medieval tower-houses and luxury palazzi, including the **Palazzo Gambacorti** and the **Palazzo Lanfranchi**. The former, erected in the mid-14th century, was named after Pietro Gambracorti, then ruler of Pisa (until he was murdered on his doorstep in 1392), while the latter (Lungarno Galilei 9-10) displays the talent of an architect, who, rather than knock down the pre-existing tower-houses, chose to incorporate them into his 16th-century design.

A SPACE FOR PISA

The Comune di Pisa (Pisa Town Hall) organizes free guided visits of the city on most Saturdays throughout the year, including cycle itineraries. Reservations must be made in advance through the tourist board or the Comune di Pisa (Palazzo Gambacorti). For further information, see www.comune.pisa.it/turismo/iniziative/aspasso.htm (Italian only).

The Ponte della Fortezza takes you back to the northern banks of the Arno. But, before you head that way, continue along Lungarno Fibonnaci to visit the pleasant **Giardino Scotto** (Scotto Gardens) and the fortezza itself, the **Citadella Nuova**.

The last major sight is just across the Arno. The **Museo Nazionale San Matteo** (National Museum, ☎ 050-541865/9711395, Tues-Fri, 8:30 am-7:30 pm, Sat-Sun, 8:30 am-1:30 pm, €4, conc. €2), which sits alongside the Romanesque church of the same name. The museum occupies a former Benedictine monastery with its vast collection of archeological remains, art (polyptych by Simone Martini, *Madonna dell'Umiltà* by Gentile da Fabriano, *San Paolo* by Masaccio, *Madonna and Child* by Fra Angelico) and sculptures (including works by Andrea Pisano, Andrea della Robbia, Michelozzo, Donatello and Tino di Camaino) taken from all over the city and the province. From here, it's just a short stroll back to the Ponte di Mezzo.

San Paolo, Masaccio

Church Crawling

Pisa has plenty more city churches worth a look.

Sant'Andrea Forisportum – This ex-church is called Forisportum (outside the walls) because it stood outside the original ring of medieval city walls. Inside the Pisan-Romanesque marble façade, the wide nave is currently used as a theater.

Sant'Antonio – Rebuilt almost entirely after WW II, the church stands near the *Mural* (1989) by Keith Haring, which decorates the whole side of a house on Via Zandonai.

Santa Caterina – Erected in 1251, the interior of this church has a remarkable trussed ceiling and a range of sculptures by Andrea Pisano and son, Nino.

Santa Cecilia – Founded by Camaldolite monks in 1103, the plain Romanesque façade of this church is jazzed up by the majolica decorations over the portal.

Santa Chiara – This small 13th-century church was almost completely rebuilt in the 18th century. It houses the *Reliquary of the Thorn*, which was transferred from the Chiesa di Santa Maria della Spina in the 1800s.

San Francesco – Designed by Giovanni di Simone, the first brick of this church was laid in 1233, although work didn't really start until 1265. In its chapel were found the bones of Ugolino della Gherardesca (see page 287). A rich polyptych by Spinello Aretino, a magnificent marble altarpiece by Tomasso Pisano, frescoes by Taddeo Gaddi and Taddeo di Bartolo, and paintings by Francesco Vanni and Ventura Salimbeni are just some of the art to be viewed.

San Frediano – Built in the Pisan-Romanesque style, this church underwent heavy restoration in the 17th century. Inside you can find early 13th-century panel paintings.

Santa Maria del Carmine – Built in a long monastic form, this church once housed the large ancona (a carved wooden altar with frames where paintings were inserted) by Masaccio, which was dismembered, with parts moved to various museums around the world, including the Museo Nazionale di San Matteo in Pisa (see page 292).

Santa Marta – Rebuilt in the mid-18th century, this church is decorated in a complex Baroque scheme.

San Martino – The *St Martin and the Pauper* that originally stood on this church's lunette has been replaced with a copy, displayed inside, along with a wall-long cycle of detached frescoes and their *sinopie* attributed to Giovanni di Nicola (early 1300s).

San Paolo all'Orto – Much altered in the 1800s from its original 12th-century form, this building is often used for exhibitions.

San Sepolcro – One of Pisa's most important examples of Romanesque architecture, this church was completely restored after flood damage in 1966.

San Sisto – Seat of the civic council during Pisa's glorious Maritime Republic, this Romanesque church is decorated with striking Islamic majolica bowls (originals in the Museo Nazionale di San Matteo, see page 292).

San Torpè – Church dedicated to the Christian saint martyred by Emperor Nero, who also gave his name to San Tropez.

Pisa

San Zeno – This church, found at the far north of the city walls, was constructed by the Benedictines from the 10th to 12th centuries. It has a beautiful tufa façade.

■ Monte Pisano

The **Rocca of Ripafratta** represents the heart of the vast defensive system that once stood between Lucca and Pisa. Thought to date back over a thousand years, the single entrance gate takes you to the central Piazza d'Armi. From there you can explore the ruins of the keep and the old lookout tower.

In the center of the Val Graziosa, **Calci** is the much-frequented home of the **Certosa di Pisa**, a vast monastic complex founded in 1366 and richly decorated both on the Baroque façade and in the sanctuary interiors where walls are covered in 16th-century frescoes by Bernardino Poccetti (Charterhouse, ☎ 050-938430, Tues-Sat, 8:30 am-6:30 pm, Sun and holidays, 8:30 am-12:30 pm, €4, conc. €2). Follow the road to Montemagno.

Inside partly preserved medieval walls, the main attraction at **Cascina** is the 12th-century **Pieve di Santa Maria Assunta**, which is considered one of the best representations of the Pisan-Romanesque style in the province. It houses a 12th-century *Madonna and Child* terracotta attributed to Benedetto da Maiano. Also worth a look is the 14th-century **Oratorio di San Giovanni** frescoed with *Stories of the Old and New Testaments* by the Sienese Martino di Bartolomeo (1398) and, just out of town, the Romanesque **Pieve dei SS. Cassiano e Giovanni**, which is embellished with friezes by Biduino.

You'll experience a leap back in time in **Vicopisano**, the ancient *Vico Auserissola*, much fought over by Lucca and Pisa. Walls built by Brunelleschi enclose the medieval old town's parish churches and towers; watch for the 11th-century **Pieve di Santa Maria e San Giovanni Battista**, constructed entirely in *verruccano* (a local stone frequently used in medieval construction), the 14th-century **Torre Quadrangolare**, known as the "four doors," and the nearby **Torri Gemelle** (twin towers).

A winding picturesque road leads the 10 miles from Calci to **Buti**. Famed for its olive oil and basket-weaving, this town is dominated by the Castel Tonni, a one-time Medici villa with a tower that gives lovely views over the town and the surrounding hills. There are also a few 17th-century palazzi and an early-medieval Chiesa di San Michele Arcangelo, a short walk away at Castel di Nocco. The town boasts a long-standing tradition known as the *Maggi*, a kind of sparring competition in words, which sees ancient plays recited in competitions on the town square.

On the southeastern slopes of Monte Pisano, **Bientina's** main square is dominated by the squat tower of the **Pieve di Santa Maria Assunta** with **Museo d'Arte Sacra** (☎ 0587-758432, Tues-Sun, 10 am-noon, 4-7 pm, closed Aug, free); its prized possession is the remains of the martyr St. Valentine. Otherwise, the town is best known for the drainage of its lake (at one time the largest lake in inland Tuscany), which represented one of the most complex stages of the area's land reclamation works in the mid-19th century. Leaving almost 300 square yards of fertile land, the WWF have since set up the **Oasi di Bottaccio** (Bottaccio Nature Reserve), where you can join guided tours (☎ 0583-955830).

Adventures

■ On Foot

 There are plenty of hikes and nature walks in Migilarino-San Rossore-Massaciuccoli Regional Park (see page 11, 251, 258, 286) to the west and the Monte Pisano (see page 294) to the east.

If you wish to join the local group of the CAI (Via Cisanello 2, Pisa, ☎ 050-578004, http://astr17pi.difi.unipi.it/CAI/index.html), you can do so every Wed and Thurs; see the website for the latest excursion information.

Migilarino-San Rossore-Massaciuccoli Regional Park

There are plenty of walking and cycling routes in the pine forests of this coastal natural park, which extends on the coast between Viareggio and Livorno. It is split into four main areas: the Macchia di Migliarino, the ex-presidential estate of Tenuta di San Rossore, the Tenuta di Tombolo and, further inland, the Tenuta di Collano.

To get here by **car** from Pisa, follow signs to Gombo and take the Viale dei Pini to Migliarino, the Viale delle Cascine to San Rossore, and head to Masaciuccoli for Lake Massaciuccoli. The nearest **train** stations are Migliarino and Pisa San Rossore.

The scrubland and man-made pine forests of the so-called **Macchia di Migliarino** (☎ 050-525500) are rich in wide compacted sand pathways good for bike riding and offer a route to the Quercia del Cinto, a 300-year-old British oak tree.

At the opening of the San Rossore canal, the 12,600-acre **Tenuta di San Rossore** can only be reached on foot, bicycle or by the park-run coach. It is open to the public every Sunday, on public holidays and for tours organized by the park agency. These tours (foot and bicycle) take place every Mon, Wed and Fri in summer (9:30-11:30 am, 2-4 pm), and every Tues and Thurs the rest of the year (9:30-11:30 am, 3:30-5:30 pm) by reservation with the **Centro Visite Guidate di San Rossore** (Visitor Center, Loc. Cascine Vecchie, ☎ 050-530101, fax 050-533755, www.parcosanrossore.it). Tours on horseback can be organized with **Fabio Tani** (☎ 033-0778623/050-539247, fax 050-539234), and visits by horse and carriage with **Federico and Antonio di Sacco** (☎ 033-0206235/033-5713793).

The estate parkways take you through a protected area inhabited by fallow deer, wild boar, wild hares, woodpeckers and migrating waterfowl in spring, including glossy ibis, greater flamingoes, bean and greylag geese, garganey, cranes and black and white-winged black terns. Marked trails take you around the beach (4a and 5c); Le Lame or the marshes (5a and 5d); and the forest, the main part of the estate, where there are seven more itineraries.

Pisa

Flora & Fauna

The fauna in Migilarino-San Rossore-Massaciuccoli Regional Park is typically Mediterranean with sand dunes that invite birds such as short-toed larks, oystercatchers, gannets, terns, black cormorants and migrating waders such as sandpipers, stints and curlews. The vast pinewood areas are occupied by fallow deer, wild boar and porcu-pines with great spotted and green woodpeckers, wood pigeons and Montagu's harriers representing just some of the bird population. The Lame (marshes) of San Rossore are your best bet for spotting marsh harriers, bitterns and black-winged stilts, with wild duck (mallard, garganey, teal and wigeon) visiting in winter.

Vegetation is equally diverse: holm oaks in the coastal forest are accompanied by ash, black alder and oak with phillyrea, alaternus and heather in the undergrowth. A vast 11,000-acre space is given up to the umbrella pine, which was planted here in the second half of the 18th century for the production of timber and pine nuts. The wetland area is mainly formed by sedge and reeds where small lakes flower in spring with water lilies, water buttercup, bladderwort and water-crowfoot. In the dunes, you'll find sand cornflower, sea holly and sand couch.

The **Tenuta di Tombolo** section of the park lies to the other side of the Arno River. It is home to a NATO military base (Camp Darby), which makes access somewhat limited. You can visit the area south of Calambrone (follow Vione dei Porcai) at the Cornacchiaia-Ulivo Nature Reserve, which is a good bird-watching site for passerines and woodpeckers.

Hitting the Coast

For relaxing sun-filled beach days, follow the Arno along the tree-lined Via d'Annunzio to **Marina di Pisa**. This is the oldest of the bathing resorts that stretch along the coast south to Tirrenia and Calambrone, and one of the best resorts for water sports with rental canoes for river adventures as well as diving and snorkeling (Piccolo Dorsean, Viale G. d'Annunzio 234, ☎ 347-8482278, www.ocean-adventures.info). The large fishing nets you'll see raised at the mouth of the river on wooden stilts are known as *bilance*. Free beaches are along Lungomare Repubblica and Lungomare P.A. da Montefeltro, where dunes are shaded by fresh pine trees and backed by restaurants, hotels and nightlife.

There are lots of free beach to the north at **Migliarino**, in the Maccha di Migliarino, where the sea is reached via 200 m (656 feet) of dunes. The road is closed during peak season, so leave your car in the car park and take the shuttle bus.

The beach is very spacious to the south at **Tirrenia**, but the only free tract is to the far north at the **WWF Dune di Tirrenia** (☎ 050-580999, www.wwf.it/oasi/schede2/tirrenia.htm, north of the Lido bathing establishment). The spacious beach to the south at **Calambrone** is your other option for much quieter bathing opportunities.

Information Sources:

APT Marina di Pisa (Marina di Pisa Tourist Office, Via Minorca, ☎ 050-311952).

APT Tirrenia (Tirrenia Tourist Office, Via Pisorno 5, ☎ 050-32510).

Monte Pisano

Hikers should head into the hills of Monte Pisano northeast of the city. An isolated group of hills that run from northwest to southeast between the Serchio and Arno rivers, the entire ridge is marked out by CAI#00, a 23-mile footpath that runs from Balbano in the province of Lucca to San Giovanni alla Vena (just north of Cascina). It can also be reached from Vecchiano (#010), Ripafratta (#011), Asciano (#015) and Agnano (#017).

Other walks will take you up Monte Verruca (#021 from Noce or #023 from Vicopisano), and there are four loop-walks for those that don't like retracing their steps: the #02 Calci ring (leaving from Foce di Calci or Castelmaggiore), the #03 Nicosia ring (which also takes you up Monte Verruca, where the rock known as *verrucano* is sourced), the #04 Vicopisano ring and the #05 Buti ring (past the Badia and up Monte d'Oro).

On the Nicosia ring watch for the Franciscan **Monastero di Nicosia** (accessible via a trail off the right of the road to Montemagno from Calci), where a church displays a *Virgin and Child with Angels* by Alvaro Pirez d'Evora and a 13th-century fresco of the *Virgin and Saints* on the lunette of the façade. Another trail leads from Montemagno itself to the medieval ruins of the **Abbazia di San Michele alla Verruca**, and on to the summit of Monte Verruca (536 m/1,758 feet) where you'll find a picturesque 13th-century castle that was once fiercely fought over between Pisa and Florence.

Cyclists will also find plenty to enjoy, whether they pick up the cycle loop from Caprona near Calci (22 miles, four hours) or one of the five well-mapped itineraries, two of which depart from Cascina up Monte Perocchio (one 25 miles, four hours; the other 22 miles, three hours), another from Cascina to Agnano and back (24 miles, three hours), one from Cascina up Monte Verruca (17 miles, two hours) and the last from Vicopisano up Monte Castellare (five miles, one hour). From Cascina, you can also join a 14-mile route along the Arno River cycle track into Pisa.

For adventures in the air, contact the **Scuola di Parapendio Monti Pisani** (San Giuliano Terme, ☎ 335-8459449, fax 0584-791360, www.montipisani.com/parapendio.htm).

Spa Days

While Montecatini and Monsummano Terme may just be a short drive away, the province of Pisa has its own thermal waters of note:

Nearest to the center, **Uliveto Terme** (Via Provinciale Vicarese, ☎ 050-789511, fax 050-788194, June-Sept), near Cascina, is noted for its gastro-intestinal benefits.

On the slopes of Monte Pisano, four miles from Pisa, **San Giuliano Terme** (Largo Shelley 18, ☎ 050-81807, fax 050-817053, www.termesangiuliano.com, €28.50) has been a spa center since Roman times with thermal-calcific waters and treatments designed to revitalize the respiratory and immune systems. It occupies an 18th-century building in a beautiful park of olive trees (Parco degli Ulivi) once frequented by the Grand Dukes of Tuscany, philosopher Montaigne, and poets Byron and Shelley. In nearby Caldàccioli (from the Latin *Calidae Aqua*) are the remains of the Roman aqueduct, which once brought water to Pisa.

Pisa

Surrounded by the vineyards and cypress trees of the Era Valley 25 miles south from Pisa, the fountain of sulfureous-calcific-carbonic waters at **Cascina Terme** (Piazza Garibaldi 9, ☎ 0587-646140, fax 0587-645154) was already known in Roman times as *Castrum de Aquis*.

■ On Wheels

Four of Pisa's most charismatic churches are a pleasant cycle ride outside the city walls. The most popular, Certosa di Pisa, is eight miles to the north, while San Piero a Grado is a three-mile cycle to the west, and the remaining two (Santa Croce in Fossabanda and San Michele degli Scalzi) are an even shorter ride to the east.

Basilica di San Piero a Grado (Via Vecchia Marina, ☎ 050-960065, daily, 8 am-7 pm, free). Heading in the direction of Marina di Pisa, this Romanesque basilica is midway between Pisa and the coast. Although much of the façade shows signs of heavy flood damage, inside the Livornese tufa and black-and-white marble walls is a grandiose interior well worth the trip. Three naves are supported by 26 beautiful classical columns and the walls are covered with three levels of early 14th-century frescoes attributed to Lucchese painter Deodato Orlandi, which were only uncovered after restorations in 2000. The frescoes, depicting the stories of Saints Peter and Paul, give some insight into the church's foundation: Apostle Peter is said to have landed here around 43 BC on his journey from Antioch to Rome.

The structure is located in prime territory for exploring the Migilarino-San Rossore-Massaciuccoli Regional Park or continuing to Marina di Pisa and exploring the Pisan coastline.

Just outside the city walls to the east, the 14th-century **Chiesa di Santa Croce in Fossabanda** has a fine 15th-century portico and, inside, a beautifully-crafted altarpiece decorated with an early 15th-century *Madonna and Child Enthroned with Angels* by Alvaro Pirez d'Evora. Farther along the street, **Chiesa di San Michele degli Scalzi** overlooks the river. It was constructed, along with the adjacent monastery, by Benedictine friars in the 11th century. Note the central portal with carved lintel representing the angelic hierarchies and, inside, a 13th-century crucifix. Its Lombardic bell tower is another of Pisa's towers to suffer from the leaning effect.

For longer cycle rides, head to into the Monte Pisano (see page 297) or the Valdera (see page 308-309).

■ On Horseback

Most of the local horseback riding takes place along the beach or in Migilarino-San Rossore-Massaciuccoli Regional Park. Contact **Centro Ippico Litorale Pisano** (Via Porcari 2, Loc. Calambrone, ☎ 050-32268), **Centro Ippico KTM** (Via F. Lanfreducci 17, Loc. Marina di Pisa, ☎ 050-311052) or **Associazione Ippica Tirrenia** (Vione dei Porcari, Tirrenia, ☎ 050-32268) for beach rides, and **Centro Ippico Equiland** (Via M. di Oratorio, Loc. Oratoio, ☎ 050-982229) and **Centro Ippico Pineta Salviati** (Via del Mare 8, Loc. Migliarino, ☎ 050-804287, fax 050-803216, http://cips.monrif.net) offer park excursions.

■ On Water

Unsurprisingly, the majority of watersports are a short drive away on the Pisan coast. There is **windsurfing** to be enjoyed at **Tirrenia** (**Scuola Wind-Surf**, Via degli Orleandri 51/3, ☎ 050-33021) and **Calambrone** (**Scuola Velica e Wind Surf**, Viale del Tirreno), and **diving** and **snorkeling** at **Marina di Pisa** (Piccolo Dorsean, Viale G. d'Annunzio 234, ☎ 347-8482278, www.ocean-adventures.info). Boat rental is available from **Circolo Nautico Marina Piccola** (Lungarno G. d'Annunzio 142, ☎ 050-960450) or the **Circolo Nautico Lega Navale Italiana** (Viale G. d'Annunzio 250, Marina di Pisa, ☎ 050-36652).

There are plenty of opportunities to **canoe** the Arno: in Pisa itself with **Canottieri Arno Pisa** (Via Bonaccorso da Padule 2, Pisa, ☎ 050-28465, fax 050-41061) and, out of town, at Calcinaia with **Canottieri Pietro Cavallini** (Via Giovanni XXIII 9, ☎ 0587-489968).

Events & Entertainment

■ Theater

The Romanesque Chiesa di Sant'Andrea was abandoned for 20 years before it was converted in 1986 by local volunteers to the **Teatro Sant'Andrea** (Via del Cuore, ☎ 050-542364, www.archicoop.it/santandrea). It hosts a range of drama and touring productions in its Nov-May season.

There's opera, drama and dance in the **Teatro Verdi** (Via Palestro 40, ☎ 050-941111, www.teatrodipisa.pi.it, €6-43, Sept-Jan). And what a venue: inaugurated in 1867 (and restored between 1985 and 1989), it is one of the most beautiful and historical theaters in central Italy.

■ Events

June is by far Pisa's most eventful month with traditional, cultural and musical entertainments known as *Giugno Pisano* (Pisa June).

On the last Sunday of June, the two rival sides of the city on either side of the Arno (Tramontana and Mezzogiorno) meet on the Ponte del Mezzo in a medieval match of strength known as the **Gioco del Ponte** (Game of the Bridge). Six teams of 20 men from each side, representing the six neighborhoods from each side of the river, compete to push a seven-ton, 12-m (39-foot) *carrello*, or iron wagon, along a sliding rail into their oppo-

nent's area. The event is opened with a costumed procession along the Lungarni (i.e., both sides of the Arno) to celebrate an event that probably dates back to medieval military training.

Every four years in June, the **Regata delle Antiche Repubbliche Marinare** (Regatta of the Ancient Maritime Republics) returns to Pisa. Archenemies, the Pisans (red with an eagle), the Amalfians (blue with a winged horse), the Genoese (white with a griffon) and the Venetians (blue with a lion) compete in this boat race. In the other three years it takes place in the lagoon at Venice, in the sea at Genoa and on the Amalfi Coast. After a procession in costume commemorating the important events in each team's maritime history, eight oarsmen and a helmsman race for 2,000 m (6,560 feet) against the current to the finishing post near Chiesa di San Matteo.

A second boat race, the **Regata Storica di San Ranieri** (Historic Regatta of St Ranieri) takes place every June 17 to celebrate Pisa's patron saint day. It is a fierce competition between the city's four historical neighborhoods as divided by the Arno River and the city's two main streets. The boats are modern versions of the frigates once used by the Medicean order of Knights of Santo Stefano. Raced by eight oarsmen, one helmsman and a climber, the race of 1,500 m (4,920 feet) departs from slightly upstream of the railway bridge and finishes in front of the Palazzo Medici where the climber must ascend to the top of the mast and grab the *paliotto* (silk banner). The event is introduced the night before by the **Luminara di San Ranieri** (Illumination of St. Ranieri), with 70,000 wax lamps placed along the Lungarni.

SOMETHING FOR THE KIDS

KID FRIENDLY Probably one of the most unusual amusement parks in Tuscany is **Ciclilandia** (Cycleland, Piazza dei Fiori, Tirrenia, ☎ 050-33573, www.ciclilandia.it, daily, summer, 3:30-8 pm, 9 pm-midnight, winter, 2:30-6 pm, €6, conc. €4, bikes for hire from €3.60). Kids can use mountain bikes, cycle-carriages, cycle-go-karts and get bicycle lessons. They even receive a special driving license! All are watched over by the traffic police. There's also a Pirates' Castle, complete with tunnels, bridges, slides and rubber forests.

Just outside of the seaside town of Tirrenia deep in the Migliarino-San Rossore-Massaciuccoli Natural Park, **Fantasilandia** is full to brimming with kiddies' attractions (Fantasyland, Viale Tirreno 42, Tirrenia, ☎ 050-30326, June-Sept, daily, 8 am-8 pm, Oct-Feb, Sat-Sun and public holidays, 9 am-8 pm, €10.50, conc. €8.50). It is split into two sectors: one free (electric car track, miniature train and mechanical bull); the other at a small charge (water slides, swings and a sky-lift).

Things get a little more educational at the **Museo di Storia Naturale** (Natural History Museum, Certosa di Pisa, Via Roma 103, Calci, ☎ 050-937751, July-Sept, daily, 10 am-1 pm, 3-7 pm (5-11 pm, Tues, Thurs), Oct-June, Tues-Sun, 10 am-1 pm, 2:30-7 pm, €3, conc. €2). Skeleton cetaceans (including a 100-foot whale) hang from invisible wires in the air, while dolphins, killer and sperm whales jostle for attention in the 350-foot-long corridor. There are also amphibians, reptiles, mammals and birds, many of which are rare or extinct.

A 20-minute drive out of Pisa, the **Museo Piaggio Giovanni A. Agnelli** (Piaggio Museum, Viale R. Paggio 7, Pontedera, ☎ 0587-27171, www.museopaggio.it, Wed-Sat, 10 am-6 pm, free) exhibits a collection of motorscooters – the Vespa, Gilera and Poggio models once produced in the factory it occupies. Kids and transport enthusiasts will enjoy the scale models, designs and publicity campaigns from the 1930s to the present day.

The ancient medieval town of Peccioli is the location of the area's **Prehistoric Park**, complete with lifelike reproductions of dinosaurs, cavemen and their habitats (Via dei Cappuccini 20, Peccioli, ☎/fax

0587-636030, www.parcopreistorico.it, daily, 9 am-noon, 2 pm-dusk, €4, conc. €3).

In Capannoli, the **Museo Zoologico** displays 1,400 species in carefully constructed natural surroundings (Zoological Museum, Villa Baciocchi, Via Volteranna 233, ☎ 0587-606611, daily, 9 am-12:30 pm, 3:30-7 pm, free).

Where to Shop

Pisa is a pleasant city for shoppers, with stores sensibly laid out from the train station along the Corso Italia and on the Ponte di Mezzo on Borgo Stretto. Shops to look out for include **Pasticceria Federico Salza** (Borgo Stretto 46, ☎ 050-580244, www.salza.it) for its beautifully-formed chocolates and pastry goods (including a chocolate Leaning Tower of Pisa) and the **Libreria Fogola** (Corso Italia 82, ☎ 050-502547, www.libreriafogola.it) with English-language books and Internet connection.

The famous **antique market** is held every second weekend of the month (except in July and Aug) under the Logge di Bianchi (Via San Martino).

Where to Eat

LOCAL FLAVORS

Bordatino: Rich bean broth with red cabbage.
Baccalà con i porri: Salt cod cooked with leeks and tomatoes.
Bavettine sul pesce: Thin, flat strips of pasta served on fish.
Cavolo strasciato: Boiled cabbage (a traditional side dish).
Cèe: Young eels sautéed with oil, garlic and sage.
Cinghiale in umido con le olive nere: Stewed boar's meat in a black olive sauce.
Coniglio alla cacciatore: Rabbit hunter-style.
Francesina in carne bollita: Onion and braised meat.
Necci: Chestnut flour flat breads.
Pappardelle alla lepre: Pasta in a rich hare's sauce.
Trippa alla pisana: Tripe served with onion, carrots and pork or minced beef.
Uova e cipolla: Eggs and onion.
Zuppa di ranocchi: Frog soup.
Traditional *dolci* include the *torta co'bischeri*, a cake made of rice, egg, chocolate, pine nuts and grapes.

It's pretty hard finding a good restaurant in the center of Pisa these days. **Da Antonio** (Via Arnaccio 105, ☎ 050-742494, $$), **L'Artilafo** (Via Volturno 38, ☎ 050-27010, $$) and **Osterio del Porton Rosso** (Via Porton Rosso 11, ☎ 050-580566, $$) are notable exceptions at the lower end of the price bracket.

Trattoria **Da Bruno** (Via Luigi Bianchi 12, ☎ 050-560818, www.pisaonline.it/trattoriadabruno, closed Tues, $$) is the best choice within walking distance of the Leaning Tower. Its menu features principally rustic country dishes such as *zuppa alla pisana*, *baccalà con i porri* (salt cod cooked with leeks and tomatoes) and a variety of grilled fish and meat dishes.

One of Pisa's most popular seafood spots, atmospheric **Al Ristoro dei Vecchi Macelli** (Via Volturno 49, ☎ 050-20424, closed Wed and Aug, $$$) serves sophisticated fish dishes and delicious homemade pasta (such as the *tortelli* stuffed with wild herbs and potato purée). Reservations recommended.

A 30-minute drive south from Pisa on the SS206, **La Gattaiola** (Via San Lorenzo 2-4, Fauglia, ☎ 050-650852, closed Mon, $$) serves a hearty menu of *risotto con fungi* (wild mushroom risotto, a speciality of the area), roasted meats and homemade pastas. Reservations recommended.

Family-run **Dante e Ivana** (Viale del Tirreno 107c, Tirrenia, ☎ 050-384882, www.danteeivana.it, closed Sun and Mon lunch, $$$) is one of the top fish restaurants in the area with a menu of seafood from the Tyrrhenian Sea. The house specialty, *catalana* (lobster), is chosen from the aquarium, rather than the menu. *Fondu delle pesce* (fish fondu) makes a tasty winter choice. Reservations recommended.

On the Trail of Local Wine

Taste your way around the region with the wines of the Colline Pisane, San Torpè and Montescudaio. Find out more about local producers by contacting:

Consorzio Vino Bianco Pisano di San Torpé DOC (Via Livornese 30, Crespina, ☎ 050-643434, fax 050-643996, www.terreditoscana.regione.toscana.it/vinitaly/ita/vini/pisano.html).

Consorzio Vini Montescudaio DOC (Via della Madonna 15, Montescudaio, ☎0586-650038, fax 0586-650236, www.terreditoscana.regione.toscana.it/vinitaly/ita/vini/montescudaio.html).

Where to Stay

Pisa's most historic hotel, the **Royal Victoria** ☆☆☆ (Lungarno Pacinotti 12, ☎ 050-940111, www.royalvictoria.it, $$$) first opened in 1837 when the Piegaja family (whose descendants still run the business) purchased an old medieval tower and turned it into the city's first hotel. Found to the right across Ponte di Mezzo, the hotel's history, frescoed ceilings and near-original furnishings (which have welcomed such illustrious names as Charles Dickens) make advance bookings necessary.

Small and friendly, **Verdi** ☆☆☆ (Piazza Repubblica 5/6, ☎ 050-598947, $$$) is one of the city's most charismatic venues, especially if you're planning on catching a performance at the nearby Teatro Verdi. It is built on the site of an old convent that was destroyed during World War II and parts of the old architecture can still be seen, including a hallway that once linked the convent to the Chiesa di San Andrea.

Within walking distance of the Piazza dei Miracoli, **Grand Hotel Duomo** ☆☆☆☆ (Via Santa Maria 94, ☎ 050-561894, fax 050-560418, www.grandhotelduomo.it, $$$$) is in one of the city's most sought-after locations, not least for the splendid views over the square from the hotel roof garden. The restaurant serves a range of Tuscan dishes.

Occupying a romantic 14th-century villa not far from the Piazza dei Miracoli, the rooms of **Relais dell'Orologio** ☆☆☆☆☆ (Via della Faggiola 12/14, ☎ 050-830361, www.hotelrelaisorologio.com, closed Jan-Feb, $$$$$) have all the low, wooden-beamed ceilings, antique furnishings and original fire places you'd probably expect in such an illustrious location. The restaurant is popular.

Within sight of the coast is **Grand Hotel Golf** ☆☆☆☆ (Via dell'Edera 29, **Tirrenia**, ☎ 050-957018, fax 050-32111, www.grandhotelgolf.it, $$$), one of the best out-of-town locations for golfing enthusiasts (it has two year-round courses). The 2½-acre grounds also have plenty to offer the non-golfing enthusiast, including luxury pools, a stretch of private beach, a piano-bar and a restaurant specializing in tasty local cuisine. Balconied rooms offer a good panorama over the coast. Bicycle rental and horseback riding by arrangement.

Your cheapest hotel options in the city are **Clio** ☆ (Via S. Lorenzino 3, ☎ 050-28446, $$), off Corso Italia, **Roseto** ☆☆ (Via Mascagni 24, ☎/fax 050-42596, $$), just beside the station, and **Villa Primavera** ☆☆ (Via B. Pisano 43, ☎ 050-23537, fax 050-27020, $$), to the east, just outside the city walls.

Pisa has a popular campground (**Torre Pendente** ☆, Via delle Cascine 86, ☎ 050-561704, fax 050-56734, $, Apr-Oct), but there is more choice along the coast at Marina di Pisa (**Internazionale** ☆, Via Litoranea 7, ☎ 050-36553, fax 050-35211, $, May-Sept), Calambrone (**Mare e Sole** ☆, Viale del Tirreno, ☎ 050-32757, fax 050-30488, $; and **Pineta** ☆, Via delle Mimose 2, ☎ 050-32028, fax 050-384721, $). There is one more at Tirrenia (**St Michel** ☆, Via della Bigattiera 24, ☎ 050-33103/348-3302190, fax 050-35211, www.campingstmichael.com, $, June-15 Sept).

There are two youth hostels in the area: **Centro Turistico Madonna dell'Aqua** near San Giuliano Terme (Via Pietrasanta 15, Loc. Madonna dell'Aqua, ☎/fax 050-890622, $) and **Ostello Sterpaia** (Viale delle Cascine, ☎ 050-523019, $). The latter is well-placed for forays into the Migilarino-San Rossore-Massaciuccoli Regional Park.

Outside of Pisa

Heading south from Pisa, the territory is split between two provinces: Pisa and Livorno. Pisa is mostly landlocked, following the Arno east to Florence and the Era south to the picturesque hill town of Volterra, the main tourist town in the province. Livorno, by contrast, is coastal, an attractive series of beaches that stretch south from the provincial capital down to the boundary with Grosseto and the Maremma. Offshore are the seven sisters of the Tuscan Archipelago.

IN THIS CHAPTER	

REGION AT A GLANCE

- **Main city:** Pisa.
- **Afternoon trips from Pisa:** Certosa di Pisa (see page 294).
- **City breaks:** Livorno (see page 317), Volterra (see page 308).

- **Rural retreats:** Valdera (see page 308-309), Valdicecina (see page 315), Val di Cornia (see page 327), San Rossore (see page 295-96), Bolgheri (see page 326).

- **Spa towns:** San Giuliano Terme (see page 297), Cascina Terme (see page 298), Uliveto Terme (see page 297).

- **Beach breaks:** Pisa's coast (see page 299), the Etruscan Riviera (see page 322), Versilia Coast (see page 249).

- **Island sorties:** Elba (see page 332), Capraia (see page 336), Gorgona (see page 337), Pianosa (see page 338).

Valdarno Inferiore

On the eastern side of Monte Pisano, Valdarno Inferiore (the Lower Arno Valley) follows the river northeast to Florence. This was an area of great importance during the Middle Ages with towns such as Santa Maria a Monte, Vicopisano, San Miniato and Montopoli in Val d'Arno growing up along the Via Francigena. To protect itself against the machinations of Florence, Pisa fortified the Arno's banks from the 12th century on, creating the towns of Castelfranco di Sotto, Santa Croce sull'Arno, Ponsacco, Cascina, Bientina and Pontedera, but the area eventually fell to the Florentines in the 16th century.

The construction in 1846 of the Florence-Pisa-Livorno railway line, and more recently of the Florence-to-Livorno *superstrada*, heralded the area's current industrial development, with busy centers producing glass, terracotta, pottery, timber and leather.

■ Getting Here & Around

By Train: The Florence-Pisa-Livorno train line (☎ 848-888088, www.trenitalia.it) runs from Firenze SMN through Empoli to Livorno stopping at San Miniato, Santa Croce sull'Arno/Montopoli in Val d'Arno and Pontedera up to five times an hour.

By Bus: From the stop in San Miniato, it is a steep two-mile climb to the historic center (San Miniato Alto); a shuttle bus runs from the station every 30 minutes (6:30-10:30 am, 3:30-7:30 pm) if you don't want to do the trek.

By Car: The valley is well placed on the road network with the Florence-Pisa-Livorno *superstrada* (SGC FI-PI-LI) and the longer winding SS67 (the old road to Florence known as the "Tosco Romagnola"), both following the river towards Pisa.

■ Information Sources

Tourist Offices: **APT Pisa** (Pisa Tourist Office) is the main tourist information center for the region, but there are smaller offices in **Montopoli Val d'Arno** (Piazza San Michele 14, ☎ 0571-449024), **Santa Croce sull'Arno** (Piazza Matteoti 41, ☎ 0571-31103), **Santa Maria a Monte** (Via dell'Orologico, ☎ 0587-26643) and **San Miniato** (Piazza del Popolo 20,

☎ 0571-42233; summer, daily, 9 am-1 pm, 4-7:30 pm, winter, Mon-Sat, 9 am-1 pm, 3-6:30 pm, Sun, 10 am-1 pm, 3-7:30 pm).

Maps: The region is well served by APT Pisa's free *Carta della Sentieristica* (trail map), which shows hiking routes and accommodation in the region.

■ Sightseeing

Castelfranco di Sotto & Santa Maria a Monte

 Across the Monte Pisano from Pisa, the small town of Castelfranco di Sotto is the first major stop on the south bank of the Arno River. The historic center is built to a typical medieval street plan, with a rectangular shape intersected at right angles by nine roads, and surrounded by fortress-style walls still in possession of four well-preserved tower gates.

Inside the walls, the main square is marked by the 15th-century porticoed **Palazzo Comunale** (Town Hall) and the heavily reconstructed **Collegiata di San Pietro** (Collegiate Church of St Pietro); only the brick lunette, the two sandstone lions and some of the façade decoration remain from the original 13th-century construction. There are a few artistic works of note: a *Raising of Tabitha* by Passignano; a 14th-century statue of *San Pietro;* and two splendid wooden statues next to the second altar.

The square is also the location for the June **Palio dei Barchini** (☎ 0571-47391), which sees the local *contrades* compete in a local version of the Ironman.

Footpaths from town take you along the Arno and up the southeastern slopes of **Monte Cerbaie**. The low ridge (its maximum elevation is 114 m/374 feet at Montefalcone) runs parallel to the Canale Usciana (one of the works built to drain the nearby Fucecchio marshes), which is crossed just before you reach Santa Maria a Monte. This now-industrial village was fortified from the 11th century on, with the Luccans adding a castle in 1252 and the Florentines three rings of walls in 1339. The latter are also to be thanked for the unusual path of the single main road, which spirals inside its remaining walls past the Palazzo Pretorio and **Collegiata di San Giovanni** (Collegiate Church of San Giovanni).

Montopoli in Val d'Arno

Hilltop Montopoli in Val d'Arno, on the Arno's south bank, is well served by foot **trails**, many of which reach down to Palaia and on to Peccioli and Lajatico in the Era Valley.

Badly damaged in the last war, the small industrial town has always borne the brunt of territorial skirmishes, located as it is midway between Pisa, Florence and Lucca. Of the original architecture, there remain only the battlement tower of the 14th-century **Chiesa di Santo Stefano**, with *Adam and Eve* after the *Original Sin* by Jacopo Vignali, the so-called **Archi di Castruccio** (Arch of Castruccio), and the 16th-century **Conservatorio di Santa Marta**, which contains a *Raising of Lazarus* by Cigoli and a *Virgin with the Souls in Purgatory* by Antonio Franchi.

A pleasant **ramble** into the Chiecina Valley to **Marti** will bring you to the 14th-century brick **Chiesa di Santa Maria Novella**, decorated with 17th-century frescoes. Take the road to the right to arrive at **Palaia**. Inside its ring of old walls (entered via the gates, Civica and Fiorentina), the center of town is marked by the 11th-century **Chiesa di Sant'Andrea** with its *Madonna and Child* in painted terracotta by Andrea della Robbia.

Just out of town, you'll find the lovely isolated **Pieve di San Martino**, a Romanesque-Gothic construction that dates back to the 13th century. You can continue

Pisa

from here to **Gello**, where the 13th-century terracotta-brick **Chiesa di San Lorenzo** contains an interesting 15th-century fresco; to **Villa Saletta**, a small fortified village that grew up around the 17th-century Villa Ricardi, with an oratory that houses a 13th-century *Virgin and Child*; or go on to **Forcoli**, where the countryside is dotted with the large *tabaccaie* (tobacco-drying buildings).

Santa Croce sull'Arno

Back on the left bank, Santa Croce sull'Arno is one of the most important towns in the area for its tanning industry. The old center has traces of the original medieval layout within its 15th-century town walls and there are two churches of note: the **parish church** with a 13th-century Byzantine wooden sculpture of Lucca's *Volto Santo*; and the Baroque **Chiesa di Santa Cristina** with vault fresco by Antonio Domenico Bamberini.

San Miniato

San Miniato marks the border with the neighboring province of Florence. A strategic hilltop site on the Via Francigena, the *Alto* (historical center) has represented since medieval times the no-man's land between the Florentine Ghibellines and the Lower Valdarno Guelphs. Today, the town conserves its medieval atmosphere dominated by the tower of the ancient *Rocca* (castle), which guides the approach to town. The town's entrance gate leads you to Piazza del Popolo, which is overlooked by the much rebuilt and incomplete façade of **Chiesa di San Dominico** (formerly dei Santi Jacopo e Lucia). Inside, the walls are

frescoed with the *Life of St Domenic* (18th century); an altarpiece with *Virgin and Child with Four Saints* by Domenico da Michelino decorates the Cappella dei Samminiati; and the marble *Tomb of Giovanni Chellini*, modeled on a tomb by Bernardo Rossellino in Florence's Chiesa di Santa Croce, is housed nearby.

The road rises to the **Piazza della Republica** (formerly Piazza del Seminario), where a spectacular view over the valley awaits behind the concave façade of the **Seminario**, whose exterior is jazzed up by 17th-century *sgraffiti* and medallions. To its left, the **Palazzo Vescovile** forms the link with the Piazza del Duomo.

Three flights of stairs lead up to the tree-lined **Piazza del Duomo** (also known as the "Prato del Duomo," the Field of the Duomo), which occupies a superb vantage point over the Arno Valley. It unites the palaces of the 13th-century ecclesiastic rulers, including the **Palazzo dei Vicari dell'Imperatore**, which incorporates a pre-existing battlement tower into the design, and was apparently the birthplace of the Countess Matilde (1046).

The Romanesque **Duomo** with polychrome terracotta and ceramic-decorated façade is itself dominated by its massive campanile, known locally as the "Torre di Matilde." Originally constructed in the 12th century (when it was dedicated to St Genesius), it was heavily altered in the 16th century when the three portals of sandstone were added to the exterior.

The adjacent **Museo di Arte Sacra** (Museum of Sacred Art, ☎ 0571-418071, Apr-Nov, Tues-Sun, 9 am-noon, 3-6 pm, Dec-Mar, Tues-Sun, 10 am-12:30 pm, 3-6 pm) displays the best bits taken from inside both the town's and province's churches, including the ceramic basins that originally decorated the Duomo façade, *Madonna of the Girdle with Saints* by Neri di Bicci and a terracotta bust of Jesus by Verrocchio called *The Redeemer*.

From the Prato del Duomo, a short walk takes you up to **Torre di Federico**, which is all that remains of the 13th-century Rocca built by Emperor Frederico II and restored after damage in World War II. It gives splendid views over the surrounding countryside as far as the Apuan Alps to the north and Volterra to the south.

To the left of the Duomo, the **Santuario del Crocifisso** was built to house a 10th-century crucifix, which, displayed in a *Risen Christ* polyptych by Francesco Lanfranchi, was thought to have saved the town from the plague of 1637. The sanctuary's dome is frescoed with the story of the *Ascension of Christ* by Antonio Domenico Bamberini. Stairs outside descend to the vast **Chiesa di San Francesco**, which was built on the site of an ancient shrine dedicated to the saint after whom the town is named.

Truffles

Nearly half of the Tuscan production of white truffles comes from the hills of San Miniato, the hamlets of the Val d'Egola and the towns of Peccioli, Montopoli, Palaia and Volterra; the white truffle capital, San Miniato, contributing approximately 220,000 lbs of truffles each year. The collection is split into three distinct stages: the first collections of truffles at the end of September, which are called "di Marca" (meaning they are found near the surface and have very little perfume); the main and best truffle collection from Oct to Nov; and the collection of the marzuolo truffle (inferior quality to the white) in Jan and Feb.

The **Mostra Mercato Nazionale del Tartufo Bianco** (National Exhibition and Market of the White Truffle, San Miniato, last three weekends of Nov) fragrantly celebrates truffle collection, with small folk and town festivals also revolving around the fungi at **Corazzano** (first weekend of Oct), **Balconevisi** (third week of Oct for a week, the event culminating in Il Palio del Papero, an old racing event), **Forcoli** (last week of Sept), **Palaia** (last week of Oct) and **Volterra** (last weekend in Oct).

The biggest white truffle in the world was found in the forests of **Balconevisi** in 1954; weighing 5½ lbs, it was donated to ex-American president Dwight D. Eisenhower.

■ Adventures

From San Miniato Basso (the new town by the train station), you can pick up **trails** across the Evola River to Montopoli in Val d'Arno and Palaia. To do the trails on **horseback**, contact **Centro Ippico San Goro** (Via San Goro 4, San Miniato, ☎ 0571-408158). To organize **canoe trips** on local rivers, contact **Canoa San Miniato** (☎ 0571-400026, http://space.tin.it/sport/ricminu/canoasm).

■ Where to Stay

 San Miniato Alto has only two hotels: **Centro Turistico San Martino** ☆☆☆ (Via Cesare Battisti 70, ☎ 0571-401469, fax 0571-403712, $$) and **Miravalle** ☆☆☆ (Piazza del Castelo 3, ☎ 0571-418074, fax 0571-419681, $$), which occupies the fortress tower of the Palazzo dei Vicari dell'Imperatore.

If you want to splurge, the best hotel in the region is in Santa Croce sull'Arno and is called **Cristallo** ☆☆☆☆ (Largo Galilei 11, ☎ 0571-366440, fax 0571-366420, $$$$). There's also the delightful **La Vecchia Fornace** ☆☆☆ (Via dell'Argine 1, ☎ 0571-36523, fax 0571-360508, $$) if Cristallo is full.

The area's campground is at Montopoli in Val d'Arno (**Toscana Village** ☆☆☆, Via Fornoli 9, ☎ 0587-449032, fax 0587-449449, $, Apr-Oct) with outdoor pool.

The majority of the *agriturismi* can be found around Palaia. Try **Ca'Solare** (Via Campagna 19, Loc. Montefoscoli, ☎/fax 0587-670190); **Il Prato** (Via Vivaldi 1, Loc. Il Prato, ☎ 0587-622076, fax 0587-622244); or **Tenuta San Michele** (Via Toiano 20, Fraz. Toiano, ☎ 0587-632128, fax 0587-632161). All have pools.

Volterra & the Colline Metallifere

The wide fertile valley of the Valdera (the Era Valley) spreads along the Era River south from Pontedera bordering the provinces of Florence and Siena. From Pontedera, you can easily access the windy SS439 (known as the "Sarzanese Valdera'), which runs through the valley to the northeastern hills of Volterra. It is your best approach to the hilltop villages, which dot the land; picturesque hamlets that descend from the ancient castles and aristocratic villas once so fiercely fought over between Florence, Pisa and Volterra.

From Volterra, the Valdicecina (and the SS68) follows the Cecina River southwest to the coast while the Colline Metallifere head south towards Massa Marittima. This is a wild area covered with woodlands and barren hills, which were once considered "hellish" because of the geothermal gases (now controlled by power stations), which once freely erupted from the soil.

■ Getting Here & Around

Heading south from Pontedera, Volterra and the Valdera are best explored by **car** and **bicycle** on the **SS439. Buses** run to Volterra from Siena (SITA, ☎ 800-373760, www.sita-on-line.it, change at Colle di Val d'Elsa), San Gimignano (SITA, change at Poggibonsi), Florence (SITA, two direct services a day or change at Colle di Val d'Elsa) and Pisa (APT, change at Pontedera); all drop you on the south side of the town, a short walk from Piazza dei Priori.

Saline di Volterra is on the Pisa-Cecina-Volterra Saline **train** line (☎ 848-888088, www.trenitalia.it); a shuttle bus will take you from the station to Volterra itself.

ATL (Via dei Parmigiani 6, Livorno, ☎ 0586-680853) run local **bus** services between the towns of Montescudaio, Guardistallo, Riparbella, Santa Luce, Castellina Marittima and Casale Marittimo.

■ Information Sources

Tourist Offices: **Consorzio Turistico di Volterra** (Volterra Tourist Office) is on the main square in Volterra (Piazza dei Priori 20, ☎ 0588-87257), it and APT Pisa are your best sources of information on the Valdera. There are also two seasonal tourist offices (summer only) at **Lari** (Piazza Matteotti 2, ☎ 0587-685515) and **Peccioli** (Via de Chirico 11, ☎ 0587-672411).

The **Parco Alta Valdera** (Valdera Park) has its own head office at Peccioli (Via de Chirico, ☎ 0587-672411, fax 0587-672450, www.valdera.org). You can find out information here about outdoor activities in the areas of Peccioli, Terricciola, Capannoli, Palaia, Lajatico and Chianni.

The main tourist office south of Volterra is in **Pomarance** (Piazza della Costituzione, ☎ 0588-63187), but there are also offices in **Casale Marittimo** (Piazza del Popolo 17, ☎ 0586-652306), **Castelnuovo Val di Cecina** (Piazza Plebiscito, ☎ 0588-20290) and **Montescudaio** (Via della Madonna 2, ☎ 0586-651942). The **Communità Montane Valdicecina** (Cecina Mountain Community) can also be found in Pomarance (Via Roncalli 38, ☎ 0588-62003)

Adventure Information: You can get further information about local nature trekking around Montescudaio from the **Gruppo Amici della Natura** (Via Provinciale Tre Comuni, ☎ 0586-630704) and around the Valdera from **Legambiente Valdera** (Via Fiumalbi 6, Pontedera, ☎ 0587-56200).

■ Sightseeing & Adventures

The Route to Volterra

Well-placed where the Era River joins the Arno, **Pontedera** is – depending on your particular interests – best-known for the motor scooters once produced in the Piaggio factory; the current furniture-manufacturing industry; or the town's most famous son, Andrea Pisano. Whatever brings you here, you'll find a town center more-or-less obliterated in World War II (the Piaggio factory was itself devastated by the retreating German soldiers) and hastily reconstructed in the 20th century. There are a few medieval frescoes still on show in the Santuario di SS Crocifisso, a well-reconstructed Torre dell'Orologio (clock tower) next to the Palazzo Pretorio, and a couple of altarpieces from the Empoli school in the Duomo, but not much else.

Pontedera is a good base for **horseback riding** into the Era Hills. Book with the **Centro Ippico Lo Scoiattiolo** (Via Vicinale della Valle, Treggiaia, ☎ 0587-476432, fax 0587-474015, www.loscoiattolo.com) for rental, lessons and guided treks. The 18-acre **Parco dei Salici** (LIPU reserve, ☎ 0587-299111) is a small riverside nature reserve on the left bank of the Arno with **bird-watching** and a short **nature trail.**

Farther south along the SS439, you'll arrive at the walled village of **Ponsacco**. The center of town – now flourishing thanks to the local furniture industry – contains the 19th-century Pieve di San Giovanni Evangelista and the nearby Oratorio della Madonna della Tosse (with a collection of 15th-century terracottas) but most stop here for the walking opportunities.

Heading west out of town toward Perignano, a **trail** takes you through the hills to Lari. Midway, you'll meet the **Castello dei Vicari** (commonly attributed to Antonio da Sangallo), whose torture chambers and prison dungeons warrant a visit, as does the enclosed **Baldinucci Civic Museum** (☎ 058-7684238, daily, 3-6 pm; €3, conc. €2), with its displays on town history.

From here, further **trails** take you to Crespina, and its rich collection of villas erected by Pisano nobility during the last centuries, or south in the direction of Crespina Terme. If you opted for Crespina's villas, watch for **Villa Belvedere**; it contains the 18th-century Oratorio dei Tarocchi, decorated with frescoes by Tempesti. The piece belonged to the family of the Ilaria immortalized by Jacopo della Quercia in Lucca's Duomo.

Adventures in the Pisan Hills

Follow the rows of cypress trees past Crespina and Lari and you'll find yourself in the Pisan Hills, an area famed for the production of olive oil and wines such as Chianti delle Colline Pisane, Chianti, Bianco Pisano, Vin Santo di San Torpè and the Rosso, Bianco and Vin Santo of Montescudaio.

Where to Go: In the hill range that stretches between Lari and Riparbella, you'll find **Santa Luce** and the ancient Pieve di Santa Luce, one of the most harmonious of Pisa's churches. Take a detour towards Rosignano and you'll reach the Lago di Santa Luce, with its nature reserve (**LIPU Oasis**, ☎ 0586-580376, www.riservasantaluce.too.it, Sat-Sun, visits on other days by appointment only, €2.60, conc. €1.55). There are **birdwatching** opportunities here (over 150 migratory and nesting birds) and an informative **guided tour** is available. There is also a two-kilometer (1½-mile) footpath, which takes you around the lake stopping at all the birdwatching hides. A mile away, you can pick up footpaths around the **Bosco di Santa Luce**, a 3,500-acre stretch of woods and Mediterranean scrub rich in flora and fauna.

More woods and Mediterranean scrub can be explored at **Riparbella**. The area is famous for the numerous wild boar. You can discover local fauna in their natural habitat at the **Fauna Oasi il Giardino** (☎ 0586-881382, May-July, Sept-Oct, Wed, Sat), where a two-hour **guided tour** will take you over the 1,300-acre territory with its beautiful views of the Maremma and the islands of the Archipelago.

Ponsacco is the site of the local **flying club**, called **Aero Club Pisa Federico Citi** (Via Pinocchio 81, ☎ 0587-608124/606859, fax 0587-608124, www.ulm.it/vend/aecpisa), which organizes lessons catering for all types of flying specialties, including parachuting and free fall.

South again and you'll arrive in **Capannoli**, another of the region's biggest furnishing towns and the starting point for many of the region's main trails. Standing on the slope of a hill overlooking the Era, it was, from the 13th century on, a fortified village of the Gheradesca family, although little remains of their original castle; the late-Baroque architecture of Villa Baciocchi has since stolen its spot. A 20-minute **trail** out of town takes you to hilltop **Santo Pietro Belvedere** – you won't be able to miss it, its castle walls dominate the valley as you approach – and onto Casciana Terme. From Casciana Terme, you can head north on trails to Lari and Crespina, or south to the Bosco di Santa Luce, where a winding path takes you up Monte Alto (397 m/1,302 feet).

In its pleasant and vineyard-covered hilltop position, **Peccioli** is on the other side of the SS67 from Capannoli. There is little that remains of the historical nucleus apart from the old city walls. They divide the town into six districts (each marked by its own towers), two entrance gates (Volterra Gate and Pisa Gate), and the ruins of the fortress of the Luccan-Ghibelline leader Castruccio Castracani. **Chiesa di San Verano** marks the main piazza; its Pisan-Romanesque façade belies some heavy reconstruction in the 19th century. Off in the oratory to its side is a carved 17th-century ceiling, three polyptychs depicting *Madonna and Child with Saints* (Jacopo Vignali and Neri di Bicci) and an early 16th-century *Crucifix*. The **Palazzo Pretorio** is home to the unusual **Museo delle Icone Russe** (Museum of Russian Icons, Piazza del Popolo 5, ☎ 0587-672877, Wed, Sat, Sun and public holidays, 10 am-1 pm, 4-8 pm), which displays Russian iconography (typically gold and silver gilded wooden panel paintings) from the last two centuries. **Trails** take you from here to Cedri (nine miles); Fabbrica di Peccioli, where the 10th-century village church contains an important circular painting by Lippo Lippi and several della Robbia terracottas; and Lajatico.

Surrounded by oak and chestnut woods, **Chianni** invites a stop for its "olio extra vergine d'oliva di Chianni" (extra virgin olive oil) and the stunning 18th-century *Virgin of the Rosary* in the village church. Lombard in origin, Chianni was fortified during the disputes between Volterra and the Pisan Republic; although, after becoming famous for its mineral mines in the 14th and 15th centuries, it wasn't that long before the Florentines became interested and took it over.

Raised on a spur above the Era Valley, **Lajatico** (also known as Laiatico) introduces the lead up to Volterra. The ruins of the *castello* mark the town's highest point, although little now remains: the Florentines destroyed both it and the town walls in their hurry to conquer the town in 1406. Even the attractive village church, dedicated to San Leonardo di Limoges, was almost completely restructured in the 19th century, making the **Palazzo Pretorio** the oldest building in town. Built in the 13th century, it at one time housed a monastery; the coats of arms you see on the front belong to the Corsini family and the friars of Camadoli.

A worthwhile diversion brings you to the fortress of **Pietracassa** (meaning broken stone), which stands majestic and solitary, on a sloping hill overlooking the Era Valley. Once mighty, this ancient fortress (the oldest in the province of Pisa) was built on a large mass of alberese stone in the seventh century. Today, though it's half-destroyed, you can still get an idea of its original appearance from the surviving lookout tower and eighth-century walls, which now encircle only three of its sides. On a clear day, there's a beautiful panorama of the coast to be enjoyed.

Walking Volterra

Introduced by the impressive **Balze**, a chasm full of ancient necropoli and churches, Volterra stands isolated on the ridge of a mountain separating the broad valley of the Cecina from that of the Era. The town was founded by the Etruscans between the fifth and fourth centuries BC when, as *Velathri,* it made up one of the 12 city-states of the Confederation of the Rasenna, as the Etruscans then called themselves.

Pisa

THE BALZE

The Colline Metallifere on which Volterra stands are a mix of clay-like rock and soft sandstone, which have suffered over the centuries from erosion and landslides. This steady erosion has produced the remarkable landscape known as the Balze (precipices) and has swept away the oldest of Volterra's cemeteries; the early medieval Chiesa di San Clemente; the first Chiesa di San Giusto (seventh century); the Monastero di San Marco (1710); and the houses on the outer edge of Borgo San Giusto. Head down to Piano della Guerraccia for a look, and you'll see on the opposite side the ruins of a Camaldoese abbey (you can still visit it along Via Pisana). Founded in 1030, it contains a vast refectory with frescoes by Donato Mascagni.

At its peak under Etruscan rule, the city had a population of 25,000, produced its own money and had a bustling artisan industry based on the production of alabaster ceramics. Traces of this past can be seen in the original city walls; the huge and rectangular stone blocks of the fourth-century Porta all'Arco (Arch Gate); the acropolis in Piano del Castello; and the vases and cinerary urns preserved in the Museo Etrusco Guarnacci.

THE CITY WALLS

Two circuits of walls surround Volterra: the four-mile circuit of Etruscan walls, built with intersecting blocks of a striking geometrical perfection in the fourth century BC; and the smaller ring of medieval walls in which the Volterra as it is recognized today can be found. From the Piano della Guerraccia along Volterra's Borgo San Giusto, a path to the right leads to the remains of the Etruscan walls, which form a loop known as the *Guardiola*.

Conquered by Rome in 260 BC (the last of the Etruscan city-states to fall), the city became the important Roman municipality known as *Volterrae*, and was developed further with the addition of the Roman baths, the enormous rectangular water cistern, and the **Teatro Romano**, now part of the Area Archeologica di Vallebuona (Viale Ferrucci, ☎ 0588-86050, Sat-Sun, 11 am-5 pm, €2). Today, Volterra conserves a predominantly medieval appearance, enclosed by

the well-preserved city walls built between 1200 and 1240, with a street plan centered on the Piazza dei Priori (or the *Prato*, as it is known). There is a variety of 14th-century buildings – the Palazzo dei Priori, the Palazzo Pretorio, the tower-houses of the Buomparenti, the Buonaguidi, Minucci and the Toscano among others – made from the local gray stone (known as *panchina*), which was particularly favored during this time.

Start your tour on the solemn Piazza dei Priori. With its large pentagonal tower, the massive **Palazzo dei Priori** (☎ 0588-86050, Sat-Sun, 11 am-3:30 pm, €1), the oldest town hall in Tuscany (1208-1254), dominates the square. It adjoins the restored **Palazzo Vescovile** which, originally used as the city granary (the building still contains the loggia that then served as the market), became the bishop's residence in 1618. The square is still the venue for the city market.

To the left, Via Turazza leads to Piazza San Giovanni and the Pisan-Romanesque flank of the **Cattedrale di Santa Maria Assunta** (cathedral), noted for its splendid marble portal with sweeping flower-motif lunette. The church itself was consecrated in 1120, amplified in the 13th century and restructured internally in the 16th century when the columns covered with pink stucco were added by Leonardo Ricciarelli. In the interior are numerous works of art, including the polychrome wooden group of the *Deposition* (1228; second chapel to the right), two marble angels by Mino da Fiesole (12th-century; Presbytery), the magnificent wooden *Virgin of the Clerics* by Francesco da Valdambrino (North Transept) and statuette of *St John the Baptist* by Andrea Sansovino (taken from the baptismal font in the Baptistery). There's also a stunning pulpit with panels by great artists such as Fra Bartolomeo, a *Nativity* terracotta attributed to Andrea della Robbia, and an *Adoration of the Magi* fresco by Benozzo Gozzoli.

Standing in front of the Duomo in the center of the piazza, the octagonal **Battistero** (Baptistery) stands proud under its green and white marble dressing. Constructed in the second half of the 13th century, the building is ornamented with a Romanesque marble portal and cupola. Inside, it's simple in design with the altarpiece designed by Mino da Fiesole and an old baptismal font by Andrea Sansovino both taking pride of place.

The **Museo Diocesano d'Arte Sacra** occupies the old refectory of the Palazzo Vescovile or Bishop's Palace (Diocesan Museum of Sacred Art, Via Roma 1, ☎ 0588-86290, summer, 9 am-1 pm, 3-6 pm, winter, 9 am-1 pm, €7, conc. €5 including entrance to Museo Etrusco Guarnacci and Pinacoteca e Museo Civico). It brings together works from the cathedral and churches in the region, including the only surviving 14th-century marble monuments from the cathedral (such as the *Virgin and Child with Praying Angels* by Giovanni di Agostino), the relief figure of the *Triumphant Christ,* a gilded bronze *Crucifix* by Giambologna and a terracotta bust of *St Linus* by Giovanni della Robbia.

Pass the tower-houses of Via Buomparenti and Via D. Riccarelli (named after the 16th-century artist better known as Danielle da Volterra) and you'll reach the **Pinacoteca e Museo Civico** (Picture Gallery and Municipal Museum, Via dei Sarti 1, ☎ 0588-87580, summer, 9 am-7 pm, winter, 9 am-1.45 pm, €7, conc. €5 including entrance to Museo Etrusco Guarnacci and Museo Diocesano d'Arte Sacra). This occupies the Renaissance Palazzo Minucci-Solaini with its collection of sculptures and paintings. Among the most notable are an altarpiece by Domenico Ghirlandaio noted for its realistic depiction of the Volterra landscape, two altarpieces by Luca Signorelli, and Rosso Fiorentino's *Descent from the Cross*, a masterpiece of Mannerism, executed for the **Chapel of the Croce di Giorno** next to the Chiesa di San Francesco (the chapel is worth a look for its early 13th-century fresco cycle representing *The Legend of the Holy Cross* by Cenni di Francesco).

Via dei Sarti, one of the most important streets in the medieval city, underwent something of a facelift in the Renaissance. On the left is the 15th-century **Palazzo Incontri** (its splendid Mannerist façade is attributed to Bartolomeo Ammannati); the **Teatro Persio Flacco** (named after the famous Volterran sati-

Pisa

rist Aulus Persius Flaccus and now a cinema); and, at the end of the street, the small Piazzetta San Michele, where the 10th-century **Chiesa di San Michele Arcangelo** can be found (look for the marble statue of the *Virgin and Child* in the lunette).

Volterra's Tower-Houses

Starting from Piazza dei Priori, you'll first meet the two 13th-century **Torre Buomparenti**, some of the most distinctive of the medieval tower-houses, linked as they are by a high arch.

On the right, a short street takes you to the **Torre Martinoli** (on the side of the Palazzo Incontri) and the 13th-century **Torre dello Sharba**. You can take a detour off onto Via D. Ricciarell to visit the 12th-century **Torre Buonaguida**.

Next to the Chiesa di San Michele Arcangelo, the **Torre Toscano** is a solid 13th-century tower-home (although much restored in recent times) made of rusticated stone.

Continue down Via di Sotto and you'll meet the **Palazzo Maffei**, an old tower-house rebuilt in the Renaissance. It links with Via Matteotti, which is lined with more 13th- and 14th-century examples (**Torre Allegretti** and **Palazzetto Rossi e Miranceli**).

Through Piazza XX Settembre, Via D. Minzoni takes you south to the **Museo Etrusco Guarnacci** (Guarnacci Etruscan Museum, Via D. Minzoni 15, ☎ 0588-86347, summer, 9 am-7 pm, winter, 9 am-2 pm, €7, conc. €5, including entrance to Pinacoteca e Museo Civico and Museo Diocesano d'Arte Sacra). This is one of the most interesting and oldest Etruscan collections in Europe for its display of urns in tufa, alabaster and terracotta. The

symbol of the museum is the enigmatic bronze from the second to first century BC, which Gabriele d'Annunzio called *Ombra della Sera* (Shadow of the Evening). But there are also artifacts from the Villanovan, Archaic and Classical Periods, black glazed pottery, funereal stele, early coins, plus mosaics and sculpture from the Roman period on.

ALABASTER

*In the area between Volterra and Castellina Marittima is one of the richest deposits of alabaster in Italy. The numerous quarries – with their range of stone, from the pure white with black veining to the most valuable flesh-colored ivory, have been in use since the fifth century BC. It was then that the Etruscans sculpted the prize funerary urns now on display in the Museo Etrusco Guarnacci. You can find out more about sculptures from the 18th century on in the **Museo Storico dell'Alabastro** (Historical Museum of Alabaster, Piazza XX Settembre 5, ☎ 0588-868868, daily, 9 am-6:30 pm, €2.50, conc. €1.50).*

A little farther down the street, the Baroque façade of the 14th-century Chiesa di San Pietro in Selci introduces the staircase up to the imposing **Fortezza**. Dominating the town's high point (also occupied by a public garden, 8:30 am-sunset, and large archeological park, Mar-Nov, 11 am-4 pm), this remarkable example of Renaissance military architecture was constructed by Lorenzo Il Magnifico after his conquest of the town in 1472. Together with the pre-existing fortification, the **Rocca Vecchia** – to which it is linked by massive curtain walls – the Fortezza forms a magnificent complex visible throughout the valley. Unfortunately, it is currently in use as a prison and cannot be visited. The archeological park includes a large complex of cisterns, of which the Augustan *piscina* is the most important example, as well as the remains of an Etruscan sanctuary.

Events

Volterra Teatro (www.volterrateatro.it, €112.60, conc. €8), the province's most interesting avant-garde theater festival, has performances of experimental drama, dance and film. It is held in the Fortezza and surrounding towns (Peccioli and Pomarance) every July.

Volterra Jazz (☎ 0588-87257) takes over Piazza dei Priori every August with performances by Italian and international greats.

The Valdicecina

The SS68 follows the river through brown clay fields (known locally as *biancana*) from Saline di Volterra to the coast at Marina di Cecina. Turn-offs and a series of **trails** head south from it to arrive at the villages of Guardistallo, Montescudaio and Casale Marittimo.

Montescudaio comes first. It is the former seat of a Benedictine monastery and guards a well-preserved 12th-century castle, which was erected by the Della Gherardesca Counts over the pre-existing Chiesa di Santa Maria; from its battlements, there is an incredible panorama, not just over the whole valley but also as far as the Tuscan Archipelago and the hills of Corsica. In the surrounding hills, the red, white and Vinsanto Montescudaio DOC wines are produced; they are celebrated annually in the wine festival at the end of September.

Guardistallo is close-by. This ancient village is Lombard in origin (when it was known by the Latin name *Stallum Gualdi*) and it guards the top of a hill above the confluence of the Sterza and Cecina rivers. The town is best-known as the birthplace of Rodolfo Siviero, who brought all the art stolen by the Nazis back to Italy after the war.

On the hills of Poggio al Bruno, **Casale Marittimo** was divided between the two towns of Casale Vecchio and Casale Nuovo before it was reunited under its present name. In the center of the fortified medieval village, is the eighth-century **Chiesa di Sant'Andrea**, including traces of the walls and two doors. Among the many Etruscan finds in the surrounding countryside is the tomb of Tholos, which is reconstructed in the Museo Archeologico in Florence.

The Colline Metallifere

Head south along the SS439 from Volterra and you'll reach the beautiful hills of the Colline Metallifere, which slope over the border into the provinces of Grosseto and Siena. The road from the train station at Saline di Volterra takes you past the salt mines that brought much wealth to the area under Florentine rule, and into

Pisa

the stretch of the landscape where fumeroles of boric acid are still generating much electricity and wealth for the province.

You'll reach **Pomarance** first. Although this industrial town retains some of its medieval fortified appearance (when it was known as Ripomarance), it is really only worth a stop if you are a fan of local-born painters Niccoló Circignani and Cristoforo Roncalli (both confusingly known as Pomerancio), who are well represented in the town Pieve di San Giovanni Battista.

Walkers should head east or west to the **Foreste di Berignone Tatti e Macchia di Monterufoli** (forest and Mediterranean scrub, Via Roncalli 38, ☎ 0588-62003, www.com-valdicecina.pisa.it), which make up part of the Area Protette della Regione Toscana (Protected Areas of Tuscany).

There are more sights on the winding road to Larderello, including the remains of the **Rocca di Silliano**, which dominates the territory from afar, and **Montecastelli Pisano**, a typical fortified village with the *Immaculate Conception* by Cosimo Daddi in the early 13th-century Chiesa dei SS Filippo e Giacomo.

This is where the "Devil's Valley" begins, the heartland of the steaming fumaroles with its tall geysers of white steam, which for centuries were considered the work of the devil. They are now mostly controlled by the huge cooling towers of the power stations. The **Museo della Geotermia** at **Larderello** (Geothermal Museum, ☎ 0588-22418, fax 0588-22555, free) offers an interesting tour on the history of geothermic energy, its research, drilling (including original equipment) and different systems of using it for energy production.

Farther to the south, **Castelnuovo Val di Cecina** is another area of intense geothermal activity. Perched on top of a hill, it has kept intact the medieval structure, which grew up around the founding church. Off toward Sasso Pisano are the ruins of an Etruscan thermal bath, and some of the most colorful of the fumaroles.

The ancient Belforti residence is marked by the powerful tower that introduces **Montecatini Val di Cecina**; it sits amid a richly wooded landscape full of wildlife and charming little village churches.

■ Where to Eat

 There are a couple of good restaurants in and around Volterra, including the eerie underground dining rooms of pizzeria **Da Beppino** (Via delle Prigioni 13/21, ☎/fax 0588-86051, closed Wed, $$) and **Etruria** (Piazza dei Priori 6, ☎/fax 0588-86064, closed Thurs, $$$).

For al fresco dining, opt instead for **Il Porcellino** (Viccolo delle Prigioni 16, ☎ 0588-85392, closed Tues, $$). It takes its name from the animal on top of the town's Torre del Podesta, which is known by locals as *Il Porcellino* (little pig).

DINING PRICE CHART	
Price per person for an entrée, including house wine & cover.	
$	Under €20
$$	€21-€40
$$$	€41-€60
$$$$	Over €60

The small two-roomed **Il Sacco Fiorentino** (Piazza XX Settembre 18, ☎ 0588-88537, $$), in typical understated Tuscan style, is one of the best eateries in the city. Everything on the menu is cooked in the house style and that means tasty starters and pastas and grilled meats with an innovative home twist.

The "Osteria of the Poets," **Osteria dei Poeti** (Via Matteotti 55, ☎ 0588-86029, closed Thurs, $$$) has spent much time and attention on its sophisticated décor. Service and menu are likewise impressive, but be sure to book ahead as the tables fill up quickly.

If you want to splash out for the best seats in town, **Etruria** (Piazza dei Priori 8, ☎ 0588-86064, $$$) is a must. In addition to tables on Piazza dei Priori, there's also a beautiful interior dining room complete with 19th-century frescoes.

Your best choice out of town is **Il Frantoio** (Via della Madonna 11, ☎ 0586-650381, $$) in the quiet streets of Montescudaio's historical center. The owners of this classic Tuscan restaurant are also key advocates of Italy's slow food movement, which ensures carefully-prepared dishes, with lots of advice on accompanying wine. Try the *salumi alle carni di cinghiale* (wild boar ham) or the *funghi ai vini della zona* (mushrooms steeped in local wine) to start.

■ Where to Stay

Hotel accommodation in Volterra is surprisingly low-priced, with **Etruria** ☆☆☆ (Via Matteotti 32, ☎/fax 0588-87377, $$), **Sole** ☆☆☆ (Via dei Cappuccini 10a, ☎/fax 0588-84000, $$) and **Villa Nencini** ☆☆☆ (Borgo Santo Stefano 55, ☎ 0588-86386, fax 0588-80601, $$) all offering three-star accommodation well within most travelers' budgets.

If you're happy to pay a little more, **Le Fonti** ☆☆☆☆ (Via di Fontecorrenti 8, ☎ 0588-85219, fax 0588-92728, $$$) and **San Limo** ☆☆☆☆ (Via S. Limo 26, ☎ 0588-85250, fax 0588-80620, $$$) are the best-located choices in the higher bracket.

HOTEL PRICE CHART	
Rates are per room with private bath, based on double occupancy, including breakfast.	
$	Under €40
$$	€41-€85
$$$	€86-€140
$$$$	€141-€210
$$$$$	Over €210

There's also a youth hostel in town: **Ostello della Gioventú** (Via del Poggetto 3, ☎/fax 0588-85577, $) and a campground within walking distance – **Le Balze** ☆☆ (Via di Mandringa, ☎/fax 0588-87880, 15 Mar-15 Dec, $).

There are more campgrounds at Casale Marittimo – **Valle Gaia** ☆☆☆☆ (Via Cecinese 87, Loc. La Casetta, ☎ 0586-681236, fax 0586-683551, Apr-Oct, $), **Centrovacanze Il Borgo** ☆☆ (Via del Poggeto, ☎ 0586-655088, fax 0586-651856, $) – and at Montescudaio, **Montescudaio** ☆☆ (Via del Poggetto, ☎ 0586-683447, fax 0586-630932, May-Sept, $).

The closest *agriturismi* to Volterra are to the south at Venzano (**Loc. Venzano**, Mazzolla, ☎/fax 0588-39095, $$) or north at Podere Orzlaese (**Loc. San Girolano**, ☎/fax 0588-42121, $$) and Podere San Michele (**Loc. Ulignano**, ☎/fax 0588-42062, $$$).

Livorno

Livorno was born in the 15th century when Ferdinando I de Medici realized his father's desire to found a new and "ideal" city here after the collapse of the Pisan Republic. Its original inhabitants came from all over Europe and the result is a mix of civilizations and religions (it is touted as Tuscany's most tolerant city

Pisa

thanks to the religious freedom law of 1593) and a decidedly Renaissance style of architecture in the historical center. The city was originally planned and built by Bernardo Buontalenti for 10,000 inhabitants. It has decidedly grown since this time with the addition of the quarter known as New Venice in the second half of the 17th century, when the population hit 80,000. Further additions were made in the 19th century in the direction of Ardenza, particularly the attractive villas and parks in typical Liberty style.

The product is a laid-back seaside town of snow-white shoreline and sea-front caffès, a historical center of narrow lanes encircled by the *fossi* (the network of canals), white-stone town houses, ochre-red coastal defenses and a bustling port, which harks back to the fishing village that once stood here.

■ Getting Here & Around

 By Train: Trains (☎ 848-888088, www.trenitalia.it) from Florence run through Pisa to Livorno Centrale, where you should also get off if arriving from Pisa's Aeroporto Galileo Galilei (☎ 050-849202, www.pisa-airport.com). If arriving from Rome, the Rome-to-Turin service stops in both Livorno Centrale and Pisa Centrale. The train station is to the east of town along Viale G. Carducci and is well-served by bus links to town.

 By Bus: Lazzi (☎ 0583-584876) runs bus services between Livorno and Florence, Lucca and Pisa. They drop you at the autostazione next to Darsena Nuova.

 By Car: Take the **A12** down from Pisa (get on it at Pisa Nord along the A11 from Lucca and Florence) or follow the toll-free **SS1 Aurelia**, which skirts almost the entire Tuscan coast. The town is has plenty of **car parks**, with day rates available at Piazza della Vittoria (€11.40/day), Scali Bettarini (€7.75/day), Porto Mediceo (€3/day), Via del Corona (€10.35/day), Stazione Marittima (€5.15/day), and Via Roma (€7.75/day).

For car rental, see **Avis** (Via Calata Carrara, Stazione Marittima, ☎ 0586-880090, www.avisautonoleggio.it), **Europcar** (Piazza XI Maggio 6, ☎ 0586-219973, www.europcar.it), **Hertz** (Via Calata Carrara, Stazione Marittima, ☎ 0586-210591, www.hertz.it), **Liberty Rent** (Via Marzocco 40, ☎ 0586-834082, www.libertyrent.it) or **Maggiore** (via Fiume 31/33, ☎ 0586-892240, www.maggiore.it).

Bikes can be rented from in front of Livorno train station, along the city walls near the Fortezza Vecchia or farther along the coast at Ardenza Mare.

 By Taxi: Taxis line up outside the train station (☎ 0586-401294) and on Piazza Grande (☎ 0586-898094). Or call **Radiotaxi** (☎ 0586-210000) or **Taxi Livorno** (☎ 0586-883377).

■ Information Sources

Tourist Offices: The main **APT Livorno** (Livorno tourist office) is on Piazza Cavour (Piazza Cavour 6, ☎ 0586-898111, fax 0586-896173, www.livorno.turismo.toscana.it), with a smaller office on Piazza del Municipio (☎ 0586-204611).

■ Sightseeing ~ The Historical Center

In an historical center neatly delineated by the *fossi* (city canals), **Piazza Grande** – also known as Piazza d'Arme – is the surprisingly substantial heart of the original 16th-century city designed by Buontalenti. It is home to the city **Duomo** (Cathedral), which was first built between 1694 and 1606, enlarged over the following century, and then rebuilt to the original plans after destruction in the last war.

To both the north and south of the square, the characteristic porticoes of **Via Grande** – under which can be found the most elegant shops of the city – lead towards the port and **Piazza Micheli** or inland to **Piazza della Repubblica**. Take the former direction first to arrive at the **Quattro Mori di Tacca**, the bronze statues of barbarians, which serve as the symbol of the city and were placed here as a monument to Ferdinando I.

Via dell'Arsenale then links you to the **Porto Mediceo**, separated from **Darsena Vecchia** (☎ 0586-897071, visits by appointment) by a pier built for and named after Cosimo I; the walls that you see hemming in the Darsena (the port terminal) from the opposite side belong to the **Fortezza Vecchia** (Old Fortress). Designed by Antonio da Sangallo Il Giovanne, it grew up in the first half of the 16th century on the old Rocca left by the Pisans.

It is linked to the **Fortezza Nuova** (New Fortress), a vast 16th-century bastion with a spacious public park, by the **Fosso Venezia** with its picturesque walkway past brightly colored boats and moorings. This is the area, which in the second half of the 17th century was heavily influenced by Venice – hence its name, Venice Nuova (New Venice). It was built at a time of fervent commercial activity made easy by the convenience of the *fossi* along which were constructed storehouses such as the Bottini dell'Olio, now transformed into prestigious art galleries and cultural exhibition centers.

The city's second spurt of growth can be traced in the Liberty architecture around the Fosso Reale. It all began in 1844 with the construction of a vast rectangular bridge above the canal, which today constitutes the **Piazza della Repubblica** (also called Piazza del Voltone). This broke the confines of the historical center and linked it to a new 19th-century town, which can be explored by following Via Buontalenti to the **Mercato Centrale** (inaugurated 1893 and still in use) or heading east to the predominantly Neoclassical quarter known as the **Ardenza**.

Alongside the panoramic **Viale Italia**, the 20th-century **Terrazza Mascagni** offers the ideal setting for a sunset or post-dinner *passegiata*, along a shoreline promenade with views of the islands of the Tuscan archipelago. It leads onto the 19th-century buildings of the **Accademia Navale**, which, surrounded by English-style lawns, still trains the Italian Navy using the 1930-built *Amerigo Vespucci*.

Finish off your visit with a trip to the **Villa Mimbelli** where the **Museo Civico G. Fattori** (Municipal Museum, Via S. Jacopo in Acquaviva 65, ☎ 0586-808001, Tuesday-Sunday, 10 am-1 pm, 4-7 pm) contains a collection of the works of local artists from the 19th and 20th centuries, such as Amedeo Modigliani and Giovanni Fattori himself. He was one of the major Italian architects of the 19th-century and the major exponent of the style known as Macchiaioli.

Pisa

HITTING THE BEACH

 Livorno has a rocky coast with a few stretches of pebbly and sandy beach. The 20th-century promenade Viale Italia offers easy access to both the city beaches (mostly controlled by majestic bathing establishments) and those farther along the coast. Heading south, the first you'll come across is the **Spiaggia della Bellana** (Bellana Beach), a handkerchief of beach on the edge of Livorno city just before the Terrazza Mascagni. This is where you'll find the **Centro Recupero Uccelli Marini** (☎ 0586-400226), a marine bird shelter center run by the LIPU with large aviaries and an interesting guided tour.

Continue along Viale Italia to pass the Accademia Navale (Italian Navy Academy, adjacent to the Chiesa di San Jacopo in Acquaviva, founded in 1881), the famous Caprilli racecourse, and **Spiaggia Roma** (Rome Beach), where on the exit of the River Banditella, you can actually surf.

Farther south, the shoreline road starts to climb again over the pinkish stone rocks of Romito, ducking down into coves popular with divers and into **Quercianella**, a quiet resort, itself popular with sailors and surfers. Both can be practiced year-round. For nature lovers, there is plenty to enjoy. The resort is set in the green of the Mediterranean scrub amid the smells and colors of the tamarisk trees, ilexes, oleanders and brooms.

■ Adventures

On Foot

 From Livorno to Rosignano, a line of gentle hills, covered by a thick Mediterranean scrub and woods of cluster pines, holm oaks and strawberry trees, stretches 60 miles along the Livorno coastline. Known as the Parco delle Colline Livornese (Park of the Livornese Hills), it has plenty of inland trails and coastal walks to enjoy, particularly down to the beach of **Romito** and through nature reserves giving shelter to roe and fallow deer, badgers and porcupines, falcons and flamingoes.

You can pick up a pleasant five-mile circular walk from Valle Benedetta to the north of Livorno in the Colline Livornesi (follow SS206). The itinerary takes you through woods to the ruins of a windmill, past Calvario and along to the 18th-century Colognole aqueduct before returning via Casa Pianone to Valle Benedetta.

Closest to the city itself is the hilltop **Santuario di Montenero,** where an important collection of pictures showing miraculous rescues at sea and a range of votive offerings from superstitious sea-goers are preserved (Galleria Ex-Voto Santuaria di Montenero, Gallery of Votive Offerings, ☎ 0586-577711, daily, 6:30 am-12:30 pm, 2:30-6:30 pm, free). A colorful cable car (Funicolare Montenero, ☎ 0586-579338, www.funicolarelivorno.it) takes you up if you don't want to walk.

On Wheels

 From the Santuario di Montenero, you can pick up a 13-mile loop itinerary into the **Valle del Chioma** (via del Poggio to the village of Castello, through the valleys of Quarata and Chioma, along the coast and back). The bike trip takes two hours.

On Horseback

 You can arrange horseback riding in the **Parco delle Colline Livornese** and the **Foresta di Montenero** though one of Livorno's riding centers: **Associazione Ippica Limone** (Via di Tramontana 22,

☎ 0586-406473) or **Centro Ippico Il Salice** (Via del Castellaccio 4, ☎ 0586-678383).

In Water

 Livorno city and coast is dotted with **diving** centers offering lessons and trips along the Etruscan Coast and Tuscan Archipelago. In **Livorno** book with **Chioma Beach Diving Center** (Via di Franco 9, ☎ 0586-754635) or **Stabilimenti Riuniti Pancaldi e Acquaviva Spa** (Viale Italia 53, ☎ 0586-805566, fax 0586-897340). Dives take you to the Secche della Meloria (Meloria sandbanks) and Torre della Meloria, a large sea reserve about a mile west from Livorno where you can discover the wrecks of ancient ships from the battles when the Pisa Maritime Republic was at its zenith, as well as plenty of coral, Neptune grass and schools of fish.

You can arrange **boat** rental from one of Livorno's *centri nautici* (nautical centers): **Circolo Ardenza** (Viale Italia 104, ☎ 0586-500295), **Circolo Borgo Cappuccini** (Via degli Asili 33, ☎ 0586-839920), **Circolo Il Passatempo** (Via del Molo Mediceo 25, ☎ 0586-895364), **Circolo Nautico Livorno** (Via del Molo Mediceo, ☎ 0586-893015) or **Circolo Nautico Quercianella** (Loc. Quercianella, ☎ 0586-491432). You can also pick up boat trips from the quay at **Via del Molo Mediceo** (Andana degli Anelli).

Surfing can be enjoyed at various points along the coast.

■ Where to Eat

LOCAL FLAVORS

Only in the province of Lucca can you find the two apparently opposite poles of Tuscan cuisine given equal importance on a restaurant menu, with meat (game from the woods and Mediterranean scrub) and fish (grilled or fried fish, mollusks and crustaceans in Livorno, octopus in Piombino) all deserving pride of place.

Baccalà and *stoccafisso*: Dried cod cooked in onion, tomato and potatoes.

Cacciucco: Fish soup, prepared with range of different fish, similar in to the Marseille *bouillabaisse* – a poor man's fish soup now cooked with olive oil, white wine, tomatoes, garlic, onions and hot pepper and served hot on pieces of toast rubbed with garlic cloves.

Cuscussù: Livorno version of couscous and one of the city's favorite dishes.

Inzimino: Squid with spinach.

Pappardelle al cinghiale: Fresh pasta with sauce made from wild boar hunted in the Mediterranean scrub.

Riso al nero di sepia: Rice with squid ink and served with dusting of Parmesan.

Riso alla scogliera: Rice with squid, octopus, prawns and mussels.

Seppie con le bietole: Squid with chard.

Stiacciata pasquale: Aniseed cake traditionally eaten at Easter.

Testina di cinghiale: Wild boar's head (increasingly rare).

Torta di ceci: Livornese chickpea cake served as a snack.

Tortelli di spinaci e ricotta con sugo di cinghiale: Spinach and ricotta pasta with wild boar sauce.

Triglie alla Livornese: Mullet cooked in tomato sauce and sprinkled with garlic and parsley.

Zuppa di arselle: Mussel soup.

Dishes should be accompanied by wine from the Costa degli Etruschi (see page 322) and finished off with a *Ponce alla Livornese* (hot black coffee laced with rum).

 Ai Paparazzi (Via Magenta 80, ☎ 0586-898802, $) is a popular lunch choice and is best know for its excellent range of pizzas, considered by many to be the best in the city. There's also an extensive wine list and a more formal dining room if you want to make an evening meal of it.

Aragosta (Piazza dell'Arsenale 6, ☎ 0586-895395, $$) is known for its delicious seafood pizza, but it's the lobster (*aragosta*), after which the restaurant is named, that brings most visitors here. Open your meal with *la frittura* (fried seafood) entrée and finish it with one of the houses' homemade desserts.

One of Livorno's most popular eateries, **Barcarola** (Viale Carducci 63, ☎ 0586-402367, $$) serves a delicious range of locally caught fish at reasonable prices. It ranks second only to Michellin-starred **Da Rosina** (Via Roma 251, ☎ 0586-800200, $$$), a charming – if slightly expensive – trattoria specializing in fish, that pairs quality service with a top menu and wine list.

There's more fish to be sampled at **Osteria del Mare** (Borgo dei Cappuccini 5, ☎ 0586-881027, $$$). It's small inside and you'll need to book ahead to ensure a table in this *osteria*, a tavern-like restaurant.

Just out of town, classy *enoteca* **Ghine' Cabri** (Loc. Castellacio, ☎ 0586-579414, $) has a carefully planned menu of dainty dishes to accompany its extensive wine list. Better still, it has a beautiful panoramic view to enjoy as you sip and nibble your way through the local produce.

■ Where to Stay

 Livorno and its coast are crammed with three- and two-star hotel accommodations, which means reservations are rarely necessary. As a result, it makes more sense to choose your hotel by location rather than price. Best picks are around Piazza Cavour, around Piazza della Repubblica or south along Viale Italia.

There are two good one-star options around Piazza Cavour: **Cavour** ☆ (Via Adua 10, ☎ 0586-899604, $) and **Goldoni** ☆ (Via E. Mayer 42, ☎/fax 0586-898705, $$). But with three-star options only slightly more expensive, go for the extra facilities at **Albergo Imperiale** ☆☆☆ (Via Carlo Bini 26, ☎/fax 0586-881326, www.albergoimperiale.it, $$).

Ariston ☆☆☆ (Piazza della Repubblica 11, ☎/fax 0586-881049, $$) and **Europa** ☆☆☆ (Via dell'Angiolo 23, ☎ 0586-888581, fax 0586-880085, www.paginegialle.it/heuropa-01, $$) are your best bets on and around Piazza Repubblica.

Along the coast close to Il Romito is the town's sole four-star option, **Hotel Rex** ☆☆☆☆ (Via del Litorle 164, ☎ 0586-580400, fax 0586-509586, www.hotelrex.it, $$$). There's plenty of luxury on the coast just outside town at **Gennarino** ☆☆☆ (Viale Italia 301, ☎ 0586-803109, fax 0586-803450, www.wel.it, $$) and **Universal** ☆☆☆ **(Viale Antignano 4, ☎** 0586-500228, fax 0586-500327, $$$).

Cheaper coastal options include **BelMare** ☆☆ (Viale Italia 109, ☎ 0586-807040, fax 0586-807276, www.hotelbelmare.com, $$), near the Terrazza Mascagni, **Etruria** ☆☆ (Viale Italia 231, ☎ 0586-802077, $$), near the Accademia Navale, and **La Capinera** ☆☆ (Via del Castello 32, ☎ 0586-580508, fax 0586-580514, $$) up by Bagni Roma.

There is also a good range of *affitacamere*: try **Mazzini** (Corso Mazzini 260, ☎ 0586-887232, $) for the cheapest, **Grossi Onorina** (Viale Rosa del Tirreno 20, ☎ 0586-809720, $) or **Piccolo Paradiso di Aleo Margherita** (Via di Quercianella 122, ☎ 0586-579186, $$).

The city youth hostel, **Villa Morazzana** (Via di Collinet 68, ☎ 0586-500076, fax 0586-502426, $) is on the Ardenza River in the Parco delle Colline Livornesi. Two campgrounds are on the coast at Antignano (**Miramare** ☆☆, Via del Littorale 220, ☎ 0586-580402, fax 0586-883338, www.campingmiramare.com, $) and up near Santuario di Montenero (**Collina** ☆, Via di Quercianella 377, Loc. Montenero, ☎/fax 0586-579573, www.collina1.it, $).

The Costa degli Etruschi

The Costa degli Etruschi (the Etruscan Riviera) stretches along the Livorno province, from Livorno in the north to Follonica (and the beginning of the Grosseto province) in the south. It is rich in ancient Etruscan cities and remains (hence the name), but there is plenty of country and seaside to explore, with Mediterranean scrub and chestnut woods, shore pinewoods and *tomboli*, rocky cliffs and long sandy beaches, islands with charming coves and crowded seaside resorts. Inland, the province is dotted with nature reserves and natural parks. The coast is the favored gateway to the Natural Park of the Tuscan Archipelago.

■ Getting Here & Around

By Bus: ATL buses (☎ 0586-847225, www.atl.livorno.it) run along the coast from Livorno, stopping at the major resorts. **ATM** services (☎ 056-5260134, www.atm.li.it) follow the same route, only departing from Piombino.

By Car: You can follow the same route along **SS1 Aurelia** south from Livorno. If arriving from Florence or Pisa, the **A12** follows the coast as far as Rosignano, where you can pick up the SS1.

Bicycle Rental: Find these on the coast at **Rosignano Solvay** (**Motonoleggio Camuzzi**, Via Aurelia 593, ☎ 0586-760123). A popular coastal cycle route can be picked up anywhere along the coast south from Vada and extends all the way to the Parco Naturale di Rimigliano.

■ Information Sources

Tourist Offices: The main **APT Costa degli Etruschi** (Etruscan Coast Tourist Office) is in Livorno (Piazza Cavour 6, ☎ 0586-898111, fax 0586-896173, www.livorno.turismo.toscana.it), but there are also offices all the way along the coast at **Castiglioncello** (Via Aurelia 967, ☎/fax 0586-752291, castiglioncello@multinet.it), **Rosignano Marittimo** (Via Gramsci 19, ☎/fax 0586-792973), **Rosignano Solvay** (Via Berlinguer, ☎/fax 0586-767215), **Vada** (Piazza Garibaldi 93, ☎/fax 0586-788373), **Marina di Cecina** (Piazza Sant'Andrea, ☎/fax 0586-620678 and Viale Galliano, ☎ 0586-622844), **San Vincenzo** (Via Alliata 2, ☎ 0565-701533) and **Piombino** (Via Ferruccio, ☎ 0565-225639 and in the port, ☎ 0565-226627, aptpiombino2@etruscan.li.it).

Maps & Guides : Pick up a copy of *Costa degli Etruschi,* free from the Livorno tourist office. With details on beaches and attractions, it also shows routes along the coast suitable for journeys by car, bicycle, horse and on foot.

Pisa

■ Sightseeing & Adventures

Livorno to Castagneto Carducci

 South of Livorno, the panoramic SS1 Aurelia makes its torturous journey south along the rocky coast, to the **Torre di Calafuria** and the remains of **Castel Sonnino**, both important **diving** locations. The harsh coast of Calafuria is the location of one of the province's most unusual sights: **Sassoscritto** (written by the rocks), a sheer rock face on which the shapes caused by wind and sea erosion look almost as if they were created by hand. Animals, skulls, exclamation marks, a diver, fish and a procession of soldiers are just some of the designs that visitors claim to see here.

On an isolated promontory covered with pinewoods, **Castiglioncello** marks the beginning of the sandy bays. Once a favorite with Italian celebrities, as the beautiful villas on the hill above testify, it is the oldest and smartest of the coastal resorts, with crystal-clear waters almost completely controlled by a chain of bathing establishments. Any fans of the *Macchiaiolo* painters will have heard of the "school of Castiglioncello"; it was here that Florentine writer and art critic Diego Martelli founded the artistic movement in the late 1800s.

FREE BEACHES

 The Costa degli Etruschi has 45 miles of almost uninterrupted beach, but with many of the larger resorts charging for access to the best sand (Quercianella, Castiglioncello, Marina di Castagneto, Vada, Cecina, Bibbona, Donoratico, San Vincenzo and Piombino representing just some of the busy bathing establishments). You may have to cough up some cash just to get a tan. Fortunately, many accessible and free beaches are just a short trip out of the center. Stretches include the shingle beaches between Livorno and Quercianella; the "Spiagga Bianche" and six miles of non-bleached bays between Rosignano Solvay and Vada; the 17-mile stretch between the Cecina River and the Gulf of Baratti; and the 18 miles of almost all free beach from the Bay of Baratti to Piombino.

A vast Etruscan necropolis comprising 11 tombs lies just outside of town. You see a wide range of the artifacts, including an impressive collection of funerary items, in the **Museo Archeologico Nazionale** in nearby **Rosignano Marittimo** (National Archeological Museum, Palazzo Bombardieri, Via del Castello 24, ☎ 058-6724287/8, summer, 9 am-1 pm, 5-10 pm, winter, 9 am-1 pm). It also houses findings from excavations farther south at San Gaetano in Vada.

Rosignano Marittimo offers plenty of trails for **horseback riders**, with itineraries along the Fine River and into the local woodland. Just over the border (12 miles) in the Pisa province, the LIPU reserve of **Lago di Santa Luce** has nature trails and bird-watching hides.

You can arrange **boat rental** in **Rosignano Solvay**, the coastal district of Rosignano Marittimo. Try **Circolo Nautico Lillatro** (Via P. Gigli 1, ☎ 0586-767523). To its south are the famous Spiagge Bianche, known as the "Caribbean of Italy" for the three miles of dazzling white sands (free access). However, do note that they are bleached this color by the calcium carbonate that is discharged from the local "Solvay" factory, producers of soda (not that the locals who crowd here seem to mind).

Above: Basilica di San Francesco e Sacro Convento, Assisi

Below: Chiesa di San Damiano, where St. Francis took refuge

Above: Basilica di Santa Chiara seen from the Rocca, Assisi (IAT Assisi)

Below: Basilica and Cupola di Santa Chiara (IAT Assisi)

Cattedrale di San Rufino in Assisi is a rare example of
Umbrian Romanesque style (IAT Assisi)

Above: Norcia's Piana Castelluccio

Below: Parco dei Sibillini in July

There are Roman ruins in the archeological area of *Vada Volaterrana* (the old low town of Volterra), as well as a few Terme Romano (spas) from the first to second centuries. These are best explored from the nearby modern resort of **Vada**, a popular **diving** spot for the Roman ships wrecked on the Secche di Vada. On these shallow sandbanks, you can find masses of coral, sea fans and fish, and a whole host of terracotta vases. Book diving trips in Rossignano Marittimo with **Nettuno Hovercraft Service** (Via Belvedere 8, ☎ 0586-787157) and in Cecina with **Centro Subacqueo Maria Giustina** (Via Fratelli Cervi 7, ☎ 330-909758).

The principal beach resort and tourist port along this coast is **Cecina**. It sits on the edge of a protected pine forest, the **Riserva Statale Tomboli di Cecina**. The reserve extends part of the way between Vada and Marina di Bibbona, and represents all that remains of extensive coastal forests artificially planted by Grand Duke Leopoldo in the 18th century. It can be explored along the Via dei Cavalleggeri, an ancient military road that once united the coastal lookout towers and is now used by cyclists, joggers and horseback riders.

TOMBOLI

The name *tomboli* is given to the strips of beachside vegetation that characterize much of the Etruscan Coast, especially the shores of Cecina, Bolgheri and Donoratico, and part of the coast of the Grosseto province. Typically found in sandy areas, they extend inland for around 800 m (2,624 feet), where the initial strip of salt-resistant vegetation is replaced by juniper scrub, then helm-oaks and pinewoods. Created in the 19th century, *tomboli* played an important role sheltering cultivated inland areas from the strong sea winds.

A few miles north of town, the 18th-century Villa Guerrazzi houses the local **Museo Archeologico Etrusco-Romano** (Etruscan-Roman Archeological Museum, San Pietro in Palazzi, ☎ 0586-669111, caesar.onlus@tin.it, summer, 4-7:30 pm, €4), with a collection of artifacts from the territory. You can visit the source of many of them by heading down to San Vincenzino (see below), where the **Villa di Albino Cecina** (Loc. San Vincenzo, ☎ 0586-260837, 4-7:30 pm) is all that remains of a 1st-century Roman complex.

Costa degli Etruschi Wine Road

The Costa degli Etruschi Wine Road departs from Cecina, winds its way 100 miles through Casale Marittima, Bibbona, Bolgheri and Castagneto Carducci and down to Sassetta and Suvereto, before finishing at Piombino. Although these hills have been covered in vineyards since the 15th century, this is a relatively new wine area, and its famed product, Sassicaia didn't emerge until the 1960s when the Marquis Mario Incisa della Rocchetta and the oenologist Giacomo Tachis created the blend. Three other DOC wines followed suit (Montescudaio, Bolgheri and Val di Cornia), and there was a boom in local food products (honey, cured meats and extra virgin olive oil among others). To organize visits to local producers, contact the **Consorzio Strada del Vino Costa degli Etruschi** (San Guido 45, Bolgheri, ☎ 0565-749705, www.lastradadelvino.com).

Situated on the top of a hill that dominates the coastal plain, **Bibbona** can trace its routes back to the medieval castle built by the della Gherardesca Counts. It's main sight is in the 15th-century **Chiesa di Santa Maria della Pietà**; the 14th-century *Pietà* from which it takes its name can be found on the main altar.

Pisa

You have to head through the fresh pinewoods to arrive at its beach on **Marina di Bibbona**. It grew up around a late 18th-century Lorraine fort.

Inland from Bibbona, the enchanting **Macchia della Magona**, (☎ 0586-672111) is a biogenetic-rich forest reserve that occupies several small hills with its typical Mediterranean scrub and chestnut woods inhabited by fallow and roe deer, wild goats and boar. Its 3,000-plus acres contain over 30 miles of well-marked paths and nature trails suitable for **hiking**, **horseback riding** and **mountain biking**. A beautiful one-mile **trail** through thick *macchia* starts at the entrance hut, Casa della Forestale. Take the unpaved road from Bibbona cemetery, following signs to the Macchia della Magona. Leave your car at the barrier and follow track #6 to the visitor center. The path passes through a small pine forest, where the Fonte al Rame (near an ancient charcoal pit) marks the trail back to the Casa.

If you don't have a car, you can **cycle (and walk)** the complete 12-mile itinerary leaving from Bibbona in two hours (five hours on foot). Trail #5 can be picked up one mile after Bibbona cemetery; it takes you through holm-oak woods to the Passo del Terminino (281 m/922 feet) where trail #10 climbs up one mile to the Poggio al Fango (340 m/1,115 feet). At this point you can choose between two routes. The first (#12, then #13) is the easier and quicker of the two, while the second (#10, #16, #12, then #13) takes you first to the panoramic Campo di Bibbona and is better for approaches on foot.

There is a short six-mile itinerary from the fork of trail #5: a right turn onto #6, then #9, will take you up to the Casetta, where you can pick up the #12 into the Macchia.

For **horseback riding** in the area, contact **Associazione La Calafornia** (Via dei Melagrani 2, ☎ 0586-600294). If you arrive in May, you can follow the 35-mile route of the national long-distance bicycle competition **Costa degli Etruschi**.

The above cycle route often goes unvisited in favor of the **WWF Rifugio Faunistico di Bolgheri** (World Wildlife Fund Wildlife Reserve of Bolgheri) to its south. Running along the coast for almost three miles, this marshland and pinewood nature reserve is justifiably famous for its wild fauna. WWF guides (WWF Piombino, ☎ 0565-224361, 9 am-noon, 2-4:30 pm) provide tours along the narrow pathways that run between the high walls of cane thickets to bird-watching huts. You can spy thousands of aquatic birds (grebes, red herons, mallards and coots), plus migratory birds such as snipes, white herons, lapwings, black storks, and the rare predatory eagle. Huts open Fri and Sat, 15 Oct-15 Apr, the beginning of the nesting season).

The town of **Bolgheri** is best approached from San Guido just outside the nature reserve. Stretching from the Oratorio di San Guido and reaching into the medieval hamlet of Bolgheri is perhaps the most famous road in the province; the bullet-straight avenue of secular cypress trees immortalized by poet, Giosuè Carducci in the ode *Davanti San Guido* (In front of St Guido). Follow it to the town, and you'll also find the small house where the poet Carducci, winner of the Nobel Prize for Literature in 1906, spent his infancy.

You'll find more about the poet in nearby **Castagneto Carducci**. Sitting on top of highland, closed in between town walls, this hamlet not only conserves the name, but also the house where the poet lived from 1848 till his death 10 years later: **Casa dei Carducci** (Via Carducci, ☎ 0565-765032, summer, Tues-Sun, 9:30 am-12:30 pm,

Giosuè Carducci

4-7 pm). It sits on the edge of the Sassetta trekking network, celebrated for its cycle routes and foot and horseback trails.

You can follow in the tracks of the poet along the 23-mile "Carducci Trail," a three-hour **cycle** route that departs from San Giusto and takes you along the Via Bolgherese (direction Bolgheri) to the junction with the famous cypress avenue, down to San Guido, up to Bibbona and then back down to Castagneto Carducci.

Mountain bikers and **walkers** should opt instead for the "Antica Via Campigliese," an eight-mile route – one hour and a bit on wheels, four hours on foot – that departs from Castagneto Carducci along the ancient Campigliese road up to Capo di Monte, down to Piano dei Brizzi and Sassetta. From here, track #1 takes you though La Fiora, where track #2 (the *Sentiero dei Molini*, the trail of the windmills) takes you back to Castagneto Carducci via the ruins of a chain of ancient windmills. **Castagneto Trekking** offers free information on trails in the area (☎ 0565-778111). You can arrange bike rental and also get local cycling information from **Cicio Sport** (Via Aurelia, 25, Donoratico ☎ 0565-777149).

From **Sassetta**, an eight-mile itinerary departs just out of town at La Cerreta (take the road to Fattoria Pian delle Vigne, direction Frassine, to pick up the trail). It takes you along a panoramic route – just over one hour on wheels; four hours on foot; 2½ hours on horseback – into the Ladano Valley and back to the starting point. **Sassetta Trekking** offers free information on trails in the area (☎ 0565-794333).

San Vincenzo to Follonica

The principal center of the Costa degli Etruschi, **San Vincenzo** is really just a small tourist resort with boutiques and a bustling seaside stretch. Its popularity is explained by the **Parco Naturale di Rimigliano** (Natural Park of Rimigliano, ☎ 0565-701970) to its south. This 270-acre sweep of beautiful holm-oak forest incorporates some of the coast's most beautiful (and free) beaches, which reach down as far as the Golfo di Baratti. The reserve is traversed by a well-marked trekking path, which skirts the juniper and honeysuckle scrub inland from the beach for six miles before heading inland to take in the varied flora and fauna of the pinewood and holm oak forests.

For **horseback riding** in the area, contact **Centro Ippico ASE** (Podere San Dazio, Via di Campiglia, San Vincenzo, ☎ 0565-702467).

Just inland, the adventure-packed Val di Cornia is introduced by the hilltop town of **Campiglia Marittima**. Built along the river, which descends to the coast from the Colline Metallifere, the historical center originally grew up as a medieval castle. Its most important sight is the Pisan-Romanesque **Pieve di San Giovanni**, where a bas-relief on the right architrave offers an interesting boar-hunting allegory.

PARKS OF THE VAL DI CORNIA

*The half-wild and barely populated hills of the Val di Cornia extend alongside the river between Campiglia Marittima and Piombino. The umbrella organization **I Parchi della Val di Cornia** (The Parks of the Val di Cornia, Via G. Lerario 90, Piombino, ☎ 0565-49430) is made up of six parks in the region: the Mediterranean scrub vegetation of the Parco Naturale di Rimigliano and the Parco Naturale di Sterpaia, the green wooded hills of the Parco Naturale di Montioni and the Parco Naturale di Poggio Neri, and the archeological parks of Populonia and San Silvestro.*

Trails take you north into the **Parco Naturale di Monte Calvi**, where routes up the mountain slopes lead first via the 10th-century fortified village of Rocca di San

Silvestro, now part of the **Parco Archeo-Minerario di San Silvestro** (Archeological and Mineral Park of San Silvestro, entrance at Madonna di Fucinaia, visitor center and parking at Temperino, ☎ 0565-838680, fax 0565-838703, parcoss@parchivaldicornia.it, June-Sept, Tues-Sun, 9 am-8 pm, Oct-May, Sat-Sun, 9 am-dusk). This veritable open-air museum traces the extraction and production of metal from Etruscan times on.

Five short trails stretch through the 1,900-acre excavation area, taking you past Etruscan and Medicean buildings, museums, the medieval Rocca and into underground grottoes. They include the Via del Temperino (40 minutes), which starts at the mine exit and stops at the park museums to show the different phases in land cultivation from the Etruscans to the present day. The second, Via delle Ferruzze (two hours, a good choice for mountain bikers) takes you through the center of the park to the most important historical sites and some iron ore known as ferruzze. The Via dei Lanzi (45 minutes) crosses the Lanzi Valley to arrive at the Rocca di San Silvestro and takes in the medieval extracting pits and buildings dating to the Medici. Via del Manienti (1½ hours) takes you around the Rocca di San Silvestro before following a track through medieval ruins once devoted to the extraction and working of copper, lead and silver. Miniera del Temperino (45 minutes) is by far the most unusual itinerary. It takes you underground to discover galleries and excavations of the Etruscan period and the modern age.

Finish off with a visit to the spa-town of **Caldana Terme**, just south of Campiglia Marittima. It has two thermal spas: Calidario, a natural open-air spring used as far back as Etruscan times (day and night; no charge); and Val di Sole (☎ 0565-851066), a bathing establishment that controls water from the same Caldana spring, and also offers mud and water therapy aimed at digestive tract and liver complaints.

Back along the coast, a winding road climbs from the calm bay of the Golfe di Baratti, with its popular crescent of sand, into the wild hills of Populonia. It is a short but tortuous journey that takes you along stunning granite cliff faces with a 50-m (164-foot) sheer drop to the sea. Make the journey at sunset to enjoy an extraordinary view over the Tyrrhenian Sea, Elba and Corsica.

The present look and feel of **Populonia** was shaped from the Middle Ages on, when it became an important coastal stronghold for the Della Gherardesca counts, but its Etruscan roots are still in evidence. The **Parco Archeologico di Baratti e Populonia** (Archeological Park, Loc. Baratti, ☎ 0565-29002, fax 0565-29107, www.parchivaldicornia.etruscan.li.it, Tues-Sun, 9 am-8 pm) encompasses the town and most of the promontory. It contains the important Etruscan tomb of Carri and monumental necropolis di San Cerbone. The remains of the Etruscan city of Populonia, which flourished as a result of the Elban iron industry, are still very much in evidence.

The coastal necropolis of **San Cerbone** has been dated as far back as the seventh century BC, but it went unnoticed under a six-meter (20-foot) layer of iron slag for centuries until it was rediscovered at the beginning of the 19th century. It includes the colossal Tomb of Carts (a tumulus 28 m/92 feet in diameter) and the important Necropoli delle Grotte (the only one of its kind in Italy), whose ancient underground stone caves had been exploited since the seventh century BC. You can find out more in Piombino's **Museo Archeologico del Territorio di Populonia** (☎ 0565-221646, fax 0565-260857, museocittadella@parchivaldicornia.it, summer, Tues-Sun, 5-11 pm).

Populonia represents the northernmost tip of the promontory of Piombino, an ex-island that has gradually been connected to the mainland by the deposits of the Cornia River. It is connected with Piombino to its extreme south via a network of **trekking paths** through the archeological zone.

- The main five-mile path takes you over the crest of the mountain, offering magnificent views over both the coast and the inland dip of the Val di Cornia (2½-hour roundtrip, 40 minutes on bicycle). It is shadowed by an easier and longer trail farther inland.

- An easier second circuit, the two-mile "Buche delle Fate" (the Fairies' Hole), allows you to descend to the isolated coves of Cala San Quirico (a popular **diving** destination), which is otherwise unapproachable except by sea (45-minute roundtrip). It also takes you past the ancient Etruscan necropolis for which the path is named and through some of the coast's most typical coastline vegetation – heather, myrtle, phillyrea, sea fennel, helichrysum, wild carrot and sea cineraia are just some of the plants you will see in the scrub. You can arrange **diving** trips in the area with the **Blue Submarine Diving Center** (Loc. Baratti, ☎ 335-5424057).

- The final undulating coastal path loops around from Salivoli via the Mediterranean scrub between Cala Moresca and Fosso alle Canne (two-hour roundtrip), with a magnificent view over the island of Elba and a chance for sunbathing on the beautiful Spiaggia Lunga (Long Beach) or the quieter pebbled beach of Fosso alle Canne.

Follow the coastal path around and you'll be able to duck down to the coves of Cala Moresca, Punta Falcone and the 12th-century Marina di Salivoli (the three main beaches of residential Piombino) before arriving in the city of Piombino itself.

Piombino was founded by survivors from the original town of Populonia after Arab destruction in 809, and is today an important iron and steel center and tourist port for Elba and the sisters of the Tuscan Archipelago. You can arrange diving tours from town with the **Moby Dick Diving Center** (Loc. Carbonifero, ☎ 0565-20414).

Although its small town center has been restored a number of times, Piombino has managed to conserve its 16th-century walls dominated by the Sant'Antonio Gate, a 13th-century tower and the lovely Renaissance Palazzo Comunale. For a beautiful panorama, head up Viale del Popolo to Piazza Bovio, which opens directly on the sea. From there you can admire the whole of the Tuscan Archipelago.

Southeast around the promontory and the Golfo di Follonica is 18 miles of small white sandy beaches and rocky bays, part of which includes the windswept vegetation of the **Parco Naturale de la Sterpaia** (☎ 0565-226445, fax 0565-226521, parchi.valdicornia@parchivaldicornia.it, spring and summer by reservation on Sats and Suns, 3-6 pm). The long strip of sand here is overshadowed by a stretch of wet forest (characterized by centuries-old oak trees) just beyond the shore. The park organizes guided tours of the reserve (Comune di Piombino, ☎ 0565-63111).

Just inland from La Sterpaia, flamingoes, ibis, storks and herons gather at the **Riserva Naturale Oasi WWF Palude Orti Bottagone** (WWF Orti Bottagone Nature Reserve, Via P Gori, 36, Piombino, ☎/fax 0565-224361, wwfpiomb@tin.it, visits from 2 Sept-31 May on Thurs, Sat and Sun, 9:30 am-2 pm). This is a mix of salt- and freshwater marshland, which comprises the last residue of the swamplands of the Cornia River after land reclamation in the 19th century. Numerous paths and lookout points in the 240-acre reserve offer the chance to view over 200 bird species, including marsh hawks, herons, bitterns and cattle egrets, white storks, occasional flamingos and nesting stilt-plovers, as well as saltmarsh vegetation, such as saltwort, and freshwater marshland flora, a thick reed bed dotted with water-lilies, bulrush and marsh orchids.

Pisa

There's one last nature reserve in the Val di Cornia before hitting Follonica and the province of Grosseto, the **Parco Naturale di Montioni** (☎ 0565-49430, fax 0565-49733, parchi.valdicornia@parchivaldicornia.it, guided tours by reservation) just inland from Riotorto.

■ Where to Stay

The coast is crammed full of campgrounds, with six options at Vada alone. You'll find the best facilities, including outdoor pools, at **Campo dei Fiori** ☆☆ (Loc. Campo ai Fiori 4, ☎ 0586-770096, fax 0586-770323, www.campingcampodeifiori.it, Mar-Sept, $) and **Rifugio del Mare** ☆☆ (Loc. I Mozzi, ☎ 0586-770091, fax 0586-770268, www.rifugiodelmare.it, May-Sept, $).

There are six more choices at Cecina. **Camping Delle Gorette** ☆☆☆☆ (Via dei Campilunghi 150, ☎ 0586-622460, fax 0586-622045, Jan-Sept, $) is the largest and most luxurious of the options, but there's also a lovely outdoor pool at the smaller **Mareblu** ☆☆☆ (Via dei Campilunghi, Loc. Mazzanta, ☎ 0586-629191, fax 0586-629192, www.monteaperto.it/mareblu, Mar-Oct, $) and sporting facilities at the cheapest of the six, **Bocca di Cecina** ☆ (Via Guado alle Vacche 2, Loc. San Pietro in Palazzi, ☎ 0586-620509, fax 0586-621326, www.ccft.it, $).

Marina di Bibbona has 12 campgrounds. Your best bets are **Le Capanne** ☆☆☆ (Via Aurelia, Fraz. La California, ☎ 0586-600064, fax 0586-600198, www.campinglecapanne.it, Apr-Sept, $); **Arcobaleno 1** ☆☆☆ (Via dei Cavalleggeri 86, ☎ 0586-600296, fax 0586-600801, www.multinet.it/arcobaleno, all year, $); its slightly cheaper sister, **Arcobaleno 2** ☆☆☆ (Via Cipressi, same phone, fax and website, all year, $); or **Il Gineprino** ☆ (Via dei Platani 56a, ☎/fax 0586-600550, www.ilgineprino.it, Jan-Sept, $). Although the cheapest option, this one still has a lovely pool and restaurant.

Farther south again at Marina di Castagneto, you can choose between **Continental** ☆☆ (Via 1 Maggio, ☎/fax 0565-744014, www.campingcontinental.it, Jan-Sept, $) and **International Etruria** ☆☆ (Via della Pineta, ☎ 0565-744254, fax 0565-744494, www.campingetruria.com, Jan-Sept, $), while inland at Castagneto Carducci, there's **Le Pinacce** ☆☆☆ (Via Bolgherese, ☎ 0565-763667, fax 0565-766085, www.campinglepinacce.it, Mar-Oct, $).

San Vincenzo has **Park Albatros** ☆☆ (Loc. Pineta di Torre Nuova, ☎ 0565-701018, fax 0565-703589, www.parkalbatros.it, Apr-Sept, $). Piombino offers **Pappasole** ☆☆☆☆ (Loc. Carbonifera, ☎ 0565-20414, fax 0565-20346, www.pappasole.li.it, Mar-Oct, $), **Orizzonte** ☆☆ (Loc. Perelli Riotorto, ☎ 0565-828007, fax 0565-28033, www.infol.it, $) and **Riotorto** ☆☆ (Loc. Perelli Riotorto, ☎ 0565-21008, fax 0565-21118, Apr-Sept, $). These are the best choices with pools.

The best of the *agriturismi* can be found around San Vincenzo. These include **Contessa Beatrice** (Via della Caduta 5, ☎ 0565-704404, agribice@infol.it, $$), the best deal close to the sea, while **Poggio ai Santi** (Via San Bartolo 100, ☎ 0565-798032, fax 0565-798090, www.terra-toscana.com/poggioaisanti, $$$$) occupies the best location. This 19th-century homestead overlooks the island of Elba from its beautiful pine forest-covered hilltop. The nearby olive groves produce the biological olive oil it sells from its welcome shop.

The Tuscan Archipelago

The Tuscan Archipelago is made up of seven islands. Five of those (Capraia, Elba, Gorgona, Pianosa and Montecristo) lie along the Livorno Coast; the other two (Giglio and Giannutri) are lower down beside the province of Grosseto. Immersed in a cobalt blue sea with white-sand beaches and coves perfect for diving, the "seven sisters" are looked after by the Parco Nazionale dell'Archipelago Toscano (National Park of the Tuscan Archipelago), established in 1989 to maintain the precious environment with its typical flora and indigenous fauna.

This area is incredibly rich in history, with the remains of Etruscan mines, Medici fortifications and the legacy of exiled Napoleon Bonaparte.

■ Getting Here & Around

 By Ferry: Toremar (Via Calafati 6, ☎ 199-123199, fax 0586-224624, www.toremar.it) runs one roundtrip ferry a day from Livorno to **Gorgona** and **Capraia** (€10.40, conc. €5.20, cars €26.40) and up to 10 a day between Piombino and the **Elba** towns of Portoferraio (€5.20, conc. €2.60, cars €20.20), Rio Marina (€3.10, conc. €1.55, cars €20.70) and Porto Azzurro €5.20, conc. €2.60, cars €20.20). There's also one roundtrip a day from Porto Azzurro and/or Rio Marina to **Pianosa** (€10.40, conc. €5.20, cars €26.40). Bicycles cost an extra €5.20 on all services.

The isle of **Giglio** is reached from Porto Santo Stefano in the Grosseto province (see page 350).

 By Train: Livorno (Harbor Office, Piazza Sanità 1, ☎ 0586-893362) and **Piombino** (Harbor Office, Piazzale Premuda, ☎ 0565-221000) are served by harbor train stations (☎ 848-888088, www.trenitalia.it) on the Pisa-to-Grosseto train line.

 By Car: Take the Firenze-Pisa-Livorno **A12** to Rosignano and then the **SS1 Aurelia** south to Venturina, where you can follow "ferry boat to Elba" signs.

 Car & Bike Rentals: Car rentals are available from **Happy Rent** (Viale Elba 5, Portoferraio, ☎ 0565-914665, www.renthappy.it). **Rent Chiappi** (Piazza Citi 5, Portoferraio, ☎ 0565-913524, fax 0565-916779, www.rentchiappi.it) rents cars, motorbikes and mountain bikes. **TWN Rent** (Viale Elba 32, Portoferraio, ☎ 0565-914666, fax 0565-914666, www.twn-rent.it) rents cars, scooters, quads and mountain bikes.

 By Bus: Once you arrive, local bus services (**ATL**, ☎ 0565-914392) connect all the towns and villages on Elba. It is also served by a good road network.

 Taxis: These can be booked in Portoferraio (☎ 0565-915112), Porto Azzurro (☎ 0565-95078), Capoliveri (☎ 0565-968533), Rio Marina (☎ 368-457487), Marina di Campo (☎ 368-496963), Marciana Marina (☎ 0565-99127) and Campo Nell'Elba (☎ 0565-976443).

■ Information Sources

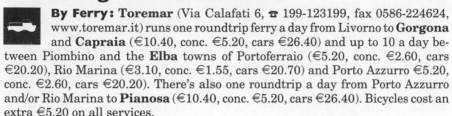 **Tourist Offices:** The main tourist office for the **Parco Nazionale dell'Arcipelago Toscano** (www.islepark.it) is in Portoferraio on Elba (Calata Italia 26, ☎ 0565-914671, www.aptelba.it) with a smaller office on **Capraia** (Via Assunzione 72, Capraia Isola, ☎ 0586-905138). Both arrange guided tours. The **Communità Montane Elba e Capraia** (Elba and Capraia Mountain Community) is also based in Portoferraio (Viale A. Manzoni 11, ☎ 0565-938111).

Parco Naturale Isola di Gorgona (Gorgona Natural Park) has its own office in Livorno (Corso Mazzini, 44, ☎ 0586-905071); the **ARDEA co-operative of Livorno** (☎ 0586-881382) provides services to day-trippers in the area.

■ The Island of Elba

Sightseeing

Elba, the "pearl of the Archipelago," is the biggest and most important of the islands. It is best known – beaches and diving apart – for the exile of **Napoleon**, who was confined here from the 4 Mar 1814 to the 26 Feb 1815, and traces of his stay can be visited as soon as you step off the ferry at Portoferraio.

Frequented from the end of the Etruscan era for the richness of its mineral mines – in particular iron (*ferro*), hence the name of its main town, Portoferraio – Elba was first colonized by the Romans, who constructed many of the villas and laid the foundations for its towns. The Middle Ages heralded Pisan rule and the addition of the majority of the defensive towers (which protected bays such as Rio Marina) and religious edifices (such as the 12th-century Pieve di San Giovanni Battista in Campo, which remains the most important Romanesque building on the island). However, it was under Medici rule and the subsequent takeover by Spain, that the island was to take on much of its present form. They added the most important of the coastal fortifications: the vast Fronte d'Attacco at Portoferraio and the grandiose Fortezza Stellare and Forte Focardo at Porto Azzurro.

All this historical background gives an extra oomph to what is one of the most popular sunbathing and watersports destinations along the Italian coast. The island boasts 150 **beaches** and isolated coves around its 147-km (91-mile) perimeter, some of which can be reached only by sea. Inland, it's a mountainous terrain, which peaks with the 1,019-m (3,342-ft) **Monte Capanne**. Along the southwest slopes runs a much-photographed **footpath**. Off this path, smaller paths will take you down to isolated bays such as Cavioli, Seccheto and Fetovaia, and the small towns of Pomonto and Chiessi.

Your arrival on the island is announced by the bastions of **Portoferraio**, a welcoming port-town encircled by walls constructed in the 16th century by Cosimo I de' Medici. It is framed by the Medicean **Forte Falcone** (the highest part of the city) and the **Forte Stella** (Star Fortress, named after the star-like design of its walls), on whose ramparts awaits a splendid panorama of the entire bay and town (both daily, 9 am-8 pm, free).

From Forte Stella, you can even see into the **Casa Napoleonica dei Mulini** (☎ 0565-915846, Mon-Sat, 9 am-7 pm, Sun and public holidays, 9 am-1 pm), the winter residence of the French emperor during his exile on the island. Surrounded by a beautiful garden, it is named for the two antique windmills that have been incorporated into the house. Remnants of his brief stay include the first Napoleonic flag of the island.

Casa Napoleonica should be followed by a visit to **Villa San Martino** (☎ 0565-914688, same hours), four miles out of town. This was Napoleon's summer house, where it is said he prepared his escape preceding his last defeat at Waterloo. It also houses the **Galleria Demidoff**, a display of 18th-century paintings, furnishings and imperial ornaments collected by Russian Prince Demidoff, which were installed here after he bought the property in 1852.

The Napoleon Trail leads you to the **Chiesa della Reverenda Misericordia**, whose museum (9 am-noon, 4-8 pm) contains the Emperor's bronze death-mask donated by his personal physician, Dr Antonmarchi. The trail also goes to the **Chiesa di SS Sacramento**, which contains a copy of the mask alongside a votive shrine dedicated to veterans of the 1915-18 war.

In front of the port, excavations have uncovered the **Resti della Villa Romana** (Promontorio delle Grotte), the remains of a Roman villa with decorations and mosaics dating back to the Hadrian era. You can find out more about local archaeology by visiting the **Museo Archeologico della Linguella** (Fortezza Medicea della Linguella, ☎ 0565-944024, Tues-Sat, 9:30 am-12:30 pm, 4-7 pm), which presents a methodical account of local history using findings from the island's main excavation sites.

The **Pinacoteca Foresiana** (Foresiana Picture Gallery, Caserma de Laugier, ☎ 0565-937380, daily, 9:30 am-noon, 4-7 pm) houses the island's major artistic offerings, with a collection of 16th- and 19th-century miniatures and paintings (including works by Signorini, Cigheri and Nomellini) decorating the walls of this former Franciscan convent.

Portoferraio can be quite chaotic in the summer months, so it's best to flee quickly to a tranquil beach. Heading west, you'll come across the first of the popular white sand bays at **Biodola** (five miles, one roundtrip bus a day). Backed by pinewoods and fronted by the transparent crystal-clear sea of the Biodola Gulf, beach establishments renting sun-loungers and umbrellas take up some of the stretch, but on the whole, the beach is free and well-served by hotels and restaurants. There is also plenty of **boat rental** and **diving**, **surf** and **canoe** facilities. A path leads across rocks to the slightly less crowded beach of Scaglieri if you arrive too late to nab a spot.

The provincial road continues from here past the picturesque fishing village of Marina di Marciana and inland to Poggio and **Marciana**, both of which sit upon natural terraces 400 m (1,312 feet) high overlooking the sea. At Marciana, you can walk the **trail** (CAI#1) to the top of **Monte Capanne**, a surprisingly woody itinerary that offers impressive views over the island as far as Corsica and Monte dell'Argentario in the province of Grosseto to the south (a chairlift departs to the peak just outside Marciana if you don't want to walk). The route first takes you through centuries-old chestnut woods to the Santuario della Madonna del Monte (on the side of Monte Giove).

But before you head off, Marciana's medieval town center is worth a look for its narrow lanes and stairways, colorful pastel buildings and relaxed ambiance. It is home to the **Museo Archeologico** (Via del Pretorio, ☎ 0565-901215, daily, 9 am-12:30 pm, 3:30-7:3:30 pm), with its collection of second-century BC relics from the coast in front of Marina di Marciana.

Continue west and you'll hit the most savage – and, therefore, least touristy – part of the island (it is also from these bays that Napoleon is said to have admired Corsica, his homeland). Framed by enormous rocks of light granite, the coastline flips between deserted little coves and wide, tranquil shingle beaches, such as the peaceful bays of **Pomonte**, **Fetovaia** and **Chiessi**. The former is the easiest to reach by car; it may be a coarse shingle beach, but it is popular with **surfers** and **scuba** divers, the latter attracted here by the wreck of the cargo ship *Pomonte*, which was shipwrecked just offshore in 1972. Sheltered by a rugged, scrub-covered promontory, Fetovaia is equally popular with surfers and scuba divers. Its beach – this time of a fine golden sand – leads into waters that hide a network of granite reefs. Chiessi is the quietest of the three; a small, shingle beach within easy reach of the village, its southerly winds ensure a steady visit of windsurfers, while its fish-filled waters make snorkeling a lazy option.

The most famous and best-loved beaches are on the southern side of the island. **Marina di Campo** has the longest stretch and is the best-equipped with **boat** rental, **diving**, **surf**, **sail** and **canoe** facilities, while the sand-dune-framed bay of **Lacona** comes a close second. It has boat rental, diving, surfing, sailing and waterskiing, while out to sea, the rocky seabed and submarine sea grass is the ideal destination for **scuba** divers. It is an area known as "German town" (even the butchers are called *metzerei* rather than the Italian *macellerie*) thanks to the yearly meeting of German surfers, attracted here by the waves of the maestrale winds from the northwest.

SOMETHING FOR THE KIDS

KID FRIENDLY

The **Acquario dell'Elba** (Elba Acquarium, Marina di Campo, ☎ 0565-977881) will entertain the kids with its collection of 150 different species of Mediterranean fishes.

The main town in this area is **Capoliveri**, the "capo dei liberi" or "free hill," so-called because it was once a Roman town inhabited by ex-slaves. It is a charming town of narrow streets (known as *chiassi*), archways and picturesque staircases, which emerges onto a gentle hilltop piazzetta (the island's "living room"). From here, **trails** lead up to Elba's second-largest mountain, **Monte Calamita** (413 m/1,200 feet). This mountain takes its unfortunate name from the unusually large number of boats that crash into the nearby rocks; local legend attributes the disasters to the mountain's magnetic pull.

Around the promontory lies another ancient town, the lively **Porto Azzurro**. This delicious beach town sits between the bright green of the Mediterranean scrub and the bright blue of the bay; its tight network of brightly colored houses link the Spanish forts of Focardo and San Giacomo. If you're here during July and Sept, the bustling night market offers the chance to peruse the wares of numerous artisans at discounted prices. Its most popular beach is in the protected bay of **Barbarossa**, less than one mile out of town and a popular **diving destination.**

If you've come here for the local minerals, you should head to the mineral park at Rio Alto and Cavo before finishing off with a tour into the island's mining history at the **Museo dei Minerali Elbani** (Mineral Museum, Rio Marina, ☎ 0565-962747, daily, 9 am-noon, 3-6 pm). Porto Azzuro also has its own reconstruction of a working Elban mine at **La Piccola Miniera** (The Small Mine, Loc. Pianetto, ☎ 0565-95350), complete with a train ride through the 250-m (820-foot) gallery. There's also a small museum of minerals at **Giannini Minerali** (Viale Italia 2, Porto Azzuro, ☎ 0565-95307).

Once round the mining promontory of Cavo, heading back towards Porteferraio, you'll see the most picturesque part of the coast with coves only reachable by sea. The beautiful beaches of **Ortano** and **Nisportino** provide the pull for those who have rented boats, as do the two tiny islands of the Canale di Piombino – the beautiful white bay of **Cerboli** (where you can't land) and the lighthouse-mounted **Palmaiola** (where you can moor to the north).

Adventures

On Foot

 Not only does Elba offer the rare chance to combine coastal and mountain walking in one easy trek, it also drops in the occasional Etruscan fortress, Roman villa, granite mine and charming fishing village, not to mention the rich variety of flora and fauna, to keep you on your sightseeing toes. There are nine itineraries crossing the island, all of which only require basic to medium fitness.

The panoramic route "In the Footsteps of Saints" takes you along a 4½-hour loop from Marciana (Marciana-San Cerbone-Valle di Pedalta-La Stretta-Marciana) through chestnut woods and Mediterranean scrub before depositing you back in town. It's your best choice for springtime rambling with the rich scent of the scrub enhancing the sea views with its pungent fragrance. To trace the effects on the landscape of Elba's rich iron mining past, opt instead for the "Land of Iron" trail, a shorter four-hour hike from Rio Elba (Rio Elba-Le Panche-Monte Capannello-Monte Strega-Santa Caterina-Torre Giove-Rio Elba), or the five-hour "Land of Granite" trail from San Piero (San Piero-Pietra Murata-Moncione-San Piero).

Other walks take you across the island (Marciana-Pomonte; 11 miles) via Monte Capanne; across the island (Marciana-Chiessi; 14 miles) via Madonna del Monte; up the slopes of Volterraio and Monte Castello (Rio nell'Elba loop; nine miles); from Capo Castello to Cavo (three miles) via Mausoleo Tonietti; and from Campo ai Peri to Acquabona (four miles) via Monte Orello.

Both the western and southern coastline of Elba offer **climbing** possibilities. On the western hills, options are the granite **"rock of the eagle"** near Madonna del Monte; parallel walls in the inlet at **Sant'Andrea**; **Monte San Bartolomeo**; and the rocky massif at **Fetovaia**. On the southern side, there are two difficult climbs on the cliffs at **Remaiolo**; and the easier sloping rock face of **Ginepro**.

You can arrange climbing excursions with **Renato Bardi** (Loc. Antiche Saline, Portoferraio, ☎ 0565-917140, freeclimbing@infoelba.it).

On Wheels

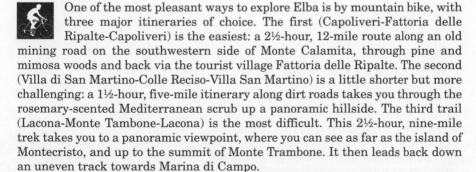 One of the most pleasant ways to explore Elba is by mountain bike, with three major itineraries of choice. The first (Capoliveri-Fattoria delle Ripalte-Capoliveri) is the easiest: a 2½-hour, 12-mile route along an old mining road on the southwestern side of Monte Calamita, through pine and mimosa woods and back via the tourist village Fattoria delle Ripalte. The second (Villa di San Martino-Colle Reciso-Villa San Martino) is a little shorter but more challenging: a 1½-hour, five-mile itinerary along dirt roads takes you through the rosemary-scented Mediterranean scrub up a panoramic hillside. The third trail (Lacona-Monte Tambone-Lacona) is the most difficult. This 2½-hour, nine-mile trek takes you to a panoramic viewpoint, where you can see as far as the island of Montecristo, and up to the summit of Monte Trambone. It then leads back down an uneven track towards Marina di Campo.

Lo Scoglio (Via Carducci 33, Portoferraio, ☎ 5 0565-914128) arranges mountain bike excursions into the island scrubland.

On Horseback

For horseback riding on the island, contact **Maneggio Country Club** (Loc. Valcarene, ☎ 0565-930811), **Ranch Antonio** (Loc. Monte Orello, ☎ 0565-933132) and **Il Fortino** (Loc. Buraccio, ☎ 0565-940245) – all near

Pisa

Portoferraio. Near Capoliveri, there is **Costa dei Gabbiani** (Loc. Ripalti, ☎ 0565-935122) and, near Porto Azzurro, try **Fattoria Sapere** (Loc. Mola, ☎ 0565-95064)

SOMETHING FOR THE KIDS

Water park **Acqua il Parco** (via Tevere 25, Cecina, ☎ 0586-623877, fax 0586-627739, www.acquailparcocecina.it, June-September, 10 am-6 pm, €13/US$16.38, conc. €11,00/US$13.86) is sure to entertain the kids with its mix of swimming pools and kamikaze slides.

Things get a little more magical at **Magiré Cavallino Matto** (Via Po 1, Marina di Castagneto, ☎ 0565-745720, fax 0565-746770) in the heart of pine forest near Castagneto Carducci. Here children can take part in African safaris, voyage through ancient Egypt, take a trip through the Fantastical Tunnel or follow fish at the aquarium.

On Water

The sea around Elba has long drawn **divers** to its rich variety of flora, shallow rock formations, underwater caves and ancient shipwrecks, but while diving locations may be numerous, three or four are the most popular among the returning crowd. These include **Scoglietto** (a rocky island, north of Portoferraio, reached by a 15-minute boat ride) and suitable for all levels, including snorkelers. There is also the **Secca di Fonza** (known as the Secca del Corallo). In its numerous dens you can see eels, lobsters and other fish. The **Relitto di** *Pomonte* (Wreck of *Pomonte*) – the 1972 relic of the Italian cargo ship – is accessible by swimming from the rocky beach. **Junker 52** is the wreck of a World War II airplane recently discovered 120 feet under water in front of Portoferraio.

Various schools on Elba organize guided dives and PADI courses. Try **Diving in Elba** (Via del Mare 10, Marciana, ☎/fax 0565-907251, www.divinginelba.com), **Il Careno** (Marciana, ☎ 0565-908125, www.ilcareno.it), **Talas Diving Center** (Loc. Lido, Capoliveri, ☎ 0565-933482, fax 0565-933572, www.subacquea.com) or **Mandel Diving Center Morcone** (Capoliveri, ☎ 0565-968528, fax 0565-935931, www.mandelclub.com).

Canoes and **sea kayaks** (along with pedal boats) can be rented on many of the beaches, but to arrange for them in advance, contact **TWN Rent** (Viale Elba 32, Portoferraio, ☎ 0565-914666, fax 0565-914666, www.twn-rent.it). The most popular kayak routes are the 47-km (29-mile) itinerary between Marina di Campo and Procchio in the north, and the shorter 15-km (nine-mile) paddle from Marina di Campo to Lacona in the south.

To explore the quieter coves, you can rent a boat with **Rent Chiappi** (Piazza Citi 5, Portoferraio, ☎ 0565-913524, fax 0565-916779, www.rentchiappi.it, motor boats and dinghies) or **Bartolini Yachting** (Loc. San Giovanni, Portoferraio, ☎/fax 0565-916957, www.bartoliniyachting.com, motor boats). The latter also doubles as a windsurfing school.

■ The Sister Islands

Capraia

For a long time closed off to tourists, Capraia was finally opened to visitors in 1986, when the penal colony, which had occupied it since 1874, was closed down. The result is a more-or-less virgin habitat where the wild goats from which its takes its name (*capra* is Italian for goats) and rare birds, such as the gabbiano corso, still have the run of the land.

The island has no real roads to speak of and so is best appreciated and visited by boat; the 30-km (19-mile) round-trip takes half a day with time to stop at the best beaches and the lookout point on Punta dello Zenobito, which commands the best views of nearby Elba and, in the distance, Corsica. For organized excursions, contact **Cooperativa ARDEA** (☎ 0586-881382) or **Cooperativa Parco Isola di Capraia** (☎ 0586-905071).

Arriving from Livorno or Elba, the ferries drop passengers off at the port-town of **Capraia Isola**. It is the island capital and has the only real tourist facilities to speak of, including the beginning of the island trail, marked with stones, which crosses the backbone of the island as far south as Punta dello Zenobito. Short walks will take you through rich scrub to the stunning **Forte di San Giorgio** (no entry), built in the 1100s by the Pisans, the ancient **Chiesa di Santo Stefano** and the idyllic bay of **Cala della Zurletta**, while more experienced hikers should clamber to the top of **Monte delle Penne** for a splendid view of the whole island.

The small lake at the base of Monte Castello offers the best bird-watching, especially during spring migrations, while the refreshing hike up **Monte Arpagna** provides some great views of the ruined tower that marks Punta dello Zenobito to the south.

The most beautiful bays are to the south with **Cala il Moreto** and **Cala Rossa**, near **Punta dello Zenobito**, providing the best sand and rays. The latter is the most visually striking of the two: it stands on the remains of an ancient volcano, which has bequeathed a glorious bay of red sand.

The coves on the west – such as Cala del Reciso, Cala del Terrain and Cala del Vetriolo – are much rockier, but deserve a visit for the *tafoni*, peculiar shapes left in the rock by the wind. **Cala della Mortola** offers the only sandy beach, which can be found right at the northern tip.

Gorgona

Unlike Capraia, Gorgona is still occupied by its penal colony, which makes visiting a little complicated – fortunately, the **Cooperativa Parco Isola di Gorgona** (☎ 0586-884522/895206, July-September, Tuesdays only, book well in advance for tours in English) arranges day-long guided tours. It is well worth going to the trouble; restrictions on visitations have ensured a relatively wild and undamaged countryside awaits.

The northernmost and smallest of the islands, Gorgona is also one of the most scenic, with an impressive blend of Mediterranean scrub, pines, cypresses, olive vines and oaks. All this supports a varied flora of up to 450 plant species – at just over one-square mile in size, that's pretty impressive – and a thriving bird community; keep your eye out for herring gulls, Corsican gulls and cormorants, greater and lesser shearwaters, buzzards and peregrine falcons.

Pisa

Now inhabited almost solely by the prisoners and their guards (the little local population that remains can be found in the old fishing village overlooking Cala de Scalo), the only real historical settlements that exist on the island are the **Torre Vecchia** (Old Tower), perched on a sheer cliff face on the western coast, and **Torre Nuova** (New Tower), near the port on the eastern side. The Pisans built the former in the 12th century; the Grand Duchy of Tuscany built the latter in the 17th century.

Pianosa

Another island to emerge untouched from years as a penal colony is Pianosa. After centuries as a maximum-security prison, this, the flattest of the seven islands, was finally opened in 1996, and continues to be well preserved thanks to limited guided tours (book though **Agenzia Arrighi**, Pianosa Isola, ☎ 0565-95000, tours on Tuesdays only).

Again, it's difficult but worth the trouble. This island houses a unique archeological treasure – a monumental complex of third- to fourth-century catacombs, which house the remains of the Christian prisoners condemned to work in the island's tufa quarries. Currently, these are being restored in preparation for visitor openings. There are more Roman ruins, including baths and the Villa of Agrippa, to be visited along the beaches of Cala Giovanna.

Apart from its 20 or so human inhabitants (mainly the families of the former guards), much of the life is supplied by nesting birds, such as the bee-eater, right; ask your guide to point out the nesting sites.

Montecristo

The fifth sister, Montecristo, is the most safeguarded island of the archipelago and still remains out of bounds to visitors (with the rare exception of scientific expeditions). Information is available from **Corpo Forestale dello Stato**, ☎ 0566-40019. A mountainous terrain now only enjoyed by its guardians (and wild goats), it was in its Benedictine monastery, abandoned since 1553, that the legend of the buried treasure was born that so inspired Dumas to write *The Count of Montecristo*. Dumas' may be the most famous of the legends, but it certainly isn't the only myth that this mysterious island has produced.

Formerly known as Oglasa, the island supposedly changed its name after San Mamiliano, patron saint of sailors, escaped to it from a pirate ship in the fifth century. The saint overcame the dragon that was then terrorizing the island, before spending the remainder of his days in solitude on the mountain he called Monte di Cristo (The Mount of Christ). The grotto he took as his home is apparently still visible today, although we may have to wait a good time yet before we can visit it.

Fortunately, you can see the huge block of granite that comprises the 545-m (1,788-foot) **Monte della Fortezza**. It is here that the endemic viper of Montecristo has made its home.

■ What to Eat & Where

The tastiest lobster in the Mediterranean is fished here.
Unsurprisingly for such a popular tourist destination, Elba has an extensive range of restaurants, many specializing in fresh-caught fish.

Trattoria la Barca (Via Guerrazzi 60, ☎ 0565-918036, $$) is one of Portoferaio's most popular restaurants thanks to its tasty fish dishes and welcoming atmosphere. Ask the waiter for the catch of the day.

In the historic center of Portoferaio, **Trattoria Lido** (Salita Falcone 2, ☎ 0565-914650, $$) is another top choice. Its house special is the *gnocchi di pesce* (potato and fish dumplings).

Moving over to Rio Marina, **Cannocchia** (Via Palestro 3, ☎ 0565-982432, $$) is the pick of the tables for seafood. Specialties center on the catch of the day, but there's also plenty of fried fish (*frittura mixta*) and fish rolls (*involtini*).

Just outside Marciana Marina is the elegant **Capo Nord** (Loc. La Fenicia, ☎ 0565-996983, $$$), serving a traditional range of fresh fish on its small riverside terrace.

On the island of Capraia, **Vecchio Scorfano** (Via Assunzione 44, ☎ 0586-9005132, $) serves its own range of traditional seafood dishes. Try the *zuppa di pesce* (fish soup) for a light lunch or the *pesce capraiese al timo* (local-style fish) for a delicious evening meal.

■ Where to Stay

Elba gets pretty busy in the summer months and there are plenty of hotels at all prices ranges to meet the rush.

Dei Fiori ☆☆ (Via della Salita 9, Marciana, ☎ 0565-906013, $), **Arrighi** ☆☆ (Via V. Veneto 18, ☎ 0565-95315, $) and **Barbarossa** ☆ (Loc. Barbarossa, ☎ 0565-95119, $) are the budget island choices. **Giardino** ☆☆ (Loc. Lacona, Capoliveri, ☎ 0565-964059, fax 0565-964363, $$), Da Renzo ☆☆ (Loc. Procchio, Marciana, ☎/fax 0565-907505, $$) and **La Conchiglia** ☆☆ (Loc. Cavoli, Campo nell'Elba, ☎ 0565-987010, fax 0565-987257, $$) cost very little more.

Things start to get a little more luxurious when you hit the three-star options: **Antares** ☆☆☆ (Loc. Lido, ☎ 0565-940131, $$$), **Bel Tramonto** ☆☆☆ (Marciana, ☎ 0565-908027, $$$), **Gabbiano Azzurro** ☆☆☆ (Viale Amedeo 48, ☎ 0565-997035, $$$), **Casa Rosa** ☆☆☆ (Loc. Biodola, ☎ 0565-969931, $$$), **Rio** ☆☆☆ (Via Palestro 34, ☎ 0565-924225, $$$) and **Pierolli** ☆☆☆ (Lungomare Kennedy, ☎ 0565-931188, $$$).

But for the best the island can offer, try **Desireé** ☆☆☆☆ (Marciana, ☎ 0565-907311, $$$$), **Locanda del Volterraio** ☆☆☆☆ (Rio nell'Elba, ☎ 0565-961236, $$$$) or the even pricier **Hermitage** ☆☆☆ (Via Biodola 1, Loc. Biodola, ☎ 0565-936911, $$$$$) or **La Fenice** ☆☆☆☆ (Via Provinciale 1, Marciana, ☎ 0565-907733, $$$$$).

If you want to stay on Capiaia, your only real option is **Beppone** ☆☆☆ (Via Assunzione 78, ☎ 0586-905001, $$).

There's camping all over Elba with options close to Portoferraio Acquaviva at **Loc. Acquaviva** (☎ 0565-915592, $), Enfola at **Loc. Enfola** (☎ 0565-939001, $) and Scaglieri at **Loc. Scaglieri** (☎ 0565-969940, $). More choices are at Porto Azzurro Arrighi with **Loc. Barbarossa** (☎ 0565-939001, $), Marina di Campo with **La Foce** (Loc. La Foce, ☎ 0565-976456, $), Ville degli Ulivi with **Loc. La Foce** (☎ 0565-976048, $) and Capoliveri Lacona with Loc. Lacona (☎ 0565-964161, $) and Stella Mare, **Loc. Lacona** (☎ 0565-964007, $).

There's also one campsite on Capraia: **Le Sughere** (Vie delle Sughere 1, Capraia Isola, ☎ 0586-905066, $).

Grosseto & The Maremma

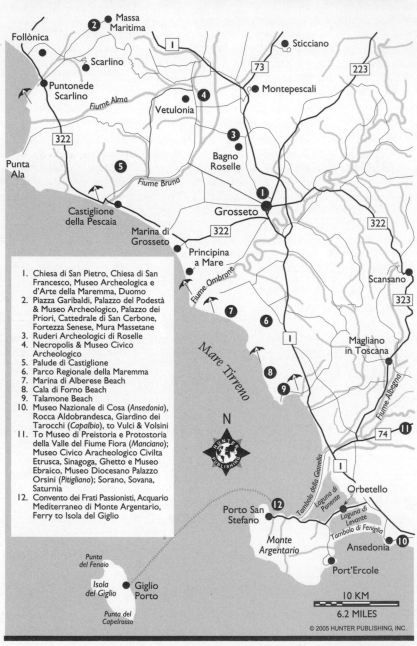

Massa Marittima · ② · Follònica · Scarlino · Puntonede Scarlino · *Fiume Alma* · Vetulonia · ④ · 322 · Punta Ala · ⑤ · *Fiume Bruna* · Castiglione della Pescaia · Marina di Grosseto · Sticciano · 73 · 223 · Montepescali · ③ · Bagno Roselle · ① · Grosseto · 322 · Principina a Mare · 322 · Scansano · 323 · *Fiume Ombrone* · ⑦ · ⑥ · Magliano in Toscana · ① · ⑧ · ⑨ · *Fiume Albegna* · 74 · ⑪ · **Mare Tirreno** · N · *Tambolo della Gianella* · Laguna di Ponente · ① · Orbetello · ⑫ · Porto San Stefano · *Laguna di Levante* · *Tambolo di Feriglia* · ⑩ · Ansedonia · Monte Argentario · Punta del Fenaio · *Isola del Giglio* · Giglio Porto · Punta del Capelrosso · Port'Ercole

1. Chiesa di San Pietro, Chiesa di San Francesco, Museo Archeologica e d'Arte della Maremma, Duomo
2. Piazza Garibaldi, Palazzo del Podestà & Museo Archeologico, Palazzo dei Priori, Cattedrale di San Cerbone, Fortezza Senese, Mura Massetane
3. Ruderi Archeologici di Roselle
4. Necropolis & Museo Civico Archeologico
5. Palude di Castiglione
6. Parco Regionale della Maremma
7. Marina di Alberese Beach
8. Cala di Forno Beach
9. Talamone Beach
10. Museo Nazionale di Cosa (*Ansedonia*), Rocca Aldobrandesca, Giardino dei Tarocchi (*Capalbio*), to Vulci & Volsini
11. To Museo di Preistoria e Protostoria della Valle del Fiume Fiora (*Manciano*); Museo Civico Aracheologico Civilta Etrusca, Sinagoga, Ghetto e Museo Ebraico, Museo Diocesano Palazzo Orsini (*Pitigliano*); Sorano, Sovana, Saturnia
12. Convento dei Frati Passionisti, Acquario Mediterraneo di Monte Argentario, Ferry to Isola del Giglio

10 KM
6.2 MILES

Maremma & Grosseto

A malaria-infested swamp until Leopoldo II brought his land reclamation processes to the area, the province of Grosseto is the least populated of the Tuscan regions and, as a result, the wildest. Its long stretches of beautiful and undeveloped coastline curl past the untamed lands of Maremma, the former island of Argentario, the lagoon of Orbetello and, out to

sea, two islands of the Tuscan Archipelago (Giglio and Giannutri). Inland, a wide fertile hinterland leads up to Monte Amiata and the Siena province along a winding road that dips first past Etruscan tombs, atmospheric ancient cities, and churches, abbeys, palaces and monasteries.

REGION AT A GLANCE

- **Main city**: Grosseto (see page 343).
- **Town breaks**: Massa Marittima (see page 342), Pitigliano (see page 354), Sovana (see page 356) and Sorano (see page 355).
- **Rural retreats**: Maremma (see page 345), Monte d'Argentario (see page 349), Laguna di Orbetello and Lago di Buruna (see page 350).
- **Spa breaks**: Saturnia (see page 358).
- **Coast**: From the Golfo di Follonica to the border with Lazio .
- **Island breaks**: Giglio and Giannutri (see page 351).

■ Information Sources

Tourist Offices: The main **APT Grosseto** (Grosseto Tourist Office, Viale Monterosa 206, ☎ 0564-462611, fax 0564-454606, www.grosseto.turismo.toscana.it) covers both the city and the region of Grosseto. The monthly *Maremma Magazine* (Italian only) is a good source of event information in the whole province.

Grosseto & Its Coast

F ollow the coast around from Follonica and the province of Pisa; the sandy bays will eventually lead to Grosseto. Its historical center may be small, but this city represents a natural capital for the province, close as it is to the sea. To the north are the Roman remains of Vetulonia and Roselle, and to the south, the rich wildlife of the Parco Naturale della Maremma.

■ Getting Here & Around

By Train: Frequent services (☎ 848-888088, www.trenitalia.it) to Grosseto run from Florence and Siena, with the slower **REG** services first stopping in Massa Marittima, Scarlino and Follonica.

By Bus: **Rama** (☎ 0564-475111, www.griforama.it) runs two daily services from Grosseto to Massa Marittima (#20), frequent services to and along the coast (Grosseto-Scarlino-Follonica (#27); Grosseto-Marina di Grosseto-Castiglione della Pescaia-Riva del Sole-Follonica (#28); Scarlino-Follonica (#29); and Follonica FS-Punta Ala (#29)) and inland from Grosseto to Vetulonia (#35).

 By Car: The **SS1 Aurelia** follows the sweep of the entire Grosseto coast from Pisa in the north to Rome in the south. If arriving from Florence and the north, the **SS223** sweeps down from Siena, although a parallel (and much fought-against) highway was under construction at the time of writing. To reach the Roman ruins at Vetulonia, follow the **SP3** (Padule) from Grosseto and turn right at Macchiascandona to pick up signs. Scarlino and other beach resorts are signposted off the SS1.

■ Information Sources

Tourist Information: The main **Grosseto APT** apart (see details on previous page), there are smaller tourist offices at **Castiglione della Pescaia** (Piazza Stefani 5, ☎ 0564-948116), **Follonica** (Via Roma 20, ☎ 0566-263332) and **Massa Marittima** (Via Ximenes 14, ☎ 0566-902243).

■ Sightseeing & Adventures

The Grosseto Coast

Just over the border from the province of Livorno, **Follonica**, in the gulf of the same name, is one of the best-known of Grosseto's resorts thanks to its spread of honey-golden sand 20 m (66-feet) wide. The (free) beach to the south is wider still, with rolling sand dunes and a thick pine forest separating it from the coastal road.

Inland, the **Riserva Naturale Integrale di Poggio Tre Cancelli** (State Nature Reserve, near Montioni, ☎ 0566-40019) is a 120-acre pocket of Mediterranean scrub, with nesting goldfinches and flycatchers, as well as domestic species at risk of extinction, such as the long-horned cattle for which Maremma is famous.

Massa Marittima

It's only a short hop from Follonica to Massa Marittima along the SS439. On the edge of the stunning Colline Metallifere, this charming "art" town is one of the major tourist draws in the region and, once you arrive in its attractive medieval center (Massa Vecchia), you'll easily see why. The heart of the old town is **Piazza Garibaldiar**, where the majority of sights are concentrated: **Palazzo del Podestà**, **Palazzo dei Priori** and the imposing Romanesque-Gothic **Cattedrale di San Cerbone**, the finest example of religious architecture in the province. The Palazzo del Podestà is the current home to the **Museo Archeologico** (☎ 0566-902289, summer, 10:30 am-12:30 pm, 3:30-7 pm, winter, 10 am-12:30 pm, 3:30-5 pm, closed Mon, €3, conc. €2). Its collection includes the Aeneolithic stone of Vado

Massa Marittima

all'Arancio, dated between 4300 and 200 BC, and Etruscan excavations from the dig at the nearby Lago dell'Accesa (Loc. Pesta, ☎ 0566-902289). The ticket includes entry to the Pinacoteca (Art Gallery, same hours) with a precious *Maestà* by Ambrogio Lorenzetti and *Angelo Annunziate* by Sassetta.

You can tour **Fortezza Senese** (Piazza Matteotti, ☎ 0566-902289, summer, 10 am-1 pm, 2-6 pm, winter, 11 am-1 pm, 2:30-4:30 pm, closed Mon) and **Mura Massetane** (guided tour, reservations required ☎ 0566-902289), both of which were built just outside the old town immediately after Siena conquered the area in the 14th century.

Scarlino

The tourist port of Scarlino is a popular choice for **scuba divers** with a reef lying just off to the south of its fine white sandy beach, and a rocky cove of interesting marine life off the rugged cliffs near Cala Violina (one of the most famous beaches in the region). A **trekking trail** leads through the pine forests of the 1,600-acre **ANPIL Costiere di Scarlino** (Coastal Fauna Oasis) along the coast as far as Castiglione di Pescaia. In addition to deer, wild boar and porcupines, it also has the sandy Cala Civette (marked by tower of the same name), a delicious four-mile stretch of beach that unites the rocky promontories of Scarlino with Punta Ala.

The promontory of **Punta Ala**, famous for its port of dream yachts and dense Mediterranean scrub-covered hills, marks the hub of the camping sites. Like the bay south of Scarlino, many of the best beaches are reached over cliff **trails** or by sea (you can drop anchor to explore the reef of the small Isola dello Sparviero). To arrange **horseback riding** in the pine forests, contact **Punta Ala Equitazione** (Via della Dogana, ☎ 0564-920121).

The fine white sandy beach of **Castiglione della Pescaia** can be reached directly from town. Surrounded by pine forests and scrub, you can **canoe** along the River Bruna, which splits the town (the river mouth is a great place to buy fresh fish directly from the fishermen), into the cane thickets of the 2,600-acre **Palude di Castiglione** (Castiglione Marsh, also known as the Diaccia Botrona Nature Reserve), a popular **bird-watching** destination for its cormorants, herons, grebes and kingfishers. The multimedia **Museo di Casa Rossa Ximenes** (Reserve Museum, Via Ettore Socci 17, ☎ 0564-933069) offers the opportunity to view the entire reserve and its wildlife via telecameras.

Between Castiglione della Pescaia and Marina di Grosseto, the coast is flanked by the **Pineta del Tombolo**, a rich coastal forest best explored by **bike**. If you cycle it from Marina di Grosseto, you can also explore the 18th-century **Forte San Rocco** built by Ferdinando III or the resort of **Principina a Mare**, a white sandy bay, just to the south.

Grosseto

Although Grosseto is mainly a modern city, it does have a small but pretty historical center, laid out between well-preserved 16th-century bastions. Corso Carducci, its principal street, takes you to its oldest Romanesque church, **Chiesa di San Pietro**, from where Piazza Indipendenza leads to the slightly younger Benedictine **Chiesa di San Francesco** (13th century). Behind its main altar there is a painted Crucifix attributed to Duccio da Bouninsegna.

The **Museo Archeologico e d'Arte della Maremma** (Piazza Baccarini 3, ☎ 0564-408750, summer, 9 am-1 pm, 4-6 pm, winter, 9 am-1 pm, closed Mon, €5, conc. €3) displays prehistoric and protohistoric findings from Maremma, includ-

ing those taken from the Etruscan centers of Roselle and Vetulonia just out of town (see page #). On the second floor, the art gallery contains a panel *Madonna of the Cherries* by Sassetta, as well as other later works.

Take Corso Carducci again to arrive at the **Duomo** on Piazza D. Alighieri – also home to a pretty Palazzo Comunale (town hall). This cathedral, dedicated to San Lorenzo, was constructed in the late 13th century, although its striking red and white façade was seriously reworked in 1845.

On the Trail of the Etruscans

The **Ruderi Archeologici di Roselle** (Roselle Archeological Park, ☎ 0564-402403, summer, 9 am-6:30 pm, winter, 9 am-5:30 pm, €4, conc. €2) is one of the most important archeological digs in Tuscany. An ancient Etruscan city, it has retained intact a two-mile stretch of city walls, part of the later Roman city, and on a hill, the remains of an amphitheater and spa.

Farther to the north, the history of the vast necropolis of **Vetulonia** can be discovered at the **Museo Civico Archeologico** (Piazza Vetluna, ☎ 0564-948058, summer, 10 am-6 pm, winter, 10 am-4 pm, €4, conc. €3) and **Zona Archeologica di Vetulonia** (Archeology Park, ☎ 0564-949587, summer, 9 am-7:30 pm, winter, 9 am-5 pm).

Finish your tour with a visit to the **Museo Civico Archeologico** in Grosseto (Palazzo del Podestà, Piazza Garibaldi, ☎ 0566-902289.

■ Where to Eat

LOCAL FLAVORS

Maremma acquacotta: Each town has its own recipe for this local soup and Grosseto is no exception. It was originally a peasant soup made using water, garlic, onions, basil leaves and celery.

Near Grosseto's Porta Vecchia (Old Gate), **Cantina** (Piazza del Mercato 16, ☎ 0564-427828, www.cantinadipiazzadelsale.com, $$$) is an atmospheric *enoteca* and contemporary art gallery in the shape of a railway tunnel with exposed brickwork and entire walls covered with wine bottles.

Just outside the city walls, **Buca di San Lorenzo da Claudio** (Via Manetti 1, ☎ 0564-25142, $$) is one of the most famous tables in town. There's another quality restaurant at Castiglione della Pescaia, **Da Romolo** (Corso della Libertà 10, ☎ 0564-933533, $$), with its great range of fish dishes caught just off the coast.

■ Where to Stay

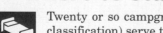

Twenty or so campgrounds (ranging from one-star to the top four-star classification) serve this stretch of coast. Generally, they are in the pine forests within about 100 m/300 feet of the beach and many arrange mountain bike rental and guided tours to the islands of the Tuscan Arcipelago. See www.camping.it/italy/toscana/grosseto for the full list.

The best camping options are **Baia Azzura** ☆☆☆ (Via delle Rocchette, Loc. Le Rocchette, ☎ 0564-941092, fax 0564-941242, www.camping.it/italy/toscana/baiaazzura, $); **Santopomata** ☆☆☆ (Strada delle Rocchette, Loc. Santapomata, ☎ 0564-941037, fax 0564-941221, www.camping.it/toscana/santapomata, $); **Maremma sans Soucis** ☆☆☆ (Loc. Casa Mora, ☎ 0564-933765, fax 0564-935759, www.maremmasanssouci.it, $); **Stella del Mare** ☆☆☆☆ (Loc. Le Rocchette, ☎/fax 0564-947100, www.stelladelmarecamping.it, $) near Castiglione della Pescaia; **Baia Verde** ☆☆☆ (Loc. Punta Ala, ☎ 0564-922298, fax 0564-923044, www.camping.it/italy/toscana/baiaverde, $), with private beach and organized bicycle tours; or **Punta Ala** ☆☆☆☆ (Loc. Torre Civette, ☎ 0564-922294, fax 0564-920379, www.campingpuntala.it, $) on Punta Ala.

The nearest youth hostel, **Rifugio Sant'Anna**, is at Massa Marittima (Viale Gramsci 7, ☎ 0566-904611, $).

Parco Naturale Regionale della Maremma

Since 1975, the Parco Naturale Regionale della Maremma (Maremma Regional Park, also known as Parco dell'Uccellina) has protected over 20,000 acres of the wildest coastline in the country. Natural highlights include the expanse of Mediterranean scrub, pine forests, the Ombrone River wetlands, ruined castles and towers, and the quiet dunes of Marina di Albarese. The hills of the Uccellina, with their highest point at Poggio Lecci (417 m/1,368 feet), represent the largest and most important part of the park, entirely covered by a mantle of vegetation with areas of true Mediterranean forest.

■ Getting Here & Around

 By Train: The Grosseto-to-Rome line (☎ 848-888088, www.trenitalia.it) runs alongside the park with three stations: Santa Maria di Rispescia (to the north), Albarese (in the center) and Talamone (to the south).

 By Bus: Rama (☎ 0564-475111, www.griforama.it) runs hourly bus services between Florence, Siena and Grosseto, (#18), and occasional services from Grosseto to Talamone Porto (#48).

 By Car: The **SS1 Aurelia** runs the length of the reserve with well-marked turnoffs to the park center at Albarese. You can rent cars in Grosseto from **Avis** (Via Telamonio 40, ☎ 0564-494682, www.avisautonoleggio.it).

■ Information Sources

Tourist Information: The **Centro Visite del Parco Regionale della Maremma** (Maremma Regional Park Visitor Center) is just outside of Albarese (Via del Bersagliere 7, Alberese, ☎ 0564-407111, fax 0564-407292, www.parcomaremma.it) and Talamone (Via del Fante, ☎ 0564-407098, fax 0564-407278).

■ Sightseeing

 Talamone, in the far south of the park, is the only real sightseeing port of call in the Maremma. While local legend attributes its foundation to Telamone, son of Eacus, who arrived here with the Argonauts, its history can more tangibly be traced back to the Etruscans. Fragments of their 150 BC terracotta sculptures have been found on the hill at Talamonccio, where the cursing of Oedipus in the war of the "Seven Against Thebes" was found depicted on the temple portico (Frontone di Talamone, Piazza della Repubblica, ☎ 0564-860447, summer, 10 am-12:30 pm, 5-9 pm, winter, Thurs-Sun, 4-8 pm, €2, conc. €1).

THE MAREMMA HERDS

Although the symbol of Maremma is the wild boar, it is more famous for its herds of cattle, wild horses and the *butteri* (Maremma cowherds) who brand the cows and break in the white horses. You can get a rare insight into this local cowboy culture by visiting the wild animal branding festival at Albarese on March 1 every year.

■ Adventures

On Foot

There are eight hiking itineraries in the park, six of which depart from the Albarese Visitor Center (whether on foot or first by coach) and two of which can be picked up at Talamone, farther south. Your park entry ticket (€2.60) includes the roundtrip coach ride to Pratini; buses leave from the office every hour.

HIKING ETIQUETTE

- Do not stray from the designated hiking trails.
- Respect the environment by not damaging or collecting rocks or minerals. Do not damage the dunes by walking on them unnecessarily.
- Respect the plants and animals – don't feed the animals or collect samples of any kind.
- Do not camp outside of the designated areas.
- Do not drop garbage.
- It is forbidden to light fires due to the high fire risk.
- Bring sufficient supplies of water, as there are no fountains or springs along the Maremma itinerares.
- Bring bug repellent and a hat.

Four trails leave from Pratini: the A1 through A4. The **A1 San Rabano** takes you on a five-hour walk through a picturesque pine forest to the 11th-century Bendictine Abbazia di San Rabano (Abbey of San Rabano). The trail includes the peak of Poggio Lecci (417 m/1,368 feet) with its great views over the park. The **A2 Le Torri** (The Towers) is the most panoramic of the itineraries. The three-hour undulating route takes you past the 12th-century Torre di Castelmarino and the 16th-century Torre di Collelungo. The four-hour **A3 Le Grotte** (The Caves) leads through dense scrubland past a series of Paleolithic caves along six miles of easy tracks. The **A4 Cala di Forno** (Bay of Forno), which goes to the rocky cove, is the longest, covering seven miles in about six hours.

Two trails leave from the Chiesa di Albarese: the A5 and A6, although they are essentially just one walk. The three-hour **A5/A6 Forestale e Faunistico** (Forest and Fauna) is an easy trail through Mediterranean scrub, which allows you to walk among fallow deer and centuries-old oak trees.

The three-hour **A7 Bocca d'Ombrone** (Ombrone River Mouth) can be picked up from the car park of Marina di Alberese. It is an easy route perfect for **bird-watching**. Finally, two trails depart from just outside **Talamone** at Podere Caprarecce: the short **T1** (two miles) and the slightly longer **T2** (three miles); both are currently being extended.

Trail routes are open from 9 am between Oct and June; during the summer, A3 and A4 are closed (due to fire regulations), A5-A7 and T1-T2 are open from 8 am, but closed from 1-4 pm, and A1 and A2 are open only for guided visits (reservations recommended). A1 guided visits leave at 8 am; A2 guided visits run between 9 am and 4 pm. (A1-A4, €8, conc. €5.50, A5-A6/T1-2, €6, conc. €4 and A7, €3.)

A three-hour **night route** (€15, reservations required) is offered throughout the year at sunset. Guides take you along a trail to point out wild boar, fallow and roe deer, fox and badgers. There's also a **bird-watching** guided itinerary (€15, conc. €13, reservations required), which takes walkers to the Palude della Trappola (Trappola Marsh) between Oct and April.

Tickets for all the guided walks can be purchased in the Visitor Office in Alberese (open from 7:30 am in summer and 8:30 am in winter) or from the office in Capracecce near Talamone (daily in summer, weekends only in winter).

The Maremma Beaches

By far the wildest beachfront along the coast, the **Marina di Alberese** is a must stop when you're in the park. Split into intimate coves by the driftwood pine, you can access it from Alberese by car (parking and entry permits are limited and must be pre-purchased in the Visitor Center, parcomar@gol.grosseto.it, €1), on a bike, or by hiking trail, which drops you lower down at Torre di Collelungo. Trail A4 takes you onto the smaller but equally splendid **Cala di Forno**. The beach at Talamone is free, but more of a pebbly affair.

On Wheels

 Il Rialto (Alberese, ☎ 0564-407102, il_rialto@katamail.com), close to the Alberese Visitor Office, is the official bicycle rental organization in the park. Rates (one-hour, €3; one day, €8; one week, €31) include your park entry ticket, guide and insurance. If you bring your own bicycle, you can pick up the route to the Marina di Alberese from just outside the Visitor Office.

On Horseback

 Il Rialto (as above) is also the official horseback riding organization for the park. Rates (two-hour tour, €29; full day, €62) include park entry ticket, guide and insurance. You can also arrange horseback riding into the park through the **Centro Ippico Grossetano** (Via delle Collacchie, Grosseto, ☎ 0564-400233) and **Centro Ippico Le Cannelle** (Loc. Cannelle, Talamone, ☎ 0564-887020).

MEDITERRANEAN SCRUB

Known in Italian as macchia (from the Corsican maquis), this dense scrub is a distinctive characteristic of the Tuscan coast. Its composition can vary considerably, but in general it consists of low aromatic plants (often thyme, rosemary, savory, lavender, wild garlic and sage) surrounded by a taller wood of trees (holm oak, maple and even hawthorn). In its natural form it is now increasingly rare. Fire and land clearance over the centuries have either removed or reduced its cover, making the Maremma one of the few places where it can still be found intact.

On Water

All **canoe** rental in the park is through **Il Rialto**. Rates (three hours, €16; full day, €26), with a tour on the River Ombrone from La Barca, park entry ticket, guide and insurance all included.

■ Where to Stay

There are *agriturismi* in and around Alberese. Try **Azienda Regionale Alberese** (Loc. Spergolaia, ☎ 0564-407077, $$$), **Montegrappa** (Via del Mulinaccio, Loc. Alberese, ☎ 0564-407237, $$$) or **Podere Oslavia** (Strada Provinciale, Loc. Alberese, ☎ 0564-407116, $$). The only campground is at Talamone (Loc. Talamone, ☎ 0564-887026, $).

Costa d'Argento

The Costa d'Argento (Silver Coast) lies south of Maremma Regional Park and its Monte Argentario is one of the most popular summer camping and walking destinations. A former island, this towering mountain is joined to the mainland by two naturally formed banks of sand (called *tomboli*) and a larger spit of land on which the ancient settlement of Orbetello stands.

■ Getting Here & Around

By Train: The Grosseto-to-Rome train (☎ 848-888088, www.trenitalia.it) runs along the Costa d'Argento, stopping at Orbetello Scalo and Capalbio.

By Bus: Rama (☎ 0564-475111, www.griforama.it) runs hourly bus services from Grosseto (#48 Grosseto-Orbetello-Porto Ercole-Porto Santo Stefano) and from Orbetello (#49 Orbetello-Ansedonia-Capalbio).

By Car: Continue down along the **SS1 Aurelia**.

You can **rent bikes** in Orbetello from **Mandragora** (Via Veneto, ☎ 0564-867790) and **Pantini** (Via Dante, ☎ 0564-860233).

■ Information Sources

Tourist Offices: There are two main tourist offices on the Monte Argentario, the main one at **Orbetello** (Piazza della Repubblica, ☎ 0564-861226, fax 0564-860648, www.proloco-orbetello.it) and a smaller branch at **Porto Santo Stefano** (Corso Umberto 55, ☎ 0564-814208, fax 0564-814052) around the bay from Orbetello. Along the coast itself, there's an office at **Magliano in Toscana** (Via Garibaldi, ☎ 0564-593440) and **Capalbio** (Via Collacchioni, ☎ 0564-896611, fax 0564-896644).

The tourist office of the Isola del Giglio is at **Gigio Porto** (Piazza del Pontile, ☎/fax 0564-809400, www.isoladelgiglioufficioturistico.com).

■ Sightseeing & Adventures

Orbetello

The ancient settlement of Orbetello rests between two salty (and strong-smelling) lagoons, one of which is a WWF Nature Reserve. The town looks like an island in its own right, joined to the mainland by one long and very narrow road.

The Spanish coat of arms that decorates the town's entrance gates remind us that this was the capital of a Spanish State, which, from 1557, extended inland to Capalbio and Talamone until absorbed back by the Grand Duchy of Tuscany in 1808. This Spanish rule (thanks to their alliance with the Medici) heralded the town's period of greatest splendor, which saw the construction of such buildings as the **Polveriera Guzman** (Former Spanish Arsenal, Viale Mura di Levante, ☎ 0564-861242), the **watchtowers** of the Monte Argentario, the **forts** of Porte Ercole, and the **Molino Spagnolo** (Spanish Windmill).

Monte Argentario

This promontory was an island until the two *tomboli* (the Feniglia and Giannella banks of sand) enclosed the lagoons (Laguna di Ponente and Laguna di Levante) and joined the mountain to the mainland some two million years ago. It is essentially a large mountain of rock that extends over 13,000 acres and reaches its peak with Monte Telegrafo at an elevation of 635 m (2,084 feet). A panoramic road circles the island, passing numerous lookout towers and taking in the main towns of Porto Ercole and Porto Santo Stefano.

An asphalt road (direction Porto Santo Stefano) leads up Monte Argentario past the **Convento dei Frati Passionisti**, with its great views over Orbetello and the two lagoons, and up to the mountain peak. Paths branching off the island road lead either up the peak or down to bays such as Cala Grande, Cala del Gesso (where there is **scuba diving** at the underwater grottoes of the island of Argentarola), Cala Piccola (another interesting diving spot around a coral reef), and the long beach of the Spiaggia Lunga. You can arrange diving trips through **Cala Galera Diving Center** (Piazza della Valle 12, Porto Santo Stefano, ☎ 0564-810145, diving@ouverture.it, and Loc. Cala Galera, Porto Ercole, ☎ 0564-832772), **Diving Club Costa d'Argento** (Porto Santo Stefano, ☎ 0564-812939), **Centro Immersioni Pelagos** (Porto Ercole, ☎ 0564-834200), **Diving Center** (L. Mare A. Doria 73, Porto Ercole, ☎ 0564-832749) and **Sub Company** (L. Mare A. Doria 78, Porto Ercole, ☎/fax 0564-832651).

Acquavision (Porto Ercole, ☎ 333-4403634, info@navimaremma.it, €10, conc. €7) offers an alternative view four times a day in its glass-bottom boat.

Porto Ercole (Port of Hercules), south of Orbetello, is the oldest of the island's towns and a former stronghold of the Spanish State. The Spanish built fortresses on the spurs of the two surrounding hills: the 16th-century **Forte Stella** (guided tours by arrangement, ☎ 0564-811925), named after its star-shaped plan, and the **Rocca Spagnola** (☎ 0564-830109, 10 am-1 pm, 4-8 pm). Both ar open to visitors.

Porto Santo Stefano, north around the coast from Orbetello, is the main town. It spreads up the hillside to Fortezza Spagnola (Piazza del Governatore, ☎ 0564-810681), but most visit the area for the **walking** and **bird-watching** opportunities along the two *tomboli*.

The 1,800-acre **WWF Oasi della Laguna di Orbetello** (☎ 0564-820297, wwwf.giannella@tiscalinet.it, Sept-Apr, visits Thurs, Sat-Sun, 10 am-2:30 pm) runs along Tombolo della Giannella, offering three nature walks on different themes – a flora and fauna walk, a botanical walk and a trip through the marsh at Casale Gianella. They also have bird-watching and photographic hides with views of white herons, black cormorants and, in winter, hundreds of flamingos.

The silver strip of sand along the **Riserva Naturale del Tombolo della Feniglia** (Feniglia Nature Reserve, ☎ 0564-834086, always open) stretches three miles between Porto Ercole and the hills of Ansedonia. You can access the strip only through the adjacent pinewood forest, where a trail suitable for **walking** and **cycling** leads to the quietest stretch. To arrange for **horseback riding** along it, contact **Maneggio da Luca** (Loc. Le Piane, ☎ 0564-862596) or **Centro Ippico Argentario** (Loc. San Rocco, ☎ 0564-881112). Establishments along the beach offer **sailing** and **windsurfing**.

THE PALIO MARINARO

The Costa d'Argento's most famous event takes place at Porto Santo Stefano every August 15. The regatta between the four districts of the town has been held here for over half a century as a re-creation of a Saracen raid in which the local fishing community managed to row their way out of trouble. The race starts at 4 pm after a colorful historical parade from the Fortessa Spagnola into town.

Giglio & Giannutri Islands

From the port at Porto Santo Stefano, frequent ferries link to the Isola del Giglio, a quiet island. It, and the nearby Isola di Giannutri, are both part of the Tuscan Archipelago.

GETTING TO GIGLIO

Two ferry companies offer daily services between Porto Santo Stefano and the island of Giglio: **Maregiglio** (Porto Santo Stefano, ☎ 0564-812920, fax 0564-801160, www.maregiglio.it and Giglio Porto, ☎ 0564-809309, fax 0564-809469) and **Torremar** (Porto Santo Stefano, ☎ 0564-810803, fax 0564-818455, http://web.tiscalinet.it/metranotoremar and Giglio Porto, ☎ 0564-809349).

Appreciated for its beaches and wild nature, **Isola del Giglio** is the second-largest of the Tuscan Archipelago after Elba (although it is actually a tenth of the size of Elba). About four million years ago it was still attached to Monte Argentario. In addition to its wild Mediterranean scrub, it is also rich in history. The **Rocca Pisana** and 15th-century **Chiesa di San Pietro Apostolo** at Giglio Castello; the **Torre del Campese** in the Baia di Campese (Campese Bay); and the two defensive towers (**Torre Medicea** and **Torre del Lazzaretto**) at Giglio Porto all warrant a visit.

Around from the sheltered semicircular bay of **Giglio Porto** (the island's only port), the remains of the fortified medieval village of **Giglio Castello** makes an attractive sight perched 400 m (1,312 feet) above the rocky bay. The lively town of narrow arched streets and winding staircases, built of the famous Giglio granite, grew between the imposing town walls and fortress towers when they were busy defending the island from Saracen raids. The nearest **beaches** are at the rocky **Cala del Corvo**, the picturesque **Cala della Cannelle**, the pretty **Calla dell'Arenella** and the most famous golden bay, the **Cala del Campese**. The latter has partly submerged remains of a Roman villa, which attracts most of the island's tourists. From Giglio Castello, a two-hour **hiking trail** takes you south across the island to the Punta del Capel Rosso. Look out for the Sardinian warbler (with a characteristic red ring around its eyes), wren, Italian hen sparrow, greenfinch and goldfinch while you're making the trip.

You can visit the remains of another Roman villa (Cala Maestra, ☎ 0564-898890) on the private island of **Isola di Giannutri** (summer only, day visits only), the most southerly of the "seven sisters." There's an easy **trekking trail** that crosses the island in about an hour, offering access to its beaches and rocky coves. It's also a popular **bird-watching** destination for spotting the peregrine hawks that nest on its rugged dolomite and limestone cliffs.

To arrange **diving** on the island, contact **Giglio Diving Club** (Via della Torre, ☎ 0564-804065), **Calus Valentin** (Via di Mezzo 14, ☎ 0564-804121, fax 0564-804123), **Gym Diving** (Via della Torre, ☎ 0564-804214) in Giglio Campese, **Dimensione Mare** (Via Tahon de Revel 26, ☎ 0564-809096), **International Diving** (Via del Saraceno, ☎ 0564-809460) or **Bus Sport** (☎ 0564-809506) in Giglio Porto. The best dives take you to two wrecks, a Roman ship from the third century BC off Giglio Porto and a more recent wreck off Giglio Campanese.

Restrictions apply for diving off Giannutri (boats can moor only in the Golfo Spalmatoio or the Cala Maestra). To reserve a boat, contact **Anna Miliani** (Via dell'Asilo 14, Giglio Porto, ☎ 0564-809149) or **Biba Boats** (Loc. Santa Liberta, Monte Argentario, ☎ 0564-820116). For boat taxis, book with **Solepizzamore** (☎ 0330-272376).

Ansedonia

Ansedonia is dominated in every sense by the ruins of the 273 BC Roman city of **Cosa** on the top of the hill. It is built on an earlier Etruscan settlement and a network of Etruscan canals built on right angles off a natural rock slit – known as the "Spacco della Regina" (Queen's Gorge) – runs the length of the beach to the east. You can find out more about both the local Etruscan and Roman heritages in the **Museo Nazionale di Cosa** (Cosa National Museum, Via delle Mimose, ☎/fax 0564-881421, 9 am-7 pm, €2, conc. €1). The nearby beach, the Spiaggia Nera, is an amazing expanse of almost black sand between Tagliata Etrusca and Capalbio Scalo accessed via trekking **trails**.

Capalbio

Inland from Ansedonia, the old hilltop town of Capalbio remains a favorite with vacationing Italians, partly because of the hunting reserve just outside of town. It is a small town dominated by the ancient **Rocca Aldobrandesca** (Aldobrandesca Fortress) and well placed for exploring the nearby coast, the WWF reserve of Lago di Burano and the **Giardino dei Tarocchi** (Tarot Garden, Loc. Garavicchio, ☎ 0564-895122, fax 0564-895700, www.nikidesaintphalle.com, 12 May-19 Oct, daily, 2:30-7:30 pm, €10.50, conc. €6), which was created by French artist Niki de Saint-Phalle in 1982 to house her tarot-influenced sculptures.

Capalbio

The four-km (2½-mile) **Lago di Burano** (☎ 0564-898829, Sept-Apr, Sun, 10 am-2:30 pm) was transformed into a zoological reserve by the WWF to protect the nesting and migratory birds that make their home in the thick vegetation. A variety of nature walks offer the chance to check out birds from the hides.

Rocca Aldobrandesca

■ Where to Stay

This is another great coast for camping with plenty of choice both along the *tomboli* and on the promontory of Monte Argentario itself.

Orbetello has the **Argentario** ☆☆☆ (Loc. Albinia, ☎ 0564-870302, fax 0564-871380, www.camping.it/toscana/argentario); Giannella has **Il Veliero** ☆☆☆ (Loc. Albinia, ☎ 0564-820201 fax 0564-821198, www.camping.it/toscana/ilveliero, $) and **Bocche d'Albegna** ☆ (Loc. Albinia, ☎/fax 0564-870097, www.camping.it/toscana/bocchedalbegna, $). If it's beach you want, opt for **Feniglia** ☆ (Loc. Feniglia, Porto Ercole, ☎ 0564-831090, www.emmeti.it/campingfeniglia, $). But you'll get better facilities (including pool) and good access to the Spiaggia Nera from **Costa d'Argento** ☆☆☆ (Loc. Montalzato, ☎ 0564-893007, $) near Capalbio.

Isola del Giglio also has its own campground, **Baia del Sole** ☆ (SS Provinciale per Campese, ☎ 0564-804036, fax 0564-804101, www.camping.it/toscana/baiadelsole, $).

■ Where to Eat

La Bersagliera (Via Roma 18, ☎ 0564-867319, closed Weds, $) is a pleasant pizzeria trattoria with outdoor terrace serving a good range of locally caught seafood.

The Southern Hilltowns

Throughout the hills of inland Maremma there is a volcanic landscape of yellow ochre tufa cut through by deep river valleys, densely covered with Mediterranean woodland. It is dotted with ancient Etruscan strongholds and crumbling medieval towns and villages. This is the old frontier territory where the last Etruscan strongholds of Vulci and Volsini met with the advancing Roman legions and fortresses and lookout towers on huge outcrops of tufa rock still oversee the land.

■ Getting Here & Around

By Bus: One of the reasons why these southern hilltowns are untouched is because they are difficult to reach. It's a pretty easy approach by car, but there are no train lines and **Rama** (☎ 0564-475111, www.griforama.it) runs only one or two bus services a day in the territory from Grosseto (#3 Grosseto-Manciano-Montermerano-Saturnia-Pitigliano, #41A Grosseto-Manciano-Pitigliano, #43 and #44 Grosseto-Pitigliano-Sovana-Sorano) and Pitigliano (#39, #40D, #45 Pitigliano-Sorano-San Quirico).

By Car: To reach Pitigliano, take the **SS74** off SS1 Aurelia. Key towns Sovana and Sorano are signposted from Pitigliano.

■ Information Sources

Tourist Information: There are helpful seasonal tourist offices in **Pitigliano** (Piazza Garibaldi 51, ☎ 0564-617111, collidimaremma@tin.it) and **Sovana** (Palazzetto dell'Archivio,

☎ 0564-614074). Both are keen to promote the area and will take the time to offer advice on both sights and accommodations.

■ Sightseeing

Manciano

 Appearing suddenly on a hilltop, the small historical center of Manciano marks the beginning of inland Maremma and the Etruscan hilltop towns. Ancient lanes spiral up through town to the walls of the large crowning Aldobrandeschi fortress, which was reconstructed by the Sienese in the 15th century but still preserves the original *Cassero* (keep). It houses the **Museo di Preistoria e Protostoria della Valle del Fiume Fiora** (River Fiora Archeological Museum, ☎ 0564-625327, Wed-Sat, 9 am-1 pm, 2:30-6:30 pm, Sun, 10 am-1 pm, €2), which documents the history of the area as far back as the five necropoli of the Aeneolithic period (3000-2000 BC).

Pitigliano

The SS74 continues through Manciano to Pitigliano, an important Bronze Age center, which led an equally industrious life under Etruscan rule. Nothing can prepare you for your first glimpse of the town from the road. It sits atop a honey-colored tufa spur flanked by tracts of the old 17th-century aqueduct and its medieval center is a pristine mix of terracotta roofs and tufa houses, which literally emerge from the rock in all shapes and sizes. You can find traces of the ancient village in the **Poggio Buco**, with its seventh-sixth century BC necropoli. In the Middle Ages, the Aldobrandeschi sited one of their principal castles here. Under their rule it built up such strategic importance that it functioned as an autonomous state from the 16th century until the Medici took over a century later.

Start your tour on **Piazza della Repubblica**, the main town square. It has seen much change since it was first constructed in the Middle Ages (not least because the original square actually lies six meters or 20 feet below the present construction), but still defines the city street plan. There are two parallel main streets – Corso Roma and Via Zuccarelli – and a third road, Via Vignoli (or Via della Fratta) found along the northern side and linked by narrow winding lanes.

The town's major features are the *cantine* (basements), which almost constitute an entire underground city, spread over three levels beneath the town and interconnected by tunnels, ancient wells and the remains of Etruscan tombs. You can find out more in the **Museo Civico Archeologico Civiltà Etrusca**, which also displays artifacts discovered in the excavation of Poggio Buco (Civic and Archaeological Museum of Etruscan Heritage, Piazza Fortezza Orsini, ☎ 0564-614067, Tues-Sun, 10 am-1 pm, 3-6 pm, €3, conc. €2).

GOING UNDERGROUND

The past comes to life with a trip into the tufa under Pitigliano. To reserve, call ☎ *338-3947455.*

The town is famous for its historic Jewish community, which flourished here until World War II after the Jews fled the persecutions of the Papal State in the 16th century. You can visit the Ghetto along Via Zuccarelli, from which a large iron gateway leads onto Vicolo Manin and the 18th-century doorway of the **Sinagoga,**

Ghetto e Museo Ebraico (Synagogue and Jewish Museum, Vicolo Marghera e Vicolo Manin, ☎ 0564-616006). The tourist office offers a tour of the Jewish sites (summer, 10 am-12:30 pm, 4-7 pm, winter, 10 am-12:30 pm, 3-5:30 pm, €2,50, conc. €1,50).

The **Museo Diocesano Palazzo Orsini** (Piazza Fortezza Orsini, ☎ 0564-616074, Tues-Sun, 10 am-1 pm, 3-6 pm, €3, conc. €2), in the old Orsini palace, displays a collection of sacred objects, including paintings by Francesco Zuccarelli, Pietro Aldi and Paride Pascucci.

The Orsini played an important role in the town's architecture, not only revamping the old Aldobrandeschi palace and nearby castle (the renovations were the work of Sangallo il Giovanne), but also commissioning work on the town **cathedral** in 1507 and the **Chiesa di Santa Maria** (from the mid-13th century), and the oldest church in town. It is situated at the meeting point of the Val del Corso and Via Zuccarelli, where Capisotto, the oldest quarter of town (with most of the *cantine*), begins. Steps lead from the small square to the La Selciata pathway, which offers a pleasant walk around the town walls past the openings of wine cellars, caves and tombs.

WALKING THE VIE CAVE

Vie Cave, mysterious narrow passageways excavated deep into the tufa rock over the years by water and foot erosion, are throughout the region, but many of the best are in Pitigliano. A fine time to see them is in the night of the Spring Equinox (March 19), when a torch-lit procession makes its way down Via Cava di San Giuseppe and the Via Cava di Fratanuti. The latter is a must-see whether you arrive in time for the procession or not; its extraordinarily high walls (some reaching 60 feet) are covered with inscriptions, carvings and graffiti of Etruscan and medieval origin. Both these and the Vie di Gradone and Poggio Cane are well signposted and easy to reach.

Sorano

The town of Sorano was declared dead in 1923 after serious landslides put its existence under threat, but the Soranese refused to move and the historical center has started to come alive again. Founded high up on a rock at the confluence of three rivers, Sorano originally developed during Etruscan and Roman times when it was built to defend the Fiora Valley from invasion. Its medieval look has survived from the rules of the Aldobrandeschi and Orsini families, but traces of the original Etruscan town, especially the necropoli excavated in the soft tufa rock, can be visited in the cliffs around town.

The center of town is marked by the natural rock formation of **Masso Leopoldino** (Via del Poggetto, ☎ 0564-633023, daily, 10 am-7 pm), which was reinforced by walls at the end of the 17th century. To the north, narrow streets descend to the Renaissance gateway "La Porte dei Merli" and into the Lente Valley. As you wander the steep streets, sharp corners give impressive views of houses hanging precipitously on the edge of the cliff. Keep your eyes out for the rusticated tufa stone and travertine doorframes along Via Selvi; the intricate labyrinth of cellars, caves and tower houses packed together on Piazza Vanni; and the *Cantinone*, one of the most interesting cellars in the old town, which consists of a series of large rooms called *bottaio* (tunnels) that extend some 30-40 feet into the tufa in the entire northeastern end of town.

You can enter the town's underground passages at the **Fortezza Orsini e Museo** (Orsini Fortress and Museum, Via San Marco, ☎ 0564-633767, 10 am-1 pm, 2-6 pm). They descend to the banks of the river and even reach as far as the Castello di Pitigliano. From the main passageway you can access the *mine*, narrow cubicles placed about six feet apart.

Leaving town, follow the road toward Sovana to visit the **Necropolis di San Rocco** and **San Rocco vie cave**, two Etruscan pathways that descend to the bottom of the valley and onto the nearby hill of **Le Rocchette**, where there are more interesting Etruscan remains. The necropolis lies nearby. It is an interesting mix of rock dwellings and *colombari* tombs similar to those at Vitozza.

THE COLOMBARI

The colombari tombs, excavated in the tufa rock sometime around the first century BC for use as dwellings and shelters, are so called for their resemblance to dovecotes. Usually large, their name derives from the square holes dug into the walls from floor to ceiling in a beehive pattern. They were probably used by the Etruscans to deposit the ashes of their dead. Many believe these caves were the dwellings of primitive peoples later transformed by the Etruscans into necropoli, and then again by the Romans who transformed them into pens for their homing pigeons. Located mostly on the outskirts of the towns of Sovana and Sorano, many can be visited along the road between the two towns.

The caves of **Vitozza** are just out of Sorano in San Quirico di Sorano (☎ 0564-614074). Lying along a rocky ridge, this is a collection of more than 200 caves, which represents one of the largest rock dwelling collections in Italy. The names of their last inhabitants – some of whom lived here up until the 17th century – are remembered on informative panels along a quiet wooded **trail**.

You can arrange **horseback riding** at Sorano through **Maneggio Belvedere** (Loc. Belvedere, ☎/fax 0564-615465). They take guided treks up to the nearby necropolis of Sovana, the Via Cava di Poggio Prisca, across the Flora River and onto Pitigliano, and along to the cliff dwellings of Vitozza and into the countryside around San Quirico.

Sovana

The ancient capital of "Maremma al di là del fiume" (Maremma on the other side of the river), Sovana was once a haughty rival to Siena. Much has changed from its heyday as an important Etruscan settlement with close ties to Vulci, and now you'll just find a quiet little village with some stunning ancient remains and beautiful terracotta architecture. Like the previous two towns, Sorana is built on a simple street plan with three principal longitudinal roads named Via di Sopra (High Road), Via di Sotto (Low Road) and Via di Mezzo (Middle Road). It can easily be explored in a few hours.

The oldest church in town (perhaps formerly a cathedral), **Chiesa di San Mamiliano** sits on the remains of an older Etruscan-Roman building. Only

Chiesa di San Mamiliano

the external walls of the church remain, and the frescoes that were removed from them are now preserved in the **cathedral**, itself an 11th-century construction built almost entirely out of tufa, except for the black-and-white striped pilasters. The most interesting church in town, however, is the 12th-century **Chiesa (and Cattedrale) di Santa Maria**, which has a travertine *ciborium* (altarpiece) supported by four ornate columns, considered one of the most important works of sculpture in Tuscany from the late Lombard period. It also has some fine 16th-century frescoes in the *Madonna and Child between Saints Sebastian and Mamiliano* and *Trinity* just beside the door.

One of the major civic constructions is the **Palazzo Pretorio**, which is covered with coats of arms of the many Sienese and Medicean commissars who governed the town between the 15th and 17th centuries. It houses the **Museo Archeologico**, which has artifacts, reconstructions and histories of the Etruscan tombs discovered in the Fiora Valley. Other important attractions include the 12th-century **Palazzo dell'Archivio**, whose tower clock still runs, with an ancient and elaborate system of balance weights using two large stones from the Fiora Valley. There is also the **House of Pope Gregory VII** (although whether or not he did actually live here is currently a subject of much debate).

The Etruscan Tombs

Heading out of town north through the main gate, there are over 100 Etruscan tombs to explore, many in the tufa cliffs along the Calesine River and its tributaries, the Folonia and the Picciolana.

Take the provincial road north and you'll soon see a signposted path leading left down to the stream and the **Tomba del Sileno** (Tomb of the Satyr). This chamber tomb of six half-columns was discovered completely intact in 1963. Next comes Costone di Sopraripa, where the **Tomba della Sirena** (Tomb of the Siren), with its famed Etruscan representation of the afterlife, is found. Continue along this path and you'll pass a series of façade tombs from the same period (third century BC) through a shady wood of oak, cherry and chestnut trees to the opening of two parallel vie cave. The first is obstructed by fallen rock, but you can explore the second – **Via Cava di San Sebastiano**.

Back on the main road in the direction of Poggio Grezzano, a stream crossing marks the trail to two *colombari* and the third-century BC **Tomba Pisa** (Pisa Tomb), the largest chamber tomb in the region. At the far end of the ridge, a via cava leads back to Sovana.

Farther along the main road, a series of paths can be picked up to the grandiose **Tomba Ildebranda** (Hildebrand Tomb), which was named after the Ildebrando of Sovana, who later became Pope Gregory VII. It's the most famous tomb of the necropolis and the most important Etruscan tomb in all Etruria thanks to its preserved condition and unique construction. The Via Cava of Poggio Prisca leads off to the left around the top of the monument, while another nearby trail takes you through to the **Tomba del Tifone** (Tomb of the Typhon), an aedicula tomb (a shrine or niche framed by two columns, piers, or pilasters carrying an entablature and pediment) that is thought to have been built in the second century BC. The last of the important tombs is back on the main road at **Tomba Pola**, a third-century BC example with a deep and long funerary corridor. For further information on any of the tombs, contact the **Tufa Archeological Park** (☎ 0564-614074).

Maremma & Grosseto

Saturnia

This is a popular hot-spring destination, with curative waters running free in a natural pool (the Cascate del Gorello) along the road south of town. Take the dirt track that continues straight ahead instead of following the road around as it veers left. If you prefer to pay for your pool, the large modern-looking villa you see to your left as you head south from town is actually the **Terme di Saturnia** (☎ 0577-600800, fax 0577-601266, www.termedisaturnia.it).

The town itself warrants a visit. The Sienese may have partially destroyed it in the 1300s, but the northern edge has the remains of a Villanovan **necropolis** (the precursors of the Etruscans); the ancient main square has a number of Roman **funerary stones**; and adjoining the **citadel** is a great **medieval arch**, which was built over an ancient and rare example of an Etruscan polygon wall (travertine stones fitted together without the need for cement). Through the arch passes a tract of the ancient Via Clodia, one of the great Imperial Roman roads that linked Saturnia with Rome.

■ Where to Eat

Pitigliano has a couple of plain local restaurants serving tasty food. Try **Osteria La Tavernaccia** (Via Roma 92, closed Wed, $) for a light lunch, or **Trattoria Il Tufo Allegro** (Vicolo della Costituzione, closed Tues and Wed lunch, $$) for a pleasant evening meal of local Maremma cuisine (wild boar, *aquacotta* and freshly-made pastas).

In Sorano, choose between **Fidalma** (Piazza Busatti 5, ☎/fax 0564-633056, closed Wed, $), with its traditional local dishes (*aquacotta,* boar stew, veal Morellino), the roasted meats and pizzas of **Il Buongustaio** (Via della Madonnina, ☎ 0564-633429, closed Mon, $), and the *enoteca*-restaurant **La Cantina del Viandante** (Via della Madonnina, ☎ 338-3500123, closed Mon, $$), which offers an extensive range of local wines.

There's plenty more typical Maremma cuisine to be sampled in Sovana. **La Tavernetta** (Via del Pretorio 12, ☎ 0564-616227, closed Thurs, $), has an outdoor terrace in summer. Or try **La Taverna Etrusca** (Piazza del Pretorio, ☎ 0564-616183, fax 0564-614193, closed Wed, $$), or **Scilla** (Via del Duomo, ☎ 0564-616531, fax 0564-614329, closed Tues, $$), which offers a hearty vegetarian menu.

■ Where to Stay

Pitigliano's popular hotel is the **Valle Orientina** ☆☆☆ (Via Valle Orientina, ☎ 0564-616661, fax 0564-616728, $$$), but you can get slightly cheaper choices with the town *affitacamere* – such as **La Magica Torre** (Piazza Petruccioli 73, ☎ 0564-616260, $$) or **Residenza d'Epoca Il Tufo Rosa** (Piazza Petruccioli 73, ☎ 0564-617019, $$).

There are also *agriturismi* in the region, including **Il Melograno** ☆☆☆☆ (Loc. La Formica, ☎ 0564-615536, $$$), with horseback riding, and **Cantinaccia di Sopra** ☆☆☆☆ (Loc. Cantinaccia di Sopra, ☎ 0564-616451, $$$), with bicycle excursions.

There is one campground near Pitigliano (Loc. Pantano, ☎ 0564-615695, six spaces, $).

Sovana hotel accommodation is slightly cheaper than Pitigliano. Try **La Taverna Etrusca** ☆☆☆ (Piazza del Pretorio, ☎ 0564-616183, fax 0564-614193, $$) or **Scilla** ☆☆☆ (Via Rodolfo Siviero 1/3, ☎ 0564-616531, fax 0564-614193, www.scilla-sovana.it, $$$). There are also plenty of *affitacamere*: **Pesna** (Via del Pretorio 9, ☎ 0564-614120, affitacamerepesna@yahoo.it, $$), **Roberto Santarelli** (Via del Pretorio 8/12, ☎ 0564-616186, $$) and **Mariella Scopetoni** (Via del Pretorio 8b, ☎ 0564-614073, $$).

Sorano probably has the nicest hotel choice with the **Hotel della Fortezza** ☆☆☆ (Piazza Cairoli, ☎ 0564-632010, fax 0564-633209, www.fortezzahotel.it, $$$), an old stone house that makes up part of the Orsini fortress and offers great views over the street on the level below and into the surrounding countryside. For *affitacamere,* contact **Antico Casale Il Piccione** (Loc. La Fratta, ☎ 0564-633398, fax 0564-632001, www.sorano.to, $) just out of town in the direction of San Quirico, or **Emilio Baldoni** (Via San Marco, ☎ 0564-633467, $$). Sorano also has one of the nicest *agriturismi* in **Casale La Fiorita** ☆☆☆ (Loc. La Fiorita, ☎ 0564-633120, $$$), where they also sell jams, pickled vegetables and wine.

Maremma & Grosseto

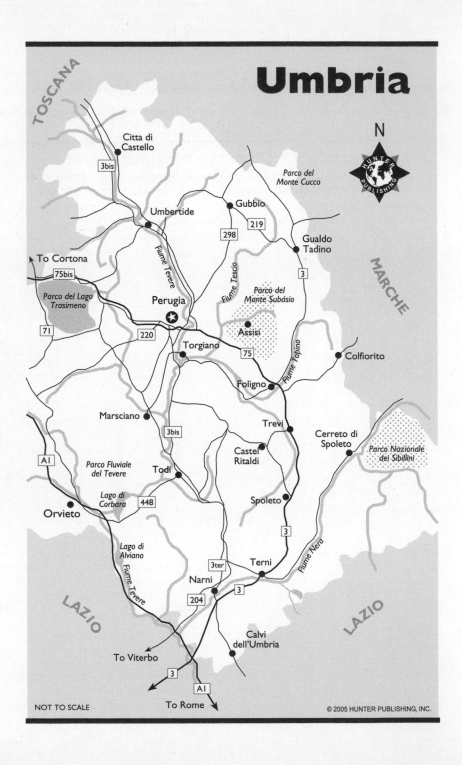

Umbria

NOT TO SCALE

© 2005 HUNTER PUBLISHING, INC.

Umbria

Perugia & Northern Umbria

The city of Perugia is the capital of the province named after it, as well as the capital city of the entire region of Umbria. To its west is Lago Trasimeno and to its north the Alta Valle del Tevere (Upper Tiber Valley), an untouched land of abbeys and monasteries and flower- and wildlife-filled hills.

REGION AT A GLANCE

- **Main city**: Perugia.
- **Afternoon trips from Perugia**: Lago Trasimeno (see page 373), Assisi (see page 435).
- **City breaks**: Assisi (see page 435), Umbertide (see page 377), Città di Castello (see page 375) and Gubbio (see page 440).
- **Rural retreats**: Lago Trasimeno (see page 373) and Monte Cucco (see page 445).
- **Spa towns**: Città di Castello (see page 375).

Information Sources

? **Tourist Office:** Servizio Turistico Territoriale IAT di Perugia (Perugia Territory Tourist Office, Via Mazzini 6, ☎ 0755-728937, fax 0755-739386, www.iat.perugia.it) is the region's main tourist center, covering the city of Perugia as well as the towns of Corciano, Deruta and Torgiano. The city

also has a smaller office in the Palazzo dei Priori (Piazza IV Novembre 3, ☎ 0755-736458).

Adventure Information: You can find out more about hiking in the area by popping into the local branch of the **CAI** (Via della Gabbia 9, Perugia, ☎/fax 0755-30334, http://utenti.tripod.it/caiperugia); they also have a caving branch on Via Santini (Gruppo Speleologico, ☎/fax 0755-847070, www.geocities.com/gspeleocaipg).

Perugia

Set in the hills 500 m (1,617 feet) above the Tiber Valley, Perugia has beautiful views over the lush Umbrian countryside that surrounds the capital city. From its perfectly preserved travertine walls, you can see Lago Trasimeno to the west and, on a clear day, Gubbio and Monte Cucco to the northeast and Monte Subasio and the Apennine chain to the east.

Surrounded by star-shaped medieval fortifications, Perugia originated in the Etruscan era, when it was thought to have been one of the 12 *lucomonies* (Etruscan city states) that controlled present-day Tuscany and Umbria. Roman rule brought further power as the city extended its dominion over the surrounding towns of Gubbio and Città di Castello, and past Lago Trasimeno into Tuscany's Val di Chiana. It was a rise that continued into the Middle Ages as Perugia expanded to rule Assisi, Nocera Umbra and Gualdo to the east, thanks to the protection of Pope Innocent III who much favored the town. This glorious era can be thanked for many of the rich monuments that remain.

The city layout – often compared to the palm of your hand – has naturally divided Perugia into five main quarters (Porta Sole, Porta San Pietro, Porta Eburnea, Porta Santa Susanna and Porta Sant'Angelo). Although these take time to explore, the majority of sightseeing destinations are within the city center, allowing for a quick and visually striking tour if you have only a day.

■ Getting Here & Around

 By Air: Most international flights arrive at Rome's **Leonardo da Vinci-Fiumicino airport** (☎ 066-5951). From there, frequent trains will deposit you in Perugia station and the ACAP-SULGA (☎ 075-5009641, www.sulga.it) bus service links the airport with Perugia's Piazzale Partigiani (Mon-Sat, 12:30 pm, 2:30 pm, 5 pm, Sun, 12:30 pm and 4:30 pm, round-trip ticket €23). However, the city does have a small airport at **Sant'Egidio** (☎ 075592141, fax 0756929562, www.airport.umbria.it) nine miles out of town. It is linked to the city by a bus (three daily services at 2:40, 5:50 and 9:50 pm, €2.50), which returns to the airport from the drop-off points on Piazza Italia (6:15 am, 12:50 pm and 4:50 pm, same fare) and the train station (15 minutes after the pick-ups on Piazza Italia, same fare), which itself lies two miles out of town.

 By Train: Trains (☎ 848-888088, www.trenitalia.it) to Perugia stop at the station on Piazza Vittorio Veneto, from where a frequent shuttle bus makes the 15-minute journey to Piazza Italia and Piazza Matteoti. If arriving from Florence or Rome, you'll need to change at Cortona Terontola station. If arriving from elsewhere in Umbria, the city is well served by the privately run Ferrovia Centrale Umbra (☎ 0755-75401, www.fcu.it) train line.

 By Bus: APM (☎ 075-5731707, www.apmperugia.it) runs 16 main bus lines (every 20-30 minutes) and 14 secondary lines (every 30-60 minutes) to the city quarters and outskirts of Perugia, including connections to Gubbio, Lago di Trasmineo, Todi and Orvieto.

By Car: This is far less complicated. Perugia sits on a well-connected road system served by the **SS3bis** (also known as the E45), which runs north to south along the Tiber Valley between Città di Castello and Terni, and the **SS75bis**, running through the city east from the A1 Rome-Florence highway across Lago Trasimeno in Tuscany (take the Val di Chiana exit from the north or the Orte exit from the south). When you arrive in Perugia, take the Perugia-Prepo exit to reach the historical center.

Parking lots are run by **SIPA** (☎ 075-5721938, www.sipaonline.it); for the best entries to the historical center try to get a space in P1 (Piazza Partigiani), P2 (Viale Pellini), P3 (Mercato) or P4 (Briglie di Braccio).

Rental cars are available at the airport from **Avis** (☎ 0756-929796, www.avisautonoleggio.it), **Europcar** (☎ 0755-731704, www.europcar.it), **Hertz** (☎ 0755-002439, www.hertz.it) and **Maggiore** (☎ 0756-929276 www.maggiore.it), or in Perugia itself from Avis (Train Station, ☎ 0755-00395), Europcar (Via R. d'Andreotto 7, ☎ 0755-002439), Hertz (Train Station, ☎ 0755-002439) and Maggiore (Piazza V. Veneto, ☎ 0755-007499).

Taxi ranks can be found outside the station (☎ 0755-010800), on Corso Vannucci (☎ 0755-721979) or Piazza Italia (☎ 0755-736092).

■ Sightseeing

The **Cooperativa Guide in Umbria** (Tourist Guide Cooperative of Umbria, Largo C. della Alpi 3b, ☎ 0755-732933, fax 0755-727235, www.infoumbria.com) organizes Saturday tours of Perugia for visitors who want to get to know the city better. Tours are free, but reservations are required.

The Historical Center

Start your tour in the center of the city at **Piazza Grande** (now also known as Piazza IV Novembre). This city square has been the center of civil and religious power in the city since it was established by the Etruscans. It became the city forum when Perugia passed into Roman rule and they constructed the five pivotal main streets (the *strade regali*), which fan out from here into each of the five city quarters.

In the center of the square stands the impressive **Fontana Maggiore**, the city symbol and one of the finest medieval fountains in Italy. It was completed in the late 13th century to welcome the water of the Monte Pacciano aqueduct and was considered so important that the Pisan father-and-son sculpture team Nicola and Giovanni Pisano were commissioned to design and decorate it. The result is a sturdy but delicate tier of white and pink stone basins, topped by a third bronze basin in which three bronze nymphs

hold the urn with water flowing. The four griffons (Perugia's heraldic symbol) that used to watch over the scene are now on display in the Galleria Nazionale dell'Umbria (see below).

A walk around the lower basin takes you past paneled scenes from the Old Testament, the story of the founding of Rome, an astrological calender that appears to relate to local farming practices, and a representation of the seven arts. Up on the top basin, the statues that top the 20 or so small columns represent a range of individuals from Perugia's history as well as important biblical figures, such as Moses, John the Baptist and the Archangel Michael.

The 14th-century **Palazzo dei Priori**, or Palace of the Priors, leads off from the left of the fountain along Corso Vannuci. It is a remarkable palace built of local white and red travertine and fronted on the fountain side by a large semi-circular staircase that was added in 1902 (the original had been destroyed at the end of the 15th century). Along the wall on Corso Vannuci there are 58 different panels representing allegories such as Generosity, Fertility and Humility, and they are topped by a lunette of statues representing the city's three patron saints.

On the third floor is the **Galleria Nazionale dell'Umbria** (☎ 0755-741247, fax 0755-741257, direzionegnu@libero.it, Tues-Sun, 8:30 am-7:30 pm), which houses an important collection of 13th- to 18th-century Umbrian art, especially the

Adoration of the Magi (detail), Perugino

detached frescoes, wooden crucifixes and tabernacles taken from churches and monasteries in the area. Prize possessions include a *Madonna with Child and Angels* by Duccio di Buoninsegna, a *Madonna with Child* by Gentile da Fabriano, an *Annunciation* by Beato Angelico and an *Adoration of the Magi* and a *Pietà* by Perugino. The collection also includes the sculptures taken from the Fontana Maggiore, including a *Scribe* and four other figures by Arnolfo di Cambio. The **Cappella dei Priori** has a late 15th-century fresco cycle by Benedetto Bonfigli, which represents scenes from the life of the city's three patron saints and views of Perugia as it was then.

The **Collegio della Mercanzia** (Chamber of Commerce, ☎ 0755-730366, Mar-Oct, daily, 9 am-12:30 pm, 2:30-5:30 pm, Nov-Feb, Tues-Sun, 9 am-2 pm) has had its seat in the palazzo since 1390, but the main draw is the **Collegio del Cambio** (Chamber of Exchange, ☎ 0755-728599, same hours), which moved here in the 15th century and whose Sala delle Udienze (Council Room) is covered with beautiful allegorical frescoes by Perugino.

Off to the right of the square, the **Cattedrale di San Lorenzo** (☎ 0755-723832) has stood on this spot since around the year 1000, although it acquired most of its current look and feel from the mid-15th century, including the Renaissance Loggia di Braccio, which stands on the remains of the earlier Roman walls. Your tour inside should combine a visit to Urbano da Cortona's sarcophagus of GA Baglioni, the Cappella di Sant'Agnolo (Chapel), which contains the "relic" of the Virgin's wedding ring and is decorated with frescoes by Pinturicchio, the Cappella di San Bernardino, which has a *Deposition* by Barocci, and the Oratorio di Sant'Onofrio (Oratory). An altarpiece by Luca Signorelli is on display in the **Museo Capitolare di San Lorenzo** (Cathedral Museum, ☎ 0755-723832, currently closed for restoration), which has the best of the cathedral's works, including triptychs by Agnolo Gaddi and Meo di Siena, a *Virgin* by Andrea Vanni, and further works by Luca Signorelli.

Between Palazzo dei Priori and Via Maestà delle Volte, the Palazzo Arcivescovile (Archbishop's residence) is the seat of the **Museo di Storia Naturale G. Cicioni** (Museum of Natural History, Piazza IV Novembre, ☎ 0755-736458), named after the Giulio Cicioni, who collected the minerals, fossils, exotic fauna, reptiles, birds and fish that it displays.

PICTURESQUE CITY STREETS

The pretty **Via Maestà delle Volte** runs downhill toward Piazza Cavallotti from the central Piazza Grande. Head down past the 16th-century Palazzo del Seminario and the Palazzo Arcivescovile and you'll see the remains of the vaulting that once supported the medieval Palazzo del Podestà, a red and white striped arch that remains from a 14th-century oratory, a fresco of the Madonna and a medieval fountain and courtyard.

Down the steps of Via C. Battisti, the steep **Via dell'Acquedotto** is another of the center's most atmospheric alleyways. It follows the end part of the two-mile-long aqueduct that brings water to the city from Monte Pacciano and remains a popular walk.

From Piazza Dante to the side of the cathedral, Via U. Rocchi (also called Via Vecchia) leads past 18th-century palazzi to the **Arco Etrusco**, one of the remaining gateways of the original city walls – you can follow a stretch of the wall by heading down Via C. Battisti. Corso Garibaldi will instead lead you past the mismatched façade of the Chiesa di Sant'Agostino; its original Gothic bottom level is topped by a Neo-Classical design added in the 18th century.

THE ETRUSCAN GATES

Of the original seven Etruscan gates, six still exist, although many were modified by the Romans or later in the Middle Ages. You've already seen the Arco Etrusco (also called the Arco di Augusto), but there's also the Arco della Mandorla on Via San Giacomo (to the west); Porta Marzia near Rocca Paolina (to the south); the Arco dei Gigli in Via Bontempi (to the northeast); the Arco di San Ercolano, on the stairs that bear the same name; and the Arco di San Luca in Via dei Priori.

Continue along Corso Garibaldi to arrive at the first of the medieval gates, the **Porta dello Sperandio**; alongside its travertine stone arch, a well-preserved stretch of city wall leads to the Paleo-Christian **Tempio di Sant'Angelo** (Via del Tempio) which, built in the late fifth century, uses 16 Roman Corinthian columns to hold up its four chapels in the shape of a Greek cross. Stairs from here lead down into the dungeons of **Porta Sant'Angelo**, the largest of the medieval gates through which can be accessed the **Convento di Monteripido**. Although it dates from 1262, it was much rebuilt to a more modern style in 1858. The Convento may not sound that exciting, but the spot does offer a marvelous view over the city of Perugia.

It's best to loop back to Piazza Grande by following Via Fuori le Mura around the exterior of the walls past the Chiesa di San Francesco, in through the gates to the Oratorio di San Francesco and on to the **Oratorio di San Bernardino** (Oratory, Piazza San Francesco al Prato, ☎ 0755-733957). It was built in 1450 to honor San Bernardino of Siena and they certainly went to a lot of trouble; the polychrome façade is covered with a vibrant mix of terracotta, limestone and white, black and red marble, and the central arch, decorated with bas-reliefs depicting the saint's miracles, is by far the most important pre-Renaissance monument in Perugia.

Pick up the charismatic Via dei Priori and you'll arrive back in the center via the **Chiesa Nuova**, called the "new church," although it was built in 1626, because it stands on the site of the Paleo-Christian Battistero di San Giovanni. When you get back to the fountain, head southwest, this time by following Corso Vannucci and ducking down to the **Rocca Paolina** (☎ 0755-728440) through Piazza Italia. This once-imposing fortress was built in 1540 by Antonio da Sangallo Il Giovanne to celebrate papal rule. Over a hundred houses are said to have been destroyed to make space for its construction on Colle Landone, one of the city center hills, but the city had its own back in 1860 when the unification of Italy brought the chance to destroy the much-hated symbol of papal power. All that remains are some of the walls along Viale Indipendenza, the eastern bastion on Via Marzia, which incorporated the Etruscan Porta Marzia, and the foundations, which were used to link the stone houses on streets such as Via Baglioni.

You can take in more atmospheric ruins by following the steps down to Corso Cavour. It's not far along here to the **Chiesa di San Domenico** (Piazza Giordano Bruno, ☎ 0755-731568), which stands on the site of the city's former cathedral, Santo Stefano in Castellare. This grand Gothic hall-church had a busy construction history; it was rebuilt and extended in the early 15th century, but was deemed unstable on its completion and had to be demolished. A second attempt also proved fruitless, and it wasn't until the complex was entrusted to Carlo Maderna that it was finally completed. Inside, a huge apse window (one of the largest in Italy) provides the light you'll need to take in the Renaissance wooden choir, 14th-century frescoes and altarpieces by Agostino di Duccio and Giannicola di Paolo.

Going Underground

The *soffitte di San Domenico* (ceilings of San Domenico) are one of Perugia's lesser-known sights. A tour, including the permanent exhibition covering the history of the building, is offered on Saturday and Sunday mornings (reserve on ☎ 0755-721469).

A second underground tour takes you to the **Pozzo Sorbello**, an Etruscan well from the third century BC, which leads under the Palazzo Sorbello (Piazza Danti 18, ☎ 0755-725778, daily, 10:30 am-1:30 pm, 2:30-5 pm, closed Tues, € 2, conc. €1) along a specially-designed walkway.

The adjacent convent houses the **Museo Archeologico Nazionale dell'Umbria** (Piazza G. Bruno 10, ☎ 0755-727141, daily, 8:30 am-7:30 pm). It contains a display of Paleolithic and Aeneolithic remains (from the Bronze and Iron Ages) and Etruscan artifacts such as urns and sarcophagi, vases and gold objects, and weapons from all over Umbria. The most important is the third-century BC Cippo di Perugia, a boundary stone bearing the longest Etruscan inscription ever found.

Just off Corso Cavour, the **Chiesa di Sant'Ercolano** (Scalette di Sant'Ercolano, ☎ 0755-722297) is announced from afar by its massive octagonal tower. Dedicated to one of the city's patron saints, the building stands close to the ancient Etruscan fortifications on the exact spot (according to local myth) where the saint was martyred after the Goth's successful siege.

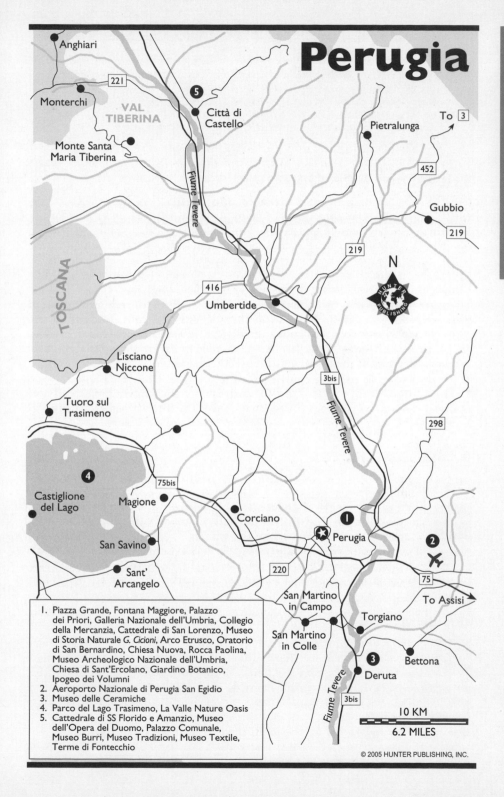

Perugia

Anghiari

221

Monterchi

VAL
TIBERINA

5

Città di
Castello

Monte Santa
Maria Tiberina

TOSCANA

Fiume Tevere

Pietralunga

To 3

452

Gubbio

219

219

N

416

Umbertide

3bis

Fiume Tevere

298

Lisciano
Niccone

Tuoro sul
Trasimeno

75bis

4

Castiglione
del Lago

Magione

Corciano

1

Perugia

2

75

To Assisi

San Savino

220

Sant'
Arcangelo

San Martino
in Campo

Torgiano

San Martino
in Colle

3

Deruta

Bettona

Fiume Tevere

3bis

1. Piazza Grande, Fontana Maggiore, Palazzo
   dei Priori, Galleria Nazionale dell'Umbria, Collegio
   della Mercanzia, Cattedrale di San Lorenzo, Museo
   di Storia Naturale *G. Cicioni*, Arco Etrusco, Oratorio
   di San Bernardino, Chiesa Nuova, Rocca Paolina,
   Museo Archeologico Nazionale dell'Umbria,
   Chiesa di Sant'Ercolano, Giardino Botanico,
   Ipogeo dei Volumni
2. Aeroporto Nazionale di Perugia San Egidio
3. Museo delle Ceramiche
4. Parco del Lago Trasimeno, La Valle Nature Oasis
5. Cattedrale di SS Florido e Amanzio, Museo
   dell'Opera del Duomo, Palazzo Comunale,
   Museo Burri, Museo Tradizioni, Museo Textile,
   Terme di Fontecchio

10 KM

6.2 MILES

© 2005 HUNTER PUBLISHING, INC.

BISHOP ERCOLANO & THE LAST CALF

It could have easily gone the other way; as a ploy to convince the besiegers that the city could withstand their attack, Bishop Ercolano is said to have taken the city's only remaining calf, fed it the last of the grain and thrown it over the city walls. The Goths had just made up their mind to give up and retreat when the bishop was betrayed by a local cleric. The Goths stormed the castle, beheaded Ercolano, and the rest is history.

The Other City Churches

It's a pretty long trek to the **Chiesa di San Pietro** (Via Borgo XX Giugno, ☎ 075-34770), further along Corso Cavour, but it's worth the walk. This former Benedictine abbey houses one of the finest Gothic wooden choirs in Italy, a remarkable gilded ceiling from 1556 and a range of frescoes and paintings by artists as prestigious as Vasari, Perugino, Parmigianino and Raphael. A door in the apse of the wooden choir leads to a tiny balcony with a fabulous view over the Valle Umbra as far as Assisi, Monte Subasio and the Apennines.

There are more frescoes by Raphael and Perugino in the 11th-century **Chiesa di San Severo** (Piazza Raffaello, ☎ 0755-733864, Mar-Oct, daily, 10 am-1:30 pm, 2:30-6:30 pm, Nov-Feb, daily, 10 am-1:30 pm, 2:30-4:30 pm, free). Its 14th-century chapel presents frescoes of the Trinity surrounded by saints and angels. Raphael is responsible for the upper section (1505-1508); Perugino for the lower (1521).

The most authentic Baroque church left in town is the **Chiesa di San Filippo Neri** (Via dei Priori, ☎ 0755-725472), designed by the Roman architect Paolo Marucelli as a simple barrel-vaulted single nave. The interior houses a beautiful *Immaculate Conception* by Pietro da Cortona above the main altar.

■ Adventures

On Foot

Perugia has plenty of green spaces perfect for a nature stroll. Try the "medieval" style **Giardino Botanico** (Botanical Garden, Via Borgo XX Giugno 74, ☎ 0755-856432, ortobot@unipg.it, Mon-Fri, 8 am-5 pm, Sat, 8 am-1:30 pm) or the **Giardino Perugia** (Perugia Botanical Garden, Via Roma 4b, ☎ 075-32643, Mon-Sat, 8 am-1 pm). For hiking in the surroundings, head east to Assisi (see page 435), northeast to Gubbio (see page 440) or south to Todi (see page 391).

On Wheels

Although you can't cycle on many of this city's streets, it's worth renting a bicycle to visit the outlying churches and the surrounding area. Perugia has two bicycle rental locations, **Ciclismo Sport** (Via Settevalli 195, ☎/fax 0755-052531, www.ciclismo.sport.it) and **Matè** (Via Trasimeno Ovest 287/289, Olmo, ☎/fax 0755-172123, mate_servizi@virgilio.it). Both are very helpful with route information.

One bike route takes you off the main road to the **Ipogeo dei Volumni** (Via Assisana, Loc. Ponte San Giovanni, ☎ 0753-93329, daily, 9 am-12:30 pm, 4:30-7 pm, €2). The Ipogeo is a second-century collection of 38 Etruscan graves that was discovered by accident in 1840 during the construction of a road. You can also take Bus #4, #92 or #93 to Ponte San Giovanni station and then a taxi.

You can rent bicycles at **Corciano** (Punto Bici, Via Brodolini 11, Loc. Ellera, ☎ 0755-181293, fax 0755-181295, www.puntobici.com), where you can pick up bike routes in full view of Lago Trasimeno.

On Horseback

There are a few locations in and around Perugia where you can arrange horseback riding. Just outside the city itself, there is **Associazione Ippica San Martino** (Strada Montebello 2, Ponte Pattoli, ☎/fax 0756-94897), **Centro Ippico Il Covone** (Strada della Fratticiola 2, Ponte Pattoli, ☎ 347-1769622, fax 0758-011012, www.covone.com) and **Club Ippico Santa Sabina** (Loc. Sodi di Santa Sabina, ☎ 335-8167953).

You can also arrange trips out of town at **Corciano** (Colleverde, Via G.B. della Porta 59, Loc. Capocavallo, ☎ 0756-05815, fax 0756-05359, www.colleverdeclub.com), **Torgliano** (Il Piccolo Ranch, Loc. Miralduolo, ☎ 339-2839477) and **Bettona** (Natura Amica, Loc. Fratta di Bettona, ☎ 0759-82922).

On Water

You don't have to head too far out of town to enjoy the watersports in Perugia; canoes for exploring this stretch of the Tiber River are available for rent from **Canoa Club Perugia** (Via della Ghisa 23, Ponte Felcino, ☎ 0756-91558, www.infinito.it/utente/canoaclubperugia).

■ Entertainment & Events

For a regional capital, you can expect a rich range of events and Perugia doesn't disappoint. Some of the best include the international **Umbria Jazz** (10 days in July), the **Sagra Musicale Umbra** (live orchestras in Sept), **Perugia Classico** (live classical music in the Rocca Paolina in Sept) and, for all gourmands, **Eurochocolate** (a delicious chocolate festival in mid-Oct). Check with Perugia Territory Tourist Office, Via Mazzini 6, ☎ 0755-728937, fax 0755-739386, www.iat.perugia.it, for details.

■ Where to Shop

In Perugia, it's all about **handwoven fabrics**. The tradition goes back as far as the 12th century, when production of the city's famous "table linen" took off. The city's special weave is a traditional combination of cotton and linen in herringbone or diamond design. Pieces are spiced up by brocaded borders in a contrasting color (usually indigo) and a geometric design.

You can purchase some of the best designs at ancient weaving studios such as **Giuditta Brozzetti** (Via T. Berardi 5/6, ☎ 075-40236, fax 0755-00236, www.brozzetti.com), who weave to the original 12th-century patterns; **Fabbri Antonio** (Via Oberdan 13, ☎ 0755-726609), who specialize in the characteristic yellow-, blue- and rust-colored designs; and **Il Telaio** (Via Rocchi 19, ☎ 0755-726603), which also sells Umbrian and Deruta pottery.

Deruta Ceramics

The decoration on the walls of the Santuario della Madonna dei Bagni in Deruta is one of the most original in Umbria. The walls are covered with hundreds of colorful majolica tiles, which were donated as votive offerings in thanks for salvation from fires, wars and floods during the 14th and 15th centuries. The design not only shows the local flair for ceramic design, but also provides a glimpse into daily life of the time.

Deruta majolicas remain a favorite with shoppers for their pure white glazes and bright orange and blue designs. You can find out more in the **Museo delle Ceramiche** (Ceramics Museum, Largo San Francesco, ☎/fax 0759-71100, www.sistemamuseo.it), which presents a history of local ceramics production from the 14th to the 20th century, and describes the refined lustre decorations, with their iridescent golden sheen, that made the city so famous.

UMBRIA'S ANTIQUE MARKETS

The main antique fair in **Perugia** (art and antiques, jewelry and other collectors' items) takes place in the Centro Espositivo della Rocca Paolina from late October to early November.

Terni has its turn (goldsmithery, clocks, jewelry and gold art) from the 12th to 14th of February.

The **Assisi** Antiques Fair reaches Bastia Umbra at the end of April-early May.

Città di Castello focuses on furniture in September and on books in March.

Todi serves up antiques during April in the Palazzi Comunali and arts and crafts in the same location during September.

Finally, crafts, handmade embroidery and antique linen go on show in **Valtopina** every September.

■ Where to Eat

LOCAL FLAVORS

Arvoltolo: Pancakes stuffed with chopped liver or truffle.

Cappelletti: Little pasta "hats" cooked in a capon broth.

Ciricole: Country-style tagliatelle.

Regina in porchetta: "Queen carp" from Lago Trasimeno baked in a wood oven in the same manner as *porchetta.*

Costolette e fegatelli di maiale: Pork ribs and liver.

Gobbi alla parmigiana: Boiled pasta "hunchbacks" fried in batter, covered with meat sauce and baked.

Minestra di ceci: Chickpea soup.

Porchetta: Pork stuffed with minced liver, heart and lungs spit-roasted in a wooden oven.

Filetti di persico alla brace: Grilled fillet of perch.

Torciglione: A snake-shaped cake also known as *serpentone* made with anything from cooked apples and dried fruit to almond paste and candied fruit.

Torta al formaggio: A *panettone*-like savory bread filled with different cheeses, popular in Perugia on Easter.

Torta al testo perugina: A type of flaky pastry often served with the local salami and hams.

Hundreds of prized vines grow on the hills throughout Perugia Province. Try the wines of the Colli Perugini, Colli Martani, Colli del Trasimeno and those of Montefalco, Torgiano and Assisi.

Perugia Enoteche (Via V. Rocchi 16, ☎ 0755-724824, Mon-Sat, 9:30 am-10 pm, Sun, 9:30 am-1 pm, $), in the heart of the city, is the perfect place to try a local aperitif or finish your evening with a whiskey or a cognac. The wine bar also serves light meals.

La Botte (Via V. della Pace, ☎/fax 0755-726104, closed Sun, $$), a short walk from the Fontana Maggiore, offers one of the most reasonably priced menus in town from its raucous underground rooms.

DINING PRICE CHART	
Price per person for an entrée, including house wine & cover.	
$	Under €20
$$	€21-€40
$$$	€41-€60
$$$$	Over €60

You'll get a warm welcome at **Locanda degli Artisti** (Via Campo Battaglia 10, ☎ 0755-735851, fax 0755-738917, closed Tues, $); the simple menu here serves some tasty local dishes, including homemade *ciricole al tartufo*, plenty of fish from Lago Trasimeno, as well as an extensive selection of pizzas.

There is more homemade fare inside the family-run **Locanda del Brigante** (Ponte d'Oddi 109, ☎ 0755-44852, fax 0755-840462, $$). Check out the freshly-made pastas and grilled meats.

Antica Trattoria San Lorenzo (Piazza Danti 19a, ☎/fax 0755-721956, www.trattoriasanlorenzo.com, $$$) is one of the city's most elegant dining establishments, with glorious vaulted ceilings and a luxurious menu of specialties based on the local porcini mushrooms.

Become a Sommelier

The Italian Sommeliers Association organizes sommelier courses in Perugia. Most are serious, but there are also light-hearted mini-courses suitable for all adventurous oenophiles. Contact **Sommelier Professionista Ricci Alunni Gabriele** (Hotel Giò Arte e Vini, Via Ruggero D'Andreotto 19, ☎/fax 0755-731100, ricciwine@tiscali.it) for further information.

■ Where to Stay

Staying in Perugia isn't particularly expensive unless you book into the **Palazzo Brufani** ☆☆☆☆☆, where prices can reach up to €350 (US$441) a night (Piazza Italia 12, ☎ 0755-732541, fax 0755-720210, www.sinahotels.com, $$$$$). The second extravagant choice, more within reach of most luxury holiday budgets, is **Alla Posta dei Donini** ☆☆☆☆ (Via Deruta 43,

Fraz. San Martino in Campo, ☎/Fraz 0756-09132, www.postadonini.it, $$$$). It's on the road out of town to the south, and its rates peak at a more reasonable €210 (US$264). Or there's the **Deco Hotel** ☆☆☆ (Via del Pastificio 8, Loc. Ponte San Giovanni, ☎ 0755-990950, fax 0755-990970, www.decohotel.it, $$$), which is cheaper still.

If you do want to stay in the historical center but don't have a five-star budget to play with, prices are reasonable at **La Rosetta** ☆☆☆ (Piazza Italia 19, ☎ 0755-720841, fax 0755-720841, www.perugiaonline. com/rosetta, $$$) and the **Sangallo Palace**

HOTEL PRICE CHART	
Rates are per room with private bath, based on double occupancy, including breakfast.	
$	Under €40
$$	€41-€85
$$$	€86-€140
$$$$	€141-€210
$$$$$	Over €210

Hotel ☆☆☆ (Via Masi 9, ☎ 0755-730202, fax 0755-730068, www.sangallo.it, $$$), next to the Rocca Paolina. Prices are better still at **Grifone** ☆☆☆ (Via S. Pellico 1, ☎ 0755-837616, fax 0755-837619, www.grifonehotel.com, $$) and **Priori** ☆☆ (Via Vermiglioli 3, ☎ 0755-723378, fax 0755-729155, hotelpriori@perugia.com, $$).

There are two campgrounds around town, the **Paradis d'Eté** ☆☆☆ (Via del Mercato 29a, Strada Fontana, Colle della Trinità, ☎ 0755-173121, fax 0755-176056, www.wel.it/cparadis, open all year, 50 spaces, $) and **Il Rocolo** ☆☆ (Strada Fontana 1n, Colle della Trinità, ☎/fax 0755-178550, www.ilrocolo.it, $).

You can also book into *affitacamere* in town at **Conservatorio Antinori** (Corso Garibaldi 226, ☎ 0755-40258, fax 0755-840784, antinoripg@libero.it, $) and out of town at **Casale Forabosco** (Loc. Forabosco, Collestrada, ☎ 0755-990840, fax 0755-999308, www.casaleforabosco.com, $) or **Le Quattro Stagioni** (Via San Sisto, Fraz. San Sisto, ☎ 0755-292386, fax 0755-295092, www.web.tiscali.it/ r4stagioni, $$).

And there is a good range of accommodation available in convents, monasteries and other religious institutions, including rooms in **Casa Santa Chiara** (Via delle Clarisse 8, ☎ 0755-735626, $), **Istituto Don Bosco** (Via Don Bosco 7, ☎ 0755-33880, fax 0755-730471, $), **Pensionato San Francesco** (Via della Cupa 4, ☎ 0755-723859, fax 0755-724711, $), **Suore della Provvidenza** (Via Francolina 18, ☎ 0755-724623, fax 0755-738700, $) and **Casa San Filippo Neri** (Via della Cupa 3, ☎ 0755-727032, due to open soon).

Finally, there is one youth hostel in town – **Centro Internazionale di Accoglienza per la Gioventù** (Via Bontempi 13, ☎ 0755-722880, fax 0755-739449, www.ostello.perugia.it, $). There are also two just out of town – **Ostello Maria Luisa Spagnoli** (Loc. Pian di Massiano, ☎ 0755-011366, fax 0755-026805, perugiahostel@tiscalinet.it, $) and **Ostello Fontignano** (Via Francesca 8b, Fontignano, ☎/fax 0755-290009, www.comune.perugia.it/ fontignano, May-Sept, $).

Monte Sibillini

Street in Assisi

Madonna fresco, Benozzo Gozzoli (1450), San Fortunato, Montefalco

Palazzo dei Canonici, Gubbio

Outside of Perugia

■ Lago Trasimeno

The largest lake on the Italian peninsula, Lago Trasimeno is also one of its most beautiful. It has been at the very center of Italian history since Hannibal defeated the Romans on its shores in 217 BC, and today there are a wealth of castles, ruins and churches to explore, as well as a variety of watersports and some of the region's most vibrant dining and nightlife.

Getting There & Around

 By Car: The lake is as easy to reach from Tuscany as it is from Umbria, lying as it does on the **SS75bis** state road, which links Perugia with the A1 highway between Florence and Rome (Val di Chiana exit).

 By Train/Bus: It is a short bus ride from Cortona's Terontola station. If you are arriving by train (☎ 848-888088, www.trenitalia.it), most hotels offer shuttle buses from the station.

 Bike Rental: In Castiglione del Lago, you can rent from **Cicli Valentini** (Via Firenze 68b, ☎/fax 0759-51663) or **Marinelli Ferrettini Fabio** (Via B. Buozzi 26, ☎/fax 0759-53126); in Passignano del Lago from **Ragnoni Brunello** (Via Pompili 61, ☎ 0758-29239); and in Tuoro sul Trasimeno from the campground at **Balneazione Tuoro** (Loc. Punta Navaccia, ☎ 328-4549766, Apr-Sept) or from **Marzano Remigio** (Via Console Flaminio 59, ☎ 0758-26269).

Information Sources

 Tourist Offices: Servizio Turistico Territoriale IAT del Trasimeno (Trasimeno Territory Tourist Office, Piazza Mazzini 10, Castiglione del Lago, ☎ 0759-652484, fax 0759-652763, www.iat.castiglione-del-lago-pg.it) provides information on all the towns that surround the lake. The **Parco Regionale del Lago Trasimeno** (Lago Trasimeno Regional Nature Park) has its head office in Passignano sul Trasimeno (Viale Europa, ☎ 0758-28059, fax 0758-299273, www.parks.it/trasimeno).

Sightseeing

It may have a maximum depth of only six meters (20 feet), but Lago Trasimeno is still the largest inland body of water on the Italian peninsula. Surrounded by a bed of reeds, dotted with nine well-tended beaches (around the resorts of Castiglione del Lago, Magione, Passignano sul Trasimeno and Tuoro sul Trasimeno) and offering a variety of watersports (including fishing), this lake continues to attract tourists and locals alike.

Remains of earlier Etruscan and Roman civilizations can be spotted around **Castiglione del Lago**, but it was the Middle Ages that left the most indelible marks on the region as fortified towns such as Castel Rigone, Passignano, Monte del Lago and Castiglione del Lago sprung up in defense. The castle for the latter sits beautifully on a promontory jutting out into the lake. It was designed by the controversial monk, St. Francis himself, who was also responsible for Assisi's Basilica di San Francesco in Assisi.

There are three islands on the lake, **Isola Polvese** to the south and **Isola Minore** and **Isola Maggiore** (the only one of the three to be inhabited) to the north. Boats run to Isola Maggiore from Tuoro del Trasimeno (APM, ☎ 075-5731707, www.apmperugia.it) and you can spend your morning exploring the island's tiny fishing villages, with the 12th-century churches of San Salvatore and San Michele Arcangelo on top of the hill, before setting off around the perimeter to take in the deserted villas and wild countryside.

Surprisingly, Maggiore is famous for its Irish lace; while you're here, you'll be able to buy a fine specimen and learn a little of the craft, which was introduced to this region when an Irish housekeeper was brought here in 1904.

TRASIMENO BLUES

*With live performances in Magione, Tuoro sul Trasimeno, Città della Pieve, Castiglione del Lago and Passignano sul Trasimeno, the international blues festival, **Trasimeno Blues** (☎ 0788-28489, www.trasimenoblues.net, some events free, other events from €5) sees the shores of the lake explode with music during the last week of July.*

Adventures

On Water

There are plenty of watersports, including **water-skiing** by arrangement with the **Sci Club Trasimeno** (Loc. Lacaioli, Castiglione del Lago, ☎ 0759-652836, fax 0759-652756) or the **Sci Club Punta Navaccia** (Loc. Punta Navaccia, Tuoro sul Trasimeno, ☎ 0758-26357, fax 0758-258147); and **windsurfing** with rental and lessons available from **Trasimeno Windsurf Club** (Loc. Monte del Lago, Magione, ☎ 349-4050200, www.trasimenowindsurfclub.com) and **Balneazione Tuoro** (Loc. Punta Navaccia, Tuoro sul Trasimeno, ☎ 328-4549766, www.spiaggiadituoro.it).

There are **sailing** schools at Passignano sul Trasimeno – **Club Velico Trasimeno** (Via Lungolago Giappesi, ☎ 0758-296021, fax 0758-29209, www.clubvelicotrasimeno.it) and **Castiglione del Lago** (Club Velico Castiglionese, Viale B. Garibaldi, ☎ 0759-53035, fax 0759-655595, www.trasinet.com/cvc). Sailboats can be rented at **Magione** (Darsena Nautica Trovati, Via F. Papini 79, San Feliciano, ☎ 0758-476032, fax 0758-479244, nauticatrovati@libero.it).

On Foot

Plenty of trails take you around parts of the lake, with the opportunity to explore the rich coastal strip of ilex wood, oak trees, olive trees and firs that make up part of the Parco Regionale del Lago Trasimeno. **Bird-watchers** should also keep their eyes out for birds of prey such as the harrier, eagle owl and osprey in the sky overhead, and herons, storks, bitterns, whooper swans, widgeons, mallards, cormorants and grebes in the rich marsh on the lake.

There are more walks and bird-watching opportunities in La Valle at **La Valle Nature Oasis** (Loc. San Savino, Magione, ☎ 0758-476007), a coastal oasis that stretches between San Savino and Sant'Arcangelo. Their visitor center supplies information as well as historical and nature itineraries. There's even an electric boat to take you onto the lake where you can see some of the coots, purple herons and little crakes.

On Horseback

Horseback riding can be arranged at **Passignano sul Trasimeno** (Poggio del Belveduto, Loc. Campori di Sopra, San Donato, ☎/fax 0758-29076, closed Mon), **Tuoro sul Trasimeno** (La Dogana, Loc. La Dogana 4, ☎ 0758-230158, fax 0758-230252), **Magione** (Associazione Ippica Arcobalengo, Case Sparse 10, Loc. Caligiana, ☎ 0758-409317) and **Panicale** (Azienda Agrituristica La Fonte, Loc. Caiolo, ☎ 0758-37122, fax 0758-37737, for *agriturismo* guests only). All require advance booking.

In the Air

For something a little different, arrange for a skydive with **Skydive Trasimeno** (Loc. Soderi, Panicale, ☎ 0758-350026).

Where to Stay

The lake has plenty of campgrounds, with choices at **Castiglione del Lago – Badiaccia** ☆☆☆ (Via Trasimeno 1, Loc. Badiaccia, ☎ 0759-659097, fax 0759-659019, www.badiaccia.com, $), and **Listro** ☆☆ (Via Lungolago, ☎/fax 0759-51193, www.listro.it, $). Both are open Apr-Sept. In Passignano sul Trasimeno, there is **Kursaal** ☆☆☆ (Viale Europa, Loc. San Donato 24, ☎ 0758-28085, fax 0758-27182, www.camping.it/umbria/kursaal, Mar-Sept, $), and **Europa** ☆☆ (Loc. San Donato, ☎/fax 0758-27405, www.camping-europa.it, Apr-Sept, $). Truro sul Trasimeno has **Punta Navaccia** ☆☆☆ (Via Navaccia 4, ☎ 0758-26357, fax 0758-258147, www.camping.it/umbria/navaccia, Apr-Sept, $).

There are even more campground options at Magione with the best of the eight or so represented by the vast **Villaggio Italgest** ☆☆☆☆ (Via Martiri di Cefalonia, Loc. Sant'Arcangelo, ☎ 0758-48238, fax 0758-48085, camping@italgest.com, Mar-Sept, 283 spaces, $) and the more intimate **Polvese** ☆☆☆ (Via Montivalle, Loc. Sant'Arcangelo, ☎ 0758-48078, fax 0758-48050, www.polvese.com, 72 spaces, $).

There are two good youth hostels at Lago Trasimeno. **Ostello Il Poggio** (Isola Polvese, ☎ 0759-659550, fax 0759-659551, www.isolapolvese.it, $) is the best option. It is located on the island of Polvese in the center of the lake (boats depart from San Feliciano every 40 minutes). **Casa del Fanciullo** (Via del Lavoro 10a, Loc. Torricella, ☎/fax 0758-43508, $) lies just outside of Magione.

■ Città di Castello & the Alta Valle del Tevere

Set in the Upper Tiber Valley among quiet and sleepy natural surroundings, the world-renowned historical and artistic treasures found in Città di Castello can come as something of a surprise. Only in Umbria can the town that contains the region's most important collection of medieval art be so difficult to reach.

Getting There & Around

By Car: From Perugia, the **SS3bis** (E45) snakes north to Città di Castello via Umbertide; if arriving from Florence and eastern Tuscany, take the **SS73** from the Arezzo exit on the A1 highway.

By Train: Trains on the private **Ferrovia Centrale Umbra** (☎ 0755-75401, www.fcu.it) run between Perugia and Città di Castello; change onto this line at Terni if arriving from Rome.

By Bus: There's a regular bus connection to the city from Arezzo.

 Bike Rental: In Città di Castello you can rent from **Giogli Antonio** (Via XI Settembre 29, ☎ 0758-557695).

Information Sources

 Tourist Offices: Servizio Turistico Territoriale IAT dell'Alta Valle del Tevere (Upper Tiber Valley Territory Tourist Office, Via San Antonio 1, Città di Castello, ☎ 0758-554817, fax 0758-552100, www.iat.citta-di-castello.pg.it) covers the Tiber Valley including the towns of Città di Castello, Pietralunga and Umbertide. The city of Città di Castello has its own office in Logge Bugalini (Piazza Matteotti, ☎ 0758-554922) and that of Umbertide can be found on Piazza Caduti del Lavoro (☎ 0759-417099).

Sightseeing in the Città di Castello

Built upon the foundations of the ancient Roman trading post of *Tifernum Tiberinum*, Città di Castello has quietly grown over the years into a city full of magnificent medieval and Renaissance churches, cathedrals, squares and palaces. The town's highlight is undoubtedly the **Pinacoteca Comunale** (Civic Picture Gallery, Palazzo Vitelli alla Cannoniera, Via della Cannoniera 22a, ☎ 0785-20656, www.cdcnet.net/pinacoteca). It lies just outside the ancient walls of the town in a bastion from where the Vitelli dynasty controlled the town. Striking frescoes by Cola dell'Amatrice, painted stairwells and *sgraffiti* by Vasari decorate the exterior walls and garden façade, while inside, *The Martyrdom of St Sebastian* by Luca Signorelli, *Trinity* by Raphael, two bronze statuettes by Lorenzo Ghiberti and works by Neri di Bicci, Ghirlandio and Andrea di Bartolo prove the biggest draws.

THE VITELLI

The Vitelli took over rule in the Città di Castello toward the end of the 15th century after a fierce battle with other local clans, and it is they who should be thanked for much of what you see in the city today. They beautified it with the Renaissance churches, palaces and monuments that can be visited.

Make your way to the medieval center of town where an 11th-century dome marks the site of the **Cattedrale di SS Florido e Amanzio**, itself constructed on the main temple from the original Roman settlement. Its present façade is divided into two parts: a lower Baroque design from 1632 and an upper Renaissance style added during later restructuring. Past its 13th-century campanile, the **Museo dell'Opera del Duomo** (Museum of Cathedral Works, Piazza Gabriotti 3a, ☎ 0758-554705, www.museoduomocdc.it) contains a rare collection of fifth- and sixth-century silver and gold works, including communion vessels, altarpieces and the *Canoscio*, a rare collection of Palaeo-Christian objects – among them 10 primitively decorated plates.

You'll also be drawn to the hulking **Palazzo Comunale**, a Gothic building in ashlar-work with portal and impressive mullioned windows that was constructed in the first half of the 14th century by Angelo da Orvieto. Immediately opposite is the **Torre Comunale**, seat of the town's medieval prison; climb its steps for beautiful views over the city and the farmland beyond its walls.

Other museums of note include the **Museo Burri** in Palazzo Albizzini (Via Albizzini 1, ☎ 0758-554649, www.cdcnet.net/museo_burri) with its collection of 130 works by painter Alberto Burri, created between 1948 and 1989; the **Museo Tradizioni** (Folk Tradition Museum, Via Garavelle 2, ☎ 0758-552119, www.cdcnet.net/museo_tradizioni), with displays on local farming culture and traditions, including blacksmithing, woodworking and crafts; and the **Museo Textile** (Via Sant'Antonio, ☎/fax 0758-554337), dedicated to Umbrian lace, embroidery and Perugian tablecloths that was created at the beginning of the century by local philanthropist Baron Franchetti.

Just out of town in Fontecchio, the spa, **Terme di Fontecchio** (☎ 0758-62851, fax 0758-628521, www.termedifontecchio.it, open all year), offers mineral water cures and mud baths aimed at treating disorders of the digestive system. You can arrange for a weekend of beauty treatments at the **Hotel delle Terme** (Fontecchio, ☎ 0785-20614, fax 0785-557236, hotel@termedifontecchio.it, $$$$).

Sightseeing in the Alta Valle del Tevere

San Giustino to the north marks the border with Tuscany and its fortified structure and central **Castello Bufalini** (Bufalini castle) harks back to the days when it was defending the region for Città di Castello. Vasari transformed the structure into a sumptuous villa and stately home after the Medici had definitively gained control of the zone. Although it can't yet be visited, plans are underway to provide tours past its period furnishings, magnificent frescoes by Gherardi and vast park grounds.

High on a hilltop east of Città di Castello, the heart of the ancient Etruscan settlement of **Pietralunga** is its 13th-century **Pieve di Santa Maria** (parish church), a must-see for its fresco of *The Martyrdom of St Sebastian* by Raffaellino del Colle. Two roads link the town to Città di Castello. One takes you past the Pieve di Saddi; the other to the Abbazia di Montemaggiore. Both are great sites for hikers, with pleasant wooded **trails** leading you into the nearby hills.

The historical town of **Umbertide** has a Rocca with a tower 40 m (131 feet) high, built in the 14th century to an imposing military design by "Trucascio" (Angeluccio di Ceccolo). Its walls are two meters (six feet) thick and it has been the local prison since the 14th century when Braccio Fortebraccio da Montone

Pietralunga

was first incarcerated here. Pleasant trips out of town take you to the Abbazia di San Salvatore and the Ermito di Montecorona, both within walking distance of one another through thick beech and chestnut groves.

Adventures in the Alta Valle del Tevere

On Foot & on Wheels

Mountainous, wooded, unspoiled and steeped in history and religion, the Upper Tiber Valley is a great destination for walking and mountain biking. Paths lead east towards the **Appenine mountains** of the Marche and west to Tuscany's Val di Chiana and the routes around Sansepolcro. Kompass 1:50,000 maps #663 *Perugia-Assisi* and #664 *Gubbio-Fabriano* cover trails in the area, including the popular routes leading into the flower-filled **Carpina Valley**.

To arrange potholing into the mountain chain north of Città di Castello, contact **Centro Escursionistico Naturalistico** (Loc. Bocca Serriola, Città di Castello, ☎ 0758-554392).

On Horseback

The main riding centers can be found around Città di Castello. Try **Centro Ippico La Valle dei Falchi** (Felicino Candeggio, ☎/fax 0758-526184), **Centro Ippico San Giovanni** (Loc. Meltina, ☎ 0758-522728), **Club Ippico San Pietro** (Loc. Il Castagneto 36, San Pietro a Monte, ☎ 0758-505005) or **Fattoria Caldese** (Caldese di Celle, Lerchi, ☎/fax 0758-510197).

There are also centers at **Pietralunga**, such as **Azienda Agrituristica La Cerqua** (Loc. San Salvatore, ☎/fax 0759-460283) and at **Umbertide – Centro Ippico Le Butulle** (Loc. Niccione, ☎ 0759-410958).

On Water

There are plenty of watersports on the Tiber River, with canoes for rent at Città di Castello through **Piazza del Mercato** (☎ 0758-553656, web.tiscalinet.it/canoacastello) and rafting by arrangement with **Centro Escursionistico Naturalistico** (Loc. Bocca Serriola, Città di Castello, ☎ 0758-554392).

ROME ALONG THE TIBER

Città di Castello has been the starting point for an annual canoe marathon to Rome for the last 25 years. The international event, which attracts professionals and amateurs to the Tiber River during the last week of April, sees seven days of sport, culture and nature as it follows the canoeists through Umbria to Lazio. To take part in any stage of the race, contact Dicesea del Tevere (☎ 329-6883135, discesadeltevere@tiscali.it, subscription €20).

In the Air

You can take part in hang-gliding north of Pietralunga. To get yourself a flight, contact **ALP Aviazione Leggera Pietralunghese** (Loc. Terzi di Pietralunga, ☎ 0759-4760082).

Where to Stay

There's one campground at Città di Castello (**La Montesca** ☆☆☆, Loc. Montesca, ☎ 0758-558566, fax 0758-520786, May-Sept, 43 spaces, $). The town also has one youth hostel (**San Florido**, Via San Florido 23, ☎ 0758-55840, $). There's also a hiking refuge at nearby Bocca Serriola (**Bocca Serriola**, ☎ 0758-554392, fax 0758-520612, larondine@tline.net, $).

Orvieto & Southwest Umbria

Close to the border where Umbria meets Tuscany and Lazio, the city of Orvieto and the western corner of Umbria occupy a stunning and uncontaminated countryside that ranges from basalt and tufa precipices in the volcanic hinterland to rolling hills and alluvial plains of the Paglia and Tiber rivers, both of which are now regional parks. It is a history-rich area, which has seen much action since the Etruscans first inhabited the area some 3,000 years ago.

REGION AT A GLANCE

Main city: Orvieto.

Afternoon trips from Orvieto: Lago di Bolsena (see page 386), Baschi (see page 386).

City breaks: Amelia (see page 400), Narni (see page 401), Terni (see page 396) and Todi (see page 391).

Rural retreats: The Amerino (see page 400), the Monti Martani (see page 394-96), the Fiume Nera and the Cascade Marmore (see page 398) and the Valnerina (see page 398).

Spa towns: Acquasparta (see page 396), Massa Martana (see page 395) and San Gemini (see page 396).

Orvieto

Halfway along the A1 highway between Florence and Rome, the unforgettable architecture of hilltop Orvieto gives a strong indication of the important role the city has played since Etruscan times. Standing on a single mass of tufa (known as *la rupe*, or the cliff), the Etruscan city of Velzna ruled here from the seventh century BC until the Romans destroyed it in 264 BC. A striking underground city still survives from that time. It was reconstructed in the fifth century, when it was called *urbs vetus* (old city). Pope Clement VIII fled here during the sacking of Rome in 1527 and thereafter it became a retreat for the popes. The above-ground settlement was during this time that the city reached its peak that saw the Gothic cathedral constructed and the town remodeled to befit its illustrious guests. The historical center is small enough to cover in a day, but it's worth hanging around to explore the lush valley, where its famous wine is produced.

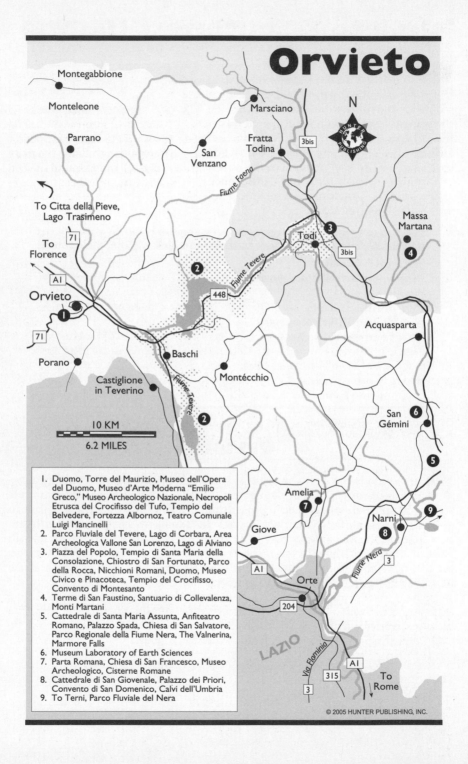

Orvieto

Montegabbione

Monteleone

Parrano

Marsciano

San Venzano

Fratta Todina

3bis

To Citta della Pieve, Lago Trasimeno

N

Massa Martana

4

Todi 3

To Florence

71

To Florence

A1

448

Fiume Tevere

3bis

Orvieto

1

Fiume Faena

71

Baschi

Montécchio

Acquasparta

Porano

Fiume Tevere

San Gémini 6

Castiglione in Teverino

Fiume Tevere

2

5

10 KM

6.2 MILES

Amelia

7

9

Giove

Narni

8

1. Duomo, Torre del Maurizio, Museo dell'Opera del Duomo, Museo d'Arte Moderna "Emilio Greco," Museo Archeologico Nazionale, Necropoli Etrusca del Crocifisso del Tufo, Tempio del Belvedere, Fortezza Albornoz, Teatro Comunale Luigi Mancinelli
2. Parco Fluviale del Tevere, Lago di Corbara, Area Archeologica Vallone San Lorenzo, Lago di Alviano
3. Piazza del Popolo, Tempio di Santa Maria della Consolazione, Chiostro di San Fortunato, Parco della Rocca, Nicchioni Romani, Duomo, Museo Civico e Pinacoteca, Tempio del Crocifisso, Convento di Montesanto
4. Terme di San Faustino, Santuario di Collevalenza, Monti Martani
5. Cattedrale di Santa Maria Assunta, Anfiteatro Romano, Palazzo Spada, Chiesa di San Salvatore, Parco Regionale della Fiume Nera, The Valnerina, Marmore Falls
6. Museum Laboratory of Earth Sciences
7. Parta Romana, Chiesa di San Francesco, Museo Archeologico, Cisterne Romane
8. Cattedrale di San Giovenale, Palazzo dei Priori, Convento di San Domenico, Calvi dell'Umbria
9. To Terni, Parco Fluviale del Nera

Fiume Nera

3

A1

Orte

204

LAZIO

Via Flaminia

A1

315

3

To Rome

■ Getting Here & Around

By Air/Train: The nearest airport to Orvieto is just outside of Perugia at **Aeroporto Sant'Egidio** (☎ 0756-929447), but the city is even easier to reach from Rome's international **Leonardo da Vinci-Fiumicino Airport** (☎ 066-5951). From there, frequent trains (☎ 848-888088, www.trenitalia.it) to Florence stop off at the bottom of Orvieto.

By Car: Orvieto is well served from both Rome and Florence via the **A1 Autostrada**. If you're coming from Perugia, the **SS448** state road passes through Orvieto on its way to Todi. There is free parking outside the main station in Orvieto Scalo (the new town at the bottom of the hill) and around the bottom of town, where escalators and lifts take you up to the historical center.

You can **rent cars** in town from **ACI** (Via Monte Vettore, Orvieto Scalo, ☎/fax 0763-305716), **Avis** (Viale 1 Maggio 46, Orvieto Scalo, ☎ 0763-393007, fax 0763-390648, www.avisautonoleggio.com), **Carpinelli** (Via di Loreto 20, ☎ 0763-344139), **Cochi Claudio** (Via Ombrone 1, ☎ 0763-390074) and **Hertz** (Str. dell'Arcone 13, c/o Fiat, Orvieto Scalo, ☎ 0763-301303, fax 0763-390506).

By Funicular/Bus: From the train station, a funicular takes you up to the historical center. Tickets (€0.80) can be purchased at the funicular office or from shops and tabacchi. Your ticket includes use of both the funicular and buses within the 60-minute validity. **ATC** (☎ 0744-402900, www.atcterni.it) run bus services, with #A and #B running every 10 minutes (7:05 am-8:35 pm) within the historical center and lines #2, #5 and #7 (twice hourly) linking the station and the old town.

By Taxi: These are available outside the **train station** (☎ 0763-301903) and in the historic center on **Piazza della Repubblica** (☎ 0763-342613).

THE ALL IN ONE CARD

*The **Carta Orvieto Unica** includes entrance to the Cappella di San Brizio, the Musei Archeologici "C. Faina" e Civico, the Torre del Moro, a guided visit to Orvieto Underground and a round-trip ticket for the minibus and funicular (or five hours of parking in Campo della Fiera). Obtain it from the Tourist Board, Piazza Duomo 24, funicular car park or any of the attractions to which it includes entry, ☎ 339-733764, €12.50, conc. ‡10.50.*

■ Information Sources

Tourist Offices: The main **Servizio Turistico Territoriale IAT dell'Orvietano** is outside the cathedral on Piazza del Duomo. It supplies tourist information both for the city of Orvieto and for its surroundings. (☎ 0763-341772, fax 0763-344433, www.iat.orvieto.tr.it, www.umbria2000.it, Mon-Fri, 8:15 am-1:50 pm, 4-7 pm, Sat, 10 am-1 pm, 4-7 pm, Sun and holidays, 10 am-noon, 4-6 pm.)

■ Sightseeing

Known as "the golden lily of cathedrals," Orvieto's Gothic **Duomo** was three centuries in the making. (Piazza Duomo, ☎ 0763-341167, Apr-Sept, 7:30 am-12:45 pm, 2:30-7:15 pm, Mar/Oct, 7:30 am-12:45 pm,

2:30-6:15 pm, Nov-Feb, 7:30 am-12:45 pm, 2:30-5:15 pm, free.) Started in the late 13th century by Benedictine monk Fra Bevignate to celebrate the Miracle of Bolsena, it was worked on by a variety of the era's leading architects and artists, including Arnolfo di Cambio, Lorenzo Maitani, Pisano, Orcagna, Signorelli and Ippolito Scalza, as the fabulous decorations on both the exterior and interior testify. The monumental Gothic façade is a riot of columns, spires, bas-reliefs, sculptures, dazzling color, colossal doorways and minute details – all held together by four enormous fluted pillars. The interior features striking basalt and limestone pillars that were brought upriver from Rome, as well as breathtaking 14th-century stained glass windows. But it's the two interior chapels that draw most visitors. The **Cappella del SS. Corporale** was built to house the relic of Bolsena, whose story is recounted in the *Miracle of Bolsena and the Sacrament of the Eucharist* fresco on the walls. It was created by Domenico di Meo, Giovanni di Buccio Leonardelli and others between 1357 and 1363. The most important chapel is **Cappella di San Brizio** (☎ 0763-342477, fax 0763-340336, opsmorv@tin.it, same hours as the cathedral, €3, tickets should be purchased in advance from the tourist office). It has its own set of frescoes. They were begun by Fra' Angelico, halted by the murder of a local patron, continued briefly by Perugino, and finally completed by Signorelli. They peak in the seven frescoes of the lunette, which depict scenes of *Last Judgment* and show a graphic picture of the damned caught in a ferocious fight with their persecutors. The piece was to have a profound influence on Michelangelo's version in the Sistine Chapel.

The clock tower that rises behind the cathedral to its left is the **Torre di Maurizio**, one of the oldest such towers in Italy. It takes its name from the bronze statue called "Maurizio" on its roof.

Next door, the 13th-century Palazzo dei Papi – itself the former monumental home to no fewer than 33 popes – is the home for many of the city's museums. You can find here the **Museo dell'Opera del Duomo** (☎ 0763-342477, closed for restoration at the time of writing), which traces the history of the cathedral's construction and includes a Simone Martini *Madonna and Saints* and a *Madonna and Child* by Pisano. The Palazzo also houses the **Museo d'Arte Moderna Emilio Greco** (☎ 0763-344605, fax 0763-344664, Apr-Sept, Mon-Fri, 10:30 am-1 pm, 2-6:30 pm, Sat-Sun, 10:30 am-1 pm, 2:30-7 pm, Oct-Mar, 10:30 am-1 pm, 2-5:30 pm, €2.50, conc. €1.50, cumulative ticket with the Pozzo di San Patrizio, €4.50, conc. €2.50). It displays a collection of sculpture by Emilio Greco. And in the same building is the **Museo Archeologico Nazionale** (☎/fax 0763-341039, Sat June-Sept only, 8:30 am-11 pm, Sun and holidays, 8:30 am-7:30 pm, €2, conc. €1, cumulative ticket with the Etruscan tombs, €3, which showcases the best finds from the surrounding necropoli.

Visiting the Etruscan Tombs

The tufa around Orvieto contains numerous Etruscan necropoli. Unfortunately, many are closed due to subsidence, but you can visit the tombale di Cannicella and the two tombs of Golini I and II. To arrange visits, contact the **Necropoli Etrusca del Crocifisso del Tufo** (SS71, ☎ 0763-343611, Apr-Sept, 8:30 am-7 pm, Oct-Mar, 8:30 am-5:30 pm, €2, conc. €1, cumulative ticket with the Museo Archeologico €3). These date from the fourth to fifth centuries BC.

Directly south of Orvieto, **Porano** is one of the most interesting archeological zones in the region with the Etruscan tombs of Golini and Hescana (Loc. Molinella, ☎ 338-2929520, open by appointment only, free).

There's another archeological museum opposite Palazzo dei Pappi in Palazzo Faina. The **Musei Archeologici C. Faina e Civico** (☎ 0763-341511, fax 0763-341250, www.systemnet.it/museo-faina, www.museofaina.it, Apr-Sept, 9:30 am-6 pm, Oct-Mar, 10 am-5 pm, closed Mon, Sept-Mar, €4.50, conc. €3, guided visits an extra €1). This museum has more Etruscan relics and a series of "Attic vases" created by Athenian ceramicists.

Over the past 3,000 years, the inhabitants of Etruscan *Velzna* and their medieval and Renaissance successors dug an unbelievable chain of caves and cavities into the soft volcanic rock beneath the present city. While you're at the tourist office, book your trip to **Orvieto Underground** (☎ 0763-344891, fax 0763-391121, www.orvietounderground.it, daily at 11 am, 12:15, 4 and 5:15 pm, €5.50, conc. €4.50). The guided visit takes you through the labyrinth of caves and tunnels hidden in the silent cliffs below Orvieto. It is an endless succession of tunnels, stairs, unexpected passageways and subterranean paths, some of which run parallel to the cliff wall, where openings offer panoramic views of the surrounding countryside.

This isn't the only opportunity for you to go underground in Orvieto; there are two cylindrical wells that can be visited. **Pozzo della Cava** (Via della Cava 28, ☎ 0763-342373, fax 0763-341029, www.pozzodellacava.it, Tues-Sun, 8 am-8 pm, €3, conc. €2), along Via della Cava, the oldest and westernmost section of the city, is the older of the two. It was built in Etruscan times to a depth of 36 m (118 feet) and later enlarged by Pope Clemente VII in 1527. The guided tour includes a visit to an Etruscan tomb, an Etruscan rainwater cistern, a medieval wine cellar and a medieval kiln with pottery and tools.

Pozzo di San Patrizio (St Patrick's Well, Viale Sangallo, ☎ 0763-343768, fax 0763-344664, Apr-Sept, Mon-Fri, 10 am-6:45 pm, Sat-Sun, 9:30 am-7:15 pm, Oct-Mar, 10 am-5:45 pm, €3.50, conc. €2.50), on the other side of the city, was itself built during the residence of Pope Clemente VII. Taking refuge in the city, he feared that Orvieto would be brought under siege and commissioned Sangallo Il Giovane to build the 62-m (203-foot) "tour de force," with two independent spiral staircases (each with 248 steps).

Opposite the Pozzo di San Patrizio, the fifth-century BC **Tempio del Belvedere**, rediscovered in 1828, is the only remaining Etruscan temple in Orvieto – the others having been replaced by Roman and Christian buildings over the years. Apart from the basement, entrance steps, the bases of a few columns and some of the perimeter blocks, very little remains; the ornamental terracottas discovered here are on display in the Musei Archeologici C. Faina e Civico.

The **Fortezza Albornoz**, on the other side of the funicular station, was commissioned by the Cardinale Egidio Albornoz during the period in which the Papal Court was moved to Avignon. Now a public park, it was torn down and restored as a military installation in the 15th century.

Via Roma leads through the Porta Roma entrance gate back to town, passing the 15th-century Chiesa di Sant'Agostino and 13th-century Chiesa di San Domenico, with the funerary monument of Cardinale De Bray by Arnolfo di Cambio on the way. It stands opposite the **Palazzo e Chiesa di San Giovanni**, which is today home to the **Enoteca Regionale** (Regional Wine Cellar, guided visits and tastings, Sat and Sun, ☎ 0763-393529, itinera.orvieto@tiscalinet). This is an important port of call on any serious wine fan's sightseeing route. The complex itself was restored to its present condition in the 17th century after serious earthquake damage, but some of the original Romanesque construction (said to have been

Orvieto & SW Umbria

started in 916) can be seen on the interior marble walls that are frescoed with a *Madonna and Child*.

The simple façade of 13th-century **Chiesa di San Francesco** belies its one important role. It is the church that saw the canonization of Luigi IX, King of France, by Bonifacio VIII in 1297. Inside, there's a wooden crucifix above the main altar attributed to Maitani, paintings by Cesare Nebbia and Gagliardi along the nave and, on the right flank, a 16th-century cloister by Ippolito Scalza.

Probably the town's former cathedral, **Chiesa di San Giovenale** is one of the oldest in Orvieto. Behind the tufa façade, the 12th-century marble altar decorated with figures of vicars and priests is one of most important examples of Romanesque Gothic art in the region.

Behind the extremely simple façade of **Chiesa di San Lorenzo de' Arari** is an ancient Etruscan altar.

The road continues onto Piazza del Popolo with its Romanesque-Gothic **Palazzo del Popolo** (now a conference venue), itself built on recently rediscovered Etruscan remains and a medieval cistern, and the **Palazzo dei Signori Sette** and adjacent **Torre del Moro**, which affords great views over the surrounding countryside (Corso Cavour, ☎ 0763-344567, Mar-Aug, 10 am-8 pm, Mar-Apr and Sept-Oct, 10 am-7 pm, Nov-Feb, 10:30 am-1 pm, 2:30-5 pm, €2.50, conc. €1.85).

Corso Cavour is the city's main shopping street. It will take you up to the quiet square of the Romanesque **Palazzo Comunale** (Town Hall), which saw extensive alterations by Ippolito Scalza in the 16th century.

Down Corso Cavour in the opposite direction, the **Teatro Comunale Luigi Mancinelli** (Corso Cavour 122, ☎ 0763-340493, fax 0763-340418, www.teatromancinelli.it) is Orvieto's famed theater. Constructed in 1844 by Vespignani in classical Renaissance style and dedicated to Luigi Mancinelli, a composer from Orvieto. It is decorated with frescoed ceilings by Cesare Fracassini, a painted drop curtain by the same artist and hall frescoes by Angelini.

TASTING TOURS

Vistando e Degustando (☎ 0763-344605, smuseo.orvieto@libero.it) offers mini-bus tours into the countryside of Alviano, the Etruscan necropoli of Montecchio and some of the most beautiful towns in Umbria with chances to "visit and taste."

■ Adventures

On Foot

More medieval castle remains are waiting at hilltop **Allerona**, around 12 miles from Orvieto. The small hamlet stands above the rich surroundings of the Parco Statale di Selva di Meana (State Park) and the Parco Publico di Villalba (Public Park). Twelve **hiking trails** take you through the Parco Publico to the ancient hamlet of **San Pietro Acquaeortus** (named after the "miraculous" spring of St Peter) and on through woods to **Fabro**. It is made up of two historical centers (Fabro and Carnaiola), which both grew up as guardposts for the River Chiana. Both the **Pro Loco di Allerona** (Allerona Tourist Office, ☎ 0763-361097) and the **Associazione Natura e Vita di Allerona** (Association for Nature and Life, ☎ 0763-624359) offer guided tours of the region throughout the year.

Immersed in green woods to the south, the picturesque medieval center of **Parrano** is a must for **cavers** and **potholers**. You can find here the **Tane del Diavolo**, a range of Paleolithic caves carved over the centuries into gorges and deep caverns by the course of the spring (Devil's Hideout, Associazione UPUPA, Contrada Bissa 9, ☎ 335-5941403, guided underground visits by appointment, €18, conc. €15.50). Guided caving tours to both the Tane del Diavolo and the caves at **Pozzi della Piana** (Loc. Roccaccia di Titignano) can be arranged with guides **Francesco Baldini** (☎ 0763-340810), **Giancarlo Papini** (☎ 0763-344784) and **Alessandro Trapassi** (☎ 0763-343246), or with **Speleo Club di Orvieto** (Orvieto Caving Club, ☎ 0763-305726).

To its southwest, the picturesque route to **Ficulle** takes you first past the beautiful Romanesque-Gothic **Chiesa di Santa Maria Vecchia**, which houses some important 15th-century frescoes and two 16th-century wooden statues. Continue through the town to **Sala** (all that remains of a Monaldeschi castle) to purchase the terracotta pottery the region is famed for. In association with the local tourist board, **Gruppo Podistico S. Vittoria di Ficulle** (Ficulle Walking Group, ☎ 0763-86414) offers guided nature **walks** though the town and surrounding countryside.

Thirty or so miles along the SS71 from Orvieto, the fortified town of **Monteleone** still conserves part of the old walls and a tower added by the Orvietani in the 11th century. Both it and nearby **Montegabbione** stand in a beautiful wooded and pre-Apennine stretch of countryside close to Tuscany's Val di Chiana towns of Chiusi and Cetona. **Cosmo di Montegabbione** (☎ 0763-837564) offers guided **walks** though the surrounding countryside as part of its campaign to safeguard the valley of Montarale. Outside the walls, you can see the "metaphysical" designs of architect Tommaso Buzzi at the Franciscan **Convento della Scarzuola e Città Buzziana** (Loc. Scarzuola, ☎/fax 0763-837463, guided group visits by appointment, €11).

Follow the SS71 around to arrive at **San Venanzo** on the slopes of Monte Peglia. It stands on striking volcanic terrain and a nature **trail** from the **Centro Museale di Vulocanologia** takes you inside the site of the lava flow (Piazza Roma 1, ☎/fax 075-875482, museovulcano@edison.it, Sat, 9 am-1 pm, €1.50, guided €2.50/$3.20, conc. €2).

On Wheels

You can easily explore Orvieto's hinterland on a bicycle. **Natura e Avventura** (Piazza del Popolo 17, ☎/fax 0763-342484, www.argoweb.it/ciclo-trekking), **Noleggio Testa Renato** (Via Montemarte 47, ☎ 0338-4760943) and **Noleggio Star Bike** (Via Monte Nibbio 35/37, ☎ 0763-301649) all offer mountain bike rental and guided tours. You can also take part in the June Gran Fondo degli Etruschi (an Etruscan-themed excursion, www.gfetruschi.it) and the occasional excursions offered by the **Unione Ciclistica Orvietana** (☎ 0763-301649, excursions from Sept to May), which depart from Orvieto's Piazza del Duomo.

On Horseback

Orvieto has two riding schools offering guided treks: **Club Ippico Orvietano** (Fraz. Canale, Loc. La Cacciata, Orvieto Scalo, ☎ 0763-301346, fax 0763-302225, www.orvienet.it/clubippicorvietano) and **New Club 2000** (Loc. Ponte dell'Adunata, Stadio de Martino, Orvieto Scalo, ☎/fax 0744-957485).

Fabro and Ficulle are both good **horseback-riding** territories. You can organize treks (guided or otherwise) with **Centro Ippico El Gaucho** (Loc. Farneta, Fabro, ☎ 0763 82170) and **Centro Ippico La Casella** (c/o Azienda Agrituristica La Casella, Strada Casella 4, Ficulle, ☎ 0763-86075, fax 0763-86684, www.lacasella.com).

On Water

You'll find many of the adventures southeast of Orvieto around **Baschi**. This town sits on a spear over the Tiber Valley and presents traces of Etruscan times, Roman ruins (including the remains of the Roman river gateway of Paliano), crumbling remnants of medieval castles and Renaissance architecture (including the Chiesa di San Nicolò by Ippolito Scalza), as well as the **watersports** afforded by the **Lago di Corbara**. You can find out more of the region's history at the town's **Antiquarium Comunale** (Piazza del Comune 1, ☎ 0744-957225, fax 0744-957333, comunedibaschi@tiscalinet.it, Sun-Mon, 3-7 pm, Thurs, 9 am-1 pm, €2.50, conc. €1). The **Centro Turistico Sportivo di Salviano** (Tourist Sports Center, Loc. Belvedere, Baschi, ☎ 329-6184767) helps organize watersports activities on the lake. Canoe rental is available from a variety of centers, including **Centro Remiero Lago di Corbara** (Loc. Belvedere, Baschi, ☎ 0744-950545), **Canoa Club di Orvieto** (☎ 0763-300878) and **Baschi Centro di Canottaggio** (☎ 0763-950545).

Heading west out of Orvieto, the SS74 brings you to **Castel Giorgio**. This town has been occupied since Etruscan times and the territory is dotted with necropoli, but its current form dates from 1477 when the Bishop of Orvieto, Giorgio della Rovere, had the castle built that bears his name. It's not far from here to **Lago di Bolsena** in the region of Lazio, where outfits like **La Spiaggetta** (Viale Cardorna, ☎ 0761-798536, mmasi@pelagus.it) offer pedallo, jet ski, banana boat and parasailing on the lake.

Lago di Corbara occupies just some of the 20,000-acre **Parco Fluviale del Tevere** (Tiber River Regional Nature Park, Baschi, ☎/fax 0744-950732, www.umbriaparchi.it), a popular **walking** and **bird-watching** destination for the buzzards, sparrow hawks and kites that can be sighted here. It's only a short trip through the park from Baschi to **Montecchio**, one of the best-preserved towns in the territory and beautifully located under the Monte Croce di Serra (999 m/3,277 feet). Hiking **trails** take you up both this and the slightly smaller Citernella (880 m/2,886 feet) and a nature trail leads into the **Area Archeologica Vallone San Lorenzo** (Archeological Area of San Lorenzo), where you can visit the pre-Roman necropolis of San Lorenzo and the seventh-century BC tombs of the Copio. **Pro Loco di Montecchio** (Montecchio Tourist Office, ☎ 0744-951443) offers guided "ecological" walks though the town and surrounding countryside.

Lago di Alviano, still part of the Tiber River Regional Natural Park, is a WWF Oasis (Loc. Madonna del Porto, Guardea, ☎ 0744-903715, Sept-May, 10 am-1 pm,

2 pm-sunset) in its own right. **Birdwatchers** should make the trip for the numerous aquatic birds (herons, cormorants, tufted ducks (right), bitterns and night herons) that make their homes in the alder and willow woods. You can also spot wild geese, kingfishers and black-tailed godwits along the two **nature trails**.

In the Air

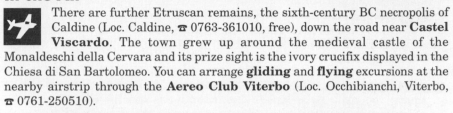

There are further Etruscan remains, the sixth-century BC necropolis of Caldine (Loc. Caldine, ☎ 0763-361010, free), down the road near **Castel Viscardo**. The town grew up around the medieval castle of the Monaldeschi della Cervara and its prize sight is the ivory crucifix displayed in the Chiesa di San Bartolomeo. You can arrange **gliding** and **flying** excursions at the nearby airstrip through the **Aereo Club Viterbo** (Loc. Occhibianchi, Viterbo, ☎ 0761-250510).

GETTING AROUND

ATC (☎ 0744-402900, www.atcterni.it) runs coaches from Orvieto FS to Allerona (four daily, single €2.40), Baschi (seven daily, single €1.60), Castel Giorgio (six daily, single €2), Castel Viscardo (five services daily, single €2), Fabro (one daily, €3.20), Ficulle (four daily, single €2), Montecchio (seven daily, single €1.60), Gabbione (six daily, single €3.20), Monteleone (four daily, single €3.20), Narni (six daily, single €4.80), Parrano (one daily, single €4), Perugia (one daily, single €6), Porano (five daily, single €1.60), Terni (seven daily, single €5.20).

■ Entertainment & Events

Orvieto's summer is livened up by a variety of shows, including **Orvieto Musica e Opera Lirica** (Opera and Lyrical Music Festival, www.orvietomusica.org, contact the tourist office for event information, July) and **Todi Music Fest** (information from Via San Fortunato 5, ☎ 0758-942526, fax 0758-943933; tickets from Teatro Comunale, ☎ 0758-956240, €15-20, conc. €10-15, first week of Sept). Both include live classical performances every night at 9 pm in the Teatro Comunale and the Sala del Consiglio. The biggest event in Orvieto is the **Umbria Jazz Winter** (www.umbriajazz.com, 27 Dec-1 Jan, from €10), which sees the town's streets, squares and theaters taken over by the vibrant and popular festival.

You'll get a taste of everything if you're lucky enough to arrive during **Orvieto con Gusto** (Orvieto with Taste, 4-12 Oct), which sees local products and wines displayed throughout the city streets.

■ Where to Shop

Arts & Crafts

You can't miss the **ceramic** stores that lead off Piazza Duomo and down Corso Cavour, with many, such as **La Torretta** (Corso Cavour 283, ☎ 0763-3440248) decorating, if not producing, the products in-house. For traditional ceramics in the Etruscan style, try **L'Arte del Vasaio** (Via Pedota 3,

☎ 0763-342022, www.viverelumbria.com) and **Cecconi Giuseppe** (Via Duomo 51, ☎ 0763-341214, www.ceramichececconi.it).

The **Associazione Arti e Mestieri dell'Area Orvietana** (Art and Artisan Association of the Orvieto Area, Via Ripa Medici 30, ☎ 0763-301473, fax 0763-390492, www.artiemestieriorvieto.com) and the local tourist board will supply a full list of the artisans working with ceramics, lace, wood, gold, silver and platinum and terracotta in the surrounding area.

Gastronomy

For local produce, including the **fine wine** that has made the area famous, visit **Consorzio Tutela Vino Orvieto Classico e Orvieto** (Orvieto Wine Consortium, Corso Cavour 36, ☎ 0763-343790) or the **Enoteca Regionale in the Palazzo del Gusto** (☎/fax 0763-393529, www.itinera2.net). They will also supply information on visiting the wine producers on the local **wine road**, Strada del Vini Etrusco Romana. Producers closest to Orvieto include **Caredeto Vini** (Loc. Cardeto, Fraz. Sferracavallo, ☎ 0763-341286, fax 0763-344123, www.cardeto.com, Mon-Fri, 8 am-12:30 pm, 2-5 pm, Sat, 9 am-1 pm), **Palazzone** (Loc. Roca Ripesena 68, ☎ 0763-344921, fax 0763-344921, www.palazzone.com, Mon-Sat, 9 am-12:30 pm, 3-6 pm), **Belloro** (Loc. Canale, ☎ 0763-29271, by appointment only) and **Tenuta Le Velette** (Loc. Le Velette, ☎ 0763-29090, fax 0763-29114, tenuta.le.velette@libero.it, Mon-Fri, 8:30 am-6 pm, Sat, 8:30 am-noon).

THE LOCAL VINE

Zesty, fruity and absolutely legendary, the white wine of Orvieto was the favorite of Pope Paul III in the 16th century, and the painter Pinturrichio, who hailed from Perugia, would work only on the condition that he had an unlimited supply. It's available in two straw-colored varieties – Orvieto Abboccato and Orvieto Secco. Production of the wine is traditional and strictly controlled, with the proportions of Tuscan Trebbiano, Verdello and Drupeggio grapes tightly monitored.

You can also visit local producers of **olive oil** (considered some of the best in Italy) by arrangement with **Consorzio Olio Extravergine di Oliva Tipico dei Colli Orvietani** (Orvieto Olive Oil Consortium, Via Filippeschi 26, ☎ 0763-832981). Those closest to the city are **Al Vecchio Frantoio Bartolomei** (Loc. Cagnano 6, Montecchio, ☎ 0744-951395, fax 0744-951655, www.oleificiobartolomei.it) and **Il Frantoio di Giulia** (Strada Comunale, Montecchio, ☎ 0744-951909, www.paginegialle.it/frantoiodigiulia).

For picnic lunches and gastronomic purchases in town, head to **Dai Fratelli** (Via del Duomo 11, ☎ 0763-343965) for its Orvietan specialties such as salami, truffles (from Fabro), pecorino, wine, oil, grappa and local pasta sauces.

■ Where to Eat

LOCAL FLAVORS

Bistecca: Thick steak from the Chianina cattle.
Cappelletti: Little pasta "hats" cooked in a capon broth.
Carbonaretto: Perch from Lago di Piediluco grilled over wood charcoal.
Cinghiale in agrodolce: Sweet and sour wild boar.

Gallina ubriaca: "Drunken chicken" – chicken in white wine sauce.
Gnocchi orvietana: Gnocchi (potato pasta) Orvieto-style, in a spicy tomato sauce with pancetta.
Lumachella: Snail-shaped buns served with ham and cheese.
Massafegate: Sweet or salty pork liver sausages.
Palomba all'amerina: Woodpigeon flavored with drippings.
Pizza di Pasqua: "Easter pizza," a cheesy bread made with parmesan and pecorino (sheep's milk) cheeses.
Tortucce: Fried bread dough.
Umbrichelli all'arabbiata/al funghi/al tartufo: A local hand-rolled pasta served in a spicy/mushroom/truffle sauce.

The picturesque vineyards and olive groves surrounding Orvieto are a sure indication of the quality of this town's wining and dining establishments.

A good central spot for lunch is **Pizzeria Charlie** (Corso Cavour 194, ☎ 0763, 344766, fax 0763-301649, www.argoweb.it/pizzeria_charlie, closed Tues, $), midway between the funicular exit and the city Duomo.

The trattoria that sits above the Poggio della Cava, **La Bottega del Buon Vino** (Via della Cava 26, ☎ 0763-342373, fax 0763-341029, www.pozzodellacava.it, $) offers a tasty and very reasonably priced simple menu of local cuisine.

Osteria Nonnamelia (Via Duomo 25, ☎/fax 0763-342402, www.evodecor.com, closed Mon, $$) is the cutest choice, with wicker chairs, tables with sofas and a mix-and-match feel. Right in the heart of the historical center, the tasty menu ranges from simple pizzas to local delicacies like *umbrichelli al tartufo* (hand-rolled pasta in truffle sauce), *ossobuco orvietano* (braised veal shanks in a spicy sauce) and *agnello all'orvietana* (spicy lamb stew).

Off a side-street of Piazza Popolo, a tiny door leads into the **Trattoria del Moro** (Via San Leonardo 7, ☎/fax 0763-342763, www.argoweb.it/trattoria_delmoro, closed Fri, $$) with its tasty menu of *umbrichelli all'amatriciana* (hand-rolled pasta in spicy tomato sauce with pancetta), *bocconcini di vitello* (veal in cognac sauce), *bistecca* and roasted wild boar.

Trattoria and *enoteca* **La Buca di Bacco** (Corso Cavour 299, ☎/fax 0763-344792, closed Tues, $$) is another good choice for modern versions of local fare, such as *umbrichelli piccanti al tartufo* (spicy pasta with truffles), s*trozzepreti fagioli e pancetta* (beans and ham), *cinghiale alla cacciatore* (wild boar hunter-style) and some fish dishes.

ENOTECHE

If you want a light snack with your wine or just an aperitif, try the light menus of the **Enoteca Regionale** (Piazza San Giovanni 1, ☎/fax 0763-393529, itinera.orvieto@tiscalinet.it, $$), **La Loggia** (Corso Cavour 129, ☎ 0763-341657, fax 0763-344371, elaloggia@tin.it, $$), **Foresi** (Piazza Duomo 2, ☎/fax 0763-341611, www.argoweb.it/cantina_foresi, closed Tues, $), **Orvieto Terra d'Umbria** (Via Duomo 23, ☎/fax 0763-343074, $$) or **Tozzi** (Piazza Duomo 13, ☎ 0763-344393, $$).

I Sette Consoli (Piazza Sant'Angelo 1a, ☎/fax 0763-343911, mstopp@tin.it, closed Wedsnesday, $$$) is the classiest and most traditional choice in town. Its menu offers *piccione nostrano arrosto e gattò di patate* (roasted local pigeon stuffed with potato) and *tortelli ai trippa al pecorino romano e mentuccia* (tortelli stuffed with tripe and pecorino).

Traveling Alone? Try a Cooking Course

A single friend of mine has spent years bemoaning the fact that she does not now have summer vacations. The idea of traveling solo hadn't even crossed her mind. But just because you fly out alone doesn't necessarily mean that you will vacation alone, as I found out on a cooking holiday in the Tolfa Mountains, near Lago di Bolsena, with **Flavours of Italy** (lorne@flavoursholidays.com, www.flavoursholidays.com, £599/$1,069 per person, all meals, wines and transportation included except flights).

The best, and in my case, riskiest, part of any cooking vacation is that you all chip in and cook for each other. There are no recipes for one; no separate ovens or hotplates; and you don't cook four recipes in the morning only to have to eaten them tepid at lunch. Flavours of Italy is all about teamwork, fine wines and, if it all goes according to plan, fine food. All in all, it's the perfect vacation choice for the gourmand singleton.

Friendships are made and, better still, not broken over lunch preparation the first full day. We stood, slightly nervous, in our Flavours' aprons, hands washed, notebook in hand, waiting for the head chef to appear. She turned out to be a lovely local woman, Anna, and most of the simple yet tasty dishes that we prepared were her's, passed down from her mother or grandmother.

It was a gentle and traditional introduction to the art of cooking, specializing in Italian regional food that you can recreate at home (the ingredients weren't of the elusive kind that you can't buy outside of Italy). Watched over by Anna's eagle eyes, we mixed and rolled the pasta base on our wooden boards, cut it into lasagne shapes, and inundated her with questions.

Unless there is enough ingredient preparation to go round, tasks are divided among the cooks on a voluntary basis. These can range from the mundane (beating eggs for the *ciambellone* or sponge, mashing potatoes for the *gnocchi*) to the visceral (kneading the pizza dough, rolling the veal meatballs), but all are accompanied by Anna's words of advice and encouragement and some aperitif-induced banter; it's all very good fun and, perhaps surprisingly, the results were very tasty!

■ Where to Stay

Historical Center

 You'll find some of the best-priced hotel rooms in town through the stately entrance foyer of the recently restored **Aquila Bianca** ☆☆☆☆ (Via Garibaldi 13, ☎ 0763-341246, fax 0763-342273, www.argoweb.it/hotel_aquilabianca, $$$). The best cheap option is at **Corso** ☆☆☆ (Corso Cavour 343, ☎/fax 0763-342020, www.argoweb.it/hotel_corso, $$), home to a lovely stone terrace with views over medieval rooftops and some simple but comfortably decorated rooms.

Palazzo Piccolomini ☆☆☆ (☎ 0763-341743, fax 0763-391046, www.hotelpiccolomini.it, $$$) is very reasonably priced given its beautiful architecture and lovely modern whitewashed rooms with their interesting wrought-iron bed frames.

The narrow terrace of **Maitani** ☆☆☆ (Via Lorenzo Maitani 5, ☎/fax 0763-342011, www.argoweb.it/hotel_maitani, $$$$) offers some great views over the Duomo, while its color-themed rooms live up to the star rating.

Out of Town

The best hotels are **Allerona** (I Ginepri, Loc. Spiagge, ☎ 0763-628020, fax 0763-629548, www.iginepri.it, $$$), **Baschi** (Villa Bellago ☆☆, Pian delle Monache, Lago di Corbara, ☎ 0744-950521, fax 0744-950524, www.argoweb.it/hotel_villabellago, $$$), **Castel Viscardo** (La Pergoletta a Castello ☆☆, Via della Piazzetta 20, ☎/fax 0763-361071, www.lapergoletta.net, $$) and **San Venanzo** (Tulliola ☆☆, Loc. Ospedaletto, ☎/fax 075-8709147, www.umbriatravel.com/hoteltulliola/in, $$).

There are also some good *affitacamere* at Baschi – **Casal Italia** (Via Italia 51, Fraz. Civitella del Lago, ☎ 0744-950178, fax 0744950455, www.primitaly.it/bb/casalitalia, $) and **Aurora** (Via della Chiesa 30, Fraz. Acqualoreto, ☎/fax 0744-958187, www.argoweb.it/bedandbreakfast_aurora, $$).

You can also book into one of the religious institutions accepting guests (monasteries, convents; minimum two days' stay) – **Casa di Accoglienza Religiosa San Lodovico** (Piazza Ranieri 5, ☎ 0763-342255, fax 0763-391380, s.lodovico@tiscalinet.it, $), **Convento San Crispino da Viterbo** (Loc. Cappuccini 8, ☎ 0763-341387, $), **Villa Mercede** (Via Soliana 2, ☎ 0763-341766, fax 0763-340119, villamercede@orvienet.it, $) and **Istituto SS. Salvatore** (Via del Popolo 1, ☎/fax 0763-342910, www.argoweb.it/istitutosansalvatore, $$).

There are two youth hostels – **Porziuncola** (Loc. Cappuccini 8, ☎ 0763-341387, $) and **Foresteria L'Umbra** (Borgo Garibaldi, Ficulle, ☎/fax 0763-86143, $$). As for campgrounds, there is **Orvieto** ☆☆ (SS448, Lago di Corbara, ☎/fax 0744-950240, Apr-Sept, 8 spaces, $), **Il Falcone** ☆☆ (Loc Vallonganino 2a, Civitella del Lago, Baschi, ☎/fax 0744-950249, www.paginegialle.it/ilfalcone, Apr-Sept, 36 spaces, $), **Scacco Matto** ☆ (Lago di Corbara, SS448, Baschi, ☎ 0744-950163, fax 0744-950373, $) and **Erbadoro** (Loc. Farnietino, Monteleone, ☎/fax 0763-835241, May-Oct, $).

Outside of Orvieto

■ Todi

Tear yourself away from Orvieto if you can and head across the Tiber River Regional Natural Park to the beautifully preserved town of Todi. On its main square, Piazza del Popolo – one of the most beautiful in Italy – a break in one of the pretty caffès offers the chance to soak up the great view over the city Duomo, palazzi and surrounding countryside.

Orvieto & SW Umbria

Getting Here & Around

By Train: Frequent trains (☎ 848-888088, www.trenitalia.it) run from Florence to Perugia (Ponte San Giovanni station), where the private **Ferrovia Centrale Umbra** (☎ 0755-75401, www.fcu.it) runs services to Todi. From Spoleto, take the train to Terni and transfer onto the same line. Todi Ponte Rio station is linked to the historical center by a shuttle bus.

By Bus: ATC (☎ 0744-492711, www.atcterni.it) services link Todi with Terni, **SSIT** (☎ 0742-670746, www.spoletina.com) with Spoleto, and **SULGA** (☎ 0755-053733, www.sulga.it) and **APM** (☎ 0755-06781, www.apmperugia.it) with Perugia. The buses drop off at two terminals in town: Piazza della Consolazione and Piazza Jacopone.

By Car: Todi is just off Umbria's central highway, the **E45**, which links to the **A1 Autostrada** near Perugia. From Orvieto, you can arrive via the **SS79bis** or the quicker but less scenic **SS448**. There is free parking south of the Porta Romana and behind Santa Maria della Consolazione.

By Taxi: You can call find taxis on **Piazza Garibaldi** (☎ 0758-942375) and **Piazza Jacopone** (☎ 0758-942525).

Information Sources

Tourist Offices: There are two tourist information points in Todi, the main **IAT del Tuderte** (Piazza Umberto 5-6, ☎ 0758-943395, fax 0758-942406, www.umbria2000.it), which serves the city and its surroundings, and the smaller **Pro Todi** (Via Condotti 5, ☎ 0758-943933).

Sightseeing

Start your walk at the far south of town. The entrance to the historical center is marked here by the calm splendor of the **Tempio di Santa Maria della Consolazione** (☎ 349-8392338, Apr-Oct, 9 am-1 pm, 2:30-6 pm, Oct-Mar, 10 am- 12:30 pm, 2:30-6 pm, closed Tues). This is one of the finest Renaissance creations of Cola di Matteuccio – and a rare example of Renaissance architecture in a town that is otherwise very much medieval in look and feel. Characterized by the five elegant and majestic domes that have crowned the building since around 1607, the door leads you into a majestic and luminous interior that houses a series of sculptures of the Apostles, culminating with the larger statue of Pope Martino I, added after the plague of 1630.

Heading north toward the center of town, the winding Viale della Serpentina takes you up to **Parco della Rocca**, from where a network of paths lead you up to the summit of the 411-m (1,348-foot) hill with its great views over the town center. Head back along the Via della Rocca – past a stretch of the original Etruscan-Roman wall – to pick up the access road to the beautifully decorated façade of the **Tempio di San Fortunato** (☎ 0758-944106, Apr-Oct, 9 am-12:30 pm, 3-7 pm, closed Mon am, Nov-Mar, 9:30 am-12:30 pm, 3-5 pm, closed Mon). This is the famous home to the remains of the Franciscan poet, Jacopone da Todi and the second-largest religious construction in Umbria. It's situated atop a fine stairway. A church has existed on this site since 1000 AD (the present building was rebuilt in the 15th century) and the two lions, which stand beside the entrance are thought to be from that time. The complex includes an imposing Gothic bell tower and the convent, which includes the **Chiostro di San Fortunato** (Cloister of St

Fortunato) with its elegant single-nave interior and finely carved choir stalls that date to the 14th century. In its crypt you will find the relics of the patron saint, San Fortunato, and the tomb of Jacopone. There's a further monument to him just outside the church on the entrance to Piazza Jacopone, but before you head here, take the steep Via di San Fortunato – past balconies covered in ivy and geraniums – in the direction of Porta Marzia (Marzia Gate) and the town's best-preserved medieval quarter.

Go left along Corso Cavour to the **Nicchioni Romani,** four Roman vaults 11 m (36 feet) high, whose origins and purpose are still shrouded in mystery. On the other side of the road, a small square leads to the **Fontana Cesia** (or "della Rua"), which was commissioned for the city by Bishop Angelo Cesi in 1606; it is his family's coat of arms on the fountain design.

Take a right off the square to arrive back on Piazza Jacopone, where Via Mazzini leads you up past the Teatro Comunale (the Municipal Theater, designed by Carlo Gatteschi in 1876, ☎ 0758-942206) to the marvelous **Piazza del Popolo**, the heart of Todi since Roman times, and the focal point of the town's major sites. The **Duomo,** dates back to the early 12th century when the delicate façade decorations were added to the cross-shaped walls. But if you think the exterior is beautiful, the interior, shown above, is even more so, embellished with classic sculptures, majestic paintings and splendid stained-glass windows, including the magnificent central rose window that was added in the 16th century. (Cathedrale di Santa Maria Annuziata, Cathedral, ☎ 0758-943041, Mar-Oct, 8:30 am-12:30 pm, 2:30-6:30 pm, Nov-Feb, 8:30 am-4:30 pm, entry to the crypt, €0.80.)

Rising opposite the cathedral, the **Palazzo dei Priori** was built in 1334 to house the priors and governors of the town, although its windows and bell tower were added over two centuries later. The nearby Gothic **Palazzo del Capitano** was constructed at the end of the 13th century in Italian Gothic style with an imposing ground-level portico. These days it marks the entrance to the **Museo Civico e Pinacoteca,** which contains Etruscan, Roman and medieval finds from in and around Todi, including pottery, coins, statues, and interesting frescoes and paintings from the 15th to 17th centuries (Civic Museum and Picture Gallery, ☎/fax 0758-944148, Apr-Aug, 10:30 am-1 pm, 2:30-8 pm, Mar/Sept, 10:30 am-1pm, 2-5 pm, Oct-Feb, 10 am-1 pm, 2-6:30 pm, €3.10, conc. €1.55).

Connected to the Palazzo del Capitano by a large staircase, the Gothic-Lombard **Palazzo del Popolo** (Palace of the People) is one of the oldest medieval buildings in Todi. It was built from 1214 on, when it was known as "Comune Vecchio," to house the Priors and then Pope Gregorio IX, before being transformed into a theater in the late 18th century. Its ground floor is characterized by a graceful portico overlooked by four-light mullioned windows, and, to the side, a 14th-century bell tower. Continue round to Piazza Garibaldi, to its side, for a wonderfully panoramic view; from here you can duck down to the Fontane di Scannabecco (Fountain of Scannabecco), which took its name in 1241 from a former Podestà of Todi.

The road leads north from here to the graceful red and white strips on the façade of **Chiesa di Santa Prassede** or south to the little Romanesque **Chiesa di San**

Illario, which was formerly Todi's cathedral. From the latter it's only a quick hop back up through Porta Marzia to reach the **Chiesa di Santa Maria in Camuccia** (☎ 0758-943120, daily, 9:30 am-12:30 pm, 3-6 pm), a Dominican convent with an attached church that contains an old and valuable wooden statue of the saint.

You have to go beyond the city walls to see the 16th-century **Tempio del Crocifisso** through Porta Romana and the **Convento di Montesanto**, reached via a long tree-lined avenue through the remains of Porta Orvietana. The latter is a fortified former convent complex, which includes an interesting 15th-century church, an enchanting convent and a large library (now used for exhibitions and conventions).

Adventures Out of Town

 Canoe trips along the River Tiber start at nearby Pontecuti. To arrange a session along the river, contact **Centro Canoistico di Pontecuti** (Pontecuti Canoe Center, Via di Mezzo Muro 5, Todi, ☎ 0758-943221).

The **Associazione Gruppo Speleologico** (Caving Group Association, same address, ☎ 347-3162381) who can take you **caving** and **potholing** at the Grotta del Chiocchio at Castagnata Cupa in the Monti Martani.

Ensconced in the center of Umbria, the territory of Todi holds an almost forgotten rural charm. It's a land of Etruscan and Roman ruins, medieval churches, Renaissance palazzi and landscapes of rare beauty, all framed by the adventure-rich Monti Martani to the east, and the Lago di Corbara and the Parco Fluviale del Tevere to the west. The River Tiber divides the territory into two parts. On the right bank is Monte Castello di Vibio, Fratta Todina and Marsciano; on the left is Collazzone, Massa Martana and Collevalenza.

Take the SS397 north out of town along the right bank first to arrive at **Monte Castello di Vibio**. Although of Etruscan origin, this town grew to its present form under the rule of the Vibia family, one of the most important dynasties in the area. Its major sight – apart from the splendid views over the entire Tiber Valley between Perugia and Orvieto – is the beautifully frescoed **Teatro della Concordia** (Piazza del Teatro 4, ☎ 0758-780737, fax 0758-780217, teatropiccolo@cronos.it, Apr-Oct, 10 am-12:30 pm, 4-7:30 pm, Nov-Mar, 10 am-12:30 pm, 3:30-6:30 pm). Built in 1808, it is one of the smallest theaters in the world, with only 30 stalls in the auditorium. Be sure to reserve well ahead if you want to get a seat.

You can pick up three **treks** out of town to explore the surrounding green of the wooded hills and the lovingly tended fields. One takes you north (four miles) along the banks of the River Faena; a second longer itinerary (six miles) heads south instead into the Parco Fluviale del Tevere; and the third trail (eight miles) leads to Santa Maria Monte via Doglio (the trail should be picked up south of Monte Castello di Vibio at Pianicoli). This last trail is also suitable for **mountain bikers**.

If you want to try **horseback riding** (or even **archery**), contact **Agrincontri** (Santa Maria Apparita, Fraz. Doglio, ☎ 0758-749610). They also rent out rooms on an *agriturismo* basis.

Fratta Todina should be your next stop (tourist information, ☎ 0758-745304, www.commune.frattatodina.pg.it). High on a hill overlooking the confluence of the Faena and the Tiber, it may be one of the smallest towns in Umbria, but it still preserves a huge section of the castle walls, a 17th-century Palazzo Vescovile (Bishop's Palace) and, just outside of town, an impressive Franciscan convent

(Convento di Santa Maria della Spineta) built in 1348. It is from the latter that you can pick up a variety of **trails** into the Monti del Peglia via pleasant medieval villages such as Montione and San Cassiano.

The final stop on the right bank is **Marsciano**, the castle remains of an old fiefdom that once controlled the fertile hinterland of vine, olive, wheat and sunflower fields, surrounded by holm-oak woods and occasional stretches of scrub. The valley of River Fersinone is your best bet for **nature walks**; the softly-flowing brook is overlooked by picturesque hilltop villages such as Morcella, Monte Vibiano and Migliano. **Bicycles** can be rented from Saccarelli Lucio (Via Tuderte, ☎ 0758-743421). But before you head into the wilderness, take some time to visit near Cerqueto, where the village parish church preserves a fresco of *St Sebastian* (around 1478), which is considered to be the first work of Perugino.

Cross over to the left bank of the Tiber to return to Todi via **Collazzone**, a small scenic village 500 m (1,640 feet) up on a hilltop overlooking woods of oak, pine and olive trees. It guards perfectly preserved medieval walls and a warren of narrow alleyways. The Romanesque **Convento di San Lorenzo**, shown at right, is the village's main sight; it was the last shelter of Jacopone da Todi, who died here on Christmas night in 1306.

Immersed in a beautiful countryside of hills and thick woods, Collazzone is a great destination for **hikers**, with a variety of sign-posted itineraries taking you around the area's flora and fauna, its ancient mineral industry and fortified castles and towers.

At the foot of the Monti Martani, which looms up 1,000 m (3,280 feet) above the town, **Massa Martana** offers by far the richest **hiking** territory around Todi. Easily accessed from town, these are glorious hills of peaceful holm oak and pine woods, dotted with ancient medieval castles and crumbling churches. You can arrange **horseback riding** through **Centro Ippico Perticara Horses** (Loc. Perticara, ☎ 0758-89506, May-Oct). The town itself is one of the most important in the region with two 13th-century pilgrimage centers (Chiesa di Santa Maria in Pantano and the Abbazia di San Faustino), the Roman remains of the Ponte Fonnaia (Fonnaia Bridge) and the only known catacombs in Umbria.

SPA BREAKS

*The **Terme di San Faustino** (Loc. Villa San Faustino, ☎/fax 0758-856421, www.sanfaustino.it, all year) has been attracting visitors for centuries to Massa Martana for its earthy spring waters renowned for their curative effects on intestinal and kidney complaints.*

The **Santuario di Collevalenza** (Sanctuary of Collevalenza) stands almost ghost-like on a hilltop just to the south of Massa Martana. Designed by the Madrid architect Giulio Lafuente in 1965, it is one of the most important examples of modern architecture in Italy.

Orvieto & SW Umbria

■ Terni

Terni is a predominantly modern town, made easy to explore by the wide, tree-lined avenues (Corso Tacito, Corso Vecchio, Via Roma and Via Cavour) that remain from the original Roman street plan. These are linked by a network of alleyways that lead to the major sights, including the important Roman remains. The local area has some of Italy's wildest natural areas with Cascade delle Marmore (Marmore Waterfall), Lago di Piediluco, and the Amerino and Valnerina areas offering the best watersports and hikes.

SIGHTSEEING & ADVENTURES EN ROUTE TO TERNI

You can approach Terni from Todi along the busy E45 (SS3bis) or the quieter SS79. Whichever you choose, you'll soon meet signs for the popular spa town of **Acquasparta**. Beautifully situated on top of a hill overlooking the lush Terni countryside, this hydrothermal resort has been popular as far back as Roman times, when it took its name from the Latin *ad aquas partas* ("by the springs"). The town preserves a large section of the medieval walls and the 16th-century Palazzo Cesi, which was built by Giovanni Domenico Bianchi, and once housed Galileo Galilei. To book into the spa, contact **Terme Amerino** (☎ 0744-943622, fax 0744-943921, www.amerino.com, May to Oct).

There's a mineral water spring at **San Gemini**, and the road that leads to it offers plenty of points to stop and take a free sip as water gurgles out of the ground. The third-century city of **Carsula** is a short drive away, with ruins still providing a visible guide. It once controlled this section of the Via Flaminia, an important communication road that joined Rome to the Adriatic Sea, and this importance can be seen in the grandeur still evident in the remains of its forum, basilica, twin temples, amphitheater and necropolis.

The small town of **San Gemini** is also on the Via Flaminia, but more medieval than Roman in design. It is these days a popular spa destination (**Terme di San Gemini e Fabia**, Via Fonte, San Gemini Fonte, ☎ 0744-630482, fax 0744-3308400, www.sangemini.it, May to Oct). You can learn more about it in the **Museum Laboratory of Earth Science** (Via della Misericordia 1, ☎/fax 0753-1293, ww.sisetmamuseo.it) and can book a tour to the stalagmites and stalactites in the **cave** from where the spring erupts (☎ 333-4715057, gianluigimonaldi@libero.it).

Closest to Terni, **Cesi** is another Roman village situated in a stunning natural location – this time on the slopes of Mt. Eolo in the southernmost part of the Martani mountain chain. But, whereas Carsulae almost died out in the Middle Ages, Cesi went on to prosper when it became the capital of the feudal land of Arnolfi. It was this role that saw the construction of its sturdy town walls, defensive town houses – many of which still preserve their "trap door" methods of resistance and escape – and luxury palazzi. It is a town well-placed for **hikes** into the nearby mountain chain, with a pleasant afternoon stroll possible to the parish church on the slopes of Monte St Erasmo and more difficult trails taking you up Monte Torre Maggiore (1,120 m/3,674 feet) and Monte Torricella (1,054 m/3,457 feet). You can also explore the interior of these mountains with the **Gruppo Speleologico Terre Arnolfe** (Arnolfe's Land Caving Group, Via C. Stocchi 3, ☎ 0744-244396).

Getting Here & Around

Forty-four kilometers (27 miles) south of Todi via **SS3bis** (E45), Terni can also be reached by **train** (☎ 848-888088, www.trenitalia.it) on the Ancona-to-Rome line; change at Orte if arriving from Florence. **ATC** (☎ 0744-492711) run **buses** throughout the territory. You can **rent cars** in town from **Avis** (Via XX Settembre 80, ☎ 0744-287170, www.avisautonoleggio.com).

Information Sources

Tourist Offices: The main **Servizio Turistico Associatio del Ternano** (Terni Tourist Office) is on Viale C. Battisti 5 (☎ 0744-423047, fax 0744-427259, www.iat.terni.it). They provide information on sightseeing in the city of Terni and the surrounding towns of Aquasparta, Arrone, Calvi dell'Umbria, Ferentillo, Montefranco, Narni, Otricoli, Polino, San Gemini and Stroncone. For information on sightseeing and adventures in the Amerino, contact **Servizio Turistico Territoriale IAT dell'Amerino** (Amerino Tourist Office, Via Orvieto 1, Amelia, ☎ 0744-981453, fax 0744-981566, www.iat.amelia.tr.it).

Sightseeing

At the confluence of the Nera and the Serra rivers, Terni sits in a beautiful natural amphitheater surrounded by green hills. A modern town much rebuilt after destruction in the last war, Terni may be best known these days for its patron saint, St Valentine, but it also has plenty of Roman remains and pretty little churches.

RIDOLFIAN TERNI

The architect Ridolfi is to be thanked for Terni's modern look and feel. He designed the spacious Piazza Tacito, Largo Villa Gloria and the Piazza and Corso del Popolo. Walk on to the end of the latter and you'll see the obelisk, *Lancia di Luce*, sculpted by Arnaldo Pomodoro.

Start your tour of the historic center on Piazza San Francesco next to the pretty church of the same name and head along Via Fratini to Piazza Duomo, home of the **Cattedrale di Sant Maria Assunta**. Although restructured in the 17th century, the cathedral has a fine portal dating back to the late 12th century. A short walk from here and you'll arrive at the remains of the **Anfiteatro Romano** (Roman Amphitheater), built in 32 AD – along with the ruins at Caesalue, one of the most important archeological remains in the territory.

From here, Via Roma will take you past the medieval Torre Barbarasa and onto **Palazzo Spada**, a massive two-storey family residence with a mezzanine, thought to have been Antonio da Sangallo il Giovanne's last work (before he died in Terni in 1546). Nearby is the beautiful little **Chiesa di San Salvatore**. This unusual church is in fact a combination of two adjacent buildings – one, circular, from the fifth century, and the other, rectangular, built next to it in the 12th century.

In Piazza della Repubblica you'll see the **Palazzo Comunale** (Town Hall), now seat of the town library, which was rebuilt to its original Renaissance design in the 19th century after World War II bombardments. Take Corso Vecchio to Piazza Carrara to reach the Augustinian **Chiesa di San Pietro**, with its marvelous

Orvieto & SW Umbria

apses and stunning Gothic portal, and the **Chiesa di San Lorenzo**, which stands on its original 13th-century foundations, although the naves were mostly restored in the post-war years.

Adventures

Terni is well placed for **hikes** into the **Parco Regionale della Fiume Nera** (Nera River Regional Nature Park. Find out about itineraries before you go by visiting their headquarters in Terni (Via Plinio il Giovanne 21, ☎ 0744-484239, fax 0744-484255, www.umbriaparchi.it). The town also has its own branch of the **CAI** (Club Alpino Italiano, Via Fratelli Cervi 31, ☎ 0744-286500) who arranges **hikes**, **caving, potholing** and **rock climbing** in the area. Further rock climbing is available from **Explore** (Via San Valentino 10, Terni, ☎ 339-2091107).

There is one **horseback riding** school just outside of the city – **Marinelli Luigi** (Loc. La Selva 17, ☎ 0744-241866, open all year); many more can be found at Montefranco, Amelia and Narni.

You can arrange **canoe** trips along the Nera River through **Gruppo Canoe di Terni** (Via Tiacci 6, ☎ 0744-407235, fax 0744-407134, gruppocanoeterni@libero.it).

■ The Valnerina

The Valnerina, "Umbria's green heart," is an adventure sports paradise: a mix of high and low land; rock and waterways; historic and artistic monuments. There is lots of sightseeing to attract your attention in between the hiking, cycling, rock climbing, rafting and other activities. The area includes the **Cascade Marmore** (the Marmore Falls), at 165 m (541 feet), the highest waterfall in Europe, the **Parco Regionale Fiume Nera** (Nera River Regional Park) and, to the south, **Lago di Piediluco** (Piediluco Lake).

While you're exploring, take time to visit the ancient suburb of **Collestatte** with its Romanesque belltower, the pretty little medieval town of **Piediluco**, dominated by its 11th-century Rocca, the fortified suburbs of **Arrone** and **Ferentillo**, the picturesque hilltop village of **Montefranco** and the Benedictine Abbazia di **San Pietro in Valle**, one of the most important medieval constructions of the Duchy of Spoleto.

THE MARMORE FALLS

In a beautiful natural setting, the Marmore Falls are actually man-made. They are the result of a Roman canal dug in 290 BC to move the stagnant waters of the Velino River into the Rieti Valley. You can visit the falls from 11 am-1 pm and 4-9 pm.

Adventures

On Foot & on Wheels

This legendary valley is crammed full with beautiful and easy-going nature walks, hikes and mountain bike trails. Kompass 1:50,000 map #644 *Gubbio-Fabriano* and #663 *Perugia-Assisi* provide details of the way-marked trails and mule tracks into the valley from Collestatte, Piediluco, Arrone, Ferentillo and Montefranco.

From the Parco Regionale della Fiume Nera you can pick up a three-day walking trail into the Monti Sibillini. And south from Terni at Stroncone, a variety of hikes and mountain bike routes lead into the *prati* (meadows), a vast elevated plateau (1,050 m/3,444 feet elevation) with breathtaking views toward Terni. A 17-km/11-mile mountain bike itinerary runs between Ferentillo and Terni.

On Horseback

A horseback riding center in Montefranco arranges trailrides throughout the year; contact **Club Eques 90** (Via della Forcella 2, ☎ 033-0646877).

On Water

Rafting is good near the Marmore Falls along two miles of the Nera River's fastest flowing and rockiest stretch, with easier options available farther into the regional park around Ferentillo and Arrone. The main canoe and **rafting** center for the Nera River is at Collestatte (**Centro Canoe e Rafting Le Marmore**, Loc. Tiro a Segno 19, ☎/fax 0686-212249, http://raftingmarmore.com), but canoe rental is also available farther up the river at Ferentillo (**Pangea**, Via Santa Valeria 2, ☎/fax 0630-887490). There's more rafting just across the border into the territory of Spoleto at **Scheggino** (☎ 333-4715057, gianluigimonaldi@libero.it); the same organization offers rafting at Arrone and **canyoning** trips around Ferentillo and Montefranco.

To arrange canoe rental on **Lago di Piediluco,** contact **Circolo Canottieri Piediluco** (Via della Pace tra I Popoli, Piediluco, ☎/fax 0744-368521). For **sailing**, contact **Circolo Velico** (Via Noceta, ☎ 0744-368266, www.trasinet.com/cvc).

On Snow

There are a few ski runs and a three-mile cross-country run at **Polino**; for information, contact the **Servizio Turistico Associatio del Ternano** (Viale C. Battisti 5, ☎ 0744-423047, fax 0744-427259, www.iat.terni.it).

On Rock

In Ferentillo, **Valnerina Verticale Sport** (Piazza V. Emanuele 9, ☎/fax 0744-244481) runs guided rock-climbing tours and gives lessons.

In the Air

 You can go **bungee jumping** on Arrone's Canale di Rosciano bridge. Contact **AS Jump Marmore** (Ponte Canale di Rosciano, Arrone, ☎/fax 0744-228105, www.comtel.it/bungee) to arrange a spectacular river jump.

■ The Amerino & Amelia

A lush green valley between the Tiber and Nera rivers, the Amerino is a striking landscape of ilex groves, vineyards, olive groves and chestnut forests centered around one of the most ancient of all Umbrian towns, **Amelia**. Commanding the Tiber Valley from within its fourth-century BC polygonal town walls, the ancient city is packed with interesting Roman and medieval remains.

Getting to Amelia: There are frequent **bus** services to Amelia from Orte train station (Tomassorri, ☎ 0744-428427, four return services daily), Narni (ATC, ☎ 0744-978260, hourly services) and Terni (ATC, hourly services).

Sightseeing

You enter the city through the **Porta Romana** (Roman Gate), which leads you to the 13th-century **Chiesa di San Francesco** (Church of St Francis), in whose cloister can be found the **Museo Archeologico** (☎ 0744-978120, Apr-June, Tues-Sun, 10:30 am-1 pm, 4-7 pm, July-Aug, Tues-Sun, 10:30 am-1 pm, 4:30-7:30 pm, €3.60, conc. €2.58), which traces the history of the town from its origins through Roman occupation to the late Middle Ages. Its prize possession is the 15-BC bronze statue of Germanico, which was discovered outside the town walls in 1963.

Porta Romana

If you're interested in Roman remains, the Associazione I Poligonali, they organize guided tours of the **Cisterne Romane**, a network of underground wells built by the Romans some 2,100 years ago. (Roman Cistern, Piazza Matteoti, ☎ 0744-978436, www.ameliasotterranea.it, Apr-Sept, Sat, 4:30-7:30 pm, Sun and holidays, 10:30 am-12:30 pm, 4:30-7:30 pm, Oct-Mar, Sat, 3-6 pm, Sun and holidays, 10:30 am-12:30 pm, 3-6 pm, €2.58, conc. €2.)

Otherwise, the town's main sights are medieval, including impressive noble palaces, such as **Palazzo Farrattini** (visits by arrangement only, ☎ 0744-981453), constructed by Antonio da Sangallo il Giovanne, the 14th-century **Palazzo Nacci** and the 16th-century **Palazzo Pertrignani** (visits by arrangement only, ☎ 0744-976220). The much-reconstructed city **cathedral** (daily, 10 am-noon, 3-6:30 pm) has frescoes by Luigi Fontana and adjacent **Torre Campanaria**, which is still in possession of its original dodecagonal walls first built in 1050 and decorated with allegories of the 12 zodiac signs and 12 apostles.

Adventures

On Foot

 Amelia is surrounded by some prime **hiking** territory with trails criss-crossing the Amerino hill range up to its peak at Monte Croce di Serra (1,000 m/3,280 feet). The best of the trails are in the **Rio Grande Valley** (trips can be organized with Amici del Rio Grande, ☎ 0744-981067); in the **Parco Matttia** near Porchiano del Monte; in the lush stretch between **Fornole and Montecampano**; and in and around **Collicello**, where the short four-mile *percorso verde* (green trail) and longer seven-mile *percorso bleu* (blue trail) take you past the ruins of the Castello di Canale and Convento Benedettino.

More **nature trails** are north of Amelia at the **Foresta Fossile** near Avigliano Umbro (Fossil Forest, Loc. Dunarobba, ☎ 0744-940348, four daily visiting times, 9:30 am, 11:30 am, 3:30 pm and 5:30 pm, €4, conc. €2.58). The guided walk around the trunks – some of which are 2,000 years old – can be followed by a session underground at the **Grotta Bella** (Beautiful Cave, tour departs from Foresta Fossile, ☎ 0744-940348, €3.60, conc. €2). It can be reached via a 20-minute *sentiero natura* (nature trail) through the chestnut forest from Casa Vecchia di Santa Restituta.

Potholing tours to karst formations (such as the Grotta del Fate near Macchia) can be arranged with the **Associazione I Poligonali** (Strada Amelia-Giove, ☎ 0744-983143).

On Wheels

 The best of the region's mountain bike routes are between **Fornole and Montecampano**, and to the north at **Collicello**. Here, a six-mile itinerary (*percorso rosso,* red trail) takes you through some of the region's most attractive natural scenery.

There are three more itineraries to the south at **Penna di Teverina**: a *percorso verde* (green route) of three miles; a *percorso rosso* (red route) of eight miles and a choice of *percorsi gialli* (yellow routes), which link onto the two main itineraries, allowing for longer or shorter routes. You can find out more and pick up maps at **AS Penna** in Bici (☎ 0744-993518, pennainbici@hotmail.com). Bicycles can be hired from **Laudi** (☎/fax 0744-993518, laudi.m@net4free.it).

On Horseback

 To organize horseback riding in the territory, contact **Maneggio San Cristoforo** (Loc. Sambucetole, Strada San Cristoforo 16m, ☎ 0744-98249, open all year), **Maneggio Totano** (Strada di Totano 8, Loc. Montenero, ☎ 0744-978497, open all year), **La Cristalla** (Loc. Toscolano, Avigliano Umbro, ☎ 0744-935018, open all year), **Le Fossate** (Loc. Le Fossate, Giove, ☎/fax 0744-992606, Feb-Dec, closed Mon) or **Umbria Resort** (Loc. Il Casaletto, Fraz. Castel dell'Aquila, Montecastrilli, ☎ 0744-935255, fax 0744-935508, www.discoveryitaly.com).

■ Narni & the South

A small hilltop village in the almost exact geographical center of Italy, Narni is only a very short trip along the Nera River from Terni. It sits in a rugged landscape of scrub, Jerusalem pines, oaks, hornbeams and maples, with outstanding views over the Nera River valley and the wide plain of Terni (Conca Ternana), all of which prove the ideal environment for a close encounter with nature.

Getting to Narni

Narni has a **train** station on the Rome-to-Ancona train line; change onto this line at Orte if arriving from Florence. The station is a little way out of town, but is linked by a frequent shuttle bus. Narni can quickly be reached by **car** from Terni along the **SS204**. You can rent cars in town at **Binnella** (Str. Calvese 40, ☎ 0744-796306), **DE.MA. Autonoleggio** (Via Tuderte 8, ☎/fax 0744-733972) or **Liberati** (Loc. Castelvecchio 6, Narni Scalo, ☎ 0744-743229).

Sightseeing

Found in the narrow gorge of the Nera River and dominated by the brooding Fortezza dell'Albornoz, Narni grew up in importance with the construction of the Via Flaminia from Rome to Rimini. The Romans also left the 27 BC **Ponte di Augusto** (Augusto Bridge); it was built to link the Via Flaminia with Carsulae. The town was favored by the Papal State in the Middle Ages, and much of its most picturesque architecture – small stone houses, arched roads, wide piazzi and brick towers –

Ponte di Augusto

remains from this time. It also heralded an era of busy artistic development as a school of painting and gold-smithery grew up and reached its peak in the Renaissance when artists such as Rossellino, Ghiriandaio, Gozzoli, Vecchietta, Antoniazzo Romano and Spagna were commissioned to produce works for local patrons. You can see some of their work in the 12th-century **Cattedrale di San Giovenale**, on Piazza Cavour, and the 13th-century **Palazzo dei Priori** (Town Hall), which is formed from three medieval tower houses and flanked by a beautiful loggia.

NARNI IN FICTION

Some believe that CS Lewis discovered his fictional Narnia as a child when he came across a mention of the Roman colony of Narnia, which stood where the town of Narni is today. The argument is fueled by a visit to the town, where you'll find adjoining the city cathedral, a shrine to a local saint known as the Blessed Lucy of Narnia (the author's main character).

One of the most interesting tours in town takes you into the subterranean rooms of the antique **Convento di San Domenico**. From this convent cellar, an underground trail leads into a Pre-Romanesque church with frescoes added in the 13th and 15th centuries, the remains of a Roman cistern, a cell decorated with graffiti by prisoners kept here in the Middle Ages, and into the remains of a Roman temple found under the eighth-century Chiesa di San Maria Impensole. From here, you can also access the subterranean remains of the Roman aqueduct Formina, a medieval cistern that stands under Piazza Garibaldi, and tunnels that lead into the San Biagio and Ippolito mountains. The volunteer group **Associazione Culturale Subterranea** (Via San Bernardo 12, ☎ 0744-722292, www.narnisotterranea.it) gives tours.

AN ANCIENT CONTEST

If you're around Narni in the last weekend of April, the **Corsa all'Anello** (the Ring Race) provides a not-to-be-missed insight into local traditions. Originally organized in the Middle Ages to celebrate the town's patron saint, the impressive competition remains as heated as ever, with each contestant attempting to outdo the other by running a spear on horseback through a ring extended from the houses along Via Maggiore.

Adventures

On Foot

An interesting walk out of town will take you to the first-century **Ponte Cardona**, part of the Roman Aqueduct Formina. Along this wooded walk you'll pass the marker indicating the "geographical center of Italy."

In addition to the tours under Narni itself, there's **potholing** and **caving** in the surrounding area with **Associazone Speleologica Italia Centrale** (Via Capitonese 385g, Capitone, ☎/fax 0744-730087) and **La Mongolfiera** (Via del Parco 27, Narni, ☎ 0744-737535, fax 0744-751976, www.lamongolfiera.net).

On Wheels

It's worth making your way on bicycle from Vigne di Narni to **Calvi dell'Umbria**. This town, known as "the blissful doorway of Umbria," stands on a rocky spur above the border with Lazio, and walks out of town take you into a rocky countryside dotted with temple remains. Another bike trail takes you along the remains of the Via Flaminia to **Otricoli**, another border town. It grew in importance in the Roman era and the remains of their settlement can be visited in Ocriculum, just outside of town.

On Horseback

Horseback riding is offered by **Centro Equestre Federale Il Viburno** (Via Capitonese 341, Capitone di Narni, ☎ 0744-730086, open all year) or **Scoccione Rolando** (Strada di Borgaria 6, Vigne di Narni, ☎ 0744-715224, open all year, closed Mon).

■ Where to Eat

Terni has a few good restaurants. **Il Melograno** (Via Bramante 2, ☎ 0744-300375, fax 0744-300414, www.gardenhotelterni.it, $$) and **Oste della Mal'Ora** (Via Tre Archi 5, ☎/fax 0744-06683, vinovip@libero.it, $$) are two I would recommend.

Orvieto & SW Umbria

A variety of restaurants in Todi serve the handmade pasta, cold meats, game and grilled meats for which the territory is known. Try **Antica Hosteria de la Valle** (Via A. Ciuffelli 19, ☎ 0758-944848, closed Mon, $$) for the closest homemade feel. Just out of town, **Trattoria Cibocchi** (Fraz. Pontemartino 67, ☎ 0758-942949, closed Wed, $$) offers a great selection of the local wine, Grechetto di Todi. **Ristorante Il Donatello** (Piazza del Mercato Vecchio, ☎ 0758-942444, closed Sun, $$$) has one of the most atmospheric locations.

DINING PRICE CHART	
Price per person for an entrée, including house wine & cover.	
$	Under €20
$$	€21-€40
$$$	€41-€60
$$$$	Over €60

If you want something light, there are a wide variety of cheap and cheerful *pizzerie* and *tavole calde* in town: **Il Capestio** (Via G. Matteotti 120, ☎ 0758-943957, closed Mon, $), **La Ruoita** (Via G. Matteotti 166, ☎ 0758-944049, closed Tues, $) and **Pizzeria Piero e Silvana** (Via G. Matteotti 97, ☎ 0758-944633, clods Wed, $$) are all within walking distance of one another.

Out in Marsciano, there's a lovely light fish menu at **Lo Scoglio del Pescatore** (Via Lenin 26, ☎ 0758-748749, closed Tues, $) and tasty more sophisticated fare at **Al Menestrello** (Fraz. Migliano, ☎ 0758-70121, $$$), with booking necessary.

The best table in and around Massa Martana is in the abbey at **San Faustino** (Loc. San Faustino, ☎ 0758-856421, closed Mon, $$), but there's also quality fare in town at **Gallo Antico** (Via XXV Aprile, ☎ 0758-89931, closed Tues, $$), as well as a fine wine list.

TRUFFLE HUNTING

The **Parco Regional Fiume Nera** in the Valnerina is another of Umbria's important black truffle centers. Watch for the precious black truffles in dishes all over the region between November and March.

In and around **Amelia**, try **Anita** (Via Roma, ☎ 0744-982146, closed Mon, $) or **Da Emma** (Loc. Montenero, ☎ 0744-882462, closed Tues, $) for typical Amerino dishes, especially game. Up in **Avigliano Umbro**, you can get tasty *agnello tartufato* (truffle-stuffed lamb) and *pollo alla cacciatore* (hunter-style chicken) in the intimate **La Casareccia** (Strada di Pian dell'Ara 69a, ☎ 0744-933482, closed Mon, $$) or excellent fresh pasta, lamb and wild boar dishes at **Meridiana** (Via Matteotti 35, ☎ 0744-933104, closed Tues $$$).

La Cerquetta (Strada di Streppara 10, ☎ 074-744122, fax 0744-744556, $$) is a good choice in **Narni**.

■ Where to Stay

Todi has five or so three- and four-star hotels. The very reasonable **Villa Luisa** ☆☆☆ (Via A. Cortesi 147, ☎ 0758-948571, fax 0758-948472, www.villaluisa.it, $$) is the luxury budget choice, while **Fonte Cesia** ☆☆☆☆ (Via L. Leoni 3. ☎ 0758-943737, fax 0758-944677, www.fontecesia.it, $$$$) is the best situated.

If you're on a really tight budget, try one of the *affitacamere* just out of town, such as **Casal Lorgnano** (Loc. Torretta 2, Fraz. Lorgnano, ☎/fax 0758-852397, www.holidaysinumbria.com/casallorgnano/i ndex.htm, $) or **Riva del Fascino** (Loc. Pontemartino 67, Fraz. San Giorgio, ☎ 0758-942949, $).

You can also book rooms in the religious centers, such as **Convento di Montesanto** (Viale Montesanto 2, ☎/fax 0758-948886, montesanto@libero.it, $), **Convento Sacro Cuore** (Via Cesia 2, ☎ 0758-942358, fax 0758-943082, www.ofmcappuccini.umbria.it, $$) and, up in Fratta Todina, **Convento Santa Maria della Spineta** (Via Clausura 15, Fraz. Spineta, ☎/fax 0758-745032, $$). The nearest campgrounds are around Terni, Spoleto and Orvieto.

HOTEL PRICE CHART	
Rates are per room with private bath, based on double occupancy, including breakfast.	
$	Under €40
$$	€41-€85
$$$	€86-€140
$$$$	€141-€210
$$$$$	Over €210

If you want an *agriturismo,* Marsciano has **Pala Antonella** (Loc. Molinella 1, Fraz. Mercatello, ☎/fax 0758-783271, $$) and **Torre Colombaia** (Fraz. S. Biagio della Valle, ☎ 0758-787381, www.terracolombaia.it, $$). In Massa Martana there's **Da Giuseppina** (Fraz. Viepri 115, ☎/fax 0758-947429, www.bellaumbria.net/agriturismo-daGiuseppina, $$) and **Orsini Carlo** (Loc. Casa Fanello 238, ☎/fax 0758-89140, www.orsiniagriturismo.it, $$).

In Terni, the budget hotel options are offered by **Villa Laura** ☆ (Strada di Cospea 50, ☎ 0744-812629, $) and **Velino** ☆☆ (Vicolo Pilastri 1, Loc. Marmore, ☎ 0744-67425, fax 0744-67164, $$), but it's not that much more for the more luxurious **Locanda di Colle dell'Oro** ☆☆☆ (Strada di Palmetta 31, ☎ 0744-432379, fax 0744-437826, www.colldelloro.it, $$) or **Valentino** ☆☆☆☆ (Via Plinio il Giovanne 5, ☎ 0744-402550, fax 0744-403335, htlvalentino@tin.it, $$).

Narni is equally well-served with the very reasonable **Terra Umbra** ☆☆☆☆ (Voc. Rosciano, ☎ 0744-750304, fax 0744-751014, terraumbrahotel@libero.it, $$) and **Dei Priori** ☆☆☆ (Vicolo del Comune 4, ☎ 0744-726843, fax 0744-726844, www.loggiadeipriori.it. $$) combining quality with price.

There's also a lot more choice for campers in this area with the **River Nera Regional Park** offering **Marmore** ☆☆ (Loc. I Campacci, Marmore, ☎ 0744-67198, Apr-Sept, 77 spaces, $), **Il Lago** ☆☆ (Loc. Piediluco, Strada di Valle Spoletina, ☎/fax 0744-369199, c.marmore@cuoreverde.com, Apr-Sept, 150 spaces, $), **Il Prati** ☆ (Loc. I Prati, ☎ 0744-336200, www.cuoreverde.com, June-Sept, 80 pitches, $) near Stroncone, and **Valnerina** ☆☆ (Loc. Calcasana, ☎ 0743-613232, fax 0743-613233, June-Sept, 80 spaces, $) near Scheggino. Farther down around Narni, there's also the **Monti del Sole** ☆☆ (Strada di Borgheria 22, Borgheria, Narni, ☎/fax 0744-796336, montidelsole@libero.it, Apr-Sept, 100 spaces, $).

You can book a room in the religious accommodation at Narni – **Suore Santa Anna**, Casa di Accoglienza Centro Speranza, Via Gattamelata 74, ☎ 0744-715217, $). And there's also a youth hostel in Amelia – **Ostello per la Gioventù Giustiniani**, Piazza Mazzini 9, ☎ 0744-978673, fax 0744-983025, ostello.giustiniani@tiscalinet.it, $). In Ferentillo, in the River Nera Regional Park, there's **Ostello Il Tiglio** (Via Abruzzo 10, ☎ 0744-388710, www.cooperativasociale.it, $). A hostel in Lugnano in Teverina is **Casale di Vallenera** (Loc. Vallenera 25, ☎ 0744-902674, www.vallenera.it, $) and there are two in Terni – **Ostello dei Garibaldini** (Loc. Collescipoli, ☎/fax 0744-800467,

Orvieto & SW Umbria

ostellogaribaldini@tiscalinet.it, $) and **Palazzo Contrelori Ostello** (Piazza I Maggio Cesi, ☎ 0744-241380, fax 0744-248410, $).

There are two hiking refuges near Acquasparta. One is **Lo Scoppio** (Loc. Lo Scoppio, ☎ 0336-607781/0744-751976, info@lamongolfiera.net, $). The other is **Rifugio Macerino** (Loc. Macerino, ☎ 0744-941797, fax 0744-302462,$), a great choice for hikers who want to make the most of the hot springs nearby.

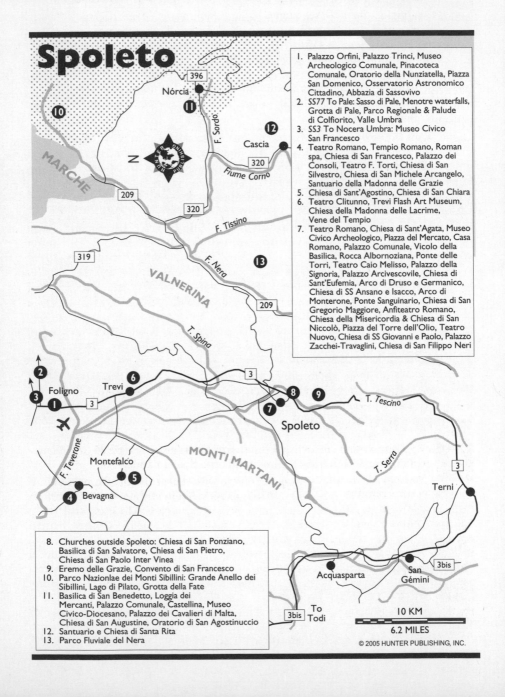

Spoleto

1. Palazzo Orfini, Palazzo Trinci, Museo Archeologico Comunale, Pinacoteca Comunale, Oratorio della Nunziatella, Piazza San Domenico, Osservatorio Astronomico Cittadino, Abbazia di Sassovivo
2. SS77 To Pale: Sasso di Pale, Menotre waterfalls, Grotta di Pale, Parco Regionale & Palude di Colfiorito, Valle Umbra
3. SS3 To Nocera Umbra: Museo Civico San Francesco
4. Teatro Romano, Tempio Romano, Roman spa, Chiesa di San Francesco, Palazzo dei Consoli, Teatro F. Torti, Chiesa di San Silvestro, Chiesa di San Michele Arcangelo, Santuario della Madonna delle Grazie
5. Chiesa di Sant'Agostino, Chiesa di San Chiara
6. Teatro Clitunno, Trevi Flash Art Museum, Chiesa della Madonna delle Lacrime, Vene del Tempio
7. Teatro Romano, Chiesa di Sant'Agata, Museo Civico Archeologico, Piazza del Mercato, Casa Romano, Palazzo Comunale, Vicolo della Basilica, Rocca Albornoziana, Ponte delle Torri, Teatro Caio Melisso, Palazzo della Signoria, Palazzo Arcivescovile, Chiesa di Sant'Eufemia, Arco di Druso e Germanico, Chiesa di SS Ansano e Isacco, Arco di Monterone, Ponte Sanguinario, Chiesa di San Gregorio Maggiore, Anfiteatro Romano, Chiesa della Misericordia & Chiesa di San Niccolò, Piazza del Torre dell'Olio, Teatro Nuovo, Chiesa di SS Giovanni e Paolo, Palazzo Zacchei-Travaglini, Chiesa di San Filippo Neri

8. Churches outside Spoleto: Chiesa di San Ponziano, Basilica di San Salvatore, Chiesa di San Pietro, Chiesa di San Paolo Inter Vinea
9. Eremo delle Grazie, Convento di San Francesco
10. Parco Nazionlae dei Monti Sibillini: Grande Anello dei Sibillini, Lago di Pilato, Grotta della Fate
11. Basilica di San Benedetto, Loggia dei Mercanti, Palazzo Comunale, Castellina, Museo Civico-Diocesano, Palazzo dei Cavalieri di Malta, Chiesa di San Augustine, Oratorio di San Agostinuccio
12. Santuario e Chiesa di Santa Rita
13. Parco Fluviale del Nera

10 KM

6.2 MILES

© 2005 HUNTER PUBLISHING, INC.

Foligno, Spoleto & Monti Sibillini

Main cities: Spoleto (see page 417) and Foligno (see page 407).
Afternoon trips from Spoleto and Foligno: Trevi (see page 416), Montefalco (see page 415).
City breaks: Assisi (see page 435), Perugia (see page 361) and Terni (see page 415).
Rural retreats: Monti Sibillini and the Piano Grande (see page 426), Valle Umbra (see page 412), Colfiorito (see page 412) and Valnerina (see page 398).

Foligno

One of the province's flattest cities, Foligno has sprawled over the banks of the Tobino River Valley since the Romans colonized and made it into an important Umbrian base. A bustling stop along the Via Flaminia during the Middle Ages, the city was also the most important Ghibelline stronghold in Umbria until 1310, when the Trinci family decided to switch the city's allegiances and establish a Guelph Seigneury here instead. Even though the new rule marked the golden age of Foligno's wealth and glory, the Seigneury came to a violent end in 1439 and the city reverted back to Papal rule. Foligno has since developed into a somewhat run-of-the-mill industrial cityscape with its main urban attractions around the Piazza della Repubblica and the adjoining Piazza Duomo, both at their best during the glorious Giostra della Quintana (Renaissance Joust) celebrations.

■ Getting Here & Around

By Car: Foligno is just to the south of Assisi along the **SS75**, which continues south of the city to Trevi and onto Spoleto and Terni.

You can arrange car rental in Foligno with **Autonoleggi Remoli** (Via F. Bettini, ☎ 0742-320975, fax 0742-329287) or **Avis** (train station, ☎ 0742-340919, www.avisautonoleggio.it). Bicycles can be rented through **Carlo Battistelli** (Via XX Settembre 88, ☎ 0742-344059).

By Train: The city is served by the privately run **Ferrovia Centrale Umbra** (☎ 0755-75401, www.fcu.it) train line, which links Perugia with Terni in the south.

By Bus: Buses link Foligno to Terni and Perugia – **APM** from Perugia (☎ 075-5731707, www.apmperugia.it) and **ATC** from Terni (☎ 0744-402900, www.atcterni.it). **Spoletina** (☎ 0743-212207, www.spoletina.com) runs the local bus network with services both within Foligno and out of the city to Assisi (four return services a day), Nocera Umbra and Gualdo Tadino (three roundtrip services a day), and Trevi (eight roundtrip services a day).

■ Information Sources

Tourist Information: The **IAT del Folignate - Nocera Umbra** (Foligno to Nocera Umbra Tourist Office, Corso Cavour 126, ☎ 0742-354459, fax 0742-340545, www.iat.foligno.pg.it) covers both Foligno and the towns of the Valle Umbra.

Adventure Information: You can get adventure advice, including details of rock climbing on the face at Grotta di Pale, from **CAI Foligno** (Via Piermarini 3, ☎/fax 0742-358804, caifoligno@tin.it).

The **Parco Regionale Colfiorito** (Colfiorito Regional Park) has offices in Colfiorito (Via Adriatica) and Foligno (Via N. Bixio 2); both share the same phone and fax (☎/fax 0742-342415, www.parks.it/parcocolfiorito).

■ Sightseeing in Foligno

Start your visit on the Piazza della Repubblica and the Piazza Duomo – two adjoining squares at the junction of four main streets that form the historical center's rectangular-shaped heart. Overlooking it is the Duomo (Cathedral), the 13th-century Palazzo Comunale (Town Hall) and adjoining Palazzo Orfini, the Palazzo Pretorio and the Palazzo Trinci. The Palazzo Trinci preserves some of the city's most valuable frescoes and wall decorations. Many of the city's museums are in this area as well.

Foligno's Romanesque **cathedral** (Piazza della Repubblica, ☎ 0742-354459, 7 am-1 pm, 4-7 pm, free) is the city's most important architectural attraction. Originally constructed in the 12th century, only the crypt remains of the ancient church; the slightly austere double façade (one looking out over Piazza Duomo; the other on to Piazza della Repubblica), enlivened by three delicate rose windows, and the three naves, all taking their form in the 15th and 16th centuries. Once inside, most tourists flock to the Cappella del Sacramento

Madonna di Foligno (detail), Raphael

(Chapel of the Sacrament), which was originally built by Antonio di Sangallo il Giovanne in the 16th century, and to a *Madonna di Foligno* by Raphael. Adjacent to the cathedral is the 13th-century Palazzo dei Canoniche (Canonical Palace), which, originally built to house the College of the Canons. It is best known for the workshops on its ground floor formerly used by the best of Foligno's painters, goldsmiths and coin makers.

The **Palazzo Comunale** was built by architect Matteo Scarscioni on the ruins of the medieval residence of the Priory. Although much of its present form was added after damage during World War II and the earthquake of 1997, the portal of **Sala Consiliare** (Council Chamber) remains from the early constructions in 1568. The room itself is decorated with works by Mariano Piervittori from 1883-7, which include four female figures painted to represent wisdom, justice, strength and prudence, and a further 12 female figures representing the arts of science. They and the 16 pictures of illustrious Foligno citizens watch over the council's meetings as inspiration for good governance. An overpass leads to the Renaissance **Palazzo Orfini**, seat of the city's first printing works opened by Emiliano Orfini around 1470. An inscription on the current façade (built in 1507) commemorates the printing of Dante's *Divine Comedy* here by Johann Neumeister.

CELEBRAZIONE DANTESCA

 After German goldsmith Johannes Gensfleisch zur Laden zum Gutenberg published the Gutenberg Bibles in 1455 (the oldest surviving example of printing with movable metal type in Europe), the skill spread quickly from Germany to Italy. It was a former pupil of Gutenberg's, Johann Neumeister, who worked one of Italy's first printing presses in Foligno in April 1472, publishing the first edition of Dante's *Divine Comedy* to great acclaim. The Celebrazione Dantesca celebrates this illustrious past with a month-long calendar of events, which includes a reading of some of the *canti* in the *Divine Comedy*. To find out about events in the year of your stay, contact the **Biblioteca Comunale** (Piazza del Grano, ☎ 0742-350734, fax 0742-340496, Mon-Fri, 9 am-1 pm, 3-7 pm, Sat, 9 am-1 pm).

The home of Foligno's ruling family between 1305 and 1439, the **Palazzo Trinci** (☎ 0742-357697, Tues-Sunday, 10 am-7 pm, €5, conc. €2.50, includes entrance to all museums) is the atmospheric hub of the city's major museums. Access is via the so-called Gothic Stairway, which leads to a loggia frescoed with legends of the foundation of Rome, a fine inner courtyard of Gothic arches, and magnificent frescoed rooms. The frescoes depict scenes from the New Testament by 15th-century artists such as Gentile da Fabriano. On the east side of the palace, the **Museo Archeologico Comunale** (Archeological Museum, guided visits in English available ☎ 0742-357989) should be your next stop. It displays the personal collection of the Trinci family (mostly marble sculptures from the Roman era), as well as artifacts, cinerary urns and sarcophagi stretching back to the city's first Umbrian and Roman inhabitants.

The **Pinacoteca Comunale** (Picture Gallery) begins with the rooms displaying paintings from the 14th century, before moving up a floor to an evocative fresco cycle, 15th-century works by local boys Bartolomeo di Tommaso, Niccolò di Liberatore and Mezzastris, and 16th-century pictorial art by Doni Doni and Bernardino di Mariotto.

Did you know? Niccolò di Liberatore is also known as l'Alunno after 16th-century painter, architect and writer Giorgio Vasari misread his signature at the base of a polptych in the Church of San Niccolò. The painter had signed himself 'Alumnus Fulginiae' (intending to mean he was a citizen of Foligno), but Vasari mistook this to mean 'pupil' in his *Lives of the Artists* and the artist has been known as Niccolò l'Alunno ever since.

Foligno, Spoleto, Monti Sibillini

THE GIOSTRA DELLA QUINTANA

This takes places on the third weekend of June and Sept every year in Piazza Grande. Seats €13-31, information, ☎ 0742-354000, www.quintana.it.

It is an equestrian competition in historic costume that coincides with Foligno's annual **Segni Barocchi** (Baroque Festival, Auditorium of San Domenico, ☎ 0742-344563) and can trace itself back to the 15th century when the city dressmakers designed the traditional costumes still in use today. Ten cavaliers, representing the 10 city *rioni* (quarters), compete on a figure-of-eight track in three successive jousts. The aim is to stick their lances through the increasingly small loop held by an ancient wooden warrior statue known as the Belli simulacrum or the Quintana. Any falls, dropped clothing or additional loops of the track subtract points.

The city *tabards* are part and parcel of the event; these atmospheric local bars, typically found in the cellars of the city's old stately homes, sprung up to provide post-Quintana celebrations, serving traditional *tenzone* menus of Renaissance fare based on the local extra-virgin olive oil, truffles, lentils and fine wine.

If you arrive out of season, you can find out more in the **Museo Multimediale dei Tornei, delle Giostre e dei Giochi** (Multimedia Museum of Tournaments, Jousts and Games), a six-room display on the history and props of medieval jousts and games next to the Porta Romana (☎ 0742-354694, fax 0742-342764, 10 am-1 pm, 3-7 pm, closed Mon, free).

To the north of Piazza della Repubblica, the **Renaissance Oratorio della Nunziatella** (Via dell'Annunziata, ☎ 0742-691424) is worth a visit for its frescoes of the *Baptism of Jesus* (1507) by Perugino, while to its south, Via G Mazzini leads to **Piazza San Domenico**, one of the oldest squares in Foligno, and one used for centuries as a place of meeting and commerce by farmers and townsfolk. It is overlooked by the **Chiesa di San Domenico**, a 13th-century Dominican church, which was deconsecrated in 1806 for use as a French military hospital, and whose adjacent convent is now used for city concerts and theater (Auditorium San Domenico, Largo F. Frezzi 8, ☎ 0742-344563, fax 0742-344563, Tues-Sat, 10 am-1 pm). Also on the square is the oldest church in Foligno, the 11th-century Benedictine **Chiesa di Santa Maria Infraportas** (Piazza San Domenico, ☎ 0742-344563). Best known for its austere belltower and stunning Romanesque cloister made up of 128 slender columns, the interior of this church also boasts frescoes by Niccolò di Liberatore, Mezzastris and Ugolino di Gisberto. The Cappella di San Pietro (Chapel of St Peter) is its oldest part; note the Byzantine-style frescoes from the first half of the 12th century.

Something Different

Foligno's **Osservatorio Astronomico Cittadino** (Observatory, Torre dei Quattro Cantoni, Via Bolletta 18, ☎ 0742-353586, Feb-Oct, Tues, 9-11 pm, Nov-Jan, Tues, 6-8 pm, by appointment only) offers star-crazed visitors the opportunity to gaze up into the heavens through the city telescope, free of charge. The tours are accompanied by an expert who provides an informative running commentary on the view, as well as a brief biography of famous local astrophysicist Paolo Maffei, who discovered, and gave his name to, two galaxies.

A few miles out of town, built on a rocky spur dominating the valley, the thousand-year-old Benedictine **Abbazia di Sassovivo** (Abbey of Sassovivo, closed for restoration at the time of writing) is well known for its mineral water spring that has brought health-conscious people here since the year 1000. Pietro di Maria built its pink marble Romanesque cloister in 1229; it leads on to a room known as Paradise, which contains important monochrome frescoes from the 1400s. A trail known as the Abbot's walk leads from outside the abbey into a forest of majestic holm oaks and up Monte Serrone.

■ Adventures

On Foot

In addition to the local branch of the CAI, Foligno has a number of walking organizations, which can provide information on or present the opportunity to join locals on walks in the local area. **Associazione Escursionistica Camminare** Liberi (Via F. Immamorati 7, ☎ 0742-320298, www.camminareliberi.it), **FIE Valle Umbra Trekking** (Via dei Preti 27, ☎ 0742-352596, www.fiefoligno.it) and **FAI Fondo per l'Ambiente Italiano** (Via B. Cairoli 19, ☎ 0742-340945, www.fondoambiente.it) are all good choices for Italian speakers or outgoing travelers.

FIE Valle Umbra Trekking have put together one of the region's most enjoyable walks, the guided **Via della Carta** (Paper Road), which takes its name from the city's printing heritage. It departs from the Benedictine Abbazia di Sassovivo and follows the route of the Menotre River through woodland and waterfalls, past ruins and ancient cloth mills, before finally winding up at the Ermito di Santa Maria di Giacobbe. This hermitage, carved directly into the cliffside, can be reached only on foot, and is a hub for walking trails throughout the entire Menotre Valley.

One path from here takes you to the to the small village of **Pale** in the Chienti Valley. Famous in the past for its paper mills, the site is now as much visited for the **Sasso di Pale** (534 m/1,753 feet), the mountain with which it shares its name. Along with the compulsory visit to the 200-m (656-ft) **Menotre waterfalls**, the area makes an ideal destination for hikes and strolls.

The most important **rock climbing** is on the cliffs of the **Grotta di Pale**; contact **CAI Foligno** (Via Piermarini 3, ☎/fax 0742-358804, caifoligno@tin.it) for information on climbing opportunities in the region.

If you take up the **caving** opportunities among the stalagmites and stalactites of the **Grotta di Pale**, you'll be following in the illustrious footsteps of Queen Catherine of Sweden and Cosimo III of Tuscany. The caves are divided into sections. The first, the Camera del Laghetto (Room of the Lake) is considered a jewel of geological architecture for its dome-shaped vault with five perfectly shaped stalactite columns at the center. The second, the "Camera delle Colonne a Terra" (Room of the Grounded Columns), has a stalagmite shaped like a lion.

On Wheels

 A 10-mile mountain bike itinerary leads from Via Bolletta, next to Foligno's 13th-century city walls, up past the Chiesa di San Sebastino, through Treggio to Chiesa di San Lorenzo Vecchio and back to Foligno. Along the route, you'll get to see the 15th-century tower of the Chiesa di Santa Lucia, the defensive fortress in Treggio and the Romanesque Chiesa di San Giovanni Profiamma built on the remains of a previous Paleo-Christian basilica. Look out for the "traveler's window," a small window on the façade near the main entrance, placed here to allow travelers passing the church to view the frescoes of the Madonna even when the church was closed.

Another itinerary (seven miles) departs from **Altolina**, just outside Pale, taking you up the Sasso di Pale (via Sostino) and back to Altolina via Lie and Belfiore. And another easy trail (also suitable on foot) leaves from **Sant'Eraclio** (12 miles), heading up past Colle Sandolaro along the Monti Martini and back down via Roviglieto.

Valle Umbra

The best of Foligno's **walks**, **mountain bike** and **horseback-riding** itineraries are in the surrounding Valle Umbra. A mix of gentle hill country and high Apennine spurs, the territory fans out from Foligno to include the Parco Regionale di Colfiorito to the north, Montefalco and Trevi to the south, Bevagna and its traditional handicrafts to the west, as well as Sellano and the enchanting Valle del Vigi to the east. Mixed in with such prime adventure territory are hot springs and mineral waters; fortresses and picturesque medieval castles; and ancient routes once trodden by saints and poets.

Nature lovers and hikers should head to the **Parco Regionale di Colfiorito** (Colfiorito Regional Park, Piazzetta del Reclusorio 1, Foligno, ☎ 0742-349714, fax 0742-680098, parco.colfiorito@parks.it), on the border with the Marches. At 500 acres, it is Umbria's smallest natural park and takes much of its form from the flat *piani* (plains), the remains of lakes that have either dried up naturally here or been drained by man. The site also incorporates the **Palude di Colfiorito** (Colfiorito Marsh), a Ramsar site, designated under the Ramsar Convention on Wetlands signed in Iran in 1971 as being of special importance for nature conservation. It's particularly noted for the wildflowers and aquatic orchids that bloom here in spring, as well as migratory wildfowl such as grey herons, purple herons, bitterns, mallards and spoonbills.

ANCIENT REMAINS

Between the base of Monte Orve and Colfiorito's cemetery is the **Esposizione Archeologica Plestini Umbri** (Via Adriatica, Colfiorito, ☎ 0742-681008, Tues/Wed, 10 am-1 pm, Fri, 3-6 pm, Sat/Sunday, 10 am-1 pm, 3-6 pm) with its display of 250 tombs and funerary objects from the 10th century BC. The Foligno Archeoclub organizes guided visits to the Colfiorito plains. To find out more contact the organization directly (Via Oberdan 123, ☎ 0742-379684).

Many of Colfiorito's walking routes take you up nearby Monte Pennino and over to Monte Tolagana. For a shorter trip (six miles, also possible on mountain bike), follow the itinerary from Colfiorito into the park and up to the top of Monte Orve for a view over the entire park.

The park is a great place for horseback riding; arrange your trip from the center at Foligno (Loc. Verchiano, ☎ 0742-632846/315273, open all year).

■ Where to Eat

LOCAL FLAVORS

Acquacotta con asparagi: "Water soup" with beans, chickpeas and asparagus.
Ciambelle di patate: Ring-shaped potato cake.
Coratella d'agnello pasquale: Lamb and rosemary stew, traditionally cooked for Easter.
Cosciotto d'agnello fracito al tartufo nero: Roasted lamb stuffed with black truffles.
Filetto di maiale con salsa all'aglio: Pork filet with a garlic sauce.
Lumache arroste: Roasted snails.
Passata di fave secche con crostini: Refried beans on toasted bread.
Penette primavera: "Spring pasta" with asparagus, ham and onions.
Sedani alla parmigiana: A specialty of Trevi, celery roasted with parmesan .
Sminuzzato di daino: Veal stew.

 There's tasty budget fare available with the pizza and pasta dishes of **Pizzeria La Tartuga** (Via Corso Nuovo 19, ☎ 0742-350926, closed Sunday, $) and the takeout roasted meats and fish of **Il Gallo Nero** (Via XX Settembre 91, ☎ 0742-344777, www.ilgallonero.it, closed Mon, $). You can step back in time with the traditional dishes of **Da Remo** (Via F Filzi 10, ☎ 0742-340522, closed Mon and most of Aug, $) at a bargain price.

Da Sparafucile (Piazzetta Duomo 30, ☎ 0368-3827246, closed Wed, $$), run by the well-reputed chef Nazzareno Brodoloni and family, offers one of the best locations in town. Its blend of innovative fish dishes and homemade time-honored fare are served in the atmospheric rooms of an historical palazzo. **Osteria del Teatro** (Via Petrucci 8, ☎ 0742-350745, closed Wed, $$), likewise, offers traditional fare in a 16th-century family palazzo.

For something a little quieter in the busy season, hotel-restaurant **Le Mura** (Via Mentana 25, ☎ 0742-354648, www.lemura.net, closed Tues, $$) is worth a stop for its spit-roasted meats and quaint exposed-brick dining rooms.

There's more tasty fare in the Valle Umbra. **Osteria del Podestà** (Corso G. Matteotti 67, ☎ 0742-361832, closed Mon, $$) is in Bevagna; **La Vecchia Cucina** (Via delle Sculoe 6, Loc. Marcellano, ☎ 0742-97237, closed Mon, $$) is in Gualdo Tadino; **Casolare della Ringhiera dell'Umbria** (Loc. Vecciano, ☎ 0742-379603, closed Thurs, $$) is in Montefalco; **Osteria la Vecchia Posta** (Via Mazzini, ☎ 0742-381690, $$) is in Trevi; and **Il Tartufaro** (Loc. Balciano, ☎ 0742-750032, closed Tues, $$) is near Valtopina. All of the above are worth the trip out of Foligno.

■ Where to Stay

There's a good choice of hotels in both Foligno and the Valle Umbra. The best budget pick in Foligno is **Hotel Bolognese** ☆ (Via Garibaldi 120, ☎ 0742-351614, fax 0742-352350, htlbolognese@freemail.it, $$). In Bevagna, it's **Il Chiostro di Bevagna**☆ (Corso Matteotti 107, ☎ 0742-361978, fax 0742-369231, www.ilchiostrodibevagna.com, $$).

Foligno has some quality mid-range options such as **Poledrini** ☆☆☆ (Viale Mezzati 3, ☎ 0742-341041, fax 0742-352973, $$$) and **Albergo Le Mura** ☆☆☆ (Via Bolletta 29, ☎ 0742-357344, fax 0742-353327, www.albergolemura.com, $$$). By far the best options are found out of town, namely **Villa Fiorita** ☆☆☆ (Colfiorito, Via del Lago 9, ☎ 0742-681326, fax 0742-681327, www.hotelvillafiorita.com, $$), **Degli Affreschi** ☆☆☆ (Montefalco, Via della Vittoria 7, ☎ 0742-379243, fax 0742-379643, $$) and **Hotel della Torre** (Trevi, Via Flaminia, ☎ 0742-391212, www.folignohotel.com, $$$). The most luxurious choice is **Hotel Ristorante Villa Pambuffetti** (Montefalco, Via della Vittoria 20, ☎ 0742-379417, fax 0742-379245, villabianca@interbusiness.it, $$$$).

There are campgrounds in the Valle Umbra at **Pian di Boccio** ☆☆☆ (Bevagna, Loc. Gaglioli, ☎ 0742-360164, fax 0742-360391, piandibosco@tiscalinet.it, April-Sept, 70 spaces, $).

A youth hostel is in Foligno – **Ostello Pierantoni** (Via Pierantoni 23, ☎ 0742-342566, fax 0742-342599, folhostel@tiscalinet.it, open all year, $) – a top choice thanks to its frescoed rooms. For religious accommodation there is **Casa Beata Angelica** (Foligno, Via San Niccolò Alunno 29, ☎/fax 0742-342688, beatangelina@box.it, $), **Casa della Gioventù** (Foligno, Fraz. Rasiglia, ☎ 0742-6432445, $), **Convento San Bartolemeo** (☎/fax 0742-357771, $) and **Locanda Emmaus** (Foligno, Via Valleverde 45, Fraz. Colforito, ☎ 0742-68117, $). Other choices include **Monstero Santa Maria del Monte** (Bevagna, Corso Matteotti 15, ☎ 0742-360133, fax 0742-369315, monastero@mclink.it, $) and **Convento San Fortunato** (Montefalco, Via San Fortunato, Fraz. Turri, ☎/fax 0742-378102, $).

■ Excursions from Foligno

Nocera Umbra

Spread on the side of a hill along the Via Flaminia, Nocera Umbra's cathedral marks the highest point of town. Of the original Romanesque construction only the large decorated vault above the portal and the octagonal apse survive; the rest was rebuilt in 1448 in the Franciscan style of large arches and exposed beams, then again in the Neoclassical style in the 18th century. The large tower behind, known as the Campanaccio, dates from the 11th century and is the only surviving portion of the town fortress.

The main attractions in town – other than the hot springs and mineral waters from which Nocera Umbra derives most of its fame – are in the ex-Chiesa di San Francesco. It currently houses the **Museo Civico San Francesco** (Civic Museum, Piazza Caprera, ☎ 0742-834011) and its displays of stone altars, wooden crucifixes and detached frescoes. The major exhibits here are a 1483 polyptych by Niccolò da Liberatore depicting the *Birth of Christ*, an oil painting by Matteo da Gualdo (1498) and paintings by Giulio Cesare Angeli, Ercole Ramazzani and

Pierino Cesarei. There's also an archeological collection with objects from the nearby necropoli in Portone.

If you want to stroll into the surrounding area, there are paths up Monte Alago and Monte Pennino and Monte Subasio Regional Park (see page 438) is not far.

Bevagna

West of Foligno, present-day Bevagna (formerly the Roman town of Mevania) is very much medieval in appearance despite the traditional Roman street plan. You enter town through the Porta Foligno. From there, a brief stroll brings you to the Roman remains of **Teatro Romano** (Roman Theater) and **Tempio Romano** (Roman Temple). Farther on is the second-century Roman **spa complex** (Via di Porta Guelfa, ☎ 0742-361667), which shelters a beautiful black-and-white Roman mosaic of marine life.

The **Chiesa di San Francesco** marks the highest point in town. Dating from the 13th century, it contains some paintings from the 14th and 16th centuries, but if it's art you're after, you're better off visiting the town's main museum inside the Palazzo Comunale (Town Hall), the **Museo Civico e Pinacoteca** (Civic Museum and Picture Gallery, Palazzo Comunale, Corso Matteotti 70, ☎/fax 0742-360031, April-May, Sept, 10:30 am-1 pm, 2:30-6 pm, closed Mon, June-July, 10:30 am-1 pm, 3:30-7 pm, closed Mon, Aug, 10:30 am-1 pm, 3-7:30 pm, Oct-March, 10:30 am-1 pm, 2:30-5:30 pm, closed Fri-Sunday). It contains both archeological remains (especially local Roman finds), as well as a collection of ecclesiastical art taken from churches in the area.

The heart of town and the site of its most important medieval monuments is on **Piazza Filippo Silvestri**. Look inside the **Chiesa dei SS Domenico e Giacomo** to find a fresco cycle from the Giotto school and two 13th-century wooden sculptures, or look into the 13th-century **Palazzo dei Consoli** to visit the recently restored **Teatro F. Torti** (☎ 0742-361667), with its drop curtain painted by Domenico Bruschi in the late 19th century. The square alo contains the Romanesque **Chiesa di San Silvestro** (1195) and the 13th-century **Chiesa di San Michele Arcangelo**.

A pleasant (if long) six-hour **walk** leads from Bevagna along rolling hills to Torre del Colle and back via Limigiano. **Cyclists** should head out of town to the 16th-century **Santuario della Madonna delle Grazie** to visit its early wooden crucifix and enjoy the great views over the countryside in the process. Or you can take a tour of one of the nearby medieval castles, such as Cantalupo, Castelbuono, Limigiano, Gaglioli, Torre del Colle or Gualdo Cattaneo. The last sits surrounded by wooded hills perfect for walks and **horseback riding**. Book these through the Associazione SIT near Gualdo (Via Roma 125, Loc. San Terenziano, ☎ 0742-98578, summer, 8 am-9 pm, winter, 8 am-4 pm).

Montefalco

It's not difficult to understand why Montefalco is known as Umbria's *Ringhiera* (balcony) when you walk along the city walls that delimit its historical center. But it's also considered an important art town for its frescoes of the Umbrian and Tuscan schools. You can see some of them in the late 13th-century **Chiesa di Sant'Agostino**; there are traces here of great painters such as Nelli, Lorenzetti, Mezzastris, Niccolò l'Alunno, Melanzio and Caporali, not to mention the remains of Beato Pellegrino (the Blessed Pilgrim).

You can find more frescoes in the **Museo Civico San Francesco** (St Francis Civic Museum, Via R. Umbra 6, ☎ 0742-379598, fax 0742-379506, June-July, daily, 10:30 am-1 pm, 3-7 pm, Aug, daily, 10:30 am-1 pm, 3-7:30 pm, Sept/Oct, March-May, 10:30 am-1 pm, 2-6 pm, Nov-Feb, 10:30 am-1 pm, 2:30-5 pm, closed Mon). Montefalco's main museum, it contains paintings from the 13th to 17th centuries, including notable frescoes by Benozzo Gozzoli (look for the cycle illustrating scenes from the life of St Francis), a Presepe by Perugino, and works by Niccolò l'Alunno, Mezzastris, Melanzio, and Tiberio d'Assisi.

The finest civil palazzi are on Piazza del Comune and along Corso Mameli. Built between the 15th and 17th centuries, grand houses here bear the imprint of grand families such as Moriconi-Calvi, Langeli, Senili, Ciardelli, Santi-Gentili and de Cuppis. There's also the civic **Palazzo Comunale** (Town Hall), which was built much earlier in the 13th century. Its tower offers another lovely view of the surrounding Umbrian countryside.

Of the churches in town, the 17th-century **Chiesa di San Chiara** is the most interesting. Inside it is the early 14th-century Cappella di Santa Croce with frescoes from the 15th-century Umbrian school.

LOCAL WINES

In the 1960s, Umbrian wine production underwent something of a renaissance with modern systems of cultivation providing a new punch. One of those to benefit was the DOCG Montefalco Sagrantino, which has been cultivated in the area since a Franciscan monk first planted vines here in the Middle Ages. Sample the sweet dessert wines and the dry table wine, known for its bouquet of wild blackberry and its intense ruby red color. To visit local vineyards, contact the **Consorzio de Tutela Vini DOC Montefalco** (Montefalco Wine Consortium), c/o Comune, Montefalco, ☎ 0742-79142/29147.

There are plenty of adventures to enjoy in the area surrounding Montefalco. From the Chiesa e Monastero di San Fortunato (with frescoes by Gozzoli and Tiberio d'Assisi), there's a pleasant **stroll** into the ancient holm oak grove. For something a little more strenuous (also possible by mountain bike), take the six-mile route from Torre di Montefalco along the Teverone River to Casevecchie and back. **Mountain bikers** should tackle the 14-mile itinerary through vineyards to the castle at Fabbri.

Trevi

Beautifully situated on a hill overlooking the Clitunno Valley, Piazza Garibaldi (formerly Piazza del Lago) marks the center of old Trevi. Of the town sights, look for **Teatro Clitunno** (Piazza del Teatro, ☎ 0742-381768), with its theater curtain decorated by Domenico Bruschi (1877), and the 13th-century **Palazzo Comunale** (Piazza Mazzini) with notable Renaissance-style windows and a municipal tower marked with the inscription "Convoco signo noto debeloo concino ploro amia dies horas nubila laeta rogos" (I assemble the troops, mark the days, toll the hours, keep storms away, celebrate festivities and mourn the dead).

Next to the Gothic Chiesa di San Francisco, the **Museo Civico San Francesco** occupies the former convent (St Francis Civic Museum, Largo don Bosco, ☎/fax 0742-381628, April-May/Sept, 10:30 am-1 pm, 2:30-6 pm, closed Mon, June-July,

10:30 am-1 pm, 3:30-7 pm, closed Mon, Aug, 10:30 am-1 pm, 3-7:30 pm, Oct-March, Fri-Sunday, 10:30 am-1 pm, 2:30-5 pm). It exhibits works by Corraduccio, Niccolò l'Alunno, Spagna and Giusto da Gand, as well as an archeological collection. Also here is the Museo della Civiltà dell'Olio (The Museum of Oil) with its displays on extra-virgin olive oil production in the area.

If it's modern art you're after, the **Trevi Flash Art Museum** (Via Lucarini 1, ☎ 0742-381818, Wed-Fri, 3-7 pm, Sat-Sunday, 10 am-1 pm, 3-7 pm) displays modern works by regional and international artists, and is home to two biannual shows, the Biennale Internazionale di Arte Contemporanea and the Biennale Nazionale di Fotografia. Finish off with some fine views in the Torrione della Neve, a triangular keep in the northern part of the town walls.

Head into the countryside on **horseback** with Trevi's riding center, **SIT** (Loc. Coste di Trevi, ☎ 0742-780823, open all year, closed Mon). Or try **mountain biking** on the 13-mile route from Trevi through Campello sul Clitunno, Cancellara, Ponze, Pissignano and back via Campello Alto. Stop off along this route at the **Chiesa della Maddona delle Lacrime**, a 14th-century church which, according to legend, was built on the site of a tabernacle where a painted Madonna shed blood-colored tears. Go inside and you'll discover frescoes by Perugino and Spagna. There's also an enjoyable **walking** route along the Clitunno River, an enchanting area that has been the source of inspiration for generations of poets from Virgil to Carducci. Start your walk from the Tempio di Clitunno to visit the springs of the **Vene del Tempio** (Fonti del Clitunno, Loc. Pissignano, ☎ 0743-521141, 9 am-1 pm, 2-6 pm, €2, conc. €1.50) emerging from the chalky limestone, or head to the summit of Monte Serano (1,429 m/4,659 feet) from Campello sul Clitunno for some great views of the surrounding area.

Spoleto

The beautiful and romantic city of Spoleto comes into its own during the *passeggiata*, the leisurely dusk-lit strolls favored by its inhabitants. This is the best time to admire the vast range of monuments, churches, castles and towers that reflect Spoleto's importance, from its early Umbrian origins, through Roman rule, self-government under the Dukes of Longobard, destruction under the Barbarians and reconstructions in both medieval and modern times. The town that once heroically repelled the advances of Hannibal is now home to one of the region's most impressive cathedrals, one of the most beautiful piazze in Italy, and a plethora of cultural and artistic traditions that reach their fullest expression in the yearly Spoleto Festival.

■ Getting Here & Around

By Car: The **SS75** drops south from Foligno to Spoleto and continues onto Terni, where it meets with the A1 highway (your best approach if arriving from Rome and the south). Arriving from Florence and the north, you should opt for the Val di Chiana-Perugia-Foligno junction of the A1. From there you can access Foligno and Spoleto along the **SS3**.

Car rental is available in Spoleto with **Avis** (Loc. S. Chiudo 164, ☎ 0743-46272, fax 0743-220840, www.avisautonoleggio.it), **Hertz** (Via Cerquiglia 144, ☎/fax 0743-46703, hertzspoleto@tin.it) and **Umbria Noleggi** (Loc. San Sabino 18e,

☎ 0743-48041, fax 0743-47680). Bicycles can be rented through **Scocchetti Cicli** (Via Marconi 82, ☎ 0743-44728).

 By Train: Frequent trains (☎ 848-888088, www.trenitalia.it) stop at Spoleto along the Rome-Ancona line and the Bologna-Firenze-Spoleto rail link, with local services supplied by the privately run **Ferrovia Centrale Umbra** (☎ 0755-75401, www.fcu.it).

 By Bus: Spoletina (☎ 0743-212207, www.spoletina.com) runs the local bus network with services both within Spoleto and out of the city to Norcia (nine roundtrips a day), Foligno and Perugia (seven roundtrips a day) and Terni (eight roundtrips a day).

 Taxis: Taxis can be picked up from Piazza Libertà (☎ 0743-44548), Piazza Garibaldi (☎ 0743-49990) and Piazza Polvani (☎ 0743-220489).

■ Information Sources

 Tourist Information: The Spoleto region has two tourist information bureaus of note, the **IAT di Spoleto** (Spoleto Territory Tourist Information, Piazza della Libertà 7, Spoleto, ☎ 0743-49890, fax 0743-46241, www.iat.spoleto.pg.it) with information on Spoleto, Campello sul Clitunno and Castel Ritaldi, and the **IAT della Valnerina-Cascia** (Valnerina-Cascia Tourist Information, Via G. Da Chiavano 2, Cascia, ☎ 0743-71401, fax 0743-76630, www.iat.cascia.pg.it) with information on sightseeing and adventures in the Cascia and Valnerina zones. Norcia has its own office (Via Solferino 22, ☎/fax 0743-828173), which it shares with that of the Parco Nationale Monti Sibillini (Mt Sibillini National Park, ☎ 0743-817090, www.parks.it/parco.nazionale.monti. sibillini).

Adventure Information: Check with **CAI Spoleto** (Via Pianciani 4, ☎ 0743-220433, www.caribusiness.it/caispoleto) for hiking and skiing advice.

■ Sightseeing

The classic hilltop town of Spoleto boasts a history that stretches back 2,000 years, so it should come as no surprise to find its streets brimming with grand remnants from the past. Best explored on foot, there are two itineraries of choice in the historical center. The first departs from Piazza della Libertà and takes you past the city's major historical and cultural monuments in the upper part of town; the second leads from Ponte Sanguinario to the churches and historical remains in its lower part. Both take around two hours to complete.

From Piazza della Libertà

Start your tour outside the tourist information office on Piazza della Libertà. It gives a great view onto the **Teatro Romano** (Roman Theater) from its west side. Head into the arcaded façade (a remnant of the Ancaiani family stables) for the best view. Originally built in the first century AD, the theater was made virtually unusable by a landslide shortly after its completion, and it wasn't properly unearthed until 1954. The marble-paved orchestra stands intact, but the theater's stage was lost. It completely disappeared with the construction of the **Chiesa di Sant'Agata** (entrance on Via delle Terme) in the Middle Ages, which was itself converted into a Benedictine convent in 1395. Although much changed since the 11th century, Sant'Agata is one of the city's oldest churches and contains the remains of a precious cycle of frescoes by the Maestro delle Palazze, a follower of Cimabue.

The complex also houses the collection of Roman and Romanesque finds that make up Spoleto's **Museo Civico Archeologico** (Palazzo Corvi, ☎ 0743-223277, daily, 8.30 am-7.30 pm, €2, conc. €1, entrance on Via Sant'Agata), from which visitors can also access the Teatro Romano. Check out the museum's prize exhibits: two third-century BC stone tablets from the sacred wood of Monteluco, the so-called "Lex Spoletina" from the same era, and a Romanesque bas-relief taken from the Chiesa di San Niccolò depicting the martyrdom of San Biagio.

Festival dei Due Mondi
(Festival of the Two Worlds)

 In late June and early July the Spoleto Festival brings a whirlwind of artistic activity, classical music, opera, theater, dance, visual arts and cinema to Spoleto's churches, theaters (including the Teatro Romano) and city squares. Launched by Italian-American composer Giancarlo Menotti in 1958 as a forum for young American artists in Europe (hence the "two worlds"), the event gives locals and visitors alike the opportunity to enjoy talented performances in stunning locations. Contact the Associazione Spoleto Festival (Spoleto Festival Association, c/o Teatro Nuovo, ☎ 0743-220321, www.spoletofestival.it) to find out about events that correspond with your stay.

Follow Corso G Mazzini north off Piazza della Libertà, before ducking down a short alley to Palazzo Rosari Spada, the former home of the Galleria Comunale d'Arte Moderna e Contemporanea and the planned home of the Museo del Tessile e dei Costumi Antichi (Textile and Ancient Clothes Museum, ☎ 0743-232537, entrance on Corso Mazzini).

Take the alley directly in front of you (as you return from Palazzo Rosari Spada to Corso Mazzini) to **Piazza del Mercato**, a charming market square (the former Roman Forum) marked by an interesting fountain, sculpted in 1746 to commemorate the site of the long-destroyed Chiesa di San Donato. Walk east from here and you'll soon stumble upon the **Casa Romana** (Roman House, Palazzo del Municipio, Via di Visiale 9, ☎ 0743-43707, 27 March-15 Oct, daily, 10 am-8 pm, 16 Oct-26 March, 10.30 am-1 pm, 3-6.30 pm, €2.10, conc. €1.50), the well-preserved remains of a house constructed in the first century, which contains a typical peristyle courtyard and an upper-level dining room (known as a triclinium), which still preserves traces of the original decorations.

HANNIBAL

Spoleto's biggest claim to fame has to be in its valiant resistance against Carthaginian General Hannibal (247-182 BC), one of the greatest military leaders in history, who arrived in Spoletium (as it was then known) fresh from his victories over the Romans at Lago di Trasimeno. While much lauded for that famous campaign – when he caught the Romans off-guard by crossing the Alps in the Second Punic War (218-202) – Hannibal was himself caught off-guard by the fierce resistance of the Spoletinos, who poured boiling oil over him and his troops. Such was the extent of the losses inflicted by Spoleto on the Carthaginian army that Hannibal changed his plan to occupy Rome and deviated towards Puglia instead.

Piazza del Municipio contains two more sights: the **Palazzo Comunale** (Town Hall) and the **Vicolo della Basilica** (the alleyway opposite the Town Hall), which is flanked by a vast Roman construction of wide stone pilasters. The Town Hall also contains the **Pinacoteca Comunale** (Picture Gallery, entrance on Via A Saffi, ☎ 0743-2181), where a number of notable 12th- and 13th-century paintings are housed.

Walking east out of Piazza del Municipio, the street takes you past Piazza Campello (the large church to your right is the Chiesa di San Simone) to one of the city's main sights: the **Rocca Albornoziana** (Piazza Campello, ☎ 0743-43707, 27 March-15 Oct, daily, 10 am-8 pm, 16 Oct-26 March, Mon-Fri, 10.30 am-1 pm,

3-6.30 pm, Sat-Sunday, 10 am-6 pm, guided visits or 45 minutes for groups of two or more only, €5, conc. €4). This vast papal bastion from the 14th century was constructed during the Great Schism under orders from Cardinal Albornoz (hence the name) on the highest point of town. This was a time when the Papacy was exiled to Avignon and Pope Innocent VI was struggling to reorder the papal state. The result, completed by architect Matteo Gattaponi, is a commanding fortress, whose great walls, topped by six regal towers, shield a surprisingly spacious rectangular interior and two beautiful courtyards. The most famous of the rooms is the Camera Pinta (Painted Room) in the main tower. It contains fresco cycles with chivalric and courtly themes that are thought to depict life in the court of Avignon.

Follow up your visit with a pleasant walk to the magnificent **Ponte delle Torri** (Bridge of the Towers), which links the hill on which the Rocca stands to the green slopes of Monteluco. This imposing bridge was constructed at the end of the 13th century on the remains of a Roman aqueduct that used to bring water from the Cortaccione springs to the city. Eighty meters (262 feet) high and 230 m (752 feet) long, the bridge is noted for its imposing pillars (two of which are actually hollow towers) linked together by 10 short arches, and is considered a marvel of medieval architecture.

Return to the center of town by following Via M Gattaponi counter-clockwise around the fortressg. Take a right after Piazza Campello up Via dell'Aringo past the Renaissance Palazzo Racani (later Arroni) and down the steps to visit the

Duomo (Cathedral of Santa Maria Assunta, ☎ 0743-44307, March-Oct, 7.30 am-12.30 pm, 3-6 pm, Nov-Feb, 7.30 am-12.30 pm, 3-5 pm, free). The city's most important religious building, this Romanesque structure was erected on the remains of a previous building, destroyed by Barbarossa in 1155. You can see the ruins of the earlier church in the carved stone along the entrance and in the crypt under the Cappella delle Reliquie (Relic Chapel). The current cathedral replaced it in 1175, but wasn't completed until around 1227 when the mosaic showing Christ between Madonna and St John the Baptist by Solsternus and the two upper rose windows were completed on the façade. The central rose window, in the final tier, depicts the four evangelists in its square frame, and is considered one of the most ornate in Umbria.

The massive bell tower is interesting not just for its size; it was put together from large square blocks mostly recycled from crumbling Roman buildings in the area. The church interior is something of a surprise – it is the work of Florentine artist Luigi Arrigucci (nephew of Pope Urban VIII, who had been bishop of Spoleto from 1608 to 1617), who was commissioned in 1644 to completely refurbish the inner hall in the Baroque style. Of the original design, only the herringbone-patterned pavement remains.

But the cathedral isn't noticeable just for its architecture; walls contain fresco cycles by Pinturicchio (Capella di Constantino Eroli) and Filippo Lippi (right transept), and a work by Filippo Lippi, a Romanesque cornice and remarkable frieze (considered the finest in town) fill the dome with their depictions of the *Annunciation*, *Death of Mary*, *Nativity* and *Coronation of Mary*. Few know that Filippo Lippi died here while working on the frescoes in the apse (1467-69); a funerary monument designed by his son, Filippino, but sculpted by an unknown Florentine, commemorating his life and works is near the Capella Orsini.

Spoleto's famous crucifix is in the Cappella delle Reliquie. This crucifix was first discovered on painted parchment and applied to wood by Alberto Sortio (1187). It was placed in the Chiesa di San Giovanni e San Paolo (see page 424) before being moved to its present location in the cathedral.

Your walking route continues past the Chiesa di Santa Maria della Manna d'Oro to the **Teatro Caio Melisso** (formerly the Nobile Teatro), one of the oldest theaters in Italy to be built with box seating. It changed its name (to honor Caius Melissus, a freed slave and friend of Maecenas, who was librarian of the imperial court under Augustus in the first century BC) after renovations in 1880 to the designs of Giovanni Montiroli. The theater ceiling and drop curtain are the work of Domenico Brushi, who also decorated the central ceiling in the foyer. After years of abandon, the theater was reopened for the inauguration of the Festival dei Due Mondi (see page 419) in 1958. From the theater you can also access the upper floor of the **Palazzo della Signoria**, a massive construction in the style of Matteo Gattapone, which housed the Museo Civico before it was moved to its current location in the former convent of Sant'Agata (see page 419).

Retrace your steps up Via dell'Aringo to explore the **Palazzo Arcivescovile** (Archbishop's Palace), including the **Museo Diocesano** (ground floor, Via A Saffi 13, ☎/fax 0743-231041, April-Sept, 10 am-1 pm, 4-7 pm, Oct-March, 10 am-12.30 pm, 3-6 pm, closed Tues, €3.10, conc. €2.50). The museum contains religious works and artifacts from the 13th to 18th centuries, including a 14th-century altarpiece by Maestro di Cesi, and a wooden crib by Domenico Beccafumi. Inside the palace courtyard is the 12th-century **Chiesa di Sant'Eufemia**, left, one of the most significant Romanesque works of art in Umbria. It stands over a previous church that is thought to have been the chapel

of the Archbishop's Palace. The church is most notable for its pure façade and delicate hanging arches that look out onto the stairway you have just climbed from the cathedral. The interior is divided into three naves with three apses. There is a woman's gallery (the only such example in Umbria) and a beautiful triptych painted by an unknown Umbria artist from the 15th century.

Return from here to Piazza del Mercato where this time you should take Via dell'Arco del Druso along to **Arco di Druso e Germanico**, the ceremonial arch that formed the entrance to the ancient Roman Forum (on which Piazza del Mercato now stands). Erected in the first century AD to honor Emperor Drusus and Germanicus from where it takes it name, the arch retains much of its original beauty and striking classical design, despite being hemmed in by more modern constructions. One of these is the **Chiesa di SS Ansano e Isacco** (Via Brignone, ☎ 0743-40305, March-Oct, 7.30 am-12.30 pm, 3-6 pm, Nov-Feb, 7.30 am-12.30 pm, 3-5 pm, free), whose structure incorporates the remains of a first-century Roman temple. First consecrated here in 1143, the church has been much altered since its construction; the earliest part is in the crypt with its cross-vaulted ceiling, narrow aisles supported by columns lifted from earlier buildings, and 12th-century frescoes depicting the life of St Isaac, whose remains are here.

Continue on Via dell'Arco and you'll soon spy another Roman arch, this time **Arco di Monterone**, the gateway to the city when the Romans built it out of the massive square blocks and strong limestone pillars you still see today. From here, Via Brignone returns you to Piazza del Libertà; there you can pick up the the second itinerary by taking Corso G Mazzini to the Chiesa di San Filippo.

From Ponte Sanguinario

The perfect itinerary for those arriving from Spoleto train station (take Viale Trento e Trieste up to the bridge), this walk begins at the ancient Roman bridge of **Ponte Sanguinario**, a first-century construction, located down some half-hidden steps next to the Porta Garibaldi gateway into town. Measuring 4½ m (15 feet) wide and 24 m (78 feet) long, the bridge is made up of three archways formed out of large blocks of travertine marble. It was originally built to cross the Tessino River, but the waterway slowly shifted, rendering the bridge obsolete. It was hidden for centuries before being rediscovered in 1817.

The gateway into town takes you onto Piazza Garibaldi and into the courtyard of **Chiesa di San Gregorio Maggiore** (Piazza Garibaldi, ☎ 0743-44140, 9 am-noon, 3:30-6:30 pm, free), which, although much renovated, was originally built in the 11th and 12th centuries to honor the Spoletino martyr from which it takes its name. The Cappella degli Innocenti, decorated with frescoes by Angelucci da Mevale, was added in the 14th century following the discovery of bones believed to belong to the saint, while the sturdy bell tower, constructed out of recycled Roman building materials, had already been added a century earlier. The church façade is preceded by a Renaissance portico with three barrel-vaults, which was added to the original construction in the 16th century (one of the few items to come through later 20th-century restorations unscathed). In its lower part are three mullioned windows and two niches containing statues of St Gregory and St Barattale. The interior has done the best job of preserving its original Romanesque look and feel with three aisles and a raised presbytery with crypt below. Look for the interesting Romanesque fresco cycle decorating the central nave.

Via dell'Anfiteatro takes you to the ruins of the **Anfiteatro Romano** (Roman Amphitheater) where 10 open arches are all that remain of its former second-century grandeur. It was almost completely destroyed in 545 under Totila, and used during the Middle Ages as a resource for much of the materials used to build Spoleto's Rocca and many of its churches. You can get the best view of the site by entering the Minervio barracks that flank your walk along Via dell'Anfiteatro.

Via S Cecili brings you toward the center of town past the early 14th-century **Chiesa della Misericordia**, which occupies the basement of the Chiesa di San Niccolò. But, before you head to the churches, follow the street the whole way around to **Piazza del Torre dell'Olio** (from where the churches can be reached up Via G Elladio) to enjoy the longest and best-preserved stretch of Spoleto's ancient **city walls**. Clearly visible for some 125 m (408 feet), this stretch of Umbrian-Roman fortifications reflects much of the city history. The largest polygonal stones date from the earliest Umbrian inhabitants in the sixth century BC; the quadrilateral blocks from Roman occupation in 241 BC; and the long and narrow blocks that run along the top are from medieval times.

THE TOWER OF OIL

Piazza del Torre dell'Olio takes its name from the Torre dell'Olio (Tower of Oil), which was built on it by one of Spoleto's richest families in the 13th century. Along with the nearby Porta Fuga (Fleeing Gate), the tower takes its name from the belief that here Hannibal's armies were driven away by Spoletinos armed with boiling oil.

The Gothic **Chiesa di San Niccolò** was constructed in the 14th century together with the lower **Chiesa della Misericordia** (linked by a steep ramp) and the adjacent ex-monastery. Together, they form one of the most interesting complexes in the city, and contain some of its finest works of art – including the 14th-century *Crucified Christ with the Madonna, St John and St Augustine* in the Cappella di San Michele of the Chiesa della Misericordia. The Chiesa di San Niccolò is best known as an important center for Humanistic studies (it was even attended by Martin Luther in 1512); unfortunately, much of it was destroyed by fires in the 1800s.

Back on Piazza del Torre dell'Olio, Via P Leoni leads up to the Dominican **Chiesa di San Domenico**. It was built in the second half of the 13th century using wide strips of red and white flint stone that give such a striking appearance to the exterior. It somehow manages to sit well next to the majestic bell tower, which is topped by a 16th-century loggia addition. You can find the entrance on the east wall marked by a magnificent portal decorated with a sadly deteriorated fresco by

Foligno, Spoleto, Monti Sibillini

Perino Cesarei. The single-nave interior contains noteworthy works of art, including an early 15th-century *Triumph of St Thomas Aquinas* on the right of the nave, episodes from the *Life of the Virgin* in the Cappella di Santa Maria Maddalena, a *Crucifixion* on the far wall, and a 15th-century *Christ with Angels* decorating the vaulted ceiling. Look for the 14th-century altar cross by Maestro di Fossa, a 14th-century *Pietà* and the altarpiece by Giovanni Lanfranco, among other pieces of interest.

On the adjacent Piazza Collicola is the new home of the **Galleria Comunale d'Arte Moderna e Contemporanea** (Modern Art Gallery, currently housed in Palazzo Collicola, Piazza Collicola, ☎ 0743-45940, fax 0743-222349, 27 March-15 Oct, daily, 10 am-8 pm, 16 Oct-26 March, 10:30 am-1 pm, 3-6:30 pm, €3.10, conc. €2.50). The pretty eclectic collection includes works by young Umbrian avant-garde artists, the vast sculpture by Alexander Calder known as *Teodolapio* (previously in the square in front of the train station), and a portable crucifix, painted on both sides, by the Mastro di Sant'Alò – one side depicts Christ surrounded by soldiers; the other, *Madonna with St John the Baptist*.

The square marks the climb to the **Teatro Nuovo** (Largo B Gigli, ☎ 0743-40265). Designed by Ireneo Aleandri according to the classical 550-seat layout of Italian theaters, it was built over 10 years, between 1854 and 1864, and today presents two of the most noteworthy cultural events in the city: the **Festival dei Due Mondi** (see page 419) and the **Teatro Lirico Sperimentale** (Experimental Lyrical Theater). The theater was built on a site once occupied by the church and monastery of Sant'Andrea and its massive facade is now marked by stuccoes and medallions representing the city's great writers and artists.

Continue along Via Filitteria to reach the **Chiesa di SS Giovanni e Paolo**, a small and simple Romanesque church from the 12th century. Inside can be seen fresco cycles from the same period, including a *Martyrdom of St Thomas à Becket* on the right wall and a *Martyrdom of Saints John and Paul* in the Presbytery. Back outside, the street curves to meet the 16th-century **Palazzo Zacchei-Travaglini** and onto Corso G Mazzini and the **Chiesa di San Filippo Neri**. This Baroque church was designed by Spoletino architect Loreto Scelli between 1640 and 1671, in the shape of a Latin cross with three aisles and a deep apse. Gaetano Lapis is responsible for much of the church's art, with a *Presentation of the Virgin at the Temple* on the second altar to the right and a *Crucifixion* in the right-hand transept. The left-hand transept has a *Holy Family* by Sebastiano Conca, a *St Francis* by Francesco Refini, and a *Descent of the Holy Spirit* by Lazzaro Baldi. From here, you can easily reach Piazza della Libertà and the sights of the upper part of town.

Four Churches on the Edge

There's plenty to be enjoyed in the immediate vicinity of town, and three hearty walks or cycle trips will bring you to four churches all too often missed on the typical Spoletino sightseeing route. The first, **Chiesa di San Ponziano** (Via della Basilica, ☎ 0743-40665, by appointment only, free), lies across the Tessino River to the northeast of town. It was built to honor the Spoletino martyr St Ponziano, who later became patron saint of the city, and it boasts a fine portal enriched with sculptured motifs, high reliefs and dramatic rose windows not unlike those of the cathedral. Inside, the walls are decorated with 14th- and 15th-century frescoes, but little else from the original construction remains after drastic remodeling in 1788. It's only a short hop from here to the Paleo-Christian **Basilica di San**

Salvatore (Via della Basilica, ☎ 0743-49606, March-Oct, 7 am-6 pm, Nov-Feb, 7 am-5 pm, free), itself a stark reminder of Spoleto's earliest origins.

Chiesa di San Pietro (Strada per Monteluco, ☎ 0743-44882, 9-11 am, 3:30-6:30 pm, free) is to the historical center's southeast at the foot of Monteluco (just north of the campground). It is one of Spoleto's oldest and most interesting churches for its steep flight of 16th century steps and magnificent Romanesque façade, complete with symbolic sculptures depicting tales from medieval folklore. It also enjoys one of the best views, with a wide panorama that stretches across all of Spoleto.

Chiesa di San Paolo Inter Vinea, is a short trip southwest of town. Recent restoration has brought the 12th-century edifice back to its former Romanesque appearance and uncovered some interesting 13th-century fresco remnants – including episodes from the *Creation* added by local painters of the era.

■ Adventures

On Foot

The forested mountain of **Monteluco** adjoining Spoleto offers the closest and easiest **walking** routes. It is connected to the town by a path along an ancient Roman road – the same road used by early Christian hermits to cross over to the mountain and establish their monasteries in the forest. Of those still intact, **Eremo delle Grazie**, the fifth-century hermitage founded by Isacco di Antiochia (now a Residenza d'Epoca, see page 432) and **Convento di San Francesco** (Loc. Monteluco, ☎ 0743-40711, 9 am-12:15 pm, 3-5:55 pm, free), the primitive convent established by St Francis in 1218 (one of his first), complete with well, small chapel and seven simple cells, can still be visited.

Farther out of town, walkers are drawn to the Clitunno River (see page 417), **Monti Martani** (see page 394-96) and the **Valnerina** (see page 398).

On Wheels

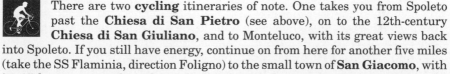

There are two **cycling** itineraries of note. One takes you from Spoleto past the **Chiesa di San Pietro** (see above), on to the 12th-century **Chiesa di San Giuliano**, and to Monteluco, with its great views back into Spoleto. If you still have energy, continue on from here for another five miles (take the SS Flaminia, direction Foligno) to the small town of **San Giacomo**, with its 15th-century castle and parish church with frescoes by Giovanni Spagna. A second cycle ride takes you from town to **Giano dell'Umbria** (head towards Monteluco but follow signs to the picturesque medieval town of Castel Ritaldi). Once in Giano, take some time to visit the town cathedral, the **Chiesa di San Francesco**, the magnificent **Abbazia di San Felice** (☎ 0742-90103, 9:30 am-1 pm, 4-7 pm, otherwise ring the doorbell, free), and the **Castello di Montecchio**.

On Horseback

You can arrange horseback riding around Spoleto with **Azienda Agrituristica Bartoli** (Loc. Patrico di Spoleto, ☎ 0743-220058, open all year), **Azienda Agrituristica Rivoli** (Loc. Uncinano, ☎ 0743-268106, open all year) and **Centro Ippico La Somma** (Fraz. Aiacugigli, Montebiblico, ☎ 0743-54370, open all year).

Monti Sibillini & the Piano Grande

The **Parco Nazionale dei Monti Sibillini** (Sibilline Mountains National Park) is one of the most popular outdoor destinations in Umbria. Full of fascinating legends and magical tales about the Sibyl fairies from which the mountain range takes its name, the territory is an adventure lover's dream for its hills and peaks full of trails for trekking, mountain biking, horseback riding and cross-country skiing (crowned by Monte Vettore). Further attractions are the flora (including the rare Alpine star), fauna (roe deer, porcupine, golden eagle and sparrow-hawk) and rocky rivers and tranquil lakes perfect for canoeing and kayaking.

Split between Umbria and the adjacent region, known as the Marches, the massive limestone block of Sibillini comprises more than 50 mountain peaks of 2,000 m (6,520 feet) or more. The side of the park in the Marches is the biggest, and wildest, but the Umbrian side offers some of its best adventure territory. This includes the western flank of Monte Vettore as well as the tamer plains of the Piano Grande and the Piano Piccolo. The Piano Grande comes into its own during the spring wildflower season at the end of June (known to locals as the "Fiorita") when two endemic plant species – *Carex buxbaumii* (Buxbaum's sedge) and *Carex disticha* (brown sedge) – rear their flowery heads.

■ Adventures

On Foot

Trails crisscross the park on the Umbria side, coming to a head on the slopes of Monte Vettore, the highest peak in the park at 2,476 m/8,072 feet. The park has historical routes into medieval villages and easier walks into the lower rural plains. Pick up a map at the visitor center. But if it's a full-on trek you want, you should opt for a stage of the nine-day **Grande Anello dei Sibillini** (Sibillini Walking Ring), a 120-km itinerary circling the entire mountain chain. The stages lead from Visso to Cupi, Cupi to Fiastra, Fiastra to the Monastero, the Monastero to Garulla, Garulla to Rubbiano, Rubbiano to Colle di Montagallo, Colle di Montagallo to Colle le Cese, Colle le Cese to Campi Vecchio and Campi Vecchio back to Visso. If you only have time for one, go for the Gola dell'Infernaccio (Gorge of Hell) walk from Montemonaco.

Myths & Legends

According to 15th- and 16th-century popular belief, **Monte Sibillini** is the kingdom of the sibyls, the fairy prophets of classical mythology, who were supposed to have predicted the coming of Christ. Legend has it that one of the sibyls was chased from the underworld and forced to hide out in the cave known as the Grotta della Fate (Cave of the Fairies), where she took her revenge by luring mortals in to join her, where they became trapped.

Lago di Pilato (reached by climbing Monte Vettore from Forca di Presta) is similarly fascinating; it is said to be the place where the body of Pontius Pilate vanished off the face of the earth, dragged into oblivion by a herd of horses.

On Wheels

There are plenty of **mountain bike** itineraries in the park, with a choice of 14 one-day circular routes (averaging 25 km/15 miles) into the Valle del Chienti (from Pievebovigliana), the Valle del Fiastrone (from Villa, near Cessapalombo), around San Liberato (from the Monastero di San Liberato), up Monte Rotondo (from Fiastra), into the Valle del Lera (from Amandola), into the Valle del Tenna at the foot of Monte Sibilla (from Montefortino), into the Valle dell'Aso (from Montemonaco), into the Valle del Fluvione (from Balzo), into the Valle del Tronto (from Arquata del Tronto) onto the Piani di Castelluccio (from Castelluccio), onto the Piano di Santa Scolastica (from Norcia), into the Val Castoriana (from Preci), up Monte Cardosa (from Visso) and into the Valle dell'Ussita (from Fluminata).

On Horseback

You can follow the trails on horseback from Cascia with **Associazione Ippica Santo Stefano** (Loc. Maltignano di Cascia (☎ 0743-75535, open July-Sept), from Norcia with **Centro Ippico Talus** (Loc. Savelli, ☎ 0743-875107, July-Sept) or **Valnido** (Loc. Ancarano, ☎ 0743-810144, July-Sept) and from Castelluccio with **Brandimarte Gilberto** (☎ 0743-817279, May-Oct) or **Prova anche tu** (☎ 0743-870212, July-Sept).

Horseback riding in the park can be organized through these *agriturismi*: **Casale nel Parco** (Loc. Fontevena 8, ☎/fax 0743-81648, www.casalenelparco.com) near Norcia; **Il Guerrin Meschino** (Loc. Castelluccio, ☎ 0743-821125); **Dimensione Natura** (Via San Cristoforo 26, Amandola, ☎ 0743-660477); **La Cittadella** (Fraz. Cittadella, ☎ 0736-856261, silvioantognozzi@tiscalinet.it); and **Le Casette** (Via Campobonomo 1, Fiastra, ☎ 0737-52571). Also **Centro Escursione Equestre** (Piazzale Pintura di Bolognola, Bolognola, ☎ 0737-520176).

Nature Notes

Once you're out and about in the park keep your eye out for the animals. The park is home to Apennine wolves, wildcats, porcupines, roe deer and martens. In the sky are golden eagles, goshawks, sparrow hawks, peregrine falcons, great owls, rock partridges, Alpine choughs and coralline choughs. Birdwatchers should also look for Arctic plovers, redstarts, Alpine chaffinches and woodpeckers.

On Water

The **Sibillini Rafting Center** (Norcia, www.asgaia.it/eng) is your best bet for watersports in the park. They have rentals and guided rafting (for groups of up to five people) along the Corno, Nera and Sentino rivers, and into the Frasassi Gorges throughout the year.

On Snow

The region's main skiing draw is the **Forca Canapine**, a mountain pass well served by ski and chair lifts, but **Ussita**, **Sarnano** and **Piobbico** also have facilities.

In the Air

The plains of Castelluccio are a well-known spot for hang-gliding and paragliding. You can book yourself a flight with **Pro Delta** (Castellucio di Norcia, ☎ 0743-821156, fax 0743-821157, www.prodelta.it).

Norcia

Founded by the Sabines (an ancient people from the Sabine Hills northeast of Rome) sometime around 1300 BC, Norcia grew into a municipium in the Roman Empire, before suffering destruction at the hands of the Goths, Franks and then Saracens. St Benedict (the patron saint of Europe) was born here around 480; he went on to form the Benedictines, the first religious order, which became one of the most influential bodies in Europe in subsequent centuries. Such a rich past has given the city some beautiful Gothic, Romanesque, Renaissance and Baroque architecture. Unfortunately, much of it has been destroyed by the seven or so earthquakes that hit the city between 1328 and 1979, resulting in an 18th-century Papal Bill forbidding any building in Norcia to surpass 12.5 m (41 feet) in height. Completely surrounded by medieval fortifications, the city's buildings are completely hidden from the arriving visitor.

■ Sightseeing

What better place to start your tour of Norcia than on its main square, marked with a statue of St Benedict by Giuseppe Pinzi (1880). It is surrounded by almost all of the town's major monuments. The Basilica di San Benedetto faces one side, with its finely sculpted, typical Gothic façade; the Palazzo Comunale is to its left; the Castellina, directly opposite; and the Duomo is by its side.

Although the existing basilica dates back to 1389, little remains of the original **Basilica di San Benedetto**. Much of it was modified following damage by earthquakes in the 17th and 18th centuries, but you can still get an idea of its early splendor. The Gothic façade is striking for its finely-sculpted entranceway and central rose window, flanked by statues of St Benedict and his twin sister, St Scolastica. The 1388 basilica bell tower managed to come through the earthquakes intact, but like other town buildings, suffered alterations under the Papal Bill, which required it to be reduced in height.

To the right of the church, the **Loggia dei Mercanti** (also known as the Portico delle Misure) is an 18th-century reproduction of the 1570 loggia that was destroyed in the 1859 earthquake. The interior suffered similar damage; of its original decorations, a 16th-century fresco of the *Madonna with Child, St Barbara and the Archangel Michael* (under the Balcone dei Cantori, the Choir Balcony) was one of the few works of art to survive. There's also a *Resurrection of Lazarus* by Michelangelo Carducci (1560) in the second altar to the left, and a *St Benedict and Totila*, by Filippo Napoletano (1621) in the left transept. The chapel in the left nave is believed to mark the place of the house where St Benedict was born.

BENEDICTINE CELEBRATIONS

On March 23, Norcia comes to life with the **Corteo Storico** (historical parade) in celebration of its patron saint, St Benedict. Accompanied by a parade in medieval costume, the ancient ceremony includes offering *ceri* (candles) to the saint, a crossbow contest between the town *guaite* (districts) and culminates in a solemn procession through the streets bearing relics of the saint himself.

The present **Palazzo Comunale** is an 18th-century reproduction of what once was; only the 14th-century doorway survives from the original (the loggia that tops it is another later renovation). Its main attraction is the 1450 reliquary kept in the palace chapel. Fortunately, the **Castellina**, which stands opposite it, has fared better. This small fortress, with its harsh corner bastions, was built under the watchful eye of Pope Julius III to the design of Vignola, over what was once the Palazzo del Podestà and the ancient Pieve di Santa Maria Argentea. The **Museo Civico-Diocesano** now occupies its first floor, with works from Norcia and surroundings. It includes artists such as Giovanni della Robbia, Nicola da Siena and Antonio da Faenza) from the 13th to 18th centuries. There's also a fine 13th-century wooden sculpture of the *Deposition* and an altarpiece by Jacopo Siculo.

Propping itself up alongside the fortress, the **Duomo** (Cathedral of Santa Maria Argentea) also bears the marks of a history of earthquakes. It has been consistently modified since the first stone was laid here in 1560, but the original wooden doors, which stand in the main doorway, have somehow managed to come through unscathed. To its side, besides the massive fortifications, lies another entrance; it comes from the early Pieve di Santa Maria Argentea, which was demolished here to make way for the castle. Inside is much of the 18th-century remodeling, but there are also a few art treasures of note which have stood the test of time – the fresco of the *Madonna della Misericordia* is the best-known, but there's also a decorated altarpiece by Duquesnoy, a *Madonna and Saints* from the brush of Pomarancio and a *St Vicenzo* by Giuseppe Paladini.

Make your way to the **Capolaterra**, the highest part of town and, as such, one of the most heavily damaged in the earthquake of 1979. Marks of the shake can be seen on its hastily reconstructed civic architecture, but the **Palazzo dei Cavalieri di Malta** and the Gothic **Chiesa di San Augustine**, with its exterior 1368 fresco and 14th- and 15th-century fresco cycles inside by Nicola da Siena and Giovannofrio di Norcia, still warrant a trip.

The very highest point of the Capolaterra is marked by the seemingly insignificant **Oratorio di San Agostinuccio**, which, despite its rather boring exterior architecture, hides a treasure of 16th-century craftsmanship inside. Its inlaid, gilded and painted wooden ceiling and richly decorated statues of the town's patron saints were crafted by the best of the region's architects.

Over toward Via Umberto is the oldest church in Norcia, the **Chiesa di San Giovanni** (renovated in the 18th century after damage by earthquakes), home to an image of the *Madonna della Palla* by Il Dalmata, which is thought to be miraculous. Nearby, on Via Umberto itself, the square **Tempietto** (small votive temple) survives from 1354. Its two entrance archways are of note for their unusual decorations of geometric, zoomorphic and anthropomorphic motifs.

The Big Daddy of Black Truffle Fairs

When Norcia's Mostra del Tartufo (Truffle Fair) hits the city streets on the last weekend of every February, stands buckle under the weight of produce brought in from near and far, and producers are heard crying the merits of their specialties and gastronomic treats – including the town's famous prosciutto, sausages and spiced salamis. But the black truffle takes pride of place. This delicious and relatively cheap truffle variety (generally considered inferior to the white truffle) provides the city streets with a potent aroma and its dishes (especially pastas) with a splash of spice. Rummage around the stands and then head into a nearby *trattoria* to try some yourself.

Cascia

O verlooking the River Corno, Cascia has its own architectural and art glories to tempt the visitor to its hilltop location. Like nearby Norcia, it too has suffered from centuries of earthquakes, and as a result nothing remains from its early foundations in Roman times. Fortunately, there's plenty of medieval splendor to enjoy from its periods of growth under rulers Frederick II of Swabia, Foligno and, later, the Papal State.

■ Sightseeing

Scenic Cascia's most famous local character is St Rita (1381-1457), a saint widely believed to grant wishes, and who is remembered in the **Santuario e Chiesa di San Rita**, a sanctuary that draws pilgrims from all over the world. The walk up from town drops you off in front of the main portal where sculptures in Carrara marble by Eros Pellini depict tales from the life of the saint. Her remains are in a glass case inside to the left, with frescoes by Montanarini, Filocamo and Ceracchini and a main altar by Giacomo Manzù.

The city's other main medieval attractions are the Gothic **Chiesa di San Francesco**, with its beautiful rose window and ogival portal, and the **Chiesa di San Antonio** (Via P Orientale, ☎ 0743-753055), which dates from the 15th century, but has since been reconstructed in Baroque style. It contains a cycle of notable frescoes depicting the *Life of St Antony* by an unknown Umbrian artist and scenes of the *Passion* by Nicola da Siena. The Gothic **Chiesa di Santa Augustine** contains more frescoes.

The **Collegiata di Santa Maria** (Collegiate Church of St Mary) is one of Cascia's oldest buildings; its origins have been traced back to Lombard times, although much has been restored after earthquake damage. Inside, it houses a 15th-century wooden crucifix and a museum of religious works.

Civic buildings reach their peak with the **Palazzo Carli**, which houses the city library and archives. The town's main museum, the **Museo di Palazzo Santi** (Piazza Aldo Moro, ☎ 0743-751010) displays archeological findings from Casica and its surroundings, including wooden sculptures dating from the 14th and 15th centuries.

Much of the town's charm, however, comes from the surrounding greenery. Follow the evocative walk to the **Roccaporena** (the birthplace of St Rita) along the River Corno, and you'll not only get to see some beautiful scenery, but you'll also be walking in the footsteps of the saint. Once you arrive, you can visit the house where she was born, with its views over the rugged peak of Monte Scoglio, which dominates the town.

■ Where to Eat

LOCAL FLAVORS

Beccacce alla norcina: Woodcock filled with giblets, sausage, thyme and, in season, black truffles.

Budellacci: Pork intestines and offal smoked on a griddle with spices and fennel.

Gnocchi dolci: Semolina gnocchi cooled and covered with pine nuts, bread crumbs and cocoa powder, traditionally served on Christmas Eve.

Porchetta: Suckling pig stuffed with aromatic herbs, garlic, pepper and wild fennel roasted or cooked on a spit.

Prosciutto di Norcia: Norcia raw ham, a protected geographical specialty still prepared using traditional techniques and easily recognizable from its typical pear shape.

Spalletta: Norcia shoulder ham, aged from one to two years.

Zuppa di Farro: Organic spelt soup made from spelt grown in Monteleone di Spoleto.

In Spoleto

Popular eateries in town include **Al Druso** (Via Arco di Druso 25, ☎ 0743-221695, closed Monday, $$) for its wild boar dishes: *pappardelle al cinghiale* (long, flat pasta with wild boar sauce) and *cinghiale al porcini* (wild boar with porcini mushrooms). There's more local wild boar at **L'Angelo Antico** (via Monterone 109, ☎ 0743-49077, closed Monday, $$). Its **cinghiale alla cacciatore** (hunter-style wild boar) is served in the traditional country fashion.

Pleasant *trattoria* **Da Sportellino** (Via Cerquiglia 4, ☎ 0743-45230, closed Thursday, $$) is another top choice; its *zuppa di farro con porcini* (spelt soup with porcini mushrooms) and *scottadito di agnella al tartufo* (grilled lamb chops with truffles) come with a real home-cooked taste.

Just off the market square, **Del Mercato** (Vicolo del Mercato 4, ☎ 0743-45325, closed Thursday, $$) serves up a more unusual range of traditional foods with *fonduta di formaggio e tartuffo* (cheese and truffle fondue), *lumache* (snails) and *piccione in salmi* (stuffed pigeon) remaining favorites, at least with the local population.

You can sample one of Tuscany's most fragrant entrées at **Il Tartufo** (Piazza Garibaldi 24, ☎ 0743-40236, closed Sunday night and Monday, $$$). Its *fiori di zucca con melanzane* (deep-fried courgette flowers and eggplant) is deliciously delicate. Follow it with the *petto di anatra con patate e tartufo* (duck breast with fried potatoes and truffles).

Welcoming *trattoria* **La Lanterna** (Via della Trattora 6, ☎ 0743-49815, closed Tuesday lunch and Wednesday, $$) serves a tasty *strangozzi rucola e pancetta* (homemade pasta with rocket and pancetta ham) and *pollo ai porcini* (chicken with porcini mushrooms). **Taverna dei Duchi** (Via A Saffi 1, ☎ 0743-40323, closed Wednesday, $$) offers an unusual *cinghiale al ginepro* (wild boar with juniper berries) and a more traditional *zuppa di farro* (spelt soup).

Out of Spoleto

Three kilometres (two miles) out of Spoleto, two-star hotel and *trattoria* **Boni Cerri** (Loc. Cortaccione, ☎ 0743-46205, closed Tuesday, $$) has a tasty seasonal menu specializing in local game and home-grown vegetables. Try the *spaghetti al tartufo* (spaghetti with truffles) or the *pappardelle al lepre* (long, flat pasta with a hare sauce).

Nearby, **Vecchio Fornio** (Loc. Cortaccione, ☎ 0743-49408, closed Monday, $$) serves a tasty *pappardelle al cinghiale* and a range of *carne alla griglia* (grilled meat) perfectly complemented by *contorni* (side dishes) such as fried potatoes, garlic spinach and deep-fried vegetables.

A little farther away (13 km/nine miles), **Castello di Poreta** (Loc. Poreta, ☎ 0743-0743-275810, closed Monday, www.ilcastellodiporetta.it, $$$) is the local gourmet choice. Occupying a restored country house, the restaurant (also selling Il Porettino, the local extra-virgin olive oil) serves some tasty homemade pasta, including a delicious *gnocchi con salsa di rapa rossa* (potato pasta with beetroot salsa).

■ Where to Stay

For hotel accommodation within the historical center of Spoleto, your best options are the following:

Dei Duchi ☆☆☆☆ (Viale G Matteotti 4, ☎ 0743-44541, fax 0743-44543, www.hoteldeiduchi.com, $$$), overlooking the Teatro Romano.

Dell'Angelo ☆☆ (Via Arco di Druso 25, ☎ 0743-222385, fax 0743-207965, hoteldellangelo@libero.it, $), alongside the Arco di Druso.

Aurora ☆☆ (Via Apollinaire 3, ☎ 0743-220315, fax 0743-221885, hotelaurora@virgilio.it, $$), on Piazza Sant'Agata.

Residenza d'Epoca Palazzo Dragoni (Via Duomo 3, ☎/fax 0743-2222220, $$$) and **Il Panciolle** ☆☆ (Via Duomo 3, ☎/fax 0 743-45677, $$), are both within a stroll of the Duomo.

Just outside of Spoleto, **Gattapone** ☆☆☆☆ (Via del Ponte 6, ☎ 0743-223447, fax 0743-223448, gattapone@mail.caribusiness.it, $$$$), has great views over the Rocca Albornoziana and the whole of the city. But if you've got the bucks, you can't beat a room in the former hermitage of **Eremo delle Grazie** (Strada per Monteluco, ☎ 0743-49624, fax 0743-49650, eremodellegrazie@tin.it, $$$$$) on the green slopes of Monteluco.

The best campgrounds in the region are at **Il Girasole** ☆☆ (Loc. Petrognano, ☎ 0743-51335, campinilgirasole@libero.it, April-Sept, 70 spaces, $) and

Monteluco ☆☆ (Strada per Monteluco, Loc. San Pietro, ☎ 0743-220358, April-Sept, 35 spaces, $).

Spoleto also has youth hostels in town. **Ostello Villa Redenta** (Villa Redenta 1, ☎ 0743-224936, villaredenta@hotmail.com, $) is just out of town in Cerreto di Spoleto. **Ostello Palazzo Nobili** (Via Umberto I, ☎/fax 0743-922147, $) is another one and, in Poggiodomo, there is **Ostello Il Sentiero** (Via del Colle 4, ☎/fax 0743-79277, $). In Cascia, try **Ostello Sant'Antonio** (Via Porta Leonina, ☎ 0743-751053, fax 0743-751053, $).

You can also book into religious accommodation in Cascia at **Casa del Pellegrino La Margherita** (Fraz. Roccaporena di Cascia, ☎ 0743-7549, fax 0743-754815, $) and **Casa Esercizi Spirituali** (Via Sant'Agostino, ☎ 0743071229). Spoleto offers **Istituto Bambin Gesù** (Via Sant'Angelo 4, ☎ 0743-40232, $) and **Monastero San Ponziano** (Via della Basilica di San Salvatore 2, ☎ 0743-225288, fax 0743-225086, san.ponziano@tiscalinet.it, $).

There's also a mountain refuge at Cascia, **Rifugio Belvedere** (Fraz. Onelli, ☎ 0743-76172, $) and two in Norcia, **Le Guide** (Fraz Forca Canapine, ☎ 0743-823012, $) and **Rifugio Perugia** (Fraz. Forca Canapine, ☎ 0743-823019, fax 0743-823006, $).

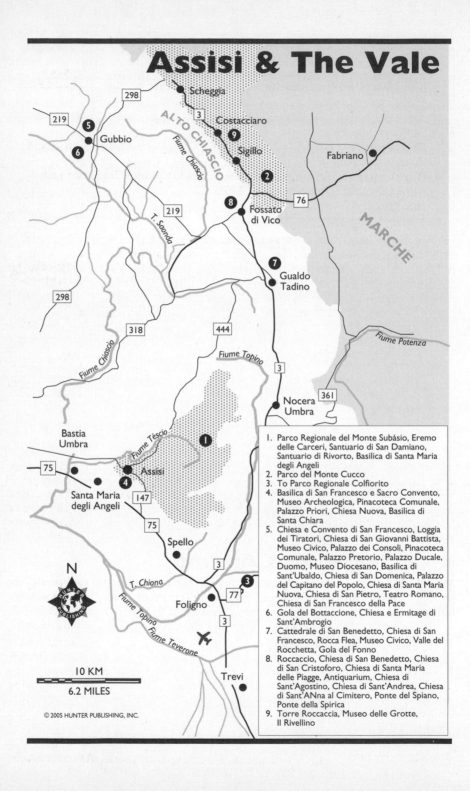

Assisi & The Vale

1. Parco Regionale del Monte Subásio, Eremo delle Carceri, Santuario di San Damiano, Santuario di Rivorto, Basilica di Santa Maria degli Angeli
2. Parco del Monte Cucco
3. To Parco Regionale Colfiorito
4. Basilica di San Francesco e Sacro Convento, Museo Archeologica, Pinacoteca Comunale, Palazzo Priori, Chiesa Nuova, Basilica di Santa Chiara
5. Chiesa e Convento di San Francesco, Loggia dei Tiratori, Chiesa di San Giovanni Battista, Museo Civico, Palazzo dei Consoli, Pinacoteca Comunale, Palazzo Pretorio, Palazzo Ducale, Duomo, Museo Diocesano, Basilica di Sant'Ubaldo, Chiesa di San Domenica, Palazzo del Capitano del Popolo, Chiesa di Santa Maria Nuova, Chiesa di San Pietro, Teatro Romano, Chiesa di San Francesco della Pace
6. Gola del Bottaccione, Chiesa e Ermitage di Sant'Ambrogio
7. Cattedrale di San Benedetto, Chiesa di San Francesco, Rocca Flea, Museo Civico, Valle del Rocchetta, Gola del Fonno
8. Roccaccio, Chiesa di San Benedetto, Chiesa di San Cristoforo, Chiesa di Santa Maria delle Piagge, Antiquarium, Chiesa di Sant'Agostino, Chiesa di Sant'Andrea, Chiesa di Sant'ANna al Cimitero, Ponte del Spiano, Ponte della Spirica
9. Torre Roccaccia, Museo delle Grotte, Il Rivellino

Scheggia
298
219
3
Costacciaro
5
Gubbio
9
Sigillo
6
Fabriano
2
Fiume Chiascio
ALTO CHIASCIO
219
76
8
Fossato di Vico
MARCHE
T. Saonda
298
7
Gualdo Tadino
Fiume Potenza
318
444
Fiume Topino
Fiume Chiascio
3
Nocera Umbra
361
Bastia Umbra
Fiume Téscio
1
75
Assisi
4
Santa Maria degli Angeli
147
75
Spello
3
N
3
77
T. Chiona
Foligno
Fiume Topino
3
Fiume Teverone
Trevi

10 KM
6.2 MILES

© 2005 HUNTER PUBLISHING, INC.

Assisi & Northeast Umbria

REGION AT A GLANCE

Main city: Assisi.
Afternoon trips from Assisi: Valfabbrica (see page 439, 442), Spello (see page 439-40).
City breaks: Perugia (see page 361), Gubbio (see page 440) and Foligno (see page 407)
Rural retreats: Monte Subasio (see page 438), Monte Cucco (see page 445) and Alto Chiascio (see page 446).
Spa towns: Nocera Umbra (see page 414).

■ Information Sources

Tourist Information: The region's main tourist office **Servizio Turistico Territoriale IAT di Assisi** (Assisi Territory Tourist Office, Piazza del Comune, Assisi, ☎ 0758-12450, fax 0758-13727, www.iat.assisi. pg.it) provides information on the towns of Assisi, Bastia Umbra, Bettona and Cannara. The information office for **Parco Regionale Monte Subasio** is just outside of Assisi (Mt Subasio Regional Park, Loc. Ca'Piombino, ☎ 0758-15181, fax 0758-15307, www.parks.it/parco.monte.subasio).

Assisi

Beautifully situated in the medieval heart of Umbria, Assisi is one of the most popular sightseeing and pilgrimage destinations in Italy. Not only does it have an historical center of distinguished monuments, collections of art and breathtaking views of the surrounding countryside, but it sits on the doorstep of the Parco Regionale Monte Subasio (Mt Subasio Regional Park). It is also tied with the legacy of its best-known son, St Francis.

■ Getting Here & Around

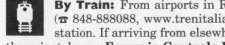

By Air: Most international flights arrive at Rome's **Leonardo da Vinci-Fiumicino airport** (☎ 066-5951). From there, air connections link to the small airport of **Sant'Egidio** (☎ 075592141, fax 0756929562, www.airport.umbria.it), located midway between Perugia and Assisi.

By Train: From airports in Rome, Pisa and Florence, frequent trains (☎ 848-888088, www.trenitalia.it) link to Assisi via Cortona Terontola station. If arriving from elsewhere in Umbria, the city is well served by the privately-run **Ferrovia Centrale Umbra** (☎ 0755-75401, www.fcu.it) train line. The train station is three miles out of town at Santa Maria degli Angeli and linked by a shuttle bus every 15 minutes.

By Car: Assisi is only a short drive from Perugia, which links to the **A1** motorway between Rome and Florence by the **SS3bis** (also known as the **E45**). Use the Val di Chiana exit if arriving from Florence and the north; the Orte exit if driving from Rome and the south.

Rental car options include **Assisiorganizza** (Via Borgo Aretino 11a, ☎ 0758-15280), **Corridoni Nicola** (Via Capobove 9, ☎ 0758-12409), **Costantini Gino** (Via degli Acquedotti 8, ☎/fax 0758-16356), **CS Autoservizi** (Via Fiorita 14, ☎ 0758-098023, fax 0758-099119, ubaldok@libero.it), **Cuppoloni Andrea** (Piaggia San Pietro 9, ☎ 0758-12777) and **Salimbeti Marco** (Via San Benedetto 99, ☎/fax 0758-12976, autoservice@edisons.it).

Bike Rental: Try **Angelucci Andrea** (Via Becchetti 31, ☎/fax 0758-042550) or **Bartolucci Bruno** outside the train station (☎ 0339-3724592).

■ Sightseeing

Historic Assisi

While the ancient Umbrian city of *Asisum* left a priceless legacy of Etruscan and Roman structures, it was the town's most famous monk who transformed Assisi into a site of immense architectural and artistic importance. Many of the greats of the high Middle Ages and the Renaissance were drawn to Assisi from all over Italy, and outstanding works of Umbrian painting and sculpture adorn every church, cathedral and palace.

Basilica di San Francesco e Sacro Convento is the city's undisputed jewel, located west of the historical center. Built just after the death of St Francis in 1228, it comprises two churches – one built above the other – and a crypt dug in 1818 to house the Saint's tomb. Entered via a courtyard built by Pope Sixtus IV with magnificent views over the surrounding countryside, the dark lower church has striking late Romanesque vaulting

St. Anthony & St. Francis, Simone Martini (Basilica di San Francesco)

and frescoes by some of the greatest painters of the 13th and 14th centuries, including Cimabue, the Lorenzetti brothers and Simone Martini; the upper church is Italy's earliest Gothic church, and is decorated with Giotto's famous cycle of 28 frescoes telling the stories and legends of the life of St Francis. Look for Giotto's *Madonna with Angels* and *St Francis*, Simone Martini's *Life of St Martin* and two Lorenzetti works – *Madonna with Saints*, and *Episodes of the Life and Passion of Christ* - while you're making the rounds. The **Treasure of the Basilica** (☎ 0758-812238) displays a goldsmithery, paintings and textiles, as well the collection of 56 Florentine and Sienese masters that make up the "Perkins Collection."

ST. FRANCIS OF ASSISI

St Francis was born in Assisi to wealthy cloth merchants around 1181. His calling first came to him in a dream in 1205 when fighting for Assisi against Perugia, and he returned to his hometown to help the sick and the poor. His parents didn't take his change of career very well, however, and he was forced to flee the city after his father imprisoned and then disinherited him for spending his money on repairing the decrepit Chiesa di San Damiano.

From this point on, he travelled the land dressed in ragged clothes, begging for food and preaching purity and peace, soon becoming celebrated for his literal interpretation of the Gospels and the example of Jesus

Christ, which the Franciscans follow to this day. After attracting numerous followers, he founded the Franciscan Order in 1209.

St Francis's is most famous as the patron saint of animals. He is also the saint of environmentalists, families, lacemakers, merchants and needle workers. The saint also watches over Assisi, Italy, Colorado and Sante Fe, New Mexico.

Walk out of the lower church and head uphill along the wonderfully preserved Via San Francesco to reach Assisi's main square, the **Piazza del Comune**. It is built on the foundations of the first century BC Roman **Tempio di Minerva** (the original portico is still visible on the left). The remains of the Roman forum are just below the piazza, with the original Roman paving and the foundations of the Temple of Minerva still visible at the **Museo Archeologico** (Via Portica, ☎/fax 0758-13053). On the Piazza itself sit the 13th-century **Palazzo del Capitano del Popolo**, the early 14th-century **Torre del Popolo**, the 14th-century **Palazzo del Priori** and the **Pinacoteca Comunale** (Municipal Art Gallery, Palazzo Vallemani, Via San Francesco, ☎ 0758-12033) which displays frescoes taken from churches and monasteries in the area.

Just behind the Palazzo del Priori, the Renaissance **Chiesa Nuova** is on the spot where St Francis's family house once stood; he was supposedly born in the nearby Oratorio di San Francesco Piccolino.

Via di San Rufino takes you away from the piazza to the 13th-century **cathedral** of the same name. Behind its beautiful Romanesque façade with three remarkable rose windows, you can still visit the font where St Francis and St Clare, one of St Francis's best-known disciples, were baptized. You can find out more about her in the Gothic **Basilica di Santa Chiara**. Designed by Filippo da Campello, it was built in 1257 and contains precious paintings from the 13th to 14th centuries, the body of St Clare preserved in the crypt, and a *Crucifix* that is said to have spoken to St Francis.

ON THE TRAIL OF ST. FRANCIS

St. Francis Preaching to the Birds, Giotto (Basilica di San Francesco)

Out of town is the peaceful **Eremo delle Carceri** (Hermitage) in the Parco Regionale Monte Subasio, where St Francis would retreat in prayer; the Franciscan **Santuario di San Damiano**, where he is said to have heard the voice of Christ through the *Crucifix* now found in Chiesa di Santa Chiara; the **Santuario di Rivotorto**, where the "hovel of St Francis" is preserved in memory of the first Franciscan community; and the Renaissance **Basilica di Santa Maria degli Angeli**, where a magnificent dome designed by Alessi marks the spot of the Oratorio di San Francesco. The cell where St. Francis died in 1226 is decorated with frescoes by Lo Spagna, while the chapel to the side of the Basilica has more frescoes by Tiberio d'Assisi. The museum annex (☎ 0578-12283) has works by the Maestro di San Francesco, Giunta Pisano and others on display.

Out of Assisi

The territory of Assisi is bound to the northeast by Mt Subasio and to the southeast by the hills that separate the region from the Tiber Valley. It is a fertile countryside, crisscrossed by softly-flowing rivers and includes the towns of Bastia Umbra, Bettona and Cannara.

These days, **Bastia Umbra** is little more than a busy agricultural and industrial center, but in the Middle Ages it was an important strategic point much fought over by the peoples of Assisi and Perugia. Unfortunately, from this time only the **Porta Sant'Angelo**, a small part of the Franciscan **Monastero di Santa Croce** (with façade formed by sparkling rows of white and pink stone from Mt Subasio) and the 11th-century **Chiesa di San Paolo** remain. The latter is all that stands of the ancient Benedictine convent where, in 1212, St Claire was housed when fleeing to the Franciscan movement.

Bettona is an active agricultural center, but its ancient origins are more visible. The Etruscan "Ipogeo," a collection of graves discovered alongside the Chiascio River in the Colle suburbs, dates from the second century BC and part of the historical center's original Etruscan ring of walls interlink with the current medieval stretches. Inside them, the 15th-century **Palazzetto Podestarile** houses an interesting **Pinacoteca Municipale** (Civic Art Gallery, Piazza Cavour, ☎/fax 0759-87306) with works from the 14th to 18th centuries by artists such as Perugino, Tiberio di Assisi and Dono Doni, terracottas by the Della Robbia brothers and an archeological collection taken from the Ipogeo.

A charming **walk** around the city walls offers a magnificent view over the valley from Torgiano to Perugia, to Assisi, to Trevi, and on to the hills that join with the Tiber Valley. Another trail takes you into the woods of Monte Lauro with its free-running hot spring, and these tracks can also be explored on **horseback**; contact **Natura Amica** (Loc. Fratta di Bettona, ☎ 0759-82922, open all year) or **Umbria a Cavallo** (Loc. Burchio, ☎ 0759-87150, open all year) to set up a ride.

A pleasant **cycle** trip will bring you to the hamlet of Passaggio, with **Abbazia di San Crispolto** and 18th-century **Villa Boccaglione** (attributed to Piermarini who designed the Teatro alla Scala in Milan) and onto Cannara. Continue through the town (in the direction of Bevagna) and you'll pass the small **Chiesa di San Giovanni** to arrive at **Pian d'Arca**, the legendary site of St Francis's sermon to the birds, which you will already have seen immortalized in Giotto's frescoes in the Basilica di San Francesco in Assisi.

■ Adventures

The Parco Regionale Monte Subasio

The Mt Subasio Regional Park on Assisi's eastern fringe takes its name from its highest mountain, Mt Subasio (1,290 m/4,231 feet) and its fame from St Francis; he wrote his famous treatise, *Praises of the Creatures,* while in meditation in its woods. Although hunting has been banned here for centuries, few animals are found on the slopes, though wolves are occasionally reported, and you may see the common grey partridge, wood pigeon, birds of prey such as buzzards and goshawks in the sky, and porcupines, badgers, foxes and wild boars on the ground.

On Foot

The karst formation of Mt Subasio was once entirely covered by tall holm oaks; today you can walk part of the woods that remain by setting out from the Franciscan hermitage of **Eremo delle Carceri**. Head up to the summit of **Mt Subasio** along the old cart tracks and you'll find a vast meadow, traversed by a beautiful scenic path. Another picturesque trail leads from Assisi to Spello along a route marked with religious retreats and medieval hamlets. You can also pick up the **Sentiero Francescano della Pace**, a "Franciscan Footpath" that follows the footsteps of St Francis from Assisi through Valfabbrica to Gubbio.

On Wheels

 From Capodaqua, a six-mile **mountain bike** trail (it can also be walked) takes you on a loop past the crumbling fortresses of Castello Salvino and Rocca Calestro with views onto the secular woods in the Piano di Colfiorito.

On Horseback

 Plenty of riding opportunities around Assisi take you into the Parco Regional del Monte Subasio or along the Chiascio River; try **Centro Equitazione Ranch Allegro** (Loc. Beviglie, ☎ 0758-16893, open all year), **Centro Ippico Assisi** (Loc. Santa Maria Maddalena, Rivotorto, ☎ 0758-042997, open all year), **Circolo Ippico Malvarina** (Loc. Capodacqua, ☎ 0758-064280, open all year), **Club Ippico La Torre** (Loc. Torchiagina, ☎ 0758-039372), **Le Querce** (Loc. Piano della Pieve, ☎ 0758-02332) or **Lo Sperone** (Loc. Castelnuovo, ☎ 0758-043257, open all year). There's a riding center close to the Aeroporto Sant'Egido, called **Club Ippico Sant'Egido** (Via Aeroporto 16, Loc. Opsedalicchio, ☎ 0758-011637).

You can also go horseback riding on the other side of the Parco Regionale del Monte Subasio from the town of Nocera Umbra with **Azienda Agrituristica Prato** (Loc. Isola, ☎ 0742-813528, open all year) or **Centro Ippico San Giorgio** (Loc. Ponte Parrano, ☎ 0338-3580019, open all year, closed Mon).

In the Air

 The winds above Mt Subasio are ideal for hang-gliding; arrange your flight with **Fly Ali Subasio** (Via Monte Subasio, Loc. Rivotorto, ☎/fax 0758-064105, www.alisubasio.com).

On Water

 Just out the other side of the park, the Topino River offers **canoeing** near Nocera Umbra. Contact **Canoa Club Topino** (Via Roma 64, Nocera Umbra, ☎ 0742-23146, fax 0742-74530, web.tiscalinet.it/rafting) to arrange outings.

■ Where to Eat

The area around Assisi is a good place to shop for **extra-virgin olive oil**. It is best tasted in *bruschetta* – a slice of local toasted bread rubbed with a clove of garlic and drizzled with olive oil. **Azienda Agraria Sasso Rosso** (Loc. Capodacqua, ☎/fax 0758-707128, www.sassorosso.it) sells it, or head up to Valfabbrica where you can taste and buy some of the best at **Molino Ceccarani** (Via Marcon 14, ☎ 0759-01611) and **Molino Serpioni** (Via del Sentino 15, Loc. Pianello, ☎ 0756-02441).

 Even three-stars in Assisi are within the reach of most budget travelers. **Beniamino Ubaldi** ☆☆☆ (Via Perugina 74, ☎ 0759-277773, fax 0759-276604, www.rosatihotels.com, $$), **Pinolo** ☆☆☆ (Via Porta

Romana 102, ☎ 0759-272747, fax 0759-272748, $$) and **Tre Ceri** ☆☆☆ (Via Benamati 7/8, ☎ 0759-222109, fax 0759-277543, $$) are all great options. Cheaper still are the **Balestrieri** ☆☆ (Via Mazzatinti 12, ☎ 0759-220650, fax 0759-220663, $) and the **Oderisi** (Via Mazzatinti 2, ☎ 0759-220662, fax 0759-220663); both are run by the same family.

■ Where to Stay

Top-rate hotel accommodation in Assisi is offered by the **Subasio** ☆☆☆☆ (Via F. Elia, ☎ 0758-12206, fax 0758-16691, $$$$), but if you're arriving out of season, book yourself into **Dei Priori** ☆☆☆ (Corso Mazzini 15, ☎ 0758-12237, fax 0758-16804, $$$$). They drop their rates considerably during the winter months. The **Fontebella** ☆☆☆ (Via Fontebella 25, ☎ 0758-12883, fax 0758-12941, $$$$$) is one of the more expensive choices, but, again, rooms become considerably cheaper when there isn't the summer demand.

In the consistently lower price bracket, nearby **Giotto** ☆☆☆ (Via Fontebella 41, ☎ 0758-12209, fax 0758-16479, $$$) and **San Francesco** ☆☆☆ (Via San Francesco 48, ☎ 0758-12281, fax 0758-16237, $$$) both offer a good location and star rating for their prices. Cheaper still are **Ancajani** ☆☆ (Via Ancajani 16, ☎ 0758-15128, fax 0758-15129, $$), **La Fortezza** ☆☆ (Vicolo Fortezza 19b, ☎ 0758-12418, fax 0758-198035, $$) and **Grotta Antica** ☆ (Via M. Vecchi 1, ☎ 0758-13467, $).

There are some campgrounds around town: **Camping Internazionale Assisi** ☆☆☆ (San Giovanni in Campiglione, Loc. Campiglione, ☎ 0758-13710, fax 0758-12335, 133 spaces, Apr-Oct, $) and **Campeggio Fontemaggio** ☆☆ (Via Eremo delle Carceri 7, Assisi, ☎ 0758-13636, fax 0758-13749, all year, 244 spaces, $).

There's another campground at Nocera Umbra, **Pian delle Stelle** (Loc. Montealago, ☎ 0742-818241, $), and one more farther south at Spello – **Subasio** ☆☆ (Loc. Sportella, ☎/fax 0742-301144, robertoroscini@tiscalinet.it, Apr-Sept, 25 spaces, $).

Out of a huge choice of religious accommodation, the best-placed are **Casa del Terziario** (Piazza Vescovado, ☎ 0758-12366, fax 0758-16337, $), **Monastero Sant'Andrea** (Vicolo Sant'Andrea, ☎ 0758-12274, fax 0758-15130, $) and **Monastero Santa Croce** (Via Santa Croce 4, ☎ 0578- 12515, fax 0578-16764). The tourist office has a full list if these three are fully booked.

Assisi has four youth hostels: **Ostello della Pace** (Via di Valecchie 177, ☎/fax 0758-16767, $) and **Fontemaggio** (Via San Rufino Campagna, ☎ 0758-13636, fax 0578-13749) in town and **Ostello Victor** (Via della Spina, Loc. Rivotorto di Assisi, ☎ 0758-064526, fax 0758-065562, $) and **Ostello Victor Center** (Via Romana 31, Loc. Capodacqua, ☎/fax 0758-065562, $) just outside.

There's a hiking shelter at Spello if you are following the Assisi-to-Spello walking route: **La Spella** (Loc. La Spella, ☎ 0742-301144, $).

Outside of Assisi

■ Gubbio

One of the most picturesque towns in Umbria, Gubbio conserves an almost intact medieval historical center and a fabulous natural location, perched on the higher reaches of a plateau at the foot of Mt Ingino. On its doorstep is the Parco Regionale Monte Cucco, a range of limestone massif popular with hikers, cavers and hang-gliders, and the lower-lying fertile river valley of the Alto Chiascio.

Getting There & Around

 By Car: Gubbio can be reached via Perugia along the **SS293**. If you prefer to wind your way up through the Alto Chiascio, take the **SS444** from Assisi and change onto the **SS219** at Gualdo Tadini.

For car rental try **Rent Car** (Via L. da Vinci, ☎ 0759-220595) or **SEL Noleggi** (Via B. Croce, ☎ 0759-220010).

 By Train: The town has a train station (Fossato di Vico/Gubbio) on the Rome-to-Ancona line (☎ 848-888088, www.trenitalia.it); the station is 10 or so miles out of town, but frequent shuttle buses run to the historical center from both this train station and the one in Perugia.

 By Taxi: These can be found on Piazza Q. Martiri (☎ 0759-273800).

Information Sources

 Tourist Information: Servizio Turistico Territoriale IAT di Gubbio (Gubbio Territory Tourist Office, Via Ansidei 32, ☎ 0759-220790, fax 0759-273409, www.iat.gubbio.pg.it) provides tourist information for the towns of Gubbio, Gualdo Tadino, Sigillo, Valfabbrica and others in the zone. **Parco Regionale Monte Cucco** (Mt Cucco Regional Park) has its own information office in Sigillo (Villa Anita, ☎/fax 0759-179025, www.parks.it/parco.monte.cucco).

There are smaller tourist information branches at **Gualdo Tadino** (☎ 0759-12172), **Sigillo** (☎ 0759-177114, sigillo@retein.net), **Costacciaro** (☎ 0759-17271, comcost@tin.it), **Fossato di Vico** (☎ 0759-14951, comfossato@tiscalinet.it) and **Scheggia e Pascelupo** (☎ 0759-259707).

Adventure Information: The **CAI** has two branches in the region, one at Gubbio (Piazza San Pietro, ☎ 0759-273618) and another at Gualdo Tadino (Via Santo Marzio 24, ☎ 0758-13119). **Centro Escursionistico Naturalistico Speleologico - CENS** (Excursions, Nature and Caving Center, Via Galeazzi 5, Costacciaro, ☎/fax 0759-170400, www.cens.it) can point you in the right direction for water and snow sports as well as hiking and underground adventures.

Maps & Guides: Your best maps for the region are *Carta dei Sentieri del Massiccio del Monte Cucco* (trail map of Mt Cucco published by CENS), *Carta dei Sentieri delle Valli Gualdesi* (trail map of the Gualdesi valleys, published by the CAI and Gualdo Tadino town hall) and *Carta dei Sentieri dei Monti di Gubbio* (trail maps of the Gubbio mountains, published by the CAI).

Sightseeing

The Historical Center

Beautifully situated on a plateau at the foot of Mt Ingino, Gubbio was already a well-established Umbrian town when the famous Eugubine Tablets referred to it in the second century BC. From then it grew with Roman rule (after becoming the first Umbrian town to be allied with Rome), was destroyed (like many towns in this area) by the armies of Goth King Totila and then re-formed in the 11th century under Ghibelline then Guelph patronage. The simple street plan makes the town easy to explore, with most of the sights dotted on the five main streets that make up the historical center, each of which runs parallel at different levels on the slopes of Mt Ingino.

THE EUGUBINE TABLETS

These seven bronze plates, housed in the **Museo Civico** (Palazzo dei Consoli), were discovered in the 15th century. They represent one of the most important texts of classical antiquity thanks to the historical-political, religious and linguistic data they have passed down to us. Written in an Umbrian language that draws on both the Latin and Etruscan alphabets, they describe the city-state structure that existed here from the third to first centuries BC.

The Gothic **Chiesa e Convento di San Francesco** marks the entrance into town. It was built in the second half of the 13th century and contains a rich range of paintings, including frescos of *The History of the Virgin* by Ottaviano Nelli and a right apse dedicated to St Francis, said to have been built exactly on the spot where Casa Spadalonga stood and where he accepted the habit. The Spadalongas were the family he stayed with when he left his hometown. The church marks the end of the **Franciscan Footpath** (Sentiero Francescano della Pace), which links Assisi to Gubbio via Valfabbrica.

The 14th-century **Loggia dei Tiratori** (Weavers' Gallery) stands in front of the Chiesa di San Francesco. The ground floor was once a hospital, while the upper loggia was used by a wool-makers to stretch out and dry freshly-dyed wool.

Cross the river and a right turn takes you to the beautiful Romanesque **Chiesa di San Giovanni Battista**, which stands behind the Loggia dei Tiratori on Piazza San Giovanni. Once the city cathedral, this striking church has a single nave with square apse and majolica font constructed and decorated in the 16th century by Benedetto Nucci.

The imposing structure of the **Palazzo dei Consoli** (Palace of the Consuls, Piazza Grande, ☎ 0579-274298, fax 0579-237530 Apr-Sept, 10 am-1 pm, 3-6 pm, Oct-Mar, 10 am-1 pm, 2-5 pm), symbol of Gubbio's medieval power, dominates – in size and beauty – the historical center. Built between 1332 and 1337 by Matteo di Giovannello, also known as "Gattapone" or by Angelo da Orvieto (according to others), the result is an elegant and majestic structure, delicately decorated with a series of hanging arches, a fan-shaped staircase and a Gothic portal. The latter leads into the city's major museums, the Museo Civico (see previous page) and the **Pinacoteca Comunale** (Civic Art Gallery) with its display of works by local painters as well as by Tuscan masters. Included are pieces by Pietro Paolo Baldinacci, Benedetto and Virgilio Nucci, Francesco Damiani and two plates by famous Renaissance ceramicist, Mastro Giorgio Andreoli. The bell tower houses the famous "campanone" (or big bell), which is rung on special occasions. The square is completed by the Gothic **Palazzo Pretorio** (Town Hall), which was built at the end of the 15th century by Gattapone as the original seat of the *Podestà* (city rulers).

Via F. da Montefeltro leads up to the ancient **Palazzo Ducale** (☎ 0579-275872, daily, 8:30 am-7 pm, closed Wed), a building of Lombard origin that was restructured at the end of the 15th century when Federico da Montefeltro transformed it into the city's most important Renaissance monument. From its rear, you can access the pleasant **Parco Ranghiasci** (Ranghiasci Park), a great spot for walks along paths that wind half-way up Mt Ingino and offer great views over the town.

The Palazzo Ducale stands opposite the **Duomo**, a Gothic 14th-century cathedral dedicated to St James and supported in the interior by 10 pointed cross Gothic arches. Just outside, the **Museo Diocesano** (Cathedral Museum, ☎ 0579-220904, summer, 10 am-1 pm, 3-7 pm, winter, 10 am-1 pm, 3-6 pm, closed Mon) occupies the old Palazzo dei Canonici with its 15th-century paintings, wooden sculptures and holy furnishing taken from the church and elsewhere in the area. Its *pièce di résistance* is the "Botte dei Canonici" (big barrel), a vast 14th-century barrel that can hold 20,000 liters (5,000 gallons).

Through Porta San Ubaldo just north of here, take the steep walk to the **Basilica di Sant'Ubaldo**, a medieval church much enlarged in the 16th century when the portal and delightful Franciscan cloister were added. The interior is divided into five aisles and its major altar displays the Renaissance urn that preserves the saint's relics. The aisle on the left leads to the *ceri,* brought out only for the yearly festivities.

Cable Car

Built in 1960 to celebrate the 800th anniversary of the death of St Ubaldo, bishop and patron saint of Gubbio, a modernized cable car will take you to the peak of Mt Ingino, if you don't want to walk. The station (Via San Gerolamo) is just beyond the city walls at Porta Romana. The ride takes six minutes and offers beautiful views over the city architecture and landscape.

Back inside the city walls, there are plenty of sights still to explore, including the Gothic **Palazzo del Bargello** (Via dei Consoli), which was built in the early 14th century as the headquarters of the town's police force. On one of its walls is a typical example of a medieval "door of the dead," and in the square in front of it is the 16th-century **Fontana dei Matti** (Fountain of the Mad); apparently you need only run around it three times to turn mad yourself.

THE DOOR OF THE DEAD

One particular feature of Gubbio's architecture is the so-called door of the dead, a narrow pointed arch door placed above street level, which, according to tradition, was reserved for the passage of coffins. Actually, it was more likely a defensive door, which could be reached only using wooden steps that could be retracted.

Other monuments to visit include the 12th-century **Chiesa di San Domenico** (Piazza G. Bruno) with its collection of important frescoes and paintings; the **Palazzo del Capitano del Popolo** (Palace of the Captain of the People), one of the oldest public buildings from the 13th century; and the 14th-century **Chiesa di Santa Maria Nuova** (Via Ottaviano Nelli) with an elegant rose window, delicate pointed arch door and fresco of *Madonna del Belvedere* by Ottaviano Nelli on the right wall.

In the old quarter of San Pietro, the **Chiesa di San Pietro** (Church of St Peter) provides a visual insight into the town's architectural history, with three levels of style on display. The first Romanesque phase can be seen in the small portal with five round arches on the church façade; the second Gothic phase is inside the church where the style's typical pointed arches and polygonal apse are on display. The third and final Renaissance phase appears in the arch-covered naves and opening side windows that were added in 1519 by Olivetan monks.

Cyclists should head outside the walls in the low-lying part of the town to the large and well-preserved **Teatro Romano** (Roman Theater, ☎ 0759-220992), which is still used for theatrical performances in the summer months. When it was built in the first century BC, the theater could hold 10,000 spectators and a 70-m (230-foot) stretch of square blocks survives from that time. Not far away, you can visit the remains of a well-preserved Roman mausoleum thought to have been built for the burial of Genzio, King of Illyria.

Other worthwhile excursions or bike rides will take you to the **Chiesa di Vittorina** (Via F. Lupo), where St Francis is said to have met the savage wolf of Gubbio. The apse in the 13th-century **Chiesa e Convento di Sant'Agostino** (just outside the Porta Romana) is decorated with frescoes depicting the life of St Augustine and a *Universal Judgment* by Nelli. The Baroque **Chiesa di Santa Croce della Foce** is just outside Porta Metauro, with a gold-leaf boxed medieval ceiling. The **Chiesa della Madonna del Prato** (Via Perugina) has a domed ceiling decorated with the *Glory of Paradise* by Francesco Allegrini. The **Chiesa di San Secondo** is on Via Tifernate, through Porta Castello, with a polygonal 14th-century apse decorated with triple arches and many 15th-century frescoes.

THE SAVAGE WOLF OF GUBBIO

After being tamed by St Francis the wolf is said to have slept the night in the seventh-century **Chiesa di San Francesco della Pace** (Via Savelli della Porta). Inside the church is a stone that St Francis is said to have preached from and the statues of the three saints – St Ubaldo, St George and St Anthony – which are placed on top of the three *ceri* on the day of the Festa dei Ceri.

The **Chiesa di Santa Maria della Piaggola** (just outside Porta Vittoria) is worth a trip; it is one of the finest examples of the Baroque style in Gubbio, complete with walls adorned by cherubs, angels and statues of saints. On the main altar is a precious painting of the *Maestà* by Ottaviano Nelli.

If you'd like to explore the natural surroundings here, make your way to **Gola del Bottaccione** (Bottaccione Gorge), an important geological research center, located out of the historical center on the steep slopes of Mt Ingino and Mt Calvo. It is here that US scientists L. and W. Alvarez found the evidence for a probable meteorite to explain the extinction of the dinosaurs 60 million years ago. On the left side of the gorge (the Mt Calvo side) is the small medieval **Chiesa e Ermitage di Sant'Ambrogio** and on the right side (the Mt Ingino side) runs a stretch of the old Roman aqueduct (with medieval extensions by Gattapone), which provided water to the whole town during the Middle Ages.

Adventures

On Foot

Trails lead from town into the pine-covered hills around Mt Ingino or south toward Assisi on the Sentiero Francescano della Pace (Franciscan Footpath). A short hike along the latter will bring you to the **Abbazia di Vallingegno** (or di San Verecondo de Spissis), a 12th-century church and monastery built on the site of a former pagan church. For trails in the Parco Regionale Monte Cucco, see below.

On Horseback

You can do horseback riding around Gubbio with **Abbazia di Vallingegno** (Loc. Vallingegno, ☎ 07589-20158, open all year), **Alcatraz** (Loc. Santa Cristina, ☎ 0759-229938, open all year), **Centro Equestre Colombu** (Loc. Castiglione Aldobrando, ☎ 0759-258045, open all year) and **La Contessa Quarter Horse** (Loc. San Bartolomeno, ☎ 0759-273790, open all year).

∎ Parco Regionale di Monte Cucco

Part of the Apennine mountain range, the 25,000-acre Mt Cucco Regional Park occupies the northeast part of the region. Crossed by the Via Flaminia and the Sentino and Chiascio rivers, the rocky slopes peak with Mt Cucco (1,556 m/5,104 feet) – one of the highest points in Umbria – and dip with the mountain pastures and deep gorges from where the rivers and mineral waters begin. The land is rich with wildlife, especially on the eastern slopes of the highest peaks. Badgers, beech-martens, foxes and grey squirrels live in the woods; chaffinches, tits, wrens, woodpeckers, larks and owls balance on the branches of the trees; and golden eagle, rock partridges and hawks fly overhead.

Adventures

On Foot

Mt Cucco offers some of the loveliest mountain walking in the province, with medium-level trails taking you through woods and meadows, and up the rounded summits of the Apennine ridge. There are over 30 trails marked in the district, many of which depart from Costacciaro, including trails up **Mt Cucco** (four hours; take #1 up to the meadow summit, Pian delle Macinarie, and #2 back down). Other trails link Pian delle Macinarie with the summit of Monte le Gronde (two hours); Pascelupo with the Pian di Rolla (four hours); and Costacciaro with the Rio Freddo canyon, the deep gorge that runs along most of the eastern border of the park. For great views of the Orrido del Balzo dell'Aquila natural canyon, take the Strada delle Scalette from Fonte Avellana to the top of Mt Catraia. Many of the 30 paths are also suitable for **mountain biking**.

Mt Cucco has one of the most important karst systems in the world, with more than 24 miles of tunnels reaching 920 m (3,018 feet) down into the ground to Italy's deepest cavern and the fifth-deepest in the world. Explored since 1889, the initial stretch of the **Grotta del Monte Cucco**, as it is known, comprises the grandiose Cattedrale and Margherita chambers and a beautiful natural arch. You can take a tour of the 40-m (130-foot) section in the cave system open to the public or organize deeper sorties (proficient amateurs and expert professionals only) by arrangement with the **Centro Escursionistico Naturalistico Speleologico - CENS** (Via Galeazzi 5, Costacciaro, ☎/fax 0759-170400, www.cens.it).

The park also contains the Valdorbia underground caves (near Scheggia), a chain of artificially produced galleries and caves that stretch for miles along the banks of the Sentino.

To arrange rock-climbing in the region contact **CAI Gubbio** (Piazza San Pietro, ☎ 0759-273618) or **Gualdo Tadino** (Via Santo Marzio 24, ☎ 0758-13119); they can tell you the best way to arrange climbs on Le Lecce, Fossa Secca and Orrido del Balzo dell'Aquila routes.

On Horseback

There are horseback-riding centers within the park near Costacciaro – **Pian d'Isola** (Loc. Pian d'Isola, ☎/fax 0759-170567, open all year, closed Mon morning) and the campground **Rio Verde** (Loc. Fornace 55, ☎ 0579-170138, fax 0579-170181, www.campingrioverde.it, open July-Aug).

On Water

CENS (Centro Escursionistico Naturalistico Speleologico, Via Galeazzi 5, Costacciaro, ☎/fax 0759-170400, www.cens.it) runs rafting trips on the Chiascio and Sentino rivers.

WATER, WATER EVERYWHERE

Water has formed the tunnels and passageways of Mt Cucco for centuries; springs surge from its rocks all over the park but most famous are the Motette spring (near Scheggia), where the water is bottled by locals, and at Rochetta (near Gualdo Tadino), where the spring still gushes out into the wild.

On Snow

In winter, the smooth terrain provides good piste and cross-country skiing opportunities with ample seasonal snow at its best in the **Pian delle Macinarie**.

In the Air

The main **hang-gliding** areas are south of Mt Cucco in the Val di Ranco (near Costacciaro), where there are a couple of organized take-off points. You can arrange a lesson or tandem flight with the **Centro di Volo Libero** (Loc. Villa Scirca, ☎/fax 0759-170761) in Sigillo.

■ Alto Chiascio

The territory of Alto Chiascio follows the Chiascio River north of Assisi between Valfabbrica and Scheggia taking in the communes of Gualdo Tadino, Fossto di Vico, Sigillo, Costacciaro and even extending up to the spectacular Serra di Burano mountain range on the border between Umbria and Mare. It is a varied landscape of low-lying valleys and gently rolling hills, dotted with towns, villages, hermitages, churches, castles and fortresses.

Sightseeing & Adventures

Gualdo Tadino

 Near the border between Umbria and Mare, the town of Gualdo Tadino sits at the foot of the Central Apennines just above the foundations of the original Umbrian, then Roman, town of *Tadinum*. This town of rich history was razed to the ground by Hannibal in 217 BC, sacked by the troops of Julius Casear in 49 BC, suffered various barbarian invasions and was the site where the Byzantine army defeated Goth King Totila, bringing the Gothic-Byzantine war to an end (552). What survived all of that was finally destroyed by fire, and the whole town was moved up the hill and rebuilt in 1273.

A walk around town will take you past the Romanesque-Gothic façade of the **Cattedrale di San Benedetto**, with three arched portals and double rose window on the exterior, a 14th-century *Crucifix*, a fresco by Matteo da Gualdo, and the relics of patron saint, Beato Angelico, in the interior. The **Chiesa di San Francesco** is another of the town's important Gothic churches. It has a simple single nave that contains works by Matteo da Gualdo, a *Madonna & Child with St Francis*, and the historical ceramic tiles of the Holy Trinity (1528) on display.

 The town's most imposing sight is the **Rocca Flea**, a majestic medieval fortress much enlarged in the 16th and 18th centuries, which now houses the **Museo Civico** (Civic Museum, ☎ 0759-16078, July-Sept, Tues-Sun, 10 am-1 pm, 3:30-6 pm, Oct-June, Thurs-Sun, same hours). The museum is divided into three sections, with displays of local antiques, ceramics (especially the local majolica) and works of art.

Trails suitable for **hiking, cycling** and **horseback riding** depart Gualdo Tadino's Rocca Flea and run up into the surrounding hills. One of the most traveled (the Sentiero Italia, the Italy Trail) passes through Valsorda along a pilgrimage trail, which leads to the summit of the Monte Serrasanta (Holy Mountain, 1,421 m/4,661 feet). The Santuario della SS Trinity contains a valuable copy of the ceramic altarpiece by Luca della Robbia on display in the Chiesa di San Francesco.

The **Valle della Rocchetta** is a nature reserve famed for its pure and refreshing mineral spring water, which you will see bottled on all restaurant tables. There are pleasant **walks** to the Gola del Fonno gorge, where you can also pick up trails to Mt Penna (1,432 m/4,697 feet). The **Gruppo Speleologico Gualdo Tadino** (Gualdo Tadino Caving Group, Loc. Rocchetta, www.gsgt.speleo.it) is based here; it is the best organization to contact if you want to try **potholing** in the area.

Fossato di Vico

Traditionally an important junction on the Via Flaminia, the modern-day Fossato di Vico is the descendant of *Helvillum Vicus,* an Umbrian center, which was closely allied with Rome and almost certainly destroyed during the wars between the Goths and the Byzantines. The latter were probably responsible for building the **Roccaccio**, the ancient castle that stands in town in ruins.

Other sights include the 13th-century **Chiesa di San Benedetto** with double pointed arched portals and a fresco of Pope Urban V; the beautiful wooden ceiling of the 13th-century **Chiesa di San Cristoforo**; the **Chiesa di Santa Maria**

delle Piagge (also known as "La Piaggiola"), which contains a 15th-century fresco cycle by Ottaviano Nelli; and the town **Antiquarium** (Via Mazzini, ☎ 0759-14951, visits by appointment only) with collections on the Roman period and the nearby excavations at Aja della Croce.

You can find the **trail** of the ancient **Via Flaminia** along the road that leads from the railway bridge about a mile to Borgo, known as *Helvillum Vicus* in Roman times. Another ancient road, the **Via Valico** can be picked up across the Roman bridge over the Rigo at the foot of Monte della Rocca on the Apennine border. Paths from here lead into the Parco Regionale Monte Cucco or across the Apennines into Marche.

Sigillo

Once the ancient Umbrian center of *Sigillum,* Sigillo was an important town along the Via Flaminia as the many Roman remains and relics in the area show. It is set in the green hills of the Parco Regionale di Monte Cucco and is a great spot to pick up **hiking** and **cycling trails** into the park. It's also a popular **hang-gliding** destination with the International Free-Fly Championships held here every July and August (for adventures from Sigillo in the air, see page 446).

Town sights include the **Chiesa di Sant' Agostino** (with *Annunciation* by local boy, Ippolito Borghese); the 13th-century **Chiesa di Sant'Andrea** (with an impressive walnut choirstall and 15 oval plaques portraying the mysteries of the rosary dotted around the walls); and the **Chiesa di Sant'Anna al Cimitero** (with splendid stone portal and rose windows on the façade). Short walks out of town will take you to the **Ponte del Spiano**, a Roman bridge of imposing sandstone blocks that was built to allow the Via Flaminia to cross the Fonturci River; and to the **Ponte della Spirca** (also known as the "Ponte dei Pietroni" due to the enormous blocks of stone), a younger bridge from the second century AD.

Costacciaro

Another of the towns along the Via Flaminia, Costacciaro grew up around the medieval fortress built here by the ruling Urbino Counts to defend the zone from attack. These days, a popular holiday destination for **hikers**, **horseback riders** and **cavers** drawn to the adventures on **Mt Cucco**, the town has the pretty **Chiesa di San Francesco** with a stunning limestone façade, the imposing defensive tower of **Il Rivellino**, and the **Torre Roccaccia**, originally the town's defensive tower. You can find out more about the local geography by visiting the **Museo delle Grotte** (The Cave Museum, Corso Mazzini 4, ☎ 0759-172723, visits by arrangement only).

Scheggia e Pascelupo

The old Roman town of Scheggia (or *Ad Ansem,* "Sword Pass") was closely linked to the Via Flaminia, and is thought to have died out during the barbarian invasions. The present town grew up on the castle of "La Schizza" during the 10th century and most of its best monuments (including the Abbazia di Santa Maria di Sitria and the Ermitario di San Emiliano in Congiuntoli) were constructed around that time. Its sister town Pascelupo is a small hill town with the remains of an ancient castle and medieval tower.

Surrounded by green mountains covered with beech forests, a network of **footpaths** and nature trails depart from both Scheggia and Pascelupo to ascend the mountains of **Catria** (1,703 m/5,586 feet), **Le Gronde** (1,373 m/4,503 feet), **Motette** (1,331 m/4,366 feet) and **Ranco Giovannello** (1,158 m/3,798 feet), as well as **Monte Cucco** itself. You can also pick up the **Sentiero Italia** (Italy Trail) that runs across the Apennine mountain chain from Monte Calvario. Guides will take you along the watercourse of the Rio Freddo canyon.

Events & Entertainment

Gubbio's **Corsa dei Ceri** (Race of the Candles) is one of Italy's most famous (and probably craziest) festivals. Celebrated on the 15th of May (patron saint, St Ubaldo's Eve), this festival is thought to have taken place here since the second half of the 12th century when the city won an important victory in battle. The "candles" are three huge octagonal wooden structures that rise four meters (13 feet) above wheelbarrows supported by brightly dressed *ceraioli* (the group of 10 townspeople on each team who race the *ceri*). Each is mounted with a statue of the district's relevant saint (St Ubaldo for the stonemasons; St George for the craftsmen and merchants; and St Anthony for the farm-workers). They raise the candles on their shoulders when the race starts at 6 pm, run along Via Dante, into Piazza della Signoria, and up the steep slopes of Mt Ingino to the Basilica di San Ubaldo. The statue of St Ubaldo must always enter the basilica first, so the race isn't judged by who gets here first, but by who gets here with the most skill – traditionally a decision of much dispute.

The last Sunday in May sees Gubbio's **Palio della Balestra**, a crossbow competition between the Gubbio and Sansepolcro crossbow societies; and in March/April, the **Procession of the Dead Christ**, carrying 17th-century statues of the Madonna and Christ, which departs from the Chiesa di Santa Croce della Foce and winds its way around town as a heart-wrenching local song of mourning, the *Miserere,* is sung. But it's Christmas that brings one of the biggest treats with the lighting of "the biggest Christmas tree in the world," a Christmas tree shape that is picked out using more than 800 lights on the slopes of Mt Ingino (Dec 7-Jan 10).

Palio della Balestra

On the last weekend in September, **Gualdo Tadino** hosts its **Giochi de le Porte** (Games of the Four Gates), which sees the town explode in medieval costume from Friday night to Sunday evening. The four districts of the city compete against one another in medieval-style games, with archery and sling-throwing competitions, plus two donkey races.

■ Where to Shop

Gubbio and the Alto Chiascio are areas known for their **majolica** ceramics. They have been manufactured here with their golden and ruby tints since the 14th century, but achieved world fame in the 15th and 16th centuries when local craftsman Mastro Giorgio Andreoli opened his workshop here. Today, the most important workshops are the **Vasellari Eugubini** (Via Baldassini, Gubbio, ☎ 0759-274235), **Fabbrica Maioliche Mastro Giorgio** (Piazza Grande 3, Gubbio, ☎ 0759-271574) and **Bottega d'Arte di Aldo Ajo** (Via della Cattedrale 20, Gubbio, ☎ 0759-273958). The Bottega sells local ceramics with an avant-garde twist. The most popular forms are the majolica with floral decorations on white backgrounds and the polished *bucchero* (a kind of *graffito* design). You can check them out in the shops or in the bi-annual ceramics exhibition, **Biennali d'arte della ceramica e dei lavori in metallo** (ceramic art and metal-working exhibition).

Ceramic History

The **Torre Medioevale** (Medieval Tower), with its fine views, is also home to Gubbio's **Porta Romana Ceramics Museum** (Via Porta Romana, ☎ 0759-221199, 9 am-1 pm, 3:30-7:30 pm). It has a collection of more than 350 pieces of majolica from the Renaissance up to the present, including important works by Maestro Giorgio Andreoli

Museo della Ceramica Contemporanea (Contemporary Ceramics Museum, Via Soprammuro, ☎ 0759-212172) displays a collection of ceramics made in the workshops of Gualdo Tadino at the end of the 19th and early 20th centuries. The zone is also known for its wood and wrought-iron furniture industries.

If you want to buy some of the local produce, there are plenty of shops selling charcuterie (pork products), extra-virgin olive oils and homemade pastas and sauces in the district. **Bottega del Buongustaio** (Via Mazzini 24, ☎ 0759-276692 and Via del Consoli 79, ☎ 0759-220302), **Gubbio Tartufi** (Via Mastrogiorgio, ☎ 0759-277579) and **Tipici Prodotti** (Via del Consoli 41, ☎ 0759-220986) in Gubbio have a bit of everything. There's tasty salami in **Frillici Francesco** (Via R. Calai, ☎ 0759-13152) and **La Commerciale Tacchi** (Via Biancospino 50, ☎ 0759-142933) in Gualdo Tadino. **Caseificio Camaggioretto** (Loc. Camaggioretto, ☎ 0759-259280), near Scheggia, is your best bet for local cheeses, including ricotta, mozzarella, caciotta, pecorino and cheese flavored with truffles.

■ Where to Eat

LOCAL FLAVORS

Bigoli di Costacciaro – A kind of thick noodles.
Borgiona – A traditional chickpea soup flavored with garlic, sage and tomato.
Cappelletti – Pasta made in the shape of little hats and stuffed with meat and cheese.
Cialde – A type of wafer prepared for the feasts of San Nicola and San Lucia as well as for Christmas.
Crescia – Flat bread made with cheese and served with salami.
Crostini di rigaglie – Chicken giblet pâté.
Fegatelli – Spit-roasted liver.
Friccò di pollo e coniglio – Chicken and rabbit meats cooked with wine, vinegar, garlic, and rosemary.

Pancaciato – Walnut bread (traditionally made in walnut season, Oct to Feb).

Porchetta – Roast pork with garlic, pepper and fennel.

Mazzafegati – Typical liver sausages.

Passatelli – Pasta made with stale bread, nutmeg and lemon rind and served in a rich broth.

Polenta – Served with a sausage sauce on a small wooden board known as the *spianatora*.

Strozzapreti di Gubbio – A kind of *gnocchi* made only with flour.

The Alto Chiascio area also produces truffles (of the *bianchetto, marzuolo* and *scorzone* varieties), sausages (*cotechino, lonza, capocollo, pepata guanciola, pancetta arrotolata,* etc.) and a wide range of salami and ham (*mortadella* from Gubbio, *prosciutto* from Pascelupo and *ciauscolo*, salami with ground fat). There's also a good choice of cheeses with *ricotta, pecorino* and *formaggio al tartufo nero* (cheese and black truffle mixed together).

In the hotel of the same name, one of the classiest places to eat in Gubbio is **Ai Cappucini** (Cia Tifernate, ☎ 0759-234, closed Mon); its large dining room serves a menu with traditional dishes like *tortino di farro al tartufo bianco di Gubbio* (savory white truffle tart). **Alla Balestra** (Via della Repubblica, ☎ 0759-273810, closed Tues) has a good *gnocchetti ai porcini e tartufo* (small potato pasta with porcini mushrooms and truffle flakes), while there are other mushroom-flavored pasta dishes at **Grotta dell'Angelo** (Via Gioia, ☎ 0759-271747, closed Tues). They do a lovely porcini mushroom risotto.

If it's something a little more meaty you want, **Emma** (Loc. Casamorcia, Gubbio, ☎ 0759-255109, closed Sat, also a two-star hotel) serves a tasty *agnella a scottaditto e carni alla brace* (lamb and spit-roasted meats). **La Cantina** (Via Piccotti, 0759-220583, closed Mon) offers a nice *filetto al tartufo* (steak with truffles) and **San Martino** (Piazza San Martino, ☎ 0759-273251, closed Tues) has a generous *coratella d'agnello* and *medaglioni di vitello al tartufo* (veal medallions in a truffle sauce).

Out of town, the **Tempio di Giove Appennino** in Scheggia (Via Flaminia, ☎ 0759-259016, closed Wed) makes a great stopping-off point for its *gnocchi tricolori al tartufo bianco* (three-colored potato pasta with white truffle shavings) and *stinco di maiale al forno con cipolle e patate al cartoccio* (pork baked with onions and foiled potatoes).

■ Where to Stay

By far the nicest hotel in Gubbio is the **Park Hotel ai Cappuccini** ☆☆☆☆ (Via Tifernate, ☎ 0759-234, fax 0759-220323, www.parkhotelaicappuccini.it, $$$$), but there are also the **Relais Ducale** ☆☆☆☆ (Via Ducale, Via Galeotti, ☎ 0759-220157, fax 0759-220159, www.relaisducale.com, $$$$) and the **Torre dei Calzolari Palace** ☆☆☆☆ (Loc. Torre dei Calzolari, ☎ 0759-256327, fax 0759-256320, www.torrecalzolari.com, $$$). A little more reasonable, the Calzolari is just out of town.

In the Alto Chiascio, **Gualdo Tadino** has a few good and cheap hotel choices in **Bottaio** ☆☆ (Via Casimiri 17, ☎ 0759-13230, $) and **Verde Soggiorno** ☆☆ (Via Don Bosco 90, ☎ 0759-16263, fax 0759-142951, sdbgualdo@pcn.net, $).

Gubbio has two campgrounds out of town in Ortoguidone – **Villa Ortoguidone** ☆☆☆☆ and **Città di Gubbio** ☆☆☆ (both ☎/fax 0759-272037, both www.gubbiocamping.com, both Apr-Sept, both $). There are more campgrounds at Costacciaro – **Rio Verde** ☆☆ (Loc. Fornace 55, ☎ 0579-170138, fax 0579-170181, www.campingrioverde.it, 50 spaces, July-Aug, $) and **Gualdo Tadino** (Valsorda ☆, Loc. Valsorda, ☎ 0759-13261, May-Sept, 40 spaces, $).

You can book into religious accommodation at **Mestre Pie Filippini** (Corso Garibaldi 100, ☎ 0759-273768, $) and there's a youth hostel just outside of Gubbio – **Ostello L'Aquilone Loc. Ghigiano**, ☎ 0759-291144, fax 0759-220197, www.aquilone.it, $). Another one is in Sigillo at the hang-gliding center, **Ostello del Volo Libero** (Villa Scirca, Via Flaminia 32, ☎/fax 0759-170761, universitadelvolo@libero.it, $) on the edge of the Parco Regionale del Monte Cucco.

There are hiking shelters near Fossato di Vico – **Il Valico** (Loc. Valico di Fossato, ☎ 338-8566578, $, with pub and pizza restaurant) and **Sigillo** (La Valleta Monte Cucco, Loc. Pian del Monte, ☎ 0759-177733, $).

Addendum
Language

■ Pronunciation

IN THIS CHAPTER
- Language   453
- Further Reading   459

Learning a few basic words and phrases is not only polite but also necessary in many of the more rural areas of Tuscany and Umbria. Fortunately, it's one of the easiest European languages to pick up (especially if you have a smattering of French or Spanish) and to get by you need only remember that every word is spoken exactly is it is written with all the letters pronounced (even if two vowels in concession).

Problem areas come with the few consonants that differ from English pronunciation:

c before e is pronounced ch, as in church

ch before e is pronounced c, as in can

g before e or i is pronounced with the soft g of geranium

gh is pronounced with the hard g of girl

gn has the ny sound of onion

gi is softened to li, as in stallion

h is deemphasized, as in honor

sce and **sci** are pronounced sh, as in she

All Italian words are stressed on the penultimate syllable unless marked by an accent.

When speaking to strangers, you should always use the polite "lei" third-person form and not the informal "tu," unless it is someone of your same age and status.

■ Basics

yes	si
no	no
all right/that's OK	va bene
all right, agreed	d'accordo
of course	volentieri
please	per favore
thank you	grazie
thank you very much	molto grazie
you're welcome	prego
sorry!	scusi!
excuse me, pardon me	permesso?
come in	avanti!
welcome	benvenuto!
hello (formal)	salve
hello (informal)	ciao
good morning	buon giorno

good evening	buona sera
good night	buona notte
see you soon	a presto
goodbye	arrivederci
pleased to meet you	piacere
well	bene
bad	male
happy birthday	buon compleanno
merry Christmas	buon Natale
happy Easter	buona Pasqua
happy New Year	buon anno
Have a good journey	buon viaggio
Mr	Signor
Mrs	Signora
Miss/Ms	Signorina
How are you?	Come sta?
Not bad, thank you	Non c'è male, grazie
Excuse me, can I ask you something?	Mi scusi, posso chiederle un'informazione?
Do you speak English?	Parla inglese?
Could you say that again?	Può ripetere per favore?
I don't understand	Non capisco
Where is Cavour Street?	Dov'è Via Cavour?
Sorry, I don't know	Non lo so, mi dispiace
Thank you for your help	Grazie dell'informazione
Wait a moment	Aspetti un momento
Come in/have a seat	Si accomodi
I like it very much	Mi piace molto
I don't like it	Non mi piace
This is Mr Brown	Le presento il signor Brown
What's your name?	Come ti chiami?
My name is Chiara	Mi chiamo Chiara
I live in	Abito a
today	oggi
yesterday	ieri
tomorrow	domani
morning	mattino
midday	mezzogiorno
afternoon	pomeriggio
evening	sera
night	notte
day	giorno
Monday	lunedí
Tuesday	martedí
Wednesday	mercoledí
Thursday	giovedí
Friday	venerdí
Saturday	sabato
Sunday	domenica
week	settimana

month	mese
January	gennaio
February	febbraio
March	marzo
April	aprile
May	maggio
June	giugno
July	luglio
August	agosto
September	settembre
October	ottobre
November	november
December	dicembre
season	stagione
spring	primavera
summer	estate
autumn	autunno
winter	inverno
year	anno
What day is it?	Che giorno è oggi?
What's the weather like?	Che tempo fa?
The sun is shining	C'è il sole
It's raining/snowing	Piove/nevica
It's very hot	Fa molto caldo

Numbers

1	uno
2	due
3	tre
4	quattro
5	cinque
6	sei
7	sette
8	otto
9	nove
10	dieci
11	undici
12	dodeci
13	tredici
14	quatordici
15	quindici
16	seidici
17	diciassette
18	diciotto
19	dicianove
20	venti
21	ventuno
22	ventidue
23	ventitre
24	ventiquattro

Language

25	venticinque
26	ventisei
27	ventisette
28	ventiotto
29	ventinove
30	trente
40	quaranta
50	cinquanta
60	sessanta
70	settanta
80	ottanta
90	novanta
100	cento
101	centuno
200	duecento
300	trecento
1,000	mille
10,000	diecimila

Time

minute	minuto
hour	ora
half an hour	mezz'ora
quarter of an hour	quarto d'ora
second	secondo
What time is it?	Che ore sono?
It's seven o'clock	Sono le sette
It's five past one	E l'una e cinque
It's almost eight o'clock	Sono quasi le otto
What time shall we meet?	A che ora ci si trova?
See you at 10 past six	Ci vediamo alle sei e dieci
In an hour	Tra un'ora
How long does the visit last?	Quanto dura la visita?
What time's dinner?	A che ora e la cena?

Emergencies

Help!	Aiuto!
Fire!	Al fuoco!
Al ladro!	Thief!
Can you help me, please?	Per favore, mi aiuti
I don't feel well	Mi sento male
Where's the hospital?	Dov'è il pronto soccorso?
I got lost	Mi sono perso
There's been an accident	C'è stato un incidente
Quick, it's very serious	Presto, è molto grave
Please call an ambulance	Chiamate un ambulanza
Where's the police station?	Dov'è il commissariato?
I lost my documents	Ho perduto i documenti
I've been robbed	Mi hanno derubato
My car has been stolen	Mi hanno rubato l'auto

I have to make an emergency phone call . . . . Devo fare una telefonata urgente

I want to phone my embassy . . . . Voglio telefonare alla mia ambasciata

Signs & Warnings

beware . . . . attenzione

do not disturb. . . . . non distubare

do not touch . . . . non toccare

drinking water . . . . acqua potabile

high voltage. . . . . alta tensione

no bathing . . . . divieto di balneazione

no entry . . . . vietato l'ingresso

non smoking . . . . non fumatori

out of order . . . . fuori servizio

work in progress. . . . . lavori in corso

Traveling

airplane. . . . . aeroplano

bicycle. . . . . bicicletta

bus. . . . . autobus/pullman

car . . . . macchina

ferry . . . . traghetto

ship . . . . nave

taxi . . . . taxi

train . . . . treno

on foot. . . . . a piedi

port . . . . porto

railway station . . . . stazione ferroviaria

bus station . . . . autostazione

customs . . . . dogana

border . . . . frontier

nationality . . . . nazionalità

passport. . . . . passaporto

work permit . . . . permesso di soggiorno

visa (tourist/transit). . . . . visto (di soggiorno/di transito)

passports please . . . . passaporti, prego

The children are on my passport. . . . . I figli sono sul mio passaporto

Have you anything to declare? . . . . Ha qualcosa da dichiarare?

Only personal effects and a few gifts . . . . Solo effetti personali e qualche regalo

Which is your luggage? . . . . Qual è il suo bagaglio?

ticket office . . . . biglietteria

ticket . . . . biglietto

one way/ return trip . . . . di andata/ andata e retorno

platform. . . . . binario

left luggage. . . . . deposito bagagli

train timetable . . . . orario ferroviario

What time does the Florence train leave? . . . . A che ora parte il treno per Firenze?

When is the next/last train to..? . . . . Quando c'è il prossimo/ l'ultimo treno per..?

When does it arrive in Perugia? . . . . Quando arriva a Perugia?

I'd like to book a seat on the fast train to . . . . Vorrei prenotare un posto sul rapido per

Which platform does it go from?. . . . . Da che binario parte?

Where do I have to change . . . . Dove devo cambiare?
Excuse me, is this the Pisa train? . . . . Scusi, è questo il treno per Pisa?
Does it stop in Lucca? . . . . Ferma a Lucca?
Is this seat free? . . . . E libero questo posto?
No, it's taken . . . . No, è occupato

Driving & Directions

Left/right . . . . sinistra/ destra
straight ahead . . . . semper diritto
driving license . . . . patente
gasoline/petrol . . . . benzina
diesel . . . . gasolio
Is there a gas station near here? . . . . C'è un distributore qui vicino
Fill it up, please . . . . Il pieno, per favore
Super or lead free? . . . . Super o senza piombio?
I'd like to rent a car . . . . Vorrei noleggiare un'auto
How much does it cost per day? . . . . Quanto costa al giorno?
Is insurance included? . . . . E inclusa l'assicurazione?
My car has broken down . . . . La mia auto è in panne
I've got a flat tire . . . . Ho una gomma a terra
highway . . . . autostrada
road map . . . . carta automobilistica
slow down . . . . rallentare
traffic lights . . . . semaforo
I'm looking for this road . . . . Cerco questa via
Is this the right road for the highway? . . . . E la strada giusta per l'autostrada?
You've come the wrong way . . . . Ha sbagliato strada
Turn right at the first traffic lights. . . . . Volti a destra al primo semaforo
Keep straight on . . . . Vada semper diritto!
Can I park here? . . . . Si può parcheggiare qui?

Accommodation

hotel . . . . albergo
room (single/double/with bathroom) . . . . . . camera (singola/matrimoniale/con bagno)
board (full/half) . . . . pensione (completa/mezza pensione)
How can I get to the Hotel Emma? . . . . Come arrivo all'hotel Emma?
Do you have any vacancies? . . . . Avete una camera libera?
For how many nights? . . . . Per quante notti?
How much does it cost per night? . . . . Quanto costa a notte?
Is breakfast included? . . . . E inclusa la prima colazione?
I don't like it. Is there another room free? . . . . Non mi piace. Ne avete un'altra?
Could you prepare my bill, please? . . . . Mi prepari il conto, per favore
Where can I pitch my tent? . . . . Dove posso pianare la tenda?

Eating Out

Che cosa desidera? . . . . What would you like?
I'd like to book a table for two this evening . . . .
. . . . Vorrei prenotare un tavolo per due per stasera
Is this table free? . . . . E libero questo tavolo?
Waiter! . . . . Cameriere!
What is the dish of the day? . . . . Qual è il piatto del giorno?

Do you have a set menu? . . . . Avete un menu a prezzo fisso?
Cheers! . . . . Salute!
The bill, please . . . . Il conto, per favore

Further Reading

■ Tuscany

Literature

The Decameron, Giovanni Boccaccio
The Divine Comedy, Dante Alighieri
Galileo's Daughter, A Historical Memoir of Science, Faith and Love, Dava Sobel
Innocence, Penelope Fitzgerald
Italian Folktales, Italo Calvino
Romola, George Eliot
A Room with a View, E.M. Forster
A Tuscan Childhood, Kinta Beevor
Valperga, Mary Shelley
War in Val d'Orcia, An Italian War Diary 1943-44, Iris Origo
Where Angels Fear to Tread, E.M. Forster

Contemporary Fiction

The Hills of Tuscany, A New Life in an Old Land, Ferenc Mate
In Maremma; Life and a House in Southern Tuscany, David Leavitt
Seasons in Tuscany, Allan Parker
Summer's Lease, John Mortimer
Too Much Tuscan Sun, Confessions of a Chianti Tour Guide, Dario Castagno with Robert Rodi
Travelers' Tales Tuscany: True Stories, James O'Reilly
Under the Tuscan Sun, Frances Mayes
Vanilla Beans & Brodo, Real life in the hills of Tuscany, Isabella Dusi
Within Tuscany: Reflections on a Time and Place, Matthew Spender

Architecture, Art & History

The Art of Florence, Glenn Andres, John Hunisak, Richard Turner, Takashi Okamura
Brunelleschi's Dome: How a Renaissance Genius Reinvented Architecture, Ross King
The Feud That Sparked the Renaissance: How Brunelleschi and Ghiberti Changed the Art World, Paul Robert Walker
The House of Medici: Its Rise and Fall, Christopher Hibbert
The Lives of the Artists, Giorgio Vasari
Renaissance Florence: The Invention of a New Art, Richard Turner

Food & Drink

A Food Lover's Companion to Tuscany, Carla Capalbo
Rosemary and Bitter Oranges: Growing Up in a Tuscan Kitchen, Patrizia Chen
Recipes and Traditions, Anne Bianchi
Foods of Tuscany, Giuliano Bugialli

■ Umbria

Fiction

After Hannibal, Barry Unsworth
The Assisi Murders, Timothy Holme
Ciao Italia in Umbria, Mary Ann Esposito
The Genesis Code, John Case
Two Lives: Reading Turgenev and My House in Umbria, William Trevor
Umbria: Italy's Timeless Heart, Paul Hofmann
A Valley in Italy: The Many Seasons of a Villa in Umbria, Lisa St. Aubin De Teran
Villa Fortuna: An Italian Interlude, Geoffrey Luck

Architecture, Art & History

Ancient Umbria: State, Culture, and Identity in Central Italy from the Iron Age to the Augustan Era, Guy Jolyon Bradley
Etruscan Art, Nigel Spivey
The Little Flowers of St Francis, Ugolino
Salvation, Scenes from the Life of Saint Francis, Valerie Martin

Natural World

Field Guide to Wild Flowers of Southern Europe, Paul Davies and Bob Gibbons
Songbirds, Truffles, and Wolves: An American Naturalist in Italy, Gary Paul Nabhan

Index